STAGE MAKEUP

Murleen Schreiner

STAGE

By the same author:

FASHIONS IN HAIR

FASHIONS IN MAKEUP

FASHIONS IN EYEGLASSES

FIFTH EDITION

MAKEUP

RICHARD CORSON

Prentice-Hall, Inc., Englewood Cliffs, New Jersey

Library of Congress Cataloging in Publication Data

CORSON, RICHARD.
    Stage makeup.

    1. Make-up, Theatrical. I. Title.
PN2068.C65 1975   792'.027   74-12197
ISBN 0-13-840496-8

STAGE MAKEUP, FIFTH EDITION
Richard Corson

© 1975, 1967, 1960, 1942 by PRENTICE-HALL, INC., Englewood Cliffs, New Jersey

Copyright renewed 1970 by Richard Corson

PRINTED IN THE UNITED STATES OF AMERICA

10   9   8   7   6   5   4   3   2

PRENTICE-HALL INTERNATIONAL, INC., LONDON
PRENTICE-HALL OF AUSTRALIA, PTY. LTD., SYDNEY
PRENTICE-HALL OF CANADA, LTD., TORONTO
PRENTICE-HALL OF INDIA PRIVATE LIMITED, NEW DELHI
PRENTICE-HALL OF JAPAN, INC., TOKYO

CONTENTS

ILLUSTRATIONS
xiii

FOREWORD   *by Hal Holbrook*
xvii

INTRODUCTION   *by Uta Hagen*
xix

PREFACE
xxi

ACKNOWLEDGMENTS
xxiii

FIGURE ACKNOWLEDGMENTS
xxv

PART ONE

PRINCIPLES OF MAKEUP   1

1

MAKEUP AND THE ACTOR
3

2

CHARACTER ANALYSIS

5

Heredity 6, Race 6, Environment 7, Temperament 8, Health 9, Age 9, Problem 12

3

PHYSIOGNOMY

13

Eyes 14, Eyebrows 15, Nose 16, Mouth 18, Problems 19

4

FACIAL ANATOMY

20

Bones of the Face 20, Construction of a Head 21, Modeling a Head in Clay 22, Problems 25

5

LIGHT AND SHADE

26

Flat and Curved Surfaces 27, Hard and Soft Edges 28, Drawing in Light and Shade 29, Problems 30

6

COLOR IN PIGMENT

31

Characteristics of Color 31, Color Mixing 33, Problems 33

7

ORGANIZING MAKEUP COLORS

34

A System of Color Classification 34, The Color Chart 35, Color Mixing 36, Problems 36

8

LIGHTING AND MAKEUP

38

Color in Light 38, Light on Pigment 38, Problems 40

PART TWO

DESIGNING THE MAKEUP 41

9

THE MAKEUP DESIGNER

43

10

SKETCHES AND WORKSHEETS
47

Preliminary Sketches 47,
Adapting the Makeup to the Actor 47,
Quick Changes 48,   Final Sketches 50,
Worksheets 51,   Problem 55

PART THREE

APPLYING THE MAKEUP 57

11

MAKEUP EQUIPMENT
59

The Makeup Kit 59,   The Makeup Room 61,
The Makeup Workshop 65,
The Makeup Morgue 66,   Problem 67

12

APPLICATION OF MAKEUP
68

Cake Makeup 68,   Creme Makeup 70,
Greasepaint 70,   Mixed Techniques 71

13

CORRECTIVE MAKEUP
74

Skin Color 74,   Facial Analysis 75,
Forehead 76,   Nose 76,
Jaw Line and Chin 77,   Wrinkles 77,
Eyes 77,   Eyebrows 80,   Cheeks 81,
Lips 82,   Neck 83,   Teeth 84,
Hair 84,   Problems 86

14

MODELING WITH PAINT
87

Foundation Colors 90,   Highlight Colors 91,
Shadow Colors 91,   Area 1: Forehead 92,
Area 2: Eyes 94,   Eye Pouches 101,
Oriental Eyes 103,   Eyebrows 104,
Area 3: Nose 109,   Area 4: Cheeks 111,
Nasolabial Folds 112,   Jaw Line 117,
Area 5: Mouth and Chin 121,
The Round Face 125,   Neck 127,
Hands 129,   Teeth 130,   Problems 130

15

THREE-DIMENSIONAL MAKEUP
133

Nose Putty 133,   Derma Wax 138,
Putty-Wax 138,   Latex 138,
Latex and Tissue 139,
Latex, Cotton, and Spirit Gum 142,
Latex and Cornmeal 144,
Syrup and Tissue 144,
Spirit Gum and Tissue 145,
Cotton and Collodion 145,
Special Constructions 146,   Problems 153

16

PROSTHESIS WITH LATEX
154

Casting for Prosthesis 154,
Types of Prosthetic Pieces 161,
Application of Prosthetic Pieces 165,
Foamed Latex 165,
Making and Applying a Foamed Latex Mask 166

17

BEARDS AND MUSTACHES
177

Crepe Hair 177,
Preparation of Crepe Hair 177,
Mixing Colors 180,
Application of Crepe Hair 180,
Beard Stubble 183,   Eyebrows 185,
Ventilated Pieces 185,
Construction of Ventilated Pieces 186,
Application of Ventilated Pieces 188,
Dressing Ventilated Pieces 189,
Removing and Cleaning Ventilated Pieces 189,
Measuring for Beards 190,
Adapting Beards 190,   Problems 190

18

HAIR AND WIGS
193

Natural Hair 193,   Soaping Out the Hair 196,
Wigs and Hairpieces 198,
Period Hair Styles 199,
Constructing the Wig 200,   Ventilating 203,
Weaving 204,   Mixing Hair 205,
Remodeling the Wig Cap 205,   Blenders 208,
Bald Wigs 209,   Toupees and Sideburns 210,
Falls 211,   Dressing the Wig 214,
Wearing the Wig 215,   Care of the Wig 216,
Renting or Buying Wigs 216,
Measuring for Wigs 216,   Adapting Wigs 217,
Problems 218

19

CREATING A LIKENESS   *Woodrow Wilson 219,   Mark Twain 220,*
219   *Stalin and Trotsky 223,   Problems 226*

20

IMAGINATIVE MAKEUP   *Problems 239*
227

21

MAKEUP FOR OTHER MEDIA   *Makeup for the Platform 241,*
241   *Makeup for Photography 242,*
    Makeup for Television 242

APPENDICES

A

MAKEUP MATERIALS
249

B

SOURCES OF MAKEUP MATERIALS
266

C

MAKEUP KITS
269

D

PLAN FOR A SHORT COURSE IN MAKEUP
273

E

RACIAL CHARACTERISTICS

275

F

FASHIONS IN MAKEUP   *Ancient Peoples 279,   The Middle Ages 279,*
279   *The Sixteenth Century 281,*
                             The Seventeenth Century 282,
                             The Eighteenth Century 283,
                             The Nineteenth Century 284,
                             The Twentieth Century 286

G

PERIOD HAIR STYLES

289

H

PICTURE COLLECTION

336

J

COLOR SECTION   *Makeups and Portraits 357,   Color Chart 365,*
357   *Tables of Equivalent Colors 373*

INDEX

383

ILLUSTRATIONS

*The numbers of the illustrations indicate the number of the chapter
or appendix in which the particular illustration appears, followed by the number of the illustration
in that chapter or appendix. The titles of the figures
are followed by the pages on which they appear.*

1-1, 1-2. Actor with and without makeup, 3

2-1. Lady in waiting, in *Elizabeth the Queen*, 6

2-2. Opar, in *Winged Victory*, 6

2-3. Queen of Hearts, in *Through the Looking Glass*, 6

2-4. Youth, 10

2-5, 2-6. Friedrich von Kaulbach, 11

2-7, 2-8. Martin Luther in youth and age, 11

3-1. Sketches from history, 14

3-2. Character in eyes and eyebrows, 15

3-3. Faces and features, 16

3-4. Profiles, 17

4-1. A human skull, 20

4-2. Diagram of prominences and depressions in the human skull, 21

4-3. Modeling a head in clay, 22

4-4. Making a severed head, 22

4-5. Planes of the face, 23

4-6, 4-7. Emperor Caesar Augustus, 24

4-8, 4-9. Livia, wife of Nero and Augustus and mother of Tiberius, 25

5-1. God, 26

5-2. Jean-Auguste-Dominique Ingres, 27

5-3. Bruce Crane, 27

5-4. Giovanni Mannozzi da San Giovanni, 27

5-5. Modeling curved and angular surfaces, 28

6-1. Color diagrams, 32

9-1. Makeup designs for *Mother Courage*, 43

9-2. Stylized makeups for *Mother Courage*, 44

9-3. Six characters from the ball scene in *The Patriot*, 45

10-1. Pencil sketches for makeup for Lizzie, in *Philadelphia, Here I Come*, 48

10-2. Lizzie, in *Philadelphia, Here I Come*, 49

10-3. Makeup worksheet, 50

10-4. Makeup worksheet for Abraham Lincoln, 51

10-5. Makeup worksheet for King Pellinore, 52

10-6. Makeups for Abraham Lincoln and King Pellinore, 53

10-7. Alternative makeup worksheet, 53

10-8. Sketches for makeup, 54

11-1. Makeup kits and containers, 60

11-2. Makeup table mirror, 61

11-3. Makeup laboratory at the California State University at Long Beach, 62

11-4. Makeup facilities, 63

11-5. Frame for portable makeup table, 64

11-6. Makeup class at the University of North Carolina, 64

11-7. Makeup artist Dick Smith in his workshop, 65

11-8. Makeup morgues, 66

12-1. The Mad Hatter, from *Alice in Wonderland*, 69

12-2. Application of greasepaint, 70

12-3. Stippling for age, 72

12-4. Materials for stippling, 72

12-5. Stippling with brush, 73

13-1. Corrective makeup, 75

13–2. Remodeling the nose with paint, 76

13–3. Corrective makeup for the nose, 77

13–4. Optical illusions in eye makeup, 78

13–5. Women's eyebrows and eyelashes, 79

13–6. Young men's eyebrows, 80

13–7. Youthful lips, male, 82

13–8. Youthful lips, female, 83

13–9. Facial lift, 84

13–10. Lifts for face and neck, 85

14–1, 14–2. Modeling with highlights and shadows, 88

14–3. Modeling with highlights and shadows, 89

14–4. Division of the face into areas, 91

14–5. Area 1: Forehead, 92

14–6. Foreheads, 92

14–7. Forehead wrinkles—light coming from above, 93

14–8. Light from below, 93

14–9. Modeling forehead wrinkles with paint, 94

14–10. Character through eye makeup, 95

14–11. Division of the orbital area into planes for shadowing and highlighting, 95

14–12. Eyes and eyebrows, 96

14–13. Eyes and eyebrows, 97

14–14. Eyes and eyebrows, 98

14–15. Male eyes and eyebrows, 99

14–16. Modeling an eye pouch with paint, 102

14–17, 14–18. Oriental eyes, 103

14–19. Eyes of an elderly Chinese, 103

14–20. Oriental actor as a Caucasian character, 104

14–21. Making plastic film for covering eyebrows, 106

14-22. Blocking out eyebrow with plastic film, 107

14–23. Queen of Hearts, 108

14–24. Sixteenth-century lady, 108

14–25. Planes of the nose, 109

14–26. Noses, 110

14-27. Cheekbone, 111

14–28. Planes of the cheek, 112

14–29. Cheekbones, 112

14–30. Cheekbones, 113

14–31. Placement of highlights and shadows for age, 113

14–32. Prisoner 7492, 114

14–33. Family Portrait, 114

14–34. Cheeks, 115

14–35. Nasolabial folds, 116

14–36. Dromio of Ephesus, 117

14-37. Dr. Frankenstein, 117

14–38. Necks and jaw lines, 118

14–39. Youthful jaw line, 119

14–40. Jaw line sagged with highlights and shadows, 119

14–41, 14–42. Jaw line sagged with crease in cheek, 119

14–43. Madwoman of Chaillot, 120

14–44. Planes of the upper and lower jaws, 120

14–45. Changing the mouth with paint, 120

14–46. Mouths, male, 122

14–47. Mouths, 123

14–48. Mouths, 124

14–49. Modeling a round cheek, 126

14–50. Round face created by modeling with highlights and shadows, 126

14–51, 14–52. Falstaff and Iago, 126

14–53. Muscles of the neck and jaw, 126

14–54. *Portrait of the Artist's Mother*, 127

14–55. Neck aged with cake makeup, 127

14–56. Hands, 128

14–57. Bones of the hand, 129

14–58, 14–59. Youthful hands aged with cake makeup, 129

15–1. Noses reshaped with putty, 134

15–2. Modeling a putty nose, 134

15–3. Portraits in makeup, 135

15–4. Noses, 136

15–5. Noses, 137

15–6. Severed hand, 138

15–7. Hand aged with latex, 139

15–8. Skin texture with latex and paper toweling, 140

15–9. Skin texture and wrinkles, 141

15–10. Makeup with tissue and latex, 142

15–11. Makeup with spirit gum, cotton, and latex, 142

15–12. Latex, cotton, and spirit gum technique, 143

15–13. Neglected mouth, 143

15–14. Hand aged with different techniques, 144

15–15. Hand aged with latex and cornmeal, 145

15–16. Blind eye with scar tissue, 146

15–17. Plastic piece for scar tissue, 146

15–18. Phantom of the Opera, 148

15–19. Diagram of Oriental eyelid made with adhesive tape, 148

15–20. Oriental eyelid made with adhesive tape, 148

15–21. Pattern for sagging eyelid, 149

15–22. Painting a plastic eyelid on glass, 149

15–23. Plastic eyelid folded and ready for use, 149

15–24. Plastic eyelid used to age the eye, 149

15–25. Scars and welts, 150

15–26. Making plastic scars with liquid plastic, 151

15–27. Plastic scars, welts, and growths, 151

15–28. Removing plastic scar from the glass, 151

15–29. Plastic growth on cheek, 152

15–30. Plastic growth near eye, 152

15–31. False teeth, 152

15–32. Scars, welt, warts, and wens, 152

15–33. Witch with warts, 153

16–1. Cast, molds, and prosthetic appliances, 154

16–2. Casting part of the face, 155

16–3. Casting a face with moulage, 156–57

16–4. Hanger for plaster cast, 159

16–5. Casting an eye pouch, 160

16–6. Molded latex piece, 162

16–7. Three-faced Girl, 162

16–8. Slush mold for partial ear, 163

16–9 to 16–30. Progressive steps in makeup for Dustin Hoffman's 120-year-old man in *Little Big Man*, 166–74

16–31. Giant, 176

16–32. Foam latex piece for Giant, 176

17–1. Mustaches and beards, 178

17–2. Preparing crepe hair, 179

17–3. Diagram for applying crepe hair beard, 180

17–4. Constructing a beard with crepe hair and spirit gum, 181–82

17–5. Captain Ahab, 183

17–6. Beard stubble, 184

17–7. Ventilated mustaches and beards, 184

17–8. Actor Mitchell Erickson as King Lear, 185

17–9. Ventilating hair onto lace, 187

17–10. Ventilating a mustache onto net or gauze, 188

17–11. Real mustache, 188

17–12. Beard blocks, 189

17–13. Full beard in sections, 190

17–14. A versatile beard, 191

18–1. Graying hair, 194

18–2. Soaping out the hair, 194–95

18–3. Making a bald head, 197

18–4. Making a bald pate, 198

18–5. Switch, 199

18–6. The lace-front wig, 199

18–7. Henvy V and the Prince of Arragon, 200

18–8. Eighteenth-century French wig styles, 201

18–9. Eighteenth-century French wig blocks and foundations, 202

18–10. Constructing the wig, 203

18–11. Wig construction, 204

18–12. Weaving hair, 205

18–13. Eighteenth-century wig shop, 206

18–14. Eighteenth-century wigmaker's tools, 207

18–15. Parts, pates, and hairlines, 208

18–16. Fitting nylon stocking over plastic head form, 209

18–17. Coating stocking with liquid plastic, 209

18–18. Ventilating hair into the nylon and plastic, 209

18–19. Plastic cap on special plastic head form, 209

18–20. Balding heads, 210

18–21. Philip IV, 211

18–22. Constructing the foundation for a Kabuki wig, 212–13

18–23. Dressing the wig, 214

18–24. Diagram for wig and beard measurements, 216

19–1, 19–2. Actor Wilson Brooks as Woodrow Wilson, 220

19–3. Actor Hal Holbrook as himself, 221

19–4. Hal Holbrook as Mark Twain, 221

19–5. Steps in the makeup for Mark Twain, 222

19–6. Final pencil sketches of Peter Falk as himself and as Josef Stalin, 224

19–7. Peter Falk to Stalin, 224

19–8. Final pencil sketches of Alvin Epstein as himself and as Trotsky, 225

19–9. Alvin Epstein to Trostky, 225

20–1. Styles of makeup, 227

20–2. Nonrealistic faces, 228

20–3. Nonrealistic makeups, 229

20–4. The Duchess from *Alice in Wonderland*, 230

20–5. Illustration from Lewis Carroll's *The Three Voices*, 230

20–6. The Mad Hatter from *Alice in Wonderland*, 230

20–7. Grotesque masks, 231

20–8. Ape makeup, 232

20–9. Tiger makeup, 232

20–10, 20–11. Bird and animal masks, 233

20–12. Parrot, 233

20–13. Tramp-clown makeup, 234

20–14, 20–15. Death, 234

20–16, 20–17. Mephistopheles, 235

20–18. Grotesque mask, 235

20–19. Devil as Jester, 236

20–20. Demon, 236

20–21. Rag doll, elf, and brownie, 236

20–22. Nonrealistic makeups, 237

20–23. Clock face, 238

20–24. Computer, 238

20–25. Witch from *Snow White and the Seven Dwarfs*, 239

21–1. Television makeup for Hal Holbrook's Mark Twain, 243–47

APPENDICES

A–1. Kryolan transparent adhesive tape, 251
A–2. Artificial blood, 251
A–3. Cake makeup, 251
A–4. Creme makeup, 251
A–5. Brushes, 252
A–6. Pencils and utensils, 252
A–7. Makeup supplies and accessories, 256
A–8. Greasepaint, 256
A–9. Liquid makeup, 257
A–10. Hair coloring, 257
A–11. Student cake-makeup kit, 259
A–12. Professional creme-makeup kit, 259
A–13. Student makeup kit, 259
A–14. Makeup palette, 259
A–15. Latex cap, 259
A–16. Makeup removers, 259
A–17. Adhesives, 262
A–18. Miscellaneous makeup, 262
A–19. Sponges, 263
A–20. Magnetic container for pins, 263
E–1. Racial variations, 277
F–1. Nefertiti, 280
F–2. Sixteenth-century lady, 281
F–3. Likeness of Mrs. Siddons, 282
F–4. Late nineteenth-century lady, 285
F–5. The Wistful Look, 1925, 287
F–6. The Lipless Look, 1963, 287
Plates 1 to 23. Period hair styles, 291–335
H–1. Medieval sculpture, French, 336
H–2. Oriental head, 336
H–3. Head of Pan, 337
H–4. Julius Caesar, 337
H–5. The Prophet Haggai, 338
H–6. King Charles II, 338
H–7. Prominent fifteenth-century Florentines, 339
H–8. Philip Melanchthon, 340
H–9. Wilibald Pirkheimer, 340
H–10. Johannes Fugger, 340
H–11. Louis XII of France, 340
H–12. Portrait of Johann Bodmer, 341
H–13. Old Man of 93, 342
H–14. Francis I, 343
H–15. Richard II, 343
H–16. Elizabeth I, 344
H–17. Mary Queen of Scots, 344
H–18. Emperor Rudolf II, 345
H–19. Heironymus Holzschuher, 345
H–20. St. Phillip, 346
H–21. St. Barnabas, 347
H–22. Portrait of Wohlgemut, 348
H–23. Jean Baptiste Camille Corot, 348
H–24. Court Jester Gonella, 349
H–25. Luther's Mother, 349
H–26. Sir Thomas More, 350
H–27. Portrait of the Artist's Father, 350
H–28. Charles Darwin, 350
H–29. William Cowper, 350
H–30. Frederick the Wise, 351
H–31. The Judge, 351
H–32. Queen Victoria, 352
H–33. John Stuart Mill, 353
H–34. Marie Tussaud, 354
H–35. Benjamin Disraeli, 354
H–36. Men of history, 355
H–37. Men and women of history, 356
J–1. Making up as Feste in *Twelfth Night*, 357
J–2. Modeling the face with paint, 358–59
J–3. Modeling apple cheeks for an aged face, 360
J–4A. Building up the nose, 361
J–4B–F. Cuts, scars, and bruises, 361
J–5. Medieval lady, 362
J–6. Leopard makeup for children's play, 362
J–7. Woman of Samoa, 362
J–8. Portrait of a sixteenth-century lady, 362
J–9. Decorative makeup based on an Oriental mask, 362
J–10. Portrait of a lady, 362
J–11. Lady Liston, 363
J–12. Francesco Saverio, Cardinal de Zelada, 363
J–13. John Tyler, 363
J–14. George Washington, 363
J–15. Mrs. Grace Dalrymple Elliott, 364
J–16. Vinnie Ream, 364
J–17. Madame de Caumartin as Hebe, 1753, 364
J–18. George Clymer, *c.* 1810, 364
J–19. Portrait of a Man, 1647, 364
J–20. Paul Wayland Bartlett, 1865–1925, 364

FOREWORD

I recall once needing a pair of ears for Abraham Lincoln. I didn't know if such a thing could be done, but I figured Dick Corson would, so I called.

"You want what?"

"Ears," I said. "For Lincoln. I'm doing Abe for the Phoenix Theatre—you know, Sherwood's play, and I'm working out the makeup."

"And you need ears."

"Yes, they were very big. Enormous, when you think about it," I said. "I figure without the ears it won't come out right."

"But with them. . . . . ?"

"Yeah."

"Why don't you come on over?"

Dick has always had a sense of humor about me. He's also been a friend ever since he helped carry a table to the theatre in Lakeside, Ohio, when I needed help and couldn't get it. That was many years ago. So I went over.

"Now, let me explain, Hal, that I've never done ears like this before. It can be done, of course, but I'm not sure that it has been. There's not a lot of call for big ears, you know. There's a little casting problem, you see—undercuts and all that. How did you want to attach them?"

"I figured I'd just slip them over mine. Like mittens."

"It's going to be rather difficult."

"Yeah, I guess so."

"Had you planned to glue them on?"

"Yeah. Once I slip them on, I'll glue them so they can't fall off. Actually, you shouldn't notice them much because his hair came out over them a lot. They shouldn't be grotesque."

"Just large."

"In case someone notices."

"I see."

Patiently he toiled over those ears. Then one night he called me. "Would you like to come down and slip them on?" I did, and they worked beautifully. It was the touch that made the makeup work, although I doubt very many people were aware of them. But Dick and I were enormously proud of them, and they made the makeup work so well in close-up that on the night we closed, the other actors in the cast waited in a local bar for me to take off the makeup so they could remember what I looked like.

Makeup requires patience. Corson is a patient man, a meticulous man, who goes about his work with the care and thought of a scientist. He is multi-talented and has used many of them in creating his books—*Stage Makeup, Fashions in Hair, Fashions in Eyeglasses*, and *Fashions in Makeup*. He's taken most of the photographs, done the intricate drawings, experimented on himself and his friends to get the many character effects, and he is a performer himself and understands the nature of the problems actors face on the stage. He's one of those totally dedicated people you sometimes meet or know in your life who make you feel that it's worthwhile to keep trying to do better.

It's been a great pleasure to see his book on makeup become established as the standard one in use wherever I go, knowing something of the toil that went to make it. In the early days when I was creating the Mark Twain makeup he would come to see the show and we would discuss its effectiveness and how it could be improved. His eye I could depend on.

He's written the best book around on the subject. To all you actors who don't feel right unless you have the ears on, trust in Dick.

Hal Holbrook

INTRODUCTION

The actor's dream is to play a wide range of characters, to explore many facets of life in roles that encompass all humanity. To fulfill this dream he requires not only talent and training but an unstinting devotion to his art.

In many areas of this endeavor the actor is assisted by the artistry and technical skills of brilliant craftsmen. From the original script to the set, lighting, and costume, every effort is made to achieve perfection. Curiously, in the field of makeup the actor is left quite to his own devices. Except for the rare production which is so exotic or stylized that a specialist is necessary, the actor must design and execute his own makeup.

It is therefore of considerable concern that many young professionals in the theater are unfamiliar with even so elementary a problem as projection of the actor's features, essential to the fullest communication of the character's inner life. Even on the rare occasions when a professional makeup artist is available, it is still the actor who is more aware than anyone else of the special problems posed by his own features and by the character he is playing. Thus, it is the responsibility of each actor to learn the craft of makeup, that final dressing of the character which will enable him to perform his role as fully and effectively as possible.

In addition to such fundamentals as the assimilation and projection of the character in terms of age, environment, and health, there is an area of psychological support which makeup can give the actor comparable only to the assistance of a perfect costume. Just as robes or rags can give the actor the "feel" of a character, so also can makeup. The visual image reflected in his dressing room mirror can be as important to the actor as it will later become to the audience.

The authority of the arch of a brow or the sweep of a profile can be as compelling as Lear's crown and scepter. The psychological effect of shadows and pallor or glowing health can be as conducive to mood and manner on stage as in life, while an impudent tilt to a nose or the simple graying of the hair will inevitably make more specific the delineation of character. The most detailed and subtle characterization can be performed only with full freedom and authority when the actor knows that the visual image supports and defines his work.

The actor untrained in makeup is deprived of an invaluable aid to his art—and little is done to remedy the situation. Large universities give courses in makeup intermittently or not at all. Drama schools often merely glance at the problem or train in outmoded techniques. And the actor must shift for himself or hope for the casual assistance and hand-me-down techniques of fellow artists.

It is therefore most exciting and encouraging to all actors when a book such as this comes to our rescue. Richard Corson's approach to makeup is meticulous and eminently practical. Perhaps even more important is his stress on the creative aspects of makeup and the avoidance of stereotypes and formulae. The insistence on supporting technical skill and imagination and individuality reflects a positive and rewarding approach. With fullest exploitation of the mind and senses, an unsuspected range of roles exists for each of us. It is through the assistance of the art and craft of makeup presented in this book that we can hope for a more complete realization of our goals in acting.

Uta Hagen

PREFACE

Makeup is often regarded as a necessary but unfortunate adjunct to dramatic productions. Too many actors and directors not only fail to realize its vast possibilities in contributing to the effectiveness of a production, but they regard it as a series of formulas to be followed blindly and mechanically. Assuredly makeup is not, or should not be, formulary or routine. Yet makeup, as it is usually learned, is frequently just that. There is a formula for middle age, one for old age, another for Irishmen, yet another for butlers. Such makeup is stultifying to the actor and an affront to the audience.

It is the purpose of this book to acquaint the student with the basic principles of the art and technique of makeup so that he may use them creatively in the design and execution of makeups which, beyond being technically commendable, will materially assist the actor in the development and projection of his character.

The book is intended for both the actor and the makeup artist, professional and nonprofessional. It is designed to be used as a text and subsequently as a reference book.

This edition includes several hundred new illustrations, many of them of student makeups. The chapter on three-dimensional makeup explains new techniques, the appendix on makeup materials and the hair-style plates have been brought up to date, and there is a completely new and expanded color chart designed to provide greater accuracy in designating colors. Information on colors suitable for dark-skinned actors, instead of being confined to a separate section, is included, where appropriate, throughout the book.

The approach of this text is based not upon learning rules, but upon understanding principles that are basic to makeup. It is therefore important, in using this book as a text, to understand each chapter thoroughly and to master the material in each chapter before proceeding to the next.

The value of recordings of students' voices in a speech class has long been recognized. In a makeup class, photographs of the students' work serve the same purpose. They not only provide a record of a student's progress, but they point up dramatically the faults in his makeup and serve as a spur to greater progress. They also demonstrate how the student can strive for greater perfection in detail. The benefits of the photographs are more immediate if a Polaroid camera is available, since this makes it possible for the student to compare the original makeup with the photograph and make any changes which seem desirable. The photographs of students' makeups in this book were taken as routine classroom procedure, using costumes and props from the costume shop. Improvised costumes which give the general effect desired are sufficient.

No matter how limited or extensive the available equipment, success in makeup is in large part the result of approaching it with a completely professional attitude. This implies an enthusiasm for learning and a refusal to settle for less than one's best. Only when the study of makeup is undertaken with such an attitude will its potentials for helping the actor be fully realized.

ACKNOWLEDGMENTS

Since the first edition of this book was in preparation, many people have given freely of their time and have made various contributions. For the current edition, I am most grateful for the cooperation of Mr. Bill Smith, Mr. Bert Roth, Mr. Alvin Cohen, Bob Kelly, Mehron's, The Makeup Center, Ben Nye, Kryolan/Braendel, and Stein's. I should also like to thank Mr. Alex Hadary, Mr. John Handy, Mr. Randy Kim, and the many students whose makeups appear in the book.

For a number of years Mr. Dick Smith, one of the most imaginative and dedicated television and movie makeup artists in the country, has been more than generous in sharing some of the results of his own experimentation. I am again indebted to him for permitting me to use not only the photographs of his television makeup for Hal Holbrook's Mark Twain, but also a new series of photographs of his remarkable film makeup of Dustin Hoffman as the 120-year-old man in *Little Big Man*.

I should particularly like to express my appreciation to Miss Uta Hagen for the Introduction and to Mr. Hal Holbrook for the Foreword.

R.C.

FIGURE
ACKNOWLEDGMENTS

Fig. 14–29 *Portait of a Man*, Dürer, p. 112, by permission of the Prado, Madrid.

Fig. 14–29 *Benjamin Franklin*, Houdon, p. 112, by permission of The Metropolitan Museum of Art, gift of John Bard, 1872.

Fig. 14–54 *Portrait of the Artist's Mother*, Dürer, p. 127, by permission of the Kupferstichkabinett der Staatl, Museen, Berlin-Dahlem.

Fig. 20–18 Grotesque mask, anonymous, p. 235, by permission of the Brooklyn Museum, gift of the Anonymous Arts Recovery Society.

Fig. F–1 *Nefertiti*, 14th c. B.C., painted limestone, p. 280, by permission of The Metropolitan Museum of Art.

Fig. H–3 *Head of Pan*, Athenian *c.* 400 B.C., p. 337 and Fig. H–26 *Sir Thomas More*, p. 350, by permission of the British Museum.

Fig. H–5 *The Prophet Haggai*, Pisano, p. 338 and and Fig. H–6 *King Charles II*, Peele, p. 338, by permission of the Victoria and Albert Museum, London.

Fig. H–12 *Portrait of Johann Bodmer*, Fuseli, p. 341, by permission of the Henry E. Huntington Library and Art Gallery.

Fig. H–14 *Francis I*, Jean Clouet, p. 343 and H–27 *Portrait of the Artist's Father*, Dürer, p. 350, by permission of the Louvre, Paris.

Fig. H–15 *King Richard II, unknown*, p. 323, Fig. H–16 *Elizabeth I*, unknown, p. 344, Fig. H–17 *Mary Queen of Scots*, unknown, p. 344, Fig. H–28 *Charles Robert Darwin*, John Collier, p. 350, Fig. H–29 *William Cowper*, Romney, p. 350, Fig.

H–32 *Queen Victoria*, after a portrait by von Angeli, p. 352, Fig. H–33 *John Stuart Mill*, G. F. Watts, p. 353, Fig. H–34 *Marie Tussaud*, attributed to F. Tussaud, p. 354, Fig. H–35 *Benjamin Disraeli*, Millais, p. 354, and Fig. 14–30 *Sir James Barrie*, Monnington, p. 113, by permission of the National Portrait Gallery, London.

Fig. H–19 *Heironymus Holzschuher*, Dürer, p. 345, by permission of Staatliche Museen Berlin, Gemäldegalerie Dahlem.

Fig. H–20 *St. Phillip*, Dürer, p. 346, Fig. H–21 *St. Barnabas* (detail), Botticelli, p. 347, and Fig. 5–1 God (detail from *Coronation of the Virgin*; currently being restored), Botticelli, p. 26, by permission of the Uffizi Gallery, Florence.

Fig. H–22 *Portrait of Wohlgemut*, Dürer, p. 348, by permission of the Germanisches Nationalmuseum.

Fig. H–24 *Court Jester Gonella of Ferrara*, Dutch, fifteenth century (no. 1840), by permission of Kunsthistorisches Museum, Vienna.

Fig. J–11 *Lady Liston*, Gilbert Stuart, p. 363, by permission of the National Gallery of Art, Washington, D.C., gift of Chester Dale.

Fig. J–12 *Francesco Saverio, Cardinal de Zelada*, Mengs, p. 363, courtesy of The Art Institute of Chicago.

Fig. J–13 *John Tyler*, Healy, p. 363, J–14 *George Washington*, Peale, p. 363, Fig. J–18 *George Clymer, c. 1810*, anonymous, p. 364, and Fig. J–20 *Paul Wayland Bartlett 1865–1925*, Pearce, p. 364, by permission of the National Portrait Gallery, Smithsonian Institution, Washington, D.C.

Fig. J–15 *Mrs. Grace Dalrymple Elliott*, Gainsborough, p. 364, by permission of The Metropolitan Museum of Art, bequest of William K. Vanderbilt, 1920.

Fig. J–16 *Vinnie Ream*, Healy, p. 364, by permission of the National Collection of Fine Arts, Smithsonian Institution.

Fig. J–17 *Madame de Caumartin as Hebe*, Jean-Marc Nattier, p. 364, by permission of the National Gallery of Art, Washington, D.C., Samuel H. Kress Collection.

Fig. J–19 *Portrait of a Man, 1647*, Helst, p. 364, by permission of The Metropolitan Museum of Art, gift of John Bard, 1872.

STAGE MAKEUP

PART ONE

PRINCIPLES OF MAKEUP

1

MAKEUP AND THE ACTOR

No makeup is complete without an actor underneath, for makeup does not in itself create character—it only helps to reveal it. And precisely the right kind of makeup can, as an integral part of the characterization, illuminate the character for the actor as well as for the audience and provide a believable character portrait.

In developing his technical skill in makeup, it is essential for the actor, first of all, to learn to observe people closely and analytically, mentally cataloging details of skin coloring and texture, bone structure, hair growth, conformation of wrinkles and sagging flesh, and so on, always matching these with the kind of person on which they are found. Then, he must understand the principles involved in recreating these effects on his own face—simple principles of light and shade and of color that have

been used by artists for centuries. And lastly, it is necessary to learn to apply his understanding and his observation to the use of specific tools and techniques of makeup in order that it may be used to accentuate and to extend what he, the actor, has already accomplished.

As stated in the preface, this book is intended for both the actor and the makeup artist. In the theater it is essential that the actor be skilled in makeup, though he may need at times to rely on the professional makeup artist when particularly difficult or unusual technical problems are presented. Like speech and body movement, makeup is part of an actor's craft, and the actor who neglects his makeup risks failure to project visually the precise and carefully drawn character-concept he has in his mind. His body is his sole means of

Figures 1–1 and 1–2. Actor with and without makeup.

3

visual communication with his audience, and neglect of a single visual aid will certainly lessen the possible impact of his performance and may spell the difference between success and failure.

Although the makeup artist can, through his great technical knowledge and skill, be of invaluable service to the actor in many ways, he should not be relied upon to do work the actor ought, more logically, to do for himself. No other person can understand the character the actor wants to project quite so well as he himself can. Therefore, the actor who must rely on the skill of the makeup artist is an artistic cripple. He may have the use of all of his faculties but one, but without that one he can never really stand on his own.

The makeup artist, on the other hand, can go beyond the actor in developing skills that the actor simply has no time or no real need to learn. It is the makeup artist and not the actor who needs to be able to ventilate beards on net, for example, to make plaster casts and latex prosthetic pieces, and, with his critical and objective eye, to appraise the completed makeup from the house under stage lights.

But whether the skill is the actor's or the makeup artist's or a combination of the two, the basis for all makeup lies in the character that is being brought to life. A makeup that functions positively in helping the actor to project his character is performing a service to the actor, to the playwright, and to the audience.

2

CHARACTER ANALYSIS

One of the basic purposes of most makeup is, by making suitable changes in the actor's physical appearance, to assist him in the creation of a character. It seems reasonable, therefore, that our study of makeup should begin with an examination of the principles of character analysis.

The first step in arriving at a suitable image for the character is to study the play. Directly through the stage directions and indirectly through the dialogue we come to know the character. We become acquainted not only with his physical appearance but with his background, environment, personality, age, and relationships with other characters in the play. Although this probing into the character is basically an acting problem, it is also essential preparation for the makeup, and it is important that we be able to translate the information into visual terms.

Take, for example, Cyrano's nose. This would appear at first glance to be the basis for Cyrano's makeup. But is it sufficient to put on a big nose and let it go at that? Without it there is no Cyrano, but there is a good deal more that we must know in order to bring the man to life.

To what extent, we may ask, is the nose comic and to what extent tragic? What elements of nobility and courage and kindness should appear in the visual impression aside from the one exaggerated feature? And from a purely practical point of view we must ask what effect any given shape of nose will have on a particular actor's face. A nose which is exactly right for Cyrano on one face may on another appear so outrageously grotesque that the visual characterization is destroyed.

Such questions as these should be asked not only about Cyrano but about any character you are analyzing. And, in answering each question, there is a choice to be made. You may not always make the right choice, but you should make a definite one. A fine makeup, like a fine painting or a fine performance, is a product of thorough preparation, intelligent selection, and meticulous execution.

You may wish, for example, to reflect specifically in an actor's face his state of health, his disposition, and his occupation. When these are specified in the script, it is essential not to deny them in the makeup. If Marguerite Gautier plays her death scene with rosy cheeks and a bloom of health, the credulity of the audience is going to be severely strained. Or if a pale, sallow-complexioned character is supposed to be a deep sea fisherman just back from a month in Florida, the more alert members of the audience may suspect a sinister twist of the plot. Therefore, it is essential, at the very least, to provide the minimum requirements of the physical appearance so as to correlate what the audience sees with what it hears. But beyond this you have an obligation to use the resources of makeup creatively to solve more subtle problems.

It is, for example, not only possible but commonplace to find members of the same family who have similar backgrounds and similar environments, as well as a family resemblance, but who are still very different—as, for example, Goneril and Cordelia in *King Lear*. Since these differences are crucial to the play, surely it will help both the actresses and the audience if they can be reflected in the makeup. This requires an analysis to determine what the character should, or might, look like.

Such an analysis can be simplified by classify-

Figure 2–1. Lady in waiting, in *Elizabeth the Queen*. **Figure 2–2.** Opar, in *Winged Victory*. **Figure 2–3.** Queen of Hearts, in *Through the Looking Glass*. Student makeups by Elaine Herman, illustrating differences in age, environment, temperament, and race. There is also a difference in style—the first two being realistic and the third, stylized.

ing the determinants of physical appearance into six groups—*heredity, race, environment, temperament, health,* and *age*. These are not, of course, mutually exclusive. Race, for example, is merely a subdivision of heredity, but it presents such a special problem that it requires individual and specific attention. Nor are the six groups usually of equal importance in analyzing a character. Race, for example, may be a basic consideration in such a play as *Raisin in the Sun* and of no significance at all in a play like *Waiting for Godot*, which was, in fact, performed on Broadway with both white and black casts. Temperament is obviously a more important consideration than environment in studying such a character as Lady Macbeth, whereas with Blanche in *A Streetcar Named Desire* both environment and temperament are basic to an understanding of the character and the play. In any character analysis, therefore, it is well to concentrate one's attention on those groups which are of most significance to the character. It is not important to know precisely in which group any specific feature or character trait belongs. The divisions are laid out merely as a practical aid in organizing one's research.

HEREDITY

Without going into problems of genetics, we can say that generally speaking this group includes those characteristics, physical and mental, with

which a person is born. The red hair of all the boys in *Life With Father* is obviously hereditary. Since it is required by the play, there is no choice to be made. But in most instances we must decide for ourselves such questions as the color of the hair, the shape of the nose, and the line of the eyebrow, and we must base our decision on a knowledge of the relationship between physical features and character and personality. We must beware of the attitude that one kind of feature will do as well as another. In the character analysis it is our problem to choose exactly the kind of feature that will tell the audience most about the character and that will best support the character portrait the actor is trying to present. Since this is the subject of the next chapter, we need not elaborate here but can merely specify it as one of the items to be noted and used in the analysis.

RACE

Racial differences bring up special makeup problems that require a solution somewhat less obvious than it might seem at first glance. In makeup in general there has been an unfortunate tendency to rely upon types rather than individuals. This is particularly pernicious in dealing with different races and nationalities. If we are Caucasians, we tend to think of Orientals, Negroes, and Indians as each belonging to a clearly defined group with an invariable set of specific characteristics involving color of skin, type of hair, form of features, and other physical traits. This is untenable simply because it is untrue. It is true that pink skins are not characteristic of Negroes, Orientals, or Indians; but within the general color limits of the race there is still variety, particularly in view of widespread intermingling of the races. Similarly, there are very definite trends in shape of features and kind of hair, and the trends are sufficiently clear-cut to make each race identifiable. But that still leaves considerable latitude for individual characterization. If we have a Japanese character in an American play, for example, how often is the Japanese character analyzed in terms of his environment? To most people a Japanese makeup is a Japanese makeup. Yet if we do a Japanese play (*Rashomon*, for example), are we to make up all the characters alike? Let us hope not. Non-Caucasion characters in a Caucasian play should be revealed as no less individual than the rest of the characters.

As the racial question becomes more subtle (in dealing with various strains of the Caucasian race, for example), it usually decreases in importance. It is true that a Norwegian must be clearly distinguished from an Italian, but the distinction can usually be made quite satisfactorily in coloring, which is hardly a major problem. To distinguish between an Englishman and an Irishman is of considerably less importance (to the makeup artist, that is—not, perhaps, to the Englishman or the Irishman).

Appendix E includes a guide to the characteristics of the various races and racial strains. These are of no particular importance now and can be referred to when needed. But the information there, brief though it is, should be used with the discussion on these pages in mind. It must be looked upon not as definitive but as a practical guide.

ENVIRONMENT

In addition to race and other hereditary factors, environment is of considerable importance in determining the color and texture of the skin. A farmer and a bookkeeper are likely to have different colors of skin, and a color which is right for one would probably look incongruous on the other. A man who has lived all of his life in the Arctic is not likely to look the same as his twin brother who has lived most of his life on the equator.

One must take into consideration not only the general climatic conditions of the part of the world in which the character lives but also the physical conditions under which he works and spends his leisure time. Offices, mines, fields, foundries, night clubs, basements, and country estates all have different effects upon the people who work or live in them. But remember that a character may have had a variety of environments. Monsieur Madeleine in Hugo's *Les Misérables* may be a wealthy and highly respected mayor, but his physical appearance will still bear the marks of his years of imprisonment as the convict Jean Valjean.

If environment is to be construed as referring to all external forces and situations affecting the individual, then custom or fashion may logically be considered a part of the environmental influences, and a very important one. Influences arising from social customs and attitudes have throughout the centuries brought about superficial and self-imposed changes in appearance.

During most of the first half of the twentieth century it was assumed that men's hair would be short and that women's hair would be longer. A man might be capable of growing long hair and might even prefer long hair, but social pressures were at work to discourage him. During other periods of history, however, customs were different, and men wore their hair long and in some periods wore wigs. The drawings in Appendix G indicate the great variety in hair styles through the centuries, and, of course, those styles must be taken into consideration in analyzing a character and planning his makeup.

Similarly, the wearing of makeup off stage has varied throughout the centuries. If an eighteenth-century fop appears to be wearing makeup, no harm is done because he might very well have done so, but if any of the men in a realistic mid-twentieth century play are obviously made up, they immediately become less believable.

Furthermore, styles in street makeup vary. The plucked eyebrows, brilliant rouge, and bizarre lips of the late twenties would seem anachronistic in most other periods. Similar eccentricities—such as the heavy, stylized eye makeup of the ancient Egyptians—can be found for other periods in history. (For information on fashions in makeup, see Appendix F.)

Remember that, on the stage, makeup should look like makeup only when the character would normally be wearing it. That means that your character must be analyzed in the light of social customs to determine not only possible hair styles but also the accepted usage in regard to makeup.

For every character that you make up, always analyze the skin color, hair style, and street makeup in terms of environmental influences.

TEMPERAMENT

An individual's temperament, which can be interpreted as including personality, disposition, and personal habits, affects his physical appearance in many ways.

The adventurer and the scholar, the Bohemian artist and the shrewd business man, the prizefighter and the philosopher—all are widely different in temperament, and these differences are to a greater or lesser degree apparent in the physical appearance. The convivial Sir Toby Belch and the melancholy Sir Andrew Aguecheek, for example, are, aside from all other differences, widely contrasting in temperament and could not conceivably look alike.

The March sisters in *Little Women* are products of the same environment and the same heredity; yet temperamental differences make them strongly individual, and their individuality should be reflected in the makeup.

In addition to these intrinsic differences, there are others that involve conscious choices by the character himself. These are related to the matter of makeup and hair discussed under "Environment." It may be, for example, that bizarre makeup was the custom in the twenties, but not every girl used it. Perhaps well-bred girls in 1900 did not wear obvious makeup, but there were not-so-well-bred girls who did.

A shy, mousy librarian in, say, 1953 would certainly not be ostracized if she wore false eyelashes, but it is most unlikely that she would do so. And the idea of her wearing green eyeshadow is preposterous. Yet green eyeshadow might be quite right for a dissolute, aging actress, such as Tennessee Williams' leading character in *Sweet Bird of Youth*. For that matter, it would be quite acceptable in the same period for any fashionable young woman, but not all fashionable young women would choose to wear it. By the mid-sixties colored eyeshadow had become nearly as commonplace as lipstick had been previously and was therefore less useful in suggesting temperament and personality.

The hair is an even more striking and obvious reflection of personality. Granted, it depends first of all on fashion, but to what extent the fashion is followed depends on personality. One would expect the mature and socially correct Mrs. Higgins in *Pygmalion* to have her hair beautifully done, not a hair out of place, perhaps not in the latest fashion but in one considered proper for a woman of her years and of her elevated social station. The Cockney flower girl, Eliza Doolittle, on the other hand, might be expected to give her hair no attention at all, except, perhaps, to push it out of her eyes. When she is transformed into a "lady," her hair, as well as everything else about her, must reflect the change. It is, in fact, an integral part of it.

There are fewer opportunities for men to express their personality in this way, but the ones which exist must not be slighted. When a beard or a mustache is to be worn, it offers an opportunity to reflect personality. First of all comes the choice of whether to wear facial hair at all. And the choice is always related to fashion. In other words, it would take as much courage not to wear a moustache or a beard in 1870 as it would to wear one in, say, 1940. In 1960 it would take less courage than in 1940, but the mere fact of wearing a beard would still be significant and a clear reflection of personality. By 1970 beards were generally acceptable—even fashionable to a degree—but certainly not obligatory.

Secondly, once the decision to wear the beard has been made, there is the equally important decision as to what kind of beard to wear. Again, this depends on fashion. We must know first of all what kind of beards were being worn in the period. If fashions were very limiting, there is less freedom of choice; if the character departs from the fashion (and there are always those who do), it is doubly significant. But there are several periods in history, especially in the late nineteenth century, for example, when facial hair was the rule and the style was limited only by the imagination, taste, and hair-growing capability of the individual. In such a period there is an extraordinary opportunity to express personality through conscious choice of style in facial hair.

The same principles apply, as well, to hair on the head. There are often limitations on styles for men, but even during periods when convention is very restrictive, as in the second quarter of the twentieth century, there is still some variation in length, in wave or absence of it, in the part, and in color.

An interesting case of temperamental differences resulting in both conscious and unconscious physical changes is found in the *Madwoman of Chaillot.* There are, in fact, four madwomen, each completely different from the others temperamentally, each showing that difference in her face. Countess Aurelia, the Madwoman of Chaillot, is calm, compassionate, clever, rather tragic, and completely charming. Mme. Constance, the Madwoman of Passy, is garrulous, argumentative, bad tempered, flighty, and quick to take offense. Mlle. Gabrielle, the Madwoman of St. Sulpice, is shy, retiring, and easily hurt. And Mme. Joséphine, the Madwoman of La Concorde, is forthright, practical, and very businesslike. A makeup that would be appropriate for one of the madwomen would be completely wrong for any of the others.

These are not problems to be faced only with certain striking characters, like the madwomen or Sir Toby Belch, or on special occasions when circumstances demand it. They should be considered and solved for every character.

An actress of 25 who is playing a contemporary character of 25 must not assume that her own hair style or her own way of making up her eyebrows or her lips will automatically be suitable for the character. The problem becomes particularly acute in stock when an actor is playing a different role every week, sometimes with very little variation in age. It is then more important than ever that ways of distinguishing among the characters be found. This means finding the most revealing ways in which the character might express himself and using these to help develop individuality in the makeup.

HEALTH

In most cases a character's state of health has nothing to do with the play. But sometimes, as with Mimi or Camille, there are noticeable changes that are important to the characterization or the plot. At other times, as with Elizabeth Barrett or with Laura in *The Glass Menagerie,* there is no specific illness, just a state of delicate health. Or a character may be undernourished and must give physical evidence of this. By contrast, there are those who are overnourished and suffer from gout. And there are others who are bursting with health and should show it in their faces.

Even when the health is not normal, a specific illness is rarely indicated. It is seldom necessary, therefore, to try to reproduce medically accurate physical symptoms. Any physical suggestion of the illness can usually be confined to changes in the skin color, the eyes, and perhaps the hair. As always, it is better to do too little than too much. Above all, avoid attributing to certain illnesses specific physical symptoms that are inaccurate and that will immediately be spotted by doctors and nurses in the audience. In certain areas of makeup it is best to curb the imagination and rely strictly on factual information.

AGE

Since age invariably affects all people in physical terms, it is an essential consideration in every makeup, but it is not necessarily the most important one. How old is Falstaff, for example, or Lady Macbeth? Is it important to know precisely? Are there not more important facts to know about those particular characters? Before beginning the makeup, there must be some definite decision made about the age, and that decision will rest with the actor and the director. But in makeup we are interested in the apparent, not the actual, age, and this depends on the kind of life the person has led and how he feels about it. Thus, the environment may have affected his apparent age, but so have his mental attitudes. Are they positive or negative? Is he cheerful or morose? Does he feel sorry for himself, or is he glad to be alive? Does he look forward or backward? And how old does he *think* he is? Is he conscious of getting older each year, or in his own mind does time seem to have stopped for him? Does he really *want* to remain young? An analysis based on such questions as these should give you some idea of the character's apparent age.

Remember also that apparent age is related to nutrition and thus involves health, which depends on both nutrition and mental attitudes. As you can see, the various factors affecting the appearance are in many cases interrelated and cannot always be considered separately.

But suppose it is already indicated in the script that a female character is supposed to look 50, regardless of what her chronological age may be. Then you may wish to use your analysis to determine the specific ways in which that particular woman will look 50. A hard-working charwoman of 40 will look 50 in quite a different way from a society woman of 65 who takes care of herself and looks 50. Obviously, in determining exactly how to express the apparent age of 50 in each case we must also deal with questions of heredity, environment, temperament, and health. And it is for that reason that the question of age has been left until last—its effects can never be determined without reference to the total character, past and present.

In discussing specific effects of age, we can only generalize and indicate the kind of changes that may take place. The conventional divisions of youth, middle age, and old age are serviceable for this discussion.

Youth. There is an unfortunate custom in the theater of referring to any youthful makeup as a *straight* makeup. This means simply that you do nothing but heighten the color and project the features. Designating a makeup as "straight" is a trap that leads to neglect of essential work. Conceivably, the term has a certain validity in the event that a specific role is so cast that the actor's features are precisely right, with not a hair to be changed. But he must be perfect. If there is anything about him that is not right, then he requires a makeup that will change him to fit the character he is playing, and this we call a *character* makeup.

Figure 2–4. **Youth.** Note smooth skin, full lips and eyebrows, and gentle curves, characteristic of youth.

Now, there are instances when there is no clearly defined character, or perhaps no character at all. In photographic portraiture, in some platform appearances, sometimes in choruses, it is expected that the actor appear as himself, but it is rare to find an actor who cannot profit by some improvement in his face. And a straight makeup does not improve—it merely projects. When we wish to improve the actor's face without relating it to a specific character, we use a *corrective* makeup. This is not, however, a term that is used to refer exclusively to youthful makeups.

Makeup for youth, then—except when an actor is appearing as himself—requires a character analysis. The physical attributes of youthfulness (see Figures 2–4 and J–16) are usually a smooth skin, a good deal of color in the face, a delicately curved mouth, smooth brows following the shape of the eye, an abundance of hair, and so on. Those are, of course, average characteristics. Heredity, environment, temperament, and health may counteract the normal effects of youth, as in the case of Richard III. Despite the fact that Richard is a young man at the time of the play, he is hardly an average, normal one. Although there may be little in the face to suggest age, it will probably not seem particularly youthful. Temperament and environment will have had strong influences on his physical appearance.

Ophelia is a young girl, but her profound unhappiness and confusion, which finally result in a complete mental breakdown and suicide, must certainly, along with other elements in her personality, be reflected in some way, however subtly, in the makeup.

Middle age. This is an indefinite period somewhere in the middle of life. It reaches its climax perhaps in the 50's or even the 60's, depending on the individual. For purposes of this discussion it can be considered as including all ages between 40 and 65. But remember that in earlier times middle age came much sooner. In any case, as has already been pointed out, it is the apparent rather than the actual age that is important in makeup.

Age can, and too often does, bring with it changes in the color of the skin and the hair, sagging muscles, falling hair, and increasing angularity in the lips, eyebrows, and cheeks, but the exact nature of these changes will depend on factors other than age. So it is important in every case to determine how seriously and in what ways age has

Figures 2–5 and 2–6. Friedrich von Kaulbach. Self-portraits at about age 32 and a few years later. Note subtle changes indicative of aging.

Figures 2–7 and 2–8. Martin Luther in youth and age. Engravings by Cranach.

affected the appearance. And remember that the effects of age are modified radically by health, environment, temperament, and mental habits. (For color portraits of middle-aged people, see Figures J–11, J–12, and J–18).

Old age. As a person advances beyond middle life, the skull structure usually becomes more prominent (Figure 14–54), especially if he is thin. If he is fat, there will be a greater tendency toward flabbiness, with pouches and puffs and double chins (Figure 2–8). Along with a general sagging of the flesh, the tip of the nose may droop (Figure 14–47B), hair may fall out (Figure 18–20), eyebrows may become bushy or scraggly (Figure 14–47D), lips almost invariably become thinner (Figure 14–47A), teeth may fall out (Figure 14–47B), skin and hair color will probably change (Figure J-13), the neck may become scrawny (Figure 14–38C) and the hands bony (Figure 14–56C), and the face may be a mass of wrinkles (Figure 14–47D). It is up to you to decide which of these effects apply to your character. Again, changes will be affected by health, environment, temperament, and mental attitudes.

The foregoing analysis is one that you should apply to most characters for which you create a makeup—with the obvious exception of such characters as goblins, fairies, devils, witches, vampires, and so on. The analysis will obviously involve some time in studying the play and discussing the character with the actor and the director. If you are an actor doing your own makeup, then your problem will be simplified. Following such a plan of character analysis means, of course, that all consideration of makeup cannot be left until the night of dress rehearsal. It is something that should be planned as carefully as the sets and the costumes.

The creative aspect of makeup lies in the mind of the artist and stems directly from his understanding of the character. If, before you sit down at your dressing table, you have intelligently planned in specific terms the physical changes you wish to make, you will have mastered the creative part of your problem and will have left only the technical one of executing your ideas.

PROBLEM

1. What impressions do you get from the faces in Figure 3–4? Perhaps it would be helpful to consider the following questions: Which looks the more intelligent—A or B? Which, the more determined—C or G? Which, the weaker—D or H? Which, the more sensitive—E or I? Which appears to have more emotional warmth—F or I? Which do you think would be the stronger leader—C or D?

3

PHYSIOGNOMY

Probably since the beginning of the human race men have observed other men and drawn conclusions from their appearance as to their probable behavior. Through trial and error, certain correlations have been found that seem to hold up with reasonable consistency. Just as people draw these conclusions consciously or unconsciously in daily life, so they continue to do it when they go to the theater and see characters on the stage. The actor, if he chooses, can turn this to his advantage by becoming consciously aware of the correlations of physical appearance with character and personality traits. The actor who chooses not to do this consciously may be doing it unconsciously. But if he isn't, he is taking the risk of assuming physical characteristics that could mislead the audience and detract from the believability of his character.

The practice of relating physical appearance to character and personality traits is defined by the dictionary as *physiognomy*. A familiarity with some of the principles of physiognomy can be enormously helpful to the actor in designing a face for his character.

Much of this you already do—most of it unconsciously. Look, for example, at the faces in Figure 3–1. Though they happen to be of real people, they might well be sketches of characters from plays. Think, if you can, of specific characters for which some of the faces would be suitable. Having found a character for a particular face, ask yourself why it suits the character. Is it a strong face or a weak one? Does it look optimistic or pessimistic? sensitive or crude? aggressive or timid? determined or vacillating? intelligent or stupid? Can you determine what there is about the face that causes you to react as you do?

Whether your response to the face is intuitive or analytical, it comes under the heading of physiognomy, and it is essentially what the audience does in relation to every character on the stage. Actors would thus do well to be aware of the ways in which an audience may relate physical appearance to personality and character traits. The purpose of this chapter, therefore, is to offer guidance in making physical changes that will support the actor's characterization and in avoiding changes that will tend to deny, in the minds of the audience, what the actor is trying to express.

In making changes in the face, remember that you are dealing with a whole face, not just a single feature, and those changes you do make will inevitably be affected by other areas of the face. For example, faces A and B in Figure 3–4 both have long, projecting noses, an indication of inquisitiveness. But the kind of inquisitiveness such a nose indicates will be affected by the kind of face it is a part of and its relationship to other parts of the face. Is it part of a reasonably harmonious whole, as in A, or is there disharmony in the face, as in B? This would suggest a positive interpretation for A —such as "intellectual curiosity"—confirmed, in this case, by the eyes and the forehead. In B the face is poorly proportioned—the forehead suggests the possibility of a fairly low intellect, and the eyes would probably collect sense impressions but there would not be much analysis or deep thought; furthermore, the mouth shows little mental control and confirms the impression of questionable intellect. The inquisitiveness of B, therefore, is more likely to be negative, perhaps excessive curiosity about other people's affairs.

This is a very simplified analysis. Its purpose is merely to alert you not only to the possibilities for interpreting faces but also to the dangers of ascribing to a particular feature a specific interpretation unrelated to the face of which it is a part.

The discussion in this chapter is confined to features that are relatively easy to change yet can have great potential for helping the actor create his character. These features are the eyes, the nose, and the mouth. In using this information, remem-

ber that it includes only a relatively small number of details that may be of practical use to the makeup artist. It is not a scientific study to be used as a basis for analyzing one's friends.

EYES

Perhaps no other feature betrays the inner man so clearly as his eyes. In general, prominent eyes (Figure 3–3F) are found on dreamers and aesthetes who live largely through their senses, whereas deep-set eyes (Figure 3–3H) are more likely to be an

Figure 3–1. Sketches from history. (A) C. M. Wieland, learned German writer and poet; (B) Miss Coutts, Englishwoman noted for her compassion; (C) Lucretia Mott, Quaker preacher; (D) Rev. John G. Lavater, Swiss poet and writer on physiognomy; (E) John Broughton, English pugilist; (F) Thomas D'Urfey, English writer of humorous poetry; (G) Rev. S. H. Tyng; (H) King George III; (I) J. B. Porta, Italian mathematician and scientific writer, inventor of the Camera Obscura; (J) Lord George Lyttleton, eminent English historian who was unable to master the multiplication table; (K) John Pierpont, New England minister and reformer; (L) George Bush, minister, professor, and theologian.

indication of an observant, analytical mind. We might say that one is the eye of a Romeo, the other of a Cassius. Many eyes will be neither strongly one nor the other, and thus the individuality might be expected to include characteristics of both types.

Small eyes, close together, with a well-developed brow tend to give a look of shrewdness.

Prominent, heavy-lidded eyes with an arching brow placed high above the eye (Figure 3–3D) may be an indication of credulity and a not-overly-active mind. This kind of eye would, in a different face, be appropriate for Bottom.

The eyes and the mouth often change markedly during one's lifetime. We usually associate the changes with the aging process, but the kind of changes that take place will depend upon the sort of mental, emotional, and physical life one leads. The kind of wrinkles which develop through frequent laughter, for example, quite logically suggest a happy, kindly disposition.

EYEBROWS

Here we have one of the most expressive and easily changed features of all. Even a slight change in the eyebrow can affect the whole face. Eyebrows vary in placement, line, thickness, color, length, and direction of the hairs. Heavy eyebrows (Figure 3–2A,H) are usually associated with energy, physical or mental, whereas faintly developed brows (Figure 3–2F) suggest less energy, sometimes even weakness and vacillation, provided other indications support this. Suppose we consider Beethoven and Mendelssohn. Judging from the music, we might assume that Beethoven was probably the more energetic of the two, and we find that his eyebrows were much the heavier. Heavy brows are also found on many military men. Julius Caesar, Hannibal, Richard Coeur de Lion, Wellington, Cromwell, Charles XII —all had heavy brows. And we find equally heavy ones on Plato, Galileo, and Cicero.

Bushy eyebrows with smooth hair (Figure 3–2A) suggest a vigorous personality. If the hairs of the brow are erratic (Figure 14–12F), they suggest an erratic mind.

It has already been noted that high, arched brows (Figure 3–3D) are associated with credulity and lack of concentration. They may also suggest a lack of initiative and a preference for following other people's ideas, and they are inconsistent with the traits of firmness and forcefulness. The heavi-

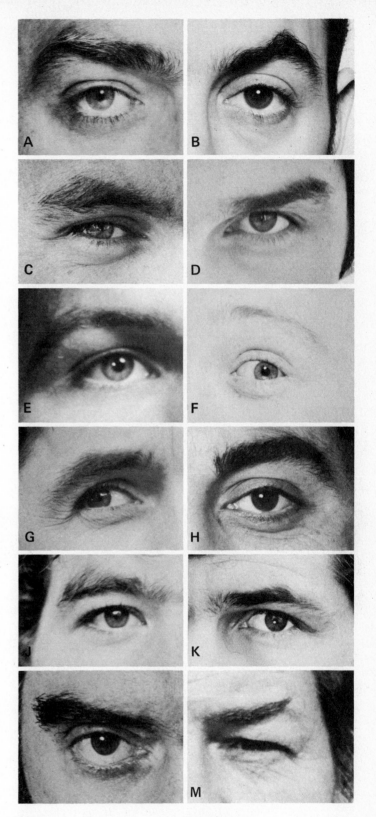

Figure 3–2. Character in eyes and eyebrows.

ness of the eyebrow has something to do with this impression of strength and so does the eye. In Figure 3–2, for example, the eyebrow in L is somewhat more forceful than the one in D, yet the deeper set eye in D results in a generally more forceful look.

15

Figure 3–3. Faces and features.

In F neither the kind of eyebrow nor its placement suggests any firmness or forcefulness at all.

Straight eyebrows (Figure 3–3H) suggest a matter-of-fact, practical personality. In general, smooth eyebrows that slant upward (Figure 3–2A) are an indication of optimism, but when the brows are knit at the inner corners, this interpretation does not apply. Brows that slant downward may, with negative indications in the face, show pessimism (Figure 14–38J) or egotism. Brows that angle upward in almost a straight line (Figure 3–2M) have an unsympathetic effect. They might be used for Scrooge.

If you want to suggest treachery or cunning, you may find it helpful to put a curve or a wave in a brow which is angled upward (Figure H–12). This would be an appropriate brow for Iago or

Richard III and is, in fact, the brow of Henry VIII. If the inside corners of the brow are drawn downward and together but the outer corners seem to be lifted (Plate 11–*l*), the impression is created of an individual who is abrupt and egotistical.

NOSE

The nose is the one bony feature that is relatively easy to remodel in three dimensions. As we all know, a very little added to or subtracted from the nose can, like a change in the eyebrows, alter the whole face. And since the change is so dramatic, it is important that the right kind of change be made.

This does not mean, for example, that a military leader must always have a large, strongly developed nose. But at the same time, if such a character is given a delicate nose with a turned-up tip, the actor may find his characterization taking a different turn from the one he had anticipated. Whereas he intended to be strong and implacable, he may seem only blustering and comic. If he wishes to be comic, fine. If not, it behooves him to choose a nose that will seem suitable to the audience.

In general, it is important to remember that beautiful, delicate modeling in the nose, whatever its size, gives an impression of a similar delicacy or sensitivity in the personality. Crudeness in the personality may well be reflected in crudeness in the nose structure. This refers largely to inherent character traits, not to superimposed ones, since the nose changes relatively little (as compared to the eyes and the mouth) and is related primarily to qualities with which one is born.

Noses can be classified as to size, length, breadth, and shape (in profile). In general, greater size suggests greater forcefulness and energy. As mentioned previously, a long nose that projects outward (Figure 3–4A) is usually a sign of inquisitiveness—intellectual or otherwise, but a long nose that lies closer to the face (Figure 15–4P) is likely to reveal a more cautious, secretive, sometimes pessimistic nature. It has been found that short noses (Figure 14–47E) tend to indicate cheerfulness and optimism.

Breadth in a nose (Figure 14–47D) adds energy and endurance. Narrow noses show greater delicacy and refinement (Figure 3–3C) but are not particularly sympathetic, though other qualities in the face may counteract this.

The Roman nose is one of authority. It is often found on military leaders, as well as on prominent men in all fields. Long or large Roman noses are more forceful than short or small ones, but any convexity on the bridge of the nose tends to add some force to the character. One that lies close to

Figure 3–4. Profiles.

the face (Figure 15–4P) tends to show more stubbornness than one that projects outward (Figure 15–4H).

The Grecian nose (Figure 3–3E) suggests refinement, taste, and sensitivity. It is now rarely found in its pure form.

The Aquiline nose (Figure H–32), which has a gradual curve from root to tip rather than a slight angle at the bridge, is more refined than the Roman. It might be considered an aristocratic and resolute nose. Breadth and length contribute to the strength of the nose.

The concave nose (Figure 15–4L) is non-aggressive and tends to be good natured but can also be capricious or stubborn. When small and delicately formed, it is considered charming or cute. With a markedly turned-up tip (Figure 15–4E), it is called *retroussé*. Whereas the convex nose adds forcefulness, the concave reduces it. Imagine, if you can, a Lady Macbeth with a small, delicate, turned-up nose or a Snow White with a large Roman one. Interpretations, as always, should be modified by size, width, length, and closeness to the face.

A straight nose turned up at the end (Figure 15–4I) seems to convey a feeling of optimism and enthusiasm and a general curiosity about life. This impression is modified considerably if the nose is coarsely formed (Figure H–10). A turned-down tip (Figure 3–1J) may accompany coldness and deliberateness and sometimes melancholy. Shortness combined with broadness (Figure 3–1K) shows vitality.

The nose does change slightly throughout life, and it is a matter of common observation that with dissipation and overindulgence the change will be in the direction of coarseness (Figure 15–5C). Fine concentration in thought and action and an active self-control may tend to refine and sharpen the lines.

MOUTH

The size of the mouth, the line of the mouth (up, down, or straight), and the thickness and color of the lips all affect the impression created. Shy, introverted, or self-centered people tend to contract the mouth, whereas genial, outgoing people tend to expand it (Figure 14–46F). Any competent actor should do this with a minimum of help from the makeup. Compare the sympathetic, compassionate Abraham Lincoln with the self-centered Henry

VIII—the one with a large, expansive mouth, the other with a tiny, contracted one.

A straight mouth gives an impression of firmness and decision. This impression is increased if the lips are thin, and softened if they are full. An upward curve to the mouth normally indicates more warmth and sociability. This, if genuine, can be confirmed by the eyes. If not genuine (Figure 3–3A, for example), it can be more calculating than friendly.

A downward curve (Figure 14–48D) suggests pessimism or severity.

Tightly closed or compressed lips (Figure 15–9I) are determined, severe, or forceful, whereas more loosely held lips (Figure 15–9K) show more emotional warmth.

Thin lips (Figure 14–47F) suggest reserve, caution, formality, precision, sometimes coldness—if confirmed elsewhere in the face. They may indicate seriousness or, if there is humor, it may be sarcastic, particularly if there are upward sweeping eyebrows. All of this might, of course, be contradicted by large, prominent eyes.

Full lips (Figure 14–46J) show greater warmth and fuller emotional expression. They are an indication of a more affectionate, sympathetic, and sociable nature, though with negative indications, they can be self-indulgent and indolent. Full lips hanging loose (Figure 3–4B) can be excessively emotional and lacking in control.

Determination and tenacity are frequently found to accompany a large mouth with the upper lip drawn down and the under one rolled outward, especially if supported by a strong chin. Abraham Lincoln (Figure H–36L) provides an excellent example.

Increased color in the lips goes with greater warmth in the personality and relates to full lips rather than thin ones.

It cannot be repeated too often that suggestions in this chapter are to be used only as guides, if you feel you need them. Use these brief suggestions with discretion and try always to correlate the features and not rely on only one to suggest the character. You will rarely be able to make all of the changes you consider ideal, but the purpose in a character analysis is to discover the determining factors in the character's behavior and then to visualize as nearly as possible what he should look like. Later you will have to meet the practical problem of recreating this image on the face of a specific actor. But always remember that a single feature should not be relied upon to define character.

PROBLEMS

1. In order to demonstrate how easily the eyebrows can be used to suggest character, draw two circles (representing eyes), and draw eyebrows over them. Then draw two more with a different kind of eyebrow. Do at least half a dozen or so. Or, if you prefer, use the same set of circles and keep changing the eyebrows.

2. Re-examine your answers to problem 1, Chapter 2. Would you now make any changes in them? If so, what? Can you now make them any more specific?

You might first study the face as a whole for general impressions, then examine the features to see which ones support that impression and which ones, if any, offer contradictions. If you are working in a class, compare and discuss your ideas. It will, of course, not be possible to reach any definite conclusions about who is right and who is wrong, but it should prove enlightening to compare reactions, and it should sharpen your awareness of faces.

3. Choose three characters from well-known plays and write brief descriptions of how you think they should look, being specific about such features as mouths, noses, and eyes. Do not be misled by photographs of actors who may have played the parts, for in those you are seeing the individual actor's interpretation, not the playwright's. Do not be concerned with practical problems of makeup.

4

FACIAL ANATOMY

The next step in preparing to make up the face is to examine the structure of bone, muscle, and cartilage that lies beneath the skin. In remodeling our own (or an actor's) face to fit a particular character, we need to know how the face is constructed. Even when we are merely trying to make our own face look its best, we need to be aware of its strong and its weak points so that we can emphasize the one and minimize the other. Thus, the makeup artist, before he ever opens his kit, should familiarize himself not only with the basic structure of a human face but with the particular structure of any face he makes up, whether it be his own or someone else's.

BONES OF THE FACE

A thorough and highly technical knowledge of anatomy, though not to be scorned, is not really essential to the makeup artist. It is not even necessary to remember the technical names of bones and muscles so long as you know where they are. There is, for example, no particular virtue in referring to the *zygomatic arch* when the term *cheekbone* is simpler and more generally understood. In a few instances, however, when the precise location of shadows and highlights is to be discussed, it is certainly advantageous to be able to refer to the exact area. The term *forehead* is useful only if we really mean the entire forehead, which in makeup we seldom do. There are two separate and distinct eminences, the *frontal* and the *superciliary*, which must ordinarily be considered separately in highlighting. In this case, then, the technical terms become useful, though it is possible to refer simply to the upper and lower forehead.

A knowledge of the bones of the face becomes increasingly important with the advancing of the character's age for the simple reason that muscles lose their tonus and begin to sag, flesh is no longer firm, and the face begins to take on the effect of a skull draped with skin. This is an effect impossible to achieve unless you know exactly where the bones of the skull are located.

Figure 4–1 shows a skull, stripped of all cartilage, muscle, and skin. This is the basic structure of all faces, though there are, naturally, variations in exact shapes of bones that provide the first step in distinguishing one individual from another.

Figure 4–2 is a diagrammatic representation of a skull indicating the names of the various bones and hollows (or fossae). The *maxilla* and the

Figure 4–1. A human skull. (From Lavater's *Essays on Physiognomy*.)

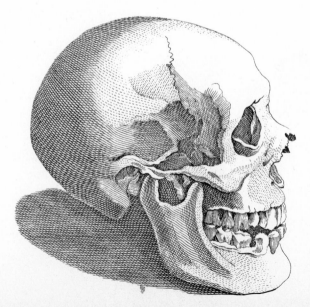

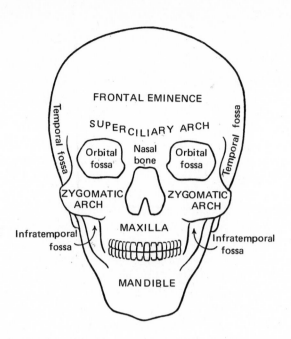

FRONTAL EMINENCE

SUPERCILIARY ARCH

Temporal fossa

Temporal fossa

Orbital fossa

Nasal bone

Orbital fossa

ZYGOMATIC ARCH

ZYGOMATIC ARCH

Infratemporal fossa

MAXILLA

Infratemporal fossa

MANDIBLE

Figure 4–2. Diagram of prominences and depressions in the human skull.

mandible are the upper and lower jaw, and the *nasal bone* is simply the bony part of the nose. But observe that only the upper section of the nose is part of the bony structure of the skull. The lower, more movable part is constructed of cartilage attached to the nasal bone.

We have already mentioned the importance of distinguishing between the two eminences of the forehead. In some individuals these are very clearly defined, especially when the source of light is from directly overhead, forming a slight shadow between the two. This can be seen in Figure 14–29A. In other individuals, the whole forehead may be smoothly rounded with no hint of a depression between the two normally prominent parts of the skull. If your own forehead is of the latter type, study someone else's so that you will understand the conformation.

The *cheekbone* or *zygomatic arch* is one of the most important bones of the face for the makeup artist. Many people have prominent cheekbones, easily located. But others may need to prod the flesh with the fingers in order to find its precise location. In studying the bones of your own face, you should locate them by feel as well as by sight. In the case of the cheekbone, prod the flesh along the entire length from the ear to the nose until you know its exact shape. It is especially important to find the top of the bone, then feel how it curves around underneath. Keep prodding until you can

locate accurately a distinct top and bottom to the bone, for it is at this point that most cheek modeling goes wrong. Figure 14–27, which shows a side view of the cheekbone, may clarify in your mind the general shape.

Then there are the hollows in the skull. The *orbital* hollows (the eye sockets) are clear-cut and easy to feel with your finger. The *temporal* hollows are what are normally referred to as the *temples.* These are not deep, but there is a slight depression which shows up increasingly with age (Figure H–8). The *infra-temporal* hollows you will have already found in the process of prodding the cheekbone. The lack of bony support here allows the flesh to sink in underneath the cheekbone, resulting in the familiar hollow-cheeked effect (Figure H–8). In extreme old age or starvation this sinking-in can be considerable.

Study the bone structure of your own face thoroughly. Then, if possible, study several different types of faces both visually and tactually.

The skull is, as you know, covered with various muscles, which operate the mandible (the only movable part of the skull) and the mouth, eyelids, and eyebrows. In order that the study of these may be made more immediately applicable, they will be discussed in Chapter 14 in connection with the individual features that they affect.

CONSTRUCTION OF A HEAD

The best way to arrive at a practical understanding of the structure of the head is actually to construct one. This should be done with artists' modeling clay (such as Plastolene) on a thin but sturdy board. A piece of Masonite about 12 × 16 inches will do very well. Only the front half of the head (from the ears forward) or perhaps the front third need be done. Figure 4–3 shows such a head being modeled.

In addition to familiarizing yourself with the construction of a human head, there are two additional advantages in working with clay. One is the actual practice in modeling features—an essential step in making any prosthetic addition to the face, whether it be of nose putty or latex. The other is having available a head that can be remodeled indefinitely. This makes it possible to study the three-dimensional form of sagging flesh, such as wrinkles or pouches, that you are trying to reproduce with paint, as well as to experiment with various shapes of noses, eyebrows, or chins in planning a makeup

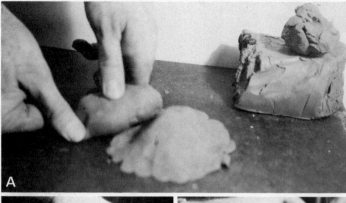

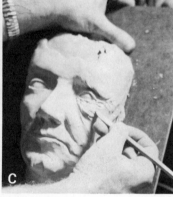

Figure 4-3. Modeling a head in clay. (A) Clay being pressed against the board to make certain that it sticks. (B) Head shaped and nose begun. (C) Completed head being aged with a modeling tool.

for a specific character. Once the original model is made, it should be kept for subsequent use. Clay heads are also useful for making papier-mâché masks or heads (Figure 4-4).

For the benefit of those who need help in modeling, the following section provides some fairly specific instructions on how to begin.

MODELING A HEAD IN CLAY

Five pounds of an oil-base clay will enable you to model a face of approximately life size. The area to be developed can be bounded by the hairline, a point just below the jaw, and a point halfway to the ear on either side (Figure 4-3C). If you wish to carry the head back as far as the ear, another three or four pounds of clay should be sufficient. The clay can be purchased in either five- or one-pound blocks. For easy working, it should be cut into half- or quarter-pound cubes. These cubes should be kneaded and worked with the hands until the mass is soft and pliable. As each piece is softened, it should be pressed to the board with the thumbs, as shown in Figure 4-3A, and additional pieces mashed onto it in the same way. If this is done properly, the completed face can be carried about or hung perpendicularly on the wall with no danger of the clay's pulling away from the board.

As each piece of clay is added, the general facial area to be developed should be kept in mind. A face about 7 to 9 inches long and about 5 or 6 inches wide works very well. Making a larger face from five pounds of clay results in too flat a construction, whereas a smaller face does not take full advantage of the material.

The softened clay (except for about half a pound, which will be used later) should be molded into a mound resembling half an egg sliced lengthwise. It is by cutting away and building up the various areas in this mound that the face is developed.

Figure 4-5A shows a stylized head construction, emphasizing its three-dimensional quality. In 4-5B you can see how this is related to a real head.

Figure 4-4. Making a severed head. Makeup instructor Bill Smith modeling a clay head (A), on which the papier-mâché head (B) was later constructed.

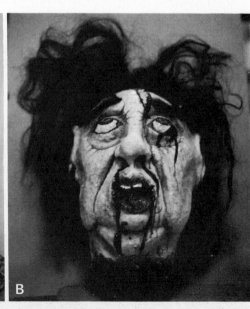

In many ways the head, especially the front half, is closer to a cube than to an egg. Although you will probably prefer to use the basic egg shape for your clay model, it is frequently helpful to visualize the cube in order to be sure that your head is really three-dimensional. It is important to be aware that the forehead, for example, has a front plane and two side planes (the temples). The depression for the eyes actually forms a sort of bottom to the forehead box, and of course the top of the head makes a rounded top.

The nose forms a smaller, elongated box with definite front, sides, and bottom. The front, sides, and bottom of the jaw should be clear-cut. Notice particularly the horseshoe shape of the teeth. Don't let your lips follow the flat plane of the forehead! Remember that there is a rounded arch of teeth that the lips must follow.

The classic face is divided into three equal parts horizontally, and that division should be your first step. The forehead occupies the top third, the eyes and nose the middle third, and the upper and lower jaws (including the mouth, of course) the lower third. It is a good idea to model the larger areas and develop the general shape of the head, defining the forehead, the jaw, and the eye sockets before starting on any detailed modeling.

Nose. This is usually the simplest single feature to model because its size and location can easily be changed without seriously disturbing the rest of the modeling. This is where you will use that extra bit of clay that was left over. In adding the clay here or elsewhere, it is best to add more than seems necessary, for it tends to be easier to cut away excess clay than to add on to a feature that has been carefully modeled and then found to be too small.

Figure 4–5C shows a breakdown of the nose into its component parts. Plane 1 represents the slender nasal bone, and 2 and 3 show the two planes of the cartilage that forms the tip. In 4 we see the roughly cylindrical flesh of the nostrils, with 5 representing the side planes. D shows the nose as it actually looks to the observer. But notice in both C and D the subtleties of shape.

The front plane of the nose (1 and 2) is not of even width all the way down. It is narrow at the bridge, then widens and narrows again slightly as it fits into the still wider cartilage of the tip (2). Examine a number of noses carefully to observe this construction. In some noses it will be quite obvious. In others the change will be so subtle that it will be difficult to distinguish it. On your clay

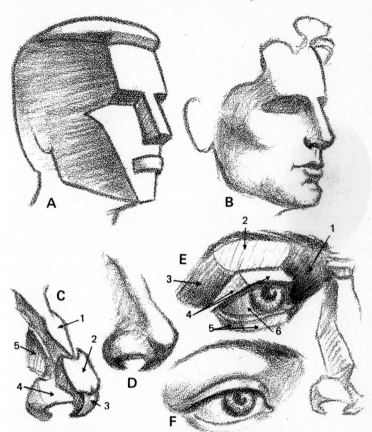

Figure 4–5. Planes of the face. A, C, and E show planes of the head, nose, and eye flattened to clarify the construction.

head, model these planes carefully to give the feeling of bone and cartilage beneath the skin. Don't let it be a shapeless lump. Since you will use this particular bit of modeling frequently in your makeup work, it becomes especially important to become proficient at it now.

Mouth. Modeling the mouth is a process of shaping and carving, working for the rounded fleshiness of the lips as opposed to a straight thin gash in the clay. As we have suggested above, start with a cylindrical shape, and model the mouth on that. Refer to Figure 4–5A. It is usually helpful in laying out the mouth to establish the exact center of the mouth with the small indention or cleft that extends from the nose down to the cupid's bow of the upper lip.

Eyes. Before beginning on the eyes, be sure the superciliary arch and the cheekbones are carefully modeled since these, along with the nose, will form the eye socket. It is usually wise to make an actual eye socket before building up an eye. This can be done quite simply by pressing with both thumbs where the eyes are to be. As we have mentioned before, this can be done during the preliminary laying out of the face. Bear in mind that eyes are normally the width of an eye apart.

As with the nose, the eyes are modeled with extra clay. A piece about the size of a walnut set into each socket should prove more than sufficient. This should give you a good start in laying out the correct planes.

Figure 4–5E shows schematically the planes of the eye, and 4–5F shows the normal eye for comparison. Planes 1, 2, and 3 represent the slope from the upper edge of the orbital fossa downward and inward to the eyeball, but this slope lies in three planes that blend gently and imperceptibly into each other. Plane 1 is the deepest part of the eye socket, formed by the meeting of the nasal bone and the superciliary arch. Plane 2 is the most prominent part of the upper socket, pushed forward by the bone of the superciliary arch. This is in essentially the same horizontal plane as the forehead. Plane 3 curves backward into the plane of the temple.

Plane 4 represents the upper lid, which comes forward over the eyeball and follows it around so that it is actually in three planes, only two of which are visible in this three-quarter view. Plane 5 represents the lower lid, which, though much less extensive than the upper, follows the same general pattern. Plane 6 represents the eyeball itself.

On your clay head it would probably be well to model the eye as if it were closed, then with the modeling tool carefully cut away a section of the lid in order to reveal the eyeball itself and give the lid thickness. It is possible, however, to model the eyeball and lay on thin pieces of clay for the lids. The important thing is to have a three-dimensional eye, correctly placed in the face, well shaped, and set properly into the eye sockets. As with all other features, avoid flatness.

When all of the features are in place, smooth out rough edges, and carefully check all planes of the face and of each feature. If the result lacks conviction, analyze it to find your missteps, and redo any problem areas.

But the best way to avoid major problems is first to lay out the proportions with great care, measuring your own features if you like, then to make sure the basic head is three-dimensional. There is a tendency among beginners to make heads that are either excessively egg-shaped or very flat. Avoid this. Develop a feeling for both roundness and squareness in the head. Both qualities are there. Be sure your individual features are carefully constructed with all of their component parts. Relate the size and placement of features to the head and to each other. A careful modeling of each feature should then result in a three-dimensional head.

The important thing is to follow through

Figures 4–6 and 4–7. Emperor Caesar Augustus.

Figures 4–8 and 4–9. Livia, wife of Nero and Augustus and mother of Tiberius.

each step logically and carefully, progressing from large areas to small ones, taking whatever time is necessary to do the job well. The skill and understanding you will gain will repay a good deal of time and effort.

PROBLEMS

1. Locate on your own face the various prominences and depressions shown in the diagram in Figure 4–2.

2. Collect photographs and works of art that can be used to illustrate the structure of the face.

3. Following the instructions in this chapter, model a head in clay. You may use yourself or someone else as a model. Use actual measurements of the real head if you like. There is no need to try for a likeness, though you may occasionally achieve one unexpectedly. The two most important objectives are to get the general proportions of the face right and to model the head as a whole and the individual features so that there is a feeling of solidity—as if there were an actual bone structure giving the whole thing form. Keep this head for future use.

5

LIGHT AND SHADE

Using modeling clay, you have now learned to model features in three dimensions as a sculptor does—and as you will be doing from time to time on the face. But more often than not, you will need to create an illusion of three dimensions using the principles of light and shade.

When we look at an object—any object—what our eye observes depends on the light that is reflected from specific areas of that object to the eye. Thus, because of its structure, your own face will reflect light in a certain pattern, and this pattern

Figure 5-1. God. Detail from Botticelli's *Coronation of the Virgin.*

of light reflection is what reveals the structure and causes you to look like you instead of like somebody else.

But suppose you *want* to look like somebody else. You can, if you wish, actually change the shape of your face with three-dimensional makeup. If you do that, the new face will reflect different patterns of light from your normal one, and you will no longer look like you.

But instead of actually reshaping your face or parts of it, you can paint on patterns of light to match those your face would reflect if you were actually to change its shape, thus causing an audience looking at your face to believe that they are seeing a face of a different shape from yours, with differently shaped features, simply through a change from the usual patterns of light reflected to their eyes.

This is essentially what the painter does. But instead of his flat, white canvas, the makeup artist has a three-dimensional head to begin with. This is not necessarily an advantage, for it means that he is limited in the effects he can achieve, whereas the painter can create any illusion he wants. Also, when the painter has determined his source of light, he knows that it will remain stationary. But on the stage, because of the actor's movements, the relationship of his face to the light is continually changing.

In spite of these differences, the principles remain the same. Both the painter and the makeup artist observe in life what happens when light falls on an object. Both see the patterns of light and shade (another name for an absence of light) that reveal to the eye the real shape of an object. Then,

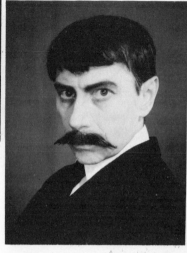

Figure 5-2. Jean-Auguste-Dominique Ingres. French painter, 1780–1867. Makeup based on a self-portrait. **Figure 5-3. Bruce Crane.** American painter, late nineteenth century. Makeup based on a photograph. **Figure 5-4. Giovanni Mannozzi da San Giovanni.** Italian painter, 1592–1636. Makeup based on a self-portrait. All three makeups done on the actor in Figure 1-1.

with colored paints of varying degrees of lightness and darkness, of brightness and grayness, both recreate the patterns. And if the artists are sufficiently skillful, the observer will be led by these painted patterns of light and shade into believing that he is seeing the real thing. In the case of painted portraits, of course, this is not strictly true, for one is always aware that he is seeing a picture. In fact, it is not normally the aim of the painter to imitate reality so closely that his work becomes photographic. But in a sense that is what the makeup artist *must* do. Although he can and should be considerably more selective than the photographer, it is really only in stylized makeup that his art should be permitted to reveal itself. In the usual realistic makeup his objective, from a strictly technical point of view, should be to deceive the audience.

Figures 5-2, 5-3, and 5-4 show three makeups recreating likenesses from portraits, following the same principles of modeling used by the painter. Figures 2-1, 2-2, and 2-3 show three student makeups of characters from plays, again using the same basic principles of light and shade.

Since the basis of actual makeup technique lies, then, in understanding and applying the prin-

ciples of chiaroscuro or light and shade, which have been used by artists for centuries, our next step is to study these principles in theory, to observe them in life, and then to apply them in monochromatic drawing.

FLAT AND CURVED SURFACES

How are we able to tell by sight alone whether a surface is flat or curved? The general outline of the object may provide a fairly reliable clue. But suppose we are trying to distinguish between a cylinder and a box of approximately the same size. If we cover up the ends, the outline will be exactly the same. But we will still have no difficulty in determining which is which simply because the patterns of light and shade will be completely different, as illustrated in Figure 5-5. What, then, is *chiaroscuro* or *light and shade?*

Perhaps the simplest way to approach it is to imagine the two forms in Figure 5-5 in total darkness, which means that both are completely black. In other words, there is a complete absence of light, and light, after all, provides the only means of our seeing these or any other objects. Now we turn on a light in the position of the arrow E right. The light hits the objects and is reflected from them to our eyes, enabling us to see them. But observe that the light does not illuminate the entire object in either case. Only those surfaces upon which the rays of light fall directly are fully visible because only they receive light rays to reflect to the eye. Surfaces that are situated away from the light source remain in darkness. This is what enables us to determine in what direction the surface planes of an object lie and whether they are flat, curved, or irregular. This information automatically tells us the shape of the object.

HARD AND SOFT EDGES

In both of the forms in Figure 5–5 part of the form is lighted, and part remains in darkness. But the shift from the lighted plane to the nonlighted or shadowed plane is entirely different in the two. In one there is a gradual shift from light through semilight (or gray) to dark. In the other the shift is abrupt and knife-sharp. Thus we know that one object has a rounded surface, the other has flat, angular ones. The sharp division between the two

flat surfaces is known as a *hard edge*, and the gradual change between planes on the curved surface, though technically not an edge at all, is known as a *soft edge*. This is a principle that is basic to all makeup, and you will be called upon to apply it repeatedly.

Observe, for example, wrinkles in the face. The largest and the easiest to analyze are the nasolabial folds, which, as the name suggests, extend from the nostrils to the mouth. If your own are not yet developed, observe someone else's. There is usually a definite crease in the flesh, forming an edge —a hard edge—which is revealed when light falls upon the wrinkle from above, lighting the top of the fold as if it were a cylinder, then fading off into shadow (a soft edge). But instead of continuing around, as a cylinder would, the flesh changes direction abruptly at the crease and moves into another plane, giving the effect of a hard edge. Understanding the principle of hard and soft edges is essential in creating convincing makeups. Observe the hard and soft edges in the faces in Figures 14–34G and 14–35A. In the painting in Figure 5–1 we see how the painter uses the same principles of lights and darks, with hard and soft edges, to create a three-dimensional effect.

Remember, then, that sharp corners result in

Figure 5–5. **Modeling curved and angular surfaces.**

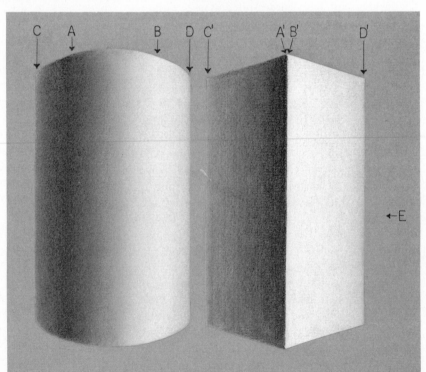

strong lights and darks being placed next to each other (Figure 5–5A′,B′), resulting in so-called hard edges, whereas curved surfaces result in lights and darks being joined by an infinite number of intermediate shades (A and B), resulting in soft edges.

DRAWING IN LIGHT AND SHADE

Now, in order to be sure that we understand the principle and can apply it, suppose we draw some simple objects, such as a cylinder and a box. Anyone can draw with a little practice. You may not have the particular type of talent necessary to become a great or even a very skillful artist, but you can become proficient enough to use the principles of light and shade to draw simple, three-dimensional objects, thus demonstrating on a fairly large scale the principles you will use in makeup.

Perhaps the simplest way to begin is to do a drawing similar to the one in Figure 5–5. It might be to your advantage to try to do the drawing at first without looking at the book, then check your mistakes. You might also do the same objects with the light from a different source.

In any event, before beginning your own drawing, pay particular attention to the areas indicated by the arrows. Arrow A designates the darkest area on the cylinder and B, the lightest. You will observe that neither of these areas is precisely at the edge of the cylinder. The edge of the dark side (C) is slightly lighter than the darkest part, while the light edge (D) is somewhat darker than the highlight (B). The reason for this is simply that on the dark side a small amount of reflected light is always seen at the extreme edge, and on the light side the surface of the edge is curving away from us so abruptly that it seems to be less brightly lighted. Try drawing a cylinder with maximum light and dark areas at the extreme edges and notice the result. The cylinder will probably seem to stop abruptly at the edges instead of continuing around to complete itself.

The source of light has been arbitrarily considered for this drawing to be in the position of the arrow E. Thus the right side of the cyinder is in direct light, resulting in a strong highlight and a gradual diminution of light from this highlight to the darkest part of the lowlight on the opposite side of the cylinder. No matter from which direction the light is coming, it will cause a highlight on the part of the object nearest it and leave a lowlight on the opposite side—a principle that must be carefully observed by the makeup artist.

This principle of light and shade holds true no matter what the shape of an object may be. In Figure 5–5, for example, we have a rectangular object illuminated from the right. Since there is a sudden change in the plane of the surface rather than a gradual one, there is a correspondingly sharp contrast in light areas, which gives us, as we have already explained, a hard edge where the surface changes direction. This hard edge is intensified in drawing by placing the lightest light next to the darkest dark. In other words, both the strongest highlight and the deepest shadow are at the edge of the rectangle nearest the eye. It is by means of this intensification of contrasts that the artist imparts solidity and third dimension to such an object. According to the principle of aerial perspective, the centralization of color value and of intensity is inversely proportional to the nearness of the color to the eye. In relation to chiaroscuro, this principle means simply that with distance both black and white become more gray—in other words, less strongly differentiated. You have undoubtedly observed this effect in distant mountains or tall buildings or even in cars or houses at a considerable distance. Thus the near edge of the rectangle is made to appear closer by intensification of its color, no matter what the hue and value may be. The far edges are made to recede by means of a decrease in color intensity and centralization of value.

Perhaps, in passing, it would be well to mention *cast* shadows as differentiated from *lowlights*, the term sometimes used to designate the kind of shadows that have already been discussed. When unidirectional light falls upon an object, it not only leaves part of the object itself in shadow, but it also casts a shadow of the object on any area around it from which the light is cut off. In other words, when an object intercepts the light, it casts a shadow. This shadow is known as a cast shadow. A cast shadow always has a hard edge, it follows the shape of the object upon which it falls, and it is darkest at the outer edge. Cast shadows are not normally used in makeup because of the continual movement of the actor and the resultant directional changes in light. Probably the only makeup for which they might be used is one in which both actor and light source are immobile, as in a tableau or for a photograph. In Figure 15–3A, for example, the makeup is copied from a painting, using the artist's lighting (from one side) instead of imagining the light to be coming from above and center and adjusting the patterns of light and shade accordingly, as would normally be done.

You would do well to spend considerable time in practicing relatively simple charcoal sketches. Since the flat-sided figure is easier, that should probably be done first. Start with your lightest light at what is to be the hard edge, and blend it gradually out toward the outer edge, allowing it to become slightly less light as you go. This can be done by applying the chalk directly as carefully as you can, then blending with the fingers or with a paper stump to achieve smooth transitions. The precise technique you use is of little importance so long as you achieve the results you want. When the light side is completed, do the dark side in the same way, starting with a heavy application of charcoal at the hard edge next to the white.

In the cylinder there is a gradual transition from light to dark. The dark can be applied in either horizontal or vertical strokes, then blended. The light can be approached in the same way. Let the gray paper serve as the middle tone between the light and the dark. In other words, the charcoal and the chalk should never quite meet since the gray of the paper is approximately halfway between and can serve as a transitional tone.

Figure 14–49 illustrates the principle of modeling a third basic shape—the sphere—and how that principle can be applied to makeup. Notice also how the same principle is used in painting the apple cheek in Figure J–3F. In the sphere all shadows and highlights fall in a circular pattern.

You might also try drawing eyes, mouths, noses, ears, and complete heads. You should be familiar with their construction from your work in clay modeling. Now see if you can create a three-dimensional illusion with charcoal and chalk. Fig-ure 4–5, and the portraits in Appendix H may be helpful, but again draw from life as much as you can.

Remember that whenever a single light falls on a three-dimensional object, those parts of the object not in the direct line of light will remain in shadow. Conversely, wherever there is a lowlight or shadow, there is a corresponding highlight. When the surface changes direction abruptly, the shadow and the highlight are immediately adjacent. But when the surface changes direction gradually, shadow and highlight are separated by a gradation of intermediate shades.

PROBLEMS*

1. With charcoal and chalk on gray paper (obtainable from your local art dealer or stationery store) sketch a number of boxes in various positions, determining each time the direction from which the light is coming. Then do a cylinder and a sphere. In each case, do the highlights first, completing them before beginning the shadows. In doing the cylinder, keep the chalk on one side and the charcoal on the other, letting the gray paper serve as a middle tone between them. The gray paper can also be allowed to show through at the outer edges of all three objects. With the box and the cylinder, this will decrease the apparent intensity of illumination on the light side and represent reflected light on the dark side.

2. Now draw a few simple objects, such as vases, books, and bottles, employing the principles of light and shade you have learned.

3. Pick out the hard and soft edges in the face in Figure 5–1. Remember that hard edges are usually very sharply defined.

4. Sketch a number of eyes, noses, mouths, and ears of various sizes and shapes in various positions. Also, do a complete head or two.

*Adequate time should be spent with the problems above, for proficiency in simple sketching in light and shade will be extremely helpful in working with makeup.

6

COLOR IN PIGMENT

In addition to understanding the principles of light and shade, you should be thoroughly familiar with the principles of color, which can then be applied specifically to makeup paints.

Scientifically speaking, color can be approached from three different points of view—those of the chemist, the physicist, and the psychologist. The makeup artist, though not primarily a scientist, must at one time or another use each of these approaches. When he mixes paints, he is a chemist. When he estimates the effect of stage lights on his makeup, he is a physicist. And when he selects a certain color of makeup pigment for the effect it will have on the audience, he is a psychologist.

All color comes originally from the source of light. White light is a mixture of light rays of all colors. Technically, pigment has no color of its own but has, rather, the ability to absorb certain rays and reflect others. The rays it reflects are the ones that are responsible for the pigment's characteristic color. A "red" dress, for example, absorbs all light rays except the red ones, which it reflects, making the dress appear red.

But since we are concerned here primarily with the artist's point of view, suppose we merely accept for the moment the existence of color in pigment and begin by examining the relationships characteristic of the various colors we see.

CHARACTERISTICS OF COLOR

In order to be able to talk intelligently about color and to approach the problem in an organized way, it is convenient to know three terms usually used to designate distinct color characteristics—*hue, intensity,* and *value.*

Hue. The hue of a color is simply the name by which we know it—red or green or blue or yellow. Pink and maroon are both variations of the basic red hue; brown is a deep, grayed orange; ivory is a tint of warm yellow.

If we take samples of all of the major hues with which we are familiar and drop them at random on a table, the result, of course, is chaos. But as we place next to each other hues that are somewhat similar, we begin to see a progression that by its very nature becomes circular—in other words, a color wheel. That is the traditional form of hue arrangement and for our purposes the most practical one.

Since, however, the progression from one hue to another is a steady one, the circle could contain an unlimited number of hues, depending only on one's threshold of perception—the point at which two hues become so nearly alike as to be indistinguishable to the naked eye and, for all practical purposes, identical. But since a wheel containing hundreds of colors would be impractical, certain hues are selected at regular intervals around the circumference. The simplified color wheel illustrated in Figure 6–1A has been chosen because it is the one familiar to most students.

Intensity. Thus far we have been speaking only of very brilliant colors. But more often than not we shall be using colors of less than maximum brilliance. A gray-blue is still blue in hue, but it is far different from the blue on the color wheel. Although of the same hue, it is lower in intensity.

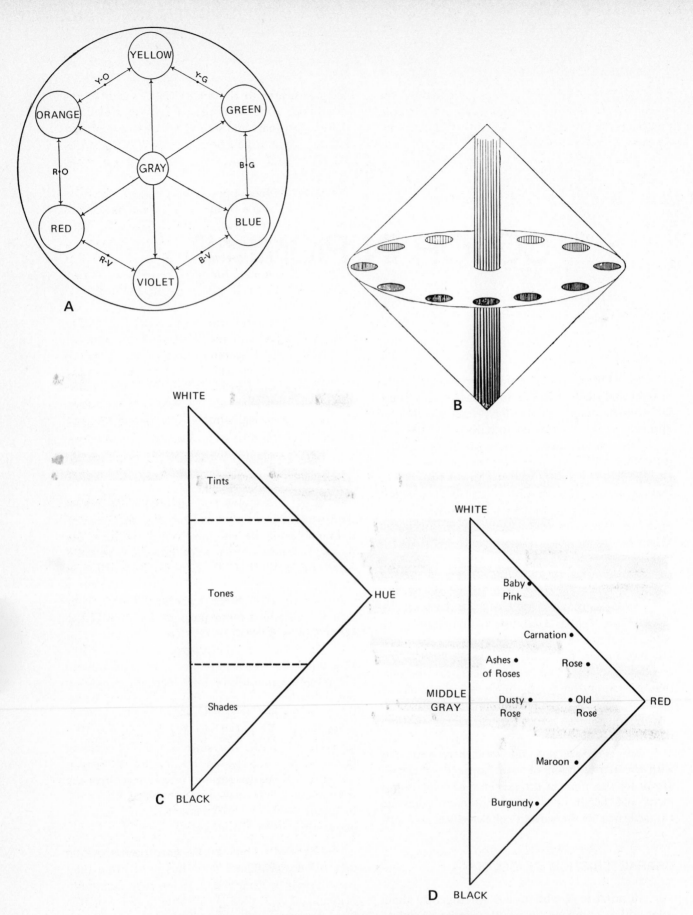

Figure 6-1. Color diagrams. (A) Color wheel. (B) Double color cone. (C) Color triangle. (D) Location of values of red on the color triangle.

32

This color would be shown as being nearer the center of the wheel—more gray, in other words. Colors on the periphery are brilliant. Colors nearer the center are less brilliant (of lower intensity) and are commonly referred to as *tones*.

Value. In addition to being blue and low in intensity, a specific color may also be light or dark—light gray-blue, medium gray-blue, dark gray-blue. This darkness or lightness of a color is called its *value*. A light value is high; a dark value is low. Pink is a high value of red; ivory is a high value of warm yellow; midnight blue is a low value of blue.

Since the color wheel is only two-dimensional, it obviously cannot be used to show values, the third color dimension. A simple way of doing it is to visualize two solid cones placed base to base with the flat round color wheel between them, as in Figure 6–1B. This gives us our third dimension.

From the color wheel we can go up or down within the cone. As we go up, we approach white, and as we go down, we approach black. Colors in the upper part of the cone are called *tints*; those in the lower part are called *shades*. (See Figure 6–1C). Straight up the center from tip to tip there is an even progression from black to white; around the periphery, an even progression from one brilliant hue to another; and from any point on the outside to the center, a similar progression from a brilliant hue to gray.

Since any given point within the color cone represents a specific color, you can easily imagine what a vast number of colors is possible. But every one can be located with reasonable accuracy in terms of *hue, intensity*, and *value*.

COLOR MIXING

If you don't have the exact color you need, you can, provided you have three primary colors to work with, mix virtually any color you want. These three primary hues are red, yellow, and blue, which can be mixed to achieve three secondary hues —orange, green, and violet, as well as an infinite number of intermediate hues. These hues will not, however, be so brilliant when obtained by mixing as when compounded directly from their sources in nature. Mixed colors always lose some intensity. A glance at the color wheel (Figure 6–1A) will show why. Blue-green, for example, lies midway on a straight line between blue and green since it is obtained by mixing those two colors. Obviously, that

brings it nearer to the gray in the center of the wheel than if it were placed on the periphery, where the primary and secondary colors are located. If the orange on the color wheel were obtained by mixing red and yellow, it too would fall nearer the center.

Colors falling opposite each other on the color wheel are called complements and when mixed will produce a neutral gray, as indicated on the color wheel. Blue and orange, for example, can be mixed to produce gray. However, if only a little blue is added to the orange, the result is a burnt orange. Still more blue will give varying intensities of brown.

The same result can be obtained by mixing black and white with the brilliant hue. Any color can be obtained by mixing three pigments—a brilliant hue, black, and white. An examination of the color triangle in Figure 6–1C will show how that is true. This triangle should be imagined as a paper-thin slice cut vertically from the outside of the cone to the center. Since the triangle bounds the complete range of any one hue, a mixture of hue, black, and white at the three points can provide a color at any point within the triangle.

Pink, for example, can be obtained by mixing white with red. Mixing black with red will give maroon. In order to achieve a dusty rose, both black and white must be added. Figure 6–1D shows where various tints, tones, and shades of red fall on the color triangle.

Practice in mixing colors with either water colors or oil paints can be very helpful as preparation for mixing colors in makeup.

PROBLEMS

1. Translate the following very general color descriptions as well as you can into terms of hue, value, and intensity: vivid pink, dull green, bright orange, pale blue, deep violet, red brown, dusty rose, peacock blue, lavender, moss green, lemon yellow, brick red, salmon, orchid, Wedgwood blue, aquamarine, mustard, chartreuse, turquoise, slate gray, cream, midnight blue, mahogany, chocolate, magenta, coral, wine.

2. Following the principle of complements, what hue would you use to gray each of the following: red-orange, blue-violet, bluish green, greenish yellow, green? Assume that all colors are of maximum intensity.

3. Using water colors, oil paints, or makeup (creme makeup or greasepaint) in red, yellow, blue, white, and black, mix the following colors: orchid, turquoise, peach, coral, rust, olive green, cerise, dark brown, ivory.

7

ORGANIZING MAKEUP COLORS

Every makeup artist, before beginning a makeup, is faced with choosing from among hundreds of available colors those that can best help him create the character. Selecting the right ones is complicated by the rather haphazard system used by the manufacturers for identifying the colors. Their color-numbering systems, each differing from the other, seem curiously devoid of logic.

What color, for example, is Leichner's 5, and how does it differ from 4½? One might reasonably expect it to be half a shade darker and fairly close in hue. Instead, it is nine shades lighter and of an entirely different hue. Stein's 12 is a fairly bright yellow, whereas 13 is a very grayed, purplish color in the tube and is much less purple on the skin. The color names applied to the various flesh colors are, on the whole, almost as unenlightening as the numbering systems and only contribute to the total picture of astonishingly complete inconsistency. No wonder the beginner is often confused.

A SYSTEM OF COLOR CLASSIFICATION

The only logical and practical solution to the problem seems to be to ignore the manufacturers' numbers and to organize all of the colors in some consistent fashion so that the paints of all of the makeup companies can be interrelated through a system of numbering that is not only logical but inherently meaningful. The chart in Appendix J represents such an organization of colors. By becoming familiar with the system used in formulating the chart, you can look at any standardized color number and tell immediately what color it represents.

In this system every makeup color is identified by a number that indicates the hue, value, and intensity of the color. In the number S-9-d, for example, S indicates the hue (scarlet); 9, the value (medium); and d, the intensity (medium).

Hue. Because of the large number of hues needed to cover the entire range of makeup colors, a few color names, such as *flame* and *chrome*, have been added to the more conventional designations, such as *red*, *yellow*, and *blue*, resulting in the following list of 39 hues, most of which are reproduced in the color chart:

Purple-Red	Chrome	Blue-Turquoise
Red	Yellow-Chrome	Turquoise-Blue
Scarlet-Red	Chrome-Yellow	Blue
Red-Scarlet	Yellow	Indigo-Blue
Scarlet	Lime-Yellow	Blue-Indigo
Flame-Scarlet	Yellow-Lime	Indigo
Scarlet-Flame	Lime	Violet-Indigo
Flame	Green-Lime	Indigo-Violet
Orange-Flame	Lime-Green	Violet
Flame-Orange	Green	Purple-Violet
Orange	Turquoise-Green	Violet Purple
Chrome-Orange	Green-Turquoise	Purple
Orange-Chrome	Turquoise	Red-Purple

For those who may not be familiar with all of the added colors, perhaps it should be pointed out that *scarlet* is a bright, orangey red; *flame*, a hot orange; *chrome*, a warm yellow; *lime*, a yellowish green; *turquoise*, a blue-green, and *indigo*, a deep violet-blue. Note that in composite color names, such as turquoise-blue and blue-turquoise, the second word represents the stronger hue and is modified by the first word. This means that turquoise-blue is a blue that is slightly turquoise, whereas blue-turquoise is a turquoise that is slightly blue.

In any particular makeup color designation in this system of color classification, the hue is indicated by the first letter of the name of the hue or the first two letters for the composite names—for example, R (red), S (scarlet), F (flame), or RS (red-scarlet), SR (scarlet-red), FS (flame-scarlet).

Value. The color values range from 0 (White) to 20 (Black). Thus, 1 is very pale, and 19 is very deep. Most makeup colors are in the range of 1–16. Numbers 7 to 9 indicate a color of medium value. Thus, FS-1 is a pale Flame-Scarlet—actually, a pale coral pink; FS-16, a deep Flame-Scarlet—actually a rusty brown; and FS–7, a warm flesh tone of medium value.

Intensity. For all colors other than the one of maximum intensity at the top of the chart (the brightest red, the brightest orange, etc.), the intensity is indicated by lowercase letters from *a* to *h, a* representing a high intensity and *h*, a low intensity approaching gray. SF-8-a, for example, would be a Scarlet-Flame of medium value and high intensity. SF-8-f would be a Scarlet-Flame of the same value but of low intensity.

GRAY is technically a neutral (N), having no hue and no intensity. But it does have value, which is indicated as for the hues—N3, N8, etc.

THE COLOR CHART

The color chart in Appendix J, though it does not include all possible variations of a single hue, does include most of the makeup colors now available, along with a number of related colors that might conceivably be available at some time in the future or that you might wish to mix from colors now available. The single block of color above each column or set of columns shows the hue in its full intensity. All of the color blocks below it are variations of this single hue. The letter designation for each hue is indicated above the single color block. Immediately above each column is a lowercase letter indicating the intensity. Values

are designated by the numbers in the margins.

In spite of the large number of hues included, it is still possible that a particular makeup hue might fall between two of the hues shown. Although this slight variation would probably not be significant from a practical point of view, greater precision in the designation of the hue can be achieved, if you want it, by combining the letter representations of the two hues on either side—thus, a hue between Blue and Turquoise-Blue would be B/TB, or between Red-Purple and Purple-Red would be RP/PR. This, in effect, doubles the number of possible hue designations.

Similarly, if a color should fall between two of the values in the chart, such as 5 and 6, it might be designated as 5½—as for example, BT-5½-a or S/F-5½-c. This doubles the potential number of values.

A color falling between two intensities, such as *a* and *b*, would be labeled *a/b*—for example, R-12-a/b, or even R/SR-7½-a/b. This doubles the number of intensities.

Thus, the potential color designations are eight times as great as the number of colors in the chart.

In using the chart, you can simply look over the colors and select the one that seems appropriate. Then, using its number, refer to Table 1 of Equivalent Colors and find the number you have selected. If it is not there, this means that there is at present no makeup color that corresponds to the color you have selected, and you can then choose the nearest available color. If the color is listed, manufacturers' numbers will be indicated. In order to find out which makeup paints correspond to these manufacturers' numbers, simply refer to Table 2, where you will find a list of those color numbers that, at the present time, are available commercially.

The most efficient way to make use of this organization of colors is to label all of your own base and shading colors in accordance with the color chart. Then you will be able to decide which number of paint you want and select it from your makeup kit immediately without consulting the Tables of Equivalent Colors. In order to determine the color number of any particular paint in your kit, consult Table 2 in Appendix J.

If you need a color you don't have, you can find out from the tables which company to obtain it from. This will save time and will make possible a more accurate color selection than would be possible from manufacturers' descriptive labels.

But suppose you have been using one brand of makeup and have recently changed to another.

You now want to know what number in the new brand corresponds to a certain number in the old. First consult Table 2, where you will find the various brands of makeup listed according to their own numbers, along with the corresponding standardized numbers. Then turn to Table 1, where you will find the list of available colors under the standardized numbers. If the color you want is not available in the brand you are using, then you might look for the nearest number with a listing for that brand.

Suppose you know the approximate color you want but don't know the standardized number. You can figure out, on the basis of the approximate hue, value, and intensity where in the chart the color is likely to be. Then, having checked the colors in the chart and decided on the specific one you want, you can note the standardized number and consult Table 1 to find out what corresponding makeup paints are available. If there are none, you can then choose the nearest one or mix colors to get exactly what you want.

COLOR MIXING

There are various approaches to mixing colors in makeup. Suppose, for example, that you decide you want an F-9-c base color. You have no F-9-c, but you do have lighter and darker F colors of the intensity (c) that you want. A mixture of the two should produce the color you need. (If your other F colors are not of the right intensity, additional mixing may be required.) If you have nothing at all in the F group, you might use an SF-9-c and an OF-9-c since both are of the same value and the same intensity, and of adjacent hues, which can be mixed to produce the color wanted. You can also mix two intensities of the same hue and the same value in order to produce an intensity somewhere between the two—as, for example, mixing F-8-a and F-8-e to get F-8-c.

To simplify your makeup kit, you can rely on mixing a few flesh colors with the more intense shading colors in order to get whatever flesh tones you want. For example, if you have an F-8-c foundation paint but find it isn't quite red enough, you can add a little red. If it is too dark, add some white. If the red makes it too brilliant, add some gray (black and white, if you don't have gray). For

a fairly grayed color, such as F-11-d, you might begin with an F-11-c and simply add a little medium gray. Or if you had an F-11-e, you could simply mix it with the F-11-c.

If, on the other hand, you have F-11-c and want F-8-c, you could add white to lighten it. Or you could get what you want by adding an F color that is lighter and of the same intensity. Different hues can be mixed in the same way. An OF-9-c mixed with SF-9-c will give F-9-c since F falls between SF and OF. Provided you have red, yellow, blue, black, and white in your kit, you can mix most of the colors you need.

Although at first reading the classification system may seem complex, once the method of classification is understood, the grouping will seem simple and logical. But it would be well to keep in mind that no system of makeup color classification can be completely accurate for three reasons. In the first place, the colors as we refer to them should look much as they do on the skin, which is rarely the same as the color in the tube, stick, or cake; and, in addition, the precise color on the skin varies with the individual. In the second place, color reproduction is seldom completely accurate. And in the third place, makeup colors are inconsistent and vary from batch to batch. Nevertheless, it must be apparent that some system is vital in organizing the many available colors.

The advantages of such organization are that the best colors and materials from various companies can be used together without confusion, that the artist can change from one brand of makeup to another without having to memorize a completely new set of numbers, that he can see at a glance what colors are available in the various brands of makeup without having to rely on vague descriptive terms, and for purposes of this textbook, that colors can be mentioned much more specifically and with less confusion than would otherwise be possible.

PROBLEMS

1. Without consulting the chart in Appendix J, indicate an approximate hue and value (such as light red, dark brown, medium yellow) for each of the following numbers in the color classification: R-2-a, V-1-b, SR-4-c, B-2-a, TB-6-a, SF-9-c, SF-8-g, FO-15-d, P-8-b, N-8, B-13-a, C-7-a, O-6-c, R-13-a, F-10-g, VI-7-a, GL-5-a.

2. Select five or six foundation paints from your kit. Then, using only red, yellow, blue, white, and black*, duplicate each of the colors.

3. Using foundation colors F-7-a or F-8-a plus red, yellow, blue, white, and black, mix in the palm of your hand an approximation of each of the following makeup colors, as shown in the color chart in Appendix J: R-2-a, R-10-d, S-5-c, RS-10-f; SF-8-g, S-6-b, FS-8-d, F-11-b, O-3-a. In judging the colors, always spread the paint very thinly on your skin.

4. If you are working in a class, mix several samples of paint; then trade samples with another student, and match his samples exactly without knowing what colors he used to mix them. This should be done until you have trained your eye to judge colors accurately. Until you can match samples, your knowledge of color is inadequate for truly effective work in makeup. If you are working alone rather than with a group, mix several colors at random without paying any particular attention to the ingredients. Then go back and try to duplicate them, not by random trial and error but by first analyzing as well as you can the colors to be matched.

*If your black paint is not a true black (not completely neutral, that is), it will throw off the color of the mixture. Most black paints in makeup tend slightly toward the blue. To find out whether or not you have a true black, mix a little with some white to make a medium gray. If the gray is entirely neutral, you have a true black, but if it seems to have a cast of any specific color (such as blue), it needs to be adjusted. This can be done by adding a tiny bit of the complementary color to the black. For example, if the gray appears bluish, add a very small amount of the darkest orange you have to the black and test again by mixing with white. If this is not done, and if the black is not true, you will not get the results you want in any mixing in which black is involved.

8

LIGHTING AND MAKEUP

Perhaps you have observed in moonlight scenes on the stage the unflattering effects of the light on the actors' faces. As the moonlight is turned on, a perfectly healthy young lady is likely very suddenly to lose her pink and ivory complexion and take on a deathly pallor, punctuated by large black spots on each cheek and one below the nose where the mouth ought to be. If she is fortunate enough to have brown or black eyes, they may withstand the sudden transformation, but blue ones are likely to disappear. Strong firelight results in similar pallor, minus the black spots.

In order to circumvent such unpleasant results of unfortunate combinations of makeup and lights, the makeup artist, in choosing his paints, must know what effects the various colors of light used on the stage will have on those paints. An understanding of the principles of color in light as well as in pigment is basic to such knowledge.

COLOR IN LIGHT

We mentioned briefly in Chapter 6 that pigment depends for its color on the light that illuminates it. In other words, trees are not green at night—unless, of course, they are artificially illuminated. Nothing has color until light is reflected from it. If all the light is absorbed, the object looks black; if all the light is reflected, we say it is white. If certain of the rays are absorbed and certain others reflected, the reflected rays determine the color.

The various colors of rays that make up what we call white light can be observed when they are refracted by globules of moisture in the air, form-

ing a rainbow. The same effect can be obtained with a prism. The colored rays are refracted at different angles because of their different lengths, red being the longest and violet the shortest. All matter has the ability to reflect certain lengths of light waves but not others, resulting in color sensations in the eye.

Just as white light can be broken up into its component hues, those hues can be synthesized to form white light as well as various other colors. As with pigments, three of the colors can be used as primaries and combined to form any other color of light as well as the neutral white. However, the three primaries are not the same in light as in pigment. In light they are *red* (scarlet), *green*, and *ultramarine* (a deep violet-blue). In mixing lights, red and green give yellow or orange, green and ultramarine give turquoise or blue-green, and ultramarine and red give purple. A mixture of all three primaries produces white light. On the stage these various colored rays are produced by placing a color medium (sheets of transparent gelatine or glass rondels) in front of some source of nearly white light, such as a spot or a flood.

LIGHT ON PIGMENT

If the colored rays fall on pigment that is able to reflect them, then we see the color of the light. But if they fall on a pigment that absorbs some of them, the color is distorted. Suppose, for example, red rays fall on a "red" hat. The rays are reflected, and the hat looks red. But suppose green rays are thrown on the "red" hat. Since the hat is able to reflect only red rays, the green rays are absorbed, nothing is reflected, and the hat looks black.

Imagine a "green" background behind the "red" hat. Add green light and you have a black hat against a green background. Change the light to red, and you have a red hat against a black background. Only white light (or both red and green lights at the same time) will give you a red hat against a green background.

The principle of light absorption and reflection can be used to advantage in certain trick effects, such as apparently changing a white man into a black one before the eyes of the audience. But ordinarily your problem will be to avoid such effects. Fortunately, since intense hues of light are seldom used on the stage, usually you need vary your makeup colors only slightly. Moonlight and firelight scenes are the most notable exceptions in realistic plays.

The problem of becoming familiar with the specific effects of the vast number of possible combinations of light and makeup is a far from simple one. It is impossible to offer a practical panacea for all of the problems one may encounter. A chart could be made, but it would be inaccurate, for not only do exact shades of makeup vary among manufacturers and from tube to tube or cake to cake, but gelatine varies, even within a given brand, from sheet to sheet. And of course light sources vary widely.

Thus the only solution seems to be to generalize and to leave details to the artist himself. The following suggestions, nevertheless, may be of some practical value.

In the first place, try to do your makeup under lighting similar to that under which it will be viewed by the audience. Ideally, dressing room or makeup room lights should be arranged to take colored gelatine slides that can be matched with those on the stage. Figure 11–2 shows a possible arrangement. Since dressing rooms are almost never so equipped, some temporary arrangement should be made if possible. A pair of small spots or floods in a central makeup room is far better than nothing.

Secondly, whenever possible, look at the makeup from the house. This can usually be done during a full dress rehearsal. If you are doing your own makeup, have someone whose judgment you trust look at you from the house and offer criticisms. Since final approval of the makeup lies with the director, he is the logical one to do this, but since he has many other problems to deal with and may, in addition, not have an extensive knowledge

of makeup, he cannot always be counted on for constructive suggestions. If a professional makeup artist is in charge of all the makeup, he will check the makeup under lights and get final approval from the director.

In the third place, you ought to have a reasonably accurate knowledge of the general effects of a certain color of light upon a certain color of makeup. Generally speaking, the following principles will hold:

1. Gelatine colors of low value will have maximum effect upon makeup; colors of high value, a minimum.

2. A given color of light will cause a similar color of pigment to become higher in intensity, while a complementary color of pigment will be lower in both value and intensity.

3. Any shade of pigment will appear gray or black if it does not contain any of the colors composing a given ray of light that falls upon it.

For a better understanding of the effects of colored light on makeup colors, you might examine the color chart and the color illustrations (Appendix J) under various colors of light. If a spotlight and colored gelatines are not accessible, the following list of the common colors of gelatine with their effects upon various colors of makeup can be used as a guide. You should remember, however, that the effects listed are only approximations and the actual effects may upon occasion vary from those indicated here.

Pink tends to gray the cool colors and intensify the warm ones. Yellow becomes more orange.

Flesh pink affects makeup less strongly than the deeper shades and has a flattering effect on most makeups.

Fire red will ruin nearly any makeup. All but the darker flesh tones will virtually disappear. Light and medium rouge become a pale orange and fade imperceptibly into the foundation, whereas the dark reds turn a reddish brown. Yellow becomes orange, and the cool shading colors become shades of gray and black.

Bastard amber is one of the most flattering colors to makeup. It may gray the cool shading colors slightly but picks up the warm pinks and flesh tones and adds life to the makeup.

Amber and *orange* have an effect similar to that of red, though somewhat less severe. Most flesh colors, except the dark browns, become more intense and more yellow. Rouges tend to turn more orange. Cool colors are grayed. Dark amber has, of course, a stronger effect than light.

Light straw has very little effect upon makeup, except to make the colors slightly warmer. Cool colors may be grayed a little.

Lemon and *yellow* make warm colors yellow, blues more green, and violets somewhat gray. The darker the gelatine, of course, the stronger the effect upon the makeup.

Green grays all flesh tones and rouges in proportion to its intensity. Violet is also grayed. Yellow and blue will become more green, and green will be intensified.

Light blue-green tends to lower the intensity of the base colors. Light red becomes darker, and dark red becomes brown. Use very little rouge under blue-green light.

Green-blue will gray medium and deep flesh tones, as well as all reds, and will wash out pale flesh tones.

Blues will gray most flesh tones and cause them to appear more red or purple. Blues and greens become higher in value, violets become more blue, and purples become more violet. The darker the blue, the stronger the effect.

Violet (*light* and *surprise*) will cause orange, flame, and scarlet to become more red. Rouge may seem more intense. Greens are likely to be a little lower in value and intensity. Be careful not to use too intense a red in either base or rouge.

Dark violet will intensify most reds, orange-reds, and oranges. Greens will be grayed.

Surprise purple will have an effect similar to that of surprise violet, except that the reds and oranges will be intensified to a much greater degree.

Dark and *rose purple* will tend to make most warm colors look orange. Rouge will turn orange. The greens will be grayed, and most blues will look violet.

One problem remains. Since stage lights are likely to change from time to time during a performance, be aware of any radical changes, especially in color, and have your makeup checked under the various lighting conditions that prevail. If such changes do affect your makeup adversely and there is no opportunity for you to adjust the makeup to the lights, try to modify your basic makeup to minimize the problem under all lighting conditions. If this is not successful, consult the director about the possibility of some adjustment of the lighting. After all, it is to the advantage of the whole production that every makeup be as effective as possible at all times.

Although you may often consider stage lighting a hindrance to your art, try to make the best of all the advantages it has to offer. Plan your makeups so that the lighting will contribute to rather than detract from their effectiveness.

PROBLEMS

1. What makeup color and what colors of light would you use to make a white man apparently change suddenly into a black man?

2. What color would each of the following appear to be under the colors of light indicated: A yellow hat under red and green lights? A green hat under red and yellow lights? A red hat under blue and green lights? A red and green hat under yellow lights? A red and yellow hat under green lights? A green and yellow hat under red lights? A red and blue hat under blue lights? A red, yellow, and blue hat under red, green, and ultramarine lights? A purple and white hat under red, green, and ultramarine lights?

3. It has been stated in the chapter that a given color of light raises the intensity of a similar color of pigment. Yet on a stage flooded with red light, all of the clear, bright reds seem to be "washed out." Why is this so?

PART TWO

DESIGNING THE MAKEUP

9

THE MAKEUP DESIGNER

It is sometimes desirable to have all of the makeups for a play designed by one person, who will first read the play, then consult with the director and the costumer, and in some cases with the set designer, before making his sketches and charts. It is helpful and sometimes essential for the makeup designer to meet the actors or, better yet, to obtain photographs of at least those playing major roles before making his sketches. Then, after the sketches have been approved by the director, the designer should make certain that the actor can do the makeup or, if the makeup for all performances is to be done by a third person, that this person can do the makeup satisfactorily. Unless the makeups are unusually simple, all of this should ordinarily be taken care of before the first dress rehearsal.

Only when he is completely satisfied that the makeups are being executed to his satisfaction should the designer leave the actors on their own, and in the case of a long run, he should check them at least once a week.

In the professional theater the makeup designer is a professional makeup artist or a costume

Figure 9–1. Makeup designs for *Mother Courage*. Preliminary sketches by student Howard Klein for Soldier, Chaplain, Eilif, and Old Colonel. For completed makeups, see Figure 9–2.

designer who may or may not be trained in makeup. In the academic theater he may be the makeup teacher, the costumer, or, ideally, one of the more advanced makeup students, who should, if possible, be given the opportunity to design the makeups for public productions. Professional or nonprofessional, the designer should start his work well in advance and have it essentially completed before dress re-

hearsals, which should be used for adjusting the makeup to the lighting and making any other necessary changes.

Although in most professional productions and in some nonprofessional ones the actors are expected to create their own makeups, there are productions that need the services of a makeup artist. The director may wish, for example, to co-

Figure 9–2. Stylized makeups for *Mother Courage.* A, B, D, and E correspond to the sketches in Figure 9–1. Charcoal-brown cake shadows used over a light yellowish cake base.

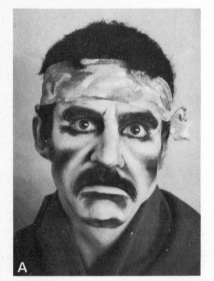

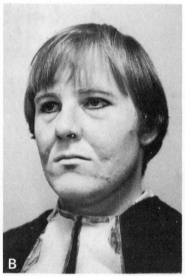

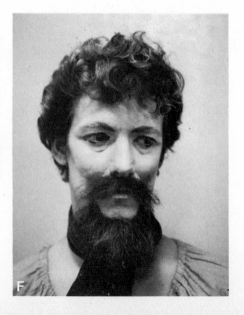

Figure 9–3. Six characters from the ball scene in *The Patriot*. (A) Peter Colley as Salome; (B) Bryan Young as the Tsarina; (C) Warren Burton as a Lady of Fashion; (D) Tom Tammi as a Medieval Lady; (E) Carl Jessop as Marie Antoinette; (F) Luis Cepero as a Shepherdess. Preliminary designs were based on the costume sketches of Freddy Wittop, following consultation with the actors and the director. Final makeups were the result of work with the actors and observation of the effects during dress rehearsals. Throughout the run of the play on Broadway, the actors did their own makeups, following the final approved designs.

ordinate the style of the makeup with the style of the sets and the costumes—as in the production of *Mother Courage* for which the makeups illustrated in Figure 9–2 were used. The makeups were designed by a student from the makeup class after consultation with the director. In some cases, minor changes were suggested and the sketches (Figure 9–1) revised. The final versions were followed carefully, some of the actors doing their own makeup and others being made up by students from the makeup class.

The six makeups in Figure 9–3 are from the Broadway production of John Osborne's *A Patriot for Me*. Although all of the actors were responsible for their own makeups for most of the play, the makeups for the actors who appeared as women in the ball scene were designed by a professional makeup artist, who then assisted those actors who needed help in learning to do their own makeup. During the run of the show, the makeup artist checked regularly on those makeups for which he was responsible. The makeup artist was needed in this case simply because not all of the actors were prepared to deal with the special problems involved.

10

SKETCHES AND WORKSHEETS

Once you have a picture of the character in your mind, the next step is to put your ideas on paper. If you are making up someone other than yourself, a sketch of your ideas is essential in order to show the actor and the director exactly what you have in mind. If you are doing your own makeup, it provides an objective image to work from. It also gives you something specific to show the director for his approval or suggestions before you actually begin to make up.

PRELIMINARY SKETCHES

The first sketches can be done in any medium you choose—pencil, charcoal, pen and ink, pastel, or conté crayon. They will usually be in black and white or sepia. If you are inexperienced at sketching, it will be easier for you to use outlines of heads with features indicated, such as those shown on the worksheet in Figure 10–3. Student drawings, using similar worksheets, can be seen in Figure 9–1. Some of these are preliminary sketches; others are working drawings. You may wish to do a number of sketches and then choose those that seem to best express the character. One or more of these might be shown to the director as a basis for discussion.

ADAPTING THE MAKEUP TO THE ACTOR

If the preliminary sketches have been conceived strictly in terms of the ideal—that is, if you

have created an image intended to fulfill both the playwright's conception and the actor's interpretation—but you have not yet taken into consideration the practical necessity of adapting this ideal conception to the face of the individual actor, this adaptation should be done before the final sketches are made. There is no use presenting to the director or the actor a visual concept of the character that simply cannot be realized.

Probably the only way to realize the ideal conception of the character is to have the actor wear a mask. This, in rare instances, can be done; but since increasing the amount of makeup tends to decrease the actor's facial expressiveness and even, in the case of a rubber mask, to further decrease his facial mobility, this is not really ideal for realistic plays.

In most instances we must accept the actor's basic bone structure and make what illusory changes we can with paint, along with any necessary three-dimensional constructions (preferably simple) and whatever changes in the hair may be most effective. The objective is to help the actor develop his character without inhibiting his facial expression.

If this is to be done with maximum effectiveness, it will be up to the director to fit the actor to the part as nearly as possible. It would be unwise, for example, for a director to cast a very thin actor as Falstaff since there is really no choice but for Falstaff to be fat. If, however, a thin actor has been cast, the makeup artist and the costumer can probably change him into a reasonably fat Falstaff.

If a director, in casting *The Barretts of Wimpole Street*, wishes to use the actor in Figure 1–1,

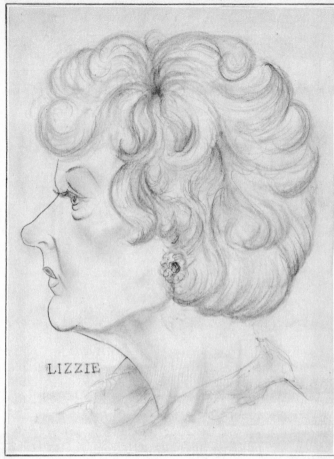

LIZZIE

LIZZIE

Figure 10–1. Pencil sketches for makeup for Lizzie in *Philadelphia, Here I Come*.

aging him and adding whiskers will not be a particularly difficult problem. But suppose the director has cast a fat actor in the part, even though he has imagined Mr. Barrett to be slender? Obviously, there is nothing the makeup artist can do but transform the fat actor into a fat Mr. Barrett. In other words, it is up to the director either to cast an actor who physically fits his conception of a particular part or to revise his conception of the part to fit a particular actor.

In either case, once the actor has been cast and is rehearsing the part, the problem then is to design a makeup to fit that specific face. One of the simplest ways of doing this is to work from photographs—front and profile—of the actor. (But make sure that the photographs are recent enough so that the face will not have significantly aged.) Place a sheet of tracing paper over the photograph and sketch the character in pencil, making sure that you do not change the actor's face in any way in which it cannot actually be changed with makeup. The sketches in Figure 10–1 were done over the photographs in Figure 10–2A,B. Figure 10–2C,D shows the final makeup. The close resemblance be-

tween the sketch and the makeup could probably be achieved only by working from a photograph of the actor. The sketches in Figures 19–6 and 19–8 were done in the same way.

QUICK CHANGES

At this point you may need to take into consideration the practical question of the amount of time and skill required for making the changes you have envisioned. If there are quick changes to be made or if your facilities or your time for making complicated prosthetic pieces are limited, then you must make sure that the requirements for the makeup are reasonable. If they are not, you will need to modify your drawing to meet practical considerations. In Peter Falk's makeup for Stalin, for example, there was a fairly fast change to be made during intermission, as indicated by the two character drawings in Figure 19–6. Fortunately, the changes could be made with cake makeup and the addition of a wig. Therefore, the requirements of the makeup as designed were reasonable.

48

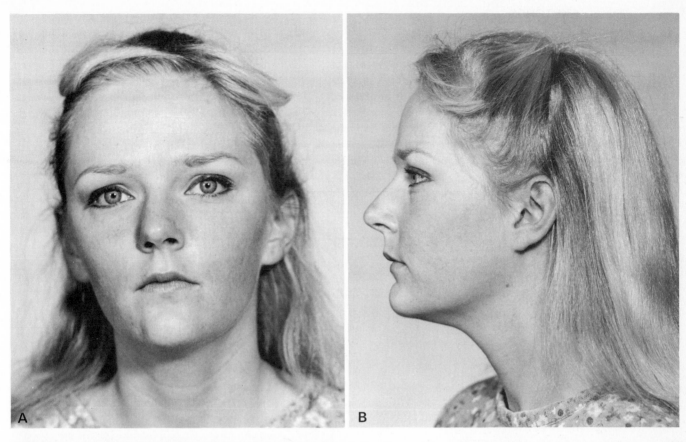

Figure 10–2. Lizzie, in *Philadelphia, Here I Come.* (A, B) Actress Bonnie
Gallup. (C, D) Final makeup based on sketches in Figure 10–1.

FINAL SKETCHES

Final sketches in either black and white or color should include both a front view and a profile (see Figure 10–1). They should be carefully rendered sketches, to give as accurate an impression as possible of what the character is to look like (Figure 10–2). For black and white sketches, the tracing-paper-over-photograph method is likely to be the most accurate. If you want a colored render-ing, it can be made by transferring the black-and-white drawing (carbon paper can be used for this if you're careful not to press too hard with the pencil) to whatever paper is to be used for the colored version. Water colors require the most experience for skillful handling. Colored pencils are easier. For a compromise, you may prefer to use water-color pencils. If you use pastels, which come in a wide range of colors, be sure to spray them with fixative to avoid smudging. It's a good idea to pro-

Figure 10–3. Makeup worksheet. Additional sketches or information can be added on back of sheet.

PRODUCTION:_____   ACTOR:_____

CHARACTER:_____   ANALYSIS:

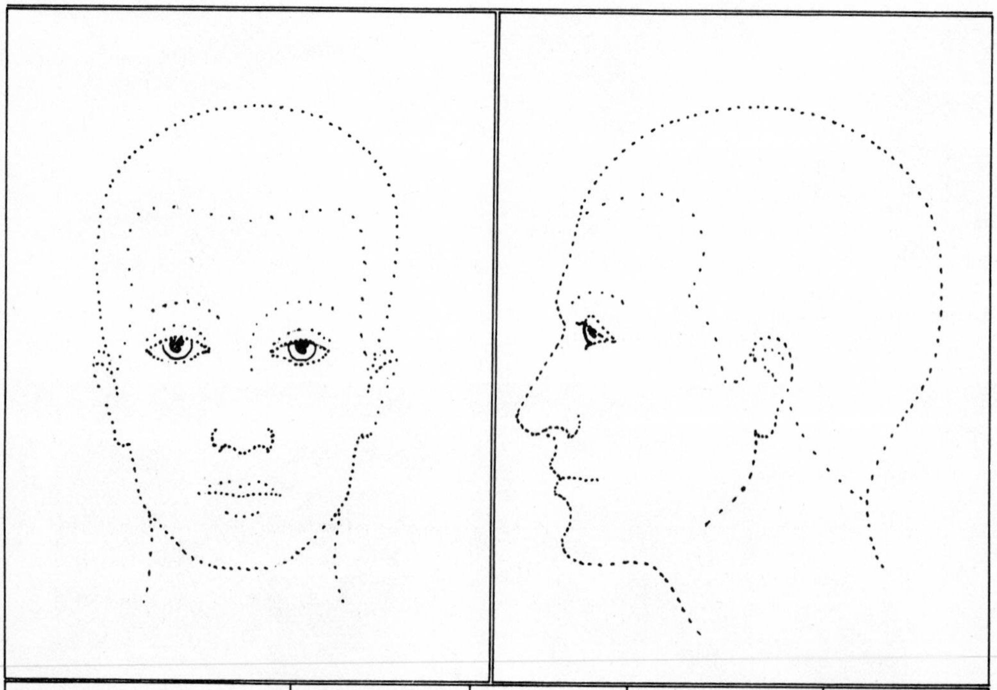

PROSTHESIS	Eye	Nose	Cheek	Mouth

Base	Highlights	Shadows	
Eye liners	Powder	Hair	
Note:			

tect all final drawings with acetate or transparent plastic sheets.

These "final" drawings are not actually final until they have been approved by the director, who may suggest changes. Pencil drawings on tracing paper are usually easy to revise. Color sketches may have to be done over. If you can get the director's approval on the black and white sketches, you may save yourself time in the revisions. Final sketches (or photocopies of them) should be made available to the actor to mount on or near his makeup mirror (see Figure 19–7).

WORKSHEETS

When the final sketch for a makeup has been approved, you should then prepare a makeup worksheet to be followed in doing the makeup. The one in Figure 10–3 is a comparatively simple form that

Figure 10–4. Makeup worksheet for Abraham Lincoln. By student Richard Brunner. For finished makeup see Figure 10–6.

1863 – Shortly before Gettysburg Address

Forehead	Eye	Nose	Cheek	Mouth
– raise forehead hairline w/ soap – suggestion of wrinkles	– deep, dark – heavy eyelids – add to natural eyebrows w/ pencil – suggestion of wrinkles rather than pouches.	– remodel w/ putty-wax – wider, slightly curved to left	– extremely deep & hollow – deep nasolabial folds – wart w/ wax	– thin dark upper lip – perhaps reshape lower lip w/ wax – shadow under lower lip

| base 4A ps w/ egyptian stipple | shadows 21, 38, Red-Brown | specials – lengthen ear lobes w/ wax | | |

| eye liners | powder | hair
– spray black (natural hair)
– crepe hair or ventilated beard (thick to compensate for firm strong jaw) | | |

| Note: – coarse stipple for skin texture | | | | |

has proved practical. The makeup can be sketched front view and profile, following the dotted lines or departing from them, using water colors, water-color pencils, drawing pens or pencils (black or colored), or conté crayon (black or sepia). When using pencils or conté crayon, the wrinkles and shadows can be blended with a paper stump or even with the fingers. When using a black lead pencil, it's possible to run the fingers lightly over the entire drawing to gray all the white areas, then to pick out

the highlights with an eraser. Precise information on makeup colors to be used, special techniques of application, hair styles, and any three-dimensional additions to the face, including beards and mustaches, can be entered in the appropriate spaces. Additional detailed sketches or diagrams can be included when necessary. Figures 10–4 and 10–5 show completed worksheets for student makeups.

Figure 10–7 shows another type of worksheet. The colors of makeup used should be listed under

Figure 10–5. Makeup worksheet for King Pellinore. By student Richard Brunner. For finished makeup see Figure 10–6.

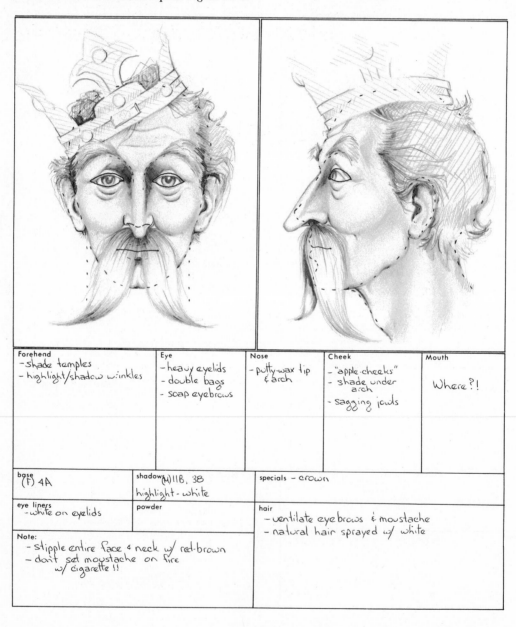

Figure 10–6. Makeups for Abraham Lincoln and King Pellinore. By student Richard Brunner. Pencil sketches for the makeups shown on the worksheets in Figures 10–4 and 10–5. (For other makeups by Mr. Brunner, see Figures 15–18, 16–7, 16–32.)

Figure 10–7. Alternative makeup worksheet.

MAKEUP WORKSHEET

Remarks:

PLAY

Actor............................. Character.............................. Age..............

PROSTHESIS...............................

	COLOR	APPLICATION
Base		
Shadows		
Highlights		
Cheek Rouge		
Lip Rouge		
Eyeshadow		
Eye Accents		
Eyelashes		
Eyebrows		
Neck		
Hands		
Powder		
Hair		

COLOR CODE
RED—Rouge, lipstick
YELLOW—Highlights
BROWN—Shadows
GREEN—Eyeshadow
BLUE—Prosthesis
BLACK—Hair, beard, eyebrows

Makeup assigned to:

Figure 10–8.   Sketches for makeups.

54

"Color," and any special remarks about application may be listed under the appropriate heading. Since any prosthetic pieces that are to be used must be applied before the rest of the makeup, there is a place at the top for indicating briefly what they are. More detailed information can be put on the back of the sheet.

The full-face and profile heads can be used to diagram hair and prosthesis and to indicate such requirements as shadows, highlights, eyeshadow, and rouge. The most practical scheme is to use colored pencils—for example, black for hair, eyebrows, and eye accents, brown for shadows, yellow for highlights, red for rouge, green for eyeshadow, and blue for prosthesis, as suggested on the chart.

The separate drawing of the eye is included to make possible a more detailed diagram of the makeup to be used. The box in the lower right-hand corner will be used only when there is a staff and the charts are made out by the makeup designer. The box in the upper left-hand corner may be used for any number of miscellaneous purposes —as, for example, to indicate that this is a quick-change makeup, that it is only one of several makeups on the same actor in the same production, that the actor has a skin condition that requires special handling, or that the makeup will be seen under unusual lighting. Additional drawings or information can be put on the back of the sheet.

After the final makeup has been approved, you should revise the worksheets so as to provide all the information necessary to reproduce the makeup exactly in its approved form. If possible, a photograph of the final makeup should be attached to the chart. Having a Polaroid camera and high speed film available at all times will make this a relatively simple matter.

PROBLEM

1. Design realistic makeups for two or more characters from a play of your choice. Use any medium you choose for the sketches. After you have studied Chapter 14, you will do worksheets for these same characters. Suggested plays: *Zoo Story, A Streetcar Named Desire, You Can't Take It With You, Who's Afraid of Virginia Woolf, Death of a Salesman, The Chalk Garden, Arsenic and Old Lace, The Effect of Gamma Rays on Man-in-the Moon Marigolds, The Wild Duck, Cat on a Hot Tin Roof, The Dock Brief,* and *Come Back, Little Sheba.*

PART THREE

APPLYING THE MAKEUP

MAKEUP EQUIPMENT

Before beginning even to experiment with the application of makeup, it is necessary to have suitable equipment with which to work. And until you have learned the tricks of doing good work with whatever equipment happens to be available, you would do well to obtain the best you can afford. This does not mean that you need a *lot* of makeup —in the beginning, a small kit will serve quite well so long as it contains what you really need. From time to time, additional supplies can be added. Materials used in makeup are listed in Appendix A. Items starred (*) should be studied now. The others can be used for reference when you need them.

THE MAKEUP KIT

The term "makeup kit" refers to a portable container of makeup or just to the makeup itself.

Individual kits. These should always be portable. Group kits may or may not be, depending on where and how they are to be used. One possible container for the individual kit is a portable, unfitted woman's makeup case, usually with a built-in mirror, obtainable in most department and leather goods stores. The case should have a tray with a few divisions. If it hasn't, then make your own tray out of plywood or other sturdy material. Since one of the purposes of the makeup case is to keep the materials in order, a divided tray is almost a necessity. The selection of the container is, of course, a personal matter, and many actors will prefer other types.

Professional kits. For touring professional actors who are sending their kits with the company luggage, a sturdy box with a good lock may prove more satisfactory. Some actors may prefer cantilever trays to the kind that must be lifted out. Professional makeup artists may want cases with trays and drawers designed specifically for makeup. It doesn't really matter what kind of makeup container you use so long as it holds the amount of makeup you need, keeps the makeup in order, is convenient to use, and is generally practical for you. Your requirements and your budget will no doubt determine your choice.

Group kits. For small group kits (or well-stocked individual ones) a large fishing-tackle box with cantilever trays (Figure 11–1A) is practical and not unreasonable in price. These boxes come in many sizes with varying numbers of trays. Similar boxes designed primarily as sample cases are also excellent. (See Figure 11–1C.)

If there is no reason to carry the makeup materials from place to place, then cabinets with small drawers or with shelves and pigeonholes are more easily accessible. The drawers or shelves can be labeled and the paints and powders arranged according to color. Dentists' cases with their many shallow trays and drawers (see Figure 11–4D) are ideal for storing makeup. They are also expensive. Metal filing cases with small drawers can also be used.

Makeup palette. You can easily make up a box palette (see Figure 11–1B), filling a plastic box of whatever size you want with sticks of paint

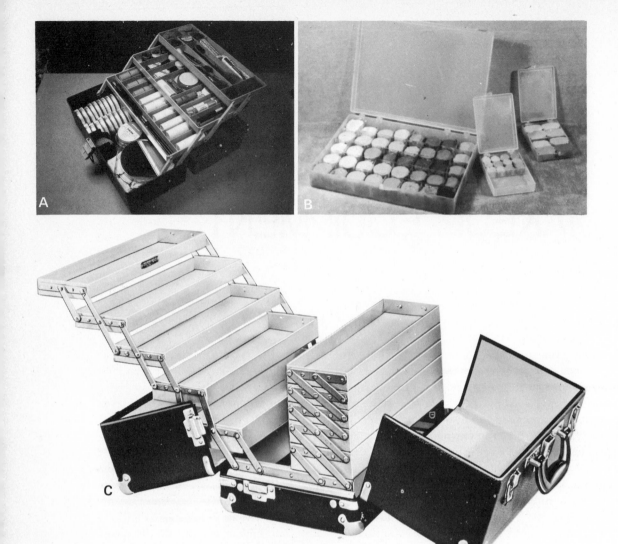

Figure 11-1. Makeup kits and containers. (A) Cantilever fishing-tackle box, available in several sizes. Shown here filled with makeup from various companies. Available from department and sporting-goods stores. (B) Plastic boxes filled with sections of creme sticks and lipsticks to provide a convenient makeup palette. (C) Ten-tray case suitable for the professional makeup artist or for use as a group kit. Available from Fibre Products Mfg. Co., which can supply other cases in various sizes. (See Appendix B for address.)

(creme sticks, greasepaints, lipsticks, eyeshadow sticks) in your choice of colors. The sticks can simply be sliced off to provide the right size for the boxes and squared off, if you like, or left round. They can be separated with strips of foil or acetate but need not be.

You may prefer to have separate boxes for your lipsticks and eyeshadow sticks. These palettes would be used for cheeks, lips, eyes, wrinkles, or stylized designs.

The advantages of such a palette are that it conserves space in the kit and makes it possible for you to have at your fingertips a large number of colors without having to take the time and trouble to open an equal number of tubes, which tend to get knocked over, resulting in general confusion, and sometimes consternation, at the dressing table. (See also *Makeup palette* in Appendix A.)

Makeup materials for the kit. After you have determined what kind of container will best fill your requirements, you will need to decide what you want in it—unless, of course, you prefer to buy a complete kit put out by one of the makeup companies—often at a considerable saving over the cost of the makeup materials purchased individually. There are a number of these available in a variety of sizes—some with cake, some with creme, and some with grease makeup. (See *Makeup kits*, Appendix A.)

The main advantage in making up your own kit is that you can combine items you particularly like from various companies and can select only those items you think you will find useful. If you decide to do this, you may wish to refer to the kits listed in Appendix C. One of them can probably be adapted, with minor changes, to your needs. The primary purpose of the student kits is to keep the price as low as possible. That means fewer colors to work with and more mixing to be done, but this can prove advantageous for the beginner.

Makeup materials for classes. For purposes of more advanced work in the makeup class the small student kits might be supplemented with additional materials as they are needed. If *all* makeup materials for a class are furnished, the dispensing of makeup from the general kit can present problems. The most practical solution, if sufficient makeup is available, is to make up a number of basic kits, which can be handed out at the beginning of the class period. Or each student may be provided with a ready-made kit from one of the makeup companies. Two or even three students can share a kit if necessary—provided each has his own brushes and, depending on the type of makeup being used, his own sponge or powder puff. If the group kit contains a small number of tubes of greasepaint, the problem can be solved by using glass slides approximately three by four inches. Each student should have one of these slides, or the whole group of slides can be kept by the instructor. When the student needs a base from the large kit, he can squeeze a small amount onto his glass slide and leave the tube in the kit for others to use. When he needs one of the shading colors, he can remove a very small amount from the container with an artist's palette knife. On the other hand, the instructor may prefer either to designate an assistant to dispense the paint or to do it himself. But no matter how the paint is distributed, the glass slide method, though rather a nuisance, does make possible the use of an average-sized kit by the whole class.

THE MAKEUP ROOM

Given the necessary materials, a makeup can be done in any surroundings, but the work can be done far more efficiently in a room designed to fill the requirements for makeup.

The focus of such a room, whether it is an individual dressing room or a large room for group makeup, is the makeup table and mirror. The average dressing room has mirrors surrounded by rows of naked bulbs. A more satisfactory arrangement would be to have the light source recessed and a slot provided for slipping in colored gelatines to approximate the stage lighting (see Figure 11–2). This will never give the same effect as the stage lights, but it will come closer to it than the usual dressing room lights. If such an arrangement is not possible, at least be sure that the amount of illumination is adequate. If fluorescent lights are used, install warm-tinted tubes if possible or else arrange for a color medium to be used over the lights.

No matter what type of illumination is used at the dressing tables, it is always desirable to have two spotlights in the general makeup room with colored gelatines to approximate the lighting used for the play. The actor can then check his makeup as often as he wishes, at a distance, under appropriately colored lights. The spots should be mounted one on each side of a full-length mirror at a sufficient height for providing a reasonable angle of illumination.

The dressing table should be about 30 inches high and should contain a drawer with a lock for storing the makeup between performances and for keeping the actor's valuables during performances. A dispenser for cleansing tissues either above or to one side of the mirror is a great convenience. Either a wastebasket or a special section built into the table should be provided for disposing of used tissues. If there is an additional space above or at the sides of the mirror, a row of small shelves or pigeonholes for makeup will help to avoid some of the usual clutter on the table. A row of cabinets

Figure 11–2. Makeup table mirror. Designed to permit the use of gelatine slides over the lights to approximate the lighting on stage.

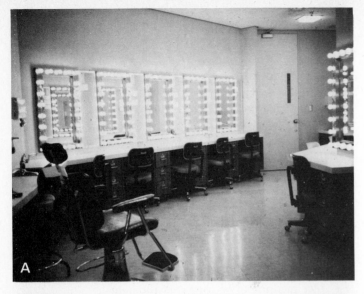

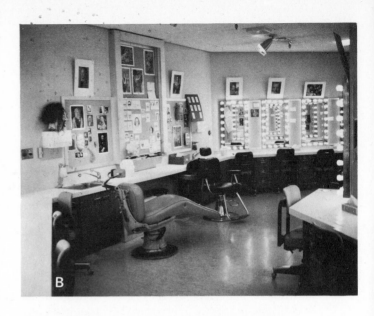

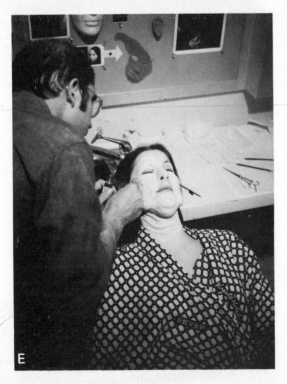

Figure 11-3. Makeup laboratory at the California State University at Long Beach. Lab is furnished with padded chairs with casters, individual drawers between the chairs, mirrors with non-heating light bulbs, spotlights in ceiling, 2 adjustable reclining makeup chairs, cork bulletin boards, colored chalk-board, 4 steel sinks, Corning-top electric range for prosthetic work, and built-in storage cabinets. (A) Laboratory in new theatre, just after completion; (B, C) room after the makeup department moved in; (D) ante-laboratory storage area with oven and sink; (E) advanced student, working under the supervision of instructor Bill Smith, applying prosthetic makeup for *The Chairs*.

above the mirrors can be very useful for getting personal belongings out of the way during performances or for storing wigs on blocks. It's a good idea to equip such cabinets with locks.

In the professional theater, actors customarily do their own makeup, but in the nonprofessional theater there is usually a makeup artist or even a makeup crew. This places an additional burden on dressing rooms, which are usually overcrowded anyway, or it necessitates moving to a vacant room that has no adequate facilities for makeup. In either case there is a loss of efficiency. All nonprofessional theaters should have a special makeup room large enough to accommodate a number of actors in addition to the makeup artists.

There should be running water in every dressing room. A makeup room should contain not only running water but also convenient facilities for storing makeup and wigs. Cases with small drawers are particularly useful. A reclining barber's or

Figure 11–4. Makeup facilities. (A) Makeup workroom. Small makeup room that has been transformed into a workroom for modeling, casting, making wigs and masks, etc. For the makeup room in the new theater at the same university, see Figure 11–3. (B) Equipment for casting. Corner of the same makeup room with dentist's chair, sink, hot plate, and double boiler. (C) Closet off makeup room transformed at minimum cost into a compact and reasonably efficient supply room. (D) Dental cabinet used for makeup storage.

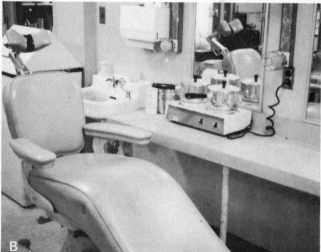

dentist's chair (see Figure 11–3) is enormously helpful to the makeup artist and should be standard equipment in any makeup room.

A general makeup room should be as near to the dressing rooms and to the stage as possible. Since makeup may need to be hurriedly touched up between acts or during an act, having the makeup room near the stage is particularly important. Good ventilation is essential, and air conditioning should be installed if possible.

It may sometimes be necessary to provide temporary or portable makeup facilities for a large number of people, such as students in a makeup class or extras in crowd scenes who are all doing their own makeup. A very simple and practical arrangement involves the construction of wooden frames (Figures 11–5 and 11–6) on which inexpensive mirrors can be hung. It is possible to use either individual small mirrors (Figure 11–5) or long, narrow mirrors (Figure 11–6) running the length of the frames. Both have their advantages. The long mirrors are less confining to the actors, but the small ones afford him access to storage space inside the frame. Both arrangements have proved very satisfactory. In either case, the frames are set on tables, the mirrors hung on nails or hooks, the lights plugged in, and chairs set up along either side.

The lighting for each unit is self-contained—that is, any unit can be plugged directly into the power source, or any number of units can be connected. The most satisfactory arrangement of lights is to have 75-watt bulbs spaced equidistant between the mirrors. This gives each actor a light source from two sides.

A number of units can be set up end to end to make a long makeup table, or they can be

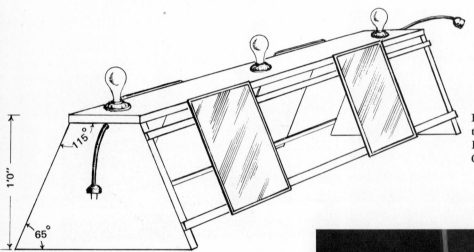

Figure 11–5. Frame for portable makeup table. Designed by Dr. Harold K. Stevens, Eastern Washington State College at Cheney.

Figure 11–6. Makeup class at the University of North Carolina. Frames are a modification of the ones designed by Dr. Stevens.

Figure 11–7. Makeup artist Dick Smith in his workshop. Shown pouring foamed latex into one of the molds for Dustin Hoffman's makeup in *Little Big Man*, Figure 16–30. (Photo by Dick Smith.)

divided into smaller sections. In order to take maximum advantage of available space, the frames should be about the same length as the tables on which they are to be used or perhaps an inch or two shorter to allow for plugging the light cords together; however, they will work just as well no matter what the length. The tables should be wide enough to allow work space for the actor on either side of the frame but not so wide that he cannot get close to the mirror.

The units can be set up and taken down very quickly, the frames can be stored or transported in a relatively small space, and any available tables can be used. For classes, the ideal arrangement is to set up as many units as needed on an empty stage. This gives the students adequate space to step back and look at themselves in the mirrors. It enables the instructor to work with much greater freedom than in a crowded dressing room, and it makes it possible to see the makeups under stage lights with maximum convenience. It is extremely useful, when possible, to have spots focused so that when the student stands back to look at himself, both he and the instructor will be seeing the makeup under stage lights.

THE MAKEUP WORKSHOP

The makeup workshop differs from the makeup room in that it is used primarily for laboratory work by the makeup artist. It may or may not be used for actual makeup. It should contain equipment and material for modeling and casting (including an oven for foam latex), for the construction and dressing of wigs, and for any experimental or preparatory work done by the makeup artist before actually applying the makeup. It should also contain ample storage facilities, allowing frequently used items to be within easy reach. The workshop may or may not be equipped with a dentist's or barber's chair for casting or with a mirror and a makeup table to be used by the makeup artist for experimental work. In other words, it should contain whatever is useful to the makeup artist in his work.

The university makeup workshop shown in Figure 11–4A was originally a small makeup room, whereas the makeup room in Figure 11–3 (in a new theater on the same campus) is actually a combination workshop and classroom. Figure 11–7 shows a corner of a professional makeup artist's workshop.

THE MAKEUP MORGUE

One of the first requisites of a good makeup artist is a keen sense of observation and the ability to apply what he observes to the creation of his makeups. To help him remember what he observes, a makeup morgue (a term used to designate a file of clippings) is indispensable. The morgue should contain, first of all, unretouched photographs of people. Illustrated magazines are a good source for these. Reproductions of works of art are useful for historical characters. Much of this can be found in secondhand bookstores. In addition, your morgue should contain makeup catalogs, price lists, and

Figure 11–8.   Makeup morgues.

any information you can collect on makeup techniques. Anything, in fact, that relates to makeup should be included. Clear acetate sheets (see Figure 11–8) are very helpful in keeping smudges off your pictures.

Below are suggested classifications for your morgue. As your collection grows, you may want to make certain changes or add subdivisions.

AGE, Male	HISTORICAL, Male
AGE, Female	HISTORICAL, Female
BALD HEADS	LATEX
BEARDS and MUSTACHES	LIGHTING
BRUISES and BURNS	MOUTHS and CHINS
CATALOGS and PRICE LISTS	NECKS and JAWLINES
COLOR	NONREALISTIC
CORRECTIVE MAKEUP	NOSES (PHOTOGRAPHY)
EARS	PROSTHESIS (Misc.)
EQUIPMENT	RACES and NATIONALITIES*
EYES and EYEBROWS	SCARS, WELTS, WARTS
FASHIONS	SKIN TEXTURE
FICTIONAL, Male	SUPPLIES
FICTIONAL, Female	TECHNIQUES (Misc.)
HAIR, Male	TEETH
HAIR, Female	WIGS, Male
HANDS	WIGS, Female

*Can be subdivided into specific ones for which you have illustrations.

The most practical form of morgue is probably a set of loose-leaf binders with 8½ × 11-inch pages for pasting up your pictures. These pages can be rearranged or temporarily removed at any time. You will probably want to start with a single binder, then expand as your morgue increases in size.

If you want a convenient way to store your pictures until you have time to paste them on to the binder pages, an expanding file (Figure 11–8) can be very useful. If you have an enormous collection of pictures and no time or inclination to paste them all up, you may find a metal filing cabinet with removable manila folders very handy. In any case, keep your pictures organized, ready for instant reference.

Keep adding to your morgue continually. It is your private library and is almost as important a part of your makeup equipment as paints and brushes.

PROBLEM

1. Start your own makeup morgue, with any photographs you may have already collected. Work out whatever filing system you find most convenient, but be sure there is adequate room for expansion. Label all material you find according to the category in which you file it. This will simplify putting it back each time you have used it. Make a point of bringing as many pictures as possible to class each day.

12

APPLICATION OF MAKEUP

Since the problems and procedures involved in the application of the various types of makeup are quite different, they will be discussed separately. Which type of makeup you choose is a matter of personal preference. The advantages and disadvantages of each will be discussed, along with their characteristics, in Appendix A.

CAKE MAKEUP

Foundation. Cake makeup is applied with a sponge for large areas and a brush for small ones. A natural silk sponge is best for the base color. The sponge should be damp but not wet. If the makeup does not come off on the sponge easily, you are not using enough water; if it seems thin and runs on the face, you are using too much water. If the paint seems to be thick and heavy, too much water may have soaked into the cake, or the sponge may have been rubbed too hard on the cake. In some brands of makeup the color comes off the cake much more readily than in others. If you use more than one brand of makeup, this difference may require some adjustment. If you have trouble getting color off the cake at all, use another brand of makeup or, as an emergency measure, scrape the surface of the cake with a knife or with your brush handle.

After the makeup has been taken up on the sponge, stroke the sponge lightly across the face until the whole area is covered smoothly with a thin film of color. Cake makeup requires no powder.

Highlights and shadows. These are normally applied over the base with cake shading colors. It is possible, however, to apply them *under* the base for subtle modeling effects or for lightening a heavy beard. Or a combination of both methods can be used. When the base is applied *over* shadows and highlights, it should be pressed on with the sponge, then smoothed over very lightly to avoid smearing the paint underneath.

Highlights and shadows are applied with brushes and appropriate light and dark cake colors, as illustrated in Figure 12–1. Although a sponge can be used for larger areas and is preferred by some makeup artists, it is somewhat easier to control the paint with brushes. For larger areas, a ½-inch or ⅜-inch flat sable brush works very well (Figure 12–1E); for smaller areas, including most wrinkles, 3/16-inch, ¼-inch, and ⅛-inch brushes can be used. Pointed Chinese brushes and eyeliner brushes are useful for small details. In general, it is best to use the largest size brush suitable for the particular job you're doing. Small brushes used for large areas are inefficient and may produce ineffective results.

If you are using a sponge to apply highlights and shadows, hold it so that only a small section of it touches the face. Apply the color directly to the face only in the area that is to be most strongly shadowed or highlighted. Then with a clean section of the dampened sponge, using a very light touch, blend the color out over the entire area to be covered, letting it fade out as you go until it blends into the base color. It may be helpful to run a clean section of the sponge very lightly over the edge of the shadow or the highlight where it meets the base in order to help merge the two.

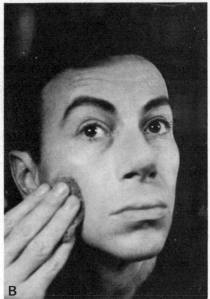

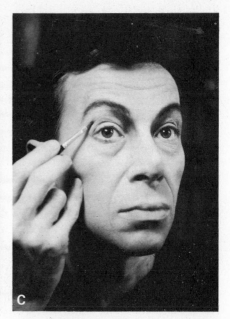

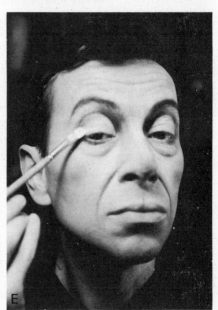

Figure 12-1 The Mad Hatter from *Alice in Wonderland.* Based on the Tenniel illustration (see Figure 20–6). Nose is built up with putty-wax (A), cake base is applied (B), face is modeled with light and dark cake makeup (C, D, E), lips and eyebrows are made up (F), hair pieces are glued down (G), and costume is added (H).

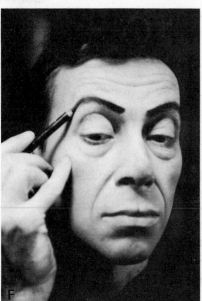

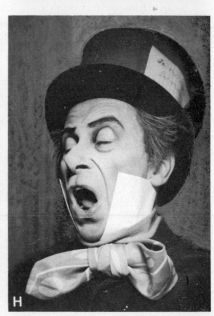

In working with brushes, the general technique is first to lay on color in the darkest area of the shadow or the lightest area of the highlight, then clean the brush and blend the edges of the shadow or the highlight with the damp brush until they blend imperceptibly into the foundation. Using separate brushes for shadows and highlights is a great time-saver.

Whether you are using a sponge or a brush, it is always best to build up a shadow or a highlight with several applications rather than trying to get just the right amount the first time. It is much easier to add color than it is to subtract it. If a shadow does become too dark, it should be lightened by lifting the color with a clean damp sponge. Never try to lighten a shadow by covering it with a highlight. The result will probably be a muddy, gray color. Shadows and highlights can, however, be toned down or softened by stippling with a sponge, using lighter colors for shadows, darker colors for highlights, or colors in between for toning down both at the same time. (For more detailed instructions in stippling, see Chapter 14.)

Rouge and eyeshadow. Cake rouge can be applied with a dry puff or with a moist sponge. Brush-on rouge and eyeshadow are normally applied dry. It is possible, however, to use damp sponges or applicators with brush-on cakes.

CREME MAKEUP

This form of makeup is usually transferred from the stick or the cake to the face with the fingers, a brush, or a sponge (rubber or synthetic). It can also be blended with any of these. Use only a thin film, just enough to color the skin and conceal minor blemishes. Then dust the base very

lightly with a neutral powder and go over the whole makeup lightly with a damp sponge. This removes excess powder and sets the makeup. If a slight sheen is appropriate, the makeup need not be powdered.

Although grease rouge and shading colors can be used with creme stick, creme rouge and shading colors are preferable. They can be applied either before or after the makeup has been powdered. If applied after, they will normally be powdered. Highlights and shadows can also be applied *under* the base for subtle modeling effects or for covering heavy beards. Or you may wish to apply shadows under the base and highlights over. The reverse is not recommended.

Dry rouge and dry eyeshadow (regular or brush-on) can both be used with creme makeup, provided the foundation has first been powdered. The dry rouge can be applied with a moist sponge instead of with a puff if you prefer.

GREASEPAINT

When soft greasepaint in tubes or jars is being used, it is important for the skin to be relatively free of grease before the paint is applied. If other makeup has been removed with cleansing cream or any kind of oil, either wash the face with soap and water or use a skin freshener to remove any greasy film before applying the greasepaint.

The paint can be taken directly from the tube onto your finger tip and applied in small dots evenly over the face, neck, and ears (Figure 12–2). If you are mixing paints, however, you may wish to mix them in your hand first to obtain the correct color, then apply the mixed paint in dots. When you have spotted the face with paint, dip your finger tips into cold water and blend the base thor-

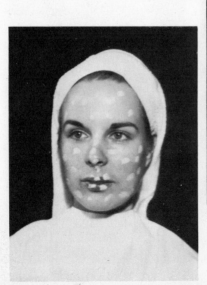 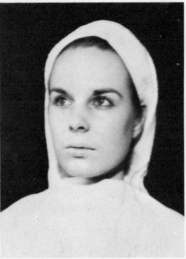

Figure 12–2. Application of greasepaint. Paint is applied from tube in dots, then blended with the fingertips dipped into cold water.

oughly, making sure that every exposed part of the flesh is covered, including the neck. Blend it into the hairline so that no line of demarcation is visible, but be careful not to get makeup into the hair. Use very little paint. The purpose of the foundation is to color the face, not to mask it. However, if there are blemishes to be covered, it may be desirable to use a somewhat heavier foundation.

When you have finished, rub a clean finger lightly across your face. If it leaves a mark or if a noticeable amount of paint comes off on the finger, you have probably used too much paint and should wipe some off. The skin should feel moist and soft to the touch but not slippery.

If you are using stick paint (this form of greasepaint is now less frequently used than the paint in tubes or jars), you should first apply a thin layer of cold cream over the entire face and neck, then wipe it off, leaving only a very thin film. Rub the stick in streaks across the face and neck—about two streaks on each cheek, two on the forehead, one down the nose, one under the nose, one across the chin, and several on the neck. Then blend the paint with your fingertips to make a completely smooth foundation—unless, of course, you want some irregularity in the color for a particular character.

Probably the most common fault in the application of greasepaint is the tendency to use two or three times too much, the result of which is a greasy makeup that does not take highlights and shadows well, rubs off easily, induces excessive perspiration, requires an abnormally heavy coating of powder, and creates a masklike effect. For most makeups the foundation color should be used sparingly.

Moist rouge and shading colors (highlights, shadows, eyeshadow) are blended into the foundation, then powdered in order to set the makeup and remove the shine. Creme rouge and shading colors can be used over a greasepaint base in the same way. Dry rouge and eyeshadow can also be used, but not until the makeup has been powdered.

MIXED TECHNIQUES

Sometimes it is advantageous to use cake makeup and creme makeup (or greasepaint, if you prefer) together. The most obvious need arises when you wish to use cake makeup but need the covering power of creme makeup or grease in blocking out eyebrows. The creme makeup or grease can be easily covered with cake and the makeup finished in the usual way. Below are a few possible techniques. It would be a good idea to try all of them in order to discover for yourself the advantages of each. As you work, you will undoubtedly develop your own modifications.

Method 1. With this method, creme or grease highlights, shadows, and rouge are applied first—much stronger than usual but still well blended. The shadows should have more red in them than usual. Then cake makeup is patted on with a sponge until the makeup underneath shows through only as much as you want it to. If highlights, shadows, or rouge require touching up afterward, this can be done over the base, preferably with cake makeup. This method can be used for very subtle aging. It would not be a good choice, however, if you want the strong three-dimensional effect shown in Figure 2–3.

Method 2. Shadows are applied under the base and highlights over. First, model the face with heavy creme or grease shadows, using no foundation. Then pat on the cake base with a sponge, letting only as much of the shadow show through as you want. Add highlights with a light cake or creme makeup over the cake base. (Creme highlights should usually be powdered.) Finally, accent the deepest parts of the wrinkles with a dark cake shading color. This technique permits a greater three-dimensional effect than is possible with Method 1.

Method 3. Do all highlights and shadows with cake makeup over a powdered creme base. You may wish to apply creme rouge before the base is powdered or dry rouge either before or after highlights and shadows have been applied.

Method 4. Use creme highlights and cake shadows over a powdered creme base. The reverse is not recommended, however, since either creme or grease makeup, even though powdered, may develop a shine, and shadows, representing areas that reflect little or no light, will thus not be convincing. However, if the skin of the character could be expected to have a slight sheen as a result of natural oils or perspiration, a slightly shiny reflection from the highlights might be acceptable.

Stippling. An effective stippling technique using either creme or grease combined with cake makeup is illustrated in Figure 12–3. The stippling is done with grease or creme makeup applied with

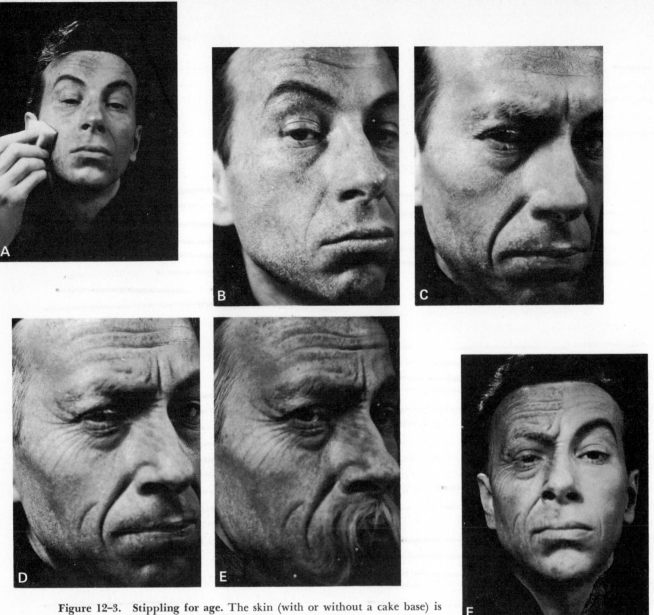

Figure 12–3. Stippling for age. The skin (with or without a cake base) is stippled first with dark brown grease or creme makeup (A), then with a light creme rouge, and finally with a light base (B). After the makeup is set with translucent powder, cake shadows are carefully laid in with sable brushes, highlights stippled on with cake, and eyebrows grayed (C). Detailed wrinkles are added with a Chinese brush and highlighted with an eyeliner brush (D). Mustache is added and makeup touched up (E). The final photograph (F) shows the stippled makeup on half of the face, flat cake makeup on the other.

Figure 12–4. Materials for stippling. Cellulose sponges cut into small pieces, with paints used for the makeup in Figure 12–3. A separate sponge is used for each color—dark brown (A), light red (B), and pale yellowish flesh tone (C). The paint is spread on a flat surface, such as glass or a plastic cake-makeup container (D), from which the sponge can pick it up evenly. Black plastic or red-rubber sponges can be used instead.

a firm, flat sponge. Although a red rubber sponge is frequently used for stippling, a special flat plastic stippling sponge, which can be cut into blocks, is easier to use and is recommended for all stippling with grease or creme makeup. (See *Sponges*, Appendix A.) An ordinary cellulose household sponge could also be used for this technique. It should be cut into small pieces (Figure 12–4), dampened with water, and then squeezed dry. The sponges illustrated are about 1¼ by 2 inches. They can be of any size or shape you find convenient—even circular if you wish. You will need, in addition, a smooth, flat, easily cleaned surface on which to spread the paint. Glass is fine, but the flat top of a plastic cake-makeup container (Figure 12–4) does very well and is usually available in the kit. Here is one possible procedure:

1. Select three colors for stippling. Which ones you choose will depend on the effect you want—healthy, sickly, tanned, sunburned, sallow. Keep in mind that colors used for men are usually darker than those used for women. And, of course, dark-skinned actors will require darker stipple colors than those with lighter complexions. The same holds true for light-skinned actors playing dark-complexioned characters. The first stipple should be quite dark—perhaps a dark brown. Even black is sometimes possible. The second might be a shade of red—a light or dark moist rouge, for example. The third should be somewhat lighter, the hue depending on what further adjustments you think should be made in the makeup—more yellow, perhaps, or more red or pink or tan or even gray.

2. Spread a small amount of your first stipple color on the smooth, flat surface you have chosen for a palette, then press your sponge lightly onto the paint, as has been done in Figure 12–4A. Be sure not to take up too much on the sponge. Then keep pressing the sponge against the face (Figure 12–3A) until you have covered all exposed areas. You may, if you wish, give the skin a base coat of cake makeup first, but this is not necessary. Since you are stippling with a very dark color, be careful not to use too much. Avoid smearing the stipple or leaving dark blotches of paint. You should set this first stipple by patting translucent powder over it very carefully so as not to smear it. Slight smears can be retouched by stippling with a small brush—an eyeliner brush does very well.

3. Follow the same procedure with your second stipple color. If this is a red stipple, you can make it heavier on areas that you wish to appear more red in the final makeup. Powder again.

4. Apply your third stipple (Figure 12–3B). With this you can control the overall lightness or darkness of the final effect. Set this final stipple with translucent powder. Now proceed with the modeling, using either cake or creme makeup.

5. Add highlights and shadows by stippling with

cake or creme makeup, using a small sponge or a brush. (See Figure 12–3C.) This must be done with extreme care since mistakes require painstaking repairs in the stippling.

6. Add detailed wrinkles with Chinese brushes or eyeliners in order to break up highlighted areas such as the cheekbones and the forehead (Figure 12–3D). If you have used creme makeup for highlights and shadows, you will need to powder again; otherwise, you will not.

7. Complete your makeup with grayed eyebrows, beard, wig, or whatever else is required.

It is also possible to model the face with strong lights and darks (cake, creme, or grease) before applying your stipple (powdering if necessary), and then merely strengthen highlights and shadows after you have finished stippling. There is probably some advantage in this, particularly for the inexperienced makeup artist, since it makes it possible to experiment with the correct placement of the highlights and shadows without ruining three coats of stippling. For the final touching up you can then follow the original pattern.

These are merely suggestions for stippling techniques. There are other possibilities, one of which will be discussed in Chapter 14. But for young actors especially, some method should be used to break up areas of smooth skin if an age makeup is to be effective. (See Hal Holbrook's Mark Twain makeup, Figures 12–5 and 19–5D.)

Figure 12–5. Stippling with brush. Detail from Hal Holbrook's makeup for Mark Twain, showing stippling used to age the skin. The three colors used were applied with a small flat brush. (For additional illustrations of Mr. Holbrook's makeup, see Figures 19–3, 4, 5.)

13

CORRECTIVE MAKEUP

Most of your work in makeup will have to do with creating characters. But there are times when an actor is to appear as himself (as in platform performances, lectures, photographs) or when it is assumed that he looks essentially right for the character but should be made as attractive as possible. This may mean only slight adjustments such as changing the shape of the mouth or the curve of the eyebrows, lowering the forehead, or shortening the nose. In the professional theater it frequently means making the actor look younger.

SKIN COLOR

Before beginning any makeup it is necessary to choose the colors you're going to work with—particularly the foundation paint, which will be used to obtain whatever skin color you want. There are two reasons for changing the color of an actor's skin. One is to counteract the effect of stage lights and stage distance; the other is to suggest character. An actor who looks perfectly healthy off stage may look ghostly on stage unless he happens to have dark skin. If the actor's skin color—no matter what his race—is dark enough to project and is of the correct color for the character, he may not need a base. In this chapter we shall assume that he does need a base and that its purpose will be to counteract the effect of stage lights and to give the actor an attractive, healthy coloring.

There are, as has been mentioned previously, a large number of foundation colors available. Perhaps the easiest way to choose which of these colors to use is to decide, first of all, what hue you want

(R, SR, RS, S, FS, etc.), then how light or dark the skin should be, choosing a number between 1 and 20 to indicate the value. In this connection it should be pointed out that men's skin is usually darker than women's. A number 7, 8, or 9, which is average for Caucasian men (English, northern European), will look dark on women, and a 4 or 5, which is average for Caucasian women, will seem pale on men. This average value is the one most frequently employed in corrective makeup, though it will vary with the actor's own coloring. For dark-skinned races the averages will be lower in intensity and usually in value and can vary widely with individuals of a particular race. The fashionable makeup colors of the day may also affect one's choice. If pale skin is in fashion, women may wish to lighten their base color. If summer tans are being worn, both men and women may want to darken it. The actor's natural skin coloring will also have some effect on the color selected. A Nigerian will naturally be considerably darker than a Norwegian. Furthermore, a given color of makeup, unless it is much too heavily applied, will not look the same on a light skin as on a dark one.

As for the hue, you will normally choose, for corrective makeup, one that will help the actor look as attractive as possible. Which color this is will depend, of course, on race. Whereas a Caucasian may look for a color in the S group, for example, an Oriental will presumably avoid the redder hues and look for something with more yellow in it. The black and brown races, if they choose to wear a foundation color at all, will usually require hues that are neither very red nor very yellow. The F, F/OF, and OF groups contain a number of suitable shades. A fairly light Negro, for example, might find an F-10-e becoming, whereas one with a darker skin might perhaps choose an F-12-f. If his skin tone had more yellow in it, he might prefer a medium dark, grayed F/OF shade. Other races will choose specific colors appropriate for them. There are no hard and fast rules about what color an actor of any race may or may not use. He should choose one that looks attractive on him in the lighting in which he will be seen.

Colors of rouge and eye makeup will be discussed under those headings.

FACIAL ANALYSIS

Before applying corrective makeup, it is necessary to analyze the actor's face to determine how it can be made more attractive. If the two sides of the face are sufficiently different to appear obviously asymmetrical, the less attractive side should be made up to match the more pleasing one. Which side is the more attractive can usually be judged by covering first one half of the face with a sheet of paper, then the other. An even more effective, though more elaborate, technique is to make a full-face photograph, and then take a reverse print. Both the normal print and the reverse one can be cut vertically in half and the halves switched and pasted together. You will then have two photographs of the face with both sides matching, but one will be based on the right side, the other on the left. The less appealing face will indicate the side that is to be corrected. It is essential, of course, that the photograph be taken absolutely straight on if the technique is to work properly.

Decisions on what is or is not to be corrected are, of course, based on personal taste, which may, in turn, be affected by current fashions. More often than not, however, fashions have to do with individual features—such as eyebrows and lips—rather than overall proportions. (Women's excessively high foreheads in the late Middle Ages and early Renaissance are a glaring exception.) But there are certain classic features and classic proportions that seem to transcend fashion and personal taste and that are, among most civilized peoples, considered beautiful.

As indicated in the chapter on facial anatomy, the classically proportioned face can be divided horizontally into three equal parts: (1) from the hairline to the eyebrows, (2) from the eyebrows to the bottom of the nose, and (3) from the bottom of the nose to the tip of the chin. If these three sections are not equal, they can be made to appear equal or more nearly so in various ways. But a face does not *have* to be classically proportioned in order to be beautiful—or to be interesting. An interesting rather than classic face may, in fact, be more effective on stage than a perfectly proportioned one; which you want to aim for will depend on the face you have to work with and what you want it to express. If you're unsure of what you want or what can be done, experiment. And keep experimenting until you're satisfied with the results.

The following suggestions are intended to help you in your experimentation.

Figure 13-1. Corrective makeup. Creme foundation, highlights, and shadows. Eyebrows filled out with brown pencil. False eyelashes used for strong emphasis on the eyes. Makeup and photographs by Bert Roth, S.M.A.

FOREHEAD

If the forehead is higher than you would like it to be, it can be darkened near the hairline with a fairly wide stripe of color about three shades darker than the rest of the base. This stripe can be blended downward very gradually so that it disappears imperceptibly into the foundation. There must be no line of demarcation. This technique works simply because light colors reflect light and attract the eye, whereas dark colors absorb light and attract less attention, often seeming to recede. Following the same principle, a low forehead can be raised by using a color about three shades lighter than the base and applied at the hairline as before. This will attract the eye upward, emphasizing the height of the forehead.

The forehead can be narrowed by shadowing the temples, blending the shadow onto the front plane of the forehead, thus apparently decreasing the actual width of the front plane by making it seem to turn sooner. Or it can be widened by highlighting the temples, carrying the highlight clear to the hairline. This will counteract the natural shadow that results from the receding of the temple areas and will appear to bring them forward. It will also seem to extend the front plane of the forehead horizontally. As always, there should be a difference of only two or three shades between the shadows and the base, since deeper shadows at the temples tend to age the face. If the frontal lobes are too prominent, tone them down with a shadow and bring forward the depression between the frontal lobes and the superciliary arch with a highlight. If the temples are normally sunken, they can be brought out with a highlight.

NOSE

If you want the nose shorter, apply a deeper color under the tip and blend it up over the tip (Figure 13–2B). This will tone down the natural highlight and take the attention away from the tip. If a short highlight is placed on the upper part of the nose, this will attract the eye to that area and help still further to give the illusion of a shorter nose. If you want the nose longer, you can carry a highlight down over and under the tip, pulling the viewer's eye downward and apparently lengthening the nose. (See Figure 13–2C.)

If you want to widen the nose, run a broad highlight down the center (Figure 13–2A). This will appear to widen the front plane of the nose—not the entire nose. You might also highlight the wings of the nostrils to attract the eye outward in both directions, thus giving an illusion of still greater width.

If you want to narrow the nose, reverse the procedure by shadowing the nostrils and the sides of the nose and running a very narrow highlight down the center (Figure 13–2C). This will give the illusion of a sharp and narrow bone and cartilage.

To flatten the nose, reverse the usual modeling by shadowing the front and highlighting the sides.

If the tip of the nose is fuller than you want it to be, shadow it on either side of the painted highlight to tone down part of the natural highlight.

If the nose is crooked, run a fairly narrow highlight down the nose, then shadow it on either side wherever there is a natural highlight that reveals the crookedness of the nose. This highlight may be straight, or it may bend slightly in the opposite direction from the real bend. Use whichever method proves the more effective for the nose you're working on. (For the procedure in making a straight nose appear crooked, see Chapter 14 and Figure 13–2D.)

In general, then, decide where you want to attract the eye of the viewer and place the highlights in that area, shadowing areas that you want to recede or to seem smaller or less conspicuous.

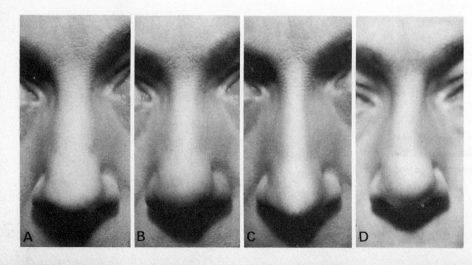

Figure 13–2. Remodeling the nose with paint. (A) Wide; (B) shortened; (C) long and thin; (D) crooked.

Figure 13-3. Corrective makeup for the nose. In B the nose has been straightened with putty-wax.

Normally, in corrective makeup, highlights and shadows are only about three shades darker than the base. But in making up the nose it is often possible and sometimes necessary to use stronger contrasts to achieve the desired effect. This applies particularly to any case in which you are using shadows to counteract strong natural highlights.

The corrective techniques just described, though effective from the front, have little or no effect on the nose in profile. This requires a three-dimensional addition. (See Chapter 15.) Obviously, the nose can't be cut down by this method, but it can be built up, as illustrated in Figure 13-3.

JAW LINE AND CHIN

If the jaw line is too square or too prominent, shadow the part that needs to be rounded off or toned down, carrying the shadow both under and over the jawbone, and blend carefully into the foundation. If you want to make the jaw line more firm and youthful, run a stripe of highlight all along the jawbone, softening the lower edge and blending the top edge imperceptibly into the foundation. A stripe of shadow can be run along under the bone and both edges blended.

If the chin is too prominent—that is, if it juts forward too much—darken the whole chin with a light shadow. If it's too long in proportion to the rest of the face, it can be shortened by shadowing the lower part. Make sure the edge of the shadow

is thoroughly blended. If you want the chin longer, highlight the lower part, and if you want it more prominent, highlight the whole chin. If it's too square, round off the corners with shadows. If it's too pointed, flatten the point with a square shadow. A double chin can be minimized by shadowing it to make it less noticeable.

WRINKLES

Wrinkles can seldom be blotted out completely any more than a double chin can, but they can be minimized by carefully brushing in highlights where you find the natural shadows and subtly shadowing the prominent part of each wrinkle where you find a natural highlight. This applies also to circles or bags under the eyes.

EYES

In making up the eyes, you should decide first of all if you are satisfied with their present placement, keeping in mind that ideally eyes are the width of an eye apart. If they are less than that, you can make them appear to be farther apart. For corrective makeup it is rare that eyes need to be brought closer together, though this may very well be done in certain character makeups. Either of these changes can easily be brought about by making use of an optical illusion. In Figure 13-4A the

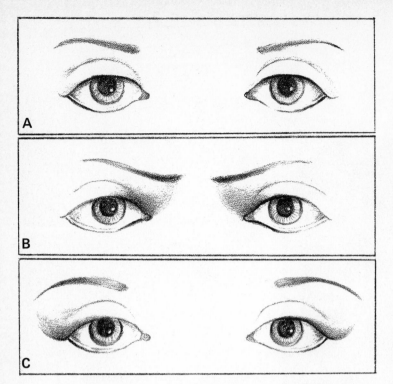

Figure 13–4. Optical illusions in eye makeup. All three pairs of eyes are the same distance apart, but in B they are made to seem closer together and in C farther apart by changing the position of the eyebrows and the shadowing.

eyes are the width of an eye apart, with normally placed eyebrows. In B the eyes are still the width of an eye apart, but pulling the eyebrows and the eyeshadow away from the outer corners and in toward the center seems to have brought them closer together. In C, although the eyes are spaced exactly the same as before, the placement of the eyebrows and the eyeshadow has apparently pulled them outward and farther apart. False eyelashes can also be used to do the same thing (see *Eyelashes*).

Eyeshadow. For women the color of eyeshadow chosen will depend on personal preference and may relate to the color of the eyes or of the costume, and it will depend to some extent on current fashions in eye makeup. The image the actress wishes to project will determine whether her eye makeup is to be high fashion, conservative, or somewhere in between. Men usually use some variation of brown or gray.

Normally the shadow is placed on the upper eyelid only. The shadow is usually heaviest next to the eye and is more or less confined to the lid itself. The occasionally fashionable practice of carrying the shadow up to the eyebrow is not to be encouraged in corrective makeup. Extreme fashions sometimes call for shadow on the lower lid as well. Since this seems hardly likely to make the eye more attractive, it should, perhaps, not be considered as corrective.

Occasionally the eyelid is highlighted instead of shadowed in order to make the eyes more prominent. The method usually used is described in detail in Chapter 14 in the discussion of highlighting the lids for glamor makeup.

A touch of rouge on the bone just below the outer end of the eyebrow will add a youthful sparkle to the eye. A red dot is sometimes placed at the tear duct for the same purpose but has less effect. It can, however, be used in addition to the rouge if you find it helpful.

Accents. Eyes are further emphasized by lining them, using a brush or a sharp eyebrow pencil. The brush can be used with cake or liquid eyeliner or with regular shading colors in cake, creme, or grease. With the brush or the pencil, a line is drawn along the upper lid close to the lashes. This line should usually start about two-thirds of the way in toward the nose or may even begin at the tear duct. The line follows the lashes and extends about a quarter of an inch beyond the outer corner of the eye. It should end in a graceful curve, not a straight line, and, when a natural effect is desired, it should fade out, not end abruptly.

A similar line is drawn on the lower lid, starting about a third of the way in from the outer corner (or possibly a third of the way out from the tear duct, as in Figure 13–5A) and moving outward along the eye, toward the top line. (A line starting in the middle of the eye, as in Figure 13–5B, is usually less becoming and tends to divide the eye in half.) This line should usually fade out before it quite meets the top line. Then both lines may be softened (for men they *should* be) by running the finger lightly over them so that they really become narrow shadows instead of lines. Their purpose is to enlarge the eye slightly as well as to emphasize it. For a natural corrective makeup, they should not completely surround the eye, though for high fashion makeup in certain periods they occasionally do. Sometimes a small amount of white is brushed or penciled in below the outer quarter inch of the top line in order to help enlarge the eye.

If the eyes are to be made to appear farther apart, the accents should be strongest at the outer ends and carried farther beyond the corner of the eye than usual (Figure 13–4C). If the eyes are to be closer together, the accents are shifted to the inner corners and should not extend to the outer corners at all (Figure 13–4B).

Eyelashes. Women's eyelashes are nearly always darkened with mascara or cosmetique (see Ap-

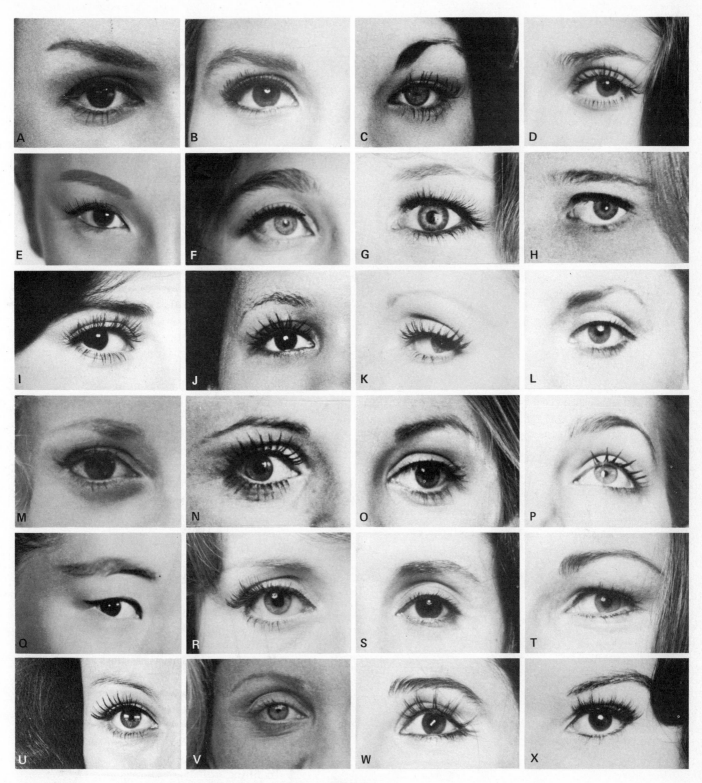

Figure 13–5. Women's eyebrows and eyelashes. Illustrates both becoming and unbecoming treatment of eyebrows and the use and misuse of false eyelashes.

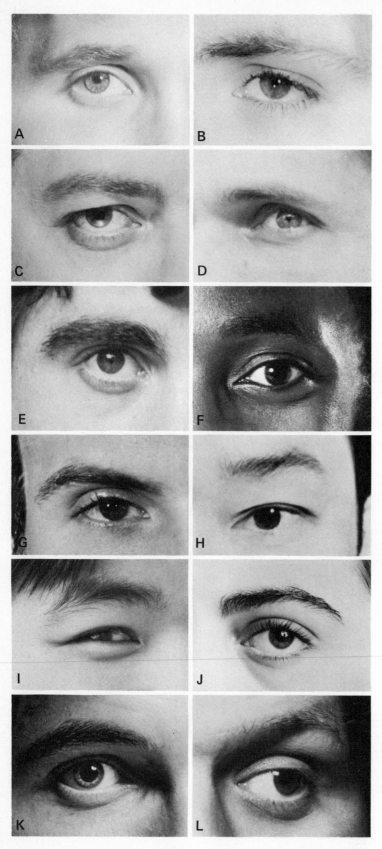

Figure 13-6. Young men's eyebrows. Natural brows without makeup. Some could be improved by darkening or reshaping for corrective makeup. Others could be left as they are.

pendix A)—usually black or brown, though other colors have occasionally been used for high fashion makeup. In applying the mascara, it is good practice to avoid clumps and to keep the lashes separated for a natural effect. C and P in Figure 13–5 illustrate a failure to avoid clumps, though the effect in P is obviously intentional. If men's eyelashes are very light or very sparse, brown or black mascara will be helpful in defining the eye. Be very careful to avoid getting mascara into the eyes, as it can be painful.

Women often wear false eyelashes on the upper lid, though seldom on the lower. Normally, one false eyelash is cut in two and the hairs cut on the bias so that when the eyelashes are applied, they are long at the outer end and relatively short at the inner. Be sure to cut the two halves of the lash in reverse so that you will have one left and one right lash. Figure 13–5B shows lashes trimmed on the bias, and G shows lashes that have evidently not been trimmed at all. Using excessively long or heavy lashes may at times be fashionable but does not necessarily make the eyes more attractive.

The eyelashes are applied with a special eyelash adhesive or with surgical adhesive (see Appendix A). If the eyes are to be made to seem farther apart, the lashes can be extended beyond the corner of the eye (Figure 13–5G). Mascara should be applied or false eyelashes put on after the makeup has been powdered.

EYEBROWS

For corrective makeup, men's eyebrows should always look natural, whereas women's need not. That does not mean that the actor's brows should necessarily be left exactly as they are. In ancient times hair between the eyebrows was considered a mark of beauty, but in these days it is not, and many men pluck these hairs. Unkempt, scraggly, or excessively heavy brows can be judiciously plucked if the actor is agreeable, but this should be done only if you are sure they will be improved by plucking. Any plucking of the brow itself should be carefully planned.

In filling out or reshaping men's brows with pencil, be sure to use short, light strokes following the direction of the hairs. It may help to soften the penciling by stroking it lightly with a finger. If the eyebrows are lighter than the hair, they should usually be darkened. In darkening men's brows, use either eyebrow pencil or mascara, being careful to maintain a natural look.

Changes in the men's eyebrows illustrated in Figure 13–6 would depend on the hair and on the entire face and even to some extent on the actor's personality or the aspects of his personality he wished to emphasize. For purposes of projection, however, B and D and possibly A should normally be darkened. In order to open up the eye area, D, for example, might be lifted slightly at the outer end. This could be done by brushing the hairs upward and reshaping the outer end of the brow slightly with a pencil, giving more of a lift to the brow and thus to the entire face. If it proved practicable, a few hairs might be plucked from the bottom of the brow in E. If one wanted a more masculine look, the brow in J might be filled out slightly with a pencil. You can judge for yourself the effect of the various brows illustrated—to what extent they enhance the eye, what quality of personality they suggest, and how they might be improved.

For women's corrective makeup, as for men's, it is not necessary to make the eyebrows fit one single pattern—rather, they should be as flattering as possible to the individual eye and to the face in general. This means that the line of the eyebrow should more or less follow that of the eye. Eyebrows that are too straight (Figure 13–5H), too arched (Figure 13–5C), too slanted (Figure 13–5A), too thick (Figure 13–5F), too thin (Figure 13–5K), too shaggy (Figure 14–35R), too close together (Figure 13–4B), or too far apart (Figure 14–12D) are probably less becoming than they might be and should be improved. Raising the eyebrow over the outer corner of the eye, as in Figure 13–5B, can be very helpful in opening up the eye and giving a slight lift to the whole face. Compare, for example, eyebrows B and H. Exaggerating this gentle curve too much, however, can become grotesque.

If the brow is well formed and well placed, it can simply be darkened with black or brown mascara or eyebrow pencil. After using mascara, you may wish to touch up the brows with petroleum jelly or cold cream to counteract the flat color of the mascara and restore a natural looking sheen. With pencils, use short, quick, light strokes, following the direction of the hair. Remember that the intention is to darken the hairs, not the skin underneath—except when the natural brow needs filling out.

If you want to change the line of the brow, this can be done by plucking, penciling, or both.

But if you're planning to pluck more than a few hairs, it would be wise to experiment with blocking out the portions of the brow to be plucked (see Chapter 14) in order to make sure you're improving the brows and not mutilating them.

CHEEKS

If the cheeks are too round, the part of the cheek to be made less prominent should be shaded with a base two or three shades darker than that used on the rest of the face. It is important, as always, to blend this lowlight imperceptibly into the lighter base. If the cheeks are too sunken, the procedure can be reversed by using a base a few shades lighter than the rest of the face to counteract the natural shadows that reveal the sunken cheeks.

Color of rouge. Rouge is usually applied after the modeling is done, though it is sometimes used as a shadow in modeling the cheeks. For women, the shade of rouge chosen will depend on skin color, fashion, costume, and personal preference. Colors suitable for pink skins will not necessarily look good on black, brown, or yellow ones, but there are too many variations to permit hard and fast rules. It is usually best to experiment with shades that you think *ought* to be suitable in order to find out which ones are actually the most effective.

Fashions in rouge colors can change very rapidly, but for corrective makeup a flattering conservative shade should always be chosen in preference to an unflattering fashionable one. Costume colors—especially reds, oranges, and purples—may determine to some extent which color should be used. A magenta rouge, for example, is not likely to be the best choice for a woman wearing an orange dress, though magenta accessories might make such a combination possible. Personal preference may be a factor, provided it does not lead one to choose an unbecoming or unsuitable color.

Placement of rouge. Normally rouge should be placed more or less on the cheekbone (Figure J–16) rather than low on the cheek, though in glamorizing the face it can be effective to use the rouge as a shadow below the cheekbone in order to sink in the cheeks. Except when used for shadowing, rouge is usually applied after any modeling with highlights and shadows has been completed. Rouge should not be placed too near the eye or the nose. If the face is narrow, it should be kept even farther from the nose and placed nearer the ears in order to increase the apparent width by attracting attention to the sides of the face. If the face is wide, keep the rouge away from the ears and apply it in a more or less vertical rather than horizontal pattern. It should not be applied in a round spot, and it should always be carefully blended.

Rouge is not always used for men, but if an actor requires color in the cheeks in order to look healthier, it should be used. When rouge is used, it should be applied with subtlety, and it should ordinarily be spread over a wider area than for women, even onto the temples if the face is not too wide. Above all, it ought to look as natural as possible. In case of doubt, use none.

LIPS

Figures 13–7 and 13–8 illustrate a number of lips of young men and women. In Figure 13–7, E represents the classical ideal—a graceful bow in the upper lip with a dip in the center, and a full lower lip not quite so wide as the upper. But the lips need not match this model of classical perfection in order to be attractive. Among the other lips in the group, some (such as A, in particular) are well shaped and well proportioned and would certainly not require correction. Others could be improved by making some changes with makeup. The lower lip in C, for example, might be made to seem less full. Although the upper lip in F is thin and out of proportion to the lower lip, the mouth is still attractive, and if it fits the face, it might better be left as it is. The lips in I do not follow classical

proportions, but they are interesting, attractive, and individual and should probably not be tampered with. Certainly it is essential that the lower lip not be darkened. The excessive fullness works only because it remains light and does not contrast strongly with the skin. Note what happens in C when the lower lip is darkened. If the red of the lips in C is their natural color, it would be well to lighten it.

In Figure 13–8, F is closest to the classical ideal. Some of the others might be improved with corrective makeup. In B, for example, the slightly crooked upper lip could easily be reshaped, perhaps giving it a more graceful curve and also widening it a bit in order to make it extend beyond the lower lip. Much the same is true of G. In E the upper lip could also be given a more graceful curve. It might be helpful in I if the upper lip were to be thinned; filling out the lower lip would also help the proportion.

Reshaping. There are various ways of reshaping lips. Thin lips can usually be corrected for women by overpainting—that is, by drawing on new lips of the shape and size wanted. This should be done for men only if the results will seem completely natural. It's usually best to make the lower lip lighter than the upper. A thin highlight over the upper lip may help to define it. Note the natural highlights over most of the upper lips in Figure 13–7. A similar highlight can be painted in over the corrected lip.

If a man's lips are too full, it is usually best to leave them the natural color (Figure 13–7G). If they are already too red, the lower one can be lightened. If the upper one is very full, it too should probably be lightened. For women the fullness can

Figure 13–7. Youthful lips, male. E is closest to the classical lip formation.

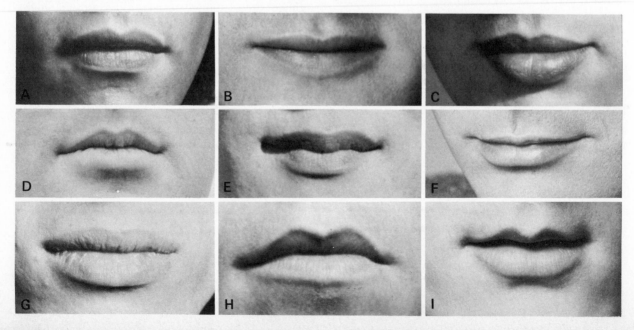

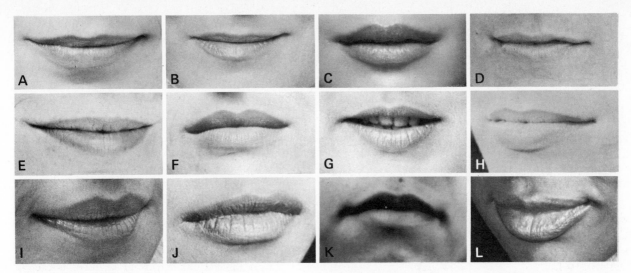

Figure 13–8. **Youthful lips, female.** F is the most nearly classical mouth.

be minimized by covering the lips with base, then using color only toward the inside of the lips and fading it outward into the base color. Deep colors should be avoided.

For too-wide lips, keep the color toward the center of the lips and cover the outer corners with base. The upper lip may be left slightly wider than the lower. If the mouth is too narrow, carry the color out to the extreme corners, particularly on the upper lip. Ordinarily, it is not possible to carry the color beyond the natural corners of the mouth with any degree of success. The artifice becomes apparent as soon as the mouth is opened.

In the case of a mouth with a heavy upper lip, a thin lower one, and the corners turned down, the solution is to overpaint the lower lip to match the upper one and to turn up the corners with paint. Or, if the outline of the upper lip is not too definite, it can be partially blocked out with base and the lower one filled in to match. This much correction may not always be possible for men.

For a mouth with a thin upper lip, the upper lip can be overpainted to match the lower.

Lip coloring can best be applied with a narrow flat brush and blotted with tissue. It is usually best not to carry the color to the extreme corners of the mouth unless you wish to widen it. It is frequently helpful, especially when overpainting, to define the lips by outlining them with a brown or, better yet, a dark red pencil. This outlining should not be left as a line, however, but should be blended inward with your brush. It is also possible to do the outline with the brush, using a darker shade of red than you have used on the lips.

For men, especially when no lipstick is used at all, the outline can be defined very subtly with a brown pencil and then blended. Further definition

is often possible by deepening the natural shadow immediately below the center of the lower lip. If the lip is naturally protruding or overhanging, this will not be necessary, but if the natural shadow is slight, it may be helpful. It should, however, be done with great care so as to look completely natural. Study the shadows under the lips in Figure 13–7.

Color. Lip coloring should be compatible with the rouge, and like rouge, it will depend on skin color, fashion, costume, and personal preference. Bizarre fashions (such as white lipstick) should not be followed for corrective makeup. For men a natural color (such as RS-13-c) is safest. Often it is best not to color the lower lip at all.

NECK

If the neck shows signs of age, this can be camouflaged somewhat by shadowing the prominent muscles and highlighting the depressions. Even a sagging neckline can be minimized at least for the front view, by shadowing. The shadow should be strongest just under the jaw line and should blend gradually into the foundation, which on the neck can be of a darker shade than that used on the face. The neck shadow must never be allowed to come up over the jaw line. The jaw line itself can be defined with a highlight, which will tend to strengthen it and take the attention away from the neck.

When the neck is seen in profile, however, no amount of paint will be really effective. The best solution, especially for women, is actually to tighten the skin under the jaw by pulling the skin in front of the ears upward, backward, or both. This can be

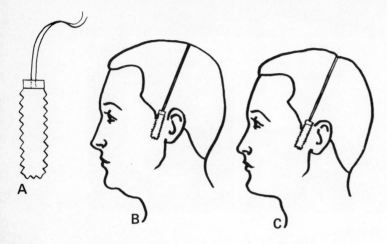

Figure 13–9. Facial lift. The lift (A) made of mousseline de soie, is attached with spirit gum to the skin in front of the ear (B), then pulled tight over the top of the head (C). The tape over the head can be concealed with a wig or sometimes with the natural hair, carefully combed. In the latter case, the tape should more or less match the color of the hair.

done by the use of *facial lifts*, constructed and applied as follows:

1. Cut two rectangles about 3 or 4 inches by ½ inch of mousseline de soie or other very thin, tough fabric. The edges may be pinked if you find that preferable. (See Figure 13–9—also Figure 13–10—which illustrate the use of three lifts.)

2. Fold over about ½ inch of the fabric at one end to strengthen it, and sew it to a length (about 8 inches) of ½-inch-wide cotton elastic. This should be done for both pieces of the mousseline. After the mousseline is attached to the face, the elastic will go over the top of the head. A dressmaker's hook should be sewn to the free end of one elastic tape (Figure 13–10B) and two or three eyes to the other so that the two ends can be hooked together at just the right tension. If you prefer, you can make the elastic slightly shorter, fold over the ends to make loops, and tie ordinary string to each loop. Then the string can be tied on top of the head to make exactly the desired tension. Whatever method is used, the construction should be completed in advance so that in making up the actor for the performance, it will be necessary only to attach the pieces.

3. For vertical lifts, the two pieces of mousseline should be attached to the dry skin, vertically in front of the ears and below the sideburns, with spirit gum. (See Figure 13–9B.) Be sure that the top of the lift, where the elastic is attached to the mousseline, is high enough so that it can be concealed by the hair. It must never, of course, fall below the natural side hair, which should be combed over it.

4. In order to conceal the edges of the fabric, stipple with Duo adhesive (or Mehron's Flexol) and allow it to dry along with the spirit gum.

5. Attach the elastic over the head and adjust the

tension. (See Figure 13–9C.) Too-great tension will result in obvious wrinkles or creases in the skin and must, of course, be avoided.

6. Cover the lifts with plastic sealer and allow it to dry. In some cases a heavy application of greasepaint or rubber-mask grease may suffice, instead of the plastic sealer. If you plan to use a cake or creme makeup for the base, powder the grease before proceeding.

7. If cake makeup is used, a brand with exceptionally good covering ability (see Appendix A) is preferable. A greasepaint or rubber-mask grease makeup is likely to prove more satisfactory, however, especially since it will also help to conceal fine wrinkles and skin irregularities.

8. If the natural hair is to be used, it can be combed over the elastic to conceal it. This, however, can be exceedingly difficult, if not impossible, for men with short hair. If the top hair is long enough to comb over the elastic, false sideburns can sometimes be used to conceal the elastic on the sides. These sideburns should be constructed on hairlace; crepe hair ones are not likely to prove satisfactory. If a wig is to be worn by either men or women, the elastic will very likely be covered, as in Figure 13–10C.

This is not the only method of constructing facial lifts, but it will serve to illustrate the principle. Each makeup artist has his own preference as to materials and exact technique of construction. You might, for example, want to experiment with the Kryolan adhesive tape shown in Figure A-1. It could replace the mousseline and would not need to be glued down.

TEETH

Dark or discolored teeth can be lightened with tooth enamel. There are several shades of white and cream available. Certain irregularities (such as very long front teeth) can be corrected by shortening the teeth with black tooth enamel, black wax, or black eyebrow pencil. More serious deficiencies, such as broken, missing, or extremely irregular teeth, require the services of a dentist. This can be very expensive, but for the professional actor, unless he is doing only certain types of character roles, it is important to have attractive teeth.

HAIR

The actor's normal hair style should be considered carefully in relation to the shape of the face, and if it can be made more becoming, it should be restyled. This can often be done merely by recombing in various ways and checking in the mirror, though it is sometimes better to consult a hairdresser whose work you know and can depend on. Medium long hair usually offers greater potential for change than does short.

If you want to make the face seem shorter and broader, avoid placing the bulk of the hairdo high on the head, which will only add length; try to keep it flat on top and wider at the sides. If you want the face longer and narrower, the reverse will apply.

Figure 13–10. Lifts for face and neck. A and C show model before and after application of lifts. She is wearing her usual street makeup in both pictures. A wig has been added to conceal the lifts. Since the purpose of these pictures is to show how much lifts alone can change the face, no additional corrective makeup has been used. One set of lifts is shown in B and the use of lifts on the cheeks, neck, and temples, in D and E. Lifts made and applied by Bert Roth, S.M.A.

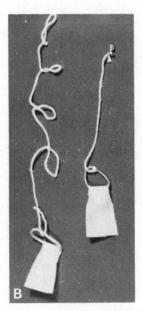

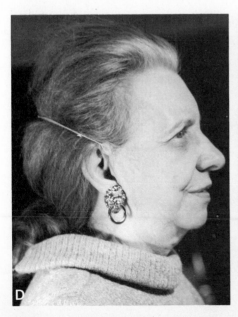
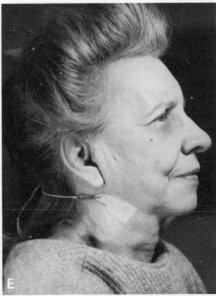

If the face is too round, avoid a round hairdo that follows the shape of the face, since this will only emphasize the roundness. But a round hairdo could be helpful for a face that is too square or too angular. If the features are sharp, the hairdo should be soft around the face, not sleek—unless, of course, you have chosen deliberately to emphasize the sharpness for an unconventional sort of beauty.

If a man's hairline is receding slightly, it can be restyled to conceal the fact, or sometimes it can be corrected, using eyebrow pencil of the appropriate color on the scalp. Never draw a hard, horizontal line; it is best to use short strokes of the pencil following the direction of the hair. These strokes should be softened and blurred with the finger so that there is no definite line, and they should also be powdered to avoid shine. Darkening the base color at the hairline will also help. Black or brown makeup can be applied to small bald spots and can also be used with some success on the hairline. If the hair has receded beyond the point where it can be corrected with paint, the actor should procure a toupee or a wig. The best ones are handmade and are expensive, but inexpensive ones, usually made with synthetic hair, are also available. No matter what you pay for a wig or a hairpiece, be sure to have it skillfully styled. (For suggestions on procuring wigs and hairpieces, see Appendix A; for instructions on wearing and caring for them, see Chapter 18.)

PROBLEMS

1. Make your forehead wider and lower, then higher and narrower.

2. Using only paint, change the shape of your nose, making it (a) longer and narrower, (b) shorter, (c) broader, (d) flatter.

3. Make your forehead more prominent and your chin less prominent, then your chin more prominent and your forehead less prominent.

4. Lengthen your entire face, then shorten it.

5. Make your eyes (a) larger, (b) smaller, (c) farther apart, (d) closer together.

6. Aside from their being currently fashionable or unfashionable, which eyebrows in Figure 13–5 do you find most attractive? Which ones would you correct and how? Which do you think would add most strength to the face? Which do you think would be most effective at stage distance? Which do you think might fail to project? Which eyelashes do you think do the most to beautify the eye? Which do you think might be effective for small theaters, for large theaters, for photography or TV?

7. Change the shape of your eyebrows as much as you can without blocking them out.

8. Make your mouth (a) wider, (b) narrower; and your lips (c) thicker, (d) thinner.

9. Analyze to the best of your ability your own face—that is, specify its general shape, prominent bones, size of eyes, nose, mouth, and chin, height of forehead, and so on. Specify which you consider your best features and which you'd like to change.

10. Do a complete corrective makeup on yourself, following your analysis.

14

MODELING WITH PAINT

We have already studied the general structure of the face. Now we must learn to modify the appearance of this structure through the use of highlights and shadows. Although this modification may involve making cheeks round, chins pointed, or noses crooked, more often than not, it will include some aging.

In youth, as we have noted, firm muscles and elastic skin fill out the hollows and smooth over the bumps in the bony structure of the skull. But with age and the accompanying sagging of muscles, this bony structure becomes increasingly evident. Therefore, the first thing we must do in aging the face is to visualize the bones of the skull and locate them by prodding with the fingers. Failure to do this is one of the primary causes of failure to achieve a realistic, three-dimensional-looking makeup.

Unquestionably, the single most important factor in learning to create the illusion of three-dimensional changes in bones and flesh through the use of two-dimensional painting techniques is a thorough understanding of what happens when directional light falls on a three-dimensional object (see Chapter 5). Once this is understood, the solution to most problems concerning realistic modeling in makeup can be reached simply by asking three questions:

1. What is the exact shape of the structure (a cheekbone, for example, or a wrinkle) that is to be represented?

2. Where is the light coming from? (On the stage it will normally be from above rather than below.)

3. What happens, in terms of light and shadow, when a light from that direction falls on a structure of that shape?

The answers to these questions will make it clear where the structure (wrinkle or cheekbone) would be light and where an absence of light would make it appear dark. These light and dark areas can then be painted onto the face, creating for the observer the illusion of prominent bones and of wrinkles where none actually exist.

In order to make the final makeup fit the actor's face, you should always be aware of how every highlight and shadow relates to the structure of the face, including bone, cartilage, muscle, fatty tissue, and skin. As an exercise to demonstrate this, suppose you cover your entire face with a deep base (cake, creme, or grease) suitable for aging–a fairly grayed color in a warm hue, such as S, FS, or SF. Then, using a white paint (or one about ten shades lighter than your foundation color), highlight areas of the face as they might look in old age, with bones becoming more prominent and flesh sagging. (See Figure 14–1.) Make the highlights *very strong*, but soften the edges except when creating the effect of creases in wrinkles. The drawings in Figure 14–3 can be used as a guide.

1. Apply your highlight to the frontal bone, emphasizing the areas marked H1.

2. Apply similar highlights to the superciliary arch, emphasizing the areas just above the eyebrows, marked H2. If you look at your forehead in profile, you may find a horizontal break or a change in direction of the planes about halfway up. If you do, this break will represent the top limit of the highlight area.

3. Since the top of the orbital bone above the outer corner of the eye (H3) nearly always catches the light, highlight it, softening all edges.

4. Highlight along the *top* of the cheekbone (H4),

Figures 14–1 and 14–2. Modeling with highlights and shadows. In Figure 14–1 the entire face has been covered with a dark base, then half of it modeled with white highlights. In Figure 14–2 a minimum of shadow color has been added, mostly as accents to deepen creases.

softening both edges of the highlight. To locate the top, lay one finger horizontally across your temple, press firmly, and move it down until you find it being pulled outward by the cheekbone. Then press *downward* against the bone. Where your finger rests will be the top of the bone. It is the top plane of the bone, not the outside or the underside, that receives the most light.

5. If you want a pouch under the eye, continue the cheekbone highlight up to the pouch and let it stop with a hard edge along the lower boundary of the pouch. It will, in fact, be strongest at the very edge of the pouch (H5).

6. Highlight the bone and cartilage that form the top or front of the nose (H6) since these invariably catch the light strongly. Keep the highlight off the sides.

7. Add a small highlight to the tops of the flared nostrils (H7).

8. Unless the chin is to be extremely receding, highlight it rather strongly. Be sure to keep the highlight below the break between the lip and the chin, making it strongest right at the break (H8), where there will be a fairly hard edge in the very center. This edge quickly softens as it moves away to the right and to the left.

9. Now you can begin to use sagging muscles and flesh along with the bone structure in placing your highlights. The flesh at the corners of the mouth often puffs out or sags with age, catching the light. Highlight this area (H9) as shown.

10. The jaw line (H10) normally catches a highlight, but in age it is usually the sagging flesh rather than the bone that is most strongly lighted, so highlight this area, keeping your edges soft and emphasizing the irregularity caused by the sagging flesh. If your own jawbone is firm and youthful, you can use photographs, paintings, or drawings to determine what might happen to it and how it might catch the light if there actually were sagging flesh.

11. The upper lip, all the way from the nose to the mouth, catches light, especially at the crease of the nasolabial fold (H11). Start your highlight at the nose, making a very sharp, clean edge along the crease, then fading it out as it moves toward the center of the lip.

12. Now observe the area marked H12. This is the top of a roll of sagging or bulging flesh called the nasolabial fold. It may not always be this pronounced, but the area is nearly always prominent in age. It catches a strong highlight with soft edges, as shown. Be sure not to carry the highlight all the way to the crease. To the outside of the crease is an area (S16) that folds under and away from the light and therefore should not be highlighted.

13. Since, with age, the sterno-cleido-mastoid muscles of the neck (H13) almost invariably become more prominent and catch the light, give them a soft-edged highlight. If your own are not obvious, you can usually find them by turning your head as far as possible to the side and feeling of the opposite side of your neck with your fingers.

14. There is likely to be a little light picked up by the larynx and the tracheal column (H14). Make the edges of the highlight soft.

Now, if you have done your painting carefully, your skull structure should be more apparent, and your flesh should seem to sag. Although the effect may be very strong, even clown-like, it should still give a striking appearance of age. Observe yourself in a spotlight at some distance from the mirror in order to get the best effect.

Although you have now brought out the bones and some of the fleshy areas, you have as yet done nothing to sink in the hollows of the face—those areas that receive relatively little light and thus appear dark to the observer. Beginners usually give these areas primary consideration in makeup and neglect the lighted areas. The result is flat, dirty-looking patches of paint on the face. Since one of the purposes of this exercise is to emphasize the primary importance of highlights and since the areas of dark foundation not covered with white will give

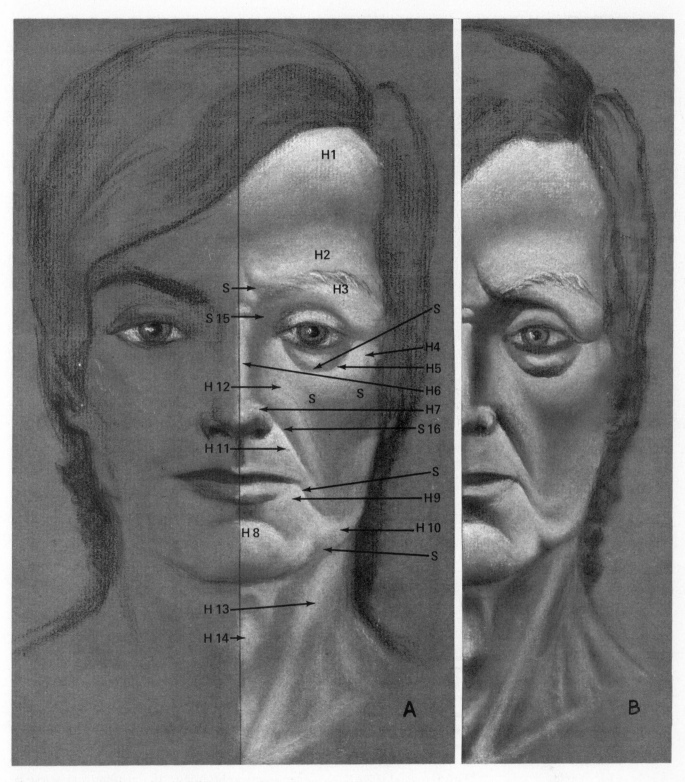

Figure 14–3. Modeling with highlights and shadows. Half of the face is modeled with highlights (A), then shadows are added (B).

the effect of light or even medium shadows, these areas will require only a touch of deep shadow or, in some cases, none at all. The objective here is to show how much can be accomplished with a very little shadow. Suppose you concentrate, therefore, on just two areas:

15. The part of the eye socket next to the nose (S15) more often than not receives the least light of any area on the face, the darkness of the shadow depending on the depth of the eye, the prominence of the brow, and the direction of the light. Normally, it can be shadowed quite heavily, but for now merely brush it lightly with a medium or dark shadow, keeping the edges soft and following the pattern shown in Figure 14–3.

16. Using the same color, merely suggest a shadow beginning at the root of the nasolabial fold just above S16. The edge of the shadow along the crease should be hard; the other edge should be soft. It is not necessary to draw in a complete fold.

Look in the mirror again and see what these two shadows have accomplished. Then, if you see other areas (such as those marked S) that obviously need deepening and you want to darken them very subtly, you may do so, but be sure to use only a light or medium shadow, not a dark one. And use very little of it. Keep the shadows at a minimum.

Now you may find that although you have achieved the beginnings of a three-dimensional effect, the results are quite stark and unlifelike. Your next step, therefore, is to counteract the ashen appearance with a touch of rouge—not on the cheeks, necessarily, but in the shadow areas. Using dry rouge (which can be applied dry with a puff or wet with a damp brush or sponge), brush-on rouge (applied with a brush), or creme rouge (applied with the fingers or a brush), touch the shadow areas marked S15 and S16, overlapping the shadow a bit. You may even wish to add a trace of rouge around the eyes to weaken them. Look again in the mirror to see how the rouge creates the effect of blood under the skin and begins to bring your makeup to life. With every realistic makeup you do, always consider the possibility of touching shadow areas with rouge for a more lifelike effect.

But the makeup is probably still too white or too contrasting. The solution to this, not only here but in any makeup that needs toning down or pulling together, is to use stippling.

Stippling. A color or colors somewhere between the highlight and the deep shadow values is best for stippling. Use your base color, if you like, or for a pinker effect, use a pinker color or add a stipple of rouge. If you want it more yellow, stipple with something yellowish. This is a good chance to experiment with different colors of stipple. In any case, stipple gently, barely touching the sponge to the face, so as to leave the pattern of the holes of the sponge, giving added texture to the skin. Keep

examining the results in the mirror as you go, and observe that as you tone down the highlights, the makeup becomes flatter and flatter and eventually you lose the three-dimensional quality you have achieved. Although this loss is normally to be avoided, it is perhaps just as well to let it happen this one time in order to familiarize yourself with the pitfalls of too much stippling. (For more detailed instructions in stippling, see Chapter 12.)

The makeup you have achieved through this purely technical approach is not necessarily complete and takes no account of character. It does not even begin to explore the intricacies of reproducing the endless variety in individual human features, but it does provide the basis for an approach to all realistic makeups. The major differences between this exercise and a finished makeup are that the finished makeup should relate to a specific character and that may require greater detail in modeling. However, this approach has the very considerable advantage of placing the emphasis in modeling where it should be—on major structural areas, which effectively project to the audience, rather than on tiny details, which do not.

Now that we have a basic modeling technique, suppose we study in greater detail the possibilities for remodeling the face to fit the individual character. This means, among other things, that we shall have to choose specific colors of paint for every makeup. The first colors we will need to use are those for foundation, highlights, and shadows.

FOUNDATION COLORS

In selecting the foundation color (unless you already know approximately what color you want), you would do well to analyze the character in terms of age, sex, temperament, environment, health, and heredity (see Chapter 2). On the basis of your analysis, decide first on the appropriate hue (yellowish, reddish, or a color in between), then on the value (the relative lightness or darkness of the skin color you want), and finally on the intensity (the brightness or grayness of the color). This should automatically lead you to the correct page of the color chart, and from the colors there you can select one that seems appropriate. If the color you select is not available, choose the nearest one that is or else mix the color you want, using the colors you have available.

If your own skin—whether it is dark or light—

is the right color for the character, then you may not need a foundation. If you choose to use one for other reasons (to cover skin irregularities, for example), it can be the color of your own skin.

HIGHLIGHT COLORS

Since highlights, in realistic makeup, represent the character's skin color seen in strong light, they will usually be of a higher value of the foundation hue. For corrective makeup they will normally be three shades lighter and for a very subtle aging effect, a bit more. For stronger contrasts, simply increase the value difference between the base color and the highlight. (See Figures J-2L, J-3E, J-12, J-13, and J-18.)

In order to achieve the sharp contrasts found in the aged face, there is some advantage in using white highlights for Caucasians and light Orientals. Dark-skinned actors can choose a color eight to ten shades lighter than their own skin. There are two reasons for using such strongly contrasting highlights. First, in using creme makeup or greasepaint, as the highlight is being applied, some of it will mix with the foundation and automatically become a high value of that color. Second, and more important, whether you are using cake, creme, or grease, you will probably stipple the highlights to help give them the texture of an aged skin and to increase the subtlety of the blending. By stippling, you can lower the highlight to whatever value you feel is appropriate. The resulting hue will depend on the stipple colors you use.

For nonrealistic makeups, when the imagination has fuller play, the only principle to be followed is the obvious one that highlights must appear lighter than the base.

SHADOW COLORS

For corrective makeup, shadow colors can be three shades darker than the base, or many shades darker for strong contrasts in age. They may be of the same intensity as the base or grayer, but they should never be brighter. They may also be of the same hue as the base or warmer, seldom cooler. In realistic makeups, shadows that are too cool for the base tend to look dirty—unless, of course, you are using creme makeup or greasepaint and the shadow mixes with the foundation to produce a grayed ver-

sion of the foundation color. If the actor is to be wearing a red costume, more red than usual can be used in the shadows. (See Figure J-12.)

If you don't have a suitable reddish shadow color to use with healthy Caucasian foundation colors, or if your shadows turn out grayer than you had expected them to, a touch of dry rouge (applied wet or dry, with brush, sponge, or puff) or a dusting of brush-on rouge will help enormously in giving the appearance of blood under the skin. This is especially useful in modeling wrinkles. (See Figure J-3B.)

There is no universal shadow color suitable for all base colors, but those in the following list are currently available ones that have proved effective for use with a variety of base colors. You may find others you will like as well or better.

SF-11-e	SF-13-d/e	FS-15-f	S-12-e
SF-12-e	SF-13-f	S-10-d	S-14-b
SF-12-f	FS-14-d	S-12-d	PR-15-d

Now that we have experimented with highlights and shadows in restructuring the face as a whole and considered the problem of choosing colors for specific characters, the face can be divided into areas so that we may examine in detail the modeling of these areas. The five area divisions—forehead, eyes, nose, cheeks, and jaws—are diagrammed in Figure 14–4. Each area will then be subdivided into planes, for more detailed analysis. The discussion of each area will indicate the various possible treatments of that area.

Figure 14–4. Division of the face into areas.

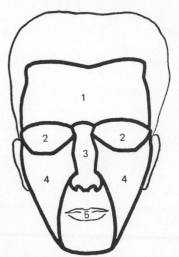

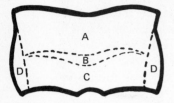

Figure 14–5. Area 1: Forehead.

AREA 1: FOREHEAD

Planes. The forehead is divided into five planes, as shown in Figure 14–5. Planes A and C are the frontal and the superciliary arches, D the temporal hollows, and B the slight depression between the two prominences.

A simple method of aging the forehead is to highlight and shadow these planes. The two prominences, A and C, catch the light and should therefore be highlighted (Figure 14–6A,C); the depression, B, falling between them, may be slightly shadowed (Figure 14–6B). Be careful, however, not to emphasize the transverse shadow too strongly or a skull-like appearance will result. If you are using a fairly dark foundation color, you would usually do better not to attempt to add any shadow at all.

The temples, D, are nearly always shadowed for age (Figures 14–6D and 14–32). These shadows are often barely perceptible in early middle age but are usually quite pronounced in later years (Figure H-8). Be sure that the shadows are always carried to the hairline; they tend to be more intense at the inner edge and to lighten as they approach the hair.

In placing the highlights, keep in mind the light source on the stage—normally above and at an angle from the face. With light coming from above, the strongest light will fall on the upper part of the frontal bone. If there is a horizontal division approximately in the middle of your forehead (most clearly observable in profile), the area coming forward below this division will catch another strong highlight, and the area immediately above the division (Figure 14–52) will be less strongly lighted. This is the area where you may or may not wish to use a very slight shadow. When there are no wrinkles to crease the skin, all edges of highlights and shadows will be soft. If you want to make the forehead more rounded or bulging, apply the highlights and shadows in a curved pattern.

Wrinkles. If you want to give the effect of a wrinkled forehead, make sure that you model the wrinkles meticulously and that you follow the natural wrinkles—otherwise, you will have a double set of wrinkles when the forehead is raised. Young people who have not yet developed any natural creases and cannot form any by raising the forehead may wish to use photographs of wrinkled foreheads as a guide.

Before beginning to model forehead wrinkles, observe your own or someone else's natural wrinkles, and with your light source from above, note where the wrinkles catch the light. Is it above or below the crease? Carefully examine photographs in your morgue and those in this chapter (especially Figure 14–7) to see exactly how the light pattern

Figure 14–6. Foreheads. A and C indicate prominences that are normally highlighted for age; B, a slight depression that may or may not be lightly shadowed; and D, a depression that is usually shadowed for age.

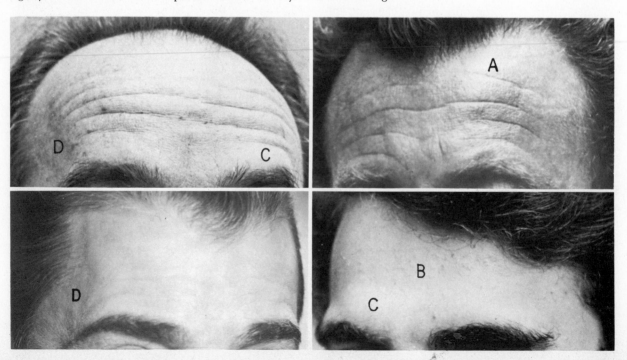

falls, giving the effect of a series of half cylinders. (Figure 14–8 shows what happens when the light source is from below.) Once you understand the principle involved, you will never make the mistake of painting wrinkles upside down, and you will always keep your hard edges crisp and clean in order to form sharp creases. Following the steps given below may be of help:

1. Using a medium flat brush with highlight color (white or very light) and holding it so that the flat end of the brush lies parallel to, and barely touches, one of the natural creases in the forehead (Figure 14–9A), draw the brush along the crease, fading the color out at each end. Make sure the paint touches the natural crease at all times but never crosses it. It is best not to try to model wrinkles with the forehead raised, since the paint is very likely to smudge in the creases, resulting in messy edges.

2. Using a clean brush, soften the lower edge of the highlight until it blends imperceptibly into the foundation. This should be done by drawing the flat of the brush along the highlight, overlapping the edge. (See Figure 14–9B.) Repeat this until you have a good blend. If you blend downward, the highlight will tend to become too wide. However, highlights for forehead wrinkles are usually wider than the shadows because of the angle of the light source. If the light were coming from directly above, highlights and shadows would be the same width. But as the light source moves forward, the light area is naturally increased and the dark diminished. Observe the relative widths of highlights and shadows in Figure 14–7.

3. Highlight and blend all of the wrinkles in the same way, making sure that hard edges are strong and crisp and soft ones fade away subtly. Make sure also that the ends of wrinkles, instead of being thick and blunt, are fine and delicate, disappearing imperceptibly into the foundation.

4. Since you must treat not only the wrinkles in a wrinkled forehead, but the entire forehead area, highlight the superciliary arch and the frontal bone, making all edges soft. (See Figure 14–9C.)

5. Using your pointed Chinese brush or your eyeliner brush, paint a very delicate shadow immediately adjacent to the hard edge of the highlight. (Figure 14–9D.) Soften the upper edge of this shadow with a clean brush, keeping the bottom edge hard and sharp. (Figure 14–9E.) If your foundation color is sufficiently dark, you may be able to skip this step. Consult your mirror before deciding.

6. In order to deepen the crease, repeat step 5 with a deep shadow color, keeping the shadow very narrow.

7. Check your wrinkles for roundness, depth, and projection—in a spotlight if possible—and make any necessary adjustments.

8. If the wrinkles seem too gray and lifeless, brush on a touch of rouge here and there in the shadows or

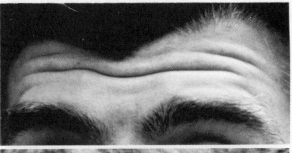
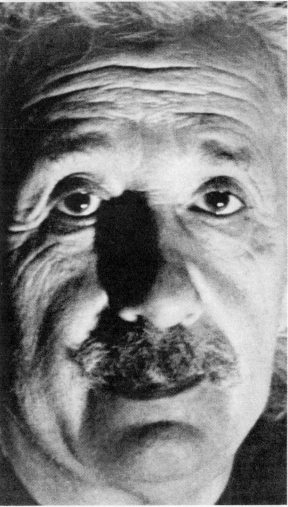

Figure 14–7. Forehead wrinkles—light coming from above. Figure 14–8. Light from below. Note the reversal of highlights and shadows as a result of the reversal of normal lighting.

between the shadows and the highlights. Your original shadow color may have enough red in it, however, in which case this may not be necessary.

9. If the wrinkles look too strong and obvious, stipple the entire forehead with the base color or any other color or colors you consider appropriate. Using more than one color tends to give a more natural effect. Stipple carefully, watching the effect as you go so that you don't wipe out everything you've done. If the stip-

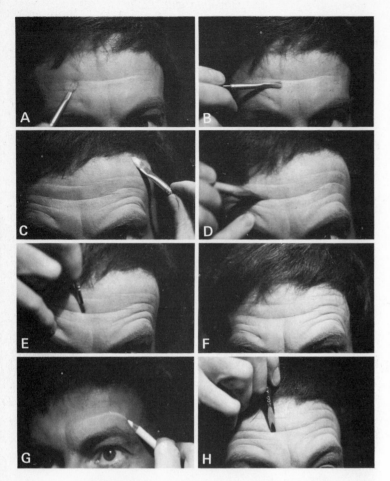

Figure 14–9. Modeling forehead wrinkles with paint.
(A) Highlighting wrinkle. (B) Blending the highlight.
(C) Highlighting frontal bone. (D) Shadowing wrinkle.
(E) Blending shadow. (F) Completed modeling. (G) Highlighting with pointed makeup pencil. (H) Shadowing with flat-cut makeup pencil.

pling grays the shadows too much, you can add a little rouge or touch up any rouge you may have added previously. If you use a red stipple, this extra rouge will probably not be necessary. Instead of brushes, you may prefer to use makeup pencils—either pointed or flat-cut, as shown in Figure 14–9G,H.

For a makeup using painted forehead wrinkles, see Figure 1–2.

AREA 2:   EYES

No feature is more important in suggesting character than are the eyes, and none can be changed in a greater variety of ways. Figure 14–10 illustrates a few of the changes that can be made in a single eye. For photographs of youthful eyes and eyebrows, see Figures 13–5 and 13–6, and for aged ones, Figures 14–12, 14–13, and 14–14. In studying these photographs, always determine the light source in the photograph and make the necessary adjustments for stage lighting.

PLANE A extends forward from the eye to the bridge of the nose and is nearly always shadowed for age. It is rarely highlighted except for Oriental makeups or for counteracting heavy shadows in deepset eyes, which would be a form of corrective makeup. The center of this plane is usually one of the darkest parts of the whole orbital area. (See Figures 14–32 and J-3E.) The lower edge fades into the shadow on the side of the nose. The outer edge is a soft one that turns into a highlight on the bridge of the nose. The inner edge is also always soft, fading into plane B. In general, the greater the age, the deeper this shadow. Shadowing plane A tends to make the eye recede without giving any particular effect of dissipation.

PLANE B is a transition area that is either left the base color or included with A. In the latter case, the shadow of A is usually lightened as it crosses B and approaches C.

PLANE C is often highlighted (or rouged) for youthful makeups (Figure 3–1) and is very important in indicating age. In old age, the skin there frequently sags and actually covers a part of the open eye. (See Figures 14–12G, 14–13I, and 14–15A.) Although we cannot do that with paint, we can approach the effect by strongly highlighting C_1 and shadowing the lower edge of C_2 (Figure 14–3B). If the light is coming from above, the lightest part of the highlight will be nearest the eyebrow—in other words, on the superciliary bone where it forms the outer edge of the eye socket. It will gradually recede into a soft shadow as it approaches the B-C division, whether or not a fold is to be made. (See Figure J-3F.)

The deepest part of the shadow is at the bottom of the area, and it turns very gradually into a highlight as it approaches C_1. The dotted line indicates only a general division of the whole plane, not a specific one. The inner edge of plane C is a very definite division, however, and should be heavily shadowed if sagging flesh is to be represented, as in Figure 14–3B. If not, then the transition to B is a gradual one.

It is usually best to use two colors for the narrow shadow that creates the impression of a fold of flesh. With the basic shading color, a medium shadow can be painted along the division between B and C and blended carefully to form two soft

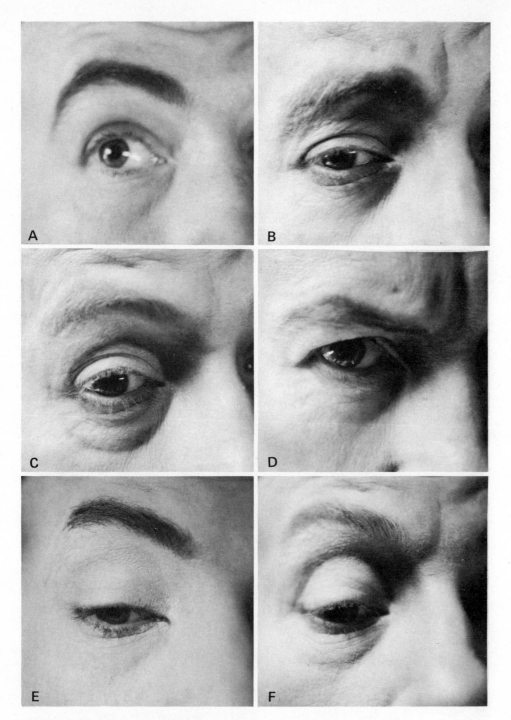

Figure 14–10. **Character through eye makeup.** All makeups on the same eye. Cake makeup used throughout, except for darkening the brows and lining the eye in E. Outer end of brow in E blocked out with spirit gum.

Figure 14–11. Division of the orbital area into planes for shadowing and highlighting.

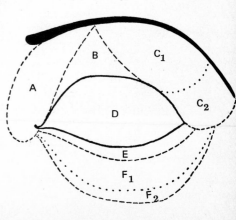

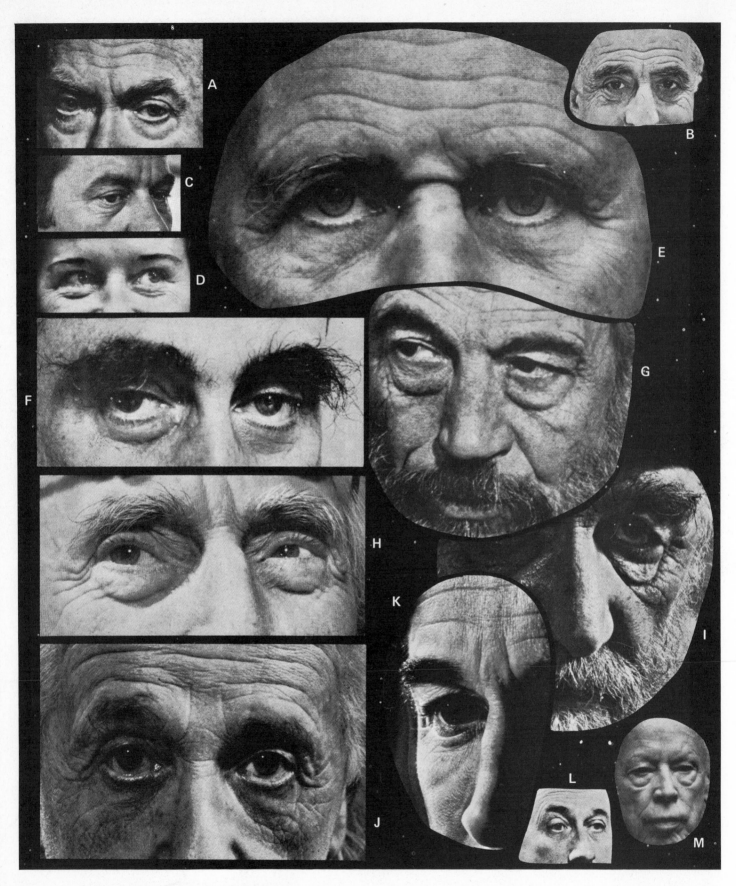

Figure 14–12.   Eyes and eyebrows.

96

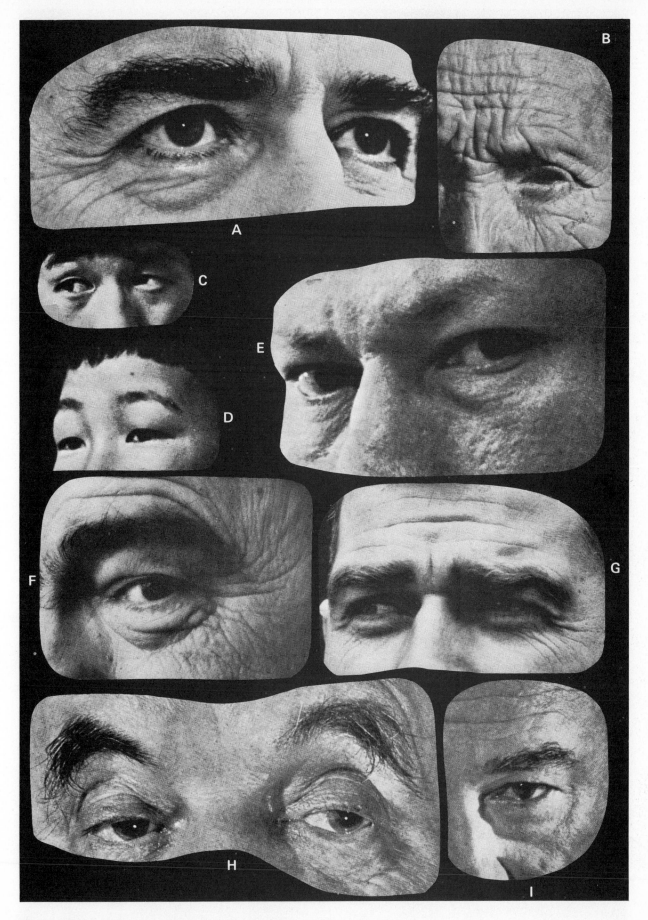

Figure 14–13. Eyes and eyebrows.

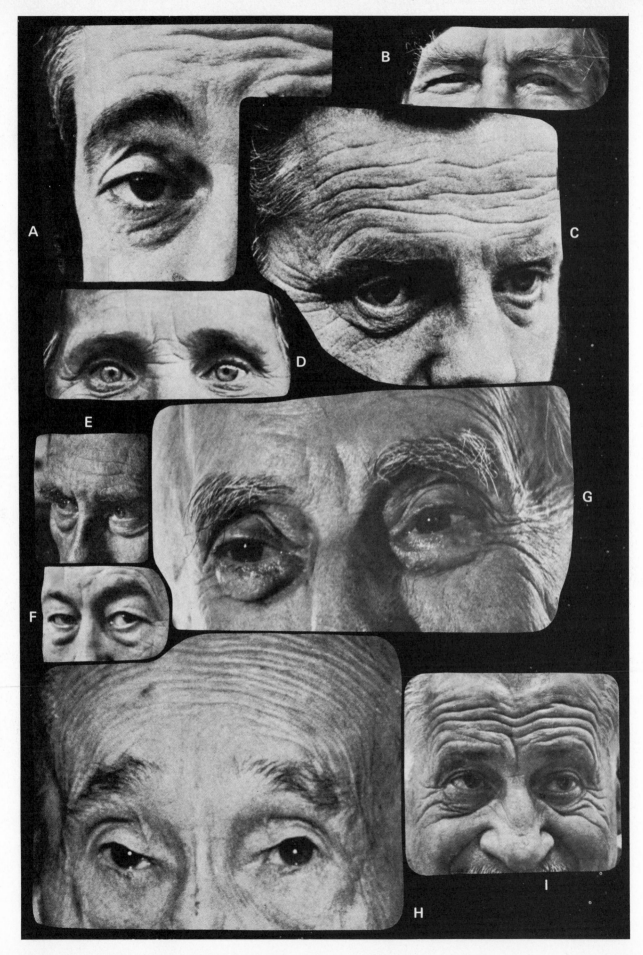

Figure 14-14. Eyes and eyebrows.

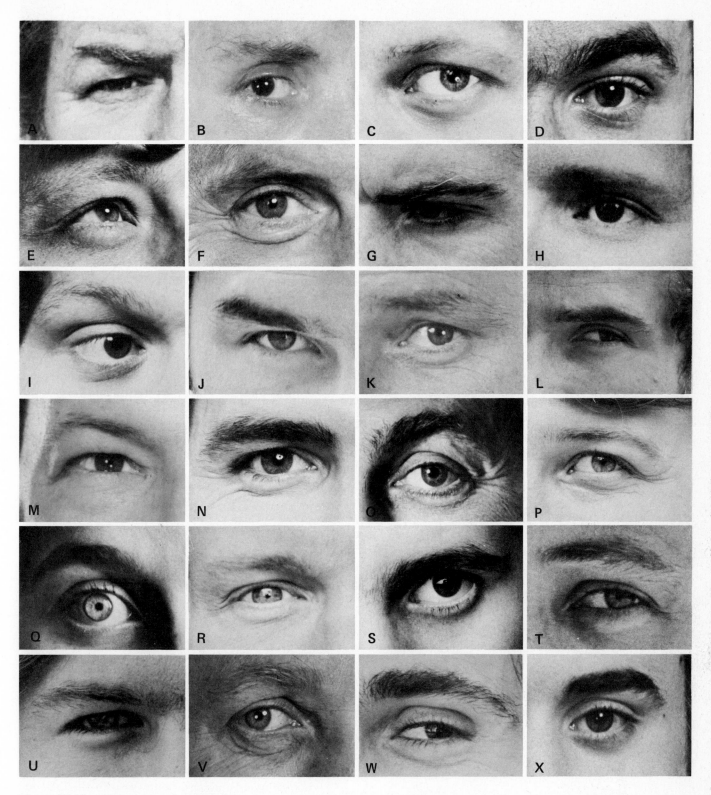

Figure 14–15. Male eyes and eyebrows.

edges. Then the simulated crease can be deepened with a darker shadow, in accordance with the suggestions given at the beginning of this chapter. This deep shadow should also be lightly blended.

Usually when there is to be a fold, it falls a little nearer the nose than does the division indicated in the diagram. That is, the fold has its inception very near the inner end of the eyebrow (Figures 14–12G and 14–15A).

If the whole orbital area is to appear sunken, then plane C may be shadowed rather than highlighted. This, however, tends to give a rather skull-like appearance and is usually done only to indicate extreme illness or emaciation. Normally, the upper part of plane C is highlighted, unless it is covered by the eyebrow. Frequently, wrinkles, commonly known as crow's-feet, cut across the outer edge of plane C_2, as in Figures 14–12H and 14–13F. If you use these wrinkles, be sure to make them true wrinkles, not lines (see discussion of forehead wrinkles). Model the wrinkles first with highlights, using a $\frac{1}{8}$-inch or an eyeliner brush, then add the shadows with an eyeliner or a pointed Chinese brush, keeping the creases very sharp and clear.

PLANE D is the eyelid itself and may be either highlighted or shadowed. If the whole eye is to appear sunken, D may be shadowed, but frequently, with age, the eyeball itself protrudes, catching the light (Figure J-10), while the skin sinks in around it. In that case, D should be highlighted and the upper division between it and the other areas deeply shadowed in the manner suggested for making a fold along the bottom edge of the B-C division. (See Figures 12–1 and 14–10F.) When D catches a highlight, C_1 normally does too (Figure 14–34E), although there may be a deep shadow between the areas.

Plane D is sometimes highlighted in the same way for glamor makeups (Figure 13–5K), with the colored eyeshadow used only on the lower part, close to the eye. For either age or glamor, the actor may, at times, want to create the effect of a more prominent lid than he has naturally. This can sometimes be faked quite successfully with paint (Figures 12–1 and 14–10F), even when the actor's own lids completely disappear under unusually prominent and overhanging A, B, and C areas. With a brush and your deepest shadow color, draw the enlarged lid on the natural eyelid in approximately the pattern shown in Figure 12–1D; then shadow upward toward the eyebrow, just as you would if there were a natural crease, and strongly

highlight the entire false lid (Figure 12–1E). The secret of modeling this false eyelid convincingly is to make the shadow edge extremely dark so that it gives the effect of a deep crease. The effect is more convincing if the eye is not opened too wide.

If the character would be wearing eyeshadow, it will usually be concentrated largely on Plane D, though fashion has sometimes decreed that the color be extended over the whole orbital area. In any case, for realistic plays, if the eyeshadow is supposed to be apparent, the placement and the color should be determined on the basis of what choice the character would make. Would she follow the latest fashion or would she not? (If she would, what *was* the latest fashion at the time?) Would she choose a conspicuous color or a conservative one? (A color that might seem conservative in one period could be conspicuous in another.) Would she take care to avoid colors that clashed with her costume or wouldn't she notice? (Eyeshadow colors that do clash with the costume can be rather jarring and should be used only when that effect is intended.) Would she wear false eyelashes or wouldn't she? (If she wouldn't, don't let the eyelashes be obviously false.)

To give the effect of weak eyes, which often accompany extreme old age, rouge the lower part of D with red. Using red around the eye opening always tends to give an effect of age or weakness of the eyes (Figures J-3E, J-10, J-11, J-13, and J-19) or may indicate the after effects of crying. Figures 14–14D, J-13, and J-14 show elderly eyes that you should be able to approximate with paint, but not all elderly eyes can be done with paint alone. For the eyes in Figure 14–14H, for example, a prosthetic piece would usually be necessary.

PLANE E is nearly always shadowed somewhat for age. (See Figure 14–10B,C,D,F.) The shadow is usually deepest at the outer end, away from the nose. The division between E and F is usually a fairly hard edge (Figure 14–16B). A strong shadow in E (Figure 14–52) tends to give the eyes a rather piercing, evil quality, which might, for example, be appropriate for Svengali, Fagin, or Richard III but hardly for Romeo, Falstaff, or Cordelia.

Since a shadow in plane E tends to strengthen the eye, it should usually not be too pronounced for old age. Rouging E helps weaken the eyes and age them (Figure J-3E).

PLANE F is seldom shadowed in its entirety. Usually the shadow is begun at the inner corner, then blended out along the lower edge, never being allowed to reach the outer corner (Figure 14–10B,D,F).

This plane is the area of dissipation. Be careful not to shadow it too heavily unless you are attempting to show the ravages of a dissipated life or illness, or lack of sleep.

The whole F plane sometimes becomes rather wrinkled (Figures 14–13F and 14–14I), and very often diagonal wrinkles cut across the lower edge of F_2 on the side away from the nose (Figure 14–13A,G).

After you have the orbital planes clear in your mind, remember that the secret of shading them effectively lies in a constant variation of intensity of shadow and highlight and in some variation in color. Not one of these areas should ever be flatly shadowed or flatly highlighted. You should start your shading at the point of maximum intensity, then decrease it gradually in other parts of the area. As suggested earlier, the use of two colors in the shadow or the addition of rouge may be helpful in achieving a convincing effect.

EYE POUCHES

In order to make a pouch (Figures 14–12 and 14–14), highlight F_1 and shadow F_2 as if you were modeling a half cylinder that ended abruptly along the bottom edge of F_2. The entire lower edge of F_2 must be hard, with a deep shadow that blends up across F_2 and turns into a highlight on F_1. The division between F_1 and F_2 must always be a soft edge. The cheek area below the pouch will always catch light coming from above and will therefore be strongly highlighted.

One of the secrets of making a convincing pouch is to keep the shadow heaviest at the bottom, where the fold of skin naturally falls, creating a deep shadow, and to let it become thinner and thinner, usually fading out almost completely before it reaches the corner of the eye (Figure J-2L). The fact that these subtle variations must be made in a very small area means that pouches, in order to be convincing, should be modeled with care and precision, keeping the hard edge clean and sharp. Always use both a medium and a deep shadow, and make sure the pouches look rounded at the bottom, where the sagging skin turns under. A flatly painted shadow will look exactly like paint, not like a pouch.

If you have the beginning of a natural pouch of your own, it will be easy to determine the correct size and shape. If you do not, then you should decide on the basis of what seems to fit in best with your eye. Use whichever brush works best for you. Although the whole pouch can be done with a single brush, you may prefer a wider one for the first highlight and a narrower one for smaller areas. You will probably find an eyeliner or a pointed Chinese brush useful for the deep shadow.

Following is a step-by-step procedure for modeling a particular form of pouch with paint, as illustrated in Figure 14–16. Other forms of pouches will require essentially the same technique, with some variations depending on the particular effect desired.

1. Very carefully highlight the area around the pouch (A), keeping the edge of the highlight next to the pouch very strong and sharp and clean. Then soften the lower edge so that it disappears into the base color. (See Figure J–2A.)

2. Highlight the inside of the pouch (B). If the lower lid (plane E) is going to be shadowed, the highlight can begin at the division between E and F, with a fairly definite edge, as in Figure 14–12I. If the lower lid is puffy and becomes part of the pouch (Figure 14–12H), the upper edge may be less definite. In either case, make the lower edge of the highlight soft in order to give a gradual transition—as if you were modeling a tiny half cylinder.

3. With a medium shadow, model the fullness at the bottom of the pouch, keeping the lower edge very clean and sharp and letting the upper one fade out toward the highlight (C).

4. With your deep shadow color and your smallest brush (D), deepen just the bottom edge (*not* the side edges) of the pouch, then pull the paint upward slightly to soften the upper edge of the shadow. Have the courage to make this shadow *extremely* dark. (Note the darkness of this lower edge in Figure 14–12G,H.)

5. Unless the shadow is already somewhat red, add a touch of rouge to the area between the shadow and the upper highlight. Use a small brush for this. This added touch of color, giving the effect of blood under the skin, can be very helpful in making your pouch believable.

6. If the lower lid (Figure 14–16E) is not actually part of the pouch itself, it is usually shadowed (Figure 14–14F). If, however, it is to be puffy (Figure 14–12I), it can be modeled like a wrinkle or a miniature pouch. Shadowing it is simpler and usually just as effective.

7. If the pouch is too smooth for wrinkled skin or if the contrasts are too strong for the rest of the makeup, stipple it very carefully with your sponge. If the stippling grays the red too much, stipple with a bit more red.

A very effective and simple variation of this technique for modeling pouches works particularly

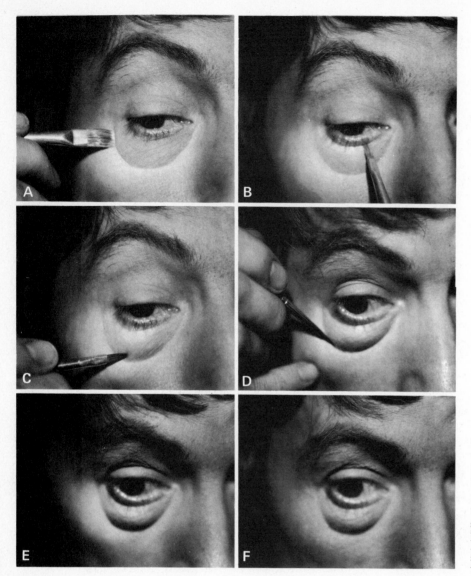

Figure 14–16. Modeling an eye pouch with paint. (A) Bony area around pouch highlighted with white cake over a dark base. (B) Upper part of pouch highlighted with a ³⁄₁₆-inch brush. (C) Pouch shadowed with medium shading color. (D) Deep shadow applied with eyeliner brush. Lower lid has been shadowed. (E) Completed pouch, without stippling. (F) Pouch lightly stippled with 3 colors.

well with makeup pencils, though brushes can also be used. The pencils can either be sharpened with an eyebrow-pencil sharpener or shaved flat with a razor blade—like an artist's shading pencil (see Figure 14–9H).

Highlights are applied as usual (steps 1 and 2). The variation comes in step 3. Instead of applying a medium shadow, model the area with a scarlet or red pencil (see Figure J-2H), bringing the color up a bit higher than you would for the shadow, since it will also serve as the red between the shadow and the highlight, thus eliminating step 5.

For step 4, instead of a brush you can use a dark pencil that will be compatible in color with your deep shadow. In working with a conventionally sharpened pencil, draw your hard edge with the point, then shade with the side of the lead (see Figure J-2I). With the flat-cut pencil, run the sharp

edge (there is no point) along the crease to form a hard edge, then pull the pencil upward, away from the crease, to complete the shadow in the same manner that you would use a flat brush. In shading with your pencil, decrease the pressure of the pencil as you move away from the hard edge. If this does not give you a soft edge, blend the edge with a clean brush to soften it.

This is the procedure for modeling a full, well-defined pouch. It can be modified according to how heavy you want the pouch and how well-defined it is to be. A pouch that is just beginning to form will obviously be less dark and less sharp. The best procedure is to check pouches in your morgue and in Figures 14–12, 14–13, and 14–14 and then adapt one of them to your own eye. Any eye can be given some kind of pouch, but not every kind of pouch is suitable for every eye.

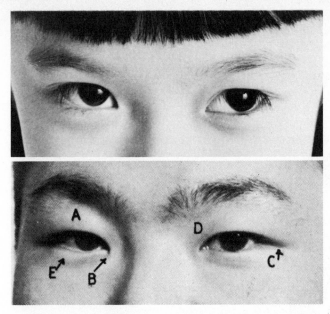

Figure 14–17 and 14–18. Oriental eyes. B is the epican-thic fold.

Also, the procedure suggested is for the simplest kind of pouch. You may wish, for example, to break up the pouch with wrinkles or to make a sort of double pouch, both shown in Figure 14–13F. A variety of possibilities can be seen in Figures 14–12, 14–13, 14–14, 14–26, 14–34, 14–47, 15–4, and 15–5. But perhaps most important of all, remember that all people do not develop pouches with age. Check the various illustrations in this book and in your own morgue for aged eyes without pouches.

ORIENTAL EYES

Since Oriental eyes require very special treatment, it will be more practical to consider them separately. An examination of photographs of Oriental eyes will show that they are occasionally quite slanted (Figure 13–5Q), more often slightly slanted (Figure 14–13E), and sometimes not slanted at all (Figure 14–13D).

The lid itself ordinarily disappears completely under a fold of flesh that is really an extension of planes A, B, and C in Figure 14–11. (See Figure 14–18A.) This fold overlaps the lower lid slightly at the tear duct (Figure 14–18B). It is this *epican-thic fold* that is particularly characteristic of Orientals. Sometimes there is also an overlap at the outer corner of the eye (Figure 14–18C).

One of the most striking characteristics of the Oriental eyes is the flatness of the orbital area. Since the eye itself is prominent and the bridge of the nose is not built up, the dip between the two (plane A) is likely to be very slight (Figure 14–18D). It is here particularly that the makeup must counteract the normal conformation of the Caucasian eye.

If the Oriental eye is to be achieved with paint alone, it is usually necessary to highlight the entire orbital area and especially plane A, in order to bring the eye forward and counteract the natural shadows. Sometimes there is a slightly puffy effect in plane E (Figure 14–18E). If you wish to create this effect you can model it as a pouch or a transverse wrinkle with the usual shadow and highlight.

In addition to the highlighting, two small shadows are necessary. One is a crescent-shaped shadow at the tear duct, which gives the illusion of the epicanthic fold. This shadow must be precisely placed, as shown in Figure 14–10E. The second shadow is placed on the outer third of the upper lid and may extend very little beyond the eye. For women who would be using makeup, a slight upward curve to this shadow is often effective.

The eyebrows normally are slanted slightly upward or are rather short and relatively straight (Figures 14–17 and E-1K). Instead of following the eye downward in a curve, as is usual for youthful brows in Caucasians (Figure 14–10A), Oriental brows may taper off quite abruptly at the ends (Figure 14–13E). There are, however, variations. (See

Figure 14–19. Eyes of an elderly Chinese. Photograph.

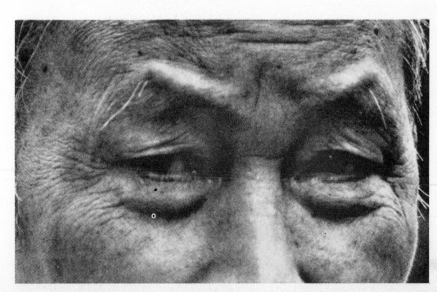

Figure 14–20. Oriental actor as a Caucasian character. Actor Randy Kim (A) in his own makeup for Titus Andronicus (B).

Figures 13–5Q, 14–18, 14–20A.) For aged Oriental eyes, see Figures 10–8D and 14–19.

For those Caucasian eyes that do not adapt easily to this painting technique, three-dimensional makeup (Chapter 15) may be required.

Orientals who wish to play Caucasians can shadow plane A, simulate a tear duct with a touch of red for the mucous membrane, and extend their eyebrows downward. They may or may not find it necessary to highlight planes B and C and shadow the division between them. Slanting eyes, unless they are very pronounced, need not be a problem, since Caucasian eyes often slant as well. If the slant

is troublesome, it can be counteracted to some extent by bringing the shadow at the outer corner of the eye downward instead of upward.

EYEBROWS

We have already discussed (Chapter 13) the problem of beautifying the brows. But besides being an adornment, eyebrows offer a great opportunity for characterization. Too frequently they are left in their natural state or merely whitened a little to suggest age. As a result, the whole makeup lacks conviction. Figure 14–10 illustrates a few simple changes that can be made with an eyebrow pencil, paint, and an eyebrow brush.

Unless your eyebrows (or those of your subject) are unusually adaptable, however, you might do well to add hair to them (Figure 19–5D), cover them completely with additional hair, or block them out with soap and greasepaint, spirit gum, spirit gum and gauze, derma wax, eyebrow cover (see Appendix A), plastic film, or by other methods that you may devise. If part of the natural brow can be used, you may prefer to block out only the part that needs to be eliminated, as was done in Figure 14–10E.

In blocking out the brows, the problem is two-fold—to flatten the hairs against the skin so that they will stay down for the duration of the performance and to cover the flattened hairs by some method that will conceal their color, using a flesh tone to match the rest of the skin. If latex pieces are used (as illustrated in Figure 16–21 and explained in Chapter 16), the flattening of the hairs is not necessary.

Blocking out with soap. In soaping, rub a moistened bar of soap repeatedly over the brows, which must be free of grease, until they are flattened down. In flattening the brows, spread the hairs with a fine-tooth comb, as shown in Figure 14–22B. When they are dry, cover them with a heavy coat of greasepaint or creme stick or, preferably, with rubber-mask grease. Make very sure that you blend the paint carefully into the skin at the edges to prevent the outline of the brows from becoming obvious when the makeup is finished. Then press powder into the paint and remove the excess with a powder brush. If the brows still show through, add alternate layers of paint and powder until they are effectively blocked out. If the brows are heavy, a coat of plastic sealer or flexible collodion can be applied over the dried soap with a brush or with the fingers. Be sure to spread the sealer beyond the soaped area, for firm adhesion. Apply the makeup over the dried sealer. Unless the brows are very light, soaping is probably the least satisfactory method of covering them, since with this method the hairs are more likely to loosen during a performance, allowing the brows to become visible. The brows in Figures 14–23 and 18–2 have been soaped out.

Blocking out with spirit gum. A more effective method than soaping is to glue down the hairs with spirit gum. Brush the gum well into the brows, then when it is very tacky, press the brows down with a damp cloth, spreading the hairs out with a fine-tooth comb, as shown in Figure 14–22B, so that they will lie flat and give as smooth a surface as possible. When the spirit gum is dry, it is wise to cover it with sealer in order to keep the paint from loosening the gum. Rubber-mask grease, greasepaint, or creme stick can then be applied over the brow, as described in the paragraph above, using more than one coat if necessary. Cake makeup will not adhere properly to sealer, though it can sometimes be used directly over dried and powdered spirit gum. If it does not adhere or cover properly, apply rubber-mask grease, greasepaint, or creme stick over the eyebrow first, powder thoroughly, then apply the cake makeup by pressing, not rubbing, with your sponge. The spirit gum can be removed with alcohol, acetone, or spirit gum remover. Be very careful, however, not to let the liquid run down into the eyes. The safest procedure is to dampen a towel with the remover, then bend over so that the eyebrow is lower than the eye. There are also makeup removers that will remove both paint and spirit gum (see Appendix A). Figure 9–3C shows eyebrows that have been partially blocked out with spirit gum.

Blocking out with derma wax. You can also mat the brows down with derma wax, blending the wax carefully into the skin at the edges, and then, if you wish, cover the wax with sealer or flexible collodion. If the brows are very heavy, it may help if you flatten them with spirit gum and let it dry before applying the wax, in order to help keep the wax from loosening. In flattening them, spread the hairs with a comb (Figure 14–22B). After the sealer over the wax is dry, makeup can be applied. Cake makeup can sometimes be used successfully over wax if it is patted on with the sponge, not rubbed. In removing the makeup, the sealer should be peeled off with the fingers, the wax massaged out with cream or makeup remover, and the spirit gum dissolved with alcohol or spirit gum remover. If you remove the wax with a liquid remover that also dissolves the spirit gum, those steps will automatically be combined. Figure 15–3B shows a makeup for which the eyebrows have been blocked out with derma wax. Eyebrow cover (see Appendix A and Figure 14–22A) can be used instead of derma wax, and it may be preferable to the wax.

Blocking out with gauze. It is also possible to block out the brow completely by painting it first with spirit gum, then laying over the sticky gum a piece of gauze, chiffon, organza de soie, or nylon stocking, trimmed only slightly larger than the brow. After it is in place, the gauze can be painted with flexible collodion or sealer, then covered with rubber-mask grease, greasepaint, or creme makeup, and powdered. Cake makeup cannot be used directly on the sealer, but it can be applied over the paints mentioned, though it has a tendency to turn lighter than the rest of the base. In order to avoid surface irregularities, the brow should be as flat as possible underneath and the gauze should not be glued down in such a way as to cause the skin to wrinkle. (See Figures 19–7 and 20–22C.)

Blocking out with plastic film. An even better method than blocking out with gauze is to use plastic film instead of the gauze, as illustrated in Figures 14–21 and 14–22. These are the steps involved:

1. Prepare the plastic film by painting liquid plastic (see Appendix A) on glass (Figure 14–21A) or any smooth surface, such as formica, that will not be affected by the plastic, or on the outside of a grapefruit (Figure 14–21C), an orange, or even a large lemon. For eyebrow covers, the fruit is preferable since it gives a simulated skin texture. The plastic can be applied with a brush (Figure 14–21A), an orangewood stick (Figure 14–21C), or a glass rod. Using a rod or an orangewood stick saves cleaning the brush. Three coats of the plastic should be sufficient. Each coat should be thoroughly dry before another coat is applied. In order to avoid trimming, paint the plastic on the glass or the fruit in the shape and size required to cover the eyebrow, overlapping it all around.

2. When the plastic is dry, powder it, then lift one end with tweezers or a fingernail. Powder the underside as you pull it up (Figure 14–21B,D).

3. Comb or brush the eyebrow upward in order to spread the hairs for greater flatness. Then flatten these hairs against the skin with eyebrow paste (Figure 14–22A), derma wax, soap, or spirit gum. Recomb (Figure 14–22B) if necessary and press the hairs flat against the skin.

4. Press powder into the flattened brows (Figure 14–22C). If the brows are dark, it may be helpful, though not absolutely necessary, to stipple the brows with a little makeup. Confine the makeup to the brows and keep it off the surrounding skin. If grease or creme makeup has been used for this stippling, powder again.

5. Apply spirit gum to the skin around the brow (Figure 14–22D) or to the plastic piece, then very carefully lay the plastic piece over the brow (Figure 14–22E), making sure there are no wrinkles or rippling of the edges. Press the plastic down firmly with a damp sponge.

6. Using a small brush dipped in acetone, go over the edges of the plastic (Figure 14–22F) in order to dissolve them and blend the plastic into the skin.

7. If you are using cake makeup, cover the plastic, overlapping a bit on to the skin, with K-Y lubricating jelly and let it dry. This will give a better surface for applying cake, which does not adhere satisfactorily to plastic.

8. Stipple your makeup (rubber-mask grease gives the best coverage) over the plastic and onto the skin area around it (Figure 14–22G). If you are using cake, you should add another coat of lubricating jelly to prevent the cake makeup from drying out completely and becoming lighter than the rest of the base. Powder, then dust off the excess powder (Figure 14–22H).

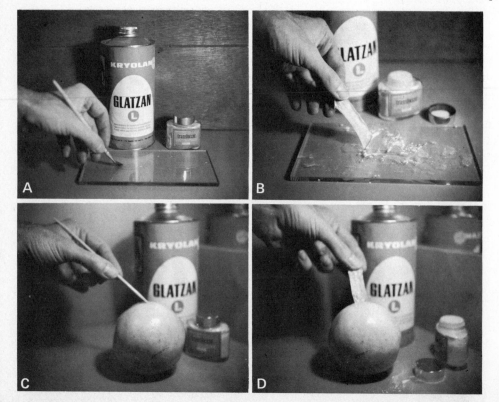

Figure 14–21. Making plastic film for covering eyebrows. (A) Painting liquid plastic on glass. (B) Removing dry and powdered film. (C) Spreading liquid plastic on grapefruit. (D) Removing dry and powdered film.

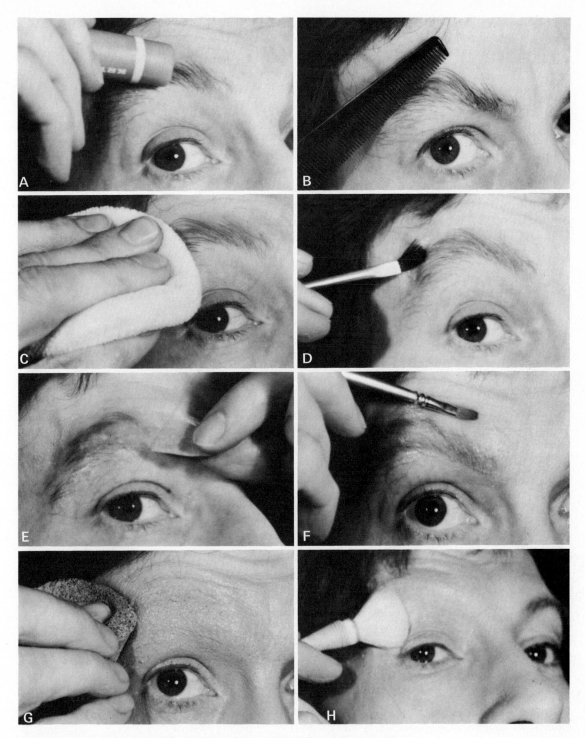

Figure 14–22. Blocking out eyebrow with plastic film. (A) Covering brow with eyebrow paste. (B) Combing hair upward to flatten it. (C) Pressing powder into the flattened brow. (D) Painting spirit gum around eyebrow. (E) Covering eyebrow with plastic film. (F) Dissolving edges of plastic film with acetone for blending. (G) Stippling rubber-mask grease over brow area. (H) Dusting powder off blocked-out brow.

If the makeup is not covering adequately, stipple on more makeup, then powder again. If you are using cake, add another coat of lubricating jelly and let it dry before repowdering.

Painted eyebrows. In addition to coloring the natural brows and filling out and reshaping them with pencil, it is possible, though not always desirable, to pencil or paint eyebrows over natural brows that have been blocked out. (See Figures 14–23 and 14–24.) Ordinarily this is done only for women who would be likely to paint their own brows or for the very thin, faint brows of the fourteenth, fifteenth, and sixteenth centuries (Figures 2–1, 14–24, and J-5) and of parts of the twentieth.

putting them in place with a pair of tweezers. The added hairs can be trimmed after the spirit gum has dried.

When the brows are to be blocked out with spirit gum, crepe hair can be attached to the whole spirit-gummed brow or to any part of it while the gum is still tacky. In fact, if any part of the natural brow is to be covered by a false brow of at least equal thickness, it is usually best to attach the crepe hair, a few hairs at a time, directly to the gummed area rather than to apply the whole false brow over a blocked-out one. The makeup to cover any exposed part of the natural brow can be applied after the false brow is securely in place.

Figure 14–23. Queen of Hearts. Natural eyebrows soaped out. Putty-wax nose. Student makeup. **Figure 14–24. Sixteenth-century lady.** Based on a portrait. Eyebrows blocked out. Putty-wax nose. Student makeup.

Painted brows can also be used for both men and women in stylized makeups (Figures 20–2C, 20–13, and 20–22A,C,F). If the penciling is to give the illusion of natural hairs, it should be carefully done with short, light, sketchy strokes, in order to avoid a flat, painted look.

Crepe-hair eyebrows. Crepe hair can be added to the natural brows or applied over brows that have already been blocked out. When using hair to fill out the natural brows, add a few hairs at a time, touching the ends with spirit gum and

For natural-looking crepe-hair eyebrows, it is usually best to mix at least two colors. If you want the hair to have a natural sheen, you can apply a small amount of brilliantine, hair dressing, petroleum jelly, or even cold cream to the surface of the brows. If you want smooth, neat-looking brows, comb very carefully, pull out loose hairs, and trim away scraggly ones. Further instructions for using crepe hair can be found in Chapter 17.

Ventilated eyebrows. When false eyebrows are to be used for a number of performances, real or synthetic hair ventilated on lace is more satisfactory than crepe hair. Detailed instructions for ventilating are given in Chapter 18.

Aging the eyebrows. In aging the eyebrows, first decide exactly what effect you want, then determine how that can best be achieved—with the natural brows, with false ones, or with a blend of the two. Sometimes you may need no eyebrows at all, a device that gives a remarkable effect of extreme age (Figure 15–11). Very light brows may sometimes be penciled on, but ordinarily, unless the character would have penciled-on eyebrows, false ones should be used.

The brows may take a wide variety of forms. They may be very sparse and irregular (Figure 14–14H) or bushy and overhanging (Figure 14–12F,H). They may be very thick (Figures 14–13F, 14–14G) or moderately thin (Figures 14–12E, 14–14I), but in suggesting age they should never look plucked unless that is really appropriate for the character (Figure 14–38J). Avoid the gentle arch in age makeup, especially when making up young actors as elderly characters. Never hesitate to cover up your own eyebrows and start afresh. Figures 14–12, 14–13, 14–14, and your own morgue should serve as source material for a number of possible variations in eyebrow treatment.

Eyebrows can be aged quickly, when that is necessary, by running a white stick liner, white creme stick, or stick hair whitener through them against the direction of hair growth (Figure 14–10B). This can also be done with clown white, cake makeup, or white mascara.

AREA 3: NOSE

If the nose tends to flatten out under lights or if it is to be altered in appearance for either corrective or character requirements, it will need a certain amount of remodeling. The nose area has seven planes (Figure 14–25).

PLANE A is the very small depression usually found, except in the classic nose, between the superciliary arch and the nose. It is shadowed for age

Figure 14–25.   Planes of the nose.

and usually contains one to three vertical wrinkles (Figures 14–12K, 14–31, 15–5H). The two appearing at the inner ends of the eyebrows have their inception in plane A of the eye socket (area 2) and become narrower as they continue upward. The center wrinkle is likely to be narrow at both ends and wider in the middle (Figure 14–34G). These are the frowning wrinkles and if made rather deep they will lend severity to the facial expression. Like all facial wrinkles, these should follow the actor's natural ones if he has any. Painted wrinkles must never conflict with an actor's natural wrinkles—including those that appear when he smiles or frowns.

PLANE B is the prominent part of the nose and is highlighted both in indicating age and in sharpening and narrowing the nose. If the nose is too long, the lower end of the plane can be left the base color or lightly shadowed (Figure 13–2B), as indicated for corrective makeup. The width of the highlight will largely determine the apparent width of the nose. (See Figure 13–2, also compare Figures 14–51 and 14–52.) If the nose is too sharp and needs to be broadened or flattened, plane B can be left the base color or lightly shadowed. If the tip is to be broadened or rounded slightly without the use of prosthesis, it can be done by rounding and broadening the highlight (Figures 13–2A,B and J-10).

The effect of a broken nose can be achieved by giving the illusion of a crook or a curve in plane B (Figure 13–2D). Since the principle involved here is the use of highlights to create prominent areas where they do not actually exist and to minimize certain prominent areas that do exist, it is important to make the highlight strongest where it overlaps plane C, which is normally shadowed, and the shadows deepest where they overlap plane B, which is normally highlighted. Avoid using more shadow than you need. A real broken nose can be straightened by reversing the procedure, as explained in Chapter 13.

PLANE C is nearly always shadowed for age (Figure 14–32). For realistic makeups, the edges between planes B and C, as well as the outer edges of plane C, must always be soft. If the nose tends to flatten out under light, as it sometimes does in youthful makeups, plane C can be subtly shadowed to give the nose greater depth.

PLANE D may be shadowed with plane C, especially if the nostrils are too wide, but usually a highlight on the upper part of the nostril, as in Figure J-13, will give the nose more form. To widen the nostrils, highlight plane D (Figures 13–2A and 14–33).

Figure 14–26.   Noses.

PLANE E is usually shadowed for age, but the fact that it receives only reflected light from the floor and sometimes a little from the footlights means that it is automatically in natural shadow. Carrying the highlight from plane B down into E will help give the nose a droopy effect.

AREA 4: CHEEKS

The use of rouge for cheeks and lips will depend on the natural skin pigmentation and on whether natural or artificial coloring is being represented. For creating natural coloring in the cheeks for youth, avoid rouges that are either too purple or too orange. The lighter values are easier to control than the deeper ones. The SR, RS, S, and FS shades from 9 to 12 (*a* or sometimes *b* intensity) are very useful for Caucasian women, and S-11-a, RS-13-c, and RS-10-b are particularly effective for Caucasian men. Whether dark-skinned races will use any rouge at all will depend on what is natural for the particular race or ethnic group. Study people to determine the natural placement. There is a great deal of variation. Rouge may be high or low, near the ear or near the nose, confined to a small area, or spread over most of the cheek. Note also other areas of the face—such as nose, forehead, and chin—that may show some color. In makeups for Caucasians, a touch of rouge in these areas can increase the realism of the makeup. (See Figures J-10, J-11, J-12, J-13, J-14, J-18, J-19, and J-20.)

In representing street makeup, ask yourself what color the character might choose, how much she would use, and where she would place it. Would she follow the fashions or be ultraconservative? Might she use too much or none at all? Would she apply it carefully or carelessly? Might she notice whether it clashed with her dress or wouldn't she care?

In other words, the problem of the addition of artificial coloring to the natural should be considered from the point of view of the character, since it is, after all, a choice over which she (or sometimes he) presumably has control. But remember one thing above all—if a character would not be wearing makeup, don't let her look as if she is. The nineteenth-century girl in Figure J-16, for example, has a natural coloring, whereas the eighteenth-century ladies in Figures J-15 and J-17 are fashionably rouged. Lady Liston's coloring (Figure J-11) is natural, healthy, and English.

Modeling.   As you have already discovered in your study of facial anatomy and in your clay modeling, the cheekbone (Figure 14–29B) is rounded, so that when light is coming from above (as we normally assume it is in makeup for the stage), the upper part of the bone receives strong light, whereas the lower part, which curves downward and inward, does not receive direct light and therefore appears considerably darker. This means that in modeling the cheeks for age or to achieve the effect of prominent cheekbones in youth, the cheekbone should be highlighted, and the hollow below it shadowed. (See Figures 2–2, 14–2, 14–29, 14–30 and 14–34A.) The following is a step-by-step procedure that you may find helpful:

1. First, prod the bone (as you have done before in the study of anatomy and possibly in corrective makeup) in order to find the underside of the bone that curves back in and does not receive direct light. Then, with a finger, brush, or sponge (depending both on what kind of makeup you are using and on your personal preference), lay on a strip of highlight along the top of the bone (Figure 14–30A$_1$), making sure that it is actually on top of the bone, where light from above would hit most strongly, and not on the side of the bone, which would be strongly highlighted only if light were coming from the side. With a clean finger, brush, or sponge, blend the upper edge out so that it disappears into the foundation, and very carefully soften the lower edge as if you were modeling a cylinder.

2. Lay on the shadow color along the lower half of the cheekbone (Figure 14–30A$_2$), taking care to leave a space between the shadow and the highlight above. (See also Figure 14–29B).

3. With a clean finger, a clean brush, or a clean

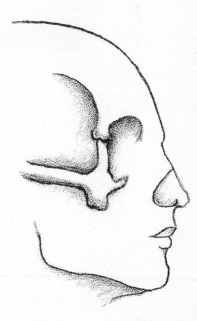

Figure 14–27.   Cheekbone.

sponge, soften the lower edge of the shadow, which should now blend into plane B of the diagram. Then very carefully soften the upper edge of the shadow so that there is a gradual transition from the light (A_1) to the dark (A_2). Avoid a definite line between the two. Now you have a completely modeled cheekbone.

How much the cheek sinks in and how prominent the bone is will depend on the intensity of the highlight and the shadow. For youthful make-ups this modeling may be very subtle, as in Figure 14–34A. For age it may be very strong.

Figure 14–28. Planes of the cheek.

A

or the one you're working on, in order to determine what treatment is likely to work best, making sure it is suitable for the character. If it isn't, you may have to compromise between the ideal cheek you have in mind and the specific potential of the face you're making up.

NASOLABIAL FOLDS

Plane C includes the nasolabial folds, the wrinkles running from either side of the nose downward to the mouth. These folds are nearly always present to some degree in middle age and old age, though the extent and exact form vary considerably.

The most important thing to understand about them is that each has one hard edge and one

B

Figure 14–29. Cheekbones. (A) Benjamin Franklin. Marble bust by Houdon, 1778. (B) *Portrait of a Man.* Painting by Dürer, 1524.

The treatment of area B varies considerably with individuals. The area under the cheekbone usually catches a little light (Figure 14–30A_3), and the bottom of the area will certainly be in shadow as it curves around under the jawbone (Figure 14–30A_4). But in between, various things may happen. Note the differences, for example, between Figure 14–30B and the other faces on the page. Study some of the faces in Figures 14–34, in Appendix H, and in your own morgue. Then analyze your own face,

soft edge. Wherever there is a crease in the flesh, as there is in the nasolabial fold, a hard edge is automatically formed (Figure 14–31E). Outward from this crease, the shadow lightens (Figure 14–31B) and turns gradually into a highlight as the crest of the fold is reached (Figure 14–31A,A'). Observe the conformation of the folds in Figures 14–34 and 14–35 and in the makeups in Figures 14–23, 14–24, 14–32, and 14–33. Here is one possible technique of application:

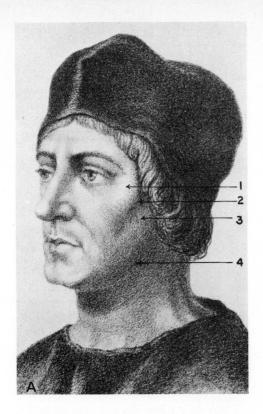

Figure 14–30. Cheekbones. (A) Thomas Wolsey, 1475?–1530. Drawing. (B) Sir James Barrie, 1860–1937. Drawing by W. T. Monnington, 1932.

Figure 14–31. Placement of highlights and shadows for age. (See text.)

1. With a wide flat brush held at right angles to the natural crease in the skin and the ends of the bristles butting up against the crease, as in Figure J–2A, move the brush downward along the crease, leaving a wide stripe of strong highlight. Make sure that the outer edge of the stripe coincides exactly with the crease and does not overlap it. This is your hard edge, and it must be kept sharp and crisp.

2. With a clean brush (also wide and flat), fade the color out across the upper lip so that the color dis-

Figure 14–32. Prisoner 7492. Student makeup by Ruth Salisbury, using the method outlined at the beginning of this chapter. Cake makeup used for dark base, white highlights, deep shadows, and final stippling. (For another makeup by the same student see Figure J-10 in the color section.)

Figure 14–33. Family Portrait. Based on a painting. The same method was used as for Figure 14-32. Student makeup by Marla Elliot.

appears entirely before it reaches the center (Figure J–2A).

3. Again with a wide or medium flat brush, starting almost at the inner corner of the eye, between the nose and the eye pouch, bring a stripe of highlight down along the fleshy area between the nose and the cheekbone. This will also serve to highlight part of the eye pouch. Make the stripe wider at the top and narrow it gradually as you go down, keeping it well away from the crease at the nostril and coming in close to it at the lower end. (See Figure J–2B.)

4. Using a medium or narrow flat brush held at right angles to the crease, with the ends of the bristles butting against it (the same way as in step 1, but from the opposite direction), paint in a narrow stripe of medium shadow color (Figure 12–1D), tapering it as you go down. The lower end should fade away into nothing. The inside edge of this stripe must follow exactly the hard edge of the highlight, touching it but never overlapping it. Instead of a shadow color here, you may wish to substitute red (Figure J–2D), carrying it out farther beyond the crease than you would the shadow, as was suggested in the instructions for modeling eye pouches. If you do this, the deep shadow (step 7) will be somewhat wider than indicated in the instructions. Makeup pencils can be used for this and for applying the deep shadow. (See Figure J–2E,F.)

5. With a clean, flat brush, soften the outside edge of the stripe so that it blends imperceptibly into the foundation. There should be just a little of the base color showing as a middle tone between the highlight and the shadow. Be sure to blend by overlapping the outside edge of the shadow with the brush and moving downward along the shadow.

6. With your pointed Chinese brush or your eyeliner and a deep shadow color, go over the hard inside edge of the shadow, fading the accent out at the bottom.

7. With a clean Chinese brush, barely touch the outer edge of the accent to soften it and keep it from looking like a stripe of paint. You should now have a sharp, clean edge with a strong contrast between light and dark. (If you have used red for step 4 instead of a medium shadow, you will need to make this deep shadow wider. You may also wish to use a pencil instead of a brush, as in Figure J–2F.)

8. If you wish to make the fold even more three-dimensional and produce a puffier effect, a touch of light or medium shadow extending downward from the eye pouch along the highlight will help (see Figures 14–30B and 14–33).

9. If the fold is three-dimensional and very sharp and crisp but looks a little too gray to be convincing, brush a touch of rouge into the shadow and into the area between the shadow and the highlight. It can, in fact, be run into the outer highlight if you want a very healthy look.

10. If the fold seems well modeled but is a little too strong, stipple it with base color or any other color or colors you think would be helpful (See p. 90). Usually it is best to keep the stipple fairly light in color so as to avoid flattening the highlight too much.

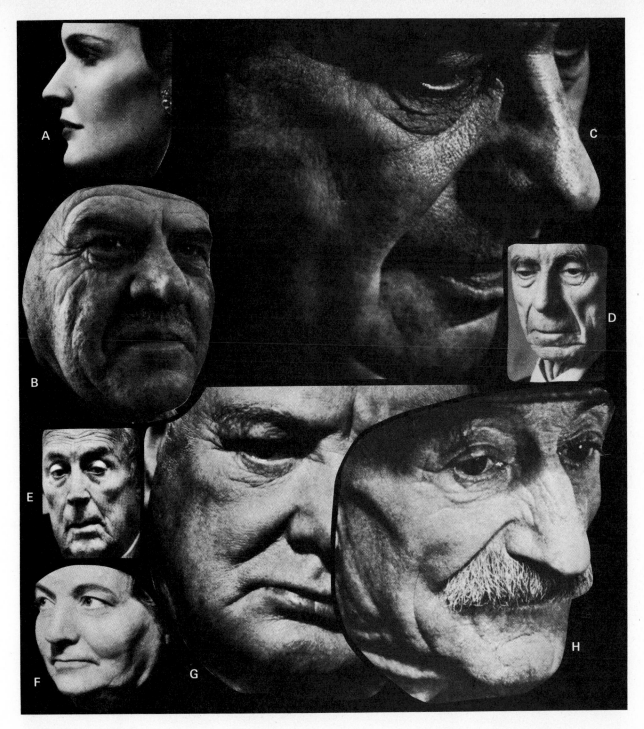

Figure 14–34. Cheeks.

This represents only one form of nasolabial fold. These folds can also be narrow at the top and wide at the bottom (Figure 14–35K), narrow at the top and bottom and wide in the middle (Figure 14–34G), short and somewhat indefinite (Figure 14–35C), short but definite (Figure 14–48H), long and sharply defined and sometimes joined to other wrinkles (Figure 14–35H), full and puffy (Figure 14–35A), or well defined but thin and flat (Figure 14–34H). They can also curve outward at the bottom and form what are often called apple cheeks.

Apple cheeks. The term as used here refers not to enormous fat cheeks, no matter how apple-like they may be, but to a nasolabial fold that spreads out and turns into a ball of flesh centered around the knob of the cheekbone. (See Figures 14–34F and 14–35D.) The nasolabial fold begins as usual, sharp and clear, but narrow at the top and widening as it goes down. As the fold turns outward, the crease disappears, and the shadow becomes very wide, so that in essence you are painting a small sphere. (See Figure J-3C.) In fact, one of the best ways of beginning the apple cheek is to smile as broadly as possible, then place a spot of

115

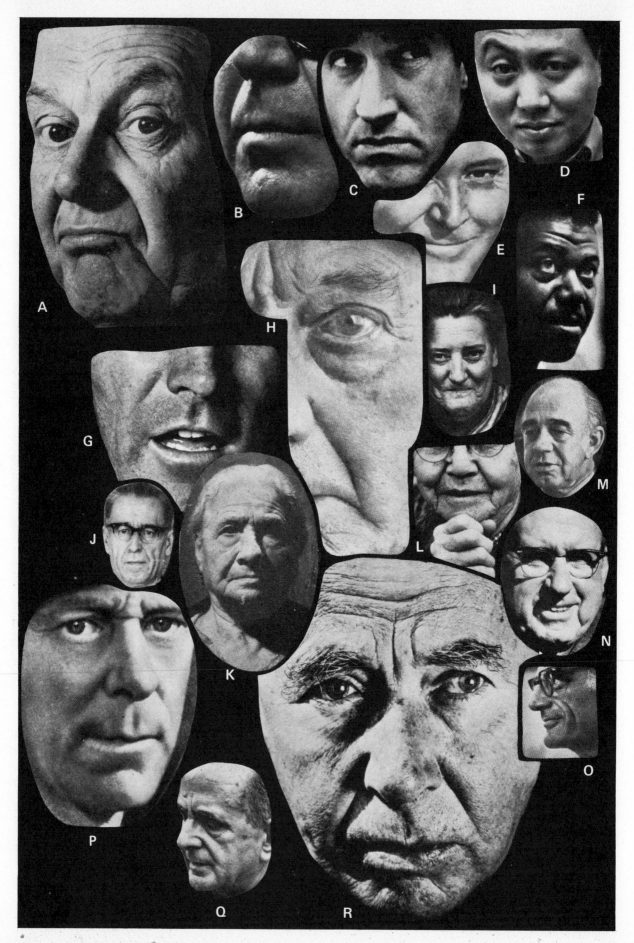

Figure 14-35. Nasolabial folds.

highlight on the most prominent part of the round fleshy area that is formed. This highlight will usually be centered on the ball of the cheekbone under the eye. Then, using a wide flat brush and a medium shadow, paint in the shadow area. The top edge of this shadow will be very soft and will fade imperceptibly into the foundation. The bottom edge will, perhaps, be a little less soft, but it will not—it *must* not—be a hard edge; a hard edge is used only to represent a crease, and there is no crease at the bottom of the shadow. Study the illustrations carefully. They will help you more than pages of instructions could.

Apple cheeks will look more apple-like with a generous touch of rouge. They are not invariably red, but more often than not there is some color. The best way to apply the color is to start at the nostril and brush downward and outward, following the form of the sphere but usually keeping the strongest color near the nose. You may want a little rouge on the nose as well. Brush-on rouge works particularly well for apple cheeks. You may wish to apply the rouge before the shadow, as shown in Figure J-3. This can be done with either a makeup pencil or a brush.

JAW LINE

PLANE D of area 4 (Figure 14–28) is the mandible, or jawbone. One of the best means of aging the face is to create the illusion of sagging jowls. The correct placement of the jowls can usually be determined by squeezing the flesh of the jaw between the fingers to see where it creases naturally, or by having the actor pull back his chin and turn his head in various ways until creases or bulges appear. (See Figures 19–5B, J-3B, J-12, J-13 and J-14.) On an extremely youthful, firm jaw it may be impossible to find the natural location of the muscular sag, in which case you can estimate the correct position from photographs in Figure 14–38B,I,K,L and in your morgue.

There are so many possible variations in jowls and sagging muscles at the jaw line that it is impossible to give precise instructions for modeling that will fit every case, but general principles can be adapted and applied to individual situations. In any case, the following is the procedure for modeling one particular kind of jowl:

1. Using a wide flat brush, sweep your highlight color down from the mouth toward the jaw line in an

arc that reaches to the bottom of the jawbone, then curves back up slightly to represent the sagging flesh (Figure 14–40). This arc extends beyond the middle of the jawbone, then curves back down and around the corner of the jawbone, giving a sort of draped effect.

2. Soften the lower edge of the highlight with a wide flat brush in the usual way, then fade the top edge upward into the cheek area, letting it disappear gradually (Figure 14–40).

3. Using a medium flat brush, paint in a triangle of medium shadow at the point where the highlight cuts the jawbone and a small arc of shadow in the middle of

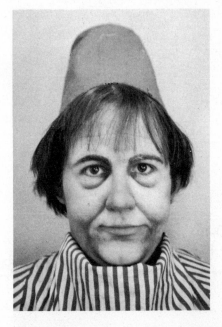

Figure 14–36. Dromio of Ephesus. Cake makeup with apple cheeks and putty nose. Student makeup by Tom Bradac.

Figure 14–37. Dr. Frankenstein. Long, heavy nasolabial folds and sunken cheeks used to thin the face. Student makeup by Pat Hadlock.

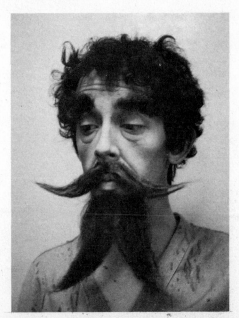

Figure 14–38. Necks and jawlines.

the jaw where the highlight rises. The correct placement for this second shadow can usually be determined by feeling for a slight indentation in the jawbone at that point. Although the two shadows may be connected by a stripe of shadow following along under the highlight, this is not always necessary.

4. Carefully soften all edges of both shadows with a clean brush (Figure 14–40).

5. In order to give the necessary depth to the little triangle of shadow, darken the center of it with a deep shadow color until it seems to sink in and the flesh appears to be curving back under. The little arc of shadow beyond the middle of the jawbone may also require some deepening but probably not as much.

6. If more color is needed in the jowl, add touches of rouge to the blend between the highlight and the shadow. (See Figure J-3B.)

With faces that tend to be muscular, there is frequently a deep vertical crease cutting up from the jaw line across the cheek. This varies with the individual, but Figure 14–42 shows how it can be suggested with paint. Here is the technique:

1. With a wide brush, sweep a highlight down from the upper plane of the chin to the bottom of the jaw line, then back up in a small curve. Blend both edges.

2. Locate any natural or potential crease in the flesh. This can usually be done either by squeezing the flesh together or by twisting the head around until a crease forms. If there is none, draw one in with highlight. This works much better on thin, bony, or muscular faces than on round or plump ones. Note that with light coming from the front, the roll of flesh behind the crease would catch the light; highlight this area, as shown in Figure 14–41B. The lower part of the highlight should be rounded to give a sagging effect. The crease edge will, of course, be hard and the other edges soft.

3. With your highlight, form another sag (C) at the turn of the jawbone. Soften all edges.

4. Using a medium shadow, form an arc (D) under the first highlight, carrying it up along the crease (E). This crease edge will be hard, the others soft. Both shadow and highlight should fade out somewhere in the middle of the cheek.

5. Add two more areas of shadow (F and G) under the two remaining highlight areas, softening the top edge. The bottom edge may be semi-hard or slightly softened. In the illustration (Figure 14–42) the area toward the chin is semi-hard, whereas further back it is slightly softer. Note the very dark triangle of shadow just below the crease in area F.

Sagging muscles in the neck (H) can contribute to the effectiveness of the sagging jawline.

In aging the jaw line it is often helpful, especially with youthful actors, to work from within as well as without. A small bit of sponge (either foam rubber or natural silk) can be placed between the lower jaw and the cheek to make the cheek pro-

Figure 14–39. Youthful jaw line. Figure 14–40. Jaw line sagged with highlights and shadows. Figures 14–41 and 14–42. Jaw line sagged with crease in cheek. (For explanation of letters in 14-41, see text.)

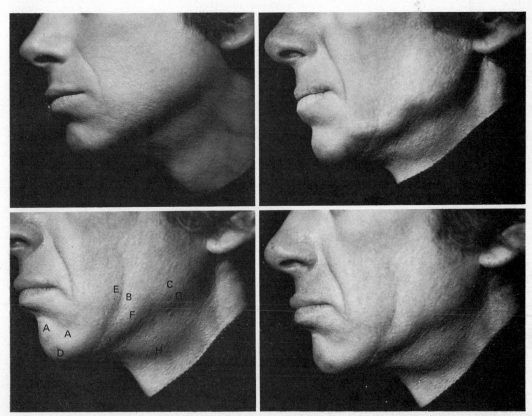

Figure 14–43. Madwoman of Chaillot. Note particularly the effect of sagging jowls created both by paint and by cotton in the cheeks. Makeup by Bill Smith, Figure 4–11. (For other makeups by Mr. Smith see Figures 15–25C and 17–5.)

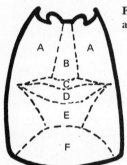

Figure 14–44. Planes of the upper and lower jaws.

trude (Figure 14–43). Absorbent cotton or cleansing tissues can also be used. Naturally, the sponge must be sanitary. A new sponge or a sponge that is reserved for this purpose, and for the one individual, should be used, and whether new or not, it should be sterilized before use. The exact size and shape can be determined by experimentation, starting with a slightly oversize piece and cutting it down. Once the pieces are cut to the right size, they can be preserved for future use. They should be thoroughly washed and dried after each wearing and kept in a tightly covered box or jar.

The actor may object at first to sponges in his mouth, but it is not difficult to adjust to them. They do not interfere with articulation or projection, though they may change the quality of the voice slightly.

For a greater effect of puffiness in the cheeks, as well as in the jowls (as for the aged Victoria, for example), a large piece of sponge or cotton can be used. It would be well to start with an entire small or medium-size sponge and then cut it down as much as necessary. The larger the sponge, of course, the more uncomfortable it is likely to be and the more difficulty it is likely to cause for the actor. If sponges are to be used at all, they must be used for a number of rehearsals to enable the actor to be-

Figure 14–45. Changing the mouth with paint. All makeups on the same actor. (A) Youthful mouth—upper lip reshaped. (B) Convex upper lip. Area from nose to mouth shaded from a white highlight to a deep shadow. Although actor's lips are pressed together, rounded effect is achieved largely with paint—with no inside padding. (C) Aged mouth. Upper lip slightly convex, lips wrinkled with highlights and shadows. (D) Lower lip thinned by painting in false shadow over bottom part of lower lip and highlighting upper part as if it were a naturally thin lip.

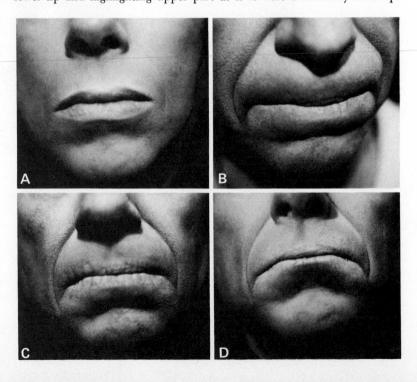

come accustomed to them. No actor can be expected to go through a dress rehearsal, let alone a performance, with a mouth unexpectedly full of sponges.

Studying people and photographs of people and modeling sagging jawlines in clay before modeling them in paint can be very helpful.

AREA 5: MOUTH AND CHIN

This area includes seven planes (Figure 14–44). When there are well-developed nasolabial folds, the outer edge of plane A is always hard (Figure 14–31E). The highlight (Figure 14–31D) decreases in intensity as it approaches plane B, which may or may not be shadowed. (See Figures 14–33 and J-2A.)

Depending on the natural formation of the actor's upper lip, it is sometimes possible to model the areas A, B, and C in such a way that areas A and B appear to curve outward, with area C sinking in, as if the character had no upper teeth. This can be done by modeling the areas like a horizontal cylinder—strongly highlighting the upper part of areas A and B, then letting the highlight fade into a medium shadow on the lower part of A and B and into a deep shadow on area C. (See Figure 14–45B.)

Conversely, the upper lip can be made to seem to protrude by highlighting the lower part of plane A and fading the highlight upward into the base color as it approaches the nose.

The treatment given the lips for a specific character can be analyzed on the basis of color, size, shape, and texture.

Lip color. In deciding on the color for the lips, determine first whether you are representing natural lips or painted ones. If natural, then choose a color that will look natural on stage. What that color is to be will probably depend on the character's age, race, sex, and state of health. In any case, it should relate to the color you have already chosen for the rouge, if any. Compare the very pale lips in Figure 2–1 with the more deeply colored but still natural ones in Figure 2–2.

If the character's lips would be painted, the decision will be made in terms of what lip coloring she would choose to wear and how heavily she would apply it. Fashion may or may not be a factor; personal taste or lack of it certainly would be. Normally the lip coloring will match the rouge unless the character would be likely to mismatch them or unless the lips would be painted and the cheeks natural (in which case, the color might or might not match).

Size of lips. The size of the lips (both width and thickness) will depend to some extent on the actor's own lips and how much they can be changed. For a realistic makeup, a very narrow mouth, for example, cannot successfully be made into a very wide one, but a wide one can often be considerably narrowed. The techniques for changing the apparent size of the lips have already been discussed as part of corrective makeup in Chapter 13.

Reshaping lips. Reshaping the lips may or may not involve a change of size. It will involve either changing the apparent natural shape (Figure 14–45) or painting on a new shape as the character would. The principles are much the same as for corrective makeup except that when you are representing lips reshaped by the character, you will not normally remodel the actor's lips with highlights and shadows but will simply—like the character—paint on a new shape. The reshaping by the character would presumably be either to produce what she considered a more becoming shape or to follow a particular fashion, such as the bee-stung lips of the twenties or the Joan Crawford mouth of the thirties.

Lip texture. Observe in Figure 14–46 the variations in lip texture, which have to do largely with age, environment, and health. In youth the texture is usually smooth, but later in life, depending on the condition of the skin generally, the lips may be rough, cracked, or wrinkled. It is, therefore, important in aging youthful faces that the lips be aged as well. This caution is based on observation of many makeups in which youthful lips in a wrinkled face have destroyed the believability of an otherwise effective makeup. (See Figure 15–13.) Suggestions for aging the lips are given below.

Aging the mouth. In addition to causing changes in texture, aging and changes inside the mouth (loss of teeth or wearing of false ones) can bring about changes in shape, size, and general conformation of the mouth. Lips are likely to become thinner (Figure 14–47A,B,I), and sometimes to virtually disappear (Figure 14–48L). And they may be cut by numerous vertical wrinkles, as in Figure 14–48G.

The most effective changes in texture can best be accomplished with three-dimensional makeup (see Chapter 15). But in using paint, you can stipple

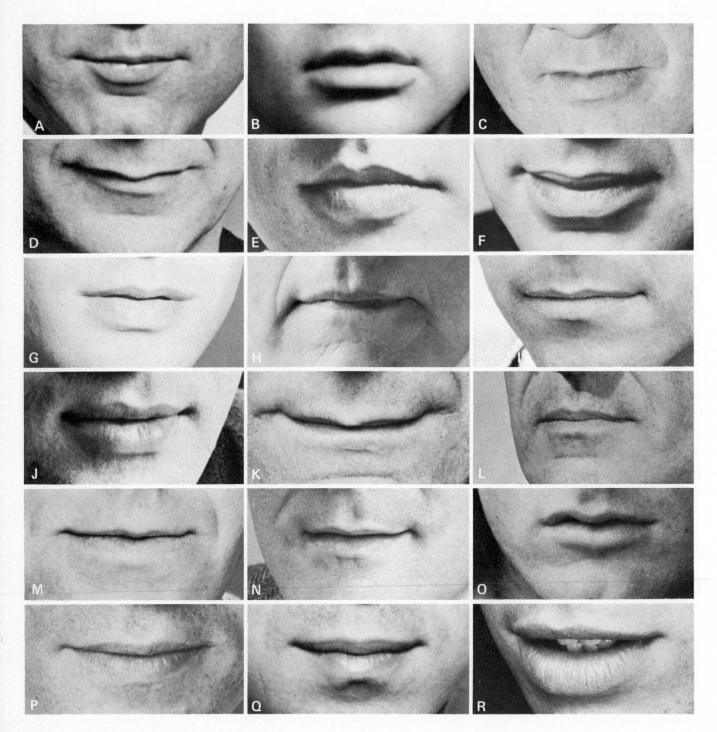

Figure 14–46. Mouths, male.

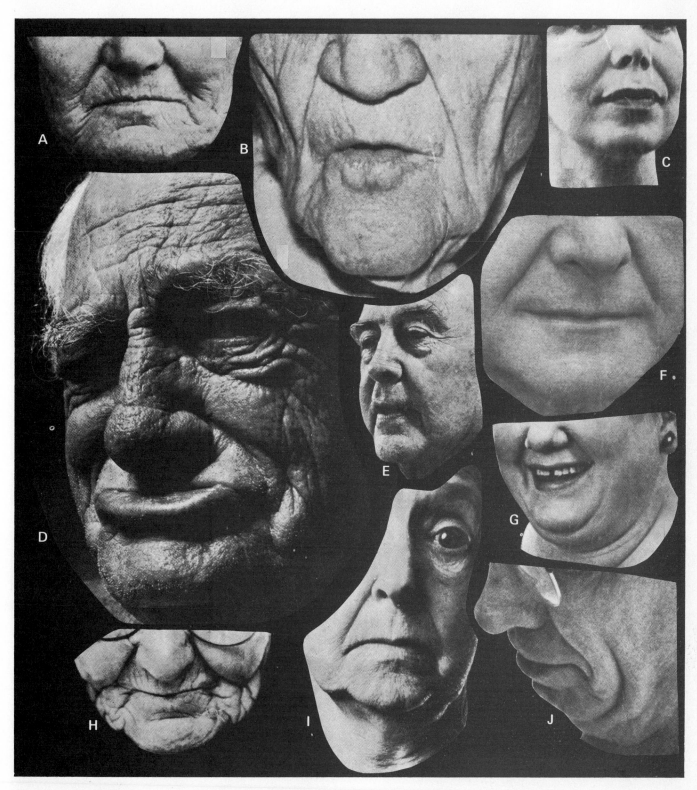

Figure 14–47. Mouths.

Figure 14–48. Mouths.

the lips or break the smoothness of the outline with wrinkles. The stippling is done along with that of the rest of the face, using the same colors. The lips should already have been reshaped, and if there are wrinkles cutting into the lip area, they should also have been done before the stippling.

If the mouth is to be wrinkled, it is helpful to make it smaller and, if possible, thinner—unless, of course, it is already small and thin. With a narrow brush, model the wrinkles carefully, using strong highlights with very narrow, deep shadows to form deep creases. Be sure each highlight has one hard edge and that the hard edge is very sharp and clean. If the wrinkles are too strong, they can be toned down with stipple. The important thing is to make them convincingly three-dimensional. Study the wrinkled mouths in Figures 14–47A,H and 14–48G.

In addition to the lips, the area around the mouth should also be aged. In old age, and sometimes in middle age, there is often considerable sagging of the muscles, particularly at the corners of the mouth. This frequently results in a crease angling downward from the corners of the mouth, with a roll of flesh above it (Figures 14–34G and 14–46H). Light falling on this roll of flesh from above will create a soft-edged highlight on top and a shadow with one hard and one soft edge below, just as it does with a nasolabial fold or a forehead wrinkle. The area immediately below the fold will be highlighted with one hard and one soft edge (Figure 14–45B).

This highlight may very well become part of a larger sagging area (Figure 14–45D) that does not usually have a sharp crease below it but often ends —in part, at least—where the chin begins. The exact conformation of this area and of the fold above varies considerably—not only with age, but with the individual. It's best to study faces and photographs, then adapt the information you have accumulated in your mind to the requirements of the specific character, relating it, as always, to the individual actor's face.

Study also the variations in plane A immediately below the lips, noticing particularly that this area can be either concave (Figure 14–47C) or convex (Figures 14–47B and J-14). Concave is normal in youth, but occasionally it becomes convex in old age.

Chin. Suggestions for changing the chin to make it more attractive have already been given in the chapter on corrective makeup. These same techniques can be used for character makeup.

The chin itself changes relatively little with age, except for the changes in the texture of the skin, which can be achieved with stippling. What is usually called a double chin is actually a sagging neckline, resulting from a relaxing of the muscles of the jaw and neck area. It begins just behind the chin and cannot be effectively simulated with paint unless the actor already has the beginnings of one that can be highlighted. Lowering the head slightly and pulling it back will help to emphasize whatever fullness is already there (see Figure 14–24).

With age, a crease sometimes develops between areas E and F (see Figure 14–48D); or there may be a fairly abrupt change of plane without an actual crease (see Figure 14–47C). In either case, the top of the chin should be more strongly highlighted than it would be in youth, in order to emphasize the increased angularity.

THE ROUND FACE

Thus far we have been discussing the average face and the problems of aging the face to represent a general sagging and sinking in. Sometimes, however, we are faced also with the problem of what to do with a round face or how to make an average face more round.

In rounding a youthful face and keeping it youthful, we follow the principles used in modeling a sphere (Figure 14–49). Drawing A illustrates the shading and highlighting for a sphere, and drawing B is the outline of a youthful face. The effect of roundness is achieved with a highlight (5) made in a round pattern in about the center of the cheek, and a thin, crescent-shaped shadow drawn in an arc from close to the eye, past the nostrils and mouth and around to the back of the jaw, as shown in Figure 14–49B4. All edges should be soft, and the shadow very subtle. This will not work, however, on a thin face with prominent cheekbones and sunken cheeks. The best you can do in such a case is to reverse the normal shadows and highlights in order to counteract the real ones that are being formed. Rouging the face in a round pattern (approximately where the highlight is located) is also helpful in rounding the face.

A round face cannot be made thin, but it can be thinned somewhat by highlighting the cheekbones and shading the whole cheek with a color two or three shades darker than the base. In aging a round face, you may wish to use apple cheeks (see Figures 14–47A,H and J-3); they can also be

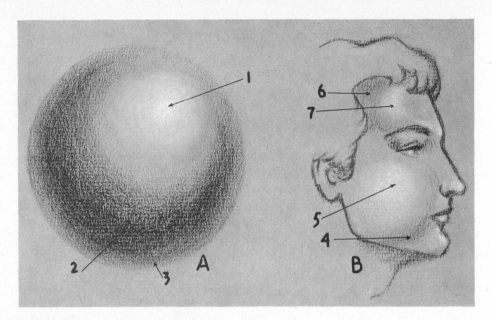

Figure 14–49. Modeling a round cheek.

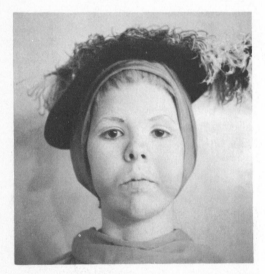

Figure 14–50. Round face created by modeling with highlights and shadows. Student makeup by Kathy Ross. (For another makeup by the same student see Figure 20–9.)

Figures 14–51 and 14–52. Falstaff and Iago. The illusion of width for Falstaff is achieved by carrying the light base from ear to ear and pulling hair and beard out horizontally. In the Iago makeup, the sides of the face are shadowed and the nose lengthened. The heavy nasolabial folds also help to lengthen the face. Cake makeup was used for both, with putty-wax for the noses, real hair beards on lace, wigs, and crepe hair for Falstaff's eyebrows. Both makeups are on the actor shown in Figure 1–1.

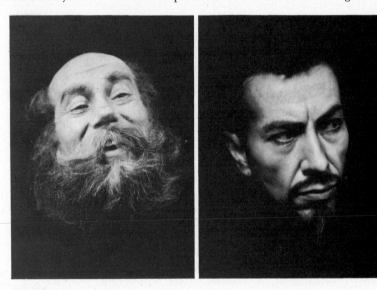

Figure 14–53. Muscles of the neck and jaw.

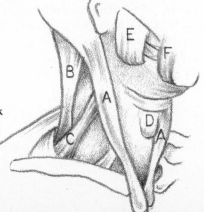

126

used to give greater roundness to an average or a thin face and usually suggest a happier disposition than would long, drooping nasolabial folds, which would tend to lengthen and sag the face. Notice in Figures 14–51 and 14–52 how the entire shape of the face has been changed with paint and crepe hair.

Sponges or absorbent cotton can be used in the cheeks to fill them out, as suggested earlier under the discussion of modeling jowls for age. The technique is the same (often using an entire small or medium sponge), but the modeling with paint will be used to suggest fullness or roundness rather than age. This modeling will, of course, be the same as without the use of sponges, which merely help the illusion. This technique is suggested only as a possibility and is not recommended as an ideal solution to every problem of making an actor's face rounded.

NECK

Remember that the neck ages along with the face and sometimes even more rapidly. A youthful neck, like youthful lips, can destroy the believability of an otherwise effective age makeup. It has already been mentioned that both the front and the back of the neck should be made up. For juveniles, nothing else is necessary. But for age, the neck requires modeling.

There are four prominences in the neck that are important in makeup. (labeled A, B, C, and D in Figure 14–53). The muscles, along with the top of the larynx and parts of the tracheal column, catch the light, and so they should be highlighted. Since all of these are roughly cylindrical in shape, they should be modeled like cylinders, with the highlight fading around to a shadow (Figure H-10). The hollow at the breastbone, where the sterno-cleido-mastoid muscles almost meet (Figure 14–55), is usually in shadow. In old age there are frequently two folds of flesh starting above the larynx and hanging down like wattles (Figure 14–38C,J,K). These can be effectively painted on for a front view (Figure 14–55) but are, of course, ineffective in profile. All of this modeling tends to give the appearance of a rather scrawny neck.

It is also possible and very effective to model the numerous wrinkles that form around the neck and extend diagonally up toward the ears. Figure 19–5D shows quite clearly how this is done and how

Figure 14–54. *Portrait of the Artist's Mother.* Drawing by Dürer, 1514. Note particularly the muscles of the neck.

Figure 14–55. **Neck aged with cake makeup.**

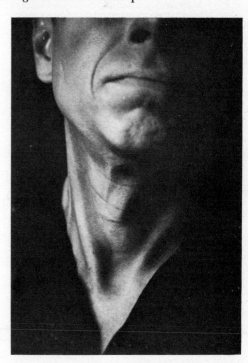

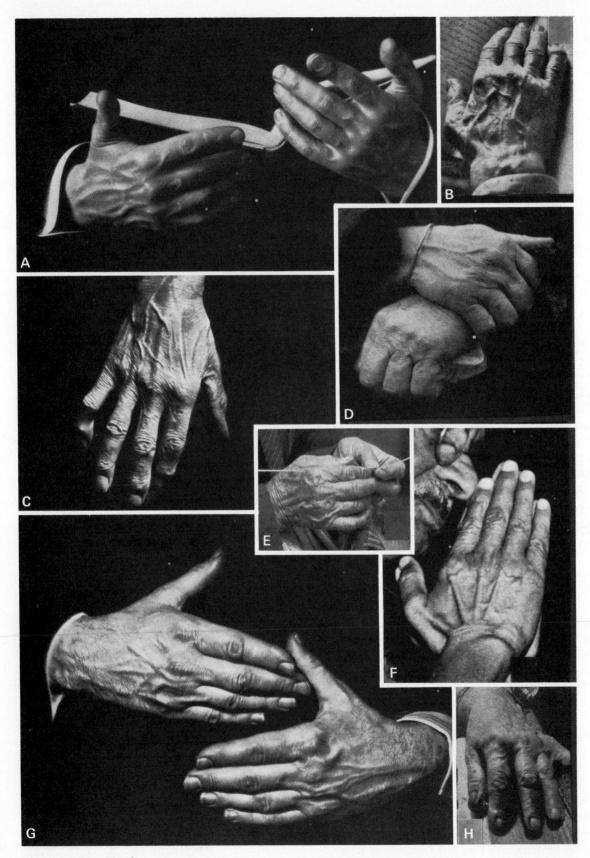

Figure 14–56. Hands.

it succeeds in breaking up the smooth, youthful neck and jaw line. It is essential that every wrinkle be carefully modeled with highlights and shadows. To determine the correct placement of the wrinkles, it is usually necessary to twist and turn the head until natural wrinkles are formed. For plumper characters, these transverse wrinkles should always be used, but they should be wider and fewer in number.

In age, the neck is often a little darker than the face. Darkening the back of the neck is a particularly good technique for dark-skinned characters, especially for outdoor people with leathery skin.

HANDS

In representing youth, the hands need only be given a coat of base color to match the face, but that base coat is very important. The effect on stage of a white hand raised to a deep tan face is, to say the least, jarring.

The extent of modeling needed for bones, knuckles, and veins will depend on both age and the care that the hands have been given. Usually, unless the character tends to be quite pudgy, the bones of the hands, in aging, become much more prominent and the veins begin to stand out (Figure 14–56). The bones, both in the back of the hand and in the fingers (Figure 14–57), should be modeled like cylinders, with highlights along the top or on one side and shadows along the other side. (Decide arbitrarily which way the light is coming from.) Often the joints may swell and redden. The swelling can be suggested by rounded highlights on top of the joint and narrow crescent-shaped shadows around them. (See Figure 14–58.) A little rouge will give the color.

The veins, if at all prominent, should appear

Figure 14–57. Bones of the hand.

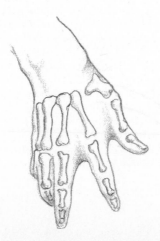

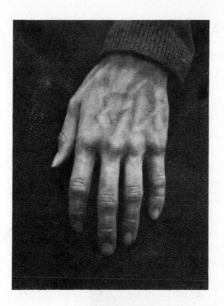

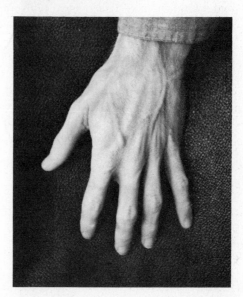

Figures 14–58 and 14–59. Youthful hands aged with cake makeup. The hand on the left can be seen without aging in Figure 15–6. Student makeup by Stuart Boss. Makeup for the hand on the right by Student Larry Kulp.

three-dimensional, not flat, which means that there should be a highlight along one side of every vein and a shadow along the other. Veins should be treated as elongated cylinders. Their roundness will be particularly pronounced as they cross over bones; at other times they may be no more than a faint bluish shadow under the skin. But they are nearly always irregular, often forking out and meandering across the hand. If the actor's natural veins are visible, they can be followed; and if his veins are prominent, they *should* be followed. Otherwise, it is possible to place the veins wherever they appear to be most effective. Be careful, however, not to use too many. A few veins carefully placed and convincingly painted will be far more effective than a complicated network. (See Figures 14–59 and 15–14A.)

The color of the veins will depend on the type and color of the hand. A pale, delicate, fine-skinned hand will naturally reveal much more blue in the veins than a deeply tanned or a black or a brown one, on which the veins may not appear blue at all and can be modeled with the normal highlight and shadow colors. Often veins that are not extremely prominent are a light greenish blue, in which case a very pale tint of blue-green can be used for highlighting and a bluish gray for the shadows. Very prominent veins under a delicate white skin are likely to be a much deeper blue, with no green cast, and would be expected to have blue-gray shadows. Observe the coloration in elderly hands—of the skin as well as the veins.

If the hand is to be delicate and not rough or reddened, it can usually best be aged with paint. If, however, it is to be rough textured, it should be stippled or, better yet, given a three-dimensional skin texture, as described in Chapter 15. The hand can also be painted to represent the blotched skin that usually accompanies age.

For aged hands, nail polish should be removed unless the character would be wearing it. If the actress has neglected to do this before coming to the theater, the acetone in the kit will remove it quickly.

TEETH

Teeth, if too white and even for the character, can be darkened with a fairly dark tooth enamel and chipped or removed entirely with black tooth enamel or black wax (see Appendix A). Black eyebrow pencil is a possible substitute for black enamel in blocking out teeth. The teeth must be perfectly dry in order to take the pencil, and they may have to be touched up occasionally during the performance.

The treatment of the teeth in age will vary greatly with the character. In some, they will be perfect, and in others, slowly rotting away.

If teeth are not as white as they should be for younger characters, they can be whitened with light tooth enamel.

If the teeth are uneven, the lower edges of the longer ones can be blocked out. If they are too even, the process can be reversed. Pointed fangs can be made in the same way.

In this chapter we have concentrated on makeup for the face, neck, and hands, but remember that other exposed parts of the body may require makeup as well. Cake makeup can be used for relatively small areas, but to cover large areas, liquid makeup is more practical. For details, see *Body Makeup* in Appendix A.

PROBLEMS

1. Make up yourself or someone else as one of the following pairs of characters. All of the characters are youthful, but the pairs have been selected to show definite contrast that should be brought out in the makeup.

Katherina and Bianca *(Taming of the Shrew)*; Olivia and Maria *(Twelfth Night)*; Barbara and Sarah *(Major Barbara)*; Ruth and Eileen *(My Sister Eileen)*; Ophelia *(Hamlet)* and Audrey *(As You Like It)*; Sally and Natalia *(I Am a Camera)*; Eliza Doolittle *(Pygmalion*, Acts 1 and 5); Gigi *(Gigi)* and Bessie Watty *(The Corn is Green)*; Laurie and Ado Annie *(Oklahoma)*; Romaine and The Other Woman *(Witness for the Prosecution)*; Canina and Colomba *(Volpone)*; Joan of Arc *(Saint Joan)* and Billie Dawn *(Born Yesterday)*; Rosalie *(Oh Dad, Poor Dad, Mamma's Hung You In the Closet and I'm Feelin' So Sad)* and Ophelia *(Hamlet)*; Lili *(Carnival)* and Electra *(Electra)*; Joan *(St. Joan)* and Hypatia *(Misalliance)*; Nancy Jones *(The Knack)* and Desdemona *(Othello)*; Frankie *(The Member of the Wedding)* and Alma *(Summer and Smoke)*; Alice *(The Killing of Sister George)* and Carol *(Black Comedy)*; Portia *(Merchant of Venice)* and Juliet *(Romeo and Juliet)*.

Charles Lomax and Bill Walker *(Major Barbara)*; Danny and Hubert *(Night Must Fall)*; Antonio and Launcelot Gobbo *(Merchant of Venice)*; Orlando and Touchstone *(As You Like It)*; Romeo and Hamlet; Oswald *(Ghosts)* and Bo Decker *(Bus Stop)*; Desmonde and Alfred *(The Happy Time)*; Dauphin *(St. Joan)* and Mosca *(Volpone)*; Billy Bigelow *(Carousel)* and Leo *(The Little Foxes)*; Lt. Cable *(South Pacific)* and Albert *(Ladies in Retirement)*; Stanley Kowalski and A Young Collector *(A Streetcar Named Desire)*; the two Gareths *(Philadelphia, Here I Come)*; Jerry *(The Zoo Story)* and Jonathan *(Oh Dad, Poor Dad)*; Albert Amundson *(A Thousand Clowns)* and Colin *(The Knack)*; Bentley *(Misalliance)* and Dromio *(Comedy of Errors)*; Joey *(The Homecoming)* and Brindsley *(Black Comedy)*; Rosencrantz and Guildenstern *(Rosencrantz and Guildenstern are Dead)*; Joey and Reg *(Butley)*.

2. Choose at least three character photographs from your morgue and analyze each face according to the

plan of areas and planes used in this chapter. Assuming that light would be falling from above, indicate whether each plane would be shadowed or highlighted.

3. Following the detailed instructions at the beginning of the chapter, model your face for aging—first with highlights only, then adding shadows, rouge, and stipple.

4. Model your own cheekbones with highlights and shadows according to the instructions in the chapter, taking care to follow your own bone structure precisely and to keep the shadow darkest on the under side of the bone. You may want to stipple with one or more colors after you have finished. The most common mistakes made in applying cheek shadows are failing to follow the natural bone structure, placing the shadow too low on the cheek (below the bone, that is, instead of on the under side of it), and making the shadow flat and patch-like instead of varying it in intensity.

5. Model a broken or a crooked nose. The most common mistakes here are failure to make the highlights strong enough, failure to counteract the natural highlights of your own nose with a sufficiently deep shadow, and the use of shadow on the sides of the nose where it is not needed.

6. Following the specific instructions in this chapter, practice doing nasolabial folds until you can do them convincingly. Use the photographs in Figures 14–35 and 14–47 and in your own morgue as a reference, always noting the direction of the light in which the photograph was taken. If you have trouble making the folds three-dimensional, model folds on your clay head and study the conformation you are attempting to model with paint. Then, in doing your painted folds, be sure to follow the natural crease precisely, to keep the crease very sharp, to start the fold at the nostril instead of below the nostril, to taper the fold, to avoid overlapping the shadow and the highlights (which can give a blurred, dirty effect) to use a dark shadow color to deepen and sharpen the crease, and to use enough red in the fold to suggest blood under the skin. If you feel that your fold can be improved, check to make sure you have done these things.

7. Do at least four different aged eyes based on, though not necessarily exact copies of, photographs of eyes in your morgue or in the book. Be sure to determine the light source in each photograph and decide how that is affecting the precise location of highlights and shadows. Make sure that at least one of the eyes has a full pouch, and keep working on the pouch until it is convincingly three-dimensional. In working for a three-dimensional effect, make sure to round the bottom of the pouch like a cylinder, to use strong lights and darks, and to taper the sides of the pouch as they approach the eye. Block out at least one eyebrow. If you are not satisfied with the results, experiment with other methods until you find one that works well for you. It would be a good idea to try more than one method even if the first one works perfectly.

8. Do Oriental eyes, using as a model a photograph from your morgue or from the book.

9. Change your mouth in several ways, for both youthful and aged characters. Use photographs of mouths as a reference, especially for age.

10. Age your forehead, using only highlights and shadows rather than wrinkles. Be very carful to avoid using too much shadow. Begin with highlights and see how little shadow you can get along with. You may need none at all.

11. Age your forehead with wrinkles, following your natural creases, if you have any, and modeling each wrinkle with extreme care. Follow suggestions in the text carefully, making sure that each highlight and shadow has both a hard edge and a soft one. Avoid letting the shadows get too wide, or making the medium shadows too strong or the deep shadows not strong enough. Make sure you model the wrinkles like half cylinders, tapering them at the ends and keeping the creases sharp. Make sure also that you follow your natural creases and that the highlights are correctly placed according to the direction of the light on stage (normally, from above). Using some red in the shadows may be helpful.

12. Age your neck and jaw line in two different ways, using photographs in this chapter and in your morgue.

13. Age your hands, deciding first what kind of character they are for. Would they be plump or bony, pale or dark, smooth or wrinkled, fine or coarse? Would veins be prominent or barely visible? How much would the blue of the veins show through the skin? Would there be blotches on the skin? Would the knuckles be red or not? Would they be swollen? Be sure to check the results for projection in a mirror some distance away.

14. Make up yourself or someone else as a specific middle-aged character from a play. Here are a few suggestions:

Alice More (*A Man for All Seasons*); Madame Rosepettle (*Oh Dad, Poor Dad*); Maxine, Hannah, Frau Fahrenkopf (*The Night of the Iguana*); Clytemnestra (*Electra*); Dolly Levi (*The Matchmaker, Hello, Dolly!*); Lizzy Sweeney (*Philadelphia, Here I Come*); Linda (*Death of a Salesman*); Blanche (*A Streetcar Named Desire*); Lola (*Come Back, Little Sheba*); Martha (*Who's Afraid of Virginia Woolf*); Medea (*Medea*); Miss Holroyd (*Bell, Book, and Candle*); Violet, Nell (*How's the World Treating You?*); George, Mrs. Mercy Croft (*The Killing of Sister George*); Elizabeth Barrett (*The Barretts of Wimpole Street*); Lady Capulet, the Nurse (*Romeo and Juliet*) Kate, Mrs. Sims (*The Twelve Pound Look*); Madame Popov (*The Boor*); Penny (*You Can't Take It with You*); Christine (*Mourning Becomes Electra*); Mrs. Bennet, Lady Lucas, Lady Catherine (*Pride and Prejudice*); Birdie, Regina (*The Little Foxes*); Mrs. Eynsford-Hill (*Pygmalion*); Mrs. Craig, Mrs. Harold (*Craig's Wife*); Mrs. Erlynne (*Lady Windemere's Fan*); Lady Bracknell (*The Importance of Being Earnest*); Vinnie (*Life with Father*); Countess Aurelia, Mme. Constance, Mlle. Gabrielle, Mme. Joséphine (*The Madwoman of Chaillot*); Miss Madrigal (*The Chalk Garden*); Margaret (*The Lady's Not For Burning*); Arkadina (*The Sea Gull*); Mme. St. Pé (*Waltz of the Toreadors*); Lady Macbeth;

Queen Gertrude *(Hamlet)*; Sophie *(White Lies)*; Marjorie, Kathleen *(Home)*; Beatrice *(The Effect of Gamma Rays on Man-in-the-Moon Marigolds).*

Pastor Manders *(Ghosts)*; Harry Sims *(The Twelve Pound Look)*; Doc Gibbs *(Our Town)*; Morrell *(Candida)*; Tyson, Tappercoom *(The Lady's Not for Burning)*; Mr. Collins *(Pride and Prejudice)*; Sir Robert Morton *(The Winslow Boy)*; Harry Brock *(Born Yesterday)*; Oscar, Horace, Ben *(The Little Foxes)*; Sir Andrew *(Major Barbara)*; Androcles *(Androcles and the Lion)*; Papa *(The Happy Time)*; Gooper *(Cat on a Hot Tin Roof)*; Morgenhall, Fowle *(The Dock Brief)*; Cajetan *(Luther)*; S. B. O'Donnell, Canon O'Byrne, Con Sweeney *(Philadelphia, Here I Come)*; Willy Loman *(Death of a Salesman)*; Mr. Bumble *(Oliver)*; Doc *(Come Back, Little Sheba)*; George *(Who's Afraid of Virginia Woolf)*; Harry *(The Collection)*; Harold Gorringe *(Black Comedy).*

15. Repeat problem 14 with two different characters, using two different techniques of application (see Chapter 12).

16. Choose, from your morgue or illustrations (photographs or works of art) in this book, three elderly people. Analyze all of the factors that make them look old rather than middle-aged. Look at them from a little distance and pick out the most prominent effects of old age.

17. Make up yourself or someone else as a specific elderly character from a play. Here are some possible choices:

Nanny *(The Effect of Gamma Rays on Man-in-the-Moon Marigolds)*; Queen Margaret *(Richard III)*; Mrs. Hanmer, Miss Hoadley, Mrs. Gross, Mrs. Sampler *(The Silver Whistle)*; Lavinia *(The Heiress)*; Duchess of Berwick *(Lady Windemere's Fan)*; Flora Van Huysen *(The Matchmaker)*; Dowager Empress *(Anastasia)*; Mrs. St. Maugham *(The Chalk Garden)*; Abby, Martha *(Arsenic and Old Lace)*; Mrs. Midget *(Outward Bound)*; Mrs. Coade *(Dear Brutus)*; Mrs. Bramson *(Night Must Fall)*; Miss Nellie *(On Borrowed Time)*; Victoria Regina (last scene); Ase *(Peer Gynt)*; Clara, Gertrude *(Save Me a Place at Forest Lawn)*; Grandma *(The American Dream)*; She *(The Chinese Prime Minister)*; Anfisa *(Three Sisters)*; Avdotya Nazarovna *(Ivanov)*; Marina, Mrs. Voinitsky *(Uncle Vanya).*

Nonno *(The Night of the Iguana)*; Bent *(The Chinese Prime Minister)*; Friar Laurence *(Romeo and Juliet)*; Lob *(Dear Brutus)*; Luka *(The Boor)*; Martin Vanderhoff *(You Can't Take It with You)*; Old Werle *(The Wild Duck)*; Gramps *(On Borrowed Time)*; Mr. Witherspoon *(Arsenic and Old Lace)*; Mr. Beebe *(The Silver Whistle)*; Archbishop of Rheims *(St. Joan)*; The Chaplain *(The Lady's Not for Burning)*; Corbaccio *(Volpone)*; Harry, Jade *(Home).*

15

THREE-DIMENSIONAL MAKEUP

In modeling with paint, there was no attempt to actually change the natural shape of the actor's features but merely to give the impression that such changes had been made. There are times, however, when a painted makeup may not be entirely convincing and a three-dimensional makeup is needed. A three-dimensional makeup involves the actual building up of the features with some substance that can be molded into any desired shape. Nose putty and derma wax are the two most commonly used materials (see Appendix A). Cotton, cleansing tissues, and paper toweling are also used. Molded latex processes will be discussed in the next chapter.

The easiest feature to change three-dimensionally is the nose. A slight change in its shape can make a tremendous difference in the appearance of a character. Yet too often an actor is content to settle for his own nose instead of the nose of the character, thus throwing away one of his most valuable means of characterization through makeup.

NOSE PUTTY

Nose putty is used primarily for changing the shape of the nose, but with practice it can also be used on the cheekbones, chin, forehead, and ears—that is, on any bony or cartilaginous structure. It is seldom practical to apply it to parts of the face in which there is a great deal of movement of the muscles, however, for bubbles will appear in the surface of the putty and ruin the effect.

The use of putty should not be restricted to fantastic noses or even to large and striking ones. There are minor changes that can easily be made

in order to give the actor a nose unlike his own and more suitable for the character (Figures 10–2, 15–1, 15–3A, 15–10). The less putty you need to use, the less difficulty you are likely to have with shaping and blending.

Building up the nose. The first step in building up the nose should be to make a profile sketch of the shape you want (Figures 10–1, 10–5, and 10–6), bearing in mind that no matter what the shape or size of the addition, it must appear to be an integral, living part of the face, not something stuck on. This means that the basic structure of the nose must give the impression of being supported by bone and cartilage. It also means that the false nose must be so carefully blended into the natural skin that it is impossible to tell where the real leaves off and the false begins.

Once you have a clear plan firmly in mind and know exactly what you intend to do, applying and shaping the nose putty is not a particularly difficult problem—provided you observe a few simple rules:

1. Keep your sketch in front of you and have available two mirrors to give you a profile view of the nose as you work.

2. Make sure the skin is free from all grease and makeup before applying the putty.

3. Coat your fingers lightly with lubricating jelly (see Appendix A) to keep the putty from sticking to them. (If you have no lubricating jelly, wave set can be substituted.) Then separate a small piece of putty from the mass and knead it with your fingers until it is very pliable. If the putty should be too stiff and the heat of the hand does not soften it sufficiently, immerse it in hot water for a few minutes or place it near a radi-

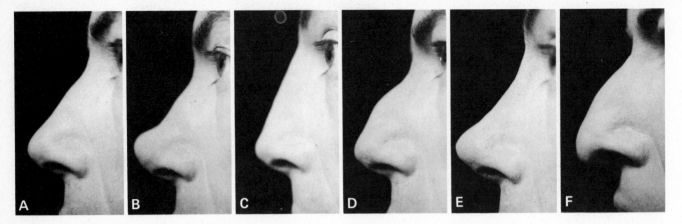

Figure 15–1.   Noses B–F show reshaping of nose A with nose putty.

Figure 15–2.   Modeling a putty nose. Ball of putty is pressed on to the nose, spread with the fingers, smoothed out with cream, given skin texture, covered with makeup, and removed with a thread.

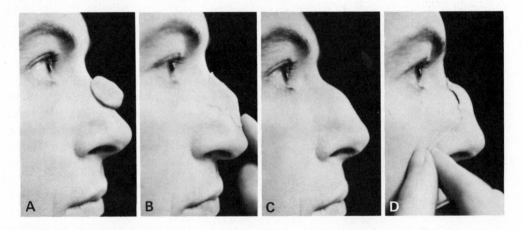

ator or some other heat source. Although it is possible to soften putty by the addition of a small amount of cold cream, the method is not recommended. There is a tendency to add too much cream, which makes the putty soft and mushy and quite unmanageable.

4. Stick the softened ball of putty on the part of the nose that is to be built up most (Figure 15–2A), pressing it into the skin for good adhesion. If it does not seem to be securely attached, paint the nose with spirit gum and let it dry before applying the putty.

5. Carefully blend the edges of the putty into the skin, shaping the nose as you work (Figures 15–2B and J–4A). Use more lubricating jelly on your fingers if the putty sticks to them. Always confine the putty to as small an area as possible, being especially careful to keep if off the cheeks and the nasolabial folds. In blending the edges, there is a tendency to keep pulling the putty outward until it has spread well away from the actual construction. In order to avoid this, it is helpful to model it *toward* the center of the nose as well as *away from* the center.

6. When the blending is finished, you can make

final adjustments in the shape. Using your sketch as a guide and a mirror to check the nose from all angles, cover your fingers with more lubricating jelly and keep pressing, prodding, and massaging the putty until you have precisely the shape you want, always keeping in mind the image of flesh and skin over bone and cartilage. A final light massaging with a generous amount of lubricating jelly will help to eliminate unintentional cracks and bumps and give a completely smooth surface.

7. When the surface of the putty is smooth, the edges perfectly blended, and the lubricating jelly dried, stipple the putty with your stipple sponge to give skin texture (Figure J–4A). Then, if the putty is lighter or less red than the skin, stipple it with rouge (dry rouge applied with a damp sponge, creme rouge, or grease rouge). (See Figure J–4A.) If creme or grease rouge is used, powder it thoroughly, then brush off the excess powder.

A method of giving three-dimensional texture to putty by using a latex negative of a grapefruit, orange, or lemon skin is explained in Chapter 16. The method is essentially the same as that for giving texture to plastic eyebrow covers, as illustrated in Figure 14–21C,D.

8. Coat the putty with plastic sealer or fixative (see Appendix A), carrying the sealer beyond the edge of the putty. It's usually a good idea to cover the whole nose with the sealer. Powder.

9. Stipple the base (cake, creme, grease) over the entire nose (Figure J–4A), and continue with the makeup. Should the base coat not completely cover the putty area, add another coat of sealer, then stipple on more base. If you are using cake makeup, it will probably dry lighter than the same makeup applied directly to the skin; this can usually be corrected by coating the light area with more lubricating jelly. The water soluble jelly will mix with the makeup and dry with a slight waxy sheen. Powdering will counteract this. If, for any reason, covering is still not satisfactory, coat the problem area with rubber-mask grease, making sure to blend the edges thoroughly into the skin, then powder. Apply the regular base over the rubber-mask grease.

10. For most characters, you will want to add rouge to the nostrils and perhaps other parts of the nose after the base coat has been applied. This will give the nose a much more natural appearance. (See Figure J–3.) This can be done after the entire makeup has been completed, when the stippling or other finishing touches are being added.

For illustrations of the use of nose putty, see Figures 15–25B, 20–25, and J-1. Figures 14–26, 14–34, 15–4 and 15–5 illustrate a variety of noses. Others are shown in Appendix H.

Removal of putty. A thread can be used to remove the putty. Starting at either the base or the bridge of the nose, run the thread along the nose under the putty (Figure 15–2D), pulling the thread tight with both hands. The putty that is removed can sometimes be used for another makeup. If you hope to do this, it would be advisable to remove the makeup before removing the putty. Any bits of putty remaining on the nose after the bulk of it has been detached with the thread can be removed by massaging with makeup remover until the putty is soft enough to be wiped off with tissues. Always do this gently, in order to avoid irritation. Any sealer remaining on the skin can either be peeled off or massaged off.

Building up the chin. When using putty on the chin, it is advisable to cover the area with spirit gum, unless you are using a putty with strong adhesive qualities. Let the gum become almost dry, then stick a ball of putty onto the tip of the chin and carefully work it outward in all directions until you have the desired shape. If at all possible, confine the building up to the bony area of the chin, keeping it off the softer parts, where muscular movement is very likely to result in wrinkling and bubbling. Blend the putty carefully into the skin so that there will be no visible edges when the makeup is finished. Massaging gently with lubricating jelly will help to smooth out any irregularities. Then apply rouge, sealer, paint, more lubricating jelly, powder, and various colors of stipple, as suggested for noses.

Figure 15–3. Portraits in makeup. (A) Johannes Fugger. Based on a portrait by Dürer. (B) Making up as Elizabeth I. Hair around face waxed back, eyebrows blocked out with derma wax, and nose built up with derma wax. (C) Elizabeth I. Both student makeups by Lee Austin. (For other makeups by Mr. Austin, see Figures 13–3, J–1, and J–9.)

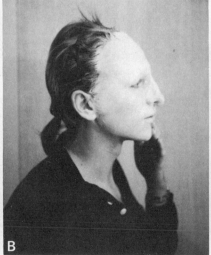

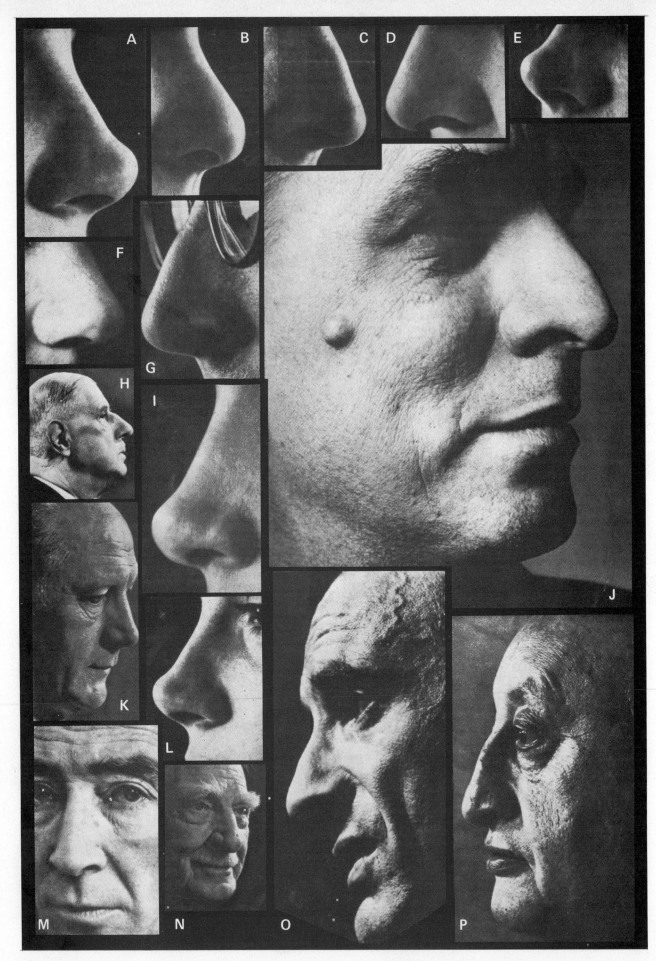

Figure 15-4. Noses.

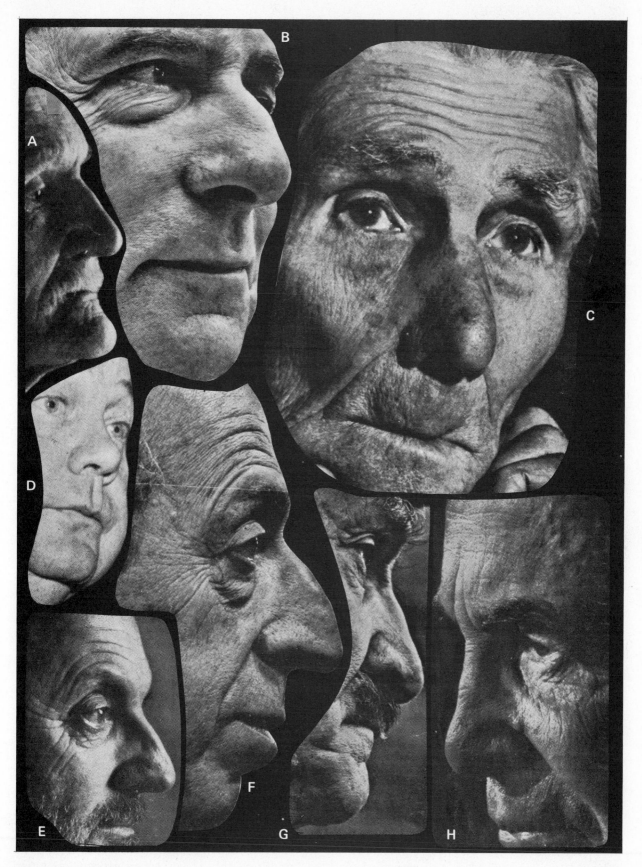

Figure 15–5. Noses.

137

Figure 15–6. Severed hand. Section of hand below wrist built up with derma wax to give illusion of being cut off.

In applying beards or goatees to a putty chin, it is best to apply sealer to the putty before applying the spirit gum. Then proceed as usual.

DERMA WAX

Derma wax (see Appendix A) is softer than nose putty. It can be shaped and blended more easily but is less stable during a performance. Before using derma wax, it is usually best to apply a coat of spirit gum to the skin in order to keep the wax from loosening. Let the spirit gum dry, then use the same procedure as for nose putty. Firm wax should be used for building up bony parts of the face (Figure 15–3B,C). Soft wax is more suitable for blocking out eyebrows (see Chapter 14) and for other techniques discussed on the following pages. For close work you may wish to blend the edges of the wax into the skin with alcohol and a soft brush.

Derma wax can also be used over nose putty to provide a smooth surface and an imperceptible blend with the skin—not that this cannot be done with putty, but doing it with wax may be easier and in some cases can save time, depending on the hardness of the putty.

For the witch in Figure 20–25, derma wax was used to build up the knuckles. This is effective for photographs, tableaus, or very short scenes in which the hands are not touched or used very much. But nose putty would give greater security.

PUTTY-WAX

A half-and-half mixture of nose putty and derma wax eliminates some of the disadvantages of each. They can be mixed manually if the putty is soft enough. It is recommended, however, that the mixture be made up a can or a box at a time by melting the two together in a double boiler. It can then be poured into a container, cooled, and used as needed. If you are mixing only a small amour.t, it's simpler to remove half the contents of a metal box of derma wax, add a piece of nose putty to the remaining half, and place the box in a shallow pan of simmering water. When the wax and the putty are both melted, they can be stirred thoroughly, then cooled. Putty-wax has been used for makeups in Figures 14–23, 14–24, and 15–10.

LATEX

In the next chapter the technique for using liquid latex in casting prosthetic pieces is discussed. It is also possible to use latex directly. Information about the material itself can be found in Appendix A.

One of the great problems in aging a young face is overcoming the natural smoothness of the skin. Methods of giving the effect of a rougher texture using only cake or creme makeup or greasepaint have already been suggested in Chapter 12.

Direct application of latex provides a simple method of creating a three-dimensional skin texture.

First, do a complete age makeup. If you use grease, use as little as possible and set it with translucent powder. If you use cake (a water-soluble paint that tends to mix with latex), you will need to be very careful not to smear the makeup.

After the makeup is completed and working on one area of the face at a time, pull the skin tight with the fingers and stipple on clear latex, or apply the latex with your fingers. When each area is dry, dust it with powder, then release the skin, which should form wrinkles. If you want deeper wrinkles, apply additional coats of latex in the same way. When the entire face has been covered, the makeup can be touched up with greasepaint, rubber-mask grease, or, preferably, with makeup pencils—provided you have suitable colors.

If you prefer, you can use the latex technique directly on the dry skin, then add any makeup that seems necessary. For this method, you may wish to use flesh-colored latex in order to provide a suitable foundation color.

Since latex is irritating to some skins, it may be advisable to coat the skin very lightly first with oil or grease. Any excess can be wiped off gently with a tissue. Powder before applying the latex.

In applying latex to the faces of women and girls or boys of pre-shaving age, using oil or grease keeps facial fuzz from becoming embedded in the latex. This could cause considerable discomfort and irritation on removal. Unfortunately, if there is much movement of the facial muscles, the latex is quite likely to separate from the skin. The likelihood of this happening is increased by the use of oil or grease, but there is always a chance that it may happen anyway—particularly around the mouth. The best solution to the problem is to loosen the edges of the latex and secure it to the skin with spirit gum, which should always be allowed to become tacky before the latex is pressed into it.

Latex can also be used to age the hands (Figure 15–7), but not if they are hairy. If there is only a small amount of fuzz or short hairs, greasing the back of the hand lightly will usually provide sufficient protection.

Plastic sealer (see Appendix A) can be used instead of latex on stretched skin to create subtle wrinkles. It can be applied directly to the skin, to skin lightly coated with oil or grease and powdered, or over makeup. If latex irritates the skin and the sealer does not, you can use plastic for the first coat, then build up coats of latex over it for deeper wrinkles.

LATEX AND TISSUE

This technique involves the use of liquid latex and cleansing tissue or a good quality of soft paper toweling (Maslinn towels—actually made of cloth fibers—are considered the best for this work). The toweling (Figure 15–8) will give much deeper wrinkles than the tissues. You can cover the entire face or only part of it. In using the toweling, however, it is usually best to cover the whole face in order to avoid unnatural contrasts in texture between the paper wrinkles and the relatively smooth skin. This is the technique:

1. Be sure the skin is clean and dry and free of grease. Then paint the area to be covered with liquid latex. *Be very careful to avoid getting latex into the hair, eyebrows, eyelashes, or beard.* If the eyebrows are to be covered, block them out first by one of the methods suggested in Chapter 14 so that there are no free hairs. Then they can be safely covered with latex. If there is fuzz on the face, either try a small area first or else lightly oil or grease and powder the skin before applying the latex, as suggested above. You may wish to use the oil or grease anyway to protect the skin, but remember that this is likely to contribute to loosening of the latex during the performance.

2. Tear (do not cut) a single thickness of tissue or toweling to the approximate size and shape of the area to be covered (Figure 15–8A), pull the skin tight with one hand, and with the other apply the tissue to the area covered with wet latex. In the case of the area around the mouth, a broad smile will take the place of pulling the skin with the hand (Figure 15–8A,B). For best results, work on only a small area at a time.

Figure 15–7. Hand aged with latex. Skin of hand on right stretched and coated with clear latex, then powdered. No other makeup used. Student makeup by Lea Stern.

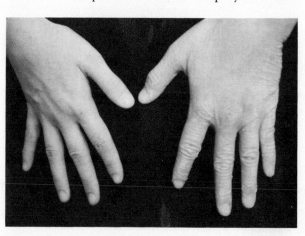

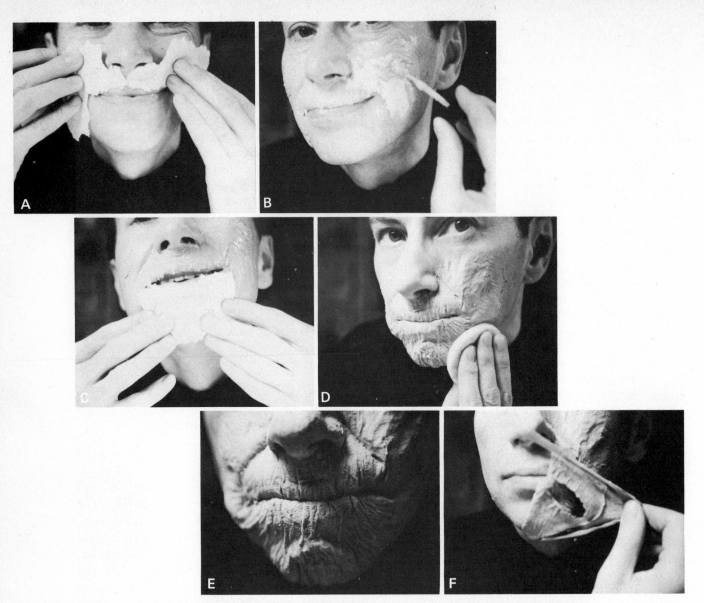

Figure 15–8. Skin texture with latex and paper toweling. (A) Paper toweling is torn to shape of smiling mouth and is pressed into wet latex. (B) Additional coat of latex is brushed or sponged over toweling. (C) Section of toweling is pressed into wet latex on chin. (D) When dry, latex is powdered. Relaxing the smile forms wrinkles. (E) Toweling is covered with foundation paint, lightly highlighted and shadowed, then powdered. Nose has been stippled with latex to give the skin a slightly roughened texture. (F) Latex and toweling removed by pulling.

3. Paint another layer of latex over the tissue or toweling (Figure 15–8B), and let it dry or force-dry it with a hair dryer.

4. Release the skin and powder the latex (Figure 15–8D). Wrinkles will form.

5. When all of the latex work is finished, cover the whole face with rubber-mask grease (or greasepaint if no rubber-mask grease is available). If you have used a fairly dark latex, apply your base (which will probably be lighter) carefully and lightly over the latex-covered tissue or toweling. Normally, there should be sufficient texture to catch the base only on top, leaving the darker latex showing through in the creases or tiny depressions. This will emphasize the texture as well as any wrinkles that may have formed.

6. Complete the makeup as usual with highlights, shadows, and powder. In order to take advantage of the texture, keep the shading subtle. Touch-ups can be done with makeup pencils if you wish.

The latex can be peeled off quite easily after the performance (Figure 15–8F).

If you wish to build up parts of the face when using this technique, it can be done with either derma wax, putty-wax, nose putty, or cotton, preferably keeping the addition small. Care should be taken to blend it smoothly into the skin. In using cotton, modify the basic method as follows:

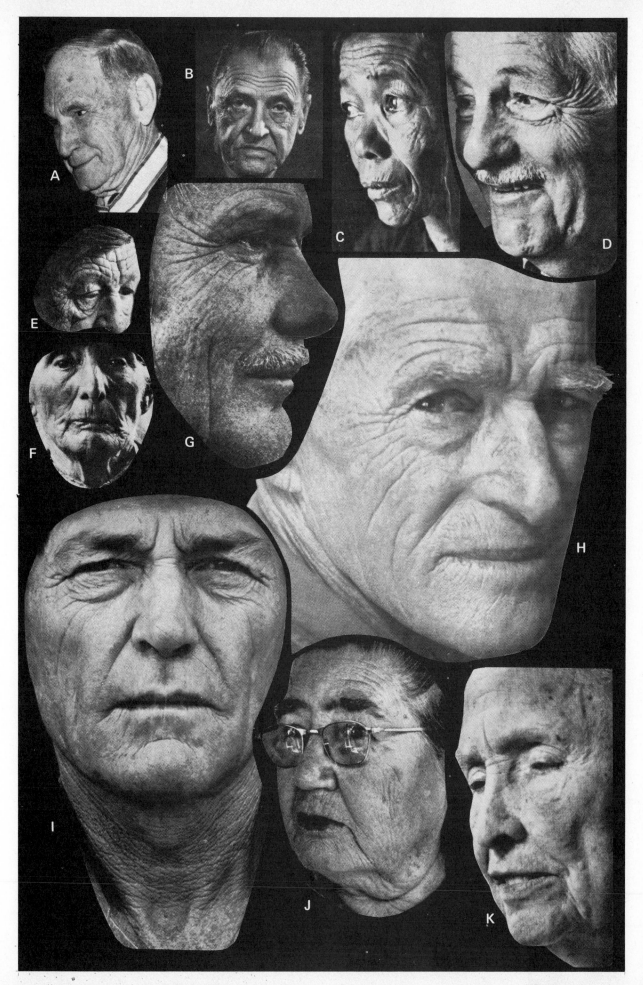

Figure 15–9. Skin texture and wrinkles.

1. Shape the cotton carefully and apply it to the wet latex on the face. This works particularly well for eye pouches.

2. Immediately apply the single layer of tissue, covering the dry cotton.

3. Apply the second layer of latex over the entire layer of tissue, and complete the makeup as usual.

For wax or putty, the following method may be used:

1. Apply small amounts of the putty or wax directly to the skin for jowls, nasolabial folds, and the like. Avoid building up the mouth area if possible. Be sure to make a good blend. Use spirit gum first if you wish. If you use putty or wax on the nose and tissue on the rest of the face, be sure to give the nose some texture by using the grapefruit rind technique (see Chapter 16) or stippling with a plastic stipple sponge or a stiff-bristled brush to create tiny holes in the surface.

2. Apply latex over the entire area to be covered, doing a section at a time, stretching the skin as you go.

3. Apply tissue immediately to the wet latex, then brush another coat of latex over the tissue. Force dry with a hair dryer before releasing the stretched skin.

4. Complete your makeup with rubber-mask grease, then powder. Stippling with about three colors of paint is usually helpful.

In removing the makeup, peel off the latex. Most of the wax or putty will probably come with it. Then use any good makeup remover. If you have used spirit gum first and it does not come off with your makeup remover, use spirit gum remover or alcohol.

It is recommended that in using this technique you begin with small areas and experiment with the effects you can obtain. In using cotton or putty, keep the constructions very small and simple, especially at first.

Latex should never be used for a performance unless it has first been tried for at least one full rehearsal, preferably more. It has a tendency to work loose from the skin, especially if the actor perspires very much or if there is considerable movement of the muscles. If it does, it can usually be pasted down with spirit gum. Also, it may irritate sensitive skin, leaving it reddened for an hour or so after the latex is removed. If there are problems in any of these areas, it would be preferable to avoid latex, to experiment with a different brand, or to use another method.

LATEX, COTTON, AND SPIRIT GUM

An effective method of achieving a leathery, wrinkled skin texture is to use latex, cotton, and spirit gum, as illustrated in Figure 15–12. This is the technique:

1. Paint the skin with spirit gum, working on one section of the face at a time. The mouth and chin area is a good place to start; the eyes should probably be done last. If you cover the eyebrows, flatten them out first with derma wax or eyebrow wax so that they will not get stuck in the latex.

2. When the gum is tacky, lay on absorbent cotton (Figure 15–12A) and let the gum dry. Be sure the fibers follow in the direction you wish the wrinkles to go—that is, vertically over the mouth, almost vertically down the cheeks, and horizontally on the forehead.

Figure 15–10. Makeup with tissue and latex. Putty-wax nose, greasepaint foundation. Student makeup by Gloria Maddock. Figure 15–11. Makeup with spirit gum, cotton, and latex. Rubber-mask grease base with cake highlights and shadows. Student makeup by Sally Palmquist.

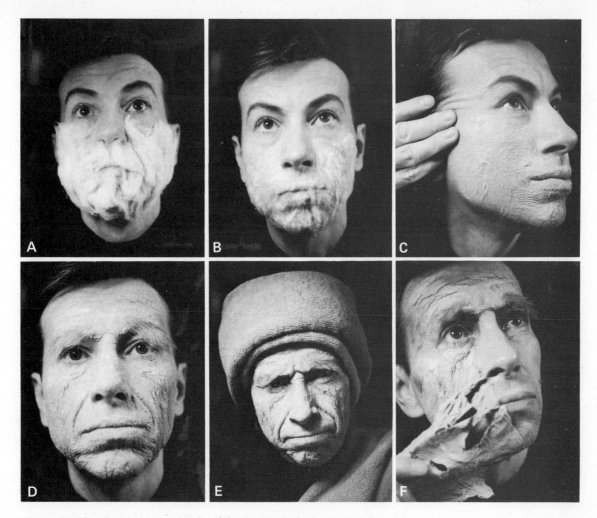

Figure 15–12. Latex, cotton, and spirit gum technique. Cotton is stuck to the skin with spirit gum (A) and the excess pulled off (B). Remaining cotton is covered with latex and dried with the skin pulled taut (C). When the skin is released (D), the latex falls into a pattern of wrinkles. Nose is covered with latex and cornmeal for texture (E). Rubber-mask grease is used as a foundation. F shows makeup being removed.

Figure 15–12A shows only the mouth and cheeks with cotton. The rest of the face was done later.

3. Pull off most of the cotton (Figure 15–12B). The less you leave on, the less pronounced the three-dimensional effect will be.

4. Cover the cotton with latex, using your finger, which will work better over cotton than would a brush. This step should be done with the skin stretched as tight as possible (Figure 15–12C). *Avoid getting latex into the hair, eyebrows, eyelashes, or beard.* Only one section of the face should be done at a time. The mouth can be stretched with a broad smile, which must be held until the latex is dry. The skin of the cheeks can be pulled taut with the fingers. A hair dryer should be used to speed the drying. When the latex is dry and the skin relaxed, it will fall naturally into wrinkles (Figure 15–12D).

5. If the eyebrows are covered, crepe hair brows can be attached with latex, as they have been in Figure 15–12D. The nose in this makeup has been covered with latex and cornmeal (see below).

6. Give the entire face a base coat of rubber-mask grease (or greasepaint if rubber-mask grease is not available) of the appropriate shade, then powder.

7. Finish the makeup with highlights and shadows of grease or creme makeup, then powder. Touch up with makeup pencils if you like. (See Figure 15–12E).

8. Most of the makeup can be peeled off (Figure 15–12F), but because of the undercoat of spirit gum, it will peel less easily than latex usually does. The remainder of the gum can be cleaned from the skin with spirit gum remover or alcohol. In pulling the latex off

Figure 15–13. Neglected mouth. Creme makeup over spirit gum, cotton, and latex. Putty-wax on nose. Note how the smooth, youthful lips counteract the effective aging of the rest of the face.

and in dissolving the spirit gum, be very careful around the eyes and the eyebrows. To avoid pulling hairs out of the brows, pull very slowly and brush a little alcohol or spirit gum remover into the brows as you go.

LATEX AND CORNMEAL

In order to give the skin a rough texture, with or without wrinkling, cornmeal can be used with the latex. It is possible either to mix the cornmeal with the latex before applying it, as was done for Figures 15–14C and 15–15, or to apply cornmeal to a wet coating of latex, then cover with another layer of latex, as was done for the nose in Figure 15–12. You then make up in the usual way, using rubber-mask grease as a foundation. For a rough, scaly texture, try wheat germ.

If you wish also to wrinkle the skin, simply apply the latex and cornmeal to the stretched skin and do not release the skin until the latex is completely dry. In this case, a hair dryer should be used to speed up the drying.

SYRUP AND TISSUE

For quick changes in which an age makeup is needed for the first scene and must be quickly removed for a subsequent scene, Karo syrup (either dark or light) provides an adhesive that can be removed quickly and easily with soap and water. The procedure is much the same as for latex and tissue.

1. Using the fingers or a stiff-bristled brush (a glue or paste brush will do), apply the syrup to a section of the skin.

2. Lay on a single thickness of peach-colored tissue (or orchid for frail old ladies), torn to the approximate size and shape of the area you are starting with. If you prefer, tear the tissue after it is on.

3. Follow the same procedure until you have covered as much of the skin as you wish. Eyebrows may be covered or not, as you choose. If you are covering most of the face, you should usually cover the neck also, particularly on a young actor.

4. You may wish to cover all of the tissue with more syrup. If you do, then let it dry or, preferably, force-dry it with an electric dryer and press powder into it to eliminate any stickiness. Remove excess powder with a soft brush.

5. Cover both the tissue and all exposed skin with creme makeup or greasepaint. If, however, the peach-colored tissue blends with the skin tone and gives a suitable color, you may be able to get along without any base—a great convenience for quick changes. It is also possible to use the syrup and colored tissue over a cake makeup. This is often done when the tissue is to be used on only part of the face (under the eyes, for example) or when there is a quick change involved.

6. With brush and fingers, add grease or creme shadows and highlights or, better yet, use fairly heavy cake shadows under the tissue and stipple on cake highlights over it. If this is done, syrup but no base color should be used over the tissue after it has been applied. This addition of highlights and shadows may or may not be necessary, depending on the amount of projection required. For arena theater particularly, the tissue alone, with or without base, may be quite sufficient. For greater projection without using highlights and shadows, simply make deeper wrinkles in the tissue.

7. Powder the makeup with neutral powder and touch up if necessary.

Although the makeup is fairly stable for short periods, it will be loosened by excessive perspiration, which dissolves the syrup. Other things being equal, the less active the muscles under the makeup,

Figure 15–14. Hand aged with different techniques. (A) Cake makeup. (B) Tissue and spirit gum. (C) Latex and cornmeal (might be used to suggest stone or decayed or diseased flesh).

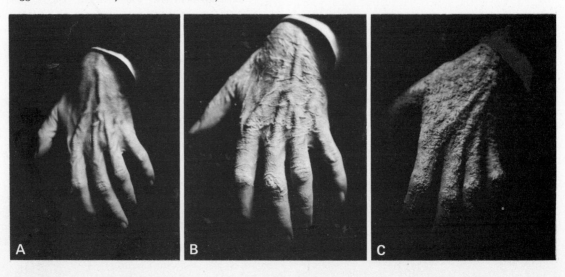

the longer it will adhere to the skin. It can be used on the hands as well as on the face and neck.

SPIRIT GUM AND TISSUE

One method of achieving wrinkled skin texture with latex and tissue has already been discussed. Essentially the same method can be used with spirit gum and either facial or bathroom tissue. This is particularly successful in aging the hands (Figure 15–14B). The following method may be used:

1. Double the hand into a tight fist, then paint the back of the hand, from knuckles to wrist, with spirit gum.

2. Place the tissue on the spirit gum, which should be fairly wet, and push it into wrinkles. Add a coating of spirit gum over the tissue.

3. Let the spirit gum dry or force-dry it.

4. Powder the spirit gum.

5. Open the hand and repeat the process for the fingers.

6. Apply the foundation paint. If you're using cake makeup, stipple or press the makeup on with your sponge rather than stroking it on. If the cake makeup turns light or chalky, cover it with lubricating jelly and let the jelly dry.

7. Shadowing and highlighting of bones and veins can be done with a brush at this point, or it can be done very heavily before the tissue is applied. Then powder.

8. If you wish to stipple the hand, this can be done by stippling one or two colors over the base, by eliminating the base color and stippling two or three colors heavily over the tissue and spirit gum, or by stippling one or two colors and letting some of the neutral color show through. Painting on the brown spots common to aged hands can also be helpful. This can be done instead of or in combination with stippling.

Be sure to carry the makeup up under the sleeve of the costume.

COTTON AND COLLODION

The traditional method of building up large areas on the face is by means of cotton and flexible collodion. This is not a very satisfactory technique at best and should be replaced whenever possible by latex prosthesis (see Chapter 16) or by one of the other methods described in this chapter. For those who may wish to use it, however, here is the technique:

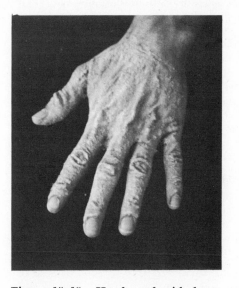

Figure 15–15. Hand aged with latex and cornmeal. Student makeup by Howard Klein.

1. Coat with spirit gum the entire area to be covered by the construction. Before attaching any cotton, allow the gum to dry slightly.

2. Then stick a tuft of cotton, which, when crushed, will almost equal the thickness of the construction, on the area at the point of maximum thickness. If there is to be more than one thick place, of course, several tufts of cotton will need to be used. All edges of the tuft should be frayed so that they will blend fairly smoothly into the foundation. If you are planning to remove the construction after the performance and use it again, soak this bottom layer of cotton with spirit gum or collodion; otherwise, leave it dry.

If there are to be two identical constructions, do them as nearly simultaneously as possible. That is, build up both as you go along rather than completing one and then starting on the other.

3. Cut or tear off a piece of cotton, which, when opened into a fairly thin sheet, will be larger than the area covered by the tuft now on the face. Carefully mold this into the shape required—usually roughly circular. The piece should be of fairly even thickness throughout. Then dampen the cotton—preferably all but the extreme edges. The water should be squeezed into the cotton so that it becomes a thin, tenuous sheet. Then pull all edges of the cotton sheet lightly so that any excess dry cotton is removed, leaving a thin fringe on all sides. This fringe is very important in blending the construction into the foundation. After you have prepared this sheet of cotton, place it near a convenient source of heat to dry while preparing a similar one for the twin construction.

4. When the cotton has dried somewhat, place it on the face so that it overlaps on all sides the tuft of cotton already there. Unless the spirit gum is too dry, the cotton will probably stick very readily.

5. If this makes a large enough construction, brush over the whole sheet very lightly with spirit gum. The

gum should be brushed on from the center out, always following the line of the imaginary radii of the circle. Special care should be taken to blend the edges very smoothly so that no join will be visible. Also, be especially careful not to roughen the surface of the cotton.

6. When the spirit gum is nearly dry, the process can be repeated, this time with flexible collodion (diluted to nearly half with alcohol or acetone) or with a plastic sealer. If no sealer or collodion is available, brush cold water over the construction while the gum is still wet. This will help to form a hard shell-like surface.

In case this first sheet of cotton should not build up the face as much as desired, continue adding dampened cotton prepared in the same manner. Be sure, however, that each new piece completely overlaps the preceding one. The under pieces may or may not be soaked with spirit gum, as you prefer. Usually gum and sealer are used only on the top layer. Derma wax can be used over the cotton construction to give it smoothness. If this is done, another layer of sealer should be painted over it.

Painting the cotton construction. After the sealer or collodion is completely dry, paint the construction carefully and lightly with a very dark shade of base in order to counteract the effect of the white cotton. This can be done with a brush or with the fingers. Then apply the base coat (preferably rubber-mask grease) to be used for the character to the skin and to all constructions. In doing this, always be very careful of the cotton applications. Complete the makeup in the usual way.

Types of cotton constructions. The best criterion of what can be done with cotton and collodion is your own ingenuity. If you are both skillful and imaginative, the range of possibilities is wide. Cheekbones, chin, forehead, and cheeks can be enlarged or remodeled. Jowls and double chins can be constructed. Such makeups are seldom effective, however, except in large theaters, where the audience is at some distance from the actor, or for certain nonrealistic makeups.

SPECIAL CONSTRUCTIONS

The following is an alphabetical listing of some special constructions that you may have occasion to use. Many of these can be done more effectively with molded latex, as described in the next chapter. Direct methods, however, are quicker.

Blindness. The actor can usually suggest blindness by keeping the eyes nearly closed (see the photograph of Helen Keller, Figure 15–9K) or by a constant stare, especially if both eyes are to be

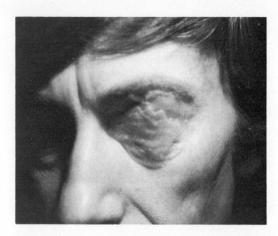

Figure 15–16. **Blind eye with scar tissue.** Plastic piece (Figure 15–17) is attached around the edge with spirit gum.

Figure 15–17. **Plastic piece for scar tissue.** Made by pouring layers of liquid plastic (see Appendix A) onto glass.

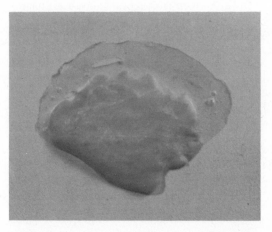

blind. For blindness involving disfigurement of the orbital area, as in Figure 15–16, latex or liquid plastic film can be painted or poured onto glass in a generally round shape to cover the orbital area. This can be a thin film, which can be glued over the bone that forms the boundaries of the orbital area. If you are using plastic, the film will be semi-transparent. It will also be flat. But with either latex or plastic, if you want to give more form to the piece, the central portion of the film can be built up to represent a distorted eyelid or a mass of scar tissue. This can be done with just the material itself, as in the scar tissue piece in Figure 15–17, or by adding face powder, cotton, or other materials. You might also model the form you want with wax, then cover the wax with more latex or plastic.

It is also possible to cast a blind eye and make

a molded latex piece (see Chapter 16 for casting methods), or if you have a plaster cast of the actor's head but don't have time to cast the blind eye, you can model what you want in clay on the cast, then paint latex over the clay instead of onto glass. Although this will not have the texture or the detail of a cast piece, it will give you a molded piece of the correct size and general form.

Whatever kind of piece you use, it can be suitably painted or made up. If you wanted a wide open, staring eye, for example, or even a partially opened one, you could paint the eye on with either makeup or acrylic paint. It would even be possible to glue on false eyelashes. If you wanted the actor to be able to see through the eye, a hole could be cut into the piece and gauze glued to the back, then painted. This would enable the actor to have at least partial vision through the painted eyeball or even the lid.

Bruises. Even when accompanied by a slight swelling, bruises are usually simulated with paint, as illustrated in Figure J-4F in the color section. The effect of swelling there has been achieved with a highlight in the center of the bruise. Bruises can be simulated by using dark reds, grays, purples, grayed greenish yellows, and white. The fresher the bruise, the more red; the older it is, the more yellow. The colors being used can be dabbed on the bruised area, then blended together with a brush. Make sure all edges are soft. Bruises tend to be generally (though not perfectly) round or oval in shape. If the bruised area is to be *very* swollen, you may wish to build it up first with derma wax, putty-wax, or nose putty. (See *Welts.*)

Burns. Minor burns can be simulated by stippling the skin with red makeup applied with a red-rubber sponge. For deeper burns, coat the skin with latex, which can be pulled loose and allowed to hang if you want it to. For the stage, a single layer of cleansing tissue placed over the latex and then covered with another layer of latex will give more body to the hanging skin. Cotton can be used with the latex for burnt flesh. Makeup can be applied over the latex. For close work you might wish to drop candle wax onto the latex to give the effect of blisters.

Cuts. Superficial cuts can be painted on, with or without the use of artificial blood. Deeper cuts usually require building up the area with wax or putty, then cutting into it with a dull instrument, such as a palette knife (Figures 15–25A and J-4D,E).

Plastic sealer can be painted over the construction at this point if you wish.

The inside of the cut can be painted red with greasepaint (Figure J-4E). For a cut that is still bleeding, a few drops or even a stream of artificial blood can be added to the cut with an eye dropper and allowed to run out onto the skin.

In some areas, such as the neck, where building up with putty or wax may not be practicable, latex can be painted directly onto the skin and allowed to dry thoroughly. The skin can then be pushed together into a crease in the middle of the strip of latex. The latex will stick to itself, forming a deep crease (Figure J-4B) that can be made to look like a cut with the addition of red makeup. Blood may or may not be running from the cut. In Figure J-4C bleeding has stopped, and most of the blood has been wiped off.

For a horizontal cut in the throat, be sure to use a natural crease in the skin if there is one. Pinching of the skin is not recommended but is often used for this purpose.

Ears. It is sometimes necessary to make pointed ears for such nonrealistic characters as sprites, leprechauns, and devils. Although latex pieces should be used for close work, the following simple, direct construction is satisfactory for most stage performances:

1. Cut a paper pattern the exact size and shape of the tip to be added.

2. Cut a small square of muslin and trace the ear pattern onto it. Cut out around this about ¼ inch beyond the edge on all sides. You will need four of these pieces.

3. Stitch two of the pieces of muslin together on the penciled line, leaving the bottom open.

4. Turn this double piece inside out, insert a bent pipe cleaner, and shape it to the pointed tip, cutting it off a fraction of an inch above the bottom of the ear construction. Two pipe cleaners can be used for a thicker piece.

5. Stitch along the inner side of the pipe cleaner to hold it in place. Then trim the bottom of the piece to fit the real ear.

6. Attach the muslin or gauze to the ear with spirit gum, making sure you let the gum become tacky before attaching the piece. Both front and back of the upper curve of the ear should be painted with gum so that the two layers of muslin can encase the ear. The muslin can be coated with latex or with plastic sealer if you like.

7. When the gum is thoroughly dry, cover the pieces with rubber-mask grease or with greasepaint along with the rest of the ear. Touching the tip and the lobe

Figure 15–18. Phantom of the Opera. Ear modeled with putty-wax. Stylized silent-screen makeup by Richard Brunner.

with rouge will give a more lifelike quality. The tip can be removed with spirit gum remover or alcohol and used a number of times.

Small additions can be made with putty (Figure 15–18). The putty should be covered with plastic sealer so as not to get stuck in the hair. Since it may not always hold its shape in hot weather on a hot stage, and since it must be made up fresh for every performance, it is less satisfactory than a latex piece or a construction of the type suggested above.

Eyelid, oriental. If the eye is so deepset as to make it difficult or impossible to create the effect of an Oriental eye with paint, and if a latex eyelid (Chapter 16) is not practicable, a satisfactory effect can usually be achieved with adhesive tape. This is one method:

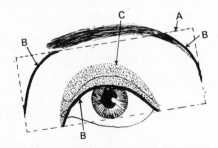

Figure 15–19. Diagram of Oriental eyelid made with adhesive tape.

1. Tear or cut slightly over 2 inches of tape from a roll at least 1 inch wide. This tape is represented by the broken line (A) in Figure 15–19.

2. Mark and cut as shown by the heavy lines (15–19B). This forms the eye opening and rounds off the upper edges so that the tape will be easier to conceal. (It is best to make a paper pattern first, then mark the tape.)

3. Cover the area indicated by C with makeup on the *back* of the tape. This gives a nonsticky area over the actor's own eyelid.

4. Attach the tape (usually slightly on the diagonal) so that the top falls just below the natural brow and covers the downward sweep of the outer end (Figure 15–20A). In order to prevent the eyebrow's appearing to be cut off too abruptly, lift a few hairs from under the tape and let them fall on the outside. Stipple the edges of the tape with latex cream adhesive (Duo or Flexol) to help conceal them.

5. When the latex is dry, cover the tape and the skin with base (Figure 15–20B), and finish the makeup. If you are using a cake foundation, cover the tape and a little of the skin around it with grease or creme makeup first; powder; then apply the cake makeup. In order to counteract the flatness of the tape, shadow the lower edge and highlight the center to give a puffy effect (Figure 15–20C).

Figure 15–20. Oriental eyelid made with adhesive tape. Tape is cut to fit the eye and attached with spirit gum, edges are stippled with latex, and tape is darkened with grease or creme makeup. Makeup is completed with eyebrow pencil and cake base, highlights, and shadows. Notice particularly how the flat tape is slightly rounded with shadowing.

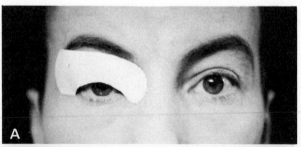

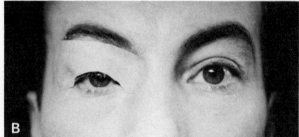

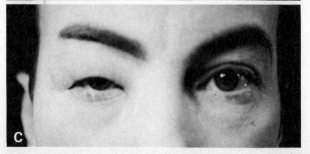

The cutting of the tape can be greatly simplified by cutting 4 inches instead of 2, folding it double, sticky sides together, marking and cutting either side, then separating the two pieces. This will insure that both eyes are exactly alike. If you place a piece of waxed paper between the two sticky sides, you will have no trouble getting them apart. Be sure the tape is not uncomfortable, that it does not interfere with the normal action of the eyelid, and that the actor can see without difficulty.

A simpler tape construction can be used with equal effectiveness on certain eyes. This consists of a crescent-shaped piece of adhesive tape, the outer edge of which is attached to the side of the nose and under the inner end of the eyebrow. The inner edge of the crescent (which should be very nearly a half moon) hangs free. The purpose of the piece is only to conceal the deep depressions (plane A, Figure 14–11) that are normal to the Caucasian eye. Plane A in the drawing represents almost exactly the shape and position of the tape.

Eyelid, sagging. A sagging eyelid (Figure 15–23) can be constructed in much the same way as an Oriental eyelid, except that the tape (Figure 15–21A) should slant down from the inner end of the eyebrow (B) to the outer corner of the eye (C). The tape should be cut as shown in Figure 15–21. The upper edge can correspond exactly to the natural brow, or the tape can be used to block out part of the brow and a new brow glued onto the tape or to the skin above the tape. The projection (A′) is folded under before the tape is attached to the skin. This gives a reasonable approximation of a fold of flesh.

Plastic film (see Appendix A) can be used instead of the tape in constructing the eyelid and is much to be preferred to tape since it will stretch slightly, is less bulky, and has thinner edges. The piece shown in Figure 15–21 can be cut from a sheet of plastic film or formed by painting liquid plastic (see Appendix A) onto glass to conform to a pattern of the piece placed under the glass (Figure 15–22).

Figure 15–21. Pattern for sagging eyelid. This is an exact pattern for the eyelid used in Figure 15–23. The size and shape can be varied to fit other eyes. The finished piece can be folded along the dotted line to give an effect of a fold of skin (Figures 23 and 24). **Figure 15–22. Painting a plastic eyelid on glass.** Pattern is placed under the glass. **Figure 15–23. Plastic eyelid folded and ready for use. Figure 15–24. Plastic eyelid used to age the eye.**

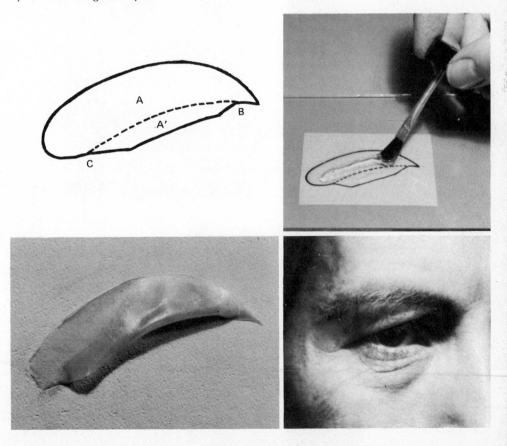

The advantage of this method is that edges can be kept very thin, whereas the center portion can be given more firmness with additional coats of plastic. Since many coats of plastic may be needed to give the desired thickness, dropping the liquid plastic onto the area to be built up instead of brushing it on will speed up the process.

When the plastic piece is dry, it should be powdered, then removed from the glass (see discussion under *Scars* and *Welts*). The tab (A′) should be folded under and glued down or secured with translucent plastic tape (see *Adhesive tapes* in Appendix A). The piece can then be applied with spirit gum. Before pressing it down into place, how-

ever, make sure that it is exactly where you want it. If you want to experiment first with various placements, coat the edges of the plastic with stubble adhesive (see Appendix A). The piece will then adhere temporarily to the skin. This experimentation should be done before any makeup is applied to the area.

In experimenting with the placement, try it with various expressions (a frown, raised eyebrows, etc.), keeping in mind the character to be played.

If any reshaping of the piece is necessary as a result of this experimentation, it can be done before the spirit gum is applied. Should this trimming result in any thickened edges, they can be thinned by

Figure 15–25. Scars and welts. (A) Welt with cut. Derma wax with blood-red creme rouge in cut. Student makeup by Paul Lynch. (B) Scar tissue. Derma wax covered with cake makeup. Student makeup by Joseph Rojas. (C) Scar tissue. Left eye partially covered with adhesive tape and left side of face, with layers of latex. Makeup by Bill Smith. (For other makeups by Mr. Smith, see Figures 14–43 and 17–5.) (D) Scar tissue. Latex, tissue and derma wax. Student makeup by Jeanne Závala.

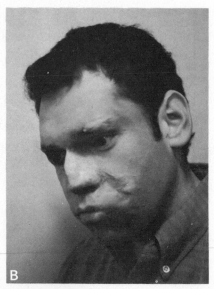

placing the piece on the glass and brushing the edges with acetone until they are thinned down.

Makeup can then be applied as usual. As with any prosthetic piece, never use this eyelid for a performance unless it has first been worn for at least one entire rehearsal—preferably more.

Clear latex can be used in essentially the same way and builds up more quickly, though it may take longer to dry.

For a more effective makeup and one that will bear closer scrutiny, use molded latex pieces (Chapter 16). Liquid plastic can also be used for molding in much the same way as latex.

Fingernails. Long fingernails can be cut out of used photographic film or sheets of acetate and glued onto the natural nails with spirit gum. They can be colored with nail polish or paint. The false fingernails available at cosmetics counters, if they are long enough, provide a simpler solution to the problem.

Scars. There are various methods for creating three-dimensional scars, the traditional one being to paint the area to be scarred with nonflexible collodion before any makeup is applied. As the collodion dries, it will wrinkle and draw the skin. If the scar thus formed is not deep enough, successive coats can be applied. Every coat should be allowed to dry completely before another is added. The makeup is then applied as usual. The scar may be accented with red, purple, brown, pink, ivory, white, or other colors. Avoid using collodion close to the eye. The scars can be peeled off or removed with acetone. If collodion irritates the skin, this method should not be used. Latex scars, which can be pasted on with spirit gum, are also effective (see Chapter 16).

Interesting scar effects can be achieved by using cleansing tissue or absorbent cotton with latex. The latex (or spirit gum, if you prefer) is applied first, then a very thin piece of cotton or tissue, then more latex. The area can be roughened as much as you like by pulling up bits of cotton. Derma wax and other materials can also be used. (See Figure 15–25B,C,D.) Makeup is applied as usual. Coloring should be fairly subtle in order not to lose the three-dimensional effect.

Another method is to pour or brush latex onto glass and, with a palete knife or an orangewood stick, swirl it and shape it into the size and kind of scar you want. Then allow it to dry or force-dry it, peel it off the glass, and apply it to the skin with

Figure 15–26. Making plastic scars with liquid plastic.

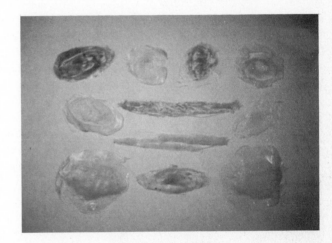

Figure 15–27. Plastic scars, welts, and growths.

Figure 15–28. Removing plastic scar from the glass.

spirit gum. Then make up in the usual way, coloring the scar appropriately. This is a variation of the molded latex scars or welts described in Chapter 16.

It is an excellent technique where closeups are involved and is particularly useful for arena staging. For greater projection, combine the latex with cotton or tissue, as suggested above (see Figure 15-32).

Similar techniques can be used to make scars with plastic sealer or, preferably, liquid plastic film (see Appendix A). The plastic is poured or smeared onto glass, then swirled with an orangewood stick to make bumps or ridges. (See Figure 15-26.) This will give a semi-transparent scar that can be applied to the skin with spirit gum. The scar can be colored and given more body by adding tinted face powder as the plastic is being swirled with the orangewood stick. For stronger coloring, powdered rouge can be used. Figure 15-27 shows scars with and without powder and rouge.

When the plastic scars are pulled off the glass (Figure 15-28), both sides should be powdered, as with latex pieces. The scars can be applied to the skin with spirit gum. The edges of the plastic can then be dissolved and blended into the skin by brushing on acetone. Makeup is applied as usual. The plastic scar can be left without makeup or can be partially or completely made up with appropriate colors. Figure 15-29 shows the scar on the skin with no makeup on either the scar or the face. The edges have not yet been blended.

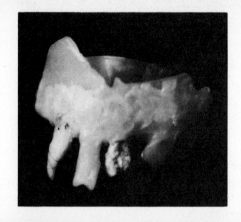

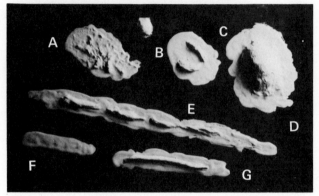

Figure 15-31. False teeth. Constructed of pink dental wax and ivory inlay wax. Made by Bert Roth, S.M.A.
Figure 15-32. Scars, welt, warts, and wens. Made on glass with latex and tissue (C, E), cotton (A, B, D), and string (G). They are three-dimensional enough to carry at some distance. For close work they should be more subtle.

As with latex, materials such as cotton or string can be used in the plastic scar.

Teeth. The method of blocking out teeth is described in Chapter 14. Enlarged or protruding teeth can be constructed from pink dental wax and ivory inlay wax (both obtainable from dental supply houses). The pink wax comes in sheets. It can be softened over heat and pressed around the teeth and the excess carved off. Then the false teeth can be molded out of ivory inlay wax, which can also be softened by heating. After the tooth is molded, it can be heated slightly and stuck to the pink wax. The pink and the ivory colors are excellent for gums and teeth, and no further coloring is necessary. Before putting in the set of false teeth, you can sprinkle a little adhesive powder for false teeth on the inside of the wax construction. (See Figure 15-31.)

Welts and warts. Welts can be constructed of nose putty or wax and appropriately painted. The latex-tissue-cotton-on-glass method described under *Scars* can also be used effectively here. The type of welt shown in Figure 15-32E (latex and

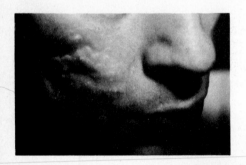

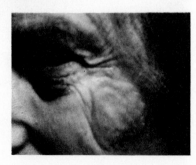

Figure 15-29. Plastic growth on cheek. Plastic piece attached with spirit gum but makeup not yet applied.
Figure 15-30. Plastic growth near eye. Same piece with some of the edges trimmed.

tissue) was used in the Broadway production of William Inge's *Natural Affection*, in which a character had to display a number of ugly welts from whip lashes across his back. The latex welts were made in long strips, cut into appropriate lengths, applied with spirit gum, and painted. After the first application, the makeup on the latex required only slight touching up. Figure 15–25A shows a welt with a cut.

Warts (see Figure 15–33 and 20–25) can be made in the same way as welts, of either wax or putty. They can also be constructed of latex and cotton, or they can be made by painting a small circle of latex or liquid plastic onto glass, placing a shaped piece of nose putty or derma wax in the middle of the circle, and covering it with additional latex or plastic. A small pill, puffed cereal, or anything of an appropriate size and shape might also be used. Hairs (real, synthetic, or wool crepe) can

be stuck into the putty or latex if desired. When wax is used directly on the skin in making warts, the skin should always be coated with spirit gum first and the wax covered with a sealer. Both welts and warts can also be made of molded latex (see Chapter 16).

PROBLEMS

1. Model three noses in putty, derma wax, and putty-wax. Be sure the noses are well constructed, smooth, and carefully blended. Then give them skin texture. Make up each nose with foundation and rouge, stipple it, then observe it carefully under a good light and from various angles to be sure that it looks real. You should take as much time as necessary to do these noses well.

2. Experiment in building up some areas of the face other than the nose by one or more of the methods suggested in this chapter.

3. Do a few special constructions, such as welts, warts, scars, burns, or ear tips, using various techniques.

4. Experiment on part of the face or hand with each of the suggested methods for creating a wrinkled skin effect.

5. Using the clay head you modeled previously, age the head to represent one of the characters in Problems 14 and 17, Chapter 14, using photographs from your morgue as guides in modeling.

6. Duplicate the clay features on your own face as nearly as possible, using three-dimensional constructions and paint.

7. Choose three other characters in Problems 14 and 17, Chapter 14, and make rough sketches of simple constructions you would ordinarily use in making up that character.

8. Remodel your clay head to represent a character for whom you would be likely to use three-dimensional makeup. Then duplicate the remodeled head with makeup. The following is a list of some possible characters: Puck *(Midsummer Night's Dream)*; Caliban *(The Tempest)*; the Trolls *(Peer Gynt)*; Evil *(Everyman)*; Falstaff; Sir Toby Belch; Lob *(Dear Brutus)*; the Witches *(Macbeth)*; Mephistopheles *(Faust)*; Bardolph *(Merry Wives of Windsor)*; Dr. Pinch *(Comedy of Errors)*; Duchess, Cook, Red Queen, White Queen *(Alice in Wonderland)*; Og *(Finian's Rainbow)*; Cyrano de Bergerac; Corbaccio *(Volpone)*.

Figure 15–33. Witch with warts. Nose and warts are of putty and eyebrows of crepe hair.

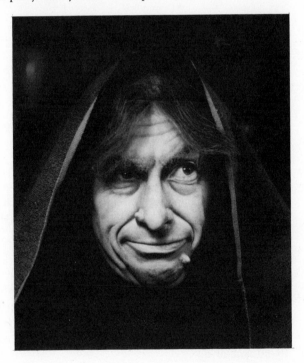

PROTHESIS WITH LATEX

The most satisfactory and professional method of building up the face is through the use of latex (or sometimes plastic) prosthesis. The latex pieces, which can be used to build up any part of the face, neck, or hands, are stiff enough in the central portions to make them hold their shape and thin enough at the edges, where they are attached to the skin, to blend imperceptibly into the foundation. The construction is a rubber shell, light in weight and not uncomfortable to wear. It can be made up in any color and can have a simulated skin texture.

Figure 16-1. Cast, molds, and prosthetic appliances. (A) Nose and sagging eyelids modeled in clay on plaster cast. (B) Negative plaster mold of left eyelid made directly from the clay model on the head. Below it is the finished latex eyelid. (C) Negative plaster mold of nose and below it the finished latex nose. (D) Latex noses for Cyrano, Disraeli, and Mr. Puff (*The Critic*). (E) Sagging neck piece.

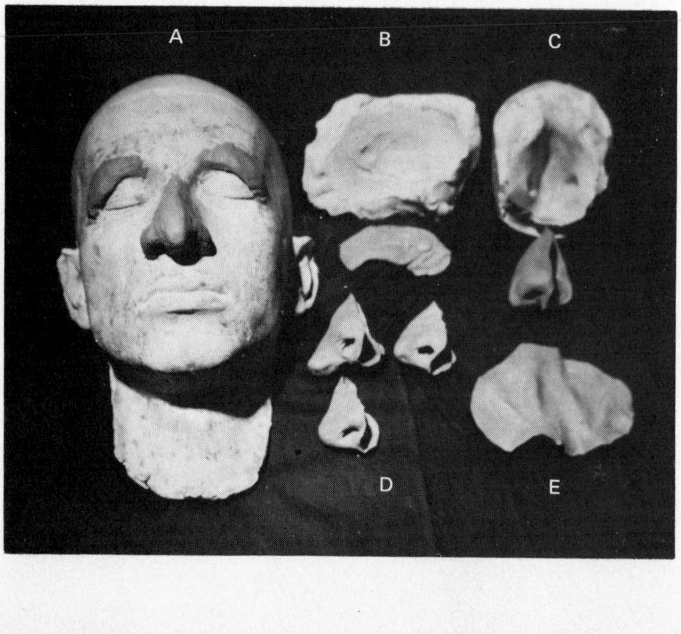

Figure 16–1 shows several latex pieces and the plaster molds from which they were cast.

The advantage of latex makeup is considerable:

1. It can provide three-dimensional additions to the face impossible to achieve with nose putty and derma wax or other direct constructions.

2. Instead of being modeled on a face before each performance, latex pieces can be modeled and remodeled on a plaster head until they are perfect.

3. Latex pieces are light and cause no discomfort to the actor, and there is little danger of their coming off once they are securely pasted down.

4. They can be quickly applied and quickly removed.

5. What is often very important, they can be used again and again. The rubber will not last indefinitely, but it should hold up for quite a long period of time if it is kept clean and in a box where it is not likely to be pressed out of shape.

Complete latex masks are possible, but they allow little change in expression and so are undesirable except for very special characters. A mask made in sections will allow more freedom. For this purpose, foamed latex is preferable. (See Figures 16–30 and 20–8.)

CASTING FOR PROSTHESIS

The first step in latex prosthesis is to reproduce the actor's own face, or some part of it, in plaster. In order to do this, a negative mold must be made. This negative mold can be made with plaster, but a flexible *moulage* (see Appendix A) is

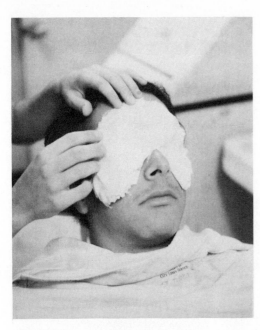

Figure 16-2. Casting part of the face. Eyes being cast in preparation for making Oriental eyelids. Moulage has been covered with plaster bandage for rigidity.

far more satisfactory. Figure 16–3 illustrates casting a face with moulage.

Preparing the subject. If the whole face is being cast, it is best to have the subject sitting up straight or reclining only slightly in order to prevent the distortion of the jaw and neck area that can result when he is lying down. A barber's or a dentist's chair is ideal. A plastic makeup cape (Figure 16–3A) or plastic sheet should be used to protect the clothing. The hardened moulage can easily be removed from the cape later. If the top of the head or the entire head is to be included in the casting, some sort of rubber or plastic cap should be used to protect the hair. It's a good idea to mark the hairline on the cap. If this is done with an indelible pencil, it will later be visible on the cast.

The face requires no special preparation, but psychologically the subject usually does. It must be made clear to him that there is no danger. If for any reason the moulage interferes with his breathing, he need only expel his breath forcefully, open his mouth and break the mold, or remove the moulage from his nose or his mouth with his hands. Most subjects, once they have confidence in the operator, find the process pleasant and relaxing.

It is important that the facial muscles not be moved while the mold is being made. A smile or the raise of an eyebrow can ruin the mold. Always arrange with the subject about signals for "yes" and

"no" so that he will be able to answer questions such as "Is the moulage too warm?" "Can you breathe easily?" "Are you comfortable?" It's a good idea, especially with nervous subjects, to let them watch a mold being made on someone else first and also to explain to them as you go along exactly what you're doing. It is usually best to work in a private room where there is not a great deal of noise or activity and where the subject does not feel he is being watched by a number of people. If others are watching (and this should be permitted only if the subject is willing), it is essential that they understand from the start that they must be quiet. Any remarks or noises that disturb the subject or tend to make him smile must not be permitted. It is also desirable for the person or persons doing the casting to avoid casual conversation unrelated to the work being done. Knowing that he has the operator's full attention tends to give the subject confidence. Never leave the subject alone until the mask has been removed—he will feel more secure knowing you are there. If a good mold is to be made, the complete cooperation of the operator, the subject, and any observers is essential.

Negative moulage mold. There are two types of moulage, one of which is reusable, the other, not. Both are used in the same way, but the preparation is different. To prepare reusable moulage for use, follow the directions that come with it. Usually you will need to add about a half cup of water per pound and heat the moulage in the top of a double boiler until it is completely liquified. It can be used as soon as it is cool enough to touch.

The second type of moulage is a dental impression powder (usually referred to as an alginate) that is mixed with cold water for a minute or less (according to directions) and used immediately. It has a much faster setting time than the reusable moulage—usually from $3\frac{1}{2}$ to 5 minutes. Using colder water lengthens the setting time and is therefore desirable in casting an entire face or head. You should either mix small amounts at a time or else work very fast. It is helpful for two people to work together, one applying the moulage while the other mixes a fresh batch. The fast mixing is a considerable advantage, whereas the fast setting may or may not be, depending on how rapidly you can work. With reusable moulage, be sure to mix enough for the entire job before you begin. Plastic mixing bowls are recommended. In using alginate, you should have available a bowl of water of the desired temperature for additional mixings.

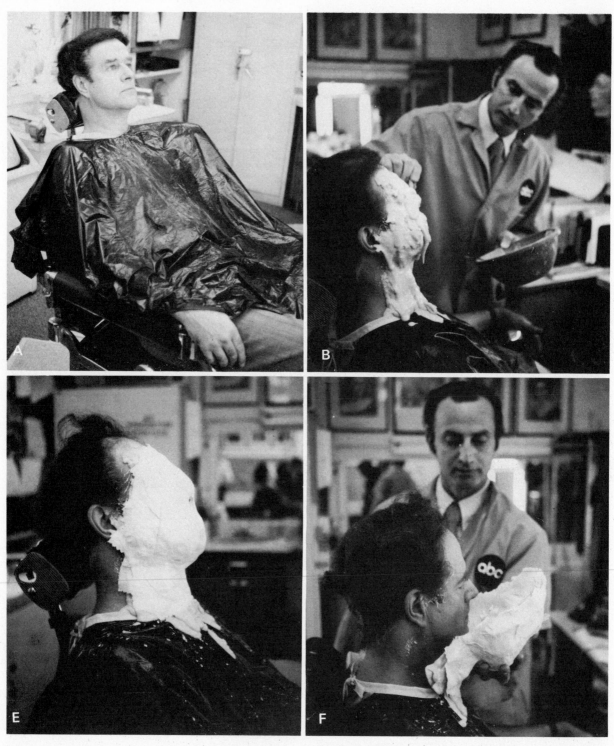

Figure 16-3. Casting a face with moulage. (A) Subject in barber's chair with protective plastic cape. (B) Moulage (alginate) being applied with brush. (C) Partially completed moulage. (D) Strips of plaster bandage being laid over solidified moulage. (E) Completed negative mold on face. (F) Re-

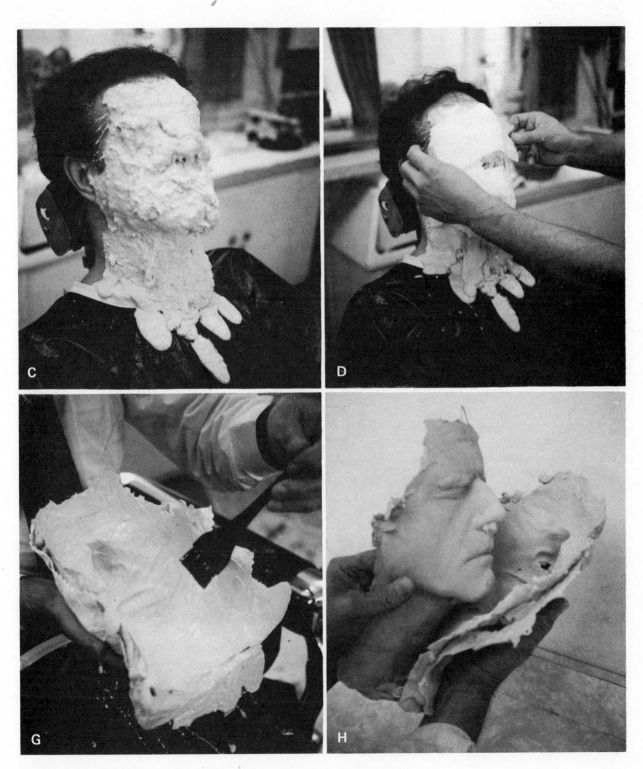

moving negative mold from face. (G) Brushing first layer of plaster or dental stone into negative mold. (H) Negative mold being removed from completed positive impression in stone or plaster. Casting by Bert Roth, S.M.A.

In using either kind of moulage, brush it quickly over the face or the facial area being cast (Figure 16–3B), making sure there is a sufficiently thick layer (¼ to ⅓ inch—more over the ears if they are being cast, and perhaps over the nose). Avoid too thick a layer (and thus too much weight) on the softer areas of the face, which may sag and distort the final cast; but make very sure there are no areas that are too thin. In building up the moulage, remember that wet moulage will not adhere to moulage that has already hardened. This is an additional reason for working rapidly.

When the nose is being cast, you can either work very carefully around the nostrils with the fingers or a small brush, making sure that both nostrils are clear *at all times,* or you can ask the subject to take a deep breath and hold it, brush moulage quickly over the nose, then ask him to expel air forcefully through the nose. This will remove moulage from the nostrils. The first method is preferable. It will give a nervous subject a greater feeling of security if you cover the nose and leave proper holes for breathing before covering the mouth. Otherwise, leave the nose until last, when the subject is likely to feel more relaxed about the whole procedure. Then, you can work around the nostrils very carefully and fill in the holes after the mold has been removed. You should explain to the subject that if moulage should cover the holes accidentally, he need only expel his breath forcefully to remove it. However, do your best to see that this doesn't happen.

It is also possible to insert straws or rolls of paper into the nostrils before beginning the casting. Derma wax around the straw will hold it in the nostril and make it impossible for the moulage to seep in. It is generally considered preferable, however, not to use straws since they may distort the shape of the nostrils. Also, it is possible for a careless swipe of the moulage brush to dislodge them.

The eyes should be kept closed. Cotton can be stuffed into the ear opening. In casting the ears, be careful of undercuts that might interfere with the proper removal of the mold and make the moulage much thicker there than on the rest of the face.

When the moulage has solidified (usually from 15 to 30 minutes is necessary for the reusable type unless you force-dry it with a hair dryer or cold cloths), it must be strengthened so that it will hold its shape when removed. The best way is to lay moistened strips of fast-drying plaster bandage (see Appendix A) over the moulage (Figure 16–3D,E).

Surgical gauze bandage dipped in wet plaster can be used instead. Four layers of bandage laid on in different directions and overlapping should be sufficient. When the plaster hardens, it will provide a rigid form to hold the shape of the moulage. (See Figures 16–2 and 16–3F,G.) Work around the nostrils carefully, crushing the bandage together as you go over the tip and between the nostrils. This will add greater strength. Do not use plaster bandage over the ears. Removal of the mask will be easier there if the thick layer of moulage is not completely rigid.

In removing the moulage, ask the subject to lean forward slightly and move his facial muscles in order to loosen the mold. Then it can be removed easily. (See Figure 16–3F.) It is best to loosen it first near the ear to let in the air. Remove it carefully and slowly, running your fingers around the edges between the skin and the moulage. The moulage does not stick to skin or hair—one of its greatest advantages over plaster. If long hair should become embedded in the moulage, however, this can require extra care in removal.

When the negative mold is finished, the positive plaster cast should be made immediately in order to prevent the possibility of shrinkage of the moulage as it loses its moisture.

Positive plaster cast. In preparing the plaster, first measure two or three cups of water into a bowl (preferably a plastic one), then slowly sift in plaster of Paris or dental stone (see Appendix A) until it reaches a level just barely below the surface of the water. Let the mixture stand without stirring until it begins to thicken. When it approaches a suitable consistency for pouring, it can be stirred very gently. It will then begin to harden quickly. After the plaster has been stirred, the bowl should be hit a few times on the bottom with the palm of the hand in order to force air bubbles to the surface.

Although plaster can be poured when it is thin and watery or as thick as mayonnaise, an in-between consistency (say, that of heavy cream) usually works best. If it is too thin, it will be hard to manage and will take longer to harden; if it is too thick, it may not conform to the shape of the mold. It should be pointed out, however, that thin plaster results in a harder, more durable cast than does thick plaster.

The wet plaster or dental stone should first be painted carefully over the inside surface of the negative mold, coating it completely. (See Figure 16–3H.) Then the rest of the stone or plaster can be either poured slowly and gently or else spooned into the mold. In order to avoid having too heavy and cumbersome a cast, brush the plaster away from the center and up along the sides of the mold, leaving a shell of plaster rather than a solid block. If the plaster is too thin to do this, let it sit until it begins to thicken. In filling the mold, be sure it is adequately supported so that the shape will not be distorted. Be very careful to protect the nose, which is especially vulnerable to damage. Having someone hold it in his lap with his hands cupped around it for support works very well, or, if you prefer, it can be set into a box of crumpled-up cloth towels.

If you plan to hang the cast on a wall for storage, form a loop from a length of wire (part of a coat hanger will do) and embed the ends in the plaster before it hardens, leaving the loop outside and near the top of the cast. (See Figure 16–4.) This can prove to be a great convenience.

When the plaster is thoroughly hardened in the mold, the moulage can be peeled or broken off. Reusable moulage can be stored indefinitely so long as it retains sufficient moisture; be sure in storing it that you add a little water to it before closing the can. The moulage mixed from powder (alginate) can usually be removed from the plaster cast in one piece (Figure 16–3H) and sometimes be used to make a second cast of the same head. But this second casting should be done immediately, before the mold begins to shrink. If the mold is set aside and allowed to shrink, it can sometimes then be used to cast a shrunken head—a miniature version of the original. If for any reason you should want to do this, make sure the edges are not allowed to curl up, since that will give a deformed head. After the castings are done, the moulage is discarded.

The plaster cast should be allowed to dry thoroughly before being used. This may take several days. Then give the cast one or two coats of white shellac. You now have a reproduction of the actor's face (Figure 16–3H), on which you can model in clay the features you want to reproduce in latex.

Clay models. The modeling of individual features is done with artists' modeling clay, which requires no special technique. You will do it largely with your fingers, though a clay modeling tool (Figure 4–3) may be helpful for details. Be sure the clay is perfectly smooth, completely blended at the edges, and modeled in exactly the form you want the latex piece to take. You can simulate skin texture by dotting the clay with tiny depressions to represent pores. Remember that the slightest mark on the clay will be reproduced on the rubber.

A useful trick for making skin texture quickly is to make a latex negative of grapefruit, orange, or lemon skin, as mentioned in Chapter 15. This is done by painting liquid latex onto a section of the outside of the fruit—preferably one with skin which is not too smooth. Three to five coats will probably be necessary. When the latex is thoroughly dry, remove it from the fruit, powder it, and you will have a textured piece that can be pressed into the clay, transferring the texture. All clay models—except those for eyelids—should be textured so as to blend with the natural skin texture.

Negative plaster cast. The next step is to make a negative cast of the clay feature just as you made a negative cast of the actor's face. This casting from the clay, however, must be done with plaster or dental stone rather than moulage.

First, with some extra clay, build up a sort of fence or dam around the modeled feature to prevent the plaster from spilling over the cast (Figure 16–5A). Then, using oil or grease (preferably castor oil), grease all exposed parts of the plaster cast that will be touched by the plaster when it is poured. When the cast has been greased, make up your

Figure 16-4. Hanger for plaster cast. Rear view of cast in Figure 16-3H. Hanger is embedded while the plaster is still wet.

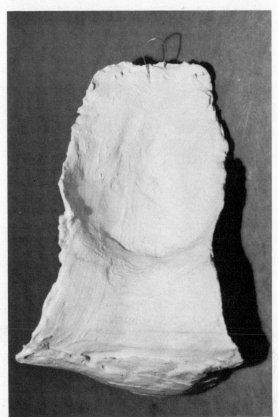

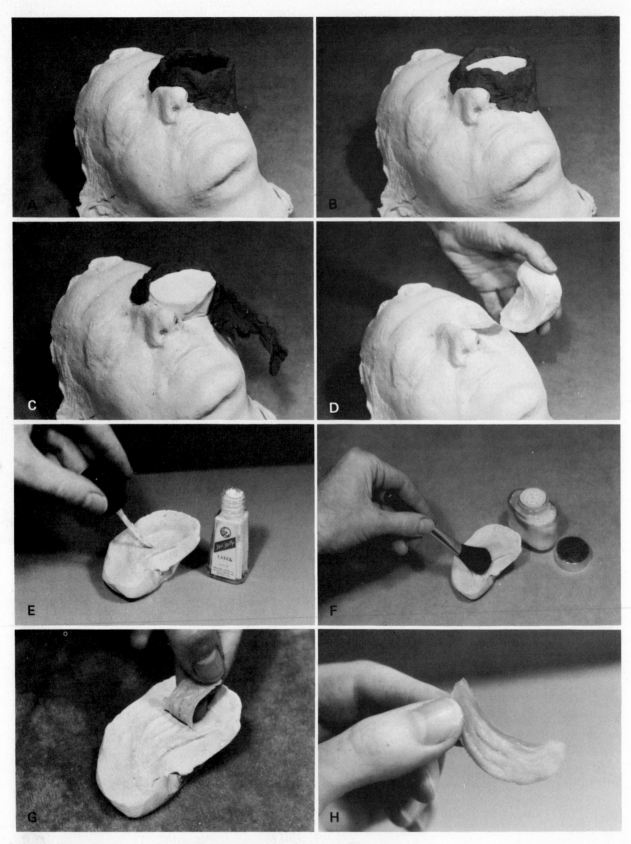

Figure 16-5. Casting an eye pouch. (A) Clay wall around eye area. (B) Plaster poured in and allowed to harden. (C) Clay wall partially removed. (D) Negative plaster mold of pouch removed. (E) Negative mold painted with latex. (F) Dried latex being brushed with powder. (G) Latex pouch being removed from mold. (H) Latex pouch trimmed and ready for use.

plaster or dental stone just as before and pour it over the new feature, giving plenty of thickness so that the cast will not break when you remove it.

When the plaster is hard, pull off the clay fence (Figure 16–5C) and maneuver the new cast around until it can be easily slipped off. Now you have a negative cast (Figure 16–5D) from which you can make any number of latex pieces. If, by chance, air bubbles have left little holes anywhere in the cast, fill them up with plaster before making the latex pieces.

Positive latex cast. There are two techniques for making the final latex prosthetic pieces from the plaster casts. One is a *painting* method, the other a *slush* method.

For either method, liquid latex is used (see Appendix A). The latex can be purchased in a few flesh tones. It can also be tinted with food coloring or with special dyes. It is not necessary for the rubber piece to match the base color, but if it is too light, it may be more difficult to cover. The solidified latex will always be considerably darker than the liquid latex.

The main requirement for a positive latex piece is to make the central parts of the piece thick enough to hold their shape and the edges thin enough to blend into the skin without an obvious line. In the brush technique (Figure 16–5E) a layer of latex is painted into the negative plaster mold (which requires no surface preparation). The type of brush used is a matter of choice. A soft bristle lets the latex flow on more easily, but it is also very difficult to clean, and unless extreme care is taken, it will probably not last very long. A stiff bristle is easier to clean but doesn't give as smooth a coat of latex. A flat, medium stiff bristle is perhaps the most generally practical. Inexpensive brushes should be used. Brushes in use should be kept in soapy water and washed out thoroughly with soap the moment you have finished with them. Once the latex has solidified, it can seldom be removed from the brush.

Before painting in the first coat, it would be well to estimate about where you want the edge of the piece to be and mark that with a pencil on the plaster. Then you can be sure to keep the latex thin along that line. On the first coat you should overlap the line slightly to allow for trimming.

Subsequent coats are painted in after the preceding coat is completely dry. Each subsequent coat can begin a little farther from the edge to provide a gradual thinning. The number of coats needed depends on the thickness of the coats. You will probably need a minimum of six and in most cases more. This you will have to learn by experience.

With the slush method, some of the latex is poured into the mold and gently sloshed around to build up layers of the latex. This is done by holding the plaster mold in the hand and moving or rocking it so that the latex runs first up to and just beyond the proposed edge, as marked with a pencil. Subsequent movements should keep the latex nearer the center and farther and farther from the edge. When you think you have built up enough thickness, drain off the excess latex or, if you like, leave a tiny bit in to dry and thus give additional rigidity.

Before removing the latex piece, be sure it is completely dry. In deep molds, such as noses, this may sometimes take several hours. Forcing hot air into the mold with a hair dryer can speed up the drying considerably. Then dust the surface of the latex with face powder or talcum to prevent its sticking to itself. (See Figure 16–5F.) Once it has been dusted, it will never stick again, even if you wash the powder off immediately. Then loosen the rubber at a spot along the edge and carefully lift it away from the plaster (Figure 16–5G). As you do so, dust more talcum inside to keep that surface of the rubber from sticking. Sometimes the piece comes away easily, sometimes it has to be pulled, but it will come. If you do have to pull hard, however, be sure not to pull it by the tissue-thin edge, which is likely to tear. Also, avoid pulling so hard that you stretch the piece permanently out of shape. As soon as you are able to loosen a little more of the piece, grasp it farther down to pull out the remainder. Tweezers can be helpful.

When the piece is out, trim any rough edges and try it on. If further trimming seems necessary, mark the desired edge with a pencil, then trim. Make sure, however, that you do not trim the piece in too far and thus lose the thin edge. If your first piece is not entirely successful, you will learn from the mistakes you make on that one how to approach the second.

The plaster cast can be used indefinitely so long as the actual casting surface remains in good condition.

TYPES OF PROSTHETIC PIECES

Noses. There are three basic criteria for a useful, workable rubber nose—it must be rigid enough to hold its shape without wrinkling or sag-

Figure 16-6. Molded latex piece. For the second face of Ionesco's Three-faced Girl.

Figure 16-7. Three-faced Girl. Latex piece attached and made up. Makeup by Richard Brunner.

ging, the blending edges must be tissue-thin, and the blend should take place on a solid, rather than a flexible, foundation (on the actor's nose, that is, not on his cheeks or his nasolabial folds).

The first two of these criteria depend on the distribution of latex in the plaster cast and have already been discussed. The third requires careful placement of the clay used in building up the nose of the plaster cast. The actual modeling of the clay corresponds closely to the modeling of a putty nose —the accurate following of natural nose structure, the careful blending of edges, the limiting of the clay addition to as small an area as possible, and the final addition of skin texture.

The principal difference between modeling a clay nose and a putty one is that putty may, if necessary, cover the sides of the nose completely, but clay should not do so. It should stop far enough short of the outer boundaries of the sides of the nose to allow for a blending edge of latex beyond the section that is being built up. The greater the latitude given for this blend, the better.

The latex piece need not cover the entire nose. On the contrary, the smaller the area it covers, the easier it will probably be to work with. A tilted tip or a small hump, for example, does not require modeling and casting a complete nose. If the piece you make involves the nostrils, they can be cut out of the piece after it has been cast in order to permit normal breathing.

Since the final rubber piece can be no better than the clay nose from which it was cast, considerable time and care should be spent in meticulous modeling. Once the model is perfected and cast, achieving an effective rubber piece is merely a matter of careful manipulation of the liquid latex in the cast.

Eyelids. Latex eyelids are particularly useful in Oriental makeups. In modeling them, be sure to give the clay sufficient thickness over the center of the eyeball so that the movement of the real eyelids will not be impeded. Before modeling Oriental lids, study the Oriental eyes in your morgue, as well as those in Figures 13–5Q, 14–13C, 14–13D, 14–13E, 14–17, 14–18, and 14–19.

Drooping eyelids for age are extremely useful and can do wonders in aging youthful eyes. Figure 16–1 shows a pair of drooping eyelids modeled in clay on a plaster head; it also shows one of the negative molds and the positive latex piece made from it. There is no standard form for such lids. It is essential to work from photographs of older people—using more than one, if you like, and combining the most useful and adaptable features of each. There are many kinds of drooping lids, and you should choose the one most appropriate for the character. (See Figures 14–12G,I,K; 14–13A,B, F,G; 14–15A.)

Although the Oriental latex eyelids usually come just to the eyebrow, it can sometimes be advantageous to let the sagging ones cover the natural brow completely. This gets rid of the youthful brow, which is usually a handicap, and makes it possible to put an aged brow onto the rubber piece itself. This can be done with crepe hair and latex or, if you prefer, by ventilating real hair into the latex (see Chapter 17). Remember that only the edges that are to be attached to the skin must be thin. The edge that falls diagonally across the eye area hangs free and should be reasonably thick.

Eye pouches. These are invaluable aids to aging and are one of the simplest pieces you can make (Figure 16–5). Again, you should work from photographs of real people (see Figures 14–12G,H, I,M; 14–13F; 14–14C,E,F,G; 15–9D,H,I). Some pouches will be fairly smooth and definitely pouch-like. Others will be rather flat and a mass of fine wrinkles. There are innumerable variations. If there is a definite line of demarcation to the pouch you wish to make, then it will not be necessary to leave a thin edge on the bottom of the piece, though there should be one at the top. As usual, remember to give it skin texture.

Ears. Rubber cauliflower ears can be slipped over the actor's real ears very simply. Rubber tips can be used for such characters as Puck or the leprechaun in *Finian's Rainbow.* Also, small ears can be enlarged—as they ought to be, for example, in a makeup for Abraham Lincoln.

The technique in making ears, partial or complete, is to make a shell that will fit over the natural ear. This requires a *split mold.* After you have modeled the clay ear on the plaster cast of the actor's natural ear and built your clay fence, place the cast so that the ear is horizontal. Then pour plaster up to the middle of the rim of the ear. It's a good idea

to let the surface of the plaster be somewhat uneven. If the plaster is fairly thick, this will happen automatically, giving a bumpy or undulating surface. When the plaster is dry, grease the surface and pour in more plaster, covering the ear. When this plaster is dry, remove the clay fence, as usual, then very carefully pry the two sections of plaster apart and remove both from the clay ear.

You can then fit the two sections back together. If the surface is uneven, this will be no problem, for there will be only one way they will fit. This will give you a deep mold with a crevice (Figure 16–8), into which you can pour the latex and slosh it around to cover all the surfaces of the negative mold. Excess can be poured back out. It is better to build the ear up with several coats rather than trying to do the whole thing at once. Be sure to keep the latex thin at the edges, which will be glued to the natural ear, and thick around the rim so that the ears will hold their shape.

When you are sure the latex is dry (it's a good idea to force dry it with a hair dryer), powder the inside, then carefully pry the mold apart, powdering as you do so. The ear should then be trimmed around the edges. After the latex ear has been slipped over the natural one and glued down, it should be made up to match the face.

In painting the cast with latex, you may have difficulty in deciding how far out to bring the latex. After you have made and trimmed your first ear, you will be able to see where the boundaries should be. Then you can mark these boundaries on the plaster cast with a pencil to serve as guidelines for all future ears. This will make it possible to keep the latex thin at all edges that are to be glued down.

Chin. Receding chins can be built up or full ones made to protrude, round chins can be made

Figure 16-8. Slush mold for partial ear. Latex is poured into closed mold (A), then mold is opened (B) to remove the ear.

more square or more pointed, or any chin can be aged by being made more irregular. Goatees can be pasted on latex chins as easily as on real ones and will not need to be remade for each performance. Frequently a chin can be combined in the same piece with a scrawny or a fat neck. If the chin addition is to be very large, a foamed latex piece (see the end of this chapter) would be preferable.

Neck. It is possible to age the neck effectively from the front with paint, but the profile is difficult to change. A latex piece will, however, produce an old neck from any angle. You can have prominent muscles and sagging flesh or transverse rolls of fat, or sagging jowls. For this type of construction, however, foamed latex is much more effective. (See the end of this chapter and Figures 16–25 and 16–31.)

Welts and warts. These are extremely simple to make and can be pasted on quickly, like any other latex piece. They can be cast on any smooth surface without having a cast of a face or even a feature to work on. They can also be made without casting, as described in Chapter 15.

Bald caps. One way of creating the effect of a bald head is to cover the hair with a latex cap. This can be worn plain, or hair can be added (see Chapter 18). Since it adapts itself to the shape of the head and fits snugly, and since it can be constructed with a very thin edge, a bald cap is considerably more satisfactory than the usual bald wig with a cloth blender.

Ideally, the latex should be slushed or painted (a combination of the two is most satisfactory) into a negative plaster head mold. This can be made from a suitably shaped wig block or millinery form. If the surface of the form is smooth, it may be possible to cast the plaster directly from the form after the usual greasing. If there is doubt about the surface, however, a thin layer of modeling clay can be used over it. If the clay is used, some reshaping can be done if that seems desirable. The normal hairline should be marked on the form with a pencil or crayon that will transfer to the plaster in order to simplify painting in the latex later. The usual clay dikes are built up and the plaster poured over the form.

Obviously, since the top of the form is larger than the bottom, it cannot be removed from the plaster cast. There are two possible solutions to this. One is to cut the plaster cast in two with a

thread while it is still soft. The two halves are allowed to dry, then they are removed and put back together again. The join can be smoothed out and touched up with additional plaster.

A better method, if you have the right kind of form, is to slice the form into sections vertically. If you cut it twice each way, you will have nine sections, including a center one that will be in contact with the cast only for a few square inches on the top. A balsa wood form is best for this purpose, since it is easily cut. Once the pieces have been cut, they are put back together, tied firmly at the base, and the form is covered with clay for a smooth surface. Then when the plaster is dry, the center section is removed from the bottom, releasing the other pieces so that they can be pulled out.

In making the cap in the negative mold, it is probably easiest to pour in a quantity of latex and slosh it around, gradually building up layers of rubber. In order to have the thin front edge of the cap correctly shaped, that area should be painted in with a brush, using only one or two coats at the very edge. The back of the cap should be left long so that it will cover all of the neck hair and can be tucked into the collar. If this back tab is not needed, it can be cut off later.

It is also possible to make a bald cap by painting the latex directly onto the form. This has several obvious disadvantages, but it can be done, though never with really high quality results. In the first place, the surface of the form must be suitable for taking the latex. If the cap is to be used shiny side out, as made, the surface must be very smooth, which is not easy to achieve. Even if the surface is not uneven, it will not take makeup well. The cap can be used inside out, but this means that the form must be free of ridges or imperfections that will be transferred to the cap.

In wearing the cap, paste down the edge and stipple it, as for any latex prosthetic piece. In making it up, use rubber-mask grease. (See also *Plastic caps* in Appendix A and *Soaping out the hair* in Chapter 18.)

Hands. Wrinkled and veined hands can be made up in the form of gloves, invaluable for quick changes. The gloves can be made by making up the hands with wax to build up knuckles, bones, and veins, then casting them, one at a time, by laying the hand, well oiled, palm down in wet plaster and pushing down until the plaster covers the lower half of the hand, including the fingers. Let the plaster set until it has solidified. Before casting the back of the hand, make sure there are no free hairs that might become embedded in the plaster. If you can't flatten the hairs sufficiently with wax and petroleum jelly or cold cream, cut them off. If the subject objects to this, make plaster casts of the hands with moulage, then make a negative plaster cast from the positive plaster cast.

Whether you are casting directly from the hand or from a positive plaster cast of it, when the bottom half of the negative cast has solidified, remove the hand and grease the exposed area of the hardened plaster, return the hand to its original position, then pour fresh plaster over the hand. When it has hardened, gently separate the two halves of the cast by moving the hand. When the cast is thoroughly dry, it can be put back together and secured with masking tape. It is then ready for the latex, which can be poured in, sloshed around, then poured out. This can be repeated three or four times, each coat being allowed to dry thoroughly or force-dried with a hair dryer before the next one is added. For each drying period, place the mold with the fingers up so that latex will not accumulate in the finger tips. Extra coats may be added just to the back of the hand in order to stiffen knuckles, bones, and veins. These coats should dry with the cast flat and the palm up. Be patient and make sure the latex is completely dry before separating the cast. Otherwise, the glove can be ruined.

Rubber pieces to be pasted on the back of the hands are, of course, much simpler to make since only the back of the hand needs to be cast. (For hands aged this way using foamed latex, see Figure 21–1I.)

It is also possible to buy thin, snug, rubber surgical gloves and to attach the pieces to the gloves instead of to the hands.

APPLICATION OF PROSTHETIC PIECES

Latex pieces should be attached to the dry skin before any makeup has been applied. This can be done with liquid latex, latex cream adhesive, or spirit gum. However, latex adhesive may become loosened during the performance and have the added disadvantage of building up on the rubber piece itself, thickening the edge, unless all traces of the latex adhesive are carefully removed after

each use. In most instances, latex should probably not be used—especially when the actor perspires freely or when there is facial activity that might tend to losen it.

Stippling the edges of the latex piece with latex cream adhesive (see Appendix A) will help to conceal them. They should then be allowed to dry before the makeup is applied.

Greasepaint should not be used on latex since it will cause it to deteriorate. Rubber-mask grease can be used instead. If cake makeup is used, either apply rubber-mask grease first, powder it, and go over it with cake makeup, or rub castor oil into the latex before applying the cake. The castor oil may not entirely keep the makeup from looking a bit lighter on the latex than on the skin, but it will help considerably. The rest of the makeup should be completed in the usual way. Figures 16–21 through 16–28 show foamed latex pieces being applied. The procedure is similar for slush-mold pieces.

The pieces can be removed by merely pulling them off. If latex adhesive was used, it should be removed from the piece immediately if possible. It can usually be pulled or rolled off with the fingers. If spirit gum has been used, the piece should be cleaned thoroughly with alcohol or acetone. It is a good idea to remove makeup from the piece with alcohol.

In addition to the great practical convenience to professional actors who repeat the same makeup night after night, the use of a few good latex pieces can make a tremendous difference in the appearance of a character makeup. This is particularly important in the nonprofessional theater, where young people often play older parts. The three-dimensional pieces, undetectable when carefully applied and made up, can age an actor by many years without relying on a myriad of painted details, which are often lost before they cross the footlights.

FOAMED LATEX

Although the hollow, shell-like latex pieces just described work well on bony parts of the face, their hollowness may become apparent on softer areas where there is much movement. This problem can be overcome through the use of foamed latex, with which it is possible to make three-dimensional,

MAKING AND APPLYING A FOAMED LATEX MASK

The photographs on the following pages illustrate the creation of the makeup for Dustin Hoffman as the 120-year-old man in the film *Little Big Man*.

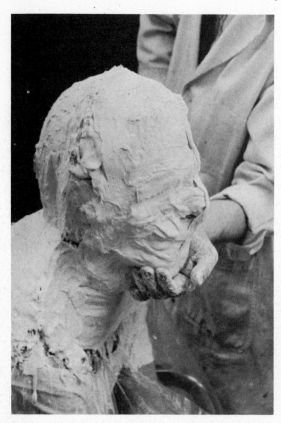

Figure 16-9. Making a plaster cast of Dustin Hoffman's head and shoulders.

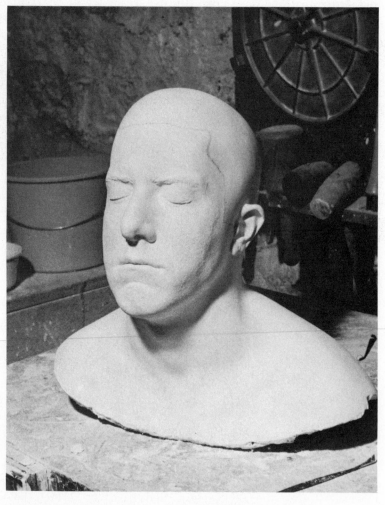

Figure 16-10. Plaster model of Dustin Hoffman's head. Clay models of every part of the latex mask were later sculpted over copies of this head or sections of it.

Makeup by Dick Smith, S.M.A.

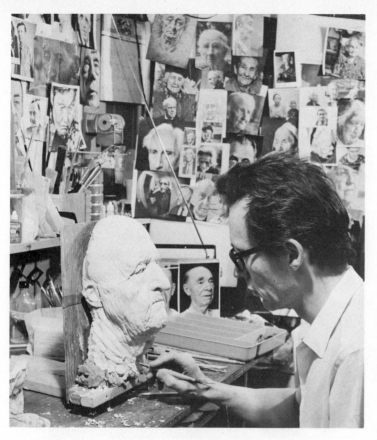

Figure 16-11. Makeup artist Dick Smith making clay model for front half of the latex mask.

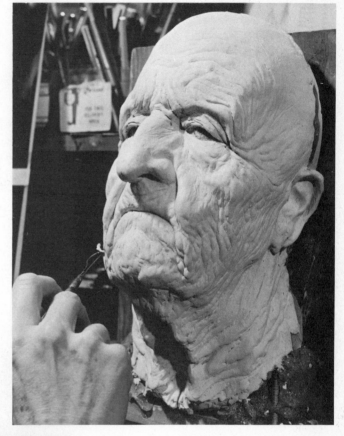

Figure 16-12. Rough model. Will later be broken down into 8 parts—brow, nose and upper lip, eyelids, bags, lower lip and chin, and sides of face and neck.

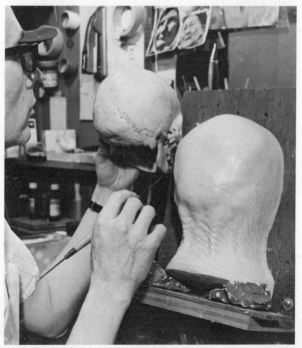

Figure 16-13. Modeling back of head on a plaster section of Dustin's head.

Figure 16-14. Making molds of clay models of bags, chin, and nose.

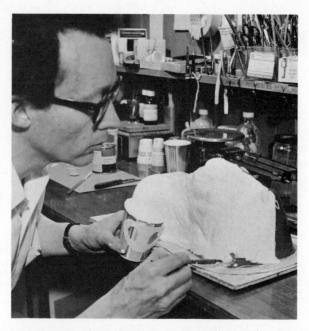

Figure 16-15. Making special epoxy mold of clay model of the largest part of the mask—sides of face and neck.

Figure 16-16. Finishing outer surface of the mold of the sides of the face and neck section. This exterior part of the mold is made of hard plaster.

Figure 16-17. Removing latex. After mold has been baked to cure latex and positive cast of Dustin's face has been lifted out, the latex mask section is then carefully removed. (Pouring latex into the mold is illustrated in Figure 11-7.)

Makeup by Dick Smith, S.M.A.

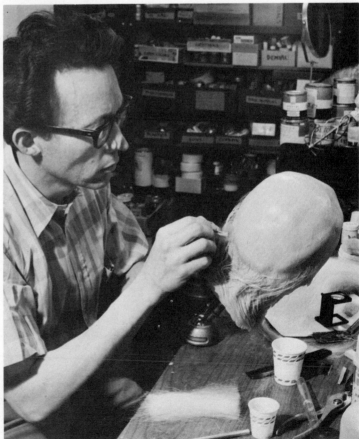

Figure 16-18. White hair being implanted bit by bit in back section of latex mask.

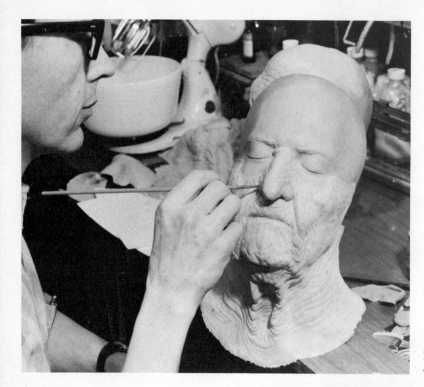

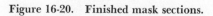

Figure 16-19. Painting "liver spots" on part of the latex mask.

Figure 16-20. Finished mask sections.

Makeup by Dick Smith, S.M.A.

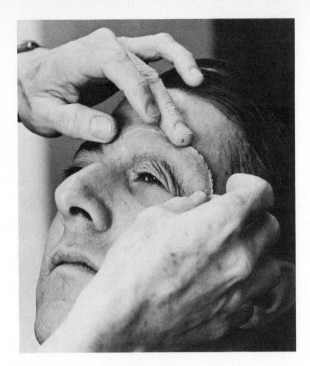

Figure 16-21. Attaching foam latex eyelid. Piece is made thin enough and with enough folds sculpted into it so that it blinks naturally.

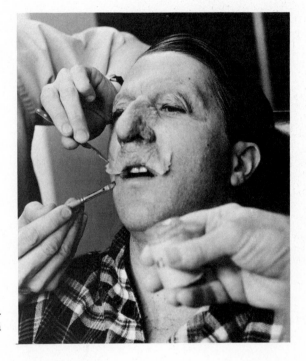

Figure 16-22. Nose and lip piece. Slomon's Medico Adhesive used near mouth for better adhesion.

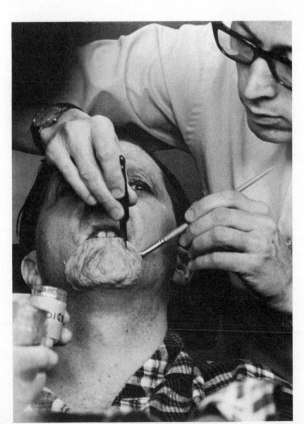

Figure 16-23. Chin and lower lip being attached. All of the pieces were pre-colored to save time, leaving only minor coloring to do after they were glued on.

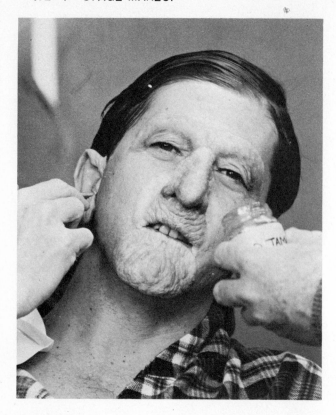

Figure 16-24. Attaching the ears. Made of slush-molded latex. All others made of foam latex.

Makeup by Dick Smith, S.M.A.

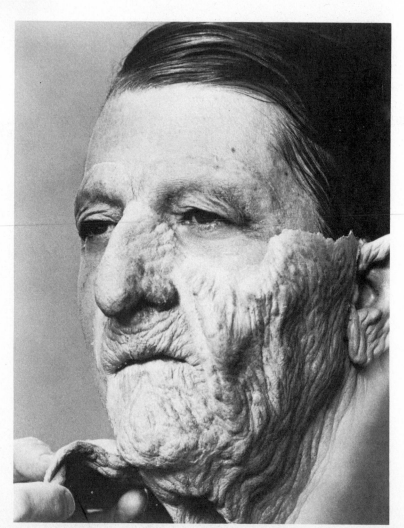

Figure 16-25. Attaching large latex piece for cheeks and neck.

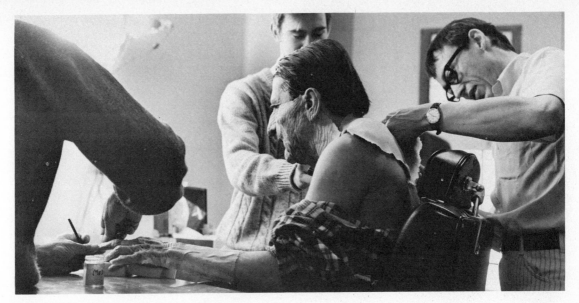

Figure 16-26.   Applying shoulder hump and hands.

Figure 16-27. Hands with latex gloves and fingernails.

Figure 16-28.   Headpiece being put on. Piece was constructed of 2 over-lapping sections of foam latex, which were glued together before being put on.

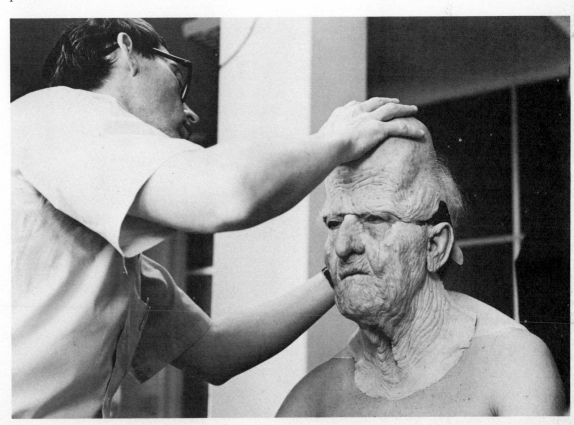

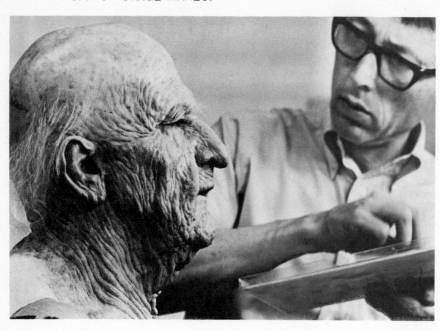

Figure 16-29. **Final touch-up of latex mask.**

Figure 16-30. **Dustin Hoffman as the 120-year-old man in *Little Big Man*.** (Photographs in Figures 16-21, 16-22, 16-23, 16-24, 16-25, 16-27, 16-28, and 16-29 by Mel Traxel, Cinema Center Films. All others by Dick Smith.)

Makeup by
Dick Smith, S.M.A.

spongy jowls and sagging necks that look and move like natural flesh. The general procedure is given below; details may vary with the particular latex formula used.

Closed molds. For foamed pieces it is necessary to use two molds—a positive and a negative—instead of the one open mold used with liquid latex. The positive mold duplicates the actor's own feature to be built up (as, for example, a nose), whereas the negative mold is taken of the projected changed feature and corresponds to the single mold used for painted-in latex pieces. The two molds reproduce the actor's own feature and the altered feature. When these two molds are fitted together, the space between will correspond precisely to the clay addition that has been built up on the plaster cast. This space is then filled with foamed latex, giving a spongy, three-dimensional piece that can be attached to the face. The casting is done with gypsum or dental stone (see Appendix A), which is harder, less porous, and more durable than plaster. Following is the procedure for making the closed mold:

1. Make a negative cast of the actor's face or any other individual feature in the usual way. This cast may be of plaster. Then make two $\frac{1}{2}$-inch balls of clay and cut them in half. This will give you four half spheres. Three of these (or all four, if you prefer) should be placed on the negative plaster cast, surrounding the face or feature. These will serve as keys or guides later in fitting the two molds together. Instead of using the semi-spherical clay pieces, you may, if you have a router bit available, drill into the positive stone cast (step 2) three depressions similar to those that would have been formed by the clay balls.

2. Build up high clay dikes around the cast, grease the cast, and pour in the stone mixture (which is handled like plaster) to make a positive cast. When the stone has hardened, pull away the clay dikes, and separate the positive stone cast from the plaster negative.

3. Now proceed as for any latex piece, modeling the character face or feature in clay on the stone positive, including skin texture as usual. (See Figures 16–11 and 16–12.)

4. Build up a high clay dike on the positive mold; grease the cast and the modeled clay features; then pour in stone to make a negative cast. This negative will be of the character face or feature.

5. When the stone has hardened, remove the dikes and separate the casts. Remove all clay and grease from the positive cast, and clean both casts thoroughly. Now you have two tight-fitting casts with semispherical keys to insure an exact fit. The air space between the positive and the negative feature will be filled with foamed latex to form the prosthetic piece. Make sure the casts are thoroughly dry before using them with the foam. Drying can be done in the oven if you wish.

Foaming the latex. Various companies that supply latex have developed their own formulas for foaming latex. The following is recommended by Uniroyal Chemical (see Appendix B) for use with their latex foam sponge compound (LOTOL L-7176), which is furnished in four parts, as follows:

Part A is the base latex compound—LOTOL L–7176 (171 grams).
Part B is the sulfur dispersion—NX–762–B (4 grams).
Part C is the zinc oxide dispersion—NX–935 (9 grams).
Part D is the gelling agent—P–4934 (5 grams), which is diluted with water (5 grams) before being added.

The three additives are normally supplied with the base compound. The amounts given above should produce about a quart of wet foam, depending on the density of foam desired. Smaller or larger quantities can be mixed using the same proportions.

Before beginning the mixing, grease the mold lightly with castor oil (preferably mixed with zinc stearate) or with rubber-mask grease. If you use the latter, the sponge will take on the color of the grease.

The mixing and foaming procedure below should be followed carefully:

1. Mix parts A, B, and C by stirring together, but do not mix more than you will use in one day. Then add any concentrated, water-soluble dye for flesh color. This dye can be obtained in red, yellow, and blue, which can be mixed to achieve any desired color. Exact amounts will have to be determined by experimentation. For flesh tones you will need the largest proportion of the dye in yellow and red (usually more yellow unless the color is to be very pink) and only a very small amount of blue (probably a maximum of 1 or 2 drops), even for grayed tones. The total amount of dye will probably not exceed 10 drops. Proceed cautiously, and note carefully each time how many drops of each color you use and the approximate color that results, so that you will have the information for future use. Since dyes vary, no exact formulas can be given here. As with any latex, remember that the color when dry is several shades darker than when wet.

2. In an electric mixer, whip the compound at high speed to approximately 5 volumes. This should take only a minute or so. The bowl in which you whip should be marked for 5 volumes in advance. For a firmer sponge decrease the volume and for a softer one increase it.

Figure 16-31. Giant. Foam latex piece for cheeks, chin, and neck, latex nose, rubber-mask grease and cake makeup. Eye pouches painted. Student makeup by Richard Brunner.

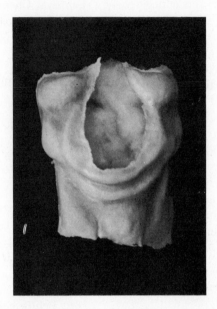

Figure 16-32. Foam latex piece for Giant. (Inside has been stuffed with cotton for the photograph.)

3. While the material is still frothing, reduce speed slightly and add Part D (diluted with water, as indicated). Mix for 30 seconds, then reduce the speed still further and continue to whip for a minute or so in order to refine the foam.

4. Pour the compound immediately into the lightly greased mold, which should then be closed and allowed to stand for about 6–8 minutes.

5. Place the mold in about a 250° F. oven (preferably air-circulated) for three to four hours, depending on the size of the mold and the thickness of the piece.

6. When it is finished curing, the latex piece can be removed immediately, if you wish, by separating the two halves of the cast and carefully lifting out the foamed piece (Figure 16–17). The mold, however, should be allowed to cool slowly in the oven. Trim any ragged edges of the latex piece, but not too closely or too evenly—they should be very thin and somewhat irregular.

Application. The foamed latex pieces can be attached with spirit gum, latex, or Duo adhesive to blend the edges (see Figure 21–1C,E,F). For areas in which there is a great deal of muscular activity, Slomon's Medico Adhesive, though more difficult to use, provides greater security. Rubber-mask grease should be applied to the pieces with a sponge (Figure 21–1L). You may then wish to adjust the color generally or locally (as with rouge, for example) by stippling on additional color with a coarse sponge. This tends to add texture and relieve the

flatness of the rubber-mask grease base. Then press a generous amount of powder into the makeup to set it and remove all shine. To suggest even greater texture and color variation (as for broken blood vessels), use a coarse sponge or a brush to stipple additional colors over the powdered makeup—red-brown, grayed purple, dull brick red, rose, gray, lavender, creamy yellow, or whatever colors seem appropriate. This stippling should then be lightly powdered. If you wish the makeup to have a slight natural sheen (as you might for a bald head, for example), simply apply a light coating of K-Y lubricating jelly and allow it to dry or force-dry it with a hair dryer. Before working with foamed latex, study the series of photographs of the TV makeup for Hal Holbrook's Mark Twain in Figure 21–1 and of the movie makeup for Dustin Hoffman in *Little Big Man*, Figures 16–9 to 16–30.*

*Difficulties that can arise in the foamed latex process may be traced to such diverse sources as the type of beater used (improper foaming), too short a curing time or too low a temperature (foam too soft), excessive baking time or temperature (hard foam with an unpleasant odor), and too much moisture in the mold (latex skin becoming detached from the foam on or after removal from the cast). Follow instructions carefully and keep a record of all experiments in order to help trace any problems that might arise and to find out what works best with the materials you're using.

17

BEARDS AND MUSTACHES

The first step in constructing a beard or a mustache is to make a rough sketch of what you have in mind. Presumably you will have done this when designing the makeup. Drawings and photographs in this book and in your morgue should be helpful. The style you choose will, of course, depend on the period of the play and on the personality of the character. Period beard styles are illustrated in Appendix G.

You can make or buy beards or mustaches of real or synthetic hair ventilated on a lace foundation. This type of beard is the quickest to apply, the most comfortable to wear, and the most convincing. It is also the most expensive, but it will last for many performances. If you will be using a beard or a mustache for only a few performances and if your budget is limited, you will probably want to use crepe hair. In any case, you should become proficient in the technique of applying it. This applies primarily to men, of course, and to women who plan to make up other people. But any actress may at some time need to use crepe hair for eyebrows.

CREPE HAIR

Wool crepe is relatively inexpensive and, if skillfully manipulated, very effective. It can be used for beards, goatees, mustaches, sideburns, eyebrows, and occasionally to add to the natural hair. It is not usually satisfactory, however, for movie or television closeups.

Various shades of hair are available, and for realistic beards or mustaches, several shades should be mixed. This can be done by straightening braids of both shades, then combing them together. This will give a far more realistic effect than would a flat color. It is especially important for realistic makeups that pure black or pure white crepe hair never be used without being mixed with at least one other color. Black usually needs some gray or brown or red; and white, some blond or light gray to make it convincingly real.

PREPARATION OF CREPE HAIR

Crepe hair comes in braids of very kinky, woolly strands, which for straight or wavy-haired actors should normally be straightened before the hair is applied. This is done by cutting the string that holds the braids together and wetting the amount of hair to be used. The portion of the hair that has been dampened can then be straightened by stretching it between the legs or arms of a chair, two clothes hooks, or any other solid objects not too far apart. Both ends of the stretched hair are tied with string to whatever moorings are being used and left to dry.

The damp hair can be straightened much more quickly with an electric iron, but one must be careful to avoid scorching the hair. Pressing under a damp cloth or using a steam iron (Figure 17–2A) is safer.

After the hair is dry, it should be carefully combed with a wide-toothed comb, then cut into lengths as needed. A great deal of the hair will probably be combed out of the braid. This extra hair should be removed from the comb, gathered

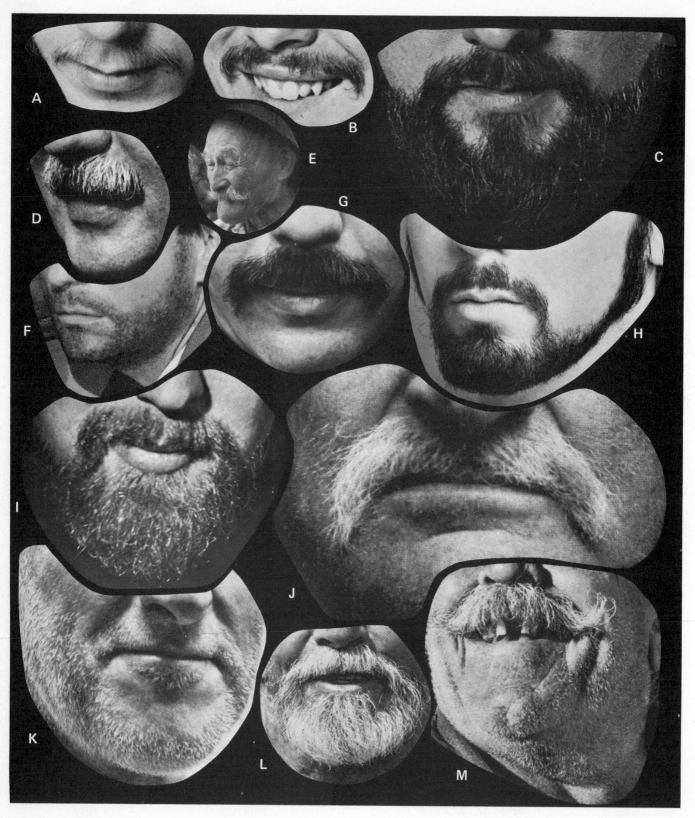

Figure 17-1. Mustaches and beards.

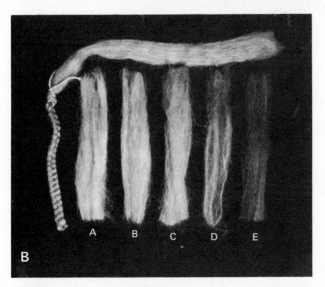

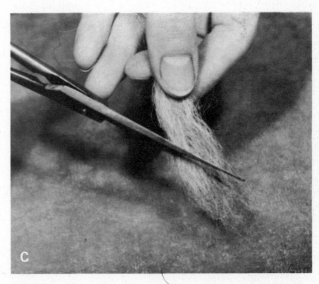

Figure 17-2. Preparing crepe hair. (A) Straightening with a steam iron. (B) Three shades of hair with two mixtures. (C) Cutting hair on the bias before applying.

in bunches, and recombed as often as necessary. It can be used for eyebrows, small mustaches, and the shorter lengths of hair needed in making beards. In combing, always begin near the end of the braid and work in, combing gently. Otherwise, you may tear the braid apart.

In case slightly wavy hair is desired, the crepe hair should be stretched less tightly while drying. Often it need only be moistened and allowed to dry without stretching. It is also possible to use straightened hair, curling it with an electric curling iron after it has been properly trimmed. Crepe hair can also be curled by wrapping the straightened hair diagonally around a curling stick (a broom

handle will do) and allowing it to dry or force-drying it with an electric dryer. Spraying the hair on the stick with hair spray or coating it with wave set will give it more body.

Occasionally it is possible to use the hair without straightening at all if a very thin, fluffy kind of beard is needed. To prepare the hair for use in this way, pull out the braid as far as it will go without cutting the string, grasp the braid with one hand, the loose end of the hair with the other, and pull in sharp jerks until a section of the hair is detached from the braid. The hair can then be spread out and manipulated with the fingers in various ways until it is fluffy. One method of fluffing is to pull the hair at both ends. Half of the hair will go with the left hand, half with the right. The two strands can then be put back together and the process repeated until there are no dark spots where the hair is thick and heavy. The curl is thus shuffled around so that it is no longer recognizable as a definitive wave. If the hair is then too fluffy, it can be rolled briskly between the palms of the hands. This is nearly always done for mustaches when straightened hair is not used. This pulling and fluffing technique is particularly useful when skin should show through the beard in spots, as sometimes happens on the chin. It can also be used in an emergency if there is no straightened hair and no iron available to straighten it.

MIXING COLORS

Since combing wool crepe, even with a wide-toothed comb, tends to waste a good deal of hair, mixing can be accomplished more economically by first cutting the various shades of hair into whatever lengths you are going to need (Figure 17–2B), always allowing extra length for the trimming. You can then proceed in one of two ways—either take strands of hair of each color and gradually put them together until the portions of the various colors you want mixed are assembled into one pile, or put together all of the hair you want mixed and keep pulling the strands apart and putting them back together until they are adequately mixed. The principle, though not the technique, is the same as for shuffling cards.

Figure 17-3. Diagram for applying crepe-hair beard. Layers of hair are applied in the order indicated by the numbers.

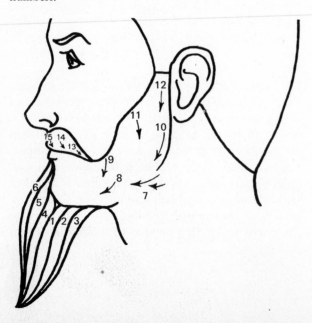

The first method will probably give you a more even mixture, particularly if you work with only a few hairs at a time. For some beards you will want to choose colors that are not too strongly contrasting in hue or value; for others you will want stronger contrasts in color. For special effects, it would also be possible to use strongly contrasting colors, such as black, white, and red.

You may wish to separate the hair into more shades and mixtures, as illustrated in Figure 17–2B, in which three shades have been used to produce two mixtures instead of one. Strands *a, c,* and *e* are the original colors from the braid; *b* is a mixture of *a* and *c;* and *d* is a mixture of *c* and *e.* This gives additional subtlety to the blending of the beard. The lightest colors should be lighter than the hair on the head and the darkest colors, darker.

APPLICATION OF CREPE HAIR

The hair is commonly applied with spirit gum over the completed makeup. If creme makeup or greasepaint is applied in a very thin coat and well powdered, the gum should stick. Over cake makeup there is not likely to be a problem.

You will already have determined the shape of beard you want. In applying the hair, always be aware of the natural line of hair growth, as shown in the diagram in Figure 17–3. The numbers indicate the most practical order of application. The procedure is as follows:

1. Paint the area to be covered by hair with spirit gum and allow the gum to become quite tacky. Lightly tapping the gum repeatedly with the tip of a finger will speed up the process. It's a good idea to have some powder handy to dust on the fingers or on the scissors whenever they get sticky. During the application, the scissors can occasionally be cleaned with acetone and the fingers with alcohol or spirit gum remover.

2. While the gum is becoming tacky, separate a dozen or so hairs from one of your darkest piles and, holding them firmly between the thumb and the forefinger of one hand, cut the ends on the bias (Figure 17–2C). The hairs should be longer than required for the finished beard or mustache; they can be trimmed later. The darker hair should usually be used underneath; the lighter, on top. In observing bearded men, however, notice that in gray or partially gray beards, certain sections of the top layer are often lighter than others. These areas normally match on both sides of the face.

3. When the gum is sufficiently tacky, apply the hair first to the underside of the chin (Figure 17–4A). Usually this application should be in three layers. Press

the first layer into the gum under the chin, about ½ or ¾ of an inch back from the tip (#1 in Figure 17–3). Press with the scissors, a towel, or a damp chamois for a few seconds (Figure 17–4B), then add a second and a third layer (#2 and #3), the latter starting from the lowest point on the neck where the hair grows naturally. The hair along the edge of this line should be very thinly spread. If you are making a full beard, the hair should be carried up to the highest point at which the beard grows on the underside of the jaw.

4. Next, apply hair to the front of the chin. The hair can first be attached in a roughly semicircular pattern, following the line of the tip of the chin (#4 in Figure 17–3). Then add thinner layers of hair (#5 and #6), following the line of the beard as outlined by the spirit gum. For full beards the hair should be built up gradually, starting at the chin and proceeding to the sideburns (Figure 17–3, #7–12; and Figure 17–4C). Since the hair is usually not so heavy on the sides of the face, a few applications will be sufficient. Each application of hair should be pressed and allowed to dry slightly before another is made. Remember that ordinarily the thin layer of hair at the edge of the beard will be somewhat lighter in color than the hair underneath.

5. When you have completed the application and have allowed the spirit gum time to dry, gently pull all of the hair in the beard in order to remove all stray hairs that are not firmly anchored. A beard that will not resist this gentle pulling is not secure enough to wear onstage.

6. Trim and shape the beard with barbers' shears according to the style required. If the beard is to be straggly, little or no trimming may be required; but a neat beard needs careful shaping. Use a hand mirror for a good profile view.

Figure 17-4. Constructing a beard with crepe hair and spirit gum. Straightened hair is built up gradually in layers, using two or more shades of hair. All loose hairs are pulled out before the final trimming. Notice how the thinner hair on the cheek blends into the skin. (Figure 17-4 continued p. 182)

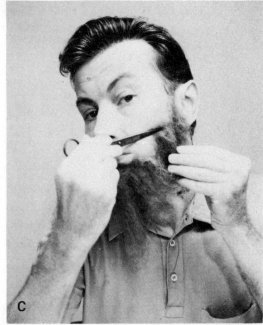

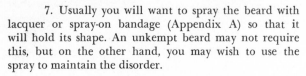

Figure 17-4. (continued)

7. Usually you will want to spray the beard with lacquer or spray-on bandage (Appendix A) so that it will hold its shape. An unkempt beard may not require this, but on the other hand, you may wish to use the spray to maintain the disorder.

Mustaches should not be stuck on in two pieces (except for distance work in which accurate detail is not necessary) but built up in the same manner as beards, starting at either end and working toward the center, letting the hair fall in the natural direction of growth (Figure 17–3, #13–15). One end of each hair should always be free. The ends of the mustache may be waxed or creamed to make them hold their shape. Better yet, the whole mustache can be sprayed with diluted spirit gum (see *Atomizer*, Appendix A), hair lacquer, or spray-on bandage.

In extending the sideburns, either separately or as part of a beard, it is sometimes possible, if the actor's hair is long and his sideburns are fairly full, to undercut the natural sideburns so that at least a quarter inch of real hair can be made to overlap the false hair, thus avoiding an obvious join. If, however, the natural sideburns are closely cropped, it will probably be more practical to continue the front edge of the false sideburns upward slightly in front of the real ones to a point somewhat above the eyebrow. There is nearly always a natural angle where the hair grows forward on the temple, then recedes. The artificial hairs can then be combed into the natural ones.

Latex base. If you need the hair construction for more than one performance, the practical thing

to do is to make it up on a latex base rather than attaching it directly to the skin with spirit gum. Before painting latex on the face, it's a good idea to protect the skin with a light coating of grease or oil. Then powder the oiled skin and brush off the excess powder. The following describes the procedure for making a mustache. Beards and sideburns would be done in the same way.

1. Paint the entire mustache area with liquid latex. If the character is to be aged, carry the latex application partially over the upper lip until the lip is

as thin as you want it to be. When the first application is dry, add successive applications—usually two or three—until the latex seems thick enough to form a firm base.

2. When your crepe hair is ready to attach, paint on a final coat of latex and immediately push the ends of the hair into it. *Do not press.* The ends will be firmly anchored when the latex dries. Since latex dries quickly, you should do only one small area at a time.

3. Pull out all loose hairs and trim the mustache.

The mustache may now seem to be anchored solidly enough to leave it on for the first performance, but if there is much movement around the mouth or excessive perspiration, the latex may well loosen and pull away from the skin. It is safer, therefore, to remove it immediately and reattach it with spirit gum. This can be done simply by lifting one edge of the latex with a fingernail, tweezers, or an orangewood stick and pulling the mustache off. The back of the latex should be powdered immediately to prevent its sticking to itself. Rough edges should be trimmed before putting the mustache back on. In trimming the latex be sure to leave as thin a blending edge as possible.

In reattaching the mustache, apply the spirit gum to the back of the latex, but only around the edges—unless there is to be so much movement that you would feel more secure with a greater area of adhesion. Let the gum become slightly tacky before attaching the piece to the skin. After the piece is in place, press with a towel for a few moments, just as in applying the hair directly with spirit gum. To conceal the edge of the piece, add a row of hair to the skin along the top edge of the mustache. This added row of hair will usually be the lightest hair you have prepared for use in making the mustache. On light-skinned actors, light hairs blend into the skin more readily than do dark ones.

In removing the mustache, apply alcohol or spirit gum remover around the edges of the latex to loosen it. Do not try to pull it off without first loosening the gum, since this may stretch or tear the latex. When the mustache has been removed, clean all the gum from the back of the latex with remover. It is possible to reattach the mustache with latex, but since the problem of security still remains, this is not advised.

In making both a beard and a mustache with a latex base, make them separately or cut them apart after they are made in order not to restrict movement of the jaw.

BEARD STUBBLE

For an unshaven effect, as in Figure J-19, crepe hair is cut into tiny pieces and applied to adhesive spread over the beard area. There are several variations in the method. This is the simplest:

1. Wash the face with soap and water or clean it with alcohol or astringent to remove all grease. If the skin under the stubble is to be made up, use transparent liquid makeup.

2. Choose the color of hair you want, then cut up tiny bits of it onto a piece of paper, your makeup table top, or any smooth surface (Figure 17–6A).

3. Cover the beard area with a special wax adhesive for stubble (see *Adhesives.* Appendix A). Mustache wax can also be used for this same purpose.

4. Push a dry rouge brush into the pile of hair bits (quite a few will stick to the brush) and, with the brush, transfer the bits to the face (Figure 17–6C). The hair bits will spread out fairly evenly and will not pile up in clumps.

Most of the stubble can be taken off with makeup remover, but a final cleansing with alcohol or astringent is helpful.

It is also possible to use matte spirit gum instead of the stubble adhesive. This can be applied

Figure 17-5. Captain Ahab. Beard constructed on latex, using 4 colors of crepe hair—light gray, light gray-brown, blond, and medium gray. Mustache of real hair ventilated on net (see Figure 17-7-E). Wig ventilated on nylon net. Makeup by Bill Smith. (For other makeups by Mr. Smith see Figures 14-43 and 15-25C.)

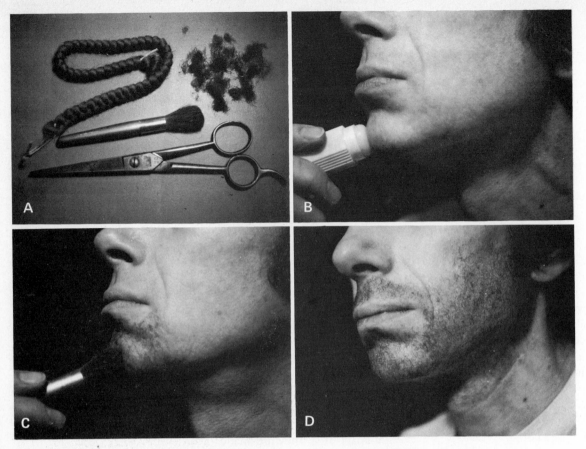

Figure 17-6. Beard stubble. (A) Crepe-hair braid, cut-up crepe hair, round brush, barber's shears. (B) Applying paste adhesive to beard area. (C) Applying hair to beard area with brush. (D) Unshaven beard.

Figure 17-7. Ventilated mustaches and beards. (A) Blending edge of a mustache. (B) Untrimmed blending edge of a beard. (C, D) Mustache ventilated onto gauze. (E) Mustache ventilated onto net, before trimming. (F) Mustache ventilated onto net, trimmed and dressed.

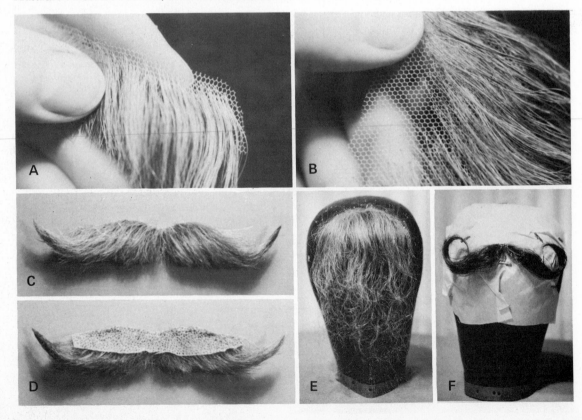

over whatever makeup you are using for the character. Regular spirit gum is not advisable because of the shine. When the gum is almost dry, the stubble can be attached by touching a fairly large clump of it to the gummed area repeatedly until the entire area is covered. Or you can spread the stubble over a towel and then apply it by pressing the towel against the gummed area of the face. In either case, loose hairs can be brushed off and final touching up can be done with the fingers or with tweezers. The spirit gum can be used over any makeup, though grease or creme makeup must, of course, be powdered. The stubble adhesive works better on the clean skin.

EYEBROWS

Crepe hair can be used to supplement the natural brows, or it can be used to make completely new ones, as suggested in Chapter 14. In adding to the natural brows, it is possible to attach the crepe hair to the skin over the brow and comb it down into the brow or to stick tufts of crepe hair into the brow. Which method is used will depend on the form and thickness of the natural brow and of the brow to be constructed. Crepe hair brows are shown in Figure 10–6.

Sometimes it is necessary to block out the eyebrows completely (see Chapter 14 for details) and build new ones with crepe hair and spirit gum or latex. In using latex, be very careful not to get it into the brows, since it may be impossible to remove the latex without removing the hairs as well. Once the hairs have been matted down with spirit gum, wax, or sealer, however, it is safe to apply latex over them.

VENTILATED PIECES

In many instances crepe hair beards and mustaches are unsatisfactory. For movie and television closeups they may not be sufficiently realistic, and for long-run plays they are a nuisance. The most realistic and convenient beards and mustaches are made of real or synthetic hairs individually knotted onto a net foundation. This knotting process is usually known as *ventilating*, though it is sometimes referred to as *working* or *knotting* the hair. Even in closeups the hair appears to be actually growing out of the skin, and the piece can be attached with

very little trouble and removed even more easily. With proper care a ventilated piece will last a long time.

Materials. Foundations may be of silk net, treated silk lace (plastic coated), nylon net, hairlace, cotton net, silk gauze, or a combination of gauze and net. The gauze is a somewhat stiff, thin, tough, closely woven fabric. The better nets are also thin, fairly stiff, and somewhat transparent, so that when they are glued to the skin they become invisible from a short distance. For many years hairlace was considered the finest type of net available, but it

Figure 17-8. Actor Mitchell Erickson as King Lear. Beard and mustache of white yak hair on net. Wig also of white yak hair. Latex nose, eye pouches, and sagging flesh over eyes. Natural eyebrows covered by latex pieces, into which white yak hair eyebrows have been ventilated.

has now been largely replaced with silk or nylon net (Figure 17–7A,B). Frequently beards and sometimes even mustaches are constructed with silk gauze for the body of the piece and edged with lace for the blend into the skin. The mustache in Figure 17–7D was ventilated onto silk gauze and the ones in Figure 17–7E,F onto net.

Both human and synthetic hair are used, but when greater stiffness is desired, yak hair may be substituted. The beard and the mustache in Figure 17–8 are made of white yak hair on net. The yak hair is less expensive, and it can be dyed any color. Yak hair does not mat, nor does it snarl as readily as human hair does.

The finest human hair comes largely from European women who let it grow long for the specific purpose of selling it. All colors are available. Beware, however, of human hair that has been dyed, since the color may fade in time. Coarser, cheaper hair is obtainable from China and Korea. Hair comes in various lengths, tightly bound with string at the cut end, and may be either straight or curled. Hair is purchased by weight, the price depending on quality and color. Grays are usually the most expensive.

Various types of synthetic hair are available in a number of colors. Some types have a high sheen, giving a rather artificial look; others have less sheen, some of them being virtually indistinguishable in appearance from real hair. Synthetic hair is suitable for ventilated beards and mustaches, but real hair can be more readily styled. Real and synthetic are sometimes mixed. Synthetic hair can also be used for direct application with spirit gum or latex. Crepe hair, however, is cheaper. For sources of all types of hair see Appendix A.

CONSTRUCTION OF VENTILATED PIECES

The first step in constructing a beard or a mustache is to draw the outline of the proposed piece on the face with an eyebrow pencil. This, of course, will indicate only the area of the skin from which the hair would normally grow—not the shape or styling of the beard or mustache. In other words, a long handlebar mustache may grow from the same basic area as a short clipped mustache. The only difference is that the hair itself is longer. The diagram in Figure 17–10 will serve as a general guide for outlining the area of growth. For individual variations in beard growth, see Figure 17–1, Appendix G, and illustrations in your own morgue.

After the area is marked on the skin, lay a piece of thin white translucent paper over the marked area and trace the outline onto the paper. Then cut out along the traced lines. This will give you an accurate paper pattern. For mustaches this is a very simple process, but for beards there is obviously a complication, since the hair grows both over and under the jawbone. The solution is to take a few tucks in the paper and crease it so that it fits the chin and the jaw snugly. Then cut with the tucks in it. After the paper pattern has been cut, open it out, lay it on the net, and cut the net flat.

The third step is to pin or tape (with masking tape) the pattern to a wig block (Figure 17–7E,F), beard block (Figure 17–12A), or plaster cast and lay a piece of net over it. The net should be about a half inch longer and wider than the pattern. It will be trimmed later. In Figure 17–10 the solid line represents the pattern of a mustache showing through the net. The net should be pinned down with large-headed pins or special T-pins (see Appendix A) if you are using a canvas-covered or styrofoam block, or with thumb tacks or staples on a wooden block. Be sure the net is secured firmly, with the head of the pin or the tack resting tightly against it so that it is not pulled out of shape in the knotting process.

The ventilating needle is shown in Figures 17–9 and 18–18. It consists of a handle about 3 inches long into which the needle is inserted. The needle is about 1½ inches long and curved with a sharp fishhook at the end. The size of this hook regulates the number of hairs that will automatically be drawn from the hank when the needle is inserted. Needle sizes are designated by number, starting with 00—the larger the number, the larger the needle. For the body of a beard, a #1 or a #2 needle can be used, but for the edges a #00 is needed so that the knots will not be obvious. Larger needles should be used only where the knots are to be covered by subsequent layers of hair. For mustaches it is best not to use a needle drawing more than two or three hairs. For the top few rows a needle drawing only one hair should be used.

Figure 17–9 illustrates the ventilating technique. Note also Figure 18–10. Practice the technique on a piece of scrap netting before you try to work on a mustache. A little practice should make you reasonably expert. This is the procedure:

A. Remove a very small bit of hair from the hank, and double it about a third of the way from the root end. Assuming you are righthanded, grasp this loop (1) between the thumb (2) and the forefinger (3) of your left hand. With the thumb (4) and the forefinger (5) of your right hand hold the needle (6), and slip it under one strand of the net (7). (In the drawing the size of the net is greatly exaggerated for clarity.) Then thrust the hook of the needle into the hair. The hook should be pointing toward you or slightly upward.

B. With the thumb and finger of the right hand twist the needle counterclockwise, as indicated by the arrow, in order to turn the hook of the needle down so that it will not catch on the net as you draw it back. In ventilating into gauze, which is closely woven, great care must be taken in withdrawing the hook to prevent its catching in the gauze. Draw back, as illustrated, but only far enough to clear the net. If you draw it too far, you will pull out the short end of the hair. Until the knot is made, you must have a double hair to work with.

C. Move the needle toward the left hand, hook it under the double hair, and give it a half-turn clockwise in order to catch the hair.

D. Continue the clockwise turn until the hook is pointing downward and draw the needle back through the loop. Continue to draw it to the right until the entire length of the hair is through. Pull the knot tight. Until you learn to do this as you pull the hair through with the needle, it may be necessary to pull it tight with the fingers.

E. The hairs will then lie in one direction, moving away from the left hand. Always move the right hand in the direction you wish the hairs to lie. Along the visible edges of your mustache you will probably place a hair in each tiny opening of the net, but when you are using a larger needle, you will space the knots in order to give you the thickness of hair you wish.

Since single knots may sometimes loosen, permitting hairs to be combed out of the piece, a double knotting process can be used for added security. In section D above, after the needle has been drawn back through the loop, but before the ends have been drawn through, the needle is once again hooked around the stems of the hair. Then the needle is drawn back through the second loop that has been formed, the ends are pulled through, and the hair is pulled tight as usual.

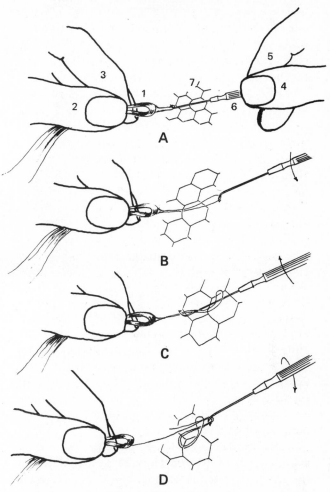

Figure 17-9. Ventilating hair onto lace. Progressive positions of the needle in relation to the hair and the lace. Size of lace is greatly magnified.

Although this knotting may sound complex, it really is not. Once you have mastered the needle technique, you will make the necessary movements automatically and will be able to work very rapidly.

In making a mustache, always begin at the outer corners and work along the bottom and upward (Figure 17–10). The top hair should always be the last to be knotted in. When the hair is in, trim the net about a quarter inch beyond the hair, as shown by the dotted line in Figure 17–10. Since the cut edges will eventually ravel and will have to be cut down further, the wider the net edge is at first, the longer the mustache will last. But at the same time, the wider net may be visible to the audience.

You may want to do some preliminary trimming of the mustache before trying it on, for when you finish the ventilating, the hair will probably

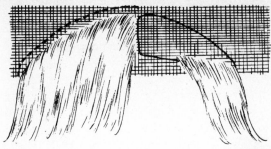

Figure 17-10. Ventilating a mustache onto net or gauze. The solid line represents the outline of the mustache, which is always drawn on paper underneath the net or, if gauze is used, on the gauze itself. The dotted line represents where the gauze or net will be trimmed.

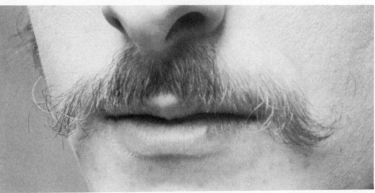

Figure 17-11. Real mustache. Note variation in color.

be as long as that in Figure 17–7E. When you are learning to trim and style beards and mustaches, carefully study photographs before you do any trimming at all. If you can find a photograph of exactly the style you want, so much the better. If you can't find a photograph, look for a drawing. Cut the hair carefully with a good pair of barber's shears, a little at a time. Be sure to try on the mustache before doing the final trimming.

In constructing a beard, place the pattern on a form (such as a beard block or a plaster cast of the head) so that the original tucks can be taken. Identical tucks can be taken in the net. These can be folded down, and you may secure them with thread if you like. However, after a little practice, you will find that you can secure the tucks simply by ventilating through the three thicknesses of net so that you are actually tying in the tucks with strands of hair.

If you wish to make the body of the beard foundation with gauze, simply lay the gauze over the beard pattern as you would the net, but trim it down ⅜ to ½ inch below the upper outline of the beard. The gauze should not show when the beard is finished. Then lay on a strip of net along the edge, overlapping the gauze about ½ inch and, of course, overlapping the edge of the pattern also. Along this edge, the hair can be ventilated through both net and gauze, tying them together.

For both beards and mustaches you should use more than one shade of hair. Facial hair is often darker underneath, lighter on top and along the edges. The lighter hair along the edge, being nearer the color of the skin, is extremely helpful in mak-

ing a subtle, realistic blend. With gray hair, the differences in color are especially marked. There may sometimes be dark brown or even black hairs underneath and white ones above. This can be reproduced very subtly in ventilating, since the hairs are put in individually. A few red or auburn hairs will frequently give a gray beard added life. Observe real beards—gray ones are rarely, if ever, the same color throughout. There may be a salt and pepper effect, with dark and light hair mixed, or the gray may be in streaks or areas, more or less matching on both sides of the face.

APPLICATION OF VENTILATED PIECES

In order that any ventilated piece with a net edge—whether wig, beard, or mustache—look natural, it must be carefully applied. This is the technique:

1. Place the piece on your face to determine the correct position. If you have a beard or a mustache with a partial gauze foundation, you can secure it to the skin with double-faced toupee tape. If you are using a mustache with no gauze, set it on the face, then observe very carefully where it goes so that you can estimate where to place the spirit gum.

2. Brush a thin coat of matte spirit gum onto the clean skin, covering the entire area beneath the lace. For beards, you will normally place the gum only under the edges of the lace, though it is possible and sometimes desirable to cover the entire area if there is to be strong muscular activity, as in singing, or if for any reason you feel the need of the additional security. *Never use latex on hair lace.*

188

3. Let the spirit gum become slightly tacky. Then press the lace into the gum with a clean, white, lintless towel, a piece of silk, or a damp chamois, being careful to press the lace straight down without letting it slide on the skin. This sliding could stretch it, causing unsightly corrugations or ripples, which could easily become permanent. Use a clean section of the cloth or chamois each time you press. Keep pressing until the lace is dry. Then with a toothbrush, a dye brush, or an eyebrow brush, lift any hairs that may have inadvertently been stuck down by the gum.

DRESSING VENTILATED PIECES

When the beard or the mustache is securely attached, it can be combed with a wide-toothed comb. But remember, in combing any hair piece, always hold the comb at an angle so that there is no possibility that the teeth will dig into the net foundation and tear it. This means holding it at the reverse angle from the one usually used in combing your own hair. This will take some getting used to, but it's very important. Also, when the hair is fairly long, always begin combing at the ends and work toward the roots. Human hair in hairpieces of any kind becomes matted and tangled much more easily than the same hair would while growing on the head. This is due to the fact that half of the hair is going against the natural direction of growth. In other words, the hair is knotted somewhere between the roots and the end, both of which are extended outward. A human hair is not quite the simple, smooth filament it appears to be—there are little scalelike projections, all going in the same direction. You can usually feel the difference by running a hair quickly between your thumb and your forefinger in the direction of growth and then against the direction of growth. When hairs are not all going in the same direction, these tiny scales catch onto each other and cause matting. Therefore, special care is needed in combing any kind of hairpiece made from human hair.

If the hair does not naturally fall just as you would like it to, comb it with water, set it, and let it dry before recombing it. You can push it into waves or even make pin curls (on the ends of beards or mustaches, for example). When the hair is dry, spray it with hair oil, hair spray, or spray bandage, then comb. Or apply one of the gel or cream dressings, then comb it into the hair. If you want the hair to look dry or unhealthy or dirty, you can use colored powder or cake makeup to dull it.

The hair can also be curled with a curling iron if you prefer. Heat should be used with great care, however, on synthetic hair. Water waving is much preferable. In order to maintain the wave in synthetic hair, it may be necessary to spray it with hair lacquer.

REMOVING AND CLEANING VENTILATED PIECES

To remove the beard or the mustache, dip a stiff brush into spirit gum remover or alcohol and press the bristles into the lace edge. Do not scrub and do not pull up the lace by force. Any good lace or net is very delicate and requires considerable care in handling to avoid stretching or tearing it.

Figure 17-12. Beard blocks. (A) Wooden beard block. (B) Ventilated beard on wooden block. (C) Ventilated beard on plaster cast of actor's face, used as a beard block.

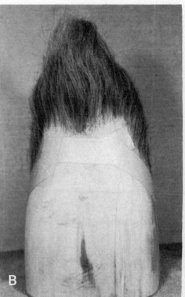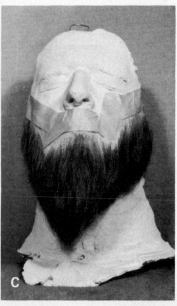

Keep flooding it with the remover until the gum is softened and the lace comes up by itself. Then dip the lace edge (or the entire piece if there is spirit gum on all of it) into a dish of acetone to remove all traces of spirit gum and makeup. The lace must be kept absolutely clean if it is to remain invisible on the skin. It may be desirable, even when gum has been used only on the edge, to soak the whole piece in acetone from time to time.

Beards and mustaches should be carefully stored so that they will be kept clean and the lace will not be damaged. It is best to keep each beard individually in a box large enough that it will not be pressed flat.

MEASURING FOR BEARDS

If you wish to order a beard by mail, the following are the necessary measurements. Letters refer to those in Figure 18–24. In the figure, the heavy dotted lines represent beard measurements; the light broken line is the beard line.

    A. From sideburn to sideburn under chin

    B. From lip to end of beard line under chin

    C. Width across the front (average measurement, 3 inches)

    D. Corner of lip to back of jawbone

If you are ordering a ready-made beard, all of these measurements may not be necessary, espe-

Figure 17-13. Full beard in sections. Sideburns, mustache, and beard made of real hair ventilated onto nylon net. These pieces can be recombed, straightened, or curled and used in various combinations, as shown in Figure 17-14.

cially if you are renting it. But better too many than not enough.

ADAPTING BEARDS

One great advantage of ventilated pieces is that they can be restyled, often merely by combing, for a variety of characters. It is possible, for greater flexibility, to make a full beard in three pieces—one center and two side sections—with, of course, a separate mustache (see Figure 17–13). Then the pieces can be used singly or in any combination, as shown in Figure 17–14, in which all eight makeups are done with a single wig and the four pieces shown in Figure 17–13. This is only a sampling of the variety that could be obtained by combining pieces and recombing.

It is most useful for an actor or any theater group to build up a stock of ventilated beards and mustaches, particularly such versatile ones as those in Figure 17–13. Real hair should be used when possible, since it can be recombed and restyled much more easily than synthetic hair. The color can be changed if necessary, though it's always better to have several colors on hand. The best way to build up a stock of hair pieces is to make whatever is required for each character you do instead of using crepe hair. Then the pieces can be saved and used in the future. This takes more time initially but pays off in the end, giving you a stock of realistic beards and mustaches to choose from.

PROBLEMS

1. Make it a point during the next few days to observe facial hair. Make sketches and notes for your file of as many types of mustaches and beards as you can find. Notice where partially grayed beards are the lightest and where the darkest in a number of individual cases, and make any generalizations that seem warranted.

2. With crepe hair, duplicate one or two beards from your morgue or from styles illustrated in Appendix G or H. If you have time, complete the makeup or use the beard for one of the characters in Problem 3 for which it would be appropriate.

3. Using suitable hair applications, make up yourself or someone else as one of the characters in each of the following groups or others of your own choice:

    a. Davies *(The Caretaker)*; Horace Vandergelder *(The Matchmaker)*; Engstrand *(Ghosts)*; Helmer *(A Doll's House)*; Constable Warren *(Our Town)*; Robert Browning *(The Barretts of Wimpole Street)*; Sergius *(Arms and the Man)*; Alfred Doolittle, Colonel Pickering *(Pygma-*

Figure 17-14. A versatile beard. Late nineteenth-century beard styles made by combining the four ventilated hair pieces shown in Figure 17-13. The same hairlace wig was recombed and used throughout.

lion, My Fair Lady); Mr. Wickham *(Pride and Prejudice);* Father *(Life with Father);* Sewer Man *(The Madwoman of Chaillot).*

b. Iago; King Richard II; Dr. Rank *(A Doll's House);* Gustave Rosenberg *(Kind Lady);* Dr. Sloper *(The Heiress);* Creon *(Antigone);* Trigorin *(The Sea Gull);* Dr. Stockman *(An Enemy of the People);* Kolenkov *(You Can't Take It With You);* Solinus *(Comedy of Errors);* Ulric Brendel *(Rosmersholm);* Macbeth; Gremio *(Taming of the Shrew);* King of Hearts *(Alice in Wonderland);* Volpone; General St. Pé *(Waltz of the Toreadors);* Vanya Astroff *(Uncle Vanya);* Firs *(The Cherry Orchard);* Fagin *(Oliver).*

c. Agmar *(The Gods of the Mountain);* King Henry IV; Baptista, Vincentio *(Taming of the Shrew);* Falstaff; King Lear; Duncan *(Macbeth);* Claudius, Polonius *(Hamlet);* Prospero *(The Tempest);* Shylock, Old Gobbo *(Merchant of Venice);* Kalchas *(Daughters of Atreus);* Teiresias *(Antigone);* The Grandfather *(The Intruder);* Angelo, Ageon *(Comedy of Errors);* Captain Shotover *(Heartbreak House);* Kublai Khan, Chu-Yin *(Marco Millions);* Gandalf *(Lord of the Rings);* Adam *(As You Like It).*

4. Using real or synthetic hair, ventilate a mustache or a beard in any style you wish. Do a sketch first or bring in a drawing, print, or photograph, or select a style from Appendix G or H.

5. Do another complete makeup for a specific character from a play, using your ventilated beard or mustache. Do a makeup worksheet first.

18

HAIR AND WIGS

The hair is nearly always a very important element in any makeup and is invaluable as a means of suggesting period, personality, and age. Rearranging the hair can often transform the actor, helping him enormously in creating his character. Conversely, failure to make the hair suit the character can ruin an otherwise skillful makeup.

NATURAL HAIR

Restyling. More often than not the actor's own hair can be used for the character he is playing, Although the makeup artist may be limited by the length of the actor's hair, within such limitations great variety can be achieved by a change in style. The same head of hair can be parted on the side, in the middle, or not at all. It can be combed straight back or straight forward. It can be well combed or mussed, straight or waved, close to the head or fluffed out. All of these transformations, unless the hair is very unmanageable, can be made with the aid of a comb and a brush, hair spray or hair dressing, and water.

For both men and women it is possible to wave the hair, if it is naturally straight, by setting it with pin curls or rollers or by curling it with a curling iron. If the hair is to look well groomed, it can be sprayed with hair oil or a commercial hair spray, or a hair dressing can be applied with the fingers and combed through the hair. A lacquer spray for keeping the hair in place is sometimes desirable, depending on how manageable the natural hair is and how well it stays combed.

For characters whose hair would be expected to look dull and lifeless, face powder the color of the hair can be dusted on, or a little cake makeup or liquid body makeup of the correct shade can be applied with a sponge to dull the hair. If the hair is to look stiff and matted, it can be heavily sprayed with a liquid hair set and shaped with the fingers rather than with a comb or a brush.

Coloring and graying. Probably the most satisfactory method of coloring the hair is by the use of a temporary spray that can be washed out (see *Hair coloring* in Appendix A). Temporary sprays are available in gold, silver, black, and a wide variety of colors. The silver is excellent for spraying when a silvery effect is appropriate. The entire head can be sprayed, or the hair can be streaked with gray or with color, then carefully combed. It is even possible to use more than one color. For example, blond hair can be changed to brown streaked with gray merely by spraying first with the brown, then when it is thoroughly dry, with silver. Black hair can be made blonde, but it is recommended that it first be sprayed with red and then with blond, since the blond spray would not cover adequately.

One must be extremely careful in using such a spray to keep it off the face and to avoid patchiness. The best way to protect the skin is to cut a piece of paper to match the hairline and hold it over the forehead as the front of the hair is being sprayed. This cutout can be kept in the makeup kit for future use. The gray should usually be combed in after spraying.

If the silvery effect is inappropriate (as, for

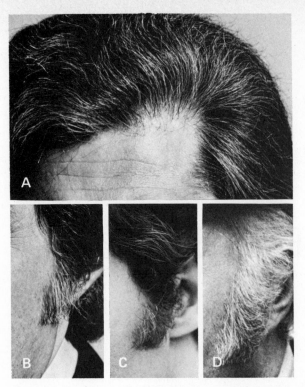

Figure 18-1. Graying hair. Photographs of naturally graying hair and sideburns.

Figure 18-2. Soaping out the hair. Hair is parted horizontally (A) at the highest point desired for the bald area, soaped down thoroughly in small sections (A–D), each section being dried with a hair dryer. Edges of the area are painted with spirit gum (E), and a piece of nylon stocking, cut approximately to size, is stretched over the soaped area (F) and pressed into the spirit gum. Any excess material around the edges is then trimmed. The spirit gum is dried (G) and the nylon covered with soap (H), which is dried, then covered with a creme or grease base (I). Powder is pressed into

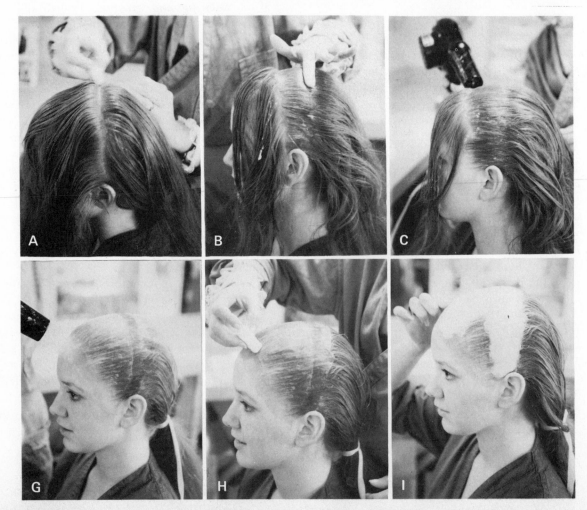

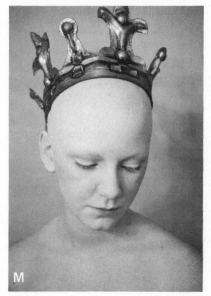

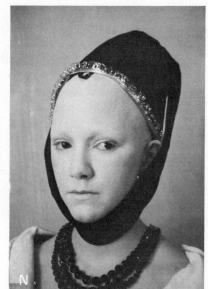

makeup with a puff and the excess removed with a powder brush (J). The whole area, including the forehead and eyebrows, is brushed with sealer (K), then another coat of creme stick (L) and powder. M and N (above) show two fifteenth-century makeups based on paintings by Jean Fouquet and Petrus Christus, illustrating the high shaved forehead fashionable at the time. Student makeup by Susan Thomas, assisted by Donna Kidder, based on a technique devised by Professor Herbert C. Camburn. For another illustration of the same technique, see Figure 18-3.

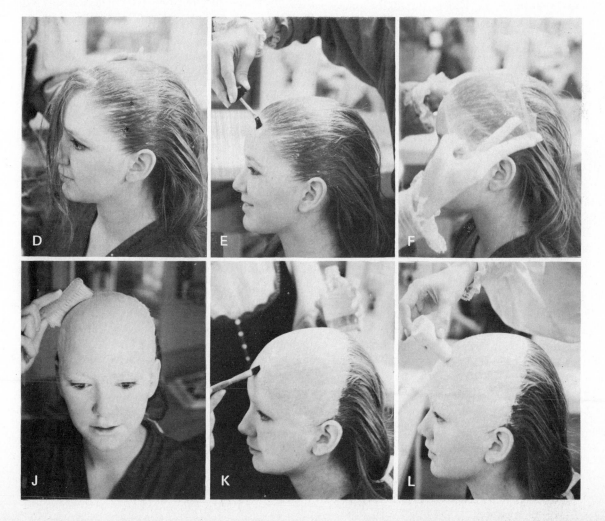

example, for a Bowery bum), there are many other methods of graying possible. Liquid or solid hair whitener (see Appendix A), white creme stick, white cake makeup, liquid white body makeup, white mascara, or white spray can be used. Any hair whitener needs to be combed into the hair, and often some color adjustment is needed. White on dark hair tends to look slightly bluish or chalky. This effect can be softened by the addition of yellow or orange food coloring to the whitener before it is applied. A little silver spray applied in streaks and thoroughly combed into the whitened hair is also helpful. If the whitener you use looks too dull or flat, a little hair oil can be sprayed on or combed in.

White powder or cornstarch should be used only in an emergency and preferably not at all. It is seldom convincing, and any unusual activity on the part of the actor sends up a cloud of white dust.

For men whose hair is thin at the crown, there are preparations for coloring the scalp (see Appendix A). Provided the spot is not completely bald, the result is usually effective enough to be used for street wear. Cake makeup of the correct color is a possible substitute. In an emergency, makeup pencils, greasepaint, or creme makeup can be used for the same purpose, but they should usually be powdered to eliminate the shine.

SOAPING OUT THE HAIR

It is sometimes possible to soap down a full head of hair to create a very convincing bald head. This technique is not suitable for hair that can't be flattened and straightened with reasonable ease; it would be exceedingly difficult, if not impossible, for an actor to do on himself (though he can do the front part of the head without help); it is time-consuming (usually from one to three hours or more, depending on one's skill and on the size of the area to be soaped out); and it must be redone each day it is to be used. But when the hair is suitable and the work is carefully done, the results can be very effective. It can be used for female characters (Figures 15–3B,C, 18–2, and J–5) as well as for males (Figures 18–4, 20–1A, and J–1), and if the hair is short enough in back, it can give the effect of a completely bald head (Figure 18–3). Here is the procedure:

1. Part the hair at the line where you wish the bald pate to begin (Figure 18–2A). For long hair, simply let the front hair hang forward over the face (Figure 18–2A). For shorter hair, pull all the top hair together, securing it with clips or pins (Figure 18–4A).

2. Using small cubes or hotel-size bars of soap that have been soaked in water (Figure 18–4D) until they are fairly soft (this may take hours or days, depending on the brand), begin soaping down a few hairs at a time (Figure 18–2A,B), confining the soap to the area that is to be bald and drying the soaped area with a hair dryer (18–2C) as you go along. An assistant who can handle the dryer as you work is very helpful. (If there is no time for softening the soap, it can be used without softening. A hair dryer is not essential but does speed up the work.)

3. When the hair is completely flattened and dried, paint spirit gum along the forehead and temples, just in front of the hairline (Figure 18–2E), then stretch a piece of nylon stocking over the area (Figure 18–2F). After pressing the front edge of the nylon into the spirit gum, glue all the other edges down with spirit gum along the borders of the soaped-out area, overlapping slightly on the forehead. Trim off the excess around the edges and press out any wrinkles with the fingers or a flat modeling tool. It can be helpful in cutting the nylon if the stocking is first placed over the head and the outline of the area to be covered is drawn on the nylon with a felt-tipped pen or a grease pencil, as shown in Figure J–1B. (The nylon is suggested because of its availability and the ease with which it can be stretched to conform to the shape of the head. For a partially bald head you might use the front section of a plastic cap or make a piece of the required size and shape by painting liquid plastic film on a suitable head form. The advantage would be in the ease of blending the front edge. Another possibility would be to cover the soaped out hair with derma wax, but this would not have the durability of the nylon or the plastic.)

4. Soap the nylon (Figure 18–2H) and let it dry or force-dry it, then coat it with plastic sealer. (The sealer can be eliminated if not available.)

5. Cover the bald pate and the forehead with rubber-mask grease to match your base (Figure 18–2I). If you are using a greasepaint base, finish the makeup, then powder. If you are using cake, be sure the rubber-mask grease is blended down over the forehead in order to avoid a line of demarcation where the grease stops; then powder the rubber-mask grease thoroughly, brush off the excess powder (Figure 18–2J), and carefully sponge on the cake (Figure 18–4C). If you are using creme makeup, it would be advisable to stipple it over the powdered rubber-mask grease when you do the rest of the face. If coverage of the bald pate is not complete, add more creme makeup and powder.

6. If the hairline is too definite, soften it by sponging lightly just above it with a cake makeup to match the hair (Figure 18–4C) or, if the hair is very dark, a shade or so lighter. Spots or skin discolorations can be sponged or brushed on if you like, and the pate can be highlighted or rouged to keep it from looking too even in color. If you are using cake makeup and want a slight sheen, cover it with K-Y lubricating jelly

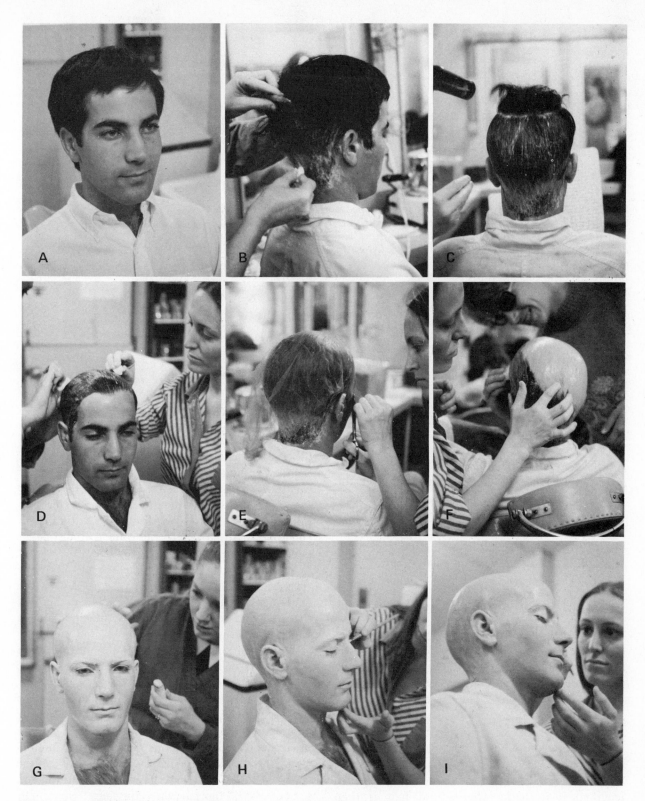

Figure 18-3. Making a bald head. The hair is soaped out, beginning at the back of the neck (B) and continuing upward and toward the front hairline (D). The entire soaped-out area is covered with a nylon stocking, which is then coated with soap, painted with creme stick (F, G), and powdered. H and I show the makeup being completed. Makeup executed by students Donna Meyer and Susan Thomas.

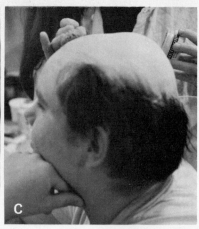

Figure 18-4. **Making a bald pate.** Hair being soaped out for a partially bald head. (A) A few hairs at a time are loosened with a brush handle and pulled to the back of the head. (B) All but the front hair has been soaped down. (C) Soaped hair has been covered with nylon stocking, more soap, greasepaint, and cake makeup. Remaining blond hair has been sprayed dark brown. (D) Soap cut into cubes and soaked overnight. Makeup being done by student Donna Meyer.

and let it dry. The natural hair can be grayed or colored if you wish (see Figure 18–4C).

If the work is properly done and the bald head is treated with care, it will hold up satisfactorily. But it is easily damaged. If hats are going to be worn, they should be put on and taken off with care and no more often than necessary; it would also be helpful to paint a coat of plastic sealer over the entire soaped-out area after the makeup is finished. To cut down on the shine, you might add a coat of K-Y and powder it. Even with this additional protection, any violent action involving the head could easily cause damage to the bald pate.

WIGS AND HAIRPIECES

If it is not possible to change the actor's own hair to achieve the effect needed for the character, a wig or a hairpiece is necessary. *Wigs* cover the entire hair area, whereas *hairpieces* are used to supplement the natural hair. Hairpieces can be divided into two kinds—*toupees*, which supply a front hairline and cover part or all of the top of the head, blending into the natural hair at the back and on the sides, and *falls*, which are attached to the natural hair, usually near the crown, in order to lengthen it in back. The natural hair is then combed over the edge of the fall and into the false hair. The fall is extremely useful for period styles, especially for men. The result is far less expensive than a wig would be and frequently more effective.

The front hairline, which is always the greatest problem in a wig, is natural; the fall provides the necessary length. In Appendix G some of the illustrated hair styles that would be particularly well suited to the use of the fall are Plates 9*t*, 14*j-n-o-q*, and 17*b*. *Switches* (Figure 18–5) are used to extend the natural hair when it is possible simply to pin them on without providing any sort of blend, as, for example, in Plates 8*a-c-i-g-k-l-n-p* and 19*b-c-d-g-h*.

Wigs can be classified by the type of construction, type of hair, and length of hair. Naturally, in choosing a particular wig, the color will also be an essential factor.

The construction of a wig involves both the type of foundation material to be used and the method by which the hair is to be added. Both of these depend to some extent on the direction in which the hair is to lie.

Foundations may be of cotton or imitation silk net, elastic net, nylon net, hairlace, silk gauze, or a combination of these.

Probably the simplest form of wig is that made of net, edged and strengthened with webbing and made to hug the head by means of short lengths of steel spring or whalebone sewn into the foundation. These are curved slightly in order to press the edges of the foundation against the skin and are used at critical spots at which the foundation might tend to pull away from the head—normally at the front center, in front of the ears, and behind the ears at the very bottom of the foundation. There should be an elastic across the back of the neck to make the wig fit snugly. Stretch wigs are constructed of a nylon net that will stretch to fit any head size. They also have a complete or a partial elastic band.

This type of wig makes no provision for a part and does not provide a realistic hairline in front, but it is quite suitable for wigs in which the hair is to be combed forward or which are meant to look like wigs rather than the natural hair—as, for example, the wigs worn in the eighteenth century (see Appendix G). This type of foundation could have a silk gauze insert to make a parting possible. When the hair is to be separated in any way to expose the scalp, silk gauze must be used unless (as is the case with toupees) there is actually a bare scalp underneath the wig, in which case silk or nylon net can be used. For close inspection a *drawn parting* is necessary. This is a painstaking and delicate technique by which the hair is knotted into gauze, then

Figure 18-5. Switch. Constructed from weft (see Figure 18-11C).

the hairs are drawn individually through another piece of gauze so that no knots will be visible and the hair will seem to be growing directly out of the scalp. (See Figure 18–15A.) The effect is very realistic but is not necessary for stage work. It is used primarily for wigs for street wear.

If the hair is to be combed away from the face, revealing a natural-looking hairline, the best solution is to put a section of nylon net or hairlace in the front of the wig (Figure 18–6). The rest of the wig may be of silk gauze, caul netting, or a combination of the two. The nylon net should extend for at least half an inch beyond the hair so that it can be glued to the skin with spirit gum. Eventually this net edge will ravel and will need to be trimmed closer. As with ventilated beards, the wider it is originally, the longer the wig will last but the more difficult it will be to conceal the net.

If the hairline of the wig is to be farther back than the actor's own hairline, a *blender* will be necessary to cover the natural hair in front (see Figures 18–15B and 19–5). The blender extends down onto the forehead, where the edge of it should be made as nearly invisible as possible with makeup. Suggestions for doing this are given under *Wearing the Wig*. Further information about blenders can be found under *Constructing the Wig*.

PERIOD HAIR STYLES

For period plays the hair styles should, of course, be correct for the period. If the natural hair

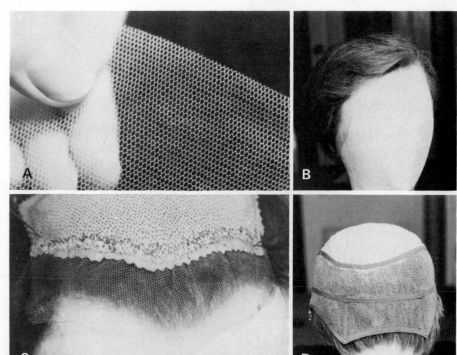

Figure 18-6. The lace-front wig. (A) Nylon net for ventilating. (B) Lace-front wig. (C) Inside of a lace-front wig. (D) Inside of a lace-front wig, back view.

can't be restyled to fit the period, false hair will need to be added.

The drawings in Appendix G illustrate representative hair styles for men and women from the early Egyptian to the present. These drawings by no means include all of the variations in style of any given period but merely show a few specific hair styles (most of them taken from paintings, sculptures, or photographs of the period) that seem to be fairly representative. All of the drawings are of styles that were worn during the period indicated but were not necessarily at the height of fashion. They are intended to provide a handy makeup guide rather than an exhaustive historical study. For such a study see *Fashions in Hair*, from which most of the drawings were taken.

Figure 18-7. Henry V and the Prince of Aragon. Hair styles fashionable at the beginning (A) and at the end (B) of the fifteenth century. In A the sideburns were blocked out with spirit gum, powder, creme stick, and cake makeup. In B the eyebrows were blocked out with spirit gum and derma wax. All highlighting and shadowing done with cake makeup. Both makeups are on the actor in Figure 1-1.

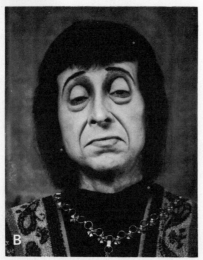

In referring to the drawings it is well to note the general style and basic silhouette of the period and adapt the characteristics of that style to the individual character. In any period it will be found that social class is reflected in the hair style as well as in the dress. When you see an elaborate hair style illustrated for past centuries (Plates 1*e*, 3*h*, 12*t*, 13*b*, 15*k-n-o-p*, and 16*a-c-d*, for example) you may be sure it was worn by a person of high social standing. Obviously, such styles would be out of place on peasants or servants. The simpler styles that require little time or care in dressing are naturally more appropriate for those people who have less interest in fashion and less time and money to indulge in it.

This does not mean that all simple styles (like those in Plates 3*o*, 8*n*, and 22*g*) are to be used for peasant classes only. Simple styles, as well as elaborate ones, may at times be fashionable.

Of course, social standing and adherence to fashion are not always synonymous. An emperor's wife may be a very simple person with simple tastes, and this will be reflected in her hair style. But chances are that her hair, though not fashionably styled, will be carefully dressed. The personality must always be considered. This is particularly true in our present society. One can no longer assume that women who work at ordinary jobs on a relatively low social level do not have the time or the money to spend on their hair. Elaborate hair styles may, in fact, be seen on sales clerks, whereas far simpler styles may be worn by women of fashion. It is largely a matter of taste.

Age is also a factor. Sometimes older people will tend to dress their hair in a style that they have worn for many years and that may once have been fashionable. This is more true in the past than in the present, and of course it does not apply to older women who are fashion-conscious. However, even if older women do follow the fashion of the moment, they do not always adopt the extremes of that fashion, which are designed primarily for younger women. As with the rest of the makeup, you should exercise your own judgment in helping the actor to reveal the character.

With the plates of drawings in Appendix G there are included brief comments on each period, indicating general characteristics of the hair styles.

CONSTRUCTING THE WIG

When the wig has been designed, you must either buy or make a foundation and then attach

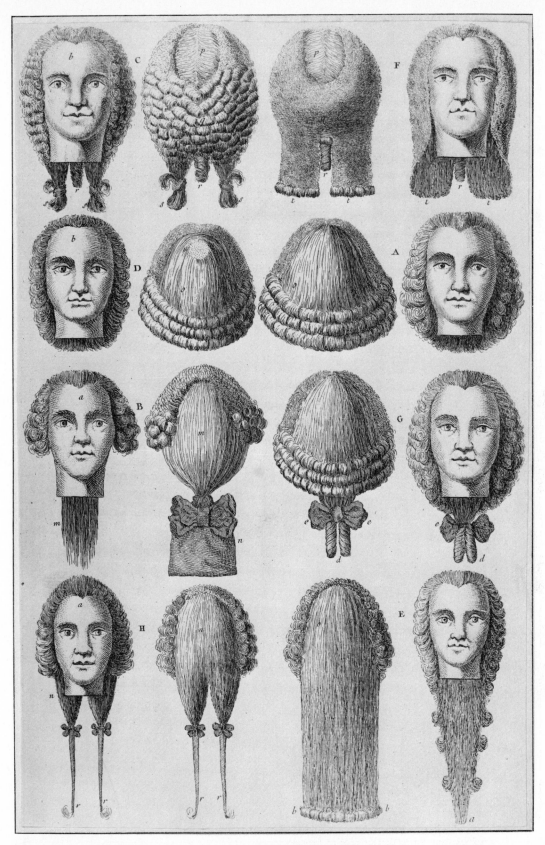

Figure 18-8. Eighteenth-century French wig styles. From Garsault's *Art du Perruquier,* 1767. (C) Knotted wig. (F) Square wig. (D) Abbot's wig. (A) Bob wig. (B) Bag wig. (G) Brigadier wig. (H) Pigtail wig. (E) Natural wig.

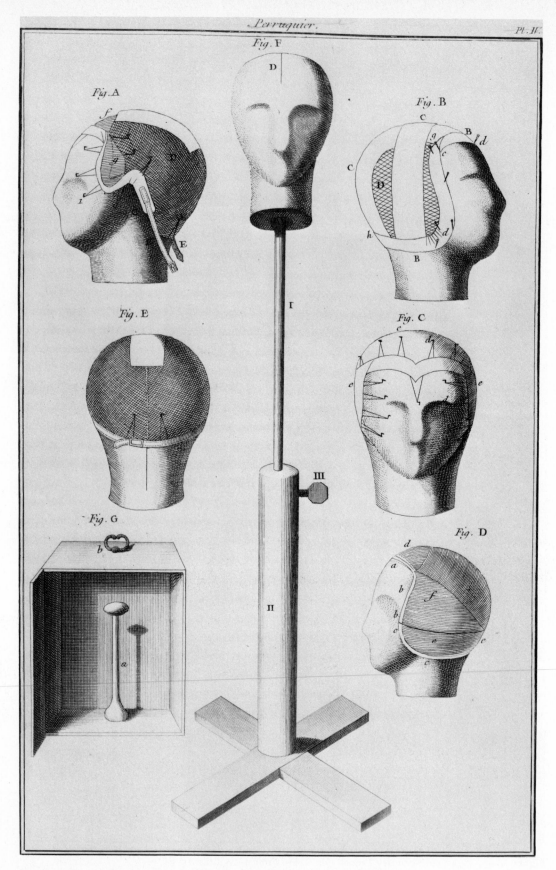

Figure 18-9. Eighteenth-century French wig blocks and foundations. In the lower left-hand corner is a wig carrying case. Garsault's *Art du Perruquier.*

the hair to the foundation. For a full wig you would do well to buy a net wig cap if it can be adapted to the type of wig you need. Such a cap is shown in Figure 18–10A. There are many types and qualities of net foundations, ranging from relatively inexpensive cotton ones, quite adequate for some types of wigs, to high quality, carefully constructed ones that fit better, look better, and are more comfortable. There are also elastic foundations for stretch wigs.

Most wigs, even those constructed on fairly simple foundations, have stays that hold the wig rather snugly to the head and an elastic at the nape of the neck to pull it tight. If the hair is to be combed back, revealing a natural-looking front hairline, a simple wig cap can't be used, at least in its original form. Individually fitted wigs with a natural hairline are expensive and require a much better quality foundation cap, as illustrated in the wig in process of construction, Figure 18–11B.

Most foundations are available in white, gray, black, brown, and sometimes various shades of blond or auburn. Choose the color nearest that of the hair you plan to use.

VENTILATING

The technique of ventilating a wig is the same as that for mustaches and beards (see Chapter 17). As with beards and mustaches, always begin with the hair that is to be underneath and finish with that which is to be on top. This means beginning at the nape of the neck and working upward toward the crown, as shown in Figure 18–11B. The wig block can be held in the lap, or it can be placed on a wig stand or holder with a tilt top and adjusted to a comfortable angle. (See Figure 18–10C,D).

As with beards, the hair can be mixed to a suitable basic color, but additional colors can be added as you ventilate—occasional hairs of another color to add interest, streaks of a different color, or a gradual lightening of the hair from the back to the front of the wig. For the latter effect you might want to mix two or more shades of hair and blend them as you ventilate. This blending of shades and making the wig lighter in front than in back is particularly effective with gray hair.

If the hair is to be combed back, you simply work forward, toward the front hairline, always pulling the hair toward the back of the wig. Brushing or combing it occasionally as you work will keep stray hairs from getting in your way. The amount of hair you use will depend entirely on how thick you want the hair to be. Ordinarily, it is desirable to keep the wig as light in weight as possible within the limits set by the effect you are trying to achieve. The hair can be knotted into the binding tapes as well as through the net.

When you approach the front hairline, use a smaller needle, and space your hair closer and very evenly. It is, in fact, usually a good idea to stop a half inch to an inch from the front edge, turn the wig block around, and work the hair from the opposite direction, beginning at the edge and letting the hair hang down as if over the face. When you

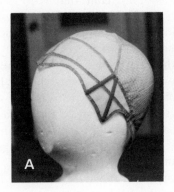
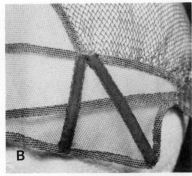
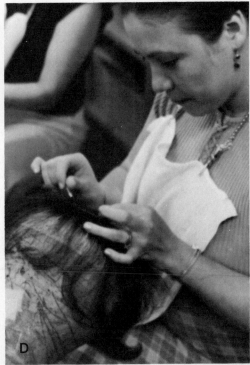
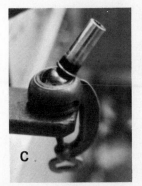

Figure 18-10. Constructing the wig. (A) Wig foundation. (B) Detail of construction. (C) Adjustable wig-block holder. (D) Ventilating a wig. (Bob Kelly Wig Creations.)

reach the previous stopping place and all the hair is in, you can comb the front section back. It will then tend to stand up away from the forehead and make the hairline somewhat less obvious. Be sure that in ventilating along the front edge you catch the needle under the edge sufficiently so that when the wig is finished, none of the binding tape will show. If necessary, you can turn the wig inside out later and add a few hairs at the hairline.

If the hair is to be combed away from the crown in all directions—as it is in styles *b, c, e,* and a majority of the others in Plate 7—you will proceed from the outer edges of the cap upward in an ever-narrowing circle so that the final hairs are knotted in at the crown. Always ventilate the hair in the direction in which it is to lie except when you deliberately reverse direction in order to make the hair stand up rather than lie flat. This should be kept in mind as you work.

WEAVING

A simple wig, such as the one just described, can be made much more quickly and easily by sewing on rows of weft, particularly across the back,

Figure 18-11. Wig construction. (A) Drawing mats with hair; (B) wig foundation in first stages of ventilating. (Bob Kelly Wig Creations.) (C) Weft.

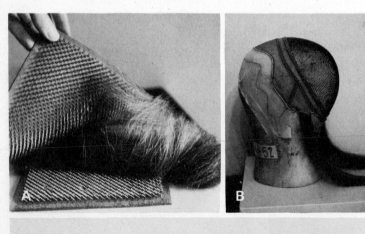

and ventilating only the front section. In fact, the entire wig can be made in this way provided the hair is to be combed back, but a much better hairline can be achieved by ventilating the front of the wig. The weft (which is made of lengths of hair woven on two, three, or four silk strands) is sewn to the wig cap, starting at the back and moving forward over the top of the head. The lengths of weft are usually about an inch apart but may be more or less. The closer they are, the heavier the hair will be. If they are too far apart, the foundation may show through. A wig made of weft is heavier to wear and much less versatile since the style of the wig can be changed very little, whereas a ventilated wig is extremely light to wear and can be recombed in many ways.

Figure 18–12 illustrates the technique for making weft. A table or bench with an overlapping edge is necessary. Two weaving sticks are clamped to it, as shown in A. You can buy weaving sticks and clamps, or you can rig up your own. The essential elements are the three threads tied as shown. For fine weft, silk is used; but any heavy, strong thread, fishline, or very light cord will do. The threads or cords should be as strong as possible without being bulky.

If you are sufficiently serious about wigmaking to be weaving hair, you should have a pair of drawing brushes or mats. The brushes have short stiff bristles. The mats, which are preferable for knotting and weaving, are made of two rectangles of tough leather into which are inserted short wires, all bent down parallel to the mat in the same direction (Figure 18–11a). Hair that is to be woven is placed on one of the mats with the ends of the bent wires pointing toward the points (not the roots) of the hair. The root ends protrude slightly over the mat. The other mat is laid on top of the first one, wire side downward. The roots should be on the side of the mats facing the weaver and extending just enough so that they can be easily grasped. The amount of hair extending beyond the other side of the mats will depend entirely on the length of hair being used and is immaterial.

The purpose of the mats is to make it possible to draw from the hank as many hairs as you wish without disturbing the remainder of the hair. Drawing mats should ideally be used in knotting as well as weaving. They have not been mentioned before since the additional equipment makes the process seem more complicated and more expensive, and it is possible to manage without them.

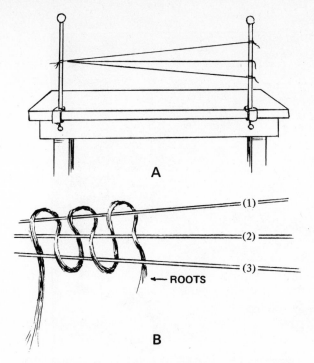

Figure 18-12. Weaving hair. (A) Weaving sticks attached to table top. (B) Threading the hair.

To weave, follow this procedure:

A. Draw a strand of hair from the braid (the more hairs you use, the heavier the weft will be), and hold it in your left hand with the root ends protruding upward.

B. Then, holding the strand of hair behind the threads, reach with the forefinger of your right hand between threads 2 and 3 (Figure 18–12B), and pull the hair through and up over the top of 1.

C. Reach between 1 and 2; grasp the hair; pull it forward (toward you, that is) between 1 and 2.

D. Reach between 1 and 2 and grasp the hair from behind. Pull it away from you under 3, then forward between 1 and 2, and back over the top of 1.

E. Reach between 1 and 2 and grasp the hair. Pull it forward between 1 and 2.

F. Reach between 1 and 2 and pull the hair under 3, away from you, and up and out toward you between 1 and 2, then over the top.

G. Reach between 1 and 2, and pull the hair forward.

H. From behind, reach forward between 2 and 3 and pull the hair back.

I. Now, holding both ends of the hair, pull it close together and tight so that it seems to be hanging from a little knot. The root ends of the hair should be short—not much more than an inch hanging down. The other end will, of course, be long.

Keep repeating this process, each time pushing the hair to the left and making sure it is as tight as you can make it. When you have the necessary length, cut the threads and tie both ends securely.

Then the weft is ready to sew onto the wig foundation. There are a number of methods of weaving (see the eighteenth-century engraving, Figure 18–13E,A,F,B,C,D), but this is one of the most common ones for making weft to be used in wigs. The technique is not nearly so complicated as it appears, and a little practice will make it possible to weave very quickly.

MIXING HAIR

You will usually do well to mix two or more colors of hair to achieve a natural look. This requires the use of a hackle (or card), which is a wooden block with numerous sharp, steel spikes projecting from it. The spikes may be either vertical or slightly angled. The design of the hackle has changed very little since the eighteenth century (see Figure 18–14K). In using the hackle, you will need to secure it to a bench or a table with clamps.

Straight hair is more easily mixed than curly. In mixing, grasp in one hand the root ends of the two hanks of hair to be mixed. Then slap the hair down onto the hackle and pull it through, mixing the two hanks with both hands as you pull. Keep repeating this process until the two colors are thoroughly blended. If you wish to add a third color, follow the same procedure. If you are not sure how much of a second color you wish to add to the first, blend in a little at a time. The purpose of the hackle in this blending process is simply to keep the hair from tangling. Hair that is already tangled can be drawn through the hackle for untangling.

REMODELING THE WIG CAP

It is always best, of course, to buy a wig foundation suitable for the wig you're making, but if this is impractical, you may be able to remodel one that you have. If you want a natural hairline, for example, the simple ready-made wig cap can still be used by cutting off the front portion and replacing it with hairlace or nylon net. (On the foundation in Figure 18–10A, you might remove everything up to the second tape.) As with beards and mustaches, a paper pattern of the desired hairline should be made first, then pinned to the wig block under the lace. Remember that the lace should extend at least 1/2 inch beyond the hairline, preferably more. It can be trimmed later, if you wish. The smallest ventilating needle, which pulls out just

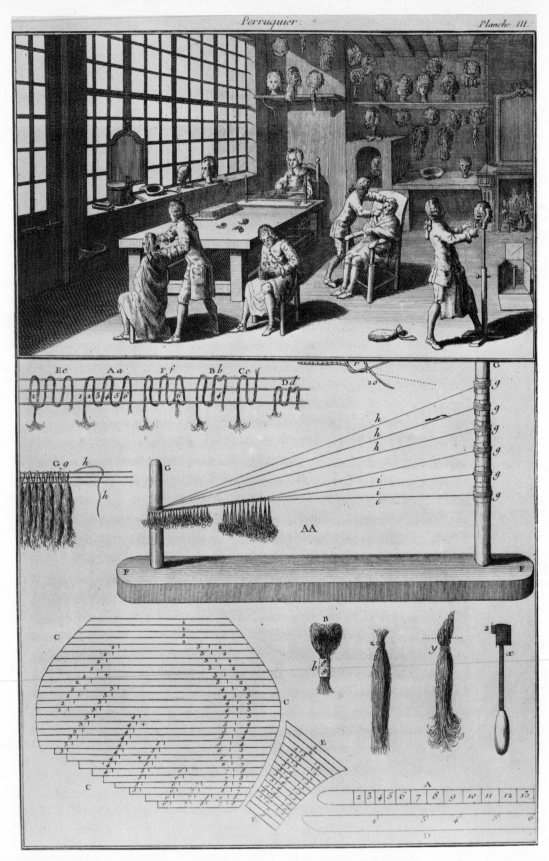

Figure 18-13. Eighteenth-century wig shop. Method of weaving hair shown
below. Diagram lower left is a white paper marked to indicate arrangement
of hair on the wig. Garsault's *Art du Perruquier*.

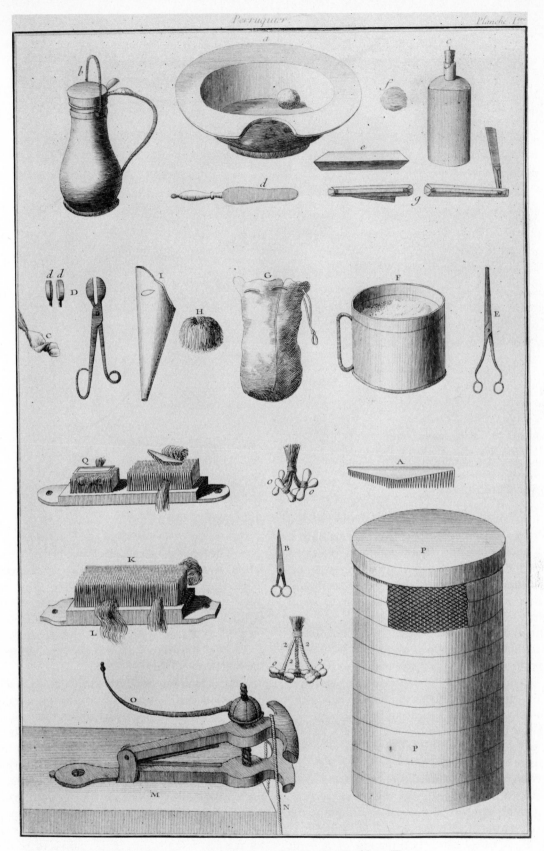

Figure 18-14. Eighteenth-century wigmaker's tools. (K, Q) Hackles. (F) Powder. (G) Powder bag. (H) Powder puff. (I) Powder cone. (C) Curl paper. (*g*) Razors. (*a*) Barber's basin. (MNO) Machine for binding pigtails. Garsault's *Art du Perruquier*.

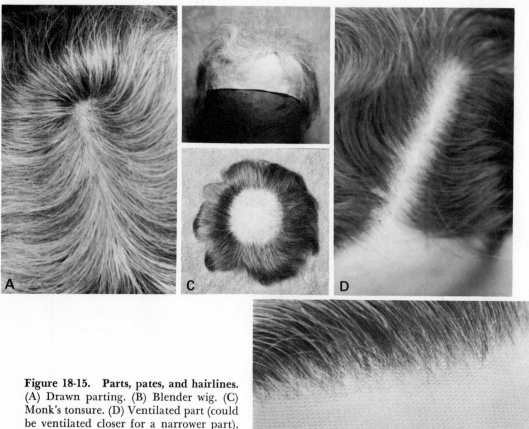

Figure 18-15. Parts, pates, and hairlines.
(A) Drawn parting. (B) Blender wig. (C)
Monk's tonsure. (D) Ventilated part (could
be ventilated closer for a narrower part).
(E) Ventilated hairline.

one hair at a time, should be used for the last few rows along the front edge if you expect to have a natural-looking hairline. If you use more than one hair at a time, the knots are likely to show. As before, you may ventilate either forward or backward, depending on whether you wish the hair to stand up slightly or lie flat.

It may sometimes be necessary to remove more of the foundation than just the front section. If you need to go farther back, you may have to resew one of the tapes so that the cap will hold its shape. When the hair is all in, trim the lace or net at the front, no closer than ½ inch from the hairline.

If you need a part in the wig, insert a section of silk gauze about an inch wide and of whatever length is necessary at the spot where you wish the part. Then ventilate toward the part from each side, using a 1-hair needle on the gauze section. Tapes should be sewn on around the edges of the section of gauze to give firmness. The gauze part will, in most cases, be a continuation of a front section of lace at the hairline. If the wig is to be used over a bald head, nylon net can be used instead of gauze so that the skin will show through, as in Figure 18–15D.

BLENDERS

These are constructed of a tightly woven, thin fabric that can be covered with greasepaint to match the foundation color on the skin. Several different fabrics are used. A high-grade shirting is satisfactory, or silk gauze (see Appendix A) can be used. Whatever your fabric, the selvage and not a raw edge must cross the forehead and be used for the blend. (See Figure 18–15B.)

It is simplest to start with a ready-made wig foundation and remove the front and as much of the top as necessary, the exact amount depending on how far back the new hairline is to go. The blender, which is attached to the side pieces of the wig foundation, must fit very tightly across the forehead. Be particularly careful at the temples to prevent wrinkling, which, of course, would ruin the entire effect. The hair is ventilated into the gauze or shirting in the usual way, using a 1-hair needle for the first few rows or, if the hair is to be thin on top, for a number of rows. A good blender wig must be very carefully fitted to be successful, and the snug fit across the forehead is essential (see Figure 19–4).

Hair and Wigs / 209

A more satisfactory blend can be achieved by using a head band or a cap (see below) of plastic or latex under a lace-front wig (see Figure 21–1). The plastic or latex will cover any natural hair that is to be concealed, and the false hairline can be made as receding as you like. The lace can be glued to the plastic (or latex), which has a much thinner edge than the fabric blender and is thus easier to blend.

BALD WIGS

The most satisfactory method of constructing a bald wig is to make or buy a snug plastic (Figure 18–19) or latex cap (see Chapter 16) and attach the necessary hair (real, synthetic, or crepe) with latex or spirit gum. But it would be advisable to ventilate the top few rows of sparse hair into the cap for a more realistic effect. Or all of the hair can be ventilated instead of being glued on. However, gluing ventilated pieces to the cap is quicker and easier than ventilating all of the hair into the cap and is preferable to gluing hairs directly to the cap.

If hair is to be ventilated into a thin plastic cap, there should be a base of woven nylon (a nylon stocking works very well) under the plastic. There are two ways in which this can be done. Either way, the first step is to stretch a nylon stocking over a plastic head (Figure 18–16). Then you can paint the nylon with at least three coats of liquid plastic (Figure 18–17), or you can slip a thin plastic cap (Figure 18–19) over the nylon. In painting the plastic over the nylon, be sure to extend it beyond the nylon to provide a thin blending edge. In using the plastic cap over the nylon, the nylon can be trimmed later, leaving the plastic cap extending beyond the nylon. The third step (Figure 18–18) is to ventilate into the plastic and nylon, whether

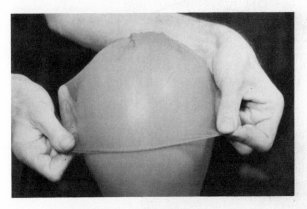

Figure 18-16. Fitting nylon stocking over plastic head form.

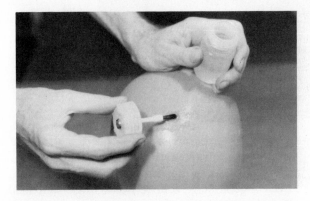

Figure 18-17. Coating stocking with liquid plastic.

Figure 18-18. Ventilating hair into the nylon and plastic.

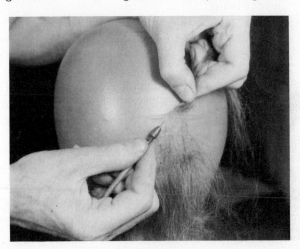

Figure 18-19. Plastic cap on the special plastic head form on which it was made. Cap can be trimmed to fit when used.

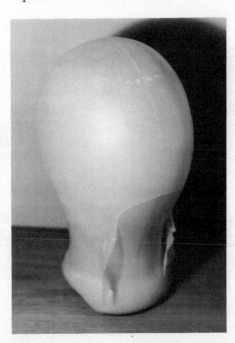

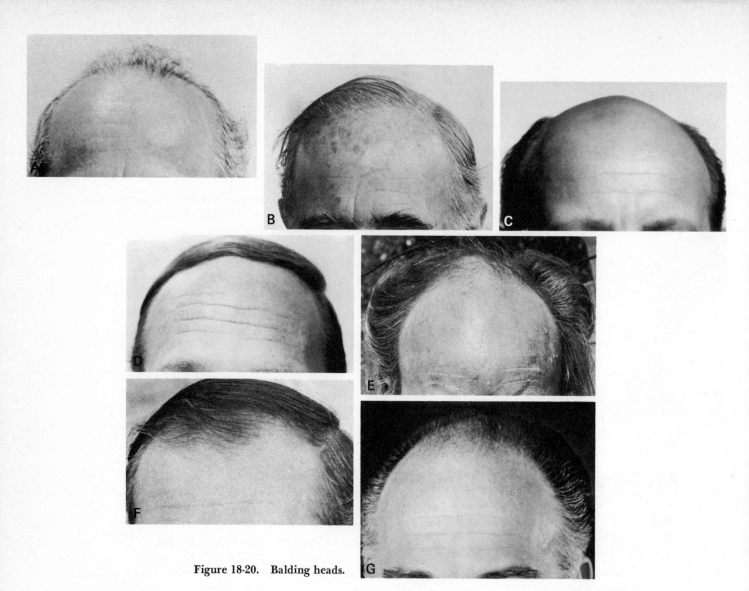

Figure 18-20. Balding heads.

they are bonded together or not. The plastic cap is particularly effective because the front edge can be dissolved with acetone to make a virtually undetectable blend. (See also *Soaping out the hair,* earlier in this chapter.)

TOUPEES AND SIDEBURNS

A toupee is usually constructed of a silk gauze piece, bound with tape slightly larger than the bald spot it is intended to cover. Toupees with the hairline showing should have a lace front and, if there is to be a part, a lace insert for the parting. Toupees made without the lace front but with the hair combed back usually look exactly like toupees. They are less expensive to have made and far simpler to put on and take off, and they last much longer; but they seldom fool anybody. A good toupee requires a lace front unless the hair is to be combed in such a way that the hairline is concealed.

Making a convincing toupee for street wear is a job requiring both skill and experience and should usually be done by professional wigmakers. Even a good stage toupee needs to be well made. But there are occasions when a satisfactory hairpiece (usually a small one) can be made by an actor or a makeup artist who has reasonable proficiency in ventilating.

In Figure 19–1, for example, we see an actor who is to be made up as Woodrow Wilson. Obviously his top hair is too sparse to be recombed in any way that would prove adequate. Therefore, a small hairpiece was made on nylon net (Figures 19–1,2). Since the hair was combed forward and only a fraction of an inch of the lace showed, great skill in wigmaking was not required. Sometimes a pointed tuft of hair—a sort of widow's peak—is needed to change the actor's hairline. That can easily be made on lace in a few minutes. The technique is the same as for beards and mustaches. First draw the new hairline on the skin with eyebrow pencil, trace and cut a paper pattern and place the hairlace or nylon net over it on the wig block, leaving the usual ½ inch or more for pasting down. Then, carefully selecting hair to match the color of the actor's own, work the hair with a small needle.

It is often necessary to conceal sharply cut sideburns, and this can easily be done with two small hairpieces with hair long enough to brush back over or behind the actor's ears and into his own hair. If his hair is long enough, these hairpieces will sometimes suffice. If not, he may need to combine the hairpieces with a fall pinned under his own hair in back. In Plate 9*v-w*, we can see hair styles that might require this treatment.

Again a pattern is made and the net placed over it on the block. The new side hair may follow the actor's natural hairline, or it may extend farther onto the face.

As is always the case in making a natural looking hairline with dark hair, it is helpful to make the last row of a lighter shade of hair, partly to soften the line and partly to avoid having a row of dark knots, which spoil the naturalness of the effect.

FALLS

Falls, as indicated earlier, are hairpieces used to lengthen the back hair while using the natural hair in front. This avoids the problem of creating a natural front hairline or of concealing the blender or the lace. Since the fall does not have a delicate lace edge, it will last far longer than a wig.

The fall can take many forms, depending on the use to which it is to be put. For a cascade of curls for women, it can be constructed of weft in a sort of basket weave—that is, the rows of weft are laid out diagonally, about 1 inch apart, sewed together where they cross, and stiffened with fine wire to give more body to the foundation. Usually, small loops are formed across the top of the piece for pinning to the natural hair, or small combs can be sewn into the piece for attaching it. The fall is then attached and the front and top hair combed back over the join and blended with the false hair, as in Figure 18–21. If the fall takes the form of a mass of curls, it is not always necessary to comb the natural hair into it—it can be pinned on top of the natural hair. (See Plate 19*m*.)

The fall may also take the form of a Juliet cap, with the front band across the top of the head from ear to ear (Figure 18–24, #3) and the bottom band around the nape of the neck. It is then constructed like the top and back of a wig. This is particularly useful for men or for women with short hair. In constructing such a piece, remember that the front of the fall must lie flat and not be too heavy.

An even smoother, flatter edge can be achieved by using a net front instead of the tape. A heavier, sturdier net can be used than would be suitable for blending at the forehead. In either case it will be necessary to pin the fall securely to the hair and then comb the natural front hair over and into it to make a perfect blend.

If the actor has very short hair and there is not time for the side hair to grow over the ears, it is possible either to add separate side pieces on lace (see preceding section on sideburns) or to make such pieces part of the fall itself. If this is done, the side pieces, when glued to the skin, serve as additional support to hold the fall in place.

The hair in a fall can be of any length and can be dressed and redressed in any style. Since it is to be blended with the actor's own hair, it should be made from real hair or a convincing synthetic. It can be constructed entirely of weft, entirely ventilated, or a combination of the two.

Figure 18–22 illustrates the traditional tech-

Figure 18-21. Philip IV. Based on Velásquez portrait. Cake makeup with putty nose. Eyebrows partially blocked out with spirit gum and putty wax. Crepe hair mustache. Natural front hair with fall. Makeup by student Larry Liles.

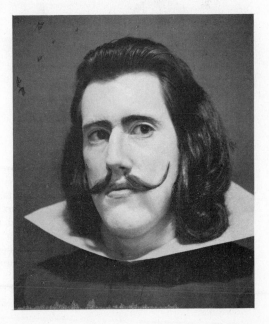

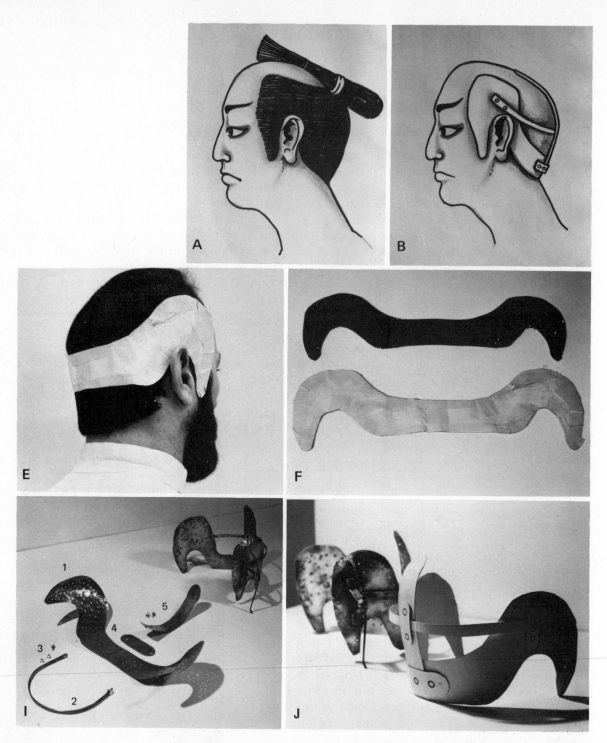

Figure 18-22. Constructing the foundation for a Kabuki wig. (A) Design for Samurai wig. (B) Design for copper under-construction, over which hair is attached. (C) Finished wig. (D) Inside view of wig. Note tip of stretcher protruding at bottom. (E) Paper pattern of main part of the foundation, fitted to the actor's head. (F) Paper pattern and piece of copper sheeting cut from it. (G) Piercing copper piece with awl to provide holes for attaching hair, which is tied and glued to the frame. (H) Three stages of basic frame piece—(1) original cutout, (2) copper piece pierced, (3) piece beaten with ping hammer to fit the individual actor's head. (I) Finished wig frame with parts from which it is constructed—(1) basic shaped piece, (2) spring steel band, which is shaped to fit over the basic piece and serves as a clamp

212

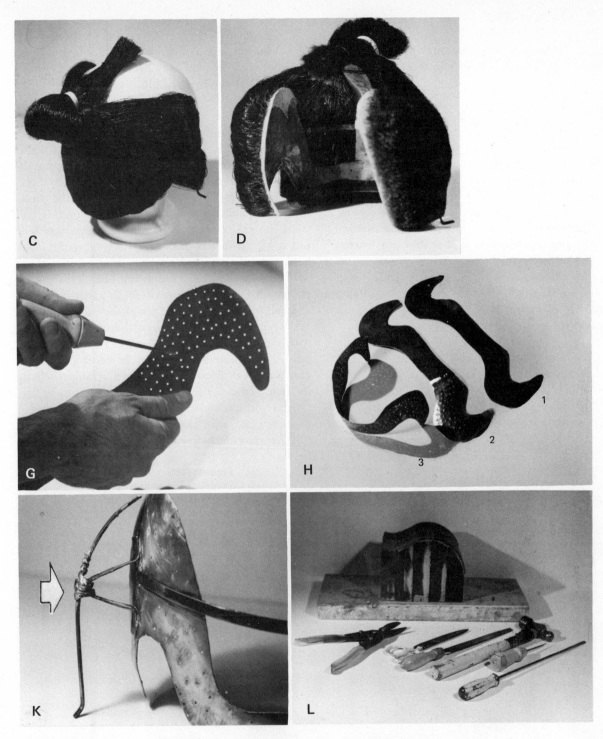

to hold on the base, (3) rivets used in assembling frame, (4) back piece, which fits the back of the head, helping stabilize the finished wig, and which is used for attaching the topknot, (5) small copper piece to hold back piece and steel spring together, allowing spring band to ride freely behind back piece. (J) Paper model of wig base, with finished copper base behind it. (K) Left side of completed wig base, showing stretcher (indicated by arrow), which gives fullness to the sides of the wig after hair is glued in front and pulled over it. (L) Tools used in making copper wig base, with leather-covered wooden shaping block in rear. (Drawings and wig construction by Bill Smith. Photographs by Ray Bingham.)

213

nique, which is still used, for making the copper foundation for a Japanese Kabuki wig.

DRESSING THE WIG

Whether you have made your own wig or rented or bought a good one, its effectiveness will depend to a great extent on how skillfully it is dressed. If a rented wig doesn't look the way you want it to, you may be able to change the styling. Cheap mohair wigs on buckram cannot be changed and are usually a waste of money, but any human hair wig or good (not necessarily expensive) synthetic one can be redressed, at least within the limits imposed by its particular construction. Although a rented wig must not be cut or damaged, there is no reason for its not being redressed.

The first step in dressing any wig is to pin or tack it to your wig block and brush and comb it out thoroughly. Bear in mind previous instructions for holding the comb in working with wigs or beards. If a very simple style is required and you are pressed for time, you can curl the ends with an electric curling iron.

You can do a more thorough job, however, by combing the hair with water until it is quite wet, then putting it up in pin curls (Figure 18–23E) or on rollers (18–23D). For those who do not already know—pin curls are made by forming a flat coil from a strand of hair and pinning it down flat to the head with a hairpin or a bobby pin. All pin curls in one row are usually coiled in the same direction though they may be coiled in opposite directions on either side of a part. Frequently the direction of the coil is reversed in alternate rows. If you want the entire head of hair to be wavy, you will put it all up in flat pin curls, starting at the front hairline and moving back and down. Often there will be some natural wave in the hair. This can be encouraged with a damp comb, and the hair may need no further curling except at the ends.

When the pin curls are thoroughly dry (the drying can be forced with a hair dryer), comb them out. A little hair dressing may be necessary to provide a natural, healthy sheen. Then arrange the hair in waves, curls, or puffs, combing it section by section as you go, and securing it with hairpins when necessary. Be sure the hairpins are inserted carefully so that they do not show. A rat-tail comb is

Figure 18-23. Dressing the wig. (A, B) Ventilated wig, dressed. (C) Inside of wig above. (D) Wig in rollers. (E) Wig in pin curls.

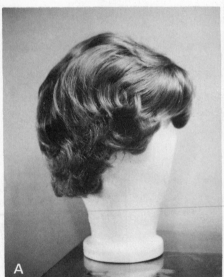
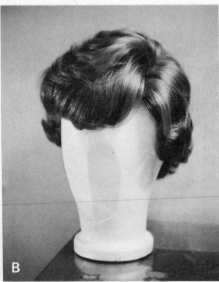
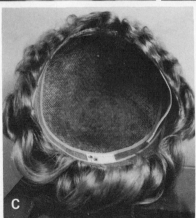

often helpful in making rolls or curls. A hair lacquer spray may be used to set the hair after it has been dressed. The basic technique for dressing a wig is extremely simple, depending on the skill you have or can develop in handling hair.

WEARING THE WIG

Wigs must be handled carefully if they are to keep their shape and fit snugly. In putting on any full wig, grasp the lower back edge of the wig foundation with both hands, slide it up over the forehead until the hairline approaches within an inch or two of its proper position, then pull the wig down snugly over the head. Then with both hands resting on the wig move it back still further till the hairline is in the correct position. If the actor's own hair is long, it should be pulled up toward the top of the head first and pinned flat. A wide band around the head is frequently helpful in making sure that no stray hairs escape. (Figure 19–5C shows a wig being put on.)

To remove the wig, grasp the back edge with both hands, and pull up and forward. *Never remove the wig by pulling on the hair.*

If the wig or toupee has a hairlace front, the procedure is the same as for applying beards on lace (see Chapter 17). Always paste down the lace edge to the dry skin before makeup is applied. In removing any hairpiece with a lace edge, always dissolve the spirit gum with spirit gum remover until the lace comes away from the skin naturally. Never pull the lace off the skin.

If the wig has a blender, it should be put on in the same way, making sure that the blender covers the natural hairline and that it fits snugly against the skin. It should be pasted down with spirit gum. You may then wish to stipple the edge of the blender at the line where it meets the skin with latex cream adhesive. This can be done with the tube itself, dotting the edge so that the adhesive overlaps both blender and skin. This will help break the line across the forehead. The stippling must be done when the skin is clean and dry and before any makeup has been applied. If the blender is too thick at the edge to be concealed by the adhesive, a small amount of derma wax or putty-wax (see Chapter 15) can be used as a filler. The skin should be coated with spirit gum and allowed to dry before the wax is applied. The wax can be coated with sealer and the makeup applied when the sealer is dry.

The filling in with wax should be done only if there is no alternative. If the blender is well made in the first place and the edge is kept clean, it will be thin enough to be concealed with adhesive and paint or, if you prefer, with paint alone. The secret of concealing the line is, first, to match the color of the blender perfectly to the color on the skin, bearing in mind that a given color of paint will not necessarily look the same on the fabric of the blender as it does on the skin. Second, it is essential to make up the blender as if it were the real forehead, with the usual shadows and highlights and wrinkles. Ordinarily it should become lighter as it approaches the hairline, at least if the hairline is a receding one. Third, the area in which the blender joins the skin should be so broken up with color that the line is lost. Shadows at the temples and highlights on the superciliary arch make a good start. A stippling technique (see Chapters 12 and 14) is almost essential. Ordinarily, grease or creme makeup should be used rather than cake when a blender is to be concealed (see Figure 19–5D). Using a plastic strap or cap, as suggested earlier, will simplify the problem of concealment.

When you remove the wig, it is not necessary to clean the entire blender each time, but you should clean the edge carefully and thoroughly with acetone. Any accumulation of adhesive and makeup will render a good blend impossible.

Toupees may or may not have a lace front. If they do, the lace is attached with spirit gum; if they do not, the front is attached with toupee tape (Appendix A). The back can be attached to the scalp with tape or to the hair in back of the crown with a French clip, which can be sewn onto the underside of the toupee.

In putting on a toupee with a lace front, place the toupee in position, then attach the lace front to the skin with spirit gum, being extremely careful to avoid corrugations in the lace. After pressing the gum dry, grasp the back edge of the toupee and gently but firmly pull it back so that it hugs the head, then press down, thus sticking the toupee tape to the skin. If a French clip is being used, it can be attached to a strand of hair about an inch wide. Since the clip makes a slight bump under the toupee (not noticeable except to the touch) and since the clip pulling on the hair may be slightly uncomfortable, the tape is preferable.

In removing the toupee, always soak the lace with spirit gum remover until it loosens, then clean it thoroughly with acetone after it is removed. Toupees without lace fronts are easier to put on and take off and require less care, but they rarely look as convincing.

When a wig is properly dressed before being worn, it should require little or no rearranging after it is on. For subsequent wearings, however, it may require some recombing. Check the wig carefully before each performance for styling and condition of the hair and do whatever redressing is necessary.

CARE OF THE WIG

Good wigs are expensive and should be given painstaking care. Any elaborately dressed wig or any wig with a lace front should be kept on a wig block between performances. At other times it should be stuffed with tissue paper and stored in an individual box.

To be effective, wigs must be kept clean. This can best be done by dipping them into wig cleaner, benzine, or naphtha. Observe the usual precautions about adequate ventilation and open flames. This type of cleaning does not materially affect the wave in the hair.

It is also possible to clean wigs by dipping them up and down in a detergent solution, then rinsing, but this removes all the wave, results in a good bit of tangling no matter how carefully the

Figure 18-24. Diagram for wig and beard measurements. The heavy broken line represents wig measurements and the heavy dotted one, measurements for a beard.

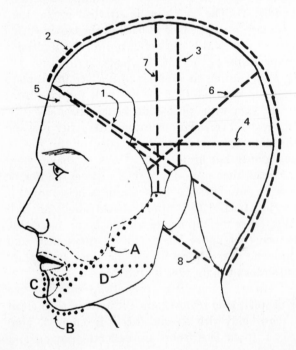

dipping is done, and is not recommended to the inexperienced. Never under any circumstances shampoo a human-hair wig. Any rubbing of the hair in water will result in hopeless matting and tangling, and the wig will be ruined.

RENTING OR BUYING WIGS

The usual means of obtaining wigs (other than making them) is to rent them if the play is to have only a few performances and to buy them if it is expected to have a longer run. Whether renting or buying, you should obtain a wig that looks good, even though it may be inexpensive. There are many synthetic stretch wigs to be had very reasonably (see Appendix A). Wigs made of mohair are available at very low cost, but they are seldom satisfactory for realistic plays.

It is not always possible to rent wigs with lace fronts, because they are too fragile and easily damaged. For the type of hairline ordinarily requiring a lace front, a blender is substituted.

In either renting or buying it is important, if ordering by mail, to send adequate measurements and to allow plenty of time for the wig to be dressed and sent through the mail. In some cases the wig will not be in stock and will have to be made up specially, in which case as much as three or four weeks' additional time may be required.

When possible it is preferable to buy a wig, unless it is a very special style which you are unlikely to use again. Buying the wig costs more for the particular play but saves money in the end—provided the wig is used for a number of subsequent productions.

For suggestions on where to obtain wigs, see Appendix A.

MEASURING FOR WIGS

If you are ordering a wig or a toupee, it is important to supply the wigmaker with accurate measurements. The numbers below refer to Figure 18–24, in which the heavy broken lines represent wig measurements. The first five measurements are the most important. The others are not always used.

1. Around the head (over the ears) from front hairline to nape of the neck and back. (The average measurement is 22 inches.)

2. From the front hairline to the nape of the neck over the top of the head. (The average measurement is 14 inches.)

3. From ear to ear over the top of the head. This is sometimes taken over the crown instead. (Average measurement, 12 inches.)

4. Temple to temple around the back of the head. (Average measurement, 16 inches.)

5. Ear to ear across the forehead at the hairline.

6. Sideburn to sideburn over crown. (Infrequently used.)

7. Bottom of sideburn to bottom of sideburn over top. (Infrequently used.)

8. Bottom of ear to bottom of ear around back of neck. (Infrequently used.)

If there is to be a part, be sure to indicate how many inches from the center and on which side. If the wig or toupee is being made, it is also important to include an exact outline of hair at the temples.

ADAPTING WIGS

Fortunately, it is not necessary to have a different wig for every different hair style. Any reasonably good wig can be redressed in various styles within the limitations set by its basic construction. The front hairline, the part or lack of one, and the length are crucial features. The color can be changed with sprays, though it is better to avoid this if possible. If the hair is too short, a fall or a switch can sometimes be added to give the necessary length.

Length and color aside, we can classify wigs generally into the following groups:

1. Hair combed forward, concealing the hairline, as in Appendix G, Plate *7b-c-d-e-f*. This is more often than not a male style. (See also Figures 5–3 and 18–7.)

2. Hair combed back, no parting, as in Plate 14*a-b-d-g* and Figures 17–14C, 17–5, 19–7, and 19–9. This ordinarily requires either a lace front or a blender except, for example, in the eighteenth-century styles that in many cases (though not all) represent wigs rather than real hair. Style *a* on Plate 14 is certainly a wig, but *n* is the natural hair.

3. Center part, as in Plate *6k-m-n-p-q*.

4. Side part, as in Plate 17*f-g-j-p*.

5. Blender front, necessitated by a receding hairline or a hairline farther back than that of the actor who is to use the wig. Styles shown in Plate 9*c-i-t*, for example, would very likely require blenders or plastic bands or caps. The hair may be combed as in 1, 2, 3,

or 4 above; but since blender wigs are not usually interchangeable with other types, they are listed separately.

6. Special styles, such as those with horizontal part (1*q*), double part (5*g*), or tonsure (5*p* and Figure 18–15C).

On the basis of this breakdown of types of wigs, it will be clear that many of the styles shown in the plates can with a little ingenuity and the use of supplementary falls and switches be achieved with a relatively small numbers of wigs. It is obvious, for example, that Plates 2*b-e*, 5*e-i-m*, and 9*a-d* could be approximated with nothing more than a simple redressing of a single wig of type 1. Among the wigs with partings there are, perhaps, even more possibilities.

It must not be assumed, however, that *every* center-part style or *every* forward-combed style, for example, can be made from one specific center part or forward-combed wig with just the addition of hair. There are other elements that must be considered such as, for example, the thickness of the hair. Although sparse hair can be fluffed up somewhat and heavy hair can be sleeked down, the possibilities are not unlimited. But they are much greater than one would suspect at first glance. If you are working with a limited budget, adapting wigs to various styles is an important part of the makeup work. For one who is able to dress a wig skillfully, the problem of adapting it requires only a little additional ingenuity.

Learning to design hair styles and dress and care for wigs is as important a part of the makeup process as learning to make a good wrinkle. If you also know how to construct wigs, so much the better. In the professional theater, actors are not usually expected to design or to dress their own wigs, but they are sometimes expected to care for them and keep them looking fresh. Professional makeup artists need to have a thorough knowledge of wigs, but they do not have to make them and do not always have to dress them. In the nonprofessional theater, however, both actors and makeup artists need to acquire as many skills as possible, and every conceivable device may need to be used to keep expenses down. A thorough knowledge of how to deal with hair, real or false, will not only contribute greatly to the effectiveness of the makeup, but it can also help trim a significant part of the makeup budget. Whether for budgetary reasons or for lack of knowledge, the hair is far too often a sadly neglected part of the makeup, and yet it is frequently one of the simplest, most important, and most effective means we have of helping the actor become the character.

PROBLEMS

1. If you have the appropriate wigs available, make yourself up as two or three of the following:

Lady Sneerwell, Lady Teazle, Mrs. Candour, Maria *(The School for Scandal)*; Mrs. Malaprop *(The Rivals)*; Lady Wishfort, Mrs. Millament *(The Way of the World)*; Polly Peachum, Lucy Locket *(The Beggar's Opera)*; Mrs. Hardcastle *(She Stoops to Conquer)*; Cleopatra, Ftatateeta *(Caesar and Cleopatra)*.

Snake, Sir Peter Teazle, Sir Oliver Surface, Sir Benjamin Backbite *(The School for Scandal)*; Dauphin, Archbishop of Rheims, Earl of Warwick *(St. Joan)*; Tetzel, Staupitz, Lucas, Knight *(Luther)*; Sir Fopling Flutter, Dorimant *(The Man of Mode)*; Sir Novelty Fashion, Sir Tunbelly Clumsey *(The Relapse)*; Mirabell, Petulant *(The Way of the World)*; Richard III.

19

CREATING A LIKENESS

For most makeups we have considerable latitude in our choice of details—the height of the forehead, the line of the mouth, the shape of the nose. But in recreating real people whose faces are well known we are obligated to achieve as accurate a likeness as possible.

We begin by comparing the face of the character with that of the actor who is to portray him, noting points of difference and of similarity. The analysis should include shape of the face; shape, length, and color of the hair and the beard; color of the skin and the eyes; and precise conformation of individual features. The points of similarity can be emphasized and the differences minimized. If the actor's nose is too small, it can be enlarged and reshaped with putty. If it is too large, it can be shadowed to make it seem less large and attention can be drawn to other features. Wigs, beards, and spectacles can be enormously helpful.

An excellent way of training yourself to observe details and to reproduce them is to copy portraits. Photographs, with their myriad of details, may prove less useful to the beginner than works of art (paintings, drawings, engravings) with their simplifications and their emphasis on significant features. In using these artists' representations, however, you should keep in mind that your objective, except when you are deliberately working with stylization, is to achieve a realistic, believable makeup. It should be your purpose to recreate in three dimensions the artist's subject, not to reproduce his technique. Whereas the artist is permitted to show brush marks and to use a cross-hatching of lines to represent shadows, the makeup artist is permitted no such license. You may also have to make certain compromises in minor features that cannot reasonably be duplicated on the actor's face. But a good likeness can usually be achieved in spite of inevitable minor variations from the original.

WOODROW WILSON

Let us consider step by step the creation of the makeup for Woodrow Wilson shown in Figure 19–2. It is apparent at a glance that the actor (Mr. Wilson Brooks, Figure 19–1) has a bone structure lending itself easily to the makeup. Since President Wilson's face was wider, Mr. Brooks' hair was puffed out a little at the sides to increase the apparent width of the head, and a small ventilated hairpiece on nylon net was used to match Wilson's hair style. Observe carefully the following relatively minor but extremely important changes in individual features:

1. Wilson's eyes have a heavy-lidded effect caused by sagging flesh that actually conceals the upper lid completely when the eye is open. For this makeup a latex piece was used over the eye. The piece was made by the method described in Chapter 16. Since Wilson's eyebrows are straighter than Mr. Brooks', the latex was allowed to cover part of the inner end of each brow. The shape of the eyebrows is always important and should be copied as accurately as possible. In this case the inner ends were raised slightly, the brows darkened, and the point just beyond the center of each brow was exaggerated. Shadows under the eye were deepened with cake makeup.

2. The nostrils were highlighted, though this does not show in the photograph, and the nose was narrowed slightly by shadowing.

Figures 19-1 and 19-2.   Actor Wilson Brooks as Woodrow Wilson.

3. The shape of both upper and lower lips was altered slightly, and the lower lip was highlighted. Shadows at the corners of the mouth were deepened. Observe also the highlights and shadows just below the mouth.

4. A slight cleft in the chin was painted in with highlights and shadows.

5. Forehead wrinkles were accentuated with highlights and shadows. The superciliary arch was highlighted.

6. The cheekbones were brought out with highlights and shadows, and the nasolabial folds were deepened. Although the line of Mr. Brooks' folds is not quite the same as Wilson's, the difference has little effect on the likeness. An actor's own wrinkles, particularly the nasolabial folds, can be deepened or flattened out, shortened or lengthened; but if they are at all pronounced, the natural line should be followed. Otherwise, a smile will reveal that the real fold does not coincide with the painted one, and the credibility of the makeup will be destroyed.

7. The ears were made to stick out slightly with nose putty.

8. The final touch was added with a pair of pince-nez.

It was observed frequently during the makeup that very slight changes in the shape of the lips or the eyebrows, a shadow here, a highlight there, made considerable difference in the likeness. Since it is impossible to have every detail perfect, it is important to make the most of what the actor's face will permit. In most cases there are one or two characteristic features that help more than anything else to identify the character. Cartoonists use these features regularly to depict people in the news.

There are relatively few people in history with faces familiar enough to require extreme accuracy of detail. Wilson is one because, like Lincoln, his picture has been frequently reproduced. Although people have a general idea of what Marie Antoinette looked like, they won't be excessively critical of details, provided the overall effect is authentic.

MARK TWAIN

Actor Hal Holbrook (Figure 19–3), in his brilliant re-creation of Mark Twain, is as meticulous in his makeup as in his acting. No detail is too small or too unimportant to be given careful attention each time the makeup is applied. And for every performance he devotes more than three hours to perfecting these details. That his makeup takes so long is perhaps less significant than that he is willing to spend that amount of time doing it.

In discussing his problems of re-creating Mark Twain physically, Mr. Holbrook says: "The jaw formation is similar, and so is the cheekbone. My eyes have the *possibility*. His eyes had an eagle sort of look, but you can create that with makeup. And, of course, his nose was very distinctive—long and somewhat like a banana. Mine's too sharp. The nose alone takes an hour. I have a smooth face, and if I don't break it up, the texture is wrong. Also, I have to shrink three and one-half inches. Part of this is done by actual body shrinkage—relaxation all the way down as though I were suspended on a string from the top of the head. Part of it is illusion —the way the suit is made and the height of the furniture on stage. The coat is a little bit longer than it should be. There's a downward slope to the padded shoulders. There's a belly, too—not much of one, but it pulls me down. The lectern, the table, and the chair are built up a little higher."

Materials. The makeup is done with a combination of creme stick, grease stick liners, pencils, and powder. Three shades of creme stick are used— SF-5-c for the base, SF-3-b highlights, and SF-12-d shadows. Three grease sticks are also used—a deep brown, a maroon, and a rose. All three are used for shadows and accents and the red for additional pink color in the cheeks, on the forehead, eyelids, and ears, for example. There are also brown and maroon pencils for deep shadows.

Application. Except for the base and the first general application of creme stick shadows to the cheeks and eye sockets and sides of the nose, all of the makeup is done with brushes, most of them flat sables in various widths. The smaller wrinkles are done with 1/8-inch and 3/16-inch brushes and some of the larger areas with a 3/8-inch brush. The makeup is taken directly from the stick. The color is sometimes taken up from the two sticks and mixed on the brush; but more frequently, the various shades are applied separately, one after the other. Mr. Holbrook uses three shadow colors—the SF-12-d, the maroon, and the dark brown—and he sometimes adds a bit of rose to give the shadow more life.

All shadows and highlights, as can be observed in Figure 19–5A, are exaggerated since they are to be powdered down. If cake were being used instead of grease, this initial heightening would not be necessary. However, once one has determined what effect the powder will have, one way is as effective as the other. For the detailed brushwork used on this makeup (the whole makeup is approached almost as if it were a painting), the creme stick and grease method is probably easier. As always, choice of materials is a personal matter.

One of the greatest problems in making up youth for age is to eliminate expanses of smooth skin. It is at this point that otherwise technically competent makeups often fail. The problem has been solved in this case by covering the smooth expanses with wrinkles, puffiness, hollows, and sagging flesh. You will notice in the accompanying photographs, especially Figure 19–5D, that the entire face and neck (except for the forehead, which is concealed by the wig blender, and the upper lip, which will be concealed by a mustache) is almost completely covered with shadows and highlights. Very little of the original base color shows through.

After the makeup has reached approximately the stage shown in Figure 19–5B, the cheek area in front of the ears is stippled (using a small brush) with dots of maroon, rose, and the creme stick base. This is then softened somewhat with a clean 3/8-inch brush. When further toned down with powder, the effect, even in the dressing room, is remarkably realistic. (See Figure 19–4.)

After the stage shown in Figure 19–5B has been reached and that much of the makeup powdered, the lower part of the forehead, across the bottom of the sideburns to the ears, is covered with spirit gum, and the wig is put on in the usual way (Figure 19–5C). Ordinarily it is safer to put the wig on first, then apply the spirit gum underneath the blender, though with a very tight wig this may be difficult. Practice makes it possible, however, to

Figure 19-3. Actor Hal Holbrook as himself. *Chicago Tribune,* photo by John Austad.

Figure 19-4. Hal Holbrook as Mark Twain. *Chicago Tribune,* photo by John Austad.

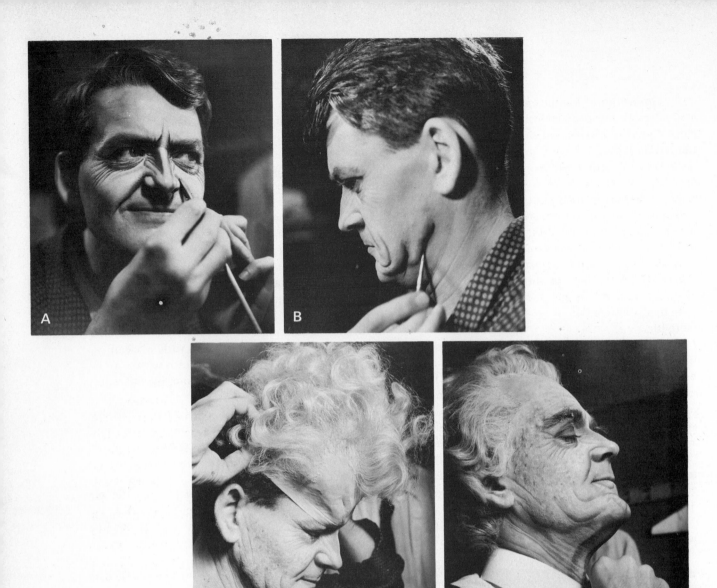

Figure 19-5. Steps in the makeup for Mark Twain. The makeup is done enitrely with paint, powder, and hair and requires 3 hours. *Chicago Tribune*, photo by John Austad.

apply the spirit gum in the right place and to put the wig on exactly right the first time so as to avoid the difficulties with the gum. The blender in this case extends down to the eyebrows.

The next problem, and a crucial one, is to adjust the blender perfectly so that there are no wrinkles, no air bubbles, nothing to destroy the illusion. This must be done quickly, before the spirit gum becomes too sticky. Again, it takes practice to know exactly how to adjust the blender and what sort of minor imperfections are likely to cause trouble later. Once the blender is perfectly adjusted, it is pressed hard with a towel all along the edge in order to stick it tight to the skin and to make it as smooth as possible. The blender is always cleaned with acetone after the performance to make sure the edge will be as thin as possible.

In concealing the edge of the blender, the creme stick base is applied to the blender somewhat irregularly with a ⅜-inch brush. Then the SF-12-d shadow is applied with a brush to the temples, crossing the edge of the blender. A little light red is worked spottily into either side of the frontal area, keeping away from the hairline. Wrinkles are then drawn on the blender with maroon and SF-12-d and highlighted with SF-3-b. Then the temples are stippled with maroon and rose and SF-5-c. This is a very important step, since it further helps to hide the blender line by breaking up the color in the area. (See Figure 19–5D.)

The eyebrows are made shaggy by sticking several tufts of gray hair with spirit gum into the natural brows. The mustache (ventilated on gauze) is attached with spirit gum, the hair is combed, and the makeup is completed. (See Figure 19–4.)

The preceding paragraphs about Mr. Holbrook's makeup were written for the third edition of *Stage Makeup*. It is interesting to note that by the time *Mark Twain Tonight* appeared on Broadway in 1966, Mr. Holbrook had made several changes in his makeup—notably, from a blender wig to one with a lace front (putting on the wig was far easier and the effect from the audience was the same) and in the use of sponges for stippling (as described in Chapter 12) instead of brushes. The effect was equally good though not quite the same. Whereas the sponge method took away the youthful smoothness of the skin, which then looked convincingly aged, the brush technique, giving equal age, suggested discolorations of the skin typical of old age. For Mr. Holbrook's television special in 1967 a three-dimensional makeup had to be created for Mark Twain using foamed latex (see Figure 21–1).

There are several lessons to be learned from Mr. Holbrook's makeup:

1. An effective makeup cannot be a hit or miss, last-minute rush job. It must be carefully planned and rehearsed. Any but the simplest sort of makeup may well require a certain amount of experimentation, sometimes a great deal. Even experienced makeup artists do careful research and planning on any makeup involving historical characters.

2. The makeup should be an integral part of the characterization. Mr. Holbrook over a period of years studied photographs and even an old film of Mark Twain, read everything he could find by or about him, and talked with people who had known or seen him. His makeup developed along with his performance and was not added as decoration before the first dress rehearsal.

3. It is important in making up to adapt the makeup to the actor's face. Mr. Holbrook does not duplicate a portrait of Mark Twain on his own face. As he makes up, he continually twists and turns and grimaces in order to make sure that every shadow or wrinkle he applies follows the natural conformations of his own face so that there is not the slightest chance that a passing movement or expression will reveal a painted wrinkle different from a real one.

4. One of the secrets of aging the youthful face is to concentrate on eradicating *all* signs of youth, including a smooth, youthful skin. This Mr. Holbrook has done. The numerous wrinkles in the Mark Twain makeup are less important individually than for their effect in breaking up smooth areas of skin with light and shade and color. Unwrinkled areas are textured with stippling. Mr. Holbrook has taken a definite, positive approach to every area of the face and has made sure that nothing remains to betray the actor beneath the makeup.

Since the remarkable recreation of Twain's likeness is essential to the effectiveness of the performance, Mr. Holbrook feels that he must cut no corners. And, significantly, he takes the attitude that even if the audience were unaware of any imperfections, *he* would know, and in his own mind the performance would suffer. This is an example of the dedicated artist to whom no amount of effort is too great or too tedious if it will in any way contribute to his performance.

STALIN AND TROTSKY

In designing the makeups for historical characters such as Stalin and Trotsky in Paddy Chayefsky's *The Passion of Josef D.*, it is helpful, as suggested in Chapter 10, to work from photographs of the actor. In doing character drawings from these photographs, one should be careful to do only that which can actually be done with makeup in the given situation. If, for example, the makeup has to be done quickly (as in the change from the young Stalin to the older one, shown in Figure 19–6), changes should be kept simple. Although it is not necessary, there is some advantage in doing a sketch of the actor as well as of the character. If you are able to draw well enough to make the sketch of the actor convincing, having both sketches for comparison, as in Figures 19–6 and 19–8, adds considerably to the effectiveness of the presentation in discussing the makeup with the director and the actor and in reassuring them that the transformation is feasible.

Two cautions should be given in connection with this method—be sure the photograph is a reasonably recent one, and use both front view and profile. If all your preliminary work is based on a firm jaw and a smooth skin, an unexpectedly wrinkled face with sagging muscles can be disastrous. Furthermore, a face that appears from the front reasonably easy to make into the likeness of a historical personage can present problems in profile.

Peter Falk as Stalin. The major elements in the change to the young Stalin were the mustache and the eyebrows. The mustache (real hair ventilated on lace) was a simple matter; the eyebrows were not. Whereas Mr. Falk's eyebrows were heavy

Peter Falk

Falk as Stalin, Acts I & II

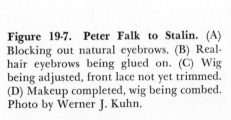
Act III

Figure 19-6. Final pencil sketches of Peter Falk as himself and as Josef Stalin. This is the first step in planning the makeup.

A

B

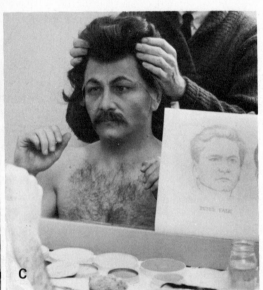
C

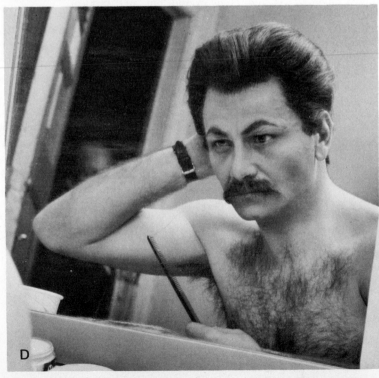
D

Figure 19-7. Peter Falk to Stalin. (A) Blocking out natural eyebrows. (B) Real-hair eyebrows being glued on. (C) Wig being adjusted, front lace not yet trimmed. (D) Makeup completed, wig being combed. Photo by Werner J. Kuhn.

Alvin Epstein

Epstein as Trotsky

Figure 19-8. Final pencil sketches of Alvin Epstein as himself and as Trotsky.

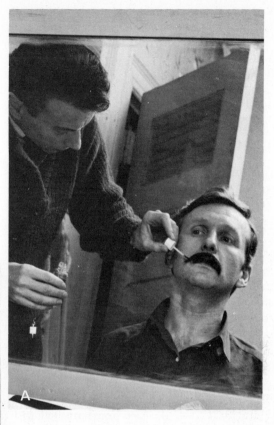

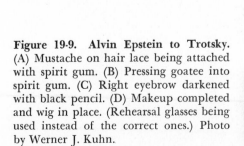

Figure 19-9. Alvin Epstein to Trotsky. (A) Mustache on hair lace being attached with spirit gum. (B) Pressing goatee into spirit gum. (C) Right eyebrow darkened with black pencil. (D) Makeup completed and wig in place. (Rehearsal glasses being used instead of the correct ones.) Photo by Werner J. Kuhn.

225

and slanting down, Stalin's had to be thin and slanting up. Thus, the actor's natural eyebrows had to be completely blocked out. After some experimentation, it was decided to use medical gauze. Although a latex or a plastic piece would have been more effective for close viewing and would have been necessary for screen or television, the use of gauze avoided the necessity for making plaster casts and molds and served well at stage distance.

The natural eyebrows were soaked with spirit gum (Figure 19–7A) and pieces of gauze cut to the appropriate shape were laid over them and brushed with more spirit gum. When this top coat was tacky, Stalin's eyebrows (real hair ventilated on lace) were placed in position on the gauze and the whole area pressed down with a dampened chamois. When the spirit gum was dry, the gauze was covered with creme stick to match cake base that was to be used. Base (SF-9e), shadows (SF-11-e), and highlights (SF-5-e) were then applied, the beard area covered with gray cake and stippled with dark brown (F-15-f) for an unshaven effect, and finally the mustache was attached with spirit gum. Mr. Falk's own hair was arranged to suit the character.

For the more mature Stalin, the wig was put on (Figure 19–7C) and the lace front attached with spirit gum. Then the lace and the rest of the youthful makeup were covered with light olive cake base (SF-5-e). Cake shadows (S-12-e, FS-15-f) and highlights (F-2-b) were added last.

Alvin Epstein as Trotsky. Alvin Epstein presented an additional problem in that he was expected not only to look like Trotsky but to achieve the likeness in a quick change. He was playing three characters, each one totally unlike any of the others; but only Trotsky needed to be a recognizable historical personage.

The major elements in the Trotsky change were the wig, the goatee, and the mustache (Figures 19–9B,D). Mr. Epstein's own blonde eyebrows (Figure 19–9B) had to be changed to Trotsky's upward-slanting dark ones, but it was possible to make the change with judicious penciling (Figure 19–9C). The pale, translucent skin that Mr. Epstein wanted for Trotsky was achieved with white cake lightly applied, then partially removed with liquid cleanser, letting the natural skin color below show through and leaving a very slight shine. The bone structure was then highly accented with cake shadows (S-11-f) and grease highlights (F/OF-2-b). The eyes were accented with black and light red pencils. A touch of red pencil was added immediately under the eyebrow.

PROBLEMS

1. Make yourself up as a historial character from a play. Here are some suggestions:

Elizabeth I, Mary of Scotland *(Elizabeth the Queen)*; Eleanor Roosevelt *(Sunrise at Campobello)*; Victoria *(Victoria Regina)*; Mary Todd Lincoln *(The Last of Mrs. Lincoln)*; Queen Mary *(Crown Matrimonial)*.

Sir Thomas More, King Henry VIII *(A Man for All Seasons)*; Martin Luther *(Luther)*; Abraham Lincoln *(Abe Lincoln in Illinois)*; Henry V *(King Henry V)*; Stalin, Trotsky, Lenin *(The Passion of Josef D.)*; Benjamin Disraeli *(Disraeli)*; Franklin D. Roosevelt *(Sunrise at Campobello)*; Richard II *(King Richard II)*; Richard III *(King Richard III)*; Oliver Wendell Holmes *(The Magnificent Yankee)*; John Adams, Thomas Jefferson, Benjamin Franklin *(1776)*; George Washington, *(The Patriot)*.

2. Reproduce as accurately as possible on your own face or someone else's one of the portraits in Appendix H or J or one from your own collection.

20

IMAGINATIVE MAKEUP

Since the conception of a makeup must first be developed in the imagination before it can be executed on the face, all makeup is to a degree imaginative. But in dealing with nonrealistic characters or with realistic characters in a nonrealistic way, the creative imagination is given greater latitude of expression.

Throughout the preceding chapters there has been an emphasis on realism in makeup, with a continual reference to nature as our guide, in order to enhance the believability of the actor's characterization. There are occasions, however, when the makeup need not and should not be completely realistic. This may be dictated by the play itself and the nonrealistic characters in it or by a style of production chosen by the director and the designer.

Figure 20-1. Styles of makeup. (A) Realistic. Front hair soaped out and hair darkened with brown spray. (B) Stylization through exaggeration of realistic features. Troll. Nose and wart of putty-wax. (C) Stylization through the use of nonrealistic designs and colors. Student makeups by Doug Massey.

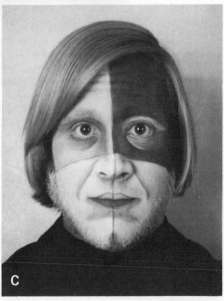

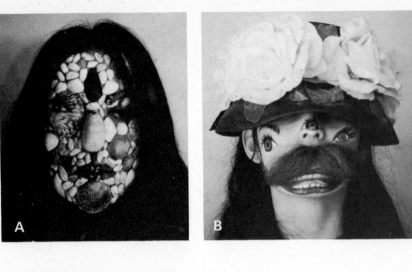

Figure 20-2. Nonrealistic faces. (A) Sea creature. Sea shells glued to the face with spirit gum. Student makeup by Christine Donish. (B) Small Person with Flowered Hat. Cake makeup, eyebrow pencil, lip rouge, ventilated mustache. Student makeup by Christine Donish. (C) Oriental mask. Cake makeup with black eyebrow pencil. Student makeup by Elaine Herman. (D) Mask for the Lincoln Center production of *The Caucasian Chalk Circle*. Designed by James Hart Stearns. (E) Scarecrow. Corn husks glued to the face with spirit gum. Student makeup by Kathy Ross. (F) Javanese porcelain mask. White, green, and black. Student makeup by Elaine Herman.

Instead of aiming for realistic accuracy, think in terms of using line, color, and form to heighten, to exaggerate, to simplify, to clarify, to satirize, to symbolize, or perhaps to amuse. Instead of consulting photographs for inspiration, consult works of art. Draw on your imagination. Instead of using hair for wigs and beards, use rope, yarn, cloth, paper, wood shavings, feathers, plastic, or metal.

Paint designs on the face (Figure 20–3) and accent them with glitter or cover the face with sea shells (Figure 20–2A). Then from the various ideas that have come to you, use those that seem best suited to the style of the production.

Makeup based on specific art forms (such as mosaics or stained glass) can be very effective when appropriate to the period, subject matter, mood,

228

and overall design of the play. Student Howard Klein's makeups for *Mother Courage* (Figure 9–2) derive from a study of works by Käte Kollwitz, Karl Schmidt-Rottluff, and other German painters of Brecht's period.

In addition to relating to the style of production and to the character, the makeup should also relate, in a very special way, to the audience. Although audiences are quite willing to go along with innovations in style, there are certain areas of resistance the makeup artist should be aware of. Our ideas about many nonrealistic characters—gnomes, trolls, fairies, elves—are somewhat vague, being based on a variety of illustrations and an equal variety of books and stories, and are thus open to fresh interpretation. But our ideas about some nonrealistic characters—such as those in *Alice in Wonderland* and *Through the Looking Glass*—are not so flexible.

Just as Gilbert Stuart determined for all time our image of George Washington, Sir John Tenniel created visual images of the characters in *Alice* that have become the definitive representations of those characters. Since we think we know and have known from childhood what the White Queen *really* looked like (based on what Tenniel thought she

Figure 20-3. Nonrealistic makeups. (A) Design based on a fabric pattern. Cake makeup with eyebrow pencil. Student makeup by Rosemary Buell. (B) Hearts and flowers. Cake makeup and eyebrow pencil. Student makeup by Lydia Lazar. (C) Metallic makeup. Gold and green. Student makeup by Donna Meyer. (D) Patterns. Putty wax nose and chin. Eyebrows blocked out with gauze. Brown, black, red, pink, yellow, blue, green, and white cake and grease.

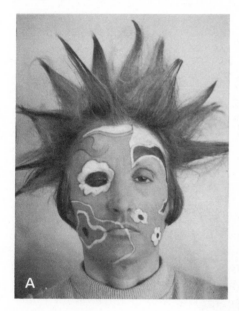

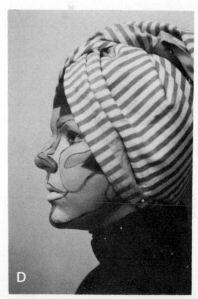

Figure 20-4. The Duchess from *Alice in Wonderland*. With Alice, Cook, Baby, and Cheshire Cat. Illustration by Sir John Tenniel.

Figure 20-5. Illustration from Lewis Carroll's *The Three Voices*. By A. B. Frost.

Figure 20-6. The Mad Hatter from *Alice in Wonderland*. Illustration by Sir John Tenniel.

looked like), any attempt to revise her image may meet with resistance. She can be presented with a slightly heightened realism (as are the Mad Hatter in Figure 12–1H and the Queen of Hearts in Figure 2-3), or she can be presented as a black and white drawing or a wooden marionette. But whatever the style of the makeup, she should probably look rather like the White Queen we know.

This is hardly a serious limitation. In the Oriental theater, however, such limitations can be much more severe. The beautifully decorative and colorful designs the actors paint on their faces look like a creative makeup artist's holiday. Actually, they are highly symbolic in both color and design and are never varied, no matter what actor is playing the part. But it is rare that the nonrealistic makeups we do will have such traditional strictures. We usually have the freedom to create new designs, though we may choose to go to works of art (such as the decorative masks in Figure 20–7) for our inspiration.

It is also possible, in doing makeups for nonrealistic characters, to combine essentially realistic makeup with purely stylized makeup through the stylistic exaggeration of certain features, as in Figures 15–33 and 20–1B. Such exaggeration is frequently needed when the character depends entirely on physical movement rather than on speech or when the character, though human, symbolizes something greater than the individual human being. A single character representing Man or the Prodigal Son or the Earth Mother requires some heightening of his makeup, some telling exaggeration of detail.

In the ballet *The Cage* the fact that human bodies are representing insect behavior should be reflected in the makeup.

In the ballet, as elsewhere, the style of the production, as well as the role, may determine the makeup—as in a production of *Firebird*, for example, in which the makeups were coordinated with the Chagall sets.

Thus, combined stylization and realism range from a simple heightening of details for better definition and projection to strong exaggerations of line or color for dramatic effect. As in all nonrealistic makeup, our primary concern should be first to free the imagination, then to select those elements that make the most positive contribution to the projection of the character and to the overall design of the production.

For those who are still in the process of freeing their creative imagination, the following suggestions may provide some ideas for dealing with a variety of nonrealistic characters. When referring to these suggestions, bear in mind that the descriptions are based largely on literature, art, and folklore, and though in many cases the characteristics of a type may be stated dogmatically, they represent only a convenient point of departure. It is up to you to vary them to suit your purpose.

Angels. First determine the style of the production and the sort of angel required. If an ethereal angel is called for, you may wish to work with pale lavenders, blues, greens, or whatever color best

fits the production scheme. Hair and eyebrows might be of metallic gold or silver. The features will probably be idealized human ones. But if you are doing *The Green Pastures*, the angels can achieve the comedy effect required only by a realistic makeup. Angels in literature come in a variety of shapes, sizes, and dispositions. Although an angel, by definition, cannot be evil, he may, some believe, be avenging.

Animals. Papier maché heads or masks (see Figure 20–10) or latex constructions (Figure 20–8)

Figure 20-7. Grotesque Masks. (1) Etruscan, terracotta. (2) Italian Renaissance, Venice. (3) Italian Renaissance, tomb of Cardinal Sforza, Rome. By Sansovina. (4) Italian Renaissance, from a frieze by Michelangelo, San Lorenzo, Florence. (5) French Renaissance, from the tomb of Louis XII, St. Denis. (6) French, more recent. From Meyer's *Handbook of Ornament.*

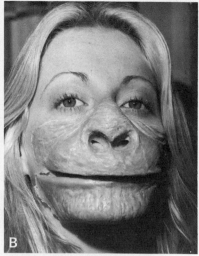

Figure 20-8. Ape makeup. Foamed latex. Face is done in 3 pieces, as shown.

Makeup by Bert Roth, S.M.A.

Figure 20-9. Tiger makeup. Student makeup by Kathy Ross. (For other make-ups by the same student see Figures 14-50, 20-2E, and 20-3D.)

can be used and sometimes should be; but if the style of the production permits, you may prefer merely to suggest animal features on a human face. This can be done in a completely nonrealistic or a modified realistic style with paint (see Figures 20–9 and J-6), or the paint can be combined with three-dimensional makeup. Crepe hair is often helpful. Split lips can be drawn on (Figure J-6), giving a remarkably animal-like effect; foreheads can be lowered; real or painted whiskers can be added.

Birds. Bird faces can be built up with three-dimensional additions, such as large beaks (Figure 20–12) or completely stylized with painted details. Sometimes the two may be combined, perhaps by using feathers with paint. Birds with small beaks and large eyes (owls, for example) are easier to do with paint than are large-beaked birds. The beak of the parrot in Figure 20–12 was molded with latex and painted a brilliant red-orange. Brightly colored

Figures 20–10 and 20–11. Bird and animal masks. Sketches and masks by makeup instructor Bill Smith.

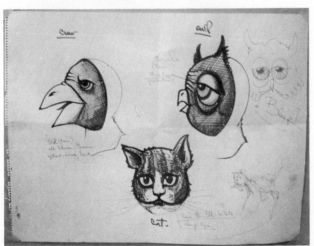

feathers were attached with spirit gum. A mask would have been far more practical for repeat performances. For smaller-beaked birds to be done with makeup rather than masks, putty might be used instead of latex. Colors can be as realistic or fanciful as can the birds themselves.

Figure 20-12.   Parrot. Beak made of latex colored coral. Gold, yellow, green, red, and purple feathers attached to face with latex. Only skin showing is around the eyes. Student makeup by Gordon Hayes.

Clowns. Since the most successful clown makeups reflect individual characteristics, the first step is to decide what sort of clown you want—sad, happy, elegant, shy, brash, drunk, suspicious, ineffectual. Then design an exaggerated, stylized makeup to fit that conception. For a sad clown, for example, you will probably want to slant the eyebrows and the corners of the mouth downward. If your clown is to be a tramp, you should think about an effect of beard stubble. For a clown with no particular personality you might paint geometric designs on the face. Sketching your design on paper first is likely to save time and result in a better makeup. There is no such thing as a standard clown. Make yours individual.

The base usually used is clown white (see Appendix A). But white creme or cake makeup with good coverage can also be used. All exposed areas of flesh should be evenly covered. Then with pencils, brushes, and shading colors, you can duplicate your design. The hair should be treated in a style harmonious with the rest of the makeup. A skull cap or a wig is commonly used. Although professional clowns frequently do nothing to block out their eyebrows beyond covering them with clown white, the makeup is likely to be more effective if natural eyebrows are not visible through the makeup. See Figure 20–13 for a student clown makeup.

Figures 20-14 and 20-15. Death. Cake makeup. Student makeups by Christine Donish (left) and Dennis Drew (right).

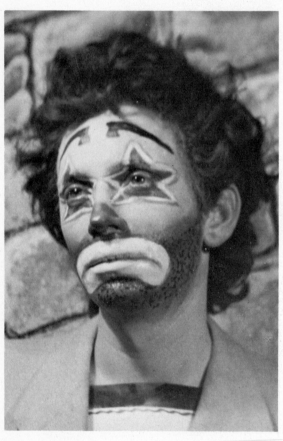

Figure 20-13. Tramp-clown makeup. By student Jan Vidra.

Death. Death is ordinarily pictured as having a skull for a head (see Figures 20–14 and 20–15). The facial bones (Figure 4–1) can be modeled with white or ivory cake, creme, or grease and shadowed with medium blue, gray, violet, or brown. The hollows can be filled in with black or charcoal brown. If the head is to show, a white skull cap or a plastic or latex cap should be worn. The cap, which should cover the ears, can be painted with the same base as the face and the edges blended carefully into the foundation. The eyebrows should always be blocked out (see Chapter 14).

If the makeup is to be luminous, the white paint can be dusted with fluorescent powder (see Appendix A) before any shading is done. Or fluorescent paint can be brushed over the completed makeup in the appropriate places. An ultraviolet ray must be used on a dark stage to cause luminosity. Phosphorescent paint or powder can be used without the ultraviolet ray. Both liquid and pigment can be obtained for either type of paint.

The same technique can be used successfully for Death in *Death Takes a Holiday* in which the Count is occasionally called upon to appear according to our conventional idea of Death. However, a normal, though pale, makeup should be used instead of white and the fluorescent paint or pigment applied only to the bones of the skull. Under normal stage lights the makeup will look normal, but

Figures 20-16 and 20-17. Mephistopheles.
Same makeup done in two different styles.
Various color combinations could be used.

under the ultraviolet ray the skull will appear. If the hands are to be seen, they should always be made up in harmony with the facial makeup. It is also possible to present Death much less conventionally—as a coldly beautiful woman, perhaps, or a black hooded figure with no face at all.

Devils and demons. The conventional devil is often made up with a bright red foundation and a long face with sharp, pointed features. The cheekbones are prominent; nose and chin, long and pointed; eyes, narrow and dark; lips, thin and well defined; eyebrows, black, close together, and slanting upward; eye sockets, dark and sunken. A small, pointed mustache may be used and a rather delicate, long and pointed goatee. Long red, yellow, green, or black fingernails may be added. Horns are commonly used, set into a skull cap over the head.

For a three-dimensional makeup the nose and chin can be extended with putty. The natural eyebrows should be blocked out and false ones either made of crepe hair or painted on, depending on the degree of stylization. If the production is to be stylized, long, upward slanting extensions of the eye lining may be used with brightly colored or metallic eyeshadow. The eye sockets, cheeks, nose, and temples can be shadowed with a very dark brownish red and highlighted with light red, pink, or yellow. Dark red or green might be used on the lips.

The base need not be red. Bright pink, red-

Figure 20-18.   Grotesque mask. Limestone, nineteenth century.

235

Figure 20-19. Devil as Jester. From an old print.

Figure 20-20. Demon. Ornament from the stalls of S. Pietro in Perugia.

dish, or yellowish foundation colors might be used effectively. Green is also a possibility, though perhaps not so logical a one as red. Blue or purple shadows and yellow highlights would be effective with a green base. A yellow base might also be used, or an extremely pale one of any tint with strong accents in black and bright colors. For that matter, there is no reason why a devil should not be made up with metallic gold or silver if that fits the overall color scheme. Figures 20–16 and 20–17 show two versions of a stylized devil makeup.

Dolls. China or porcelain dolls should usually be made up with white, ivory, or pale pink foundations. The rouge, preferably of a pinkish or bluish-pink variety, should be applied in a round spot in the center of each cheek, and the spot should be blended at the edges. The lips should be small with a pronounced cupid's bow. The eyelashes can be blackened with mascara or cosmetic (or false ones used) and the eyes lined with brown or black and shadowed with blue or lavender. The eyes should be made to look as round as possible. (See Figure 20–22A). A wig may be helpful. In this case, an inexpensive wig with shiny synthetic hair may well be preferable to an expensive one.

Other types of dolls (see Figure 20–22C) will, of course, require different techniques.

Elves. An elf or a brownie is considered to be a kind of fairy sympathetic to man and living in the woods and fields. Elves are imagined to be very small and to have pointed, butterfly-shaped ears, small turned-up noses, and quite round, open eyes. They may wear caps that partially or completely cover the hair; on the other hand, the hair may show and be either short or long. The hair is usually rather casually dressed and is likely to fall

Figure 20-21. Rag doll, elf, and brownie. Drawings by John Gee.

over the forehead. Brownies, it seems, may have normal ears. (See Figure 20–21.)

The skin of either may be of human flesh color, though the reddish shades should probably be avoided. They may have red cheeks and lips and should usually be cheerful and pleasant. The nose can be shaped with nose putty.

Fairies. Fairies other than elves, sprites, gnomes, and the like (Titania and Oberon, for example) should always be slender and graceful, unless otherwise specified for a particular character.

The base color might be ivory, light pink, pale blue, lavender, silver, gold, or any color fitting into the general scheme. The red shades, being more human, should be avoided. Metallic flakes or sequins can be used with good effect on exposed parts of the body. The flakes usually adhere to greasepaint, and the sequins can be attached with a latex adhesive or spirit gum.

The features can be delicate, well formed, mortal ones. The ears may be pointed or not. Some lip coloring may be used but usually no cheek rouge. The eyes should be as beautiful as possible.

Figure 20-22. Nonrealistic makeups. (A) Marionette. Eyebrows blocked out. Cake makeup with black eyebrow pencil. Student makeup by Sarah Barker. (B) Flower in *Through the Looking Glass*. Pink cake base. Eyebrows made of black sequins, eyelashes of lilac paper. Paper petals in crimson and fuchsia. Student makeup by Carol Gackowski. (C) Rag doll. Eyebrows blocked out with spirit gum and gauze. Black, white, and red cake makeup. Red yarn wig. Student makeup by Jeanne Zavala. (D) Puck. Student makeup by Jon Freeman. (E) Flower with caterpillar. Rice, popcorn, and beans attached with spirit gum. Student makeup by Lorie Ponzuric. (F) Pinocchio. Putty nose, eyebrows blocked out, greasepaint with black eyebrow pencil. Student makeup by Debra Burgess.

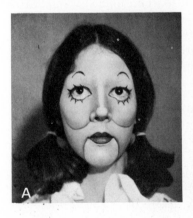

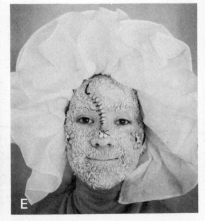
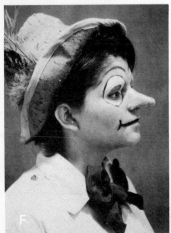

Gold, silver, or bronze eyeshadow might be used. Gold or bronze could also be used for the lips instead of pink or red. The women's hair is usually long and wavy and more often golden than dark.

It is also possible to use a flat, decorative, stylized makeup, as in Figure 20-3 or 20-22D.

Flowers. These obviously cannot be given a realistic treatment. They are usually created by surrounding the face with petals, but there can be a variety of approaches to the face itself. Two possibilities are illustrated in Figure 20-22B,E.

Gnomes. Gnomes, goblins, and trolls (Figure 20-1B) are commonly thought of as living underground. They are always mischievous and nearly always unfriendly toward mortals. Usually they are grotesque and often very ugly, even deformed.

A long ugly nose, prominent cheekbones, prominent brow and receding forehead, pointed chin, receding chin, fat cheeks, sunken cheeks, large and wing-shaped ears, peculiarly shaped eyebrows, very bushy eyebrows, no eyebrows, pop eyes, small and beady eyes, and bulging forehead are characteristics that may be considered in doing a makeup of this sort. Very long and flowing pointed beards are appropriate for older gnomes. The skin should be darker than for other types of fairies—possibly green, yellow, or other colors. The head may be entirely bald except for a tuft or two of hair, or else well supplied with unkempt hair.

Inanimate objects. Just as the cartoonist may humanize inanimate objects by giving them human features, the makeup artist can sometimes dehumanize people by designing a makeup to represent an inanimate object. This may be done quite liter-

ally, as with the clock face in Figure 20-23, or more stylistically, as in the representation of a computer spewing a punched card out of its mouth in Figure 20-24.

Monsters. This category covers a variety of creatures, from mechanical men to werewolves. If the monster is to be animalistic, the hair should grow low on the forehead and perhaps cover a good deal of the face. The nose usually needs to be widened and flattened. False teeth made to look like fangs will make the monster more terrifying. But if the creature is to appear in a children's play, it should be conceived with some discretion. Gory details, such as blood streaming from an open wound and eyes torn out of their sockets, might well be saved, if they are to be used at all, for adult horror plays. Foreheads can be raised and heads squared off, eyes rearranged, teeth made large and protruding, and so on. Skin texture techniques—towel or tissue with latex, tissue and spirit gum, latex and cornmeal—can be used to good effect.

Ogres. An ogre is usually conceived to be a hideous monster who feeds on human beings. Prosthetic applications will undoubtedly be needed. You might consult the suggestions for making up a gnome and then greatly exaggerate them. Helpful pictures of ogres can be found in books of fairy tales.

Pierrot. Pierrot and Pierrette are often made up with a white foundation covering all exposed flesh. Ivory or very pale pink may be used if preferred, and they are, perhaps, more desirable. The lips should be small and quite red with a pronounced cupid's bow. The natural brows should

Figure 20-23. Clock face. Student makeup by Christine Augsburger.

Figure 20-24. Computer. Student makeup by Christine Augsburger.

be blocked out with soap and high arched ones painted on with black eyebrow pencil. Blue, green-blue, blue-gray, blue-violet, or violet eyeshadow could be used. The eyes should be well defined. Pierrette may have two small, well-blended dots of rouge. Her eyeshadow could be blue, lavender, or pale blue-green. A thoroughly stylized makeup may be even more effective. Rouge, lips, and eyebrows might all be in the shape of diamonds or other simple geometric figures. The design of the costume should harmonize.

Statuary. All exposed flesh should be made up, the color depending on the color of the material of which the statue is supposedly made. Grays, grayed blues, grayed greens, and grayed violets are useful for shadowing. Avoid warm tones unless the statue is of a color that would require warm shadows. Whether or not the makeup should be powdered will depend on the material of which the statue is supposedly made. If the finish would naturally be shiny, a creme or a grease base without powder can be used. A dull finish requires a water-soluble base or powdered creme or grease one. For large areas, liquid makeup is most practical.

Gold, silver, or bronze statues can be made with metallic body makeup. The effect is excellent, but the technique should be used with care (see discussion in Appendix A under *Metallic makeup*).

Toys. Makeup for toys other than dolls—as, for example, tin or wooden soldiers or marionettes (see Figure 20–22A,F)—can best be copied from the actual toys. Their unreality should be stressed in order to counteract the obvious lifelike qualities of the actor.

Trolls. In Scandinavian folklore, trolls are supernatural beings, either very large or very small, living underground or in caves. Trolls are usually thought of as being ugly, though not necessarily repulsive, and not very friendly. The trolls in *Peer Gynt* slit their eyeballs and proposed to do the same to Peer. They can be green, yellow, gray, puce, or any color that seems appropriate. But they should look grotesque in some way and usually not kindly. (See Figure 20–1B.)

Witches. In much the same way as gnomes and goblins, witches provide an opportunity for originality in makeup. Sharp, hooked noses, prominent cheekbones, sunken cheeks, thin lips, small sunken eyes, prominent pointed chins, and numerous wrinkles are comon characteristics (see Figure 15–33). Traditional witches have straggly hair, claw-

Figure 20-25. Witch from *Snow White and the Seven Dwarfs*. Derma wax on chin, nose, and knuckles. Student makeup by Nancie Underwood. (For another makeup by the same student see Figure F-3.)

like hands, and seldom more than one or two good teeth. The complexion may be light or dark, but in either case it usually tends to be sallow. It might even be gray, blue, green, or other colors. Prosthetic applications on the nose, chin, and cheekbones are usually helpful. Warts and hair on the face are common.

Witches can, however, be good or bad, young or old, ugly or beautiful. And each of these could be realistic or stylized. Whereas a wicked old witch might have a face the texture and color of a dried apple, a good young witch might have a face of alabaster with hair of metallic gold. A bad (but sophisticated) young witch, on the other hand, could have a face with a glint of steel, slashed with jet black eyebrows over heavily lashed, slanted eyes. And then there are those witches who look exactly like everybody else and not like witches at all.

PROBLEMS

1. Make clay models of several different types of heads for nonrealistic characters. Create makeups on the basis of these.

2. Make up yourself or someone else as several of the following characters: Pierrot; Oberon, Titania, Puck, Peaseblossom (*A Midsummer Night's Dream*); Manikin, Minikin (*Mannikin and Minikin*); Mephistopheles; one of the Witches (*Macbeth*); The Magistrate (*Liliom*); Ivan

Borolsky (*Captain Applejack,* Act II); The Green Thing (*The Gods of the Mountain*); Red Queen, White Queen, King of Hearts, Queen of Hearts (*Alice in Wonderland*); He (*He Who Gets Slapped*); Ariel, Caliban (*The Tempest*); Elvira (*Blithe Spirit*); Pagliacci; Ghost (*Hamlet*); Trolls (*Peer Gynt*); Insects (*The Insect Comedy*); Arturo, Old Hindborough, Roma, Ragg, Givola, Giri (*Arturo Ui*); one of the Orcs (*Lord of the Rings*). Do at least one of the characters in two different styles—one, heightened realism; the other, a flat, decorative style.

3. Make yourself up as any character you wish following the style of a not-too-realistic artist with whose work you are familiar. It would usually be best to choose a character from a play that might logically be given a stylized production.

4. Do a nonrealistic makeup for a character you have already done in a realistic style; or, if you prefer, do a realistic and a nonrealistic makeup for the same character. Choose a character that might possibly be done on stage in either style.

21

MAKEUP FOR OTHER MEDIA

Although this book is primarily concerned with makeup for the theater and is not intended to cover other fields, there are times when it may be convenient or necessary to adapt a stage makeup for photographs, for platform appearances, or for television. Since there are available books covering these areas of makeup, the brief discussions in this chapter are intended only as practical aids for the stage artist who may be working temporarily in other media.

MAKEUP FOR THE PLATFORM

Platform appearances are frequently made on a stage, of course, but the term "platform" is used to refer to occasions when the performer is appearing as himself at least part of the time. Monologists, interpretive readers, singers, pianists, magicians, and others are considered platform artists, but since they do frequently appear on a stage, they usually wear makeup. The makeup must, however, be relatively subtle, especially if the program is in an intimate hall or theater or if the performer appears primarily on the stage apron, close to the audience.

There is an additional problem that occasionally comes up. Sometimes there are no dressing rooms, no adequate lighting off stage (or even on stage for that matter), no opportunity before the performance to apply makeup, and none afterward to take it off (tea with the ladies immediately following the program, for example). It may, therefore, be wise to apply makeup before going to the theater or the club. The problem, then, is to apply

it subtly enough that one can meet people without being uncomfortable and still not look washed-out on stage. The difficulty is not too great for women but is rather an imposing one for men. For them the best solution is a natural tan, but if that is impractical, a transparent liquid makeup (see Appendix A) or one of the men's skin toners for street wear works quite well. For women, a cake or creme makeup in not too dark a shade is satisfactory. Either cake or creme makeup is preferable to a grease foundation.

The principles of corrective makeup should be followed, though very subtly. White lights are much more commonly used in platform performances than in legitimate shows. You should, therefore, be very careful with the reddish hues frequently used on stage. Colors in the F or SF group are safest. The value will depend largely on how dark you want to look. If you decide you want a good suntan, be sure your hands and your neck are tanned too.

For men, very little else is usually necessary unless the eyes need accenting. For women, eyeshadow should be chosen with both the costume and the eyes in mind, and rouge in relation to costume and complexion.

For platform makeup there is no necessity for carrying a large kit. Platform artists who travel a great deal, as many do, should try to condense their makeup kits as much as possible.

For character makeup in platform work the two things to be kept in mind are the proximity of the audience (there is not always a significant difference from the usual theater situation, but there may be) and the lighting. A carefully executed, subtle makeup done with the particular lighting situation in mind will usually serve the purpose. You might refer to the discussion of Hal Holbrook's Mark Twain makeup, which is as effective on the lecture platform as in the theater.

MAKEUP FOR PHOTOGRAPHY

The principles of makeup for photography are essentially the same as those for stage makeup except that in making up you must work specifically for your mirror and not for an imagined audience many feet away. If you have been following the suggestions in this book and doing carefully modeled, realistic makeups that are convincing to the front row, you will have no trouble in toning down the contrasts just a little and exercising special care in blending. Never delude yourself into thinking that what you see in your mirror won't show up in the camera. The camera will, in fact, pick up details your eye may miss.

If you are working on makeup for black-and-white photography, you should remember that red tends to photograph dark and it should therefore not be used as rouge. There is no objection to using red in shadows if you normally use it, but if used on the cheeks it is likely to photograph as a shadow. If a dark lipstick is being worn for the performance, it should be lightened for the photograph. In doing makeup specifically for black-and-white photography, one ordinarily uses a panchromatic scale of colors, but it is not usually necessary to change your regular makeup colors for photographs.

Photographs are frequently taken after a performance or a rehearsal. This, of course, is the worst possible time. Aside from the fact that the actors are tired, the makeups will certainly not be at their best, and the pictures will probably suffer. If, however, they must be taken at this time, be sure to touch up the makeup, remove dark rouge for black-and-white pictures, and take a fresh look at the makeup with the camera in mind. Portraits should, if possible, be taken at a special time with the makeup done specifically for the camera.

MAKEUP FOR TELEVISION

Television makeup is both like and unlike makeup for the stage. The principles of modeling with paint and with prosthetic pieces are basically the same and vary only in the matter of color, in the lack of necessity for projection to a theater audience, and in the extreme care that must be taken with details in order to permit close-ups. Nose putty and crepe hair are less frequently used. Wigs and beards are usually ventilated on silk or nylon net. Rubber prothesis is used extensively, and plastics are occasionally used. In television, as for photography, you make up for the mirror in front of you, not for an imaginary audience many feet away.

Creme stick and cake makeup are usually used for the foundation color. Greasepaint is seldom used, though rubber-mask grease is used over latex prosthetic pieces. The usual colors for women are those designated as Fair, Medium, Olive, and Deep Olive. Men usually use CTV-6W, 7W, 8W, and 9W or their equivalents. In selecting foundation colors, remember that when a group of men in straight or corrective makeup are to be seen together on camera, as in a talk show, it is a good idea to make sure there are no strongly contrasting skin colors—such as one very red, another yellowish—that can cause difficulties in adjusting the color in the control room and may result in none of them looking their best.

Some corrective makeup is nearly always necessary for television appearances for both men and women. The principles are the same as for stage makeup. However, the overhead lighting in television may tend to accentuate the shadows in deep-set eyes, in which case a highlight should be used to offset the natural shadow. As for the stage, facial proportions should be carefully checked and improved, if possible, and other corrections made. (See Chapter 13.)

Highlights are usually three or four shades lighter than the base, and shadows three to six shades darker. The greater the contrast, the greater the care needed in blending. It is easier to get a subtle blend if you apply the shadows and highlights first to the clean skin, then carefully cover the entire face with foundation. If any of the shadows and highlights need to be intensified, they can easily be touched up over the base. If there are pouches or dark circles under the eyes, an even lighter highlight may be necessary.

Bronze rouge is usually used for women and amber for men, though rouge should be used sparingly for men if at all. Be careful of strong reds. For women, subtle lipstick shades are used—bronze, cinnamon, coffee, amber. Lip color is not used for men. Naturally red lips on men are usually toned down with the base color.

Men's eyes are not ordinarily lined, since the makeup would probably be visible in closeups. In making up men, be extremely careful that the makeup does not show on the screen.

For eliminating shine, Corn Silk Micron Pressed Powder O-23 is more effective than the usual face powder.

For character makeups, highlights may be much lighter and shadows much deeper. CTV-1W may be used for strong highlights and dark brown for deep shadows. The base color may be lighter or darker than the shades usually used for corrective makeup. Since texture is more important than it is in stage makeup, a dark stipple (sponge and cake makeup) over the completed makeup may sometimes be helpful in suggesting an aged skin if a darker-than-normal effect is desired.

Special techniques for three-dimensional textured effects (such as latex or sealer and tissue) are more widely used in television work than they are for stage purposes because of the closer work.

Quality wigs should always be used. Crepe hair may sometimes be used, but usually not for characters who will have close-ups.

Figure 21-1. Television makeup for Hal Holbrook's Mark Twain. The series of photographs on the following pages shows the step-by-step creation of Dick Smith's makeup for the CBS-TV special of *Mark Twain Tonight*. Although Mr. Holbrook does his own Mark Twain makeup for the stage (see Figures 19-3, 19-4, 19-5), three-dimensional constructions were required for television. Mr. Smith spent 8–10 weeks preparing for the makeup. This involved making more than 50 casts (A) and a number of experimental tests. Three complete makeups were created before the final one was chosen. With the help of an assistant, Mr. Smith was able to cut the 5-hour application time to 4½ hours and removal time to 1 hour. The method of making casts and foam-latex pieces like those on the following pages is described in Chapter 15.

The makeup involved both expected and unexpected problems. In order to prevent the smearing of makeup when Mr. Holbrook put his hands into the pockets of his white suit, Mr. Smith painted the backs of the hands (after the foam-latex pieces had been attached) with a mixture of latex and acrylic paint. Then at the dress rehearsal it was discovered that the edges of the large latex appliances were working loose around the mouth because of muscular activity—a common problem with any prosthetic application in that area. The use of Slomon's Medico Adhesive in troublesome spots successfully prevented any loosening of edges during the performance.

Although the three-dimensional television makeup shown here would obviously not be practical for regular use in the theater, some of the techniques used might very profitably be incorporated into makeups for the stage.

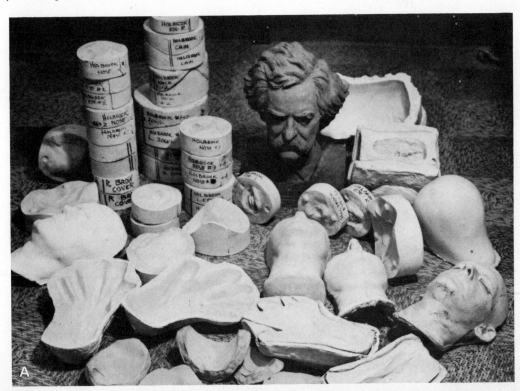

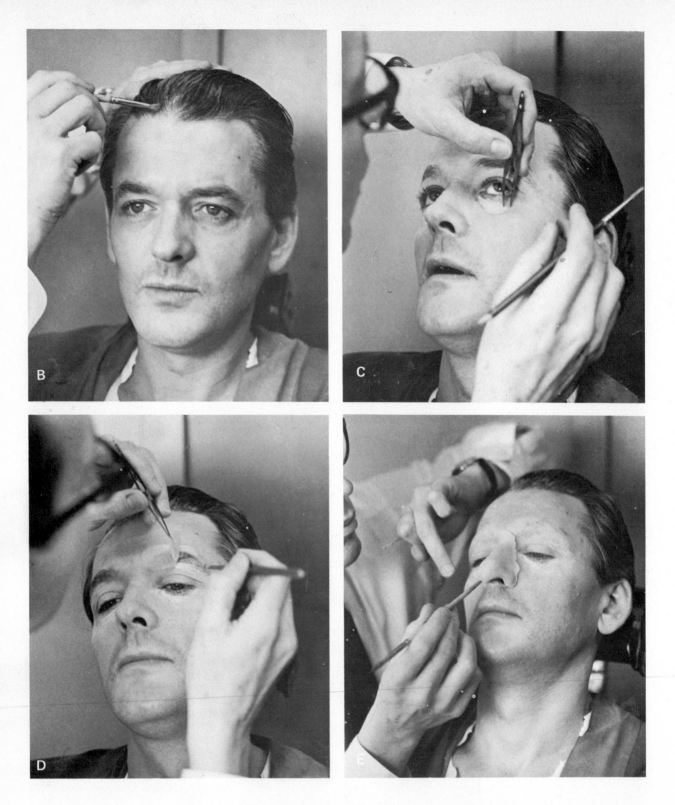

The first step was to flatten Mr. Holbrook's front hair with spirit gum. After the gum was brushed on (B), it was pressed down with a wet towel. Stipple-latex was then applied to the eyelids, dried with a hair dryer, and powdered to prevent sticking. Foam-latex eye pouches were attached with stipple-latex and adjusted with tweezers (C). Eyebrows were flattened with spirit gum and covered with foam-latex pieces (D). The foam-latex nose was attached with spirit gum and stipple-latex (E). The large foam-latex ap-

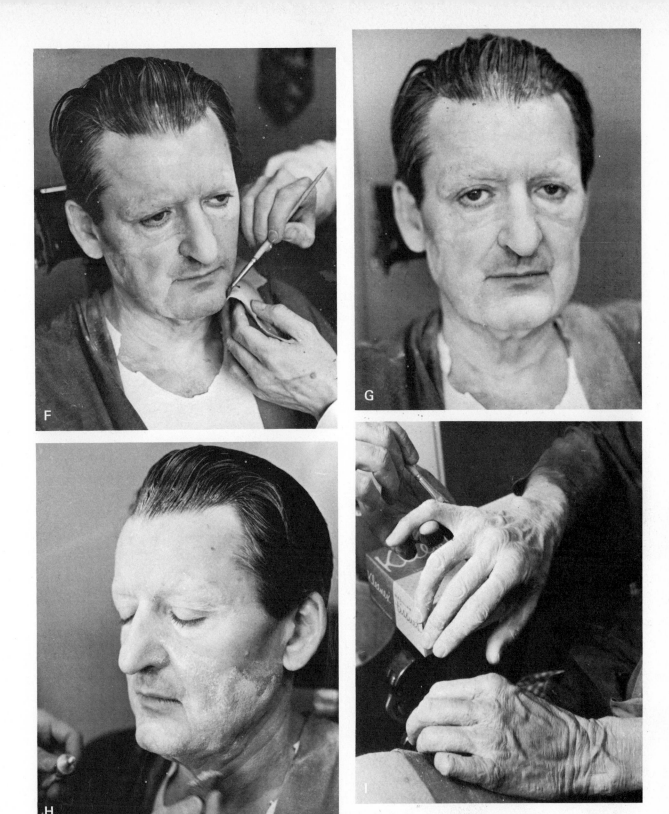

pliance (neck, jowls, nasolabial folds) was set in place and attached with spirit gum on the lower parts and stipple-latex on the top edges (F). The edges were blended with Scar Plastic Blending Liquid. Photograph G shows the piece completely attached. Duo adhesive was then applied as a sealer (H). Meanwhile, foam-latex pieces were being attached to the backs of the hands by an assistant.

Makeup by Dick Smith, S.M.A.

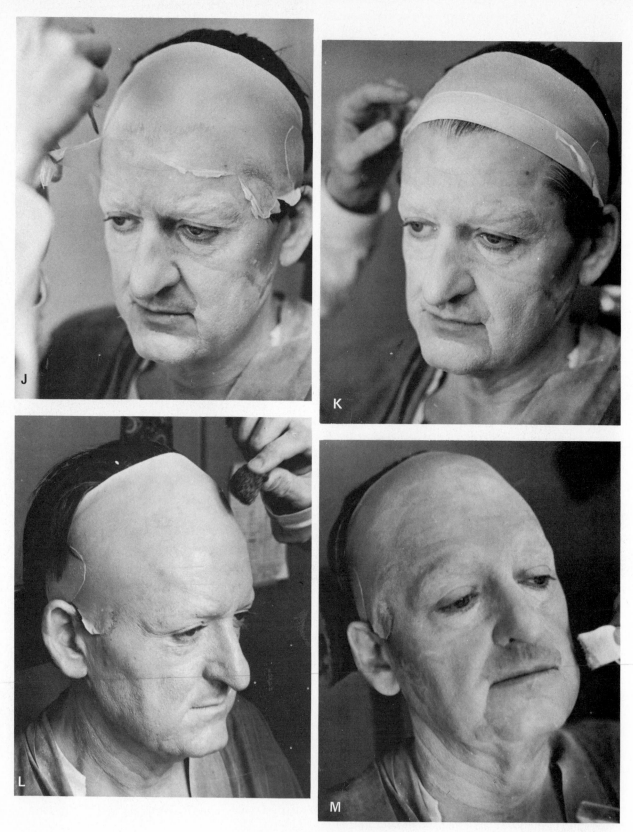

A plastic forehead piece (J) was needed to give an effect of seeing the scalp through the thin and fluffy front hair of the wig. After it was attached with gum, the edge of the plastic piece was dissolved with acetone (K) to blend it imperceptibly into the natural skin. A light rubber-mask grease-paint base was applied over the entire face (L), then stippled with other

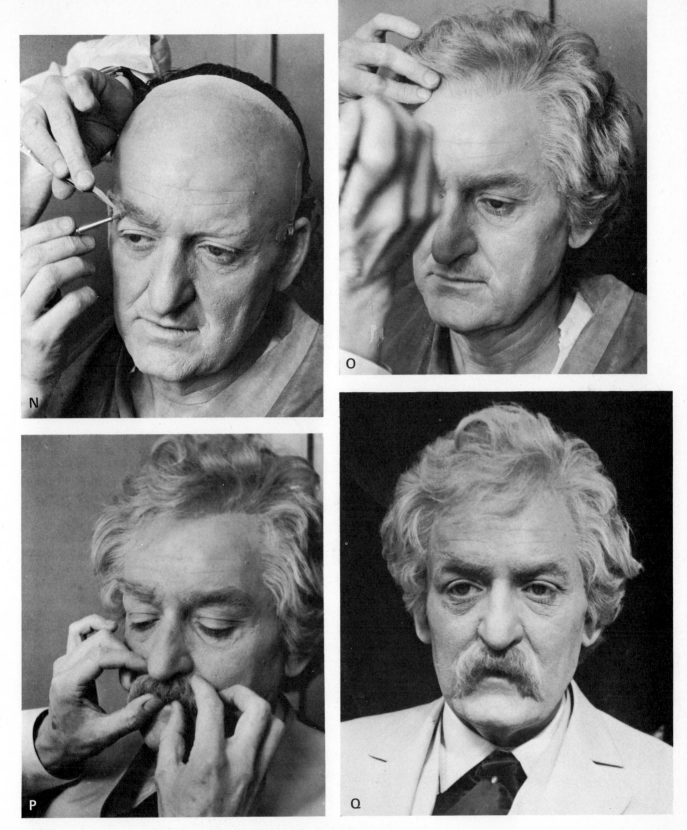

colors, using a coarse sponge (M) and in some cases a brush. Eyebrows were attached over the latex covers (N). The wig was then put on, the front lace glued down with matte plastic (O), and the hair brushed. After the mustache (ventilated on a net foundation) was attached (P), the entire makeup was touched up wherever necessary. Photograph Q shows the final result.

Makeup by Dick Smith, S.M.A.

Three-dimensional makeup is used to a much greater extent in television than it is in stage makeup, and there is of necessity much greater emphasis on precision of detail. Rubber prosthesis is extensively used, especially foamed rubber, which makes it possible to construct jowls, double chins, and the like, far more successfully than by other methods (see Chapter 16). Special plastics that require double molds, heat, and pressure are sometimes used. Although these give excellent results for close-up work, they are hardly practical for stage use. Not only is the procedure long and exacting, but the edges of the pieces may be destroyed in blending them into the skin. This is not an insurmountable problem for television or movie work, but for stage use it usually is. Furthermore, the perfection of blending to be achieved with plastic prosthesis is less important on the stage. But for the benefit of those who may wish to do some advanced experimentation and those who are curious about some of the special effects used in television and films, an abbreviated explanation of the process is included in Chapter 16.

MAKEUP MATERIALS

On the following pages are listed all of the makeup materials you are likely to use. The list is reasonably complete at the present time (1974), but since makeup products are continually being improved in form, quality, effectiveness, and packaging, the comments here will not be completely accurate indefinitely. A conscientious actor or makeup artist will want to keep abreast of all new developments and to formulate his own opinions on the basis of actual experimentation with new products.

The foremost manufacturers of theatrical makeup today are Mehron, Bob Kelly, Kryolan/Braendel, Ben Nye, Leichner, and Stein. The brand selected for use depends largely on personal preference and in some cases on local availability. There is, however, no particular advantage in using one brand of makeup exclusively. Since available products—and especially colors—vary from brand to brand, you may wish to use a combination of brands.

Mehron's makeup is of exceptionally high quality. Their excellent cake makeup comes in glass jars in double the amount of Factor's cake. Their foundation makeup—also in jars—has a lanolin rather than a grease base. Rouges and shading colors are packaged in plastic containers.

Bob Kelly has a complete line of quality makeup, including creme sticks and cake makeup in an unusually wide range of colors. The creme makeup is available in small flat containers for shading colors and rouges. He also has a variety of makeup kits (see *Makeup kits*).

Kryolan/Braendel is a very high quality German makeup with a great variety of items, including several new and useful products. Some of the makeup carries the Kryolan label, some the Braendel.

Ben Nye has a hypo-allergenic creme makeup packaged in flat containers for foundation, shading colors, and rouge, as well as an excellent hair whitener, stipple sponges, and many other useful makeup items.

Leichner's makeup, available in sticks, tubes, tins, and bottles, is high in quality and has a good color range. Emphasis seems still to be on sticks, which are used for lip, cheek, and eye makeup as well as for the foundation color. There are plastic jars of eye makeup, however, and some foundation colors are available in tubes.

Stein's makeup, in use for many years, is available in tubes, sticks, and flat plastic containers, in a wide range of colors. They have excellent brushes and an extensive line of other makeup needs.

At the present writing, Factor has discontinued so many stage colors that their stage line appears to be no longer competitive.

Makeup materials can be obtained directly from the manufacturer, from your local drugstore (which seldom has an adequate supply—if they handle stage makeup at all), from most costumers, or from a makeup supply house.

If you are ordering by mail and you are using one brand exclusively, you may wish to order directly from the makeup company. If you wish to order more than one brand, however, a good source is Paramount Theatrical Supplies in New York. They handle all brands of makeup as well as some items of their own, and will supply, if they can, most of the items mentioned in this book.

The Makeup Center in New York carries most brands, including their own (On Stage), and specializes in personal service to actors, models, makeup artists, and others who can visit their shop, though they will also fill mail orders.

Kryolan/Braendel is available from the Makeup Center and from Paramount. Bob Kelly sells directly at his New York establishment, by mail, and through distributors, including Paramount. Mehron sells by mail and directly from their factory in New York, as well as through Paramount, the Makeup Center, and other distributors. Ben Nye sells by mail and through distributors; his makeup can be obtained from Paramount in New York and from Robinson Plays and Costumes in Toronto. Leichner's makeup is available from the Makeup Center in New York; in London, they have a conveniently located studio offering personal service. Stein sells only through retail outlets, including Paramount, or by mail. All addresses are listed in Appendix B.

In the following alphabetical listing the starred (*) items are those with which you should become familiar first.

Absorbent cotton. Used for stuffing in the cheeks to enlarge them and for building up the face, neck, or hands in combination with spirit gum, collodion, latex, or sealer (see Chapter 15).

Acetone. A clear liquid solvent for spirit gum and collodion. Since it evaporates very rapidly, it must be kept tightly sealed. Obtainable at drugstores in pound bottles (it is usually measured by the pound rather than the pint) or much more reasonably by the gallon from beauty supply houses, which sell it as nail polish remover. If you are buying it at a drugstore, try to get the cheapest brand available. If your local store does not have one of the less expensive brands, they may be willing to order it for you.

*Adhesives. There are several adhesives of various types used in makeup. Spirit gum is used to attach beards, mustaches, hairpieces, and sometimes rubber prosthetic pieces. Johnson and Johnson's Duo Surgical Adhesive and Mehron's Flexol Adhesive (cream latex types) are used to attach prosthetic pieces and for stippling to conceal edges of prosthetic pieces and wig blenders.

Braendel's *Stoppelpaste* is a wax adhesive for beard stubble. (See *Stubble paste.*)

Dicor Adhesives 209 (paste) and 210 (liquid) are used largely in prosthesis. Slomon's Medico Adhesive is sometimes used to attach latex or plastic pieces to the skin, but it may often prove irritating. Kryolan has an extra strong spirit gum.

Regular spirit gum is obtainable from any makeup supply house, Duo Adhesive from drugstores, Flexol from Mehron or Paramount, *Stoppelpaste* from the Makeup Center or Paramount, Dicor and Medico from the sources listed in Appendix B. (See also *Spirit gum.*)

Adhesive tape. Occasionally used to draw the skin in order to change the shape of the eyes or the mouth or to construct false Oriental or sagging eyelids. For drawing the skin, a transparent plastic tape, available in drugstores, is effective.

Kryolan has a wide, semi-transparent tape with a very strong adhesive (see Figure A-1A) and also an unusually effective double-faced adhesive (toupee tape), which comes in a large roll and is made with a very thin layer of strong adhesive on a brown paper tape. When the tape has been pressed into place, the brown paper is peeled off, leaving the adhesive. Both Kryolan tapes are available from Paramount.

Bob Kelly and the Makeup Center have thin plastic tape in strips, called Top Stick. The conventional cloth double-faced adhesive is available from Paramount, the Makeup Center, and most makeup companies. Double-faced adhesive tape can be used to attach mustaches and beards for quick changes, as well as to secure toupees.

Alcohol. Common rubbing alcohol can be used to remove spirit gum. Obtainable at drugstores.

Alginate. A non-reusable impression powder for making molds. Available from Paramount and from dental supply houses. (See also *Moulage.*)

Atomizers. Useful for spraying brilliantine on the hair, diluted spirit gum onto crepe hair to help it hold its shape, and alcohol onto the face and onto rubber pieces to remove spirit gum. Hair lacquer atomizers with rubber stoppers are recommended for the makeup kit, since they are not easily clogged and do not spill. Brilliantine, however, will eventually rot the rubber stoppers.

Bandoline. A thick hair-setting liquid.

Beard block. (See Figure 17–12A.) A shaped wooden block for use in ventilating beards. Available from wigmakers' supply houses. A plaster cast of the actor's head can be substituted if no beard block is available or if a more perfect fit is required. The hairlace can be taped to the plaster with masking tape. (See Figure 17–12C.) If you want to attach

Figure A-1. Kryolan transparent adhesive tape.

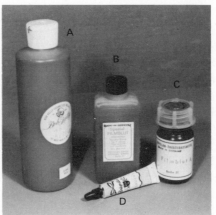

Figure A-2. Artificial blood. (A) Bob Kelly, (B, C) Kryolan, (D) Braendel.

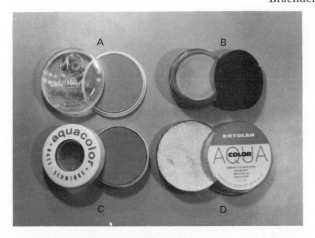

Figure A-3. Cake makeup. (A) Bob Kelly, (B) Mehron, (C) Kryolan, (D) Kryolan metallic.

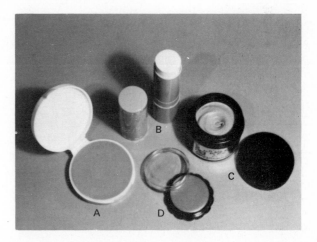

Figure A-4. Creme makeup. (A) Ben Nye, (B) Bob Kelly, (C) On Stage, (D) Ben Nye.

the plaster head to a wig-block holder, embed a 1-inch pipe into the plaster while it is still wet; the pipe will fit over a standard holder. For temporary use, a pipe might be taped to the back of the cast.

Beards. There are instructions for making beards in Chapter 17. Ready-made beards can be purchased from Paramount and from some wigmakers and costumers. Made-to-order beards are available from Bob Kelly.

Black wax. A preparation for blocking out teeth. It must usually be first softened by holding it in the palm of the hand or next to a warm light bulb, then molded into a thin sheet and placed over the teeth that are to be blocked out. The teeth must be dry before the wax is applied. Preparing the wax is sometimes a slow process, depending on its hardness, and the actor may find the wax uncomfortable. Black tooth enamel serves the same purpose and has neither of these disadvantages, but it possesses certain others that may occasionally prove even more undesirable (see *Tooth enamel*). Black eyebrow pencil can sometimes be used as a substitute (see Chapter 14). Black wax can be obtained from Mehron, Kelly, Stein, or Paramount. Kelly's comes conveniently packaged in a lipstick case.

Blending powder. See *Face powder.*

Blood, artificial. (See Figure A-2.) Used in any situation calling for visible blood. It is usually a heavy, viscous liquid with the consistency of real blood. For specific purposes, gelatin capsules (obtainable from your local pharmacist in various sizes) can be filled with it and at the right moment crushed by the actor in the hand or the mouth to release the blood. Obtainable from Kryolan, Kelly, Stein, Leichner, Paramount, or the Makeup Center. Kryolan has four kinds—regular theater blood, film blood, blood to be used in the mouth, and plastic blood in tubes (called *Fixblut* or Fixed Blood) for a dried blood effect. The *Fixblut* dries quickly, does not rub off, and is removed with acetone. Available from the Makeup Center and Paramount. For blood from the mouth, red toothpaste can be used. Mixing it with adhesive powder for false teeth will produce an effect of dried blood.

Body makeup. See *Liquid makeup, Metallic makeup,* and *Texas Dirt.*

Brilliantine. Useful for giving a pleasing sheen to the hair and keeping unruly hair in place. Any good brand is satisfactory for stage purposes. After the brilliantine has been sprayed on, the hair should be combed or brushed. Obtainable from Stein, dime stores, drugstores, and elsewhere. Also available in solid form. Aerosol sprays and commercial hair dressings are more frequently used.

Brushes, Chinese (or ***Japanese).*** (See Figure A-5.) Water-color brushes with a fine, sharp point, useful in accenting wrinkles. Obtainable at art supply stores.

Brushes, dye. (See Figures A-5 and 16–3G.) Available in various forms. Some are shaped like toothbrushes and can be used for applying spirit

Figure A-5. Brushes. (A) Hair brush, (B, C) eyebrow brushes, (D) dye brush, (E) rouge brush, (F) rouge or powder brush, (G) long-handled sable makeup brushes, (H) short-handled makeup brushes, (I) brush for spirit gum or collodion, (J) Chinese water-color brush.

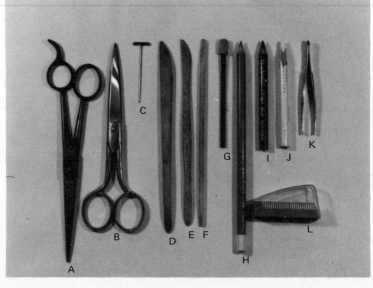

Figure A-6. Pencils and utensils. (A) Barber's shears, (B) utility shears, (C) T-pin, (D, E) modeling tools, (F) orangewood stick, (G) sponge applicator for eyeshadow, (H, I) pointed makeup pencils, (J) flat-cut makeup pencil, (K) tweezers, (L) Maybelline pencil sharpener.

gum remover to hairlace in removing wigs, toupees, beards, and mustaches. Obtainable from beauty supply shops.

Brushes, eyebrow. (See Figure A-5.) For brushing the eyebrows. Available from the makeup companies and cosmetics counters.

Brushes, moulage. For applying moulage in casting. Obtainable from Paramount. Other kinds of brushes, however, can be used for the same purpose.

Brushes, powder. Usually of camel's hair or nylon. Available in various shapes and sizes from the Makeup Center, Mehron, Kryolan, and Paramount. Figure A-5F shows a rouge brush that can just as well be used as a powder brush. The actual powder brush in this particular style is slightly larger.

*Brushes, shading or *tinting.* (See Figure A-5.) Several flat sable brushes (or the cheaper camel's hair or oxhair) are indispensable in doing character makeups. The bristles should be soft and smooth, yet springy; they must lie flat and not spread too much. Mehron, Kelly, Kryolan, and Stein all have excellent shading brushes in various widths. Sable brushes can be obtained from art supply stores, but the handles are often inconveniently long. Paramount has a good variety of both sable and oxhair, and the Makeup Center has an excellent selection of quality brushes. Their stubby powder and rouge brushes (Figure A-5F) are particularly handy.

Brushes, stiff-bristled. These are flat brushes, usually about ⅜-inch or wider, useful for applying spirit gum or latex. Obtainable in art stores, dime stores, and sometimes stationery stores.

Brushes, water-color. (See Figure A-5I.) Used to apply collodion or sealer. Either round or flat camel's hair brushes are satisfactory. They should be cleaned in acetone immediately after use. Obtainable in various sizes at artists' supply stores or dime stores. Moulage brushes can be used instead.

Burnt cork. Used for minstrel makeup only. It is available from Paramount or the makeup companies. Stein has nongreasy Blackface Makeup in tubes. It is available in Indian, Hawaiian, and Creole as well as black.

*Cake makeup. (See Figure A-3.) A greaseless, water-soluble foundation that is applied with a dampened sponge. Its chief advantages consist of simplicity of application, comparative cleanliness, and smoothness of the completed makeup. It does not encourage perspiration as a grease foundation does. The only serious disadvantage is the near impossibility of mixing colors. It is obtainable in plastic cases (Kelly, Kryolan, Stein) or jars (Mehron). In judging costs, be sure to check the net weight, which varies considerably with the brand. One cake may weigh twice as much as another and last twice as long. All cakes are available in a wide range of stage colors. Kryolan's comes in three sizes and more than 200 shades. Mehron's, Kelly's, and Kryolan's cakes are particularly recommended.

Castor oil. Used on latex pieces when they are to be covered with cake makeup. Can also be mixed with ground-up cake makeup to make rubber-mask grease.

Chamois. Used to press down the net in attaching hairlace wigs, beards, and mustaches with spirit gum. Can also be used in applying crepe hair. Obtainable at art supply, paint, or hardware stores.

Cleansing cream. See *Makeup removers.*

Cleansing tissues. Indispensable for removing makeup. The large boxes are the most economical. Pocket-size packs of tissues, however, are especially handy for the individual makeup kit. Nearly any brand is satisfactory.

Clown white. A thick white paint used for such characters as clowns, statuary, and dolls. It can be obtained from Paramount, Mehron, Kelly, or Stein. Kelly's is water-soluble.

Collodion. There are two kinds of collodion used by the makeup artist—flexible and nonflexible. They should not be confused. The flexible type is painted over absorbent cotton to build up the face and neck (see Chapter 15). Liquid sealer serves the same purpose. Either can be diluted with acetone. Nonflexible collodion is used directly on the dry skin for making scars (Chapter 15). Both types of collodion are obtainable at most drugstores or from Paramount or the Makeup Center. Kelly carries the nonflexible type and calls it Scarring Material. Mehron also has plastic sealer (called Fixative A), as does Ben Nye (called Old Age Plastic and Sealor). Collodion can be peeled off the skin or removed with acetone.

Combs. A wide-toothed comb is used for combing out crepe hair and wigs. The kit should also contain a comb to be used for hair with temporary coloring in it, one to be used with clean hair, and a rat-tail comb.

Cornstarch. Formerly used for graying the hair. One of the hair whiteners (see *Hair whiteners*) should be used instead. For quick-change makeups or when the gray must be removed during the play, it may be necessary to use white blending powder, which, though not satisfactory, is preferable to cornstarch.

Cosmetic or ***cosmetique.*** Used for beading the eyelashes when very heavy ones are required. False eyelashes are usually used instead, but cosmetic can serve as a cheap substitute. The cosmetic must be heated before use. Available from Paramount, Stein, or Mehron. Mehron's is called Beadex.

Cover stick. A paint in lipstick form for covering blemishes and skin discolorations. Available from Kelly, Kryolan, and Factor. Kelly's is called Blot-Out and Factor's is called Erace.

*Creme makeup. (See Figure A-4.) A velvety, nongreasy makeup base applied with the fingers or (for shadows and highlights) with a brush. Bob Kelly's is called Creme Stick and Stein's is called Velvet Stick. Ben Nye's makeup is of the same type but not in stick form. Kelly's is slightly drier than the others, thus requiring less powder. On Stage foundations (from the Makeup Center) are available in Mousse for medium coverage and Cream for heavy coverage. Both the Kelly and the On Stage foundations are pleasantly scented. Nye's is unscented. Kelly and Nye also have a complete line of creme shadows, highlights, and rouges.

Unless you want the natural sheen of creme makeup, a little neutral powder can be applied over it to give a matte finish. Creme makeup has some of the advantages of both cake makeup and greasepaint. It does not have the greasiness of greasepaint but is as easily mixed, giving it a slight advantage over cake. The necessity for powdering, however, is a slight drawback. Both creme and cake makeup are more expensive than greasepaint. Creme makeup is available from Bob Kelly, Ben Nye, the Makeup Center, Paramount, Kryolan, and Stein.

Creme rouge. See *Rouge, creme.*

*Crepe hair. (See Figure 17–2.) Indispensable for male character makeups. Crepe wool, as it is sometimes called, comes in tightly woven braids and is purchased by the yard. It can be obtained in a number of colors, such as blond, auburn, light brown, medium brown, dark brown, light gray, and medium gray, and in some very useful shades that are a mixture of gray and brown. Crepe hair is available from Paramount, the Makeup Center, and from most of the makeup companies. Crepe hair must usually be dampened and straightened before use.

Dep. A thick hair-setting liquid. Available from beauty supply houses.

*Derma wax. A soft wax for building up areas of the face. It is easier to apply and to remove than nose putty but is less adhesive. It can also be mixed with nose putty as explained in Chapter 15. It is available from Paramount, Stein, Kryolan, or the Makeup Center. Nye's is called Nose and Scar Wax. Kryolan's is called Soft Putty. Paramount has Naturo Plasto, a high quality wax, in both firm and soft consistencies.

Drawing mats. Used in wigmaking for drawing hair (Figure 18–11A). See description and explanation in Chapter 18. Available from Jaari or Paramount.

Duo adhesive. A Johnson and Johnson cream latex adhesive obtainable in drugstores or from Paramount. Will eventually deteriorate in the tube. See *Adhesives.*

Dye brushes. See *Brushes, dye.*

Dye colors. Liquid food coloring is a useful and inexpensive dye for tinting liquid latex or for changing the usual tan color of transparent liquid makeup. Obtainable at grocery stores. It can also be mixed with water as a substitute for commercial transparent liquid makeup.

*Eyebrow pencils. (See Figure A-6.) Wooden pencils with soft grease lead used for darkening eyebrows. (See *Makeup pencils.*)

Eyebrow-pencil sharpeners. Ordinary pencil sharpeners are not usually satisfactory for eyebrow pencils. Paramount has a tiny sharpener, and Maybelline has an even better one (Figure A-6L), obtainable at most dime-store cosmetics counters. The Maybelline sharpener catches its own shavings so that you don't have to be near a wastebasket when you sharpen your pencil. Bob Kelly supplies a small sharpener in every kit. For giving pencils a flat cut (Figure A-6J), a single-edged razor blade or a sharp mat knife is usually used.

Eyebrow wax. A wax for blocking out the eyebrows. Kryolan makes a stick called Eyebrow Plastic (Figure A-7D), which is harder than derma wax and has the convenience of the stick form. It can be applied simply by rubbing it over the brows. Makeup is applied over it as usual. It can be removed quite easily with makeup remover. Available from the Makeup Center and from Paramount. A similar wax is available from Bob Kelly.

Eyelashes, artificial. Widely used by women for straight or corrective eye makeup or when the character requires heavy lashes. To some extent they can be used to change the shape of the eyes, though that is not their normal function. They are sold in pairs and must usually be trimmed before using. Ordinarily each lash can be cut in half to make a pair (see Chapter 13). It is possible to buy ready-trimmed lashes with a "feathered" look. Artificial eyelashes can be obtained at any cosmetics counter or from Paramount. The Makeup Center has a large selection. Very high quality ones are made by Mehron (Figure A-7E). Stein has natural hair lashes as well as self-sticking nylon ones. Artificial eyelashes are fairly expensive, but with proper care they should last a long time. They are applied with special adhesive or with Flexol or Duo adhesive.

Eyeliner brush. (See Figure A-5.) A narrow brush suitable for lining the eyes. Mehron, Kelly, Stein, and the Makeup Center have excellent sable ones.

Eyeliners. Special water-soluble, cake eyeliners are available, mostly in brown and black. The color is applied with an eyeliner brush. Liquid eyeliners are also available. Eyeliners can be obtained from most of the makeup companies, from Paramount and the Makeup Center, and at cosmetics counters. The Makeup Center also has an Eyeliner Seal to prevent smearing.

*Eyeshadow. A variety of colors, including iridescents, is available from all of the makeup companies and from Paramount and the Makeup Center. Some of these are specifically labeled as eyeshadow—others are the regular shading colors. Kelly's are available in creme and brush-on cake, Nye's in creme, Mehron's in their lanolin-base makeup, Stein's in grease, cake, and sticks, Leichner's in sticks, and Kryolan's in both sticks and flat plastic containers. All types and forms of eyeshadow are available from Paramount.

*Face powder. Used over foundation paint to set it. It comes in a wide variety of tints and shades, most of which are unnecessary. A translucent face powder, which causes less distortion in makeup colors than do other powders, is obtainable from most of the makeup companies. Mehron's is called Colorset, Kelly's is called Translucent, and Stein's, Leichner's, and Paramount's are called Neutral. When a tinted face powder is used, the shade of powder should be lighter than the lightest paint on the face. Deeper shades are useful for dark-skinned actors. The very dark shades are sometimes useful for crowd scenes when large numbers of makeups must be done very quickly—the skin can be darkened merely by the application of the dark powder without using any foundation.

Fishskin. Can be used to draw the skin into various shapes. One end may be attached to the skin with spirit gum and the other tied over the head with a string. Fishskin is semitransparent and very strong. Obtainable from music stores, particularly those specializing in repairing. It is no longer widely used in makeup; transparent plastic adhesive is more convenient.

Fixative spray. (See Figure A-18A.) For setting makeup so that it will not rub off. Made by Kryolan (Fixier Spray). It dries quickly but leaves a shine and therefore usually requires powdering. Available from Paramount. The Makeup Center has a liquid Liner Seal for use over any eyeliner that might tend to smear.

Fluorescent paints. See *Luminous paints.*

Gauze, silk. A thin, tough foundation material for wigs and beards (see Chapters 17 and 18). It is available in three qualities—domestic, imported, and Swiss—and in various grades. Obtainable from wigmakers' supply houses.

Gauze, surgical. Can be used for blocking out eyebrows or dipped in plaster for use in making negative moulage molds. Obtainable from drugstores.

Glatzan. (See Figure 14–21.) Kryolan's liquid plastic. See *Plastic caps* and *Plastic film.*

Glycerine. May be brushed or sponged on the body to make it shine or used as a base for metallic powders. The powders can be either patted on over the glycerine or mixed with it before it is applied (see *Metallic makeup*). Obtainable at drugstores.

Greaseless makeup. See *Cake makeup* and *Liquid makeup.*

*Greasepaint. (See Figure A-8.) The traditional foundation paint used to give the basic skin coloring. It is manufactured in a great variety of colors and in both a soft and a hard consistency. Most artists find the soft paint more satisfactory than the stick because it is more sanitary and keeps fresh longer. Mehron's foundation paint is not strictly a greasepaint since it contains a pure lanolin base, but since it is used for the same purpose, it will be included under this heading. It is packaged in jars (Figure A-8A). The Mehron foundation paint does not separate as some soft greasepaints do. Kryolan's greasepaint comes in plastic cases (Figure A-8I,J) in three sizes. They also have sticks in two sizes. Leichner and Stein supply greasepaint in sticks and tubes.

The chief advantages of greasepaint over cake makeup are that the colors are easily mixed, skin blemishes and irregularities in prosthetic applications are easily covered, and the paint is inexpensive. The chief disadvantages are that it is messy to use, rubs off easily on clothing, encourages perspiration, and requires powdering, which modifies the character work, often obliterating detail.

The more intense hues of greasepaint are called shading colors, lining colors, or liners. They are used for shadows and highlights, eye makeup, rouge, and lip rouge, and are of a firmer consistency than greasepaint foundation. The paint is of a consistency that makes it easily applicable with a brush. Leichner and Stein have shading color sticks.

Hackle. (See Figure 18–14K.) An instrument combining the qualities of a comb and a brush, constructed of metal spikes in a wooden block, used for combing or untangling skeins of hair (See Chapter 18.)

Hair, crepe. See *Crepe hair.*

Hair, human. Used for fine wigs, toupees, falls, and other hairpieces, and for ventilated beards and mustaches. Waved hair comes in a loose corkscrew curl, which forms a natural wave in the wig. Unlike crepe hair, real hair should not normally be straightened before use. It is usually available in lengths from 10 to 24 inches, in a variety of colors, and is sold by the pound (or the ounce). The price per pound varies with the length and the color. It is also possible to have a sample of hair matched perfectly. Available from Jaari (address in Appendix B).

Hair, synthetic. See discussion in Chapter 17. Synthetic hair with a high sheen is suitable largely for stylized wigs. That which is more nearly like real hair can be ventilated or made into weft for wigs, beards, and mustaches. Synthetic hair can also be blended with real hair. The cheaper synthetics are sometimes used instead of crepe hair. Available from Paramount and from Kryolan in a number of colors. The colors can easily be mixed. Synthetic hair is sold by the ounce, and the cost is considerably less than that of the cheapest human hair.

Hair, yak. Sometimes used for wigs but more often for beards and mustaches. It is also less expensive than human hair.

Hair coloring. Various manufacturers of beauty products also have temporary hair-coloring products as well as permanent dyes. Mascara (black, white, brown, blond, for example) can be used for small areas but is less effective. Colored powders can be used in an emergency but are not really satisfac-

Figure A-7. Makeup supplies and accessories. (A) Kryolan's Tuplast, (B) Kryolan's nose putty, (C) Kryolan's soft nose putty, (D) Kryolan's Eyebrow Plastic, (E) Mehron's false eyelashes, (F) Braendel's plastic glitter.

Figure A-8. Greasepaint. (A) Mehron's foundation paint, (B) Mehron's Mask Cover, (C) Kryolan's rubber-mask grease, (D, E, F) Leichner's greasepaint sticks, (G) Mehron's Shado-Liner, (H) Mehron's lip rouge, (I) Braendel's shading color, (J) Kryolan's shading color.

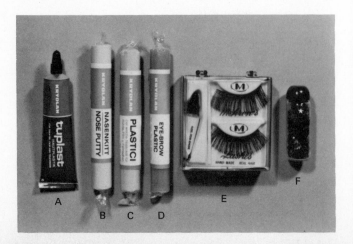

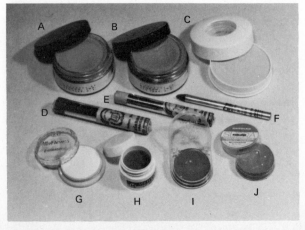

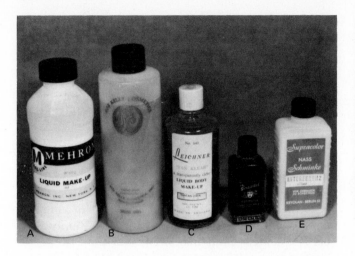

Figure A-9. Liquid makeup. (A) Mehron's Liquid Make-up, (B) Bob Kelly's Body Makeup, (C) Leichner's Body Makeup, (D) Braendel's transparent liquid makeup, (D) Kryolan's liquid makeup.

Figure A-10. Hair coloring. (A) Bob Kelly's hair whitener, (B) Paramount's Color Sprae, (C, D) Braendel's Color Spray, (E) Ben Nye's Silver Hair Gray.

tory. Temporary color sprays, such as Streaks n' Tips, are available from the Makeup Center, from drugstores, and at cosmetics counters. Paramount and Kryolan also have sprays in a number of shades for coloring and graying the hair (Figure A-10). All can be removed by shampooing the hair.

Hair dryer. Useful in force-drying molded latex and such materials as plastic, sealer, spirit gum, collodion, and moulage—also for drying hair. Obtainable from drugstores, appliance shops, department stores, and elsewhere.

Hairlace. (See Figure 18–6.) A netlike foundation used in making quality wigs, toupees, beards, and mustaches. See Chapters 17 and 18. Obtainable from Jaari or Paramount.

Hair spray. Any spray used for keeping the hair in place. See also *Hair coloring.* Colorless aerosol hair sprays in a variety of brands are available in drugstores, at cosmetics counters, and from Paramount.

*Hair whiteners. (See Figure A-10.) Liquid or solid whitener for graying the hair. It is brushed on, then combed into the hair. In the liquid form, the pure white can be modified by the addition of food coloring. Removable with soap and water. White cake mascara, or white cake makeup can also be used. The mascara is applied with a brush, the cake makeup with a sponge. Hair whitener is obtainable from Paramount or from any of the makeup companies. Ben Nye's liquid Silver Hair Gray produces a particularly natural effect and is

highly recommended. Bob Kelly's stick whitener in two shades is convenient to use and quite effective. If you are in doubt about which to use, try the yellowed white. Braendel has a stick whitener called Temple White, available from the Makeup Center.

Kalginate. An alginate impression powder that can be used effectively for making face masks. See *Moulage.*

Knotting needles. See *Ventilating needles.*

K-Y Lubricating jelly. (See Figure A-18E.) Useful for blending nose putty and derma wax. Can also be used as a protective film over a grease makeup, then removed for a quick change. Since the K-Y is water soluble, it and the makeup covering it can be removed with water, leaving the grease makeup more or less intact, though some detail is likely to be lost. Available in large and small tubes at drugstores.

*Latex, liquid. A liquid rubber used for building up flexible prosthetic pieces (see Chapter 16), attaching crepe hair (Chapter 17), or creating wrinkles and texture for age (Chapter 15). Obtainable from Paramount, Mehron, Kelly, Stein, or Kryolan. Latex is normally an off-white but can easily be colored by the addition of small amounts of concentrated dye, food coloring, or even makeup powders to arrive at whatever flesh tone is needed. When dry, however, the latex is normally darker than when wet. The Paramount latex is available in two colors, in addition to clear. The clear is pref-

erable for aging and is also good for casting. Latex can be obtained in small bottles with a brush and larger bottles without a brush. The larger bottles are, naturally, much more economical. If a bottle with a brush is used, the brush must always be returned to the bottle immediately and not be exposed to the air any longer than absolutely necessary. Once latex dries on the brush, the brush is usually ruined.

Latex foamed sponge compounds can be obtained from Paramount or from Uniroyal Chemical in four parts to be combined when used. See Chapter 16 for details. Kryolan has an easy-to-use combination of plastic foam and latex in three parts, listed as "Foam Components, Hagen, #2594." The foam sets in 15 minutes, with no heat required.

Latex caps. (See Figure A-15.) For bald heads. Available from Kryolan or Paramount. See also *Plastic caps.*

Latex pieces. A few ready-made latex pieces (noses, chins, wrinkled foreheads, pouches, scars, warts, burns, etc.) are available—some from Bob Kelly, some from the Makeup Center, and some from Kryolan. With certain pieces, such as chins and noses, getting a perfect fit cannot really be expected. Other pieces, such as eye pouches, are more easily adaptable. Warts, burns, and scars should cause no problem. For instructions in making your own latex pieces, see Chapters 15 and 16.

Lipsticks. They are usable in the individual makeup kit but for sanitary reasons have no place in group kits. Bob Kelly, On Stage, Ben Nye, Kryolan, and Stein have a variety of colors.

Liquid makeup. (See Figure A-9.) This is a greaseless foundation comparable to cake makeup except that it comes in liquid form. It can be obtained from Paramount or from most of the makeup companies in a wide variety of colors paralleling their other foundation colors.

Liquid makeup is applied with a sponge and is removable with soap and water or makeup remover. It can be used for the face but is most useful as a body makeup.

Kryolan has a special makeup called Liquid Brightness—a nonmetallic makeup that can be mixed with other liquid body makeups to make the skin glisten. For water-soluble body makeup in powder form, see *Texas Dirt.*

There is also a transparent liquid made by Braendel (Exotenteint) and one by Leichner (Tan Klear) in two shades. Transparent liquid makeup is intended only for coloring the skin and does not cover blemishes or provide a foundation for other makeup. The color can be varied by adding food coloring, or a satisfactory transparent liquid can be made by adding food coloring to water.

Liquid plastic. See *Plastic, liquid.*

Luminous paints. Occasionally it is necessary to have a makeup glow in the dark, as, for instance, Death in *Death Takes a Holiday.* The transition from the makeup of the Count to that of Death can be very simply accomplished by the use of luminous paints or pigments. For the exact technique see Chapter 20. Both fluorescent and phosphorescent paints and pigments can be used. The fluorescent ones must be excited by an ultraviolet light. The phosphorescent ones require no ultraviolet light but are less brilliant. A number of shades are obtainable in both kinds of paints and pigments. The yellow is perhaps the most effective. The paints are expensive, but only a small amount is required for an ordinary makeup. Obtainable from Paramount.

Makeup cape. For protecting clothing. Paramount has an excellent translucent white plastic cape. Sheets of plastic can also be used.

*Makeup kits. (See Figures A-11, A-12, A-13.) Bob Kelly has a choice of 11 kits—for students, professionals, groups, and light- and dark-skinned actors. These are available in creme or cake makeup. Ben Nye has student kits in creme makeup for both light- and dark-skinned actors. Since each Nye kit contains only two foundation colors, more mixing is required than with the Kelly kits. Mehron has a student male and female kit with their foundation and shading colors. Greasepaint kits are available from Paramount and from Stein.

Makeup palette. Kryolan has available a makeup palette (Figure A-14) with 132 samples of their makeup colors. This palette makes it possible to try various colors on the face before buying them. Each color sample is sufficient for several makeups.

*Makeup pencils. (See Figure A-6.) Wooden pencils with soft grease lead used for darkening eyebrows and also for accenting eyes and wrinkles, outlining lips, and drawing designs on the face. When used for eyebrows, they are usually called eyebrow pencils. They are available in a wide variety of colors in addition to the usual brown and

Figure A-11. Student cake-makeup kit. By Bob Kelly.

Figure A-12. Professional creme-makeup kit. By Bob Kelly.

Figure A-13. Student makeup kit. By Mehron.

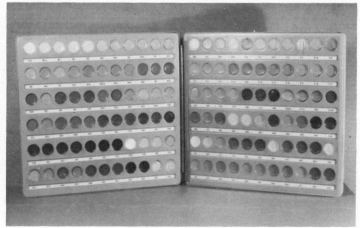

Figure A-14. Makeup palette. By Kryolan.

Figure A-16. Makeup removers. (A) Bob Kelly's Makeup Remover, (B) Mehron's Liquefying Cream, (D) Mehron's Spirit Gum Remover, (E) Ben Nye's Makeup Remover.

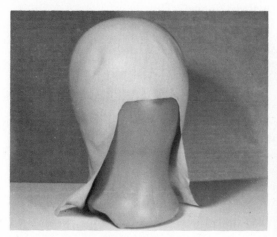

Figure A-15. Latex cap. By Kryolan.

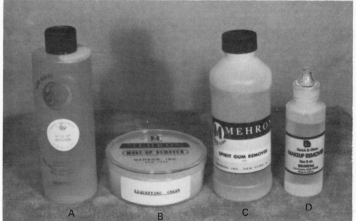

259

black. Bob Kelly has more than 20 shades, including turquoise, lilac, gold, silver, yellow, ash, and six shades of red.

Pencils to be used for shading can be sharpened flat with a razor blade, rather like an artist's shading pencil (see Figure 14–9H and the discussion in Chapter 14 in the section on eye pouches).

*Makeup removers. (See Figure A-16.) Available in solid or liquid form. Cleansing creams are available from all makeup manufacturers, drugstores, dime stores, and cosmetics counters. Mehron has two excellent removers, called Makeup Remover and Liquefying Cream. Bob Kelly has a very effective liquid remover that removes both paint and spirit gum. Ben Nye also has a liquid remover. Stein has a good liquefying cream called Makeup Remover Cream as well as other types of creams. Some actors use McKesson's Albolene; others prefer baby oil. For cake makeup, some use soap and water. Special spirit gum removers are also available. The choice of remover is a matter of personal preference. Removers are available from Paramount, the Makeup Center, makeup companies, and drugstores.

*Mascara. Used primarily for coloring the eyelashes, sometimes the eyebrows, and occasionally the hair. It is made in brown, black, white, and various colors, such as blue, green, blond, and henna. Available from Paramount, the makeup companies or at any cosmetic counter. It comes in cake, liquid, and cream and is applied with a brush or, when in wand form, with a special applicator.

Masslinn towels. Disposable cotton and rayon (nonwoven) towels which can be used with latex for skin-texture effects (Chapter 15). Obtainable in department stores.

Metallic makeup. Greasepaints are available in gold and silver in flat plastic containers from Kryolan and in stick form from Leichner. Metallic shading colors or eyeshadow are available from Mehron, Kryolan, Stein, the Makeup Center, and Paramount, and makeup pencils from Kelly. Stein has body makeup in gold and silver. It is easily removable with soap and water.

Kryolan has an extremely effective water-soluble gold and silver makeup (Aquacolor, Figure A-3), which can be applied with the fingers or with a damp sponge or a brush. Normal application gives a solid metallic effect, but it can also be applied lightly over other makeup to give a slight metallic sheen. Available from the Makeup Center or Paramount.

Gold and silver powders can be used on the hair for graying or adding brilliance. The effect is usually striking, but the powder is exceedingly difficult to remove and is ruinous to any grease or creme makeup upon which it happens to fall. Silver and gold sprays (see *Hair sprays*) are preferable. The powders can be mixed with glycerine and isopropyl alcohol and applied to the body for special effects. The powders are usually available in silver (aluminum), gold, copper, red, blue, and green. Mehron has gold and silver. Try art or paint stores for other colors. Flakes or sequins are also available. These are useful for certain scintillating, sparkling effects in stylized makeups. Obtainable at paint stores, art supply stores, theatrical costumers, and elsewhere. Braendel has glitter (they call it Glimmer) in various colors, as well as tiny stars. The glitter is made of plastic to prevent any discomfort in wearing it. It is packaged in a convenient glass bottle with a shaker top (Figure A-7F).

No metallic paint should remain on the entire body longer than necessary and not used at all unless the actor is in good health. It is considered harmless for very short periods, but if it is left too long on the entire body or a large portion of its area, the effects could be extremely serious. As a precaution, at least a few square inches of skin—even if the actor is completely nude—should be free of the makeup to allow that much of the skin to "breathe." Should the actor wearing the metallic makeup show any sign of faintness—no matter what you *think* the cause may be—the makeup should be removed immediately.

Mineral oil. Can be sprayed on the face to simulate perspiration. It can also be used as a makeup remover.

Mirror. A round, double-faced mirror (one side magnifying) is very useful in the makeup kit. Whenever possible, of course, makeup should be done before a large, well-lighted mirror, but the small mirror is essential in getting back and profile views. Obtainable at dime stores, drugstores, and cosmetics counters. Portable lighted makeup mirrors are very useful—especially those that allow for adjusting the color of the light. The ones with triple mirrors (two adjustable side panels) are the most useful.

Modeling clay. Oil-base modeling clay, which

does not dry out, is used in modeling heads when studying facial structure and also in modeling features for prosthesis. Obtainable at art supply stores, usually in 1-pound or 5-pound blocks. Various colors are available.

Modeling wax.   See *Derma wax.*

Modeling tools.   (See Figure A-6.) Shaped orangewood sticks used in clay modeling, also in modeling nose putty or derma wax. Available from art supply stores in a variety of styles.

Moist rouge.   See *Rouge, moist.*

Moulage.   A gelatinous material used in making plaster or stone casts for prosthesis (see Chapter 16). A reusable type has been largely replaced by an alginate that is much faster but is not reusable. Obtainable from Paramount and dental supply houses.

Mousseline de soie.   A gauzelike silk or rayon cloth often used in making facial lifts. Obtainable at dry goods counters.

Mustaches.   Can be purchased ready-made on gauze in various forms and colors from Paramount or made to order by Bob Kelly. Instructions for making beards and mustaches are given in Chapter 17.

Mustache wax.   Available from the Makeup Center and from Bob Kelly.

Needles, knotting or **ventilating.**   See *Ventilating needles.*

Netting.   Foundation for wigs, toupees, beards, and mustaches. Available in silk, nylon, plastic, and cotton. The English silk vegetable netting is usually the most expensive and the English cotton vegetable netting the cheapest. The more expensive nettings (or hairlace) should be used on good wigs, toupees, and beards. Cotton netting can be used for practice work. All nettings and laces are available from Jaari.

*Nose putty.   (See Figure A-7B, C.) A sticky, pliable material used for building up the nose and other bony parts of the face. Mehron and Kelly have excellent nose putty. Kryolan has a high quality putty, which comes in two degrees of stiffness, the softer of which is called *Plastici*, the other *Nasenkitt* or Nose Putty. Both are highly recommended. They are easy to work with and very adhesive. The Makeup Center has Kryolan putty. All brands are available from Paramount.

Orangewood sticks.   (See Figure A-6.) Can be used for modeling nose putty, derma wax, or modeling clay. Also used for applying cosmetic to the eyelashes. Obtainable from dime stores, drugstores, and art stores.

Pan-Cake.   Factor's trade name for cake makeup.

Pan-Stik.   Factor's trade name for creme stick.

Pencils.   See *Makeup pencils.*

Phosphorescent paints.   See *Luminous paints.*

Plaster bandage.   Rolls of gauze impregnated with plaster for use in making molds with moulage. Obtainable from art stores—also from drugstores and medical supply houses. Surgical gauze dipped into plaster can be substituted.

Plaster of Paris.   Used in making both positive and negative casts in rubber prosthesis (see Chapter 16). Obtainable at paint and hardware stores.

Plastic, liquid.   See *Plastic film.*

Plastic caps.   (See Figure 18–19.) Used for bald heads. See Chapter 16 for instructions in making. Kryolan makes a convenient liquid plastic (*Glatzan L*) that can simply be painted on a smooth head form to make a cap. *It must not be used directly on the skin!* Available from the Makeup Center and from Paramount. Kryolan plastic head forms (see Figure 18–19) for making the caps are available from Paramount. Kryolan also has ready-made plastic caps. Available from Paramount. See also *Latex caps.*

Plastic film, liquid.   The Kryolan liquid plastic mentioned above can also be painted on glass to make a plastic film in any shape or size. The film is useful for making eyebrow covers (see Chapter 14) as well as scars and sagging eyelids (see Chapter 15).

A plastic that *can* be used on the skin is available in tubes (Kryolan's *Tuplast*) for making scars (see *Scar plastic*).

Plastic head forms.   (Figure 18–19.) For use in making plastic caps (see above). A Kryolan product, available from Paramount.

Plastici.   (See Figure A-7C.) A soft nose putty made by Kryolan. See *Nose putty.*

Putty.   See *Nose putty.*

Putty-wax. A soft putty made by melting nose putty and derma wax together (see Chapter 15).

Rabbit's paw. Formerly used for applying dry rouge or for removing excess powder. Now rarely found in the makeup kit.

*Rouge, creme. Various shades of red and orange creme makeup. Available from Kelly, Nye, the Makeup Center, and Paramount.

*Rouge, dry. A cake or powder rouge that can be applied dry with a puff or a soft brush for touching up completed makeups or with a damp sponge in the same manner as any cake makeup. A good variety of colors is available from Paramount, the Makeup Center, the various makeup companies, or—more reasonably—from dime stores. Brush-on rouge—a somewhat powdery cake—is applied dry with a soft brush. It is available in natural, subtle colors that can be used by both men and women. Can be purchased at cosmetics counters, at dime stores, from Bob Kelly, or from Para-

Figure A-17. Adhesives. *(top)* (A) Braendel's empty spirit gum bottle, (B) Kryolan's spirit gum, (C) Bob Kelly's Hairlace Adhesive, (D) Bob Kelly's latex, (E) Stein's latex.

Figure A-18. Miscellaneous makeup. *(bottom)* (A) Kryolan's Fixier Spray, (B) Bob Kelly's Scar Material, (C) Ben Nye's Old Age Plastic and Sealor, (D) Mehron's Fixative A, (E) K-Y Lubricant.

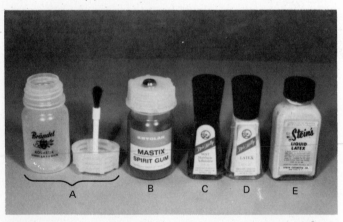

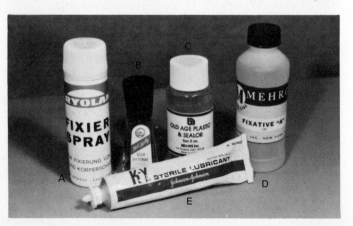

mount. The lighter colors are not usually strong enough for the stage.

*Rouge, moist. Shades of red and orange makeup with a grease or lanolin base. Available from Mehron, Kryolan, Leichner, Stein, and Paramount.

Rubber. See *Latex.*

Rubber-mask grease. A special castor-oil-base paint for use on latex. Mehron has developed a new formula, which eliminates the separation and general messiness of the old rubber-mask grease. It comes in six shades, which can be mixed. Bob Kelly's is also made in six shades and Kryolan's in more than eighty. Available from Mehron, Kelly, Kryolan, the Makeup Center, and Paramount.

Scar plastic. A liquid plastic applied directly to the skin for making scars. Ben Nye's, in bottles, is called Old Age Plastic and Sealor (Figure A-18C). Kryolan's, in tubes, is called *Tuplast* (Figure A-7A). It is much thicker than Nye's and can be used to build up a 3-dimensional scar with a single application. It is available from the Makeup Center. Both are available from Paramount.

Scissors. (See Figure A-6.) Necessary for trimming crepe hair and frequently useful for other purposes, such as trimming latex pieces. Barbers' shears are best for hair work.

Sealer. A liquid plastic skin adhesive containing polyvinyl butyral, castor oil, and isopropyl alcohol, sometimes used medically as an adhesive and as a protective coating. It is especially useful in makeup to provide a protective surface for derma wax constructions, for blocking out eyebrows, and often in place of flexible collodion with cotton. Can be obtained from Mehron, Ben Nye, or Paramount. Mehron's (Figure A-18D) is called Fixative A; Ben Nye's (Figure A-18C) is called Old Age Plastic and Sealor.

If you wish to make your own sealer, you can do it very simply by dissolving 1 oz. VYNS (a vinyl chloride-acetate resin) and $\frac{1}{2}$ oz. DOP (dioctyl-phthalate, a plasticizer) in 10 oz. acetone. Materials obtainable from Bakelite. This will give a fairly stiff film and a fast drying one. For a softer film the amount of plasticizer can be increased two or three times. The sealer does not deteriorate but must be kept in a tightly closed container to prevent evaporation. It is applied with a soft brush.

Shading colors. See *Greasepaint.*

Silk gauze. See *Gauze, silk.*

Skin freshener. For oily skins and for removing any traces of grease after the makeup has been taken off. Available from Bob Kelly, the Makeup Center, and cosmetics counters.

Slomon's Medico Adhesive. A strong adhesive, useful for attaching latex pieces to areas of the skin where there is likely to be a great deal of muscular activity. May prove irritating to some skins.

Soap. For blocking out the eyebrows or the hair. See Chapters 14 and 18. Any small bar of toilet soap is satisfactory.

*Spirit gum. (See Figure A-17.) A liquid gum adhesive used to attach crepe hair, hairlace, or latex prosthetic pieces. Also to paste down eyebrows in blocking them out. There are differences in spirit gums and in drying time among the various brands. Regular spirit gum is shiny when dry. For use with hairlace, a matte gum (dull surface when dry) is preferable. If the brush that comes in the bottle is too small, a larger brush can be used instead. In applying crepe hair, you should wipe the brush from time to time with an old cloth to remove the hair that sticks to it. And it's a good idea to tape the bottle to your makeup table to avoid the possibility of knocking it over. Spirit gum is available from all of the makeup companies, from the Makeup Center, and from Paramount. Kryolan's comes in regular, matte, and quick-drying; theirs is the best bottle and the best brush available. Empty bottles with brushes (Figure A-17A) can be purchased. In ordering Kryolan spirit gum, be sure to specify the plastic bottle with brush if that's what you want. Only one size (Figure A-17B) comes with a brush.

*Sponges. Natural silk sponges (Figure A-19C) are used primarily for applying cake or liquid makeup. Large ones can be cut into smaller ones. They are irregular in shape but roughly round or oval. Red-rubber sponges (Figure A-19B) can be used for creating skin texture effects with stippling and also for applying rubber-mask grease. But the best sponge for stippling is a flat-surface, black nylon sponge (Figure A-19D,E,F) used in humidifiers. It is available from Ben Nye and from Bob Kelly. Foam sponges (Figure (A-19A) are sometimes used with creme makeup. Flat, synthetic sponges (stiff when dry, soft when wet) can be used with

Figure A-19. Sponges. *(top)* (A) Foam-latex sponge, (B) red-rubber sponge, (C) natural silk sponge, (D, E, F) black plastic sponges.

Figure A-20. Magnetic container for pins. *(bottom).* By Kryolan.

cake makeup when natural sponges are not available. The natural silk sponges can also be used in the cheeks for making them fatter or for creating jowl effects. Sponges can be obtained from Paramount, the Makeup Center, from the various makeup companies, in drugstores and dime stores, and at cosmetics counters.

Stone, dental. Comes in powder form to be mixed with water and is used for making casts in the same way as plaster. The resulting cast is harder than plaster and must be used when the cast is to be subjected to considerable pressure. Can be obtained from dental supply houses.

Spray-on bandage. Packaged in aerosol cans under the trade name of Safeguard. Sprays on a thin plastic film that is useful in setting beards or mustaches or as an adhesive. Obtainable at drugstores.

Stoppelpaste. See *Stubble paste*.

Stubble paste. (See Figure 17–6.) An adhesive wax in convenient stick used to attach beard stubble for an unshaven effect. Made by Braendel under the name of *Stoppelpaste*, it is available from the Makeup Center and from Paramount. Bob Kelly has a similar stubble stick.

Stumps. Paper stumps are small, pointed, pencil-like rolls of paper sometimes used for shadowing and highlighting. Brushes should be used instead, but stumps are useful for drawing with charcoal and chalk. They can be obtained from Stein, Paramount, or any artists' supply store. Chamois stumps are more expensive but last much longer.

Tape, adhesive. See *Adhesive tape*.

Temple White. A hair-graying stick made by Braendel. Available from the Makeup Center.

Texas Dirt. An effective body makeup that comes in powder form and is applied quickly and easily with a damp sponge. It is easily removable with soap and water. Obtainable from Paramount and Mehron. Mehron's Plain dries with a dull finish. Their Gold is about the same color but has a gold sheen. Mehron's Texas Dirt, Silver and Paramount's Texas Dirt are similar in color. Paramount's has a very subtle silvery sheen. Mehron's has a slightly more definite silver sheen. Since the effects of the various versions of Texas Dirt are quite dissimilar, you should decide whether or not you want the slightly metallic sheen and if so, whether you want the strong suntan color with gold or the silvery bronze.

Thread. Common cotton or silk thread is useful in removing nose putty. When the thread is passed between the skin and the putty, most of the putty will come off easily.

Toupee tape. See *Adhesive tapes*.

T-pins. (See Figure A-20.) T-shaped pins for securing wigs to wig blocks. They come in various sizes and can be obtained from Jaari or any wig supply company. Kryolan sells a very convenient magnetic pin container, shown with T-pins in Figure A-20.

Tuffy head. A life-size rubber head (face and neck only) that can be used for making beards with a latex base rather than doing them directly on the face. If the beard is to be sprayed, it can be done more conveniently on the Tuffy head than on the actor's face. The head can also be used instead of a beard block for ventilating beards and mustaches. It fits on to any standard wig-block holder. It works best, of course, for faces with average proportions. A plaster cast of the actor's face can be used in the same way and for a perfect fit the cast is preferable. The Tuffy head is available from Kryolan.

Tuplast. (See Figure A-7A.) A thick liquid plastic that can be used on the skin to build up 3-dimensional scars. Made by Kryolan. Available from the Makeup Center and from Paramount.

Tweezers. Handy for removing stray hairs in dressing crepe hair applications or in attaching small latex pieces. Any good tweezers will do.

Velvet Stick. Stein's trade name for creme stick.

Ventilating needles. For knotting hair into net or gauze for wigs or beards. See Chapters 17 and 18. Obtainable from Jaari or any wigmakers' supply company. Should be ordered by number, the smallest usually being 00. The needle holder is ordered separately. One holder is sufficient, but you should have several sizes of needles.

Wax, black. See *Black wax*.

Wax, derma. See *Derma wax*.

Weaving frames. For weaving hair. See Chapter 18. Available from Jaari, Paramount, or any wigmakers' supply house.

Wig blocks. Available in various materials, wood perhaps being the most common for professional use. Canvas-covered ones are also useful. They will take T-pins, whereas wooden blocks require tacking or taping for securing the wig. Available from Jaari, Paramount, or any wigmaker's supply house.

Wigs. Instructions for wigmaking can be found in Chapter 18. Wigs can be rented or bought from Bob Kelly or other wigmakers or from most theatrical costumers. A variety of ready-made wigs can be bought from Paramount. In general, buying wigs is more satisfactory than renting, but you might better rent a good wig than buy a poor one. Bob Kelly will make or rent wigs to match any style illustrated in Appendix G. You need only give the plate number and letter of the style, specifying

Stage Makeup, 5th edition, or *Fashions in Hair*, depending on which book you order from. Be sure to include the usual wig measurements (see Chapter 18). Paramount will also have wigs made to order from the sketches in Appendix G. These are for sale only.

   Wig springs.   Used only if you make your own wig foundations. They hold the wig snugly to the head. Obtainable from Jaari or other wigmakers' supply houses.

   Wig stands and ***holders.***   (See Figure 18–10C.) For holding wig blocks in place when wigs are being dressed. They can be in the form of floor stands, table clamps, or a small rubber stand with a suction cup, which can be attached to any smooth surface. Floor stands are cumbersome to have around unless you have plenty of space, but they do make it possible to work on your wig anywhere in the room. The table clamps usually allow tilting the wig block to any convenient angle, but they require a suitable table or bench to which they can be attached. The suction cup stand is a handy portable gadget, useful for attaching to makeup or dressing-table tops and for carrying about. Wig stands and clamps are available from Jaari or other wigmakers' supply houses or from Paramount.

Appendix B

SOURCES OF MAKEUP MATERIALS

A. JAARI HAIR PROCESSING CORPORATION, 12 East 22nd Street, New York City 10010.
Hair in bulk and wigmakers' supplies, including ventilating needles, hairlace, etc.

BAKELITE COMPANY (Division of Union Carbide Corp.), 270 Park Avenue, New York City.
Materials for prosthesis with plastics, including XYSG, VYNS, and Flexol DOP. Ask for pamphlets and price lists on vinyl resins.

FACTOR, MAX, MAKEUP STUDIOS, 1655 North McCadden Place, Hollywood, California 90028.
Write for price list.

FIBRE PRODUCTS MFG. CO., 601 West 26th Street, New York City.
Variety of sample cases suitable for makeup kits. Write for catalog, specifying particular interest in makeup.

JEVNIKAR CORPORATION, 1030 Euclid Avenue, Cleveland, Ohio.
Toupees and wigs for street wear only. Write for quotations. *No theatrical wigs of any kind.*

KELLY, BOB, 151 West 46th Street, New York City 10036. Phone: 212 CI 5-2237.
Has a complete line of stage makeup, including both creme stick and cake makeup—also a variety of kits. Makes wigs, hairpieces, beards, and mustaches for the professional theater, television, movies, and street wear. One of the most reliable sources of rental wigs for the nonprofessional theater. Write for brochure. If you are in New York, you can purchase makeup, have wig fittings, or rent wigs at the address above, in the same building as the Eaves Costume Company.

KRYOLAN/BRAENDEL GmbH, 1 Berlin 51, Papierstrasse 10, Federal Republic of Germany.

Complete line of theatrical makeup. Their products are available through New York distributors—the Makeup Center and Paramount Theatrical Supplies (see addresses below). Also through London distributors—Charles Fox and the Theatre Zoo (see *Sources in Great Britain*).

MAKEUP CENTER LTD., 150 West 55th Street, New York City. Phone: 212 CI 7-1166.
A convenient source of makeup—including Kryolan/Braendel, Mehron, Stein, Leichner, and Factor—for New York customers or visitors to the city. The owners are very helpful and allow professional customers to try various shades of makeup in their makeup room. A makeup service (especially valuable for models) is also available. Mail orders are accepted. Write for brochure.

MEHRON, INC., 325 West 37th Street, New York City 10018. Phone: 212 524-1133.
Complete line of stage makeup, including both cake makeup and a lanolin-base foundation. Write for price list. If you are in New York, you can buy Mehron's products at the address above—also from the Makeup Center and Paramount.

NYE, BEN, INC., 11571 Santa Monica Blvd., Los Angeles, California 90025. Phone: 213 478-1558.
Complete line of creme makeup, along with other makeup supplies. Write for brochure. Their makeup is also available through Paramount.

OLESON COMPANY, 1535 Ivar Avenue, Hollywood, California 90028.
Makeup supplies.

PARAMOUNT THEATRICAL SUPPLIES (Alcone), 32 West 20th Street, New York City 10011. Phone: 212 CH 3-0765.
The most complete mail-order source of makeup

of all brands, as well as hair supplies, with fast air-mail service when needed. Write for catalog. The owner, Mr. Alvin Cohen, will do his best to supply most of the makeup and hair items listed in this book.

PLASTODENT, INC., 2881 Middletown Rd., New York City.
Dental supplies.

ROBINSON PLAYS AND COSTUMES LTD., 47 Simcoe Street, Toronto 1, Ontario, Canada.
They have their own Roll-On Cosmetic, as well as a variety of makeup of other brands, including Ben Nye. Write for brochure.

SLOMON'S LABORATORIES, 43–28 Van Dam Street, Long Island City, New York 10001.
Medico adhesive.

M. STEIN COSMETIC COMPANY, 430 Broome Street, New York City 10013.
Complete line of stage makeup, including greasepaint (tubes and sticks) and cake makeup. Write for catalog. Mail orders only.

UNIROYAL CHEMICAL, Elm Street, Naugatuck, Connecticut 06770.
Latices, including their compound for foaming, LOTOL L-7176. (See Chapter 16 for formula and instructions for use.) Sold in minimum quantity of 1 gallon. Also available from Paramount.

VERNON-BENSHOFF COMPANY, 929 Ridge Avenue, Pittsburgh, Pennsylvania.
Dicor Adhesives #209 and #210.

S. S. WHITE DENTAL MFG. COMPANY, 211 S. 12th Street, Philadelphia, Pennsylvania.
Dental supplies.

SOURCES IN GREAT BRITAIN

AMALGAMATED DENTAL CO. LTD., 26 Broadwick St., London, W. 1.
Dental plaster.

ASH, CLAUDIUS, SONS & CO., LTD., 26 Broadwick St., London, W. 1.
Inlay wax, tooth plastics.

BAKELITE LTD., 12 Grosvenor Gardens, London, S.W. 1.
Sealers, VYNS.

BATEMANS, Young Corner, British Grove, London, W. 4.
Latex adhesives.

CAFFERATA & CO. LTD., Newark-on-Trent, Nottingham.
Casting plaster.

DENTAL FILLINGS LTD., 49b Grayling Road, London, N. 16.
Tooth plastics.

DENTAL MANUFACTURING CO. LTD., Automotive House, Great Portland St., London, W. 1.
Dental plaster.

EYLURE LTD., 60 Bridge Road East, Welwyn Garden City, Herts.
Eyelashes, brushes, pencils, sponges, false nails, brush-on eyeshadow.

FOX, CHARLES H., LTD., 25 Shelton Street, Upper St. Martin's Lane, London, W.C. 2.
Kryolan/Braendel makeup.

GEMEC CHEMICALS CO., 120 Moorgate, London, E. C. 2.
Plasticizer (DOP).

GOTHAM CO. LTD., Bentinck Buildings, Wheeler Gate, Nottingham.
Casting plaster.

HOECHST CHEMICALS LTD., Portland House, Stag Place, London, S.W. 1.
Polyvinyl butyrals.

LEICHNER'S CREATIVE STUDIOS, 44a Cranbourn St., London, W.C. 2.
Complete line of makeup materials, studio for consultation, and advisory service. Inquiries from outside Great Britain are welcomed. Open 9:30 A.M. to 5:30 P.M. weekdays. Phone REGent 7166 for appointments.

MACADAM & CO., 5 Lloyd's Ave., London, E.C. 3.
Latex.

MAX FACTOR, 16 Old Bond St., London, W. 1.
Makeup materials.

MONSANTO CHEMICALS LTD., Monsanto House, Victoria St., London, S.W. 1.
Sealing compounds, plasticizers.

NAGELE'S, 8 Broadwick St., London, W. 1.
Hairdressing supplies.

REVERTEX LTD., 51 Strand, London, W.C. 2.
Latex.

RUBBER LATEX LTD., Mosley Road, Trafford Park, Manchester, 17.
Latex adhesives, Easifoam #457.

RUBBER TECHNICAL DEVELOPMENTS LTD., 78 Bridge Road East, Welwyn Garden City, Herts.
Latex.

SERVENTI, HENRY, LTD., 61 Beak St., London, W. 1.
Human hair.

STATHAMS, Uttoxeter, Staffs.
Casting plaster.

THEATRE ZOO, Bert Broe, 28 New Row, St. Martin's Lane, London, W.C. 2.
Kryolan/Braendel makeup.

VINYL PRODUCTS LTD., Butler Hall, Carshalton, Surrey.
Sealing compounds.

WHITE, S. S., CO. OF GREAT BRITAIN, LTD., 126 Great Portland St., London, W. 1.
Tooth plastics.

WIG CREATIONS LTD., 22 Portman Close, Baker St., London, W. 1.
Wigs and hairpieces.

WIG SPECIALTIES, 173 Seymour Place, London, W. 1.
Wigs.

WITCO CHEMICAL CO. LTD., Bush House, Aldwych, London, W.C. 2.
Latex.

Appendix C

MAKEUP KITS

The following are suggested kits for those who prefer to make up their own. They should be revised and supplemented to suit individual needs. All makeup color numbers refer to those used in this book. For equivalents in commercial brands, see Table 1 following the color chart.

No single brand of makeup is superior in every way to all other brands, though certain specific materials or colors made by one company may be of higher quality, more practical, more conveniently packaged, more economical, or more dependable. There is no particular advantage in using one brand of makeup exclusively. By choosing items individually, you can select the best each manufacturer has to offer.* For sources of makeup materials, see Appendix A.

Good professional makeup boxes can be obtained from a variety of sources (see Chapter 11). For complete makeup kits for students and professionals, see *Makeup kits* in Appendix A.

*Foundation colors in both creme and cake makeup can also be used for highlights and shadows when appropriate.

STUDENT MAKEUP KIT: Caucasian Male

Creme	*Cake*	*Creme or Cake*
Foundation colors: FS-5-d *or* SF-5-e SF-8-e/f SF-12-d/e *or* FS-12-e OF-3-b *or* OF-2-a White Shading colors: S-12-d *or* FS-14-d F/OF-17-b OC-9-a N-13 *or* N-11 Creme rouge: RS-10-b Dry rouge: RS-10-b *or* RS-11-a Face powder: neutral Powder puff Powder brush Stipple sponge	Cakes: S-10-d FS-9-c *or* SF-8-c FS-15-f SF-8-e/f *or* FS-9-d/e SF-12-d/e *or* S-12-e OF-3-b White Dry rouge: RS-10-b Creme rouge: RS-10-b Natural silk sponge Stipple sponge *Optional:* Cake OC-9-a Creme shading colors S-12-d and PR-15-d Face powder: neutral Powder puff Powder brush	1 eyeliner brush 1 flat shading brush, 3/16-inch 1 or 2 flat shading brushes, 3/8-inch Makeup pencils: dark brown, black, maroon, red Nose putty Spirit gum Spirit gum remover Scissors Comb Eyebrow-pencil sharpener Makeup remover Tissues

STUDENT MAKEUP KIT: Caucasian Female

Creme	*Cake*	*Creme or Cake*
Foundation colors:	Cakes:	1 eyeliner brush
FS/SF-6-c	S-10-d	1 flat shading brush, 3/16-inch
SF-8-e/f	FS/SF-6-c or SF-5-c	1 or 2 flat shading brushes,
SF-12-d/e or FS-12-e	FS-15-f	3/8-inch
OF-3-b or OF-3-c	SF-8-e/f or FS-9-d/e	Makeup pencils: dark brown,
White	SF-12-d/e or S-12-e	black, maroon, red
Shading colors:	OF-3-b	Nose putty
S-12-d or FS-14-d	White	Spirit gum
F/OF-17-b	Dry rouge:	Spirit gum remover
OC-9-a	RS-11-a or SR-10½-a	Scissors
N-13 or N-11	RS-10-b	Comb
Creme rouge:	Creme rouge:	Eyebrow-pencil sharpener
RS-10-b	RS-10-b	Makeup remover
R-11-a or R-11-a/b	Eyeshadow and lip rouge:	Tissues
Dry rouge:	Personal choice of colors	
RS-10-b	Natural silk sponge	
Face powder: neutral	Stipple sponge	
Powder puff	*Optional:*	
Powder brush	Cake OC-9-a	
Stipple sponge	Creme shading colors S-12-d	
	and PR-15-d	
	Face powder: neutral	
	Powder puff	
	Powder brush	

STUDENT KIT: Dark-Skinned Male or Female

Creme foundation colors:	RS-10-b	1 flat shading brush, 3/16-inch
SF-11-e	SF-11-a or SF-13-a	1 or 2 flat shading brushes,
SF-14-d or SF-13-d	Dry rouge:	3/8-inch
F-9-c or F/OF-9-c/d	RS-10-b or S-11-a	Makeup pencils: dark brown,
OF-2-a or OF-3-b	FS-10-a	black
Creme shading colors:	Eyeshadow: personal choice of colors	Nose putty
PR-15-d	Stipple sponge	Spirit gum
OC-7-b	Face powder: suitable shade	Spirit gum remover
White	for your own coloring	Scissors
Black	Powder puff	Comb
Creme rouge:	Powder brush	Eyebrow-pencil sharpener
S-11-a	1 eyeliner brush	Makeup remover
		Tissues

PROFESSIONAL MAKEUP KIT: Caucasian Male

Creme	*Cake*	*Creme or Cake*
Foundation colors:	Cakes:	Face powder: neutral
FS-9-c	S-10-d	Powder puff
FS-5-d *or* SF-5-e	FS-9-c	Powder brush
SF-8-e/f	FS-5-d *or* SF-6-c	1 eyeliner brush
SF-8-c *or* SF-8-d	SF-8-e/f *or* FS-9-d/e	1 flat shading brush, 3/16-inch
SF-12-d/e *or* FS-12-e	FS-11-d *or* S-10-d	2 flat shading brushes, 3/8-inch
OF-3-b *or* OF-2-a	FS-15-f	Makeup pencils: dark brown,
White	SF-12-d/e *or* S-12-e	black, maroon, red
Shading colors:	F-7-c/d	Nose putty
PR-15-d	OF-3-b	Derma wax (firm)
S-12-d *or* FS-14-d	CO-2-a	Sealer
FO-16-b/c	White	K-Y Lubricating jelly
OC-10-b	Dry rouge:	Crepe hair: assorted shades
LG-13-c *or* G-11-b	RS-11-a *or* SR-10½-a	Spirit gum
N-13 *or* N-11	RS-10-b	Spirit gum remover
IB-13-a *or* I-12-a	Creme rouge:	Latex (clear)
Black	R-11-a	Hair spray
Creme rouge:	Creme shading colors:	Hair cream
RS-10-b	PR-15-d	Hairpins
S-11-a	S-12-d *or* FS-14-d	Hair whitener
Dry rouge:	LG-13-c *or* G-11-b	Scissors
RS-11-a *or* SR-10½-a	OC-10-b	Combs
RS-10-b	IB-13-a *or* I-12-a	Eyebrow-pencil sharpener
	N-13 *or* N-11	Makeup remover
	White	Tissues
	Black	Lintless towel or chamois
		(Plastic makeup apron)
		(Toupee tape)

PROFESSIONAL MAKEUP KIT: Caucasian Female

Creme	*Cake*	*Creme or Cake*
Foundation colors:	Cakes:	Face powder: neutral
RS-1-b	S-10-d	Powder puff
FS/SF-6-c	RS-1-b *or* S-2-a	Powder brush
SF-8-e/f	FS-15-f	1 eyeliner brush
F-4-b/c	SF-4-c	1 flat shading brush, 3/16-inch
SF-12-d/e *or* FS-12-e	SF-8-e/f *or* FS-9-d/e	2 flat shading brushes, 3/8-inch
OF-3-b *or* OF-2-a	F-4-b/c	Makeup pencils, dark brown,
OC-10-b	SF-12-d/e *or* S-12-e	black, maroon, red
White	OF-3-b	Nose putty
Shading colors:	CO-2-a	Derma wax (firm)
PR-15-d	OC-10-b	Sealer
S-12-d *or* FS-14-d	White	K-Y Lubricating jelly
FO-16-b/c	Dry rouge:	Crepe hair: assorted shades
OC-10-b	S-11-a	Spirit gum
LG-13-c *or* G-12-b	SR-10½-a *or* RS-11-a	Spirit gum remover
IB-13-a *or* I-12-a	Creme rouge:	Latex (clear)
V-11-b *or* P-11-b	S-11-a	Hair spray
Black	RS-10-b	Hair cream
Creme rouge:	Creme shading colors:	Hairpins
R-11-a	PR-15-d	Hair whitener
RS-10-b	S-12-d *or* FS-14-d	Artificial eyelashes
S-11-a *or* S-10-a	LG-13-c *or* G-11-b	Mascara
Dry rouge:	IB-13-a	Scissors
S-11-a *or* FS-10-a	N-13 *or* N-11	Combs
RS-11-a	Black	Eyebrow-pencil sharpener
RS-10-b	White	Makeup remover
	Natural silk sponge	Tissues
	Stipple sponge	Lintless towel or chamois
		Plastic makeup apron

PROFESSIONAL MAKEUP KIT: Dark-Skinned Male or Female

Creme	*Cake*	*Creme or Cake*
Creme foundation colors:	Dry rouge:	Sealer
F-14-d	RS-10-b	K-Y Lubricating jelly
SF-14-d *or* SF-13-d	S-11-a	Crepe hair: assorted shades
SF-11-e	FS-10-a	Spirit gum
F/OF-9-c/d *or* F-9-c/d	Eyeshadow: personal choice of colors	Spirit gum remover
OF-2-a *or* OF-4-b *or* OF-3-b	Stipple sponge	Latex (clear)
F/OF-6-d *or* F-8-f	Face powder: suitable shade	Hair spray
Creme shading colors:	for your own coloring	Hair cream
PR-15-d	Powder puff	Hair whitener
OC-7-b	Powder brush	Scissors
White	1 eyeliner brush	Combs
Black	1 flat shading brush, ³⁄₁₆-inch	Eyebrow-pencil sharpener
Creme rouge:	2 flat shading brushes, ³⁄₈-inch	Makeup remover
S-11-a	Makeup pencils: dark brown,	Tissues
RS-10-b	black	Lintless towel or chamois
SF-13-a *or* SF-11-a	Nose putty	(Plastic makeup apron)
	Derma wax (firm)	

GROUP MAKEUP KIT

Creme	*Cake*	*Creme or Cake*
Foundation colors:	Creme rouge:	Spirit gum remover
RS-1-b *or* S-2-a	R-11-a	Latex (clear)
FS-5-d *or* SF-5-e	S-11-a *or* S-10-a	Hair sprays (for coloring, graying,
SF-8-e/f	RS-10-b	and holding)
FS-11-d	SF-11-a	Hair cream
SF-12-d/e *or* FS-12-e *or*	Dry rouge:	Hairpins
SF-13-d	S-11-a	Hair whitener
F-4-b/c *or* SF-5-e *or* SF-4-c	RS-10-b	Mascara
F-7-c/d *or* SF-6-e *or*	RS-11-a	Scissors
SF-6-c	R-10-c	Combs
F/OF-9-c/d *or* F/OF-9-c	Face powder: neutral; colored	Eyebrow-pencil sharpener
F-15-d *or* F/OF-13-d	powders if desired	Toupee tape
F/OF-16-b	Powder puffs	Stipple sponges
OF-2-a *or* OF-3-b *or* OF-4-b	Powder brushes	Red-rubber sponges
F/OF-8-d *or* F/OF-8-c	Shading brushes: ³⁄₁₆-inch,	Rubber-mask grease: assorted
Creme shading colors:	³⁄₈-inch, eyeliners	colors
PR-15-d	Dye brushes	Absorbent cotton
S-12-d *or* FS-14-d	Makeup pencils: medium brown,	Clown white
FO-16-b/c	dark brown, black, maroon, red	Black tooth wax
LG-13-c *or* G-11-b	Nose putty	Lintless towels or chamois
IB-13-a *or* I-12-a	Derma wax (firm)	Makeup remover
V-11-b *or* P-11-b	Sealer	Tissues
N-13 *or* N-11	K-Y Lubricating jelly	Plastic makeup aprons
Black	Crepe hair: assorted shades	Liquid body makeup:
	Spirit gum: regular and matte	assorted shades
		(Texas Dirt)

Appendix D

PLAN FOR A SHORT COURSE IN MAKEUP

The following plan for a condensed workshop course can be used when time does not permit covering the entire book in detail. You will probably be able to complete the first half of the material outlined in about thirty hours of laboratory work, preferably divided into five 6-hour sessions or ten 3-hour sessions.

Since this is an extremely condensed course, it is absolutely essential that you study the text in advance of each class, *including the first one.* There will be no lectures and no demonstrations covering text material, but you will have an opportunity to ask questions. Since this is a workshop course, you will spend your time actually making up. By following the assignments below, you will be able to progress at your own speed. When one assignment has been approved, you will be free to proceed to the next. It is more important to master fundamentals, however, than to cover a lot of ground.

MAKEUP WORKSHOP
ASSIGNMENT SHEET*

1. PREPARATION. Study Chapters 1 through 14 before the first class.

2. LIGHT AND SHADE. Chapter 5, problem 1.

3. CORRECTIVE MAKEUP. Chapter 13, problems 1, 2, 5, 6, 7, 8, 9, 10.

*The student kits listed in Appendix C contain most of the materials you will require. If you already have a kit, make sure it contains colors similar to those listed. If you prefer to get a larger kit, see the professional kits listed. If you would rather buy a kit already made up (you can sometimes save money that way), the Bob Kelly creme and cake kits are very similar to those in Appendix C.

4. MODELING WITH PAINT. Chapter 14, problem 3. Repeat this makeup till you are satisfied with the results. You may add details (eye pouches, forehead wrinkles, different forms of nasolabial folds) as your skill increases. If, after a few complete makeups, you should have difficulty with any particular area of the face or neck, concentrate on that area till you have solved the problem, then return to the complete makeup.

5. MODELING WITH PAINT. Chapter 14, problems 5, 7, 13, 14.

6. THREE-DIMENSIONAL MAKEUP. Chapter 15, problems 1 (two noses) and 4 (three methods). Do one or more complete makeups, using any three-dimensional techniques.

7. BEARDS AND MUSTACHES. Chapter 17, problem 2. Experiment with both latex and spirit gum.

8. CREATING A LIKENESS. Chapter 19, problem 2. Before you begin the makeup, be sure that you will be able to do the appropriate hair style with either your own hair or a wig and that any necessary headdresses, hats, and partial costumes are available so that the likeness can be as close as possible. For this assignment, a painting or an engraved portrait is preferable to a photograph. If you wish to do a second likeness, do a famous historical character, possibly from a play. There are suggestions in problem 1. Use any portraits (works of art or photographs) you can find. Your makeup may be a composite of more than one portrait if you wish.

9. NONREALISTIC MAKEUP. Chapter 20, problem 2, two different styles. Do sketches before beginning the makeup.

10. VENTILATING BEARDS. Chapter 17, problem 4.

11. MAKEUP WITH BEARD. Chapter 17, problem 5.

12. EXPERIMENTAL MAKEUP. Do a complete makeup, using an original technique or a material not usually used in makeup. This may require some experimentation and should be carefully planned.

13. MAKEUP FOR A PERIOD PLAY. Do a makeup for a specific character from a period play, making sure be-

273

fore you begin that you can obtain a suitable wig or that you can dress your own hair appropriately. The makeup should be carefully planned in advance, with sketches. (This should be for a fictional character, not a historical one.) Appendix F can be used for reference.

14. RUBBER PROSTHESIS. Chapter 16. Using a plaster cast of a face (preferably your own), model, cast, and complete at least one successful latex piece—more if you wish and have time.

15. MAKEUP WITH PROSTHETIC PIECE. Do a complete makeup (specific character) using the prosthetic piece you have made. (This may be combined with your beard and mustache if you like.)

Appendix E

RACIAL CHARACTERISTICS

The purpose of the following information is to provide a guide in making up characters of races other than your own. Nowadays, however, there is such an intermingling of the races and of ethnic groups that it is frequently impossible to pinpoint specific features and skin colors as being truly characteristic. The following suggestions, therefore, should be taken as generalizations and not followed slavishly.

Alpine. Includes Swiss, Russian, Czech, Balkan, and northern French peoples. Faces tend to be broad and short with straight noses, either medium or narrow in width. Brown, wavy hair is typical. Skin color is largely in the F, F/OF, and SF groups, light to medium in value, with relatively high intensity (mostly *a* or *b*).

Arabian. (Figures 10–8J and E-1L.) The face is usually narrow with a medium or narrow, straight or convex nose. Hair is black or brown and likely to be wavy. Skin colors tend to range from fairly light to medium dark in the middle intensities of the F, F/OF, and SF groups.

Armenoid. Includes Turkish, Syrian, Persian, Russian, and Greek. Faces tend toward the long and narrow, with long, convex noses. Dark, wavy hair is typical. Skin color ranges from light to medium in the F through OF groups, mostly in the middle intensities.

Celtic. Includes the English, Scottish, Irish, and Welsh. The pure type has a long face with a straight, narrow nose, but there is much variation. Light to medium brown hair, as well as reddish is

typical. Complexions tend to be light. The S through F groups can all be used. Rosy cheeks are common.

Chinese. (Figures 10–8D and E-1H,K.) Faces tend to be broad, with short, broad, somewhat flat noses, concave or straight. Eyes have the epicanthic fold and are often oblique. Hair is straight and black. The skin color ranges from light to medium in the OF, FO, and O groups and tends to be slightly grayed.

Czech. See *Alpine.*

Danish. See *Nordic.*

Dutch. (Figures H-24 and J-19.) See *Nordic.*

East Baltic. This includes Balkan, Finnish, and some Russian and German. Faces tend to be broad. In the pure type, the nose is concave and of medium width. Hair is likely to be ash blond or brown. Complexions range from light to medium, mostly in the warm groups—S through F—with fairly high intensity.

East Indian. See *Indian, East.*

Egyptian. The ancient Egyptians (Figures F-1 and H-37D,G,H) ranged from narrow to broad. Noses were usually broad and straight or sometimes convex. Natural hair was mostly brown, but wigs were usually darker. Complexions ranged from medium light to dark, largely in the SF and F groups, with low (*f*) intensity.

English. (Figures H-33 and H-37F,J,O.) See *Celtic* and *Nordic.*

Eskimo. (Figure E-1B). Faces tend to be broad with concave noses of medium width. Eyes may be almond-shaped. The hair is black and straight. Complexions range from medium light to medium dark, mostly in the middle and low intensities of the F through OF groups.

Finnish. (Figure 10–8A.) See *East Baltic.*

French. (Figures H-14 and H-37L.) For northern French, see *Alpine*; for southern, see *Mediterranean.*

German. (Figure H-36D,M.) For north German, see *Nordic*, and for south German, see *East Baltic.*

Greek. See *Armenoid.* The ancient Greeks (see Figure 3–3E) were evidently lighter than the present-day ones and are typified by the classic Greek nose.

Hawaiian. See *Polynesian.*

Indian, American. (Figure E-1D.) Faces are broad in the middle with prominent cheekbones and straight or convex noses of medium width. Hair is black and straight. The skin is usually medium dark and quite grayed. The F and F/OF groups are suggested. Avoid making Indians brick red!

Indian, East. (Figure E-1M,N,P.) The Dravidian faces are of medium width with a broad, convex nose and curly black hair. The skin is dark (F group, very grayed). Aryans have narrower faces, wavy dark hair, and lighter complexions.

Irish. See *Celtic.*

Italian. (Figure H-36B.) See *Mediterranean.*

Japanese. (Figure E-1Q.) Some faces are long, some broad, with convex, straight, or concave noses, narrow, medium, or broad. Eyes have the epicanthic fold and tend to be almond-shaped. Hair is black and usually straight. Skin colors vary from light to medium. Medium grayed colors in the OF group are perhaps the most generally useful, though the FO group is also possible. You may have to mix colors to get what you want.

Mediterranean. This includes French, Spanish, Portugese, and Italian. Faces vary but tend more toward the narrow than the wide, with noses medium or wide and straight or convex. Among southern Italians, convex noses seem to predominate. The hair ranges from ash blond or light brown to black. The usual complexion is medium

light to medium olive (F or SF, with *e* or *f* intensity). Southern Italians tend to be darker than northern.

Mexican (Indian). (Figure E-1D.) Faces tend toward broadness, though this is variable. Noses may be concave, convex, or straight. Hair is black and either straight or wavy. Complexions also vary from medium light to dark. The *c* and *d* intensities in the F/OF and OF groups are good possibilities.

Mongolian. (Figure E-1G.) Complexion is similar to Chinese.

Negro. (Figure E-1A.) There is great variation through intermingling of the races, but the more nearly pure Negro characteristics tend toward flat, broad, concave noses, wooly black hair, and very dark skins, which may appear close to black but are actually a low value and low intensity of brown. The mixture of races has resulted in skin coloring ranging from medium light to very dark—some low in intensity, some medium, mostly in the F through OF groups.

Nordic. This includes Scandinavian, North German, Dutch, and some English and Scottish. Faces tend to be long and narrow, with broad or convex noses (medium or narrow), and wavy gold or ash blond hair. Complexions are light, sometimes pale, sometimes pink. Light colors of *a* and *b* intensity in the F, SF, FS, and RS groups can be used.

Norwegian. See *Nordic.*

Persian. (Figure E-1R.) See *Armenoid.*

Polynesian. (Figure E-1F.) This includes Samoan (Figure E-1-O), Tahitian, and Hawaiian. Faces tend to be long and narrow, with broad or medium noses. Hair may be wavy or straight, black or brown. Skin color varies from medium light to medium dark, in grayed tones of the SF through OF hues.

Portuguese. See *Mediterranean.*

Roman. See *Mediterranean.* For ancient Romans, see Figures 4-6 through 4-9.

Russian. (Figure H-37K.) See *Alpine, Armenoid*, and *East Baltic.*

Samoan. (Figure E-1-O.) See *Polynesian.*

Scandinavian. See *Nordic.*

Figure E-1. Racial variations. A—Negro, B—Eskimo, C—Korean, D—Mexican, E—American Indian, F—Tahitian, G—Mongolian, H—Chinese, J—Turk, K—Chinese, L—Arab, M,N—East Indian, O—Samoan, P—East Indian (Aryan), Q—Japanese, R—Persian.

Scottish. See *Celtic* and *Nordic*.

Siamese. The typical face is broad, with a concave nose of medium width and almond-shaped eyes. Hair is straight and black. The skin color ranges from medium light to medium, in grayed tones of the OF, FO, and F groups.

Swedish. See *Nordic*.

Swiss. See *Alpine*.

Syrian. See *Armenoid*.

Tahitian. See *Polynesian*.

Tibetan. Faces tend to be broad, with almond eyes and medium wide, concave noses. Hair is straight and black. The skin colors range from light to medium, in grayed tones of the F through FO groups.

Turkish. (Figure E-1J.) See *Armenoid*.

Welsh. See *Celtic*.

Yugoslav. See *Alpine* and *East Baltic*.

Appendix F

FASHIONS IN MAKEUP

One of the determining factors in any realistic makeup for the stage is the historical period to which the character belongs. This applies not only to the hair style but, in many cases, to the facial makeup as well. The kohl-lined eyes of the ancient Egyptians, the whitened faces of eighteenth-century ladies, the fashionably pale lips of the early 1960s—all must be taken into consideration in creating makeups for those periods.

The brief notes in this chapter are intended to give an overall view of the subject and to serve as a reference in doing period plays. Although hair styles are mentioned from time to time along with the makeup, more extensive information can be found in the twenty-three plates of hair-style drawings in Appendix G.

ANCIENT PEOPLES

Among the Egyptians, both men and women used makeup. The eyelids were frequently colored with green malachite and the eyes heavily lined and the eyebrows darkened (Figure F-1) with black kohl (powdered antimony sulfide). Carmine was used on the lips; for coloring the cheeks, red clay was mixed with saffron. Veins, especially on the bosom, were sometimes accented with blue. White lead was occasionally used for whitening the skin. Both men and women shaved their heads and wore wigs. The hair was usually dark brown or black, though at the height of Egyptian civilization it was sometimes dyed red, blue, or even green. Beards were often false and tied on with a ribbon or a strap; no attempt was made to make them look natural.

Sometimes they were even made of gold or other metal.

The Assyrians and the Persians also dyed their hair and their beards, the Assyrians preferring black, the Persians, henna color. The eyes were lined with kohl, though not so heavily as those of the Egyptians. The brows, however, were often made very heavy and close together. Both natural hair and wigs were worn, and the hair was curled with tongs. On special occasions it was sometimes decorated with gold dust and intertwined with gold threads.

Upper-class Greek women sometimes painted their cheeks and lips rose or earthy red, whitened their faces, darkened their eyebrows, shadowed their eyelids, and, upon occasion, dyed their hair or wore wigs. Red hair was popular, and blue, it is reported, was not unknown.

Fashionable Roman women and some men whitened their faces, rouged their cheeks and lips, darkened their eyebrows, and sometimes dyed their hair blond or red. During the period of the extremely elaborate and rapidly changing hair styles for women, wigs were frequently worn. Men sometimes wore wigs or painted on hair to cover their baldness. Both sexes sometimes wore beauty patches made of leather.

THE MIDDLE AGES

Upper-class medieval women liked a pale complexion and in the late Middle Ages frequently used white lead to achieve it. Cheek and lip rouge were often used. In the thirteenth century, rouge

Figure F-1. **Nefertiti.** Queen of Egypt, fourteenth century B.C. Painted limestone.

was in general use among women; often rose or pink was worn by the upper classes and a cheaper brownish red by the lower. Fifteenth-century French women sometimes painted their cheeks and their lips with a crimson rouge. Throughout the Middle Ages, rouge seems usually to have been applied in a round spot with some attempt at blending.

Various colors of eyeshadow were used to some extent in the Middle Ages, and the upper lid was sometimes lined with black. Eyebrows were natural until the late Middle Ages and early Renaissance, when women of fashion (and in England, at least, even lower-class women) plucked their brows to a fine, arched line (Figures F-2, H-7, H-16, H-17). Sometimes, it seems, the brows were shaved off completely. The hairline was also plucked so that little or no hair would show below the headdresses. The plucking was even done in public.

Both black and blond hair were fashionable, but red was not and would not be until Elizabeth I made it so.

THE SIXTEENTH CENTURY

The Renaissance brought a marked increase in the use of cosmetics but not, unfortunately, much improvement in the knowledge of how to make them safe for the skin. Frequently, irritating and poisonous artists' pigments were used to paint the face as if it were a living canvas. The skin was whitened and the cheeks and lips rouged. In *Love's Labours Lost* Biron says:

> Your mistresses dare never come in rain,
> For fear their colours should be washed away.

Spanish wool and Spanish papers (wool or small leaves of paper containing powdered pigment) were popular for rouge (and sometimes for the white as well) and continued to be used for several centuries.

By the end of the sixteenth century the artificially high forehead for women was no longer in fashion. Women had stopped plucking their eye-

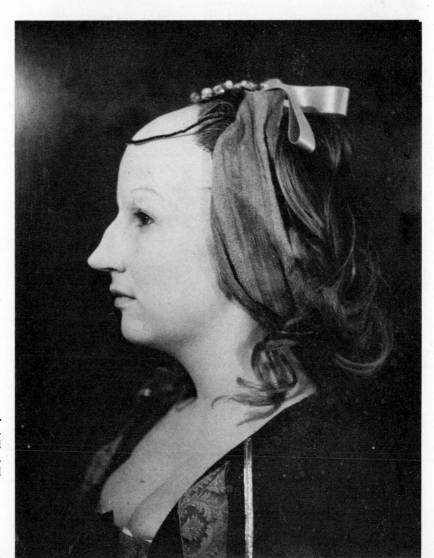

Figure F-2. Sixteenth-century lady. Based on a contemporary portrait. Front hair soaped out, brows blocked out with spirit gum and derma wax, latex nose. Student makeup by Carol Doscher.

Figure F-3. Likeness of Mrs. Siddons. Based on Gainsborough portrait. Putty-wax nose, cake makeup, crepe hair, wig. Student makeup by Nancie Underwood. (For another makeup by the same student, see Figure 20-25.)

brows to a thin line, and some of them had begun to spot their faces with black patches.

Although some men painted their faces, this was not looked upon with favor by either sex. Nonetheless, Henri III is said to have gone about the streets of Paris "made up like an old coquette," his face plastered with white and red, his hair covered with perfumed violet powder.

Wigs were sometimes worn (both Elizabeth I and Mary Queen of Scots had large numbers of them); false hair was used; and beards, as well as hair and wigs, were sometimes dyed. Elizabeth favored red hair and thus made it a popular color. White or tinted powder was sometimes used on the hair. Venetian women in particular sat for days in the sun bleaching their hair and, according to contemporary reports, occasionally suffered severe reactions from overexposure to the sun. Blonde wigs were sometimes worn instead.

Elizabeth's teeth, like so many people's of the time, were yellow, spotted, and rotting away.

THE SEVENTEENTH CENTURY

Cosmetics were more widely used in the seventeenth century, and with somewhat more delicacy. Spanish papers in red and white were still in use. Samuel Pepys in his diary referred to his cousin, Mrs. Pierce, as being "still very pretty, but paints red on her face, which makes me hate her." On the other hand, the Earl of Chesterfield wrote to his well-painted Miss Livingston: "Your complexion is none of those faint whites that represents a Venus in the green sickness, but such as Apollo favours and visits most."

It is important to remember in doing Restoration plays that country girls still relied on their natural coloring but that ladies who wore makeup made no attempt to conceal the fact. Faces were usually whitened with powder or washes. Dark complexions were considered common.

Rouge worn by the upper classes was usually rose colored, whereas that used by lower-class women was an ochre red, often applied excessively.

Eyebrows were occasionally darkened, and a creme eyeshadow in blue, brown, or gray was sometimes worn by upper-class women. It was usually concentrated on the upper lid near the eye but might occasionally, in a burst of enthusiasm, be allowed to creep up toward the eyebrow.

Rouge, pink or flesh powder, and sometimes a touch of lip rouge were worn by men of fashion in the last decade of the century. Patches were worn by some fashionable men—whether or not they wore makeup—and in profusion by fashionable ladies. Some, according to Beaumont and Fletcher, were "cut like stars, some in half moons, some in lozenges." There were other shapes as well. Their placement was not without significance—a patch close to the eye was called *la passionée*, one beside the mouth, *la baiseuse*, on the cheek, *la galante*, and so on. Ladies were seldom content with one patch. According to John Bulwer, writing in 1650 in his *Anthropometamorphosis*, "Our ladies have lately entertained a vaine custom of spotting their faces out of an affectation of a mole, to set off their beauty, such as Venus had; and it is well if one black patch will serve to make their faces remarkable, for some fill their visages full of them, varied into all manner of shapes and figures." Bulwer includes an illustration of a "visage full of them." Eight years later, in *Wit Restored*, there appeared a few lines on the subject:

> Their faces are besmear'd and pierc'd
> With severall sorts of patches,
> As if some cats their skins had flead
> With scarres, half moons, and notches.

The patches were usually made of black taffeta or Spanish leather (usually red) or sometimes of gummed paper. It was also suggested in *Wit Restored* that patches might be of some practical use in covering blemishes. It is reported, in fact, that the Duchess of Newcastle wore "many black patches because of pimples around her mouth." Plumpers, made of balls of wax, were sometimes carried in the mouth by aging ladies to fill out their sunken cheeks.

The fashion of wigs for men was begun by Louis XIII; black wigs were popularized by Charles II. At the end of the century, light powder (mostly gray, beige, and tan, but not white) was used on the hair. Hair styles even developed political significance for a time—whereas the Cavaliers wore their hair long, the Puritans cut theirs short and were called Roundheads. Beards and mustaches were carefully groomed with special combs and brushes and kept in shape with perfumed wax.

Teeth were still poorly cared for and often looked it.

THE EIGHTEENTH CENTURY

Face painting and patching continued to flourish in the eighteenth century. In Wycherly's *Love in a Wood*, published in 1735, Dapperwit, who is trying to arouse Miss Lucy, says to Ranger, "Pish, give her but leave to gape, rub her Eyes, and put on her Day-Pinner, the long Patch under the left Eye, awaken the Roses on her Cheeks with some Spanish Wool. . . . Doors fly off the Hinges, and she into my Arms."

As for patches, a prominent marquise is reported to have appeared at a party wearing sixteen of them, one in the shape of a tree on which were perched two love birds. Sometimes the patches had political significance—Whigs patching on the right side and Tories on the left. Ladies who had not made up their minds patched on both sides.

Face painting became more garish in the second half of the eighteenth century. The ladies "enamelled" their faces with white lead and applied bright rouge heavily and with little subtlety. Horace Walpole, in writing of the coronation of George III, mentions that "lord Bolingbroke put on rouge upon his wife and the duchess of Bedford in the Painted Chamber; the Duchess of Queensberry told me of the latter, that she looked like an orange-peach, half red, half yellow."

In *The Life of Lady Sarah Lennox* we read that a contemporary of Lady Caroline Mackenzie remarked that she wore "such quantities of white that she was terrible" and that the Duchess of Grafton "having left red and white quite off is one of the coarsest brown women I ever saw." A guest at a party in 1764 was described as wearing on her face "rather too much yellow mixed with the red; she . . . would look very agreeable if she added blanc to the rouge instead of gamboge."

The white paints, according to *The Art of Beauty* (written anonymously and published in 1825),

> affect the eyes which swell and inflame and are rendered painful and watery. They change the texture of the skin, on which they produce pimples and cause rheums; attack the teeth, make them ache, destroy the enamel, and loosen them. . . . To the inconveniences we have just enumerated, we add this, of turning the skin black when it is exposed to the contact of sulphureous or phosphoric exhalations. Accordingly, those females who make use of them ought carefully to avoid going too near substances in a state of putrefaction, the vapours of sulphur . . . and the exhalation of bruised garlic.

The latter problem conjures up interesting possibilities.

The warnings about the white lead paints were hardly exaggerated. Walpole wrote in 1766 that the youthful and attractive Lady Fortrose was "at the point of death, killed like Lady Coventry and others, by white lead, of which nothing could break her." At least they did not lose their lives through ignorance of the dangerous nature of their paints.

Despite the seemingly excessive makeup used by English ladies, they still lagged behind the French. Walpole reported that French princesses wore "their red of a deeper dye than other women, though all use it extravagantly." Lady Sarah Lennox found the Princess de Condé to be the only lady in Parisian society who did not "wear rouge, for all the rest daub themselves so horribly that it's shocking."

Casanova was of the opinion that the rouge, though excessive, had its attractions and that the charm of the ladies' painted faces lay in the carelessness with which the rouge was applied, without the slightest attempt at naturalness.

The rouge was sometimes applied in a round pattern (Figure J-17), sometimes triangular (Figure J-15). About 1786 hairdresser William Barker described French fashions in makeup:

> From a little below the eye there is sometimes drawn a red streak to the lower temple and another streak in a semicircular form to the other line. If the eye-brows are not naturally dark, they make them so. . . . Sometimes the French ladies . . . put on rouge of the highest color in the form of a perfect circle, without shading it off at all.

But Mr. Barker added that Marie-Antoinette had introduced a more natural application of rouge. A red pomade was used on the lips as well. One recipe for lip pomade suggested that the lady might add some gold leaf if she wished.

But it was not only the women who used cosmetics. In 1754 a correspondent wrote to *Conoisseur*:

> I am ashamed to tell you that we are indebted to Spanish Wool for many of our masculine ruddy complexions. A pretty fellow lacquers his pale face with as many varnishes as a fine lady. . . . I fear it will be found, upon examination, that most of our pretty fellows who lay on carmine are painting a rotten post.

Wigs were almost universally worn by men, much less frequently by women. Powdered hair was in fashion until near the end of the century. White powder was introduced in 1703; but tinted powder —gray, pink, blue, lavender, blond, brown—continued to be worn. Facial hair was never fashionable and rarely worn except, in some instances, by soldiers. Military hair styles were strictly regulated.

The wigs and high headdresses and powdered hair passed, however, and with them the garish makeup. At the end of the century a more-or-less natural makeup was in vogue.

THE NINETEENTH CENTURY

In the early years of the nineteenth century, fashionable cheeks were rouged. A portrait by Sir Thomas Lawrence, painted about 1803, shows the rose-colored rouge applied in a round pattern. The lips were also rose. But excessive rouging was not always looked upon with favor. The Countess of Granville wrote disapprovingly to her sister of ladies whose makeup she considered ill-bred: "Mrs. Ervington, dressed and rouged like an altar-piece but still beautiful . . . Miss Rodney, a very pretty girl, but with rather too much rouge and naivete . . . Lady Elizabeth Stuart by dint of rouge and an auburn wig looks only not pretty but nothing worse." A Mrs. Bagot she described as being "rouged to the eyes."

The Art of Beauty, published in 1825, noted that it was "not the present fashion to make so much use of red as was done some years ago; at least, it is applied with more art and taste. With very few exceptions, ladies have absolutely renounced that glaring, fiery red with which our antiquated dames formerly masked their faces."

In Victorian England there was a reaction

against any form of paint on the face, though creams and lotions and a little powder were acceptable. Makeup was used nonetheless, but so subtly (by "nice" women, that is) that it was often undetectable. A woman who would not dare buy rouge in a public shop was often not above rubbing her cheeks with a bit of red silk dipped in wine or trying some other home-made artifice.

As the Victorian influence became more pervasive, the use of cosmetics became more furtive, particularly in the United States. Despite the example of George Washington, who was perfumed and powdered along with other men of his class, sentiment against any use of cosmetics by men was becoming exceedingly strong—so much so, in fact, that the revelation that Martin Van Buren used such cosmetic aids as Corinthian Oil of Cream, Double Extract of Queen Victoria, and Concentrated Persian Essence helped to end his political career. But in other countries, essential items for the gentleman's toilet included hair oil, dye for the hair and beard, perfumed chalk for sallow complexions, and a little rouge, which was to be used with great care so as to avoid detection.

The use of cosmetics was revived to some extent in the 1860s, and it was reported that rouge was "extensively employed by ladies to brighten the complexion" and to give "the seeming bloom of health to the pallid or sallow cheek." Eyebrows were dark, full, moderately thick, and attractively curved. The Empress Eugénie is believed to have introduced the use of mascara, and Charles Meyer, a German teenager trained in wigmaking, introduced Leichner's theatrical makeup—the first greasepaint to be made in America.

By the end of the century the shops were well supplied with fascinating and irresistible cosmetics. Not only did women not resist them, but they were known brazenly to repair their makeup in public. In 1895 the editor of the *London Journal of Fashion* wrote:

> Rouge, discreetly put on, of course, forms a part of every toilet as worn by fashionable women, and some among these are beginning to use their toilet-powders somewhat too heavily. Even those who do not use rouge aim at producing a startling effect of contrast by making the lips vividly red and the face very pale, with copiously laid on powder or

Figure F-4. Late nineteenth-century lady. Natural look, with full eyebrows. Pencil drawing by Friedrich von Kaulbach.

enamel—which when badly put on is of very bad effect, and, in point of fact, greatly ages a woman. Still, the entirely unaided face is becoming more and more rare, almost everybody uses other makeup effects, if not rouge, and an almost scarlet lipsalve.

It should be particularly noted, in planning your own makeup for a Victorian woman, that well-bred young girls never used makeup, though they did pinch their cheeks occasionally. Married women might resort to a delicate rouge, very subtly applied so as to look like natural color; but they did not rouge their lips. They might, however, employ various methods of bringing the blood to the surface, such as biting; and they might soften the lips with cream. But lipstick was used only by actresses when on stage and by courtesans.

Early in the century, wigs for women were fashionable. Black and blonde were both popular colors. By the 1820s black was favored. *The Art of Beauty* included a recipe for "Grecian Water for Darkening the Hair," which, the reader was warned, was not only dangerous to the skin, but might eventually turn the hair purple. In the second half of the century the preference was for brown or black hair, and dyes were freely used by both men and women—the men for their beards as well as their hair.

In 1878 Mrs. Haweis wrote that red hair was all the rage; and in 1895 the *Journal of Fashion* announced that "the coming season will be one of complexions out of boxes . . . and the new colour for the hair a yellow so deep as to verge on red. It is not pretty, it is not becoming, and it is somewhat fast-looking because manifestly unreal."

THE TWENTIETH CENTURY

At the turn of the century, many women were using henna to turn their hair fashionably auburn. The purpose of makeup was still to enhance the natural beauty rather than to look frankly painted. Some women, including Queen Alexandra, tended to defeat their purpose by applying their makeup quite heavily, though the colors used were delicate. The English and the Americans lagged behind the French in the frank and open application of paint. In the second decade the use of eyeshadow, eyebrow pencil, mascara, and lipstick became widespread.

As the twenties dawned, beauty experts in England and America were still advising natural-looking makeup, but it was a losing battle. In the mid-twenties, geranium or raspberry lips and a pale complexion were fashionable, and eyebrows were being plucked into a thin, hard line. In 1927 it was reported, with marked disapproval, that some women actually used eyeshadow. They were also lining their eyes with black and painting their lips cerise. By the end of the decade, heavily painted, bee-stung lips, plucked eyebrows, and short hair were the mark of the emancipated woman.

It was in the late twenties that sun-tanned faces became popular, and dark powders were made available for those who did not tan well or had no time to lie in the sun. Orange rouge and lipstick were in fashion, and the lips were overpainted with an exaggerated cupid's bow. Beauty experts recommended that eyeshadow be applied close to the lashes, then blended out to elongate the eye. Brown was recommended for day use, blue for night. Rouge and lipstick also came in day and evening colors—light for day, dark for evening.

Early in the thirties, orange lipstick went out and raspberry came in. Even schoolgirls used makeup. Their older sisters bleached their hair platinum, and their mothers or even their grandmothers rinsed away their gray. Hollywood set the styles. For the first time in history women made their mouths larger—Joan Crawford style. The bee-stung lips were gone. Fingernails and toenails were painted various shades of red, gold, silver, green, blue, violet, and even, for a time, black. Polish had been used for some years previously, but it was either colorless or natural pink.

In the forties and fifties, extremes of artificial makeup subsided somewhat, though lips were still heavily painted. Rouge became less and less used and eventually was omitted entirely by fashionable women. Makeup bases in both water-soluble cake and cream form were available in a variety of shades, ranging from a pale pink to a deep tan, and were often applied rather too heavily. Eye makeup was still more or less natural. Eyebrows were no longer plucked to a thin line, colored eyeshadow was used mostly for evening wear, and mascara and false eyelashes were usually intended to deceive the viewer.

In the early half of the sixties, however, the natural look was out. Makeup became as extreme as the hair styles, with a shift of emphasis from the mouth to the eyes. Lips were not only pale (either unpainted or made up with a pale lipstick), they were, for awhile, even painted white. This fashion, like most others, began in Paris. Eye makeup be-

Figure F-5. The Wistful Look, 1925. Plucked and penciled eyebrows, shadowed eyes, and painted rosebud mouth. From *Fashions in Makeup.*

Figure F-6. The Lipless Look, 1963. Emphasis on the eyes and off the mouth. From *Fashions in Makeup.*

came heavier and heavier, with colored eyeshadow generously applied for daytime wear and the eyes heavily lined with black in a modified Egyptian style. False eyelashes became thick and full, and sometimes several pairs were worn at once. It was a time for restless dissatisfaction and experimentation. White and various pale, often metallic, tints of eyeshadow were tried. Eyebrows were even whitened to try to focus attention on the eye itself, and extremely pale makeup bases were worn. The objective seemed to be great dark eyes staring out of a colorless blob. Hair was tinted, rinsed, dyed, teased, ironed, and wound on enormous rollers, which were even, on occasion, worn in public. Sometimes the hair was just left to hang (possibly a beatnik influence), framing a pale face with great black furry-lashed eyes.

The 1970s began with a flurry of artificiality—red eyelashes, green hair, colored polkadots around the eyes, doll-like makeup on the cheeks, heavy black eyelashes painted on the skin, eyebrows blocked out with makeup. No innovation seemed too bizarre. But reaction set in, and a greater naturalness in makeup took over. In 1972, however, severely plucked eyebrows were once again in fashion—sometimes no more than the thin line of the twenties. But rouge was natural, and lip color varied with the season. By 1974 the variations included stronger colors—both very bright and very dark—than had been worn for a number of years.

Appendix G

PERIOD HAIR STYLES

The twenty-three plates of hair styles that follow are intended as a general guide for period plays. The captions opposite each plate date each style as specifically as possible, often identifying the wearer. This does not mean that the style was confined to that year or that decade, but only that it is known to have been worn then. How fashionable it was can usually be determined by observing other styles of the period or from the social status of the person identified as the subject. A style worn by Marie Antoinette may be assumed to be in the latest fashion, whereas a style worn by a French peasant would not be. In general, young women are more likely to wear extremes in fashion than older ones, though social status and personality must always be considered.

In preparing to do any period play, you will need to study fashions in both makeup and hair styles. Appendix F, though it is devoted primarily to period makeup, contains occasional supplementary notes on hair styles. (See also the portraits in Appendix H and J.)

Keep in mind always that the closer you come to the present, the more precise you should be in dating a hair style. Whereas a few hundred or even a thousand years' discrepancy in ancient Egyptian styles may not be noticed, a year or two is the most you should allow in the mid-twentieth century. You may deliberately choose a hair style that is ten or fifteen years out of date for a character who might wear it, but you should never select a style that is even so much as a year ahead of its time. Such carelessness reflects on the quality of the whole production.

The drawings on the following plates are extracted from *Fashions in Hair—The First Five Thousand Years*, revised edition published (1971) in London by Peter Owen Limited and in New York by Humanities Press. In the more than 700 pages of text, reproductions of works of art, and plates of drawings you will find detailed information on all periods of history.

PLATE 1: ANCIENT PEOPLES, MEN

a. c.2800 B.C., Sumerian. The bundle of hair at the back is typical of the Sumerian hairdo.

b. c.2700 B.C., Egyptian. The hair is braided and the braids stitched to a woven foundation to keep them firmly in place. The ends of the braids are fringed.

c. c.2500 B.C., Egyptian. Senodem, a magistrate. This style was quite common. Rows of small, tight, spiral curls were stitched onto a well-ventilated cap or woven foundation.

d. c.2500 B.C., Egyptian.

e. c.2500 B.C., Sumerian. Wig and false beard. The beard style strongly resembles both the Assyrian and the Greek, but the hair seems more closely related to the Phoenician and the Semitic Akkadian.

f. c.1875 B.C., Egyptian. Sehetep-Ib-Rē'-'Ankh, steward of the king. The body of the hair is slightly waved and is curled only at the ends. The beard is presumably real.

g. c.1500 B.C., Hittite warrior from Carchemish.

h. c.1450 B.C., Egyptian. Kha'-Em-Wēset. Black wig in typical tile-like arrangement of hundreds of tiny curls.

i. c.1420 B.C., Egyptian. Roy, Scribe and Steward of the Queen. The fullness of the wig results from many layers of curls.

j. c.1400 B.C., Egyptian. The hair is stitched down from forehead to crown to form a center parting.

k. c.1250 B.C., Egyptian. The curls in the top layer radiate from a central point. The lower side sections are formed of tile-like layers of tiny curls.

l. c.860 B.C., Phoenician. The binding up of the hair in back is typical and distinguishes the hair style from that of the Assyrians, which it otherwise resembles.

m. c.740 B.C., Assyrian king. Hair and beards were always carefully curled.

n. c.740 B.C., Assyrian. Bearer of the king's bow.

o. c.700 B.C., Assyrian.

p. Late seventh century B.C., Etruscan.

q. c.600 B.C., Etruscan.

r. c.525 B.C., Etruscan. The shaved upper lip was not uncommon among bearded men.

s. Late sixth century B.C., Etruscan youth.

t. c.500 B.C., Persian.

a   *b*   *c*   *d*

e   *f*   *g*   *h*

i   *j*   *k*   *l*

m   *n*   *o*   *p*

q   *r*   *s*   *t*

Plate 1

PLATE 2: ANCIENT PEOPLES, MEN

a. Late sixth century B.C., Greek. Young men were beginning to wear shorter hair, though older ones often let theirs grow. A braid sometimes replaced the fillet and was arranged in various ways. Here the ends of the braid are concealed under the front hair.

b. Sixth century B.C., Greek.

c. 440–400 B.C., Greek. Back hair looped over fillet.

d. 470–450 B.C., Greek. The fillet here is in the form of a braided cord.

e. Fifth century B.C., Greek. The style of turning the hair over the fillet was followed by both men and women. The long, hanging ends come from both the front and the back hair.

f. Dionysius the Elder, 430(?)–376 B.C. Tyrant of Syracuse. The hair radiates from the crown, and the ends are curled.

g. Fourth century B.C., Greek.

h. Fourth century B.C., Greek.

i. Caius Julius Caesar, 102(?)–44 B.C.

j. Marcus Junius Brutus, 85–42 B.C.

k. Julius Caesar, 102(?)–44 B.C. Later than *i* above.

l. Pompey, 106–48 B.C.

m. c. A.D. 10, Roman boy.

n. Claudius, 10 B.C.–A.D. 54. Emperor, A.D. 41–54.

o. Vespasian, A.D. 9–79. Emperor, A.D. 69–79.

p. End of the first century A.D., Roman.

q. c.134, Roman. L. Julius Ursus Servianus, Hadrian's brother-in-law.

r. Lucius Verus. Died A.D. 169.

s. Second century A.D., Egyptian. Natural hair, resulting from Roman influence.

t. Third century A.D., Roman.

u. Constantine I (the Great), 280(?)–237.

v. Early fifth century, Roman.

w. Fifth century.

x. c. A.D. 400, Roman.

a

b

c

d

e

f

g

h

i

j

k

l

m

n

o

p

q

r

s

t

u

v

w

x

Plate 2

PLATE 3: ANCIENT PEOPLES, WOMEN

a. c.2900 B.C., Egyptian. The braids are stitched firmly onto a foundation. Braids were usually smaller than this.

b. c.2800 B.C., Sumerian.

c. c.2500 B.C., Semitic Akkadian. Wig.

d. c.2200 B.C., Egyptian servant. Notice the lack of a center part in the wig.

e. c.1500 B.C., Egyptian. Wig.

f. c.1450 B.C., Egyptian. Metal headband. Hair of the wig is crimped for fullness and the ends tightly curled.

g. c.1450 B.C., Egyptian. Metal headband decorated with blossoms and belonging to a lady of the court. The body of the hair is frizzed and puffed out and the curled ends tightly bound and waxed.

h. c.1350 B.C., Egyptian. Queen Mutnezemt.

i. c.1250 B.C., Egyptian. Wig of a queen or a princess. Long, elaborately dressed wigs were worn only by persons of high rank.

j. c.1025 B.C., Egyptian. Princess Na-ny, daughter of King Pinedjem. The wig, now in the Metropolitan Museum of Art, consists of a long, narrow braid of human hair over linen thread, from which numerous plaits, set with beeswax, hang. The braid is sewn together loosely with a faggoting stitch to form a skull cap or caul. The size was adjusted by linen drawstrings fastened at each temple, which also held the plaits at the forehead in place.

k. Late sixth century B.C., Etruscan girl.

l. Second half of the sixth century B.C., Greek. Sections of the hair running the length of the head are separated and curled, then arranged in parallel rows. The style was still worn in the fourth century and was later popular in Rome.

m. Probably late fifth century B.C., Greek.

n. About fifth century B.C., Greek.

o. Early fifth century B.C., Greek.

p. Probably late fifth century B.C., Greek.

q. Greek. Persephone. Since high foreheads were considered ugly, the hair was usually dressed low.

r. Fourth century B.C., Greek.

s. Fourth century B.C., Etruscan.

a   b   c   d

e   f   g   h

i   j   k   l

m   n   o

p   q   r   s

Plate 3

PLATE 4: ANCIENT PEOPLES, WOMEN

a. Late fifth or fourth century B.C., Greek.

b. Between 206 and 30 B.C., Egyptian. Wig of one of the Cleopatras.

c. Between 300 B.C. and A.D. 100, Greek. The higher forehead and the knot were popular after Alexander.

d. Mid-first century B.C., Roman. Fulvia, wife of Marc Antony. Died 40 B.C. The puff at the forehead and the coil at the neck are typical of the fashion of the period. Sometimes the hair behind the front puff was braided and the braid carried over the top of the head and down to the coil on the neck. Braids were also worn around the head and over the head.

e. Late first century B.C. or early first A.D., Roman. The fringe at the forehead is probably a development of the puff of the Fulvia style. The hair is beginning to get a little fuller.

f. Early first century A.D., Roman. Livia, 55(?) B.C.–A.D. 29. Typifies early Empire style.

g. Early first century A.D., Roman.

h. Livia. Front view of *f* above.

i. Late first century A.D., Roman.

j. Late first or early second century, Roman. A modification of the *orbis.*

k. Late first century, Roman. Style of Julia, daughter of Titus. *Orbis.* The curls are arranged on crescent-shaped wire frames. The back hair is divided into sections, braided, then curled. Sometimes the hair was coiled without braiding.

l. End of the first century, Roman. Modification of the *orbis.*

m. Early second century, Roman. The large crown of braids is typical of the Hadrian period.

n. Second quarter of the second century, Roman. Hadrian period.

o. A.D. 195, Roman.

p. Early third century, Roman. Julia Domna, wife of Septimus Severus. Typical of the padded hair style of the period, with massive braids or coils at the back of the head. Wigs were common.

q. Third century, second quarter. Roman. Orbiana, wife of Alexander Severus. The hair is less massive, and the coil at the back has shrunk. Hair is lower in back. Later it rose again.

r. Third century, Roman.

s. Fourth century, Roman.

t. Fourth century, Roman.

a *b* *c* *d*
e *f* *g* *h*
i *j* *k* *l*
m *n* *o* *p*
q *r* *s* *t*

Plate 4

PLATE 5: MEDIEVAL MEN

a. Sixth century, Gaul.

b. Byzantine.

c. c. 547, Byzantine. A dignitary in the court of Justinian. Some of the members of the court were bearded, some not. Although Justinian's hair style was much like this one, he was clean-shaven. An earlier mosaic shows him bearded.

d. c.750.

e. c.879. Long hair, full mustaches, and shaven chins seem to be typical of many of the barbaric tribes.

f. Late tenth century.

g. 1130–1135. Although beards were commonly worn by older men, young men were usually beardless. The front hair was ordinarily combed forward and cut relatively short; but the back was sometimes left long, as it is here, or cut shorter.

h. c.1150, Italian. Note that the hair radiates from a point on the natural hairline rather than at the crown. This was not an unusual style among the Italians.

i. French.

j. c.1150, French. The hair was occasionally plaited in the eleventh century as well.

k. c.1160, French.

l. c.1235, French.

m. c.1245.

n. Mid-thirteenth century.

o. Thirteenth century, last quarter. The ends of the hair were curled with irons.

p. Early fourteenth century, Italian. Monk wearing tonsure of St. Peter.

q. Fourteenth century, second quarter.

r. Fourteenth century, English. Richard II, ruled 1377–1399.

s. Fourteenth century, last quarter, French.

t. c.1376, French. Fashionable young man.

u. c.1390.

v. 1390, French. Fashionable young man.

w. c.1400, English.

a   b   c   d   e
f   g   h   i   j
k   l   m   n
o   p   q   r
s   t   u   v   w

Plate 5

PLATE 6: MEDIEVAL WOMEN

a. c.400, Byzantine. Athenais Endocia, wife of Emperor Theodosius.

b. Sixth century, Byzantine. The hair was built up over rolls and pads. Often it was studded with jewels.

c. Sixth century, Byzantine.

d. 1083, French. Queen Mathilde.

e. 1180, French queen. The braids were worn very long and extended with artificial hair if necessary.

f. About twelfth century, German.

g. Thirteenth century, Italian.

h. Late thirteenth century, Italian.

i. Thirteenth century.

j. Late twelfth or early thirteenth century.

k. c.1340, French.

l. French.

m. Fourteenth century, first quarter, French. Woman wearing a *gorgière*.

n. c.1310, French.

o. Mid-fourteenth century, German.

p. After 1320. It was in the fourteenth century that women began plucking or shaving the hairline to give a higher forehead, as shown here.

q. 1364, English.

r. Fourteenth century, French.

s. c.1360.

a

b

c

d

e

f

g

h

i

j

k

l

m

n

o

p

q

r

s

Plate 6

PLATE 7: FIFTEENTH-CENTURY MEN

a. Louis II, Duc d'Anjou, Comte de Provence, 1377–1417.

b. 1412. This style remained fashionable until about 1460 and was still worn somewhat later.

c. Henry V, 1387–1422. King of England, 1413–1422. This was the fashionable and popular hair style during the first half of the century. Frequently the ends were curled under, as in *b* above.

d. 1416. The pointed or forked beard without side-whiskers was worn at the beginning of the century but in 1416 was disappearing.

e. Charles VII, 1403–1461. In 1429 Joan of Arc had him crowned king at Rheims.

f. German.

g. c.1440, French.

h. 1448. Alfonso V (the Magnanimous), 1396–1458. King of Aragon and Sicily, 1416–1458, and of Naples, 1443–1458.

i. 1445.

j. Mid-century, French king. Beards were not fashionable, but long ones were sometimes worn by dignitaries as a symbol of their importance and to set them apart.

k. Johann Fust, c.1400–1466, German printer, partner of Gutenberg. Issued first dated book in 1457.

l. 1480, French.

m. 1476, Italian.

n. 1491, Italian. Lorenzo de' Medici, 1449–1492.

o. 1488.

p. Italian. Piero de' Medici, 1471–1503.

q. Last quarter, Italian. Fashionable young man.

r. 1486, Italian. Fashionable young man.

s. Giovanni Pico della Mirandola, 1463–1494. Brilliant Italian humanist. Fashionable hair style.

t. c.1490. Long bangs were fashionable in the last decade.

u. Italian. Probably a wig.

v. c.1495, German. Fashionable style.

w. Last quarter, Italian. Young gentleman.

a *b* *c* *d* *e* *f* *g* *h* *i* *j* *k* *l* *m* *n* *o* *p* *q* *r* *s* *t* *u* *v* *w*

Plate 7

PLATE 8: FIFTEENTH-CENTURY WOMEN

a. c.1400, probably Italian.

b. First half, Italian.

c. Mid-century or third quarter, French.

d. First half, Italian.

e. c.1440, French. Jeanne de Saveuse, wife of Charles d'Artois.

f. 1447, Italian. Cicilia Gonzaga.

g. c.1470, German.

h. Last quarter.

i. 1488, Italian. Fashionable lady.

j. Last quarter (before 1491), German.

k. Last quarter, German.

l. Last quarter, German.

m. Last quarter, Italian. Fashionable style.

n. Last quarter.

o. Last quarter, Italian.

p. 1495, Italian. Elisabetta Gonzaga, wife of Guidobaldo da Montefeltro, son of the Duke of Urbino.

q. Noble Italian lady. Back hair is probably false.

r. 1492, Italian. Worn only by fashionable upper-class ladies.

s. Italian.

t. c.1500, Italian. Isabella d'Este, 1774–1539, wife of Francesco Gonzaga.

a *b* *c* *d* *e* *f* *g* *h* *i* *j* *k* *l* *m* *n* *o* *p* *q* *r* *s* *t*

Plate 8

PLATE 9: SIXTEENTH-CENTURY MEN

a. French. Louis XII, 1462–1515. Succeeded Charles VIII in 1498.

b. 1510, German. Unusually large *round* or *bush* beard.

c. Francis I, 1494–1547. King of France, 1515–1547. For later hair style see *k* below.

d. 1520, German. Hieronymus Holzschuher.

e. 1520, German. Martin Luther, 1483–1546. For later hair style see *l* below.

f. German.

g. 1529, German. Philip Künstler, age 7.

h. 1530, German.

i. 1530, German. Martin Luther's father.

j. 1535, German. Count Ulrich von Württemberg.

k. Francis I. For earlier style see *c* above.

l. Martin Luther. For earlier style see *e* above.

m. Gustavus I, 1496–1560. King of Sweden, 1523–1560.

n. German. Martin Bucer, 1491–1551. Reformer.

o. Flemish. Gerardus Mercator (Gerhard Kremer), 1512–1594. Geographer.

p. English. Cornelius Vandun, 1483–1577. Soldier with King Henry, Yeoman of the Guard and usher to King Henry, King Edward, Queen Mary, and Queen Elizabeth.

q. Italian. *Marquisette* beard.

r. c.1575, Scottish.

s. French. Henri de Lorraine, duc de Guise, 1550–1588. *Pique devant* beard with inverted mustache.

t. Henri II, 1519–1559. King of France, 1547–1559.

u. c.1594, Italian. Small *bush* beard.

v. 1596, English. *Swallow-tail* beard.

w. 1599, English. Sir Henry Neville.

Plate 9

M. Schreiner

PLATE: 10: SIXTEENTH-CENTURY WOMEN

a. c.1512, Italian.

b. Italian. Lucrezia Borgia, 1480–1519.

c. c.1515, Italian.

d. Before 1520, Italian.

e. 1520, Italian.

f. First quarter, Italian.

g. Mid-century.

h. c.1550, French.

i. c.1550, Italian.

j. Mid-century, Italian.

k. c.1560, probably English.

l. 1560.

m. German peasant.

n. c.1575, French. Hair dressed over pads.

o. Last quarter, French. Probably a wig.

p. English. Hair dressed over pads.

q. Marguerite de Valois, 1553–1615. Queen of France and Navarre, wife of Henri IV. Wig.

r. Probably French.

s. Elizabeth I, 1533–1603. Queen of England, 1558–1603. Wig.

t. c.1595, French. Wig.

u. 1597, Italian. The same treatment of the front hair was also used without the cone-shaped arrangement at the back. This was a short-lived style worn in Italy. Hair dressed over wire frames.

a

b

c

d

e

f

g

h

i

j

k

l

m

n

o

p

q

r

s

t

u

Plate 10

PLATE 11: SEVENTEENTH-CENTURY MEN

a. William Shakespeare, 1564–1616. (The drawing is based on the Chandos portrait.)

b. 1614, Italian. Francesco de' Medici, brother of the Grand Duke.

c. 1614, German. *Pique devant* beard.

d. 1628, Spanish peasant.

e. Christian IV, King of Denmark and Norway, 1577–1648. Notice the small braid in front of the ear. The fashion of wearing a single pearl earring was started by Henri de Lorraine, duc d'Harcourt, who subsequently became known as *le Cadet à la perle.*

f. Bavarian. Gottfried Heinrich, 1594–1632. Imperialist general in the Thirty Years War. *Stiletto* beard.

g. Captain John Smith, 1579–1631. English adventurer. *Round* beard.

h. English. William Slater, D.D.

i. c.1630, Dutch. Crispin Van de Passe the Younger. *Square* cut beard.

j. English. John Endicott, 1589–1665. Governor of Massachusetts colony. *Needle* beard.

k. Anthony Van Dyck, 1599–1641. Stiletto beard, later called a *Van Dyck* or *Vandyke.*

l. English. Thomas Howard, Earl of Arundel, 1586–1646.

m. 1632, Spanish. Charles of Austria, son of Philip III.

n. 1633, French. Fashionable gentleman with *lovelock.*

o. c.1635.

p. 1645, English. Fop with two *lovelocks.*

q. 1645, English. Oliver Cromwell, 1599–1658.

r. 1649, English. Cavalier with *lovelock.*

s. c.1650, French. Molière, 1622–1673.

t. c.1650, French.

u. Charles II, 1630–1685. King of England, 1660–1685.

v. Louis XIV, 1638–1715. King of France, 1643–1715. Wig.

a *b* *c* *d* *e* *f* *g* *h* *i* *j* *k* *l* *m* *n* *o* *p* *q* *r* *s* *t* *u* *v*

Plate 11

PLATE 12: SEVENTEENTH-CENTURY WOMEN

a. c.1610, French. Probably a wig.

b. 1610, French. Wig.

c. 1615, probably Spanish.

d. c.1630, French.

e. c.1630, Dutch. Hélène Fourment, wife of Peter Paul Rubens.

f. c.1635, French.

g. 1640, French.

h. c.1640, Dutch.

i. German.

j. 1643, French.

k. c.1650, Spanish.

l. French. Anne of Austria, 1601–1666. Queen of France, mother of Louis XIV.

m. c.1650, Dutch.

n. c.1650, Spanish.

o. 1660, Dutch. Catherina Horft.

p. 1665, French. Side curls are wired to stand out.

q. 1680, English. *Hurluberlu.* The style was created by Martin in 1671 in Paris.

r. English. Nell Gwynn, 1650–1687. Actress and mistress of Charles II after 1669.

s. 1680's, French. Early *fontange.*

t. 1690's, French. *Fontange* with *tour,* decorated with jeweled pins.

Plate 12

PLATE 13: EIGHTEENTH-CENTURY MEN

a. Baron Gottfried Wilhelm von Leibnitz, 1646–1716. German philosopher and mathematician. *Full-bottom wig.*

b. c.1718. *Full-bottom wig.*

c. King George II, reigned 1727–1760. *Full-bottom wig.* This was no longer a fashionable style, and the enormous full-bottoms had disappeared completely.

d. c.1735, English clergyman. *Long bob*—sometimes called a *minister's* or *clergyman's bob.*

e. *Campaign wig* or *knotted wig.* This bushy version was also known as a *physical tie.*

f. 1735, English. Composer. Powdered *knotted wig.*

g. 1736, English.

h. 1750, English. *Scratch wig* or natural hair.

i. 1747, English. Alderman's clerk. *Bob wig.*

j. 1735, English.

k. Henry Fielding, 1707–1754. *Physical bob.*

l. 1761, English. *Physical bob*, worn by bishops. The foretop was not always so high.

m. *Full-bottom* or *square wig*, worn mostly by gentlemen of the Law.

n. Voltaire, 1694–1778. *Long bob.*

o. c.1750, English. *Physical bob*, very popular with the medical profession.

p. c.1760, English. *Short* or *minor bob.* Ends of the hair are frizzed into a bush and the wig powdered. (See other versions of long and short bobs.)

q. c.1763, English. Gentleman wearing *cauliflower* or *cut wig.*

r. 1758, English. *Short bob.*

s. 1762, English. Natural hair.

t. 1770's, French soldier. Wig with *horseshoe toupee* and *twisted queue*, raised and secured with comb.

u. 1773, *Bob wig.*

v. 1773, English. *Major wig*, sometimes a *brigadier.*

w. Johann Sebastian Bach, 1685–1750. *Square wig.*

x. 1745, English marriage broker. *Knotted wig* or *physical tie.*

a

b

c

d

e

f

g

h

i

j

k

l

m

n

o

p

q

r

s

t

u

v

w

x

Plate 13

PLATE 14: EIGHTEENTH-CENTURY MEN

a. 1772, English. Variation of *cadogan* or *club wig.*

b. 1771, German. *Bag wig.* The high toupee was very fashionable at this time.

c. 1772, German. *Bag wig.* The bag tended to be quite large in the 1770's.

d. 1776, French. Gentleman at home. The back hair is pulled up and secured with a comb. It would be worn this way only at home.

e. 1770's, French. *Wig à l'enfant* or *à la naissance* or *naissante*, popular primarily in France in the last quarter of the century. Style *d* above might be worn this way in public.

f. c.1775. Double *pigtail wig* with *grecque.* The double queue was largely French. The *grecque* is the horseshoe-shaped toupee.

g. Jean d'Alembert, 1717–1783. French mathematician and philosopher. *Bag wig.* Note the large and elegant bow.

h. Benjamin Franklin, 1706–1790. Natural hair.

i. John Howard, 1726(?)–1790. Powdered *cadogan* or *club wig*, popular after the late 1760's.

j. Wolfgang Amadeus Mozart, 1756–1791. Powdered *tie wig.*

k. Marquis de Lafayette, 1747–1834.

l. Jacques Necker, 1732–1804. French banker and financial expert, minister of state under Louis XVI. *Bag wig.*

m. 1782, English.

n. Late 1780's. *Pigtail.* Probably natural hair.

o. 1789, French. *Tie wig.*

p. 1786, Italian. *Club wig.*

q. 1786, Italian. *Pigtail wig.*

r. c.1790, French. *Cadogan.*

s. 1790's, French.

t. 1794. William Bligh, British admiral, captain of the *Bounty.* Natural hair.

u. John Adams, 1735–1826. Became president of the United States in 1796. Natural hair with queue.

v. 1796, French. Natural hair in the Napoleonic style.

a *b* *c* *d*

e *f* *g* *h*

i *j*

k *l* *m* *n*

o *p* *q* *r*

s *t* *u* *v*

Plate 14

PLATE 15: EIGHTEENTH-CENTURY WOMEN

a. c.1700, French. *Fontange* style with pearls, jeweled pins, and *favorites* (curls at temple).

b. c.1702, English. Queen Anne.

c. 1732, English.

d. c.1730, French. Known as the "Dutch coiffure." Usually powdered. Popular into the 1750's.

e. c.1735, French.

f. c.1750.

g. 1750's. Style worn by Marie Joseph of Austria.

h. 1760's, French.

i. 1764. Style of Madame de Pompadour.

j. c.1770, French. Madame du Barry.

k. c.1770, French.

l. 1774, French.

m. 1773, German. Hair in this period was dressed back and low with a fairly high toupee and a number of small puffs or curls down the sides. Most coiffures were powdered.

n. 1774, French. *A la Venus.*

o. c.1776, French. Coiffures at this time were high and narrow.

p. Marie Antoinette.

q. 1776, French. Coiffure *à la Syrienne*, originated in 1775.

r. 1778, French. Coiffure *en rouleaux.* The high coiffures were built up on elastic cushions or sometimes stuffed with horsehair or wool, teased (although that term was not used), thoroughly greased with pomatum, and heavily powdered.

a *b* *c* *d* *e* *f* *g* *h* *i* *j* *k* *l* *m* *n* *o* *p* *q* *r*

Plate 15

PLATE 16: EIGHTEENTH-CENTURY WOMEN

a. 1778, French. *Chien couchant.* Coiffures were decorated with ropes of pearls, jewels, ribbons, plumes, flowers, fruit, vegetables, chiffon kerchiefs, ornaments of blown glass, reproductions of gardens, parks, carriages, ships, planets, tombstones, and almost anything else one can imagine.

b. 1780, French. Marie Antoinette.

c. 1780, French. Frizzed toupee and side hair.

d. 1780, French. *Le bandeau d'amour.* Frizzed toupee and sides. The hanging curls were always smooth. Later in the 1780's the side curls were not always worn.

e. c.1782, French.

f. 1781, English. *Hérisson* or *hedgehog.* Originated in Paris, it was an extremely popular style and lasted for some years in both France and England, in many versions. The essential was the bouffant frizzle, which gives the style its name.

g. 1788, French. *Hérisson.*

h. 1798, English.

i. 1794, English.

j. 1796, French. *Titus cut.* This style signalled the end of long hair.

k. Late 1790's, French.

l. c.1788, French.

m. 1797, French. Wig *à la grecque.*

n. 1798, French. "Garland of flowers and moss."

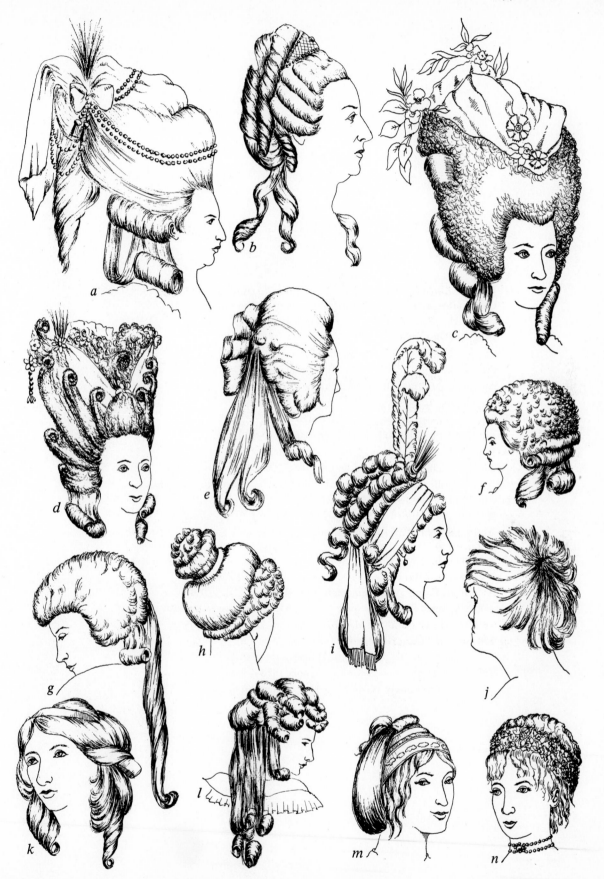

a

b

c

d

e

f

g

h

i

j

k

l

m

n

Plate 16

PLATE 17: NINETEENTH-CENTURY MEN

a. Early years, English.

b. Joseph McKeen, 1757–1832. First president of Bowdoin College, 1802–1807. Long hair was still worn by conservative men but was not fashionable.

c. George IV, 1762–1830. King of England, 1820–1830.

d. 1820, English.

e. English. Benjamin Disraeli, 1804–1881.

f. Frédéric Chopin, 1810–1849.

g. American. Matthew Brady, 1823–1896. Pioneer photographer.

h. Napoleon III, 1808–1873.

i. German. Robert Schumann, 1810–1856.

j. Benjamin Franklin Kelley, 1807–1891. *Uncle Sam* beard.

k. Johann Peter Eckermann, 1792–1854. German writer.

l. c.1860. E. A. Sothern as Lord Dundreary in *Our American Cousin*.

m. American. Benson John Lossing, 1813–1891. Historian and journalist.

n. Algernon Charles Swinburne, 1837–1909.

o. Russian. Alexander II, 1818–1881.

p. Andrew Adgate Lipscomb, 1816–1890. Author and educator. *Billy whiskers* or *billies*.

q. English. Benjamin Disraeli, 1804–1881. In America this small beard was called a *breakwater*.

r. American. Ralph Waldo Emerson, 1803–1882.

s. 1880's. Watson Robertson Sperry, born 1842. American journalist.

t. 1880's. John Meredith Read, 1837–1896. U.S. Minister to Greece.

u. 1880's. Washington C. DePauw, 1822–1887. Founder of DePauw University.

v. 1880's, American. Richard Grant White. *Dundrearies.*

w. 1880's, American. General George Crook, 1828–1890.

x. 1880's. Irving Ramsay Wiles, born 1861. American artist.

Plate 17

PLATE 18: NINETEENTH-CENTURY MEN

a. 1890's, Norwegian. Fridtjof Nansen, 1861–1930. Explorer, scientist, statesman, humanitarian, and first Norwegian minister to Great Britain.

b. 1890's, American. Edward Mitchell. Lawyer.

c. 1890's, American.

d. 1890's, Scottish. Robert Louis Stevenson, 1850–1894.

e. 1892, American. William Collins Whitney, Secretary of the Navy, 1885–1889.

f. 1890's. Armand Capdervielle. American editor and publisher.

g. 1890's, American merchant, soldier.

h. 1890's, American. John Mason Loomis.

i. 1890's, American. H. M. Alexander. Attorney.

j. 1890's, American. James Roosevelt. Steamship official.

k. 1890's, American. Rev. Charles K. Parkhurst.

l. 1890's. Charles Carroll Walcutt, 1838–1898. American soldier.

m. 1890's, American. John Philip Sousa, 1854–1932. Composer.

n. 1890's, American merchant, philanthropist. *Imperial* beard.

o. 1890's, American journalist.

p. 1890's. Edward Gay. Irish-American artist.

q. English. Sir Arthur Sullivan, 1842–1900.

r. 1890's, American. Business executive. *Burnsides.*

s. 1890's, American. John F. Shera. Stockbroker.

t. 1890's, American banker.

u. 1890's, American. Paul L. Thebaud. Shipping merchant. *Swallow-tail* beard.

v. 1890's, American broker. *Dundrearies.*

w. 1890's, American. Thomas S. Hastings. President of the Union Theological Seminary.

x. 1890's. Daniel Smith Lamb, 1843–1929. American pathologist and anatomist. A variation of the *imperial.*

y. Hermann Sudermann, 1857–1938. German dramatist and novelist.

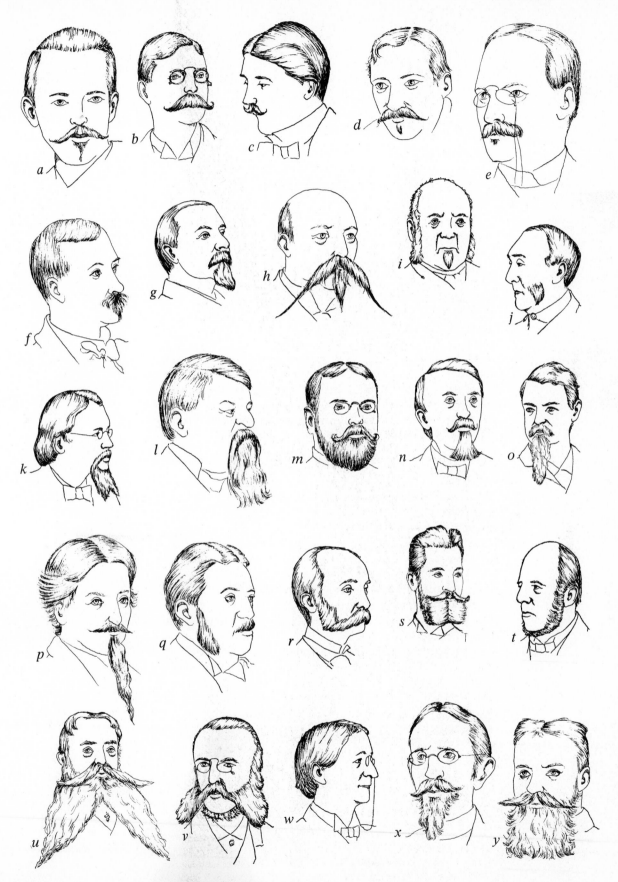

Plate 18

PLATE 19: NINETEENTH-CENTURY WOMEN

a. 1803, French.

b. 1808, French.

c. 1813, French.

d. c.1820, American. Maria Monroe Gouverneur, daughter of James Monroe.

e. 1827. Coiffure for a ball.

f. 1831. The high, lacquered bows were wired in place and the coiffure decorated with feathers, flowers, leaves, ribbons, beads, or jewels.

g. 1841, English. Queen Victoria, 1837–1901. Hair was worn flat to the head and parted in the center. Ears were exposed, and braids and spiral curls were popular.

h. 1848. Hair was still straight, front and back sections of the hair were usually separated, and braids were more popular than ever.

i. 1855. Slight waves were beginning to appear. Braids were less popular.

j. 1860. Hair was much fuller. Curls and braids were popular. Feathers were worn in the evening.

k. 1862. Low chignons, often false, were in fashion.

l. 1865, French.

m. 1869, French. Curls probably false. Sometimes an entire coiffure was made up of false hair pieces.

n. 1869, French. Coiffures were becoming higher.

o. 1874, French. Most of the hair is probably false.

p. 1877, French. Hair at the temples is natural, but the rest may be a combination of various pieces of false hair.

q. 1879, French. Top hair was lower and nearly always waved or curled.

r. 1880. Combs were very fashionable.

s. 1885, French. Back hair entirely false. Wispy bangs softened the line of the forehead.

t. 1888. The hair was heading upward again.

u. 1894, French. Tight marcels were no longer fashionable, and the hair was beginning to puff out.

v. 1894, French. Topknots vied with puffs.

w. 1894, French.

x. 1899, French.

a *b* *c* *d* *e*

f *g* *h* *i*

j *k* *l* *m* *n*

o *p* *q* *r* *s*

t *u* *v* *w* *x*

Plate 19

PLATE 20: TWENTIETH-CENTURY MEN

a. 1905, American engineer.

b. John Philip Sousa, 1854–1932. American bandmaster and composer. Beards were not fashionable but were still being worn by older men.

c. Georg Morris Cohen Brandes, 1842–1927. Danish writer.

d. Piotr Kropotkin, 1842–1921. Russian anarchist.

e. Rupert Brooke, 1887–1915. English poet.

f. Woodrow Wilson, 1846–1924. 28th U.S. President.

g. c.1922, American senator.

h. 1926, American actor. Most fashionable men were clean-shaven. Mustaches, when worn, were small.

i. 1929. John Barrymore.

j. 1930's, English. Military hair style. The American military cut was much the same.

k. 1937, American actor.

l. 1940, American.

m. 1953, American. *Crew cut.*

n. 1956, American. Elvis style. Long hair, rising in a high wave in front, often worn with sideburns. Worn by Elvis Presley, American entertainer.

o. c.1958, British. *English cut.* Hair long on top and sides, full over the ears and in back, and combed back from the forehead.

p. 1959, American actor.

q. 1961, American college student.

r. 1961, French. *Caesar cut.* Hair combed down over forehead. Very popular with young men.

s. 1961, French. *Caesar cut.* Small beards were being seen increasingly on young men, even in the United States.

t. 1962, American. *Caesar cut.*

u. 1962, English.

v. 1963, English.

w. 1965, English. Beatle style.

x. 1966, American college student. Not typical but indicative of the trend toward longer hair.

y. 1966, American. The majority of teen-agers and young men were combing the hair forward and letting it grow fuller.

Plate 20

PLATE 21: TWENTIETH-CENTURY MEN

a. 1965. *Sosh* style. Always carefully combed and greased.

b. 1966, American university student.

c. 1966, English. Working class. Also worn in other countries.

d. 1968. Full sideburns and mustache.

e. 1968. Facial hair was sometimes false.

f. 1968, American. False beard and mustache. Natural hair. Ready-made false beards, mustaches, and sideburns were available in a variety of styles, singly or in sets.

g. 1968, American. False sideburns. Most men who wanted long sideburns grew their own, unless prevented from doing so by a conservative employer.

h. 1969, French.

i. 1970.

j. 1971.

k. 1971, American. *Afro* style. Worn first by Blacks, later in various colors by others.

l. 1971.

m. 1970, French.

n. 1972, American. *Natural* style. An outgrowth of the *Afro;* see *k* above.

o. 1972.

p. 1972.

q. 1972. Same style could be worn loose.

r. 1972.

s. 1973.

t. 1973.

u. 1973.

v. 1973.

w. 1973.

x. 1973.

y. 1973.

z. 1973.

aa. 1973.

Plate 21

PLATE 22: TWENTIETH-CENTURY WOMEN

a. 1904, American. Fashionable. Gibson girl style.

b. 1910, American.

c. 1914, French. Fashionable.

d. 1917, American. Ornate tortoise-shell combs were fashionable.

e. 1919, American. Hair turned under to look like a bob. A style designed for women who hesitated to take the plunge and have their hair cut off.

f. 1919. The latest bob from Paris.

g. 1924. *Egyptian bob.*

h. 1923, American.

i. 1925. *Marcelled bob.*

j. 1925. The latest *shingled bob*. The *boyish bob*, a bit shorter at the crown, was equally fashionable.

k. 1934, American. Soft waves were back, hair was longer, and the full face was exposed.

l. 1940, American. Front hair up and back hair down was the fashionable style.

m. 1940, American.

n. 1941, American. Side part, hair long and slightly waved, partially concealing one eye. Style popularized by Veronica Lake.

o. 1945, American.

p. 1948. A popular and durable style.

q. 1954, French. Zizi Jeanmaire. Singer and dancer. The vogue for very short hair did not last long.

r. 1959, American.

s. 1961, American. *Beehive* style. Hair was teased to give it volume.

t. 1961, American. Jacqueline Kennedy style.

u. 1964, English. Fashionable and popular style.

v. 1964, English. False topknots had been worn for several years. Hair partially concealed the forehead.

w. 1965, English and American. A Vidal Sassoon style. Sassoon's chunky, boyish cuts, reflecting the men's style popularized by the Beatles, had considerable influence on young sophisticates.

x. 1966, American. Hair was worn both up and down, short and long. When up, a good deal of it was false.

Plate 22

PLATE 23: TWENTIETH-CENTURY WOMEN

a. 1967. *Page-boy* style, with hair poufed from center crown.

b. 1967. Natural hair or wig.

c. 1968. *Shirley Temple* style. Natural hair or wig.

d. 1969. Natural hair.

e. 1969. Natural hair with fall.

f. 1969. Natural hair poufed in *Gibson-girl* style, topped with false curls.

g. 1969. Short-clipped natural hair or wig.

h. 1970. Style known as the *Ape* or *Shag*. Hair short on top, long in back, with a shaggy look. Could be either straight or curly.

i. 1970. Natural hair with long fall.

j. 1970. Natural hair. Front and crown set with large rollers, back and side with medium ones. Hair is brushed back and held with elastic, then ends are back-brushed to make pouf, which is shaped with the fingers.

k. 1970. Natural hair.

l. 1970. Natural hair.

m. 1970. Natural hair.

n. 1970. Natural hair or wig.

o. 1971. Natural hair.

p. 1971. Natural hair or wig.

q. 1972. Natural hair or wig.

r. 1972.

s. 1973. Natural hair.

t. 1973. Natural hair.

u. 1973. Version of a braided style popular with Blacks.

v. 1973. Natural hair or wig.

w. 1973. Natural hair.

x. 1973. Natural hair or wig.

y. 1973. Natural hair.

Plate 23

PICTURE COLLECTION

The pictures on the following pages are included for easy reference when your personal picture morgue is not available or if your own is not yet extensive enough. It can be used as a source of ideas for making up specific characters or as portraits for you to copy. For portraits in color, see Appendix J. For creating likenesses from portraits, see Chapter 19.

Figure H-1.   Medieval sculpture, French.

Figure H-2.   Oriental head.

Figure H-3. **Head of Pan.** Athenian, c. 400 B.C.

Figure H-4. **Julius Caesar.** Marble bust.

Figure H-5. The Prophet Haggai. Marble bust by Giovanni Pisano.

Figure H-6. King Charles II. Marble bust by Honoré Pelle, 1684.

Figure H-7. Prominent fifteenth-century Florentines. Engraving.

339

Figure H-8. Philip Melanchthon. Engraving by Dürer, 1526.

Figure H-9. Wilibald Pirkheimer. Engraving by Dürer, 1524.

Figure H-10. Johannes Fugger. Early sixteenth-century engraving.

Figure H-11. Louis XII of France.

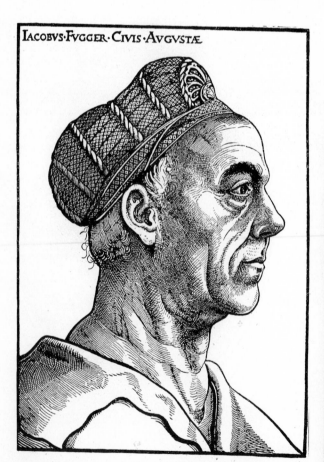

IACOBVS·FVGGER·CIVIS·AVGVSTÆ

Figure H-12. Portrait of Johann Bodmer. Pencil drawing by Henry Fuseli, 1741–1825.

Figure H-13. **Old Man of 93.** Brush drawing by Dürer, 1521.

Figure H-14. **Francis I, 1494–1547.** Painting attributed to Jean Clouet.

Figure H-15. Richard II, 1367–1400. Painting by an unknown artist.

Figure H-16. Elizabeth I, 1533–1603. Painting by an unknown artist.

Figure H-17. Mary Queen of Scots, 1542–1587. Painting by an unknown artist, after Nicholas Hilliard.

Figure H-18. Emperor Rudolf II.
Painting by Hans van Aacken, 1552–
1615.

**Figure H-19. Heironymus Holz-
schuher.** Painting by Dürer, 1526.

Figure H-20. St. Philip. Painting by Dürer, 1516.

Figure H-21.   St. Barnabas. Detail of painting by Botticelli.

347

Figure H-22. Portrait of Wohl-gemut. Painting by Dürer, 1516.

Figure H-23. Jean Baptiste Ca-mille Corot, 1796–1875.

Figure H-24. Court Jester Gonella. Dutch, fifteenth century (no. 1840).

Figure H-25. Luther's Mother. Painting by Lucas Cranach the Elder.

Figure H-26. Sir Thomas More, 1478–1535.

Figure H-28. Charles Darwin, 1809–1882. Painting by the Hon. John Collier.

Figure H-27. Portrait of the Artist's Father. Painting by Dürer, 1493.

Figure H-29. William Cowper. Drawing by George Romney, 1792.

Figure H-30.   Frederick the Wise. *(top)* Sixteenth century. Engraving by Albrecht Dürer. **Figure H-31. The Judge.** *(bottom)* Eighteenth century. Engraving by Hogarth.

Figure H-32.   Queen Victoria, 1819–1901. Painting after a portrait by H. von Angeli, 1899.

Figure H-33.   John Stuart Mill, 1806–1873. Painting by G. F. Watts.

Figure H-34.   Marie Tussaud, 1760–1850.
Attributed to Francis Tussaud.

Figure H-35.   Benjamin Disraeli, 1804–
1881. Detail of painting by Sir J. E. Millais.

Figure H-36.   Men of history. (A) John Calvin, (B) Savanarola, (C) Winston Churchill, (D) Adolf Hitler, (E) Lenin, (F) Thomas Jefferson, (G) Napoleon, (H) John Adams, (I) George Bernard Shaw, (J) Prince Vlad, the real Dracula, (K, L) Abraham Lincoln, (M) Prince Albert, (N) George Washington.

Figure H-37.   Men and women of history. (A) Socrates, (B) Lord Byron, (C) Galileo, (D) Cleopatra, (E) Oscar Wilde, (F) Charles I, (G, H) Cleopatra, (I) Queen Victoria, (J) William Shakespeare, (K) Catherine the Great, (L) Robespierre, (M) Ulysses S. Grant, (N) Theodore Roosevelt, (O) Sir Walter Raleigh, (P) Franklin D. Roosevelt, (Q) Woodrow Wilson.

Appendix J

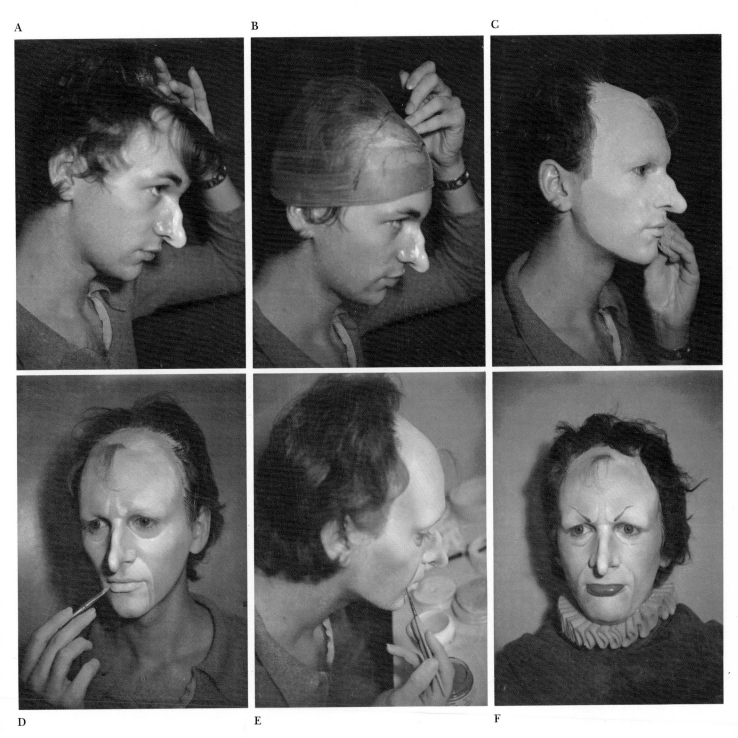

A   B   C

D   E   F

Figure J-1. Making up as Feste in *Twelfth Night.* (A) Soaping out front hair. Nose built up with putty. (B) Making outline of bald area on nylon stocking, which will cover soaped-out hair. (C) Applying the foundation with a sponge. Eyebrows have been blocked out. (D) Modeling the face with highlights. (E) Applying shadows. (F) Completed makeup, with painted eyebrows, rouge, and full lower lip. Makeup by Lee Austin. (For other makeups by Mr. Austin, see Figures 13-3, 15-3, and J-9.)

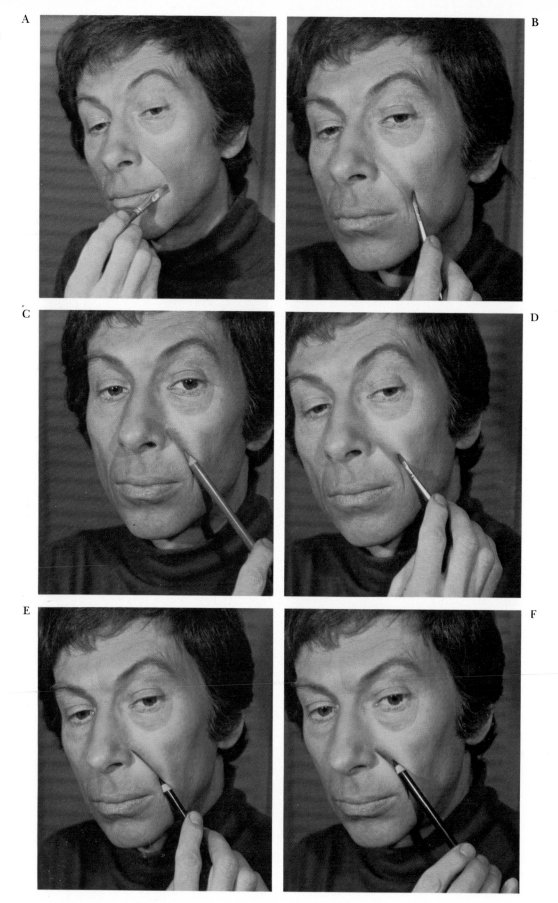

Figure J-2. Modeling the face with paint. (A) Modeling a hard-edged highlight for the nasolabial fold, using a ⅜-inch brush. (B) Highlighting top of nasolabial fold. (C) Penciling shadow area with bright red. (D) Blending soft edge of the red. (E) Adding a hard-edged shadow with a dark brown pencil in order to deepen the crease. (F) Filling out the shadow area with a brown pencil. (G) Blending the soft

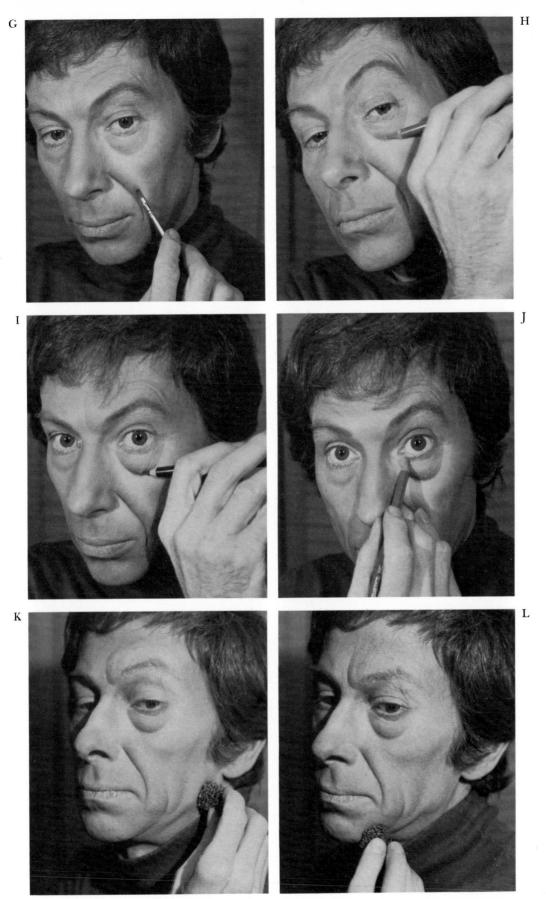

edge of the shadow with a 3/16-inch brush. (H) Filling in the shadow area of the eye pouch with a red pencil. (I) Deepening the bottom of the pouch shadow with a dark brown pencil. (J) Outlining the eye with red to age and weaken it. (K) Modeled jaw area being stippled with red. (L) Entire makeup being carefully stippled with a dark shadow color for texture.

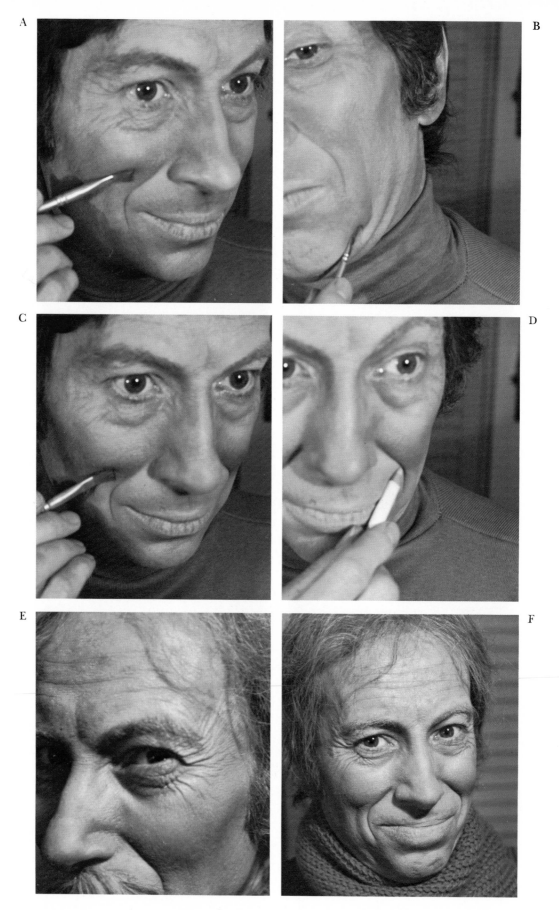

Figure J·3. Modeling apple cheeks for an aged face. (A) Rouging the apple cheek with a ⅜-inch brush. (B) Adding rouge to jaw-area wrinkles. (C) Shadowing the apple cheek. (D) Highlighting the hard edge of the apple cheek. (E) Closeup of modeled apple cheek and eye area. Note liver spots on forehead and in temple area. (F) Completed makeup.

J-4 A

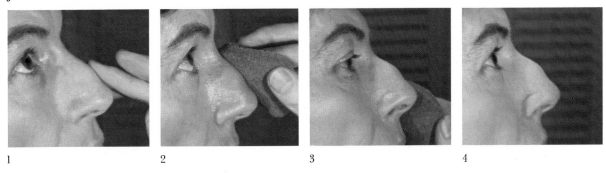

1   2   3   4

J-4 B   **J-4 C**

J-4 F

J-4 D   **J-4 E**

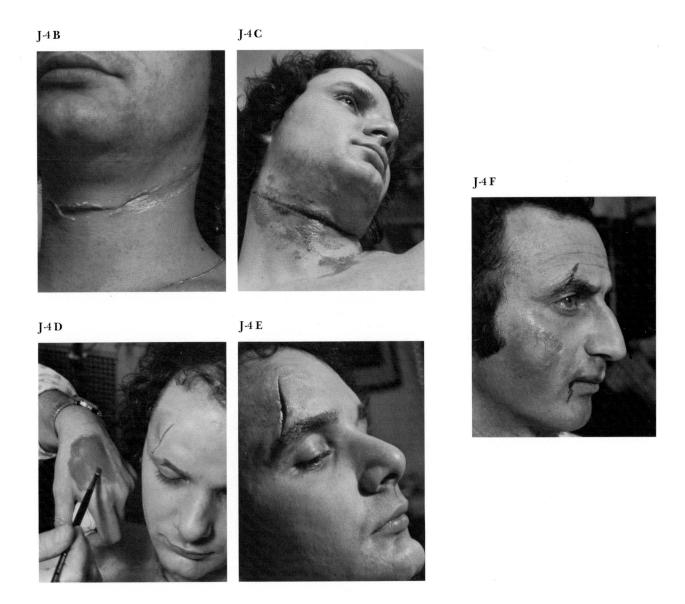

Figure J-4A. Building up the nose. (1) Smoothing out the derma wax. (2) Stippling the nose with rouge. (3) Applying creme-stick foundation. (4) Finished nose, powdered and rouged.

Figure J-4 B, C. Making a deep, bleeding cut. Latex is brushed on and allowed to dry, then pinched together (B) to form a crease. Blood is then added and wiped off (C). Makeup by Bert Roth, S.M.A.

Figure J-4 D, E. Making a deep cut. Forehead area built up with derma wax, then cut with palette knife. Grays, purples, and reds (D) are mixed to create a bruise. Moist rouge is then painted into cut (E).

Figure J-4 F. Scar and bruise. Makeup artist Bert Roth with collodion scar, artificial blood running from his mouth, and a bruised cheek made to look swollen by highlighting.

J-5 **J-6** **J-7**

J-8 **J-9** **J-10**

Figure J-5. Medieval lady. Inspired by a fifteenth-century painting by van der Weyden. Eyebrows and front hair soaped out. Lips reshaped. Student makeup by Rondi Hillstrom.

Figure J-6. Leopard makeup for children's play. Entire makeup painted on with cake. Student makeup by Dianne Harris.

Figure J-7. Woman of Samoa. Facial shape changed by modeling with lights and darks. Note effect of broad cheekbone area and narrow chin. Student makeup by Dianne Harris.

Figure J-8. Portrait of a sixteenth-century lady. Inspired by a painting by Leonardo da Vinci. Creme makeup used for foundation, highlights, shadows, and rouge. Student makeup by Gaye Bowan.

Figure J-9. Decorative makeup based on an Oriental mask. Student makeup by Lee Austin. (For other makeups by Mr. Austin, see Figures 13-3, 15-3, and J-1.)

Figure J-10. Portrait of a lady. Inspired by a painting by Chardin. Creme makeup used for foundation, highlights, shadows, and rouge. Student makeup by Ruth Salisbury.

Figure J-11. Lady Liston, detail. Painting by Gilbert Stuart, 1755–1828. Note the large amount of natural red in the face. In makeup this would be achieved by using rouge over a much lighter foundation.

Figure J-12. Francesco Saverio, Cardinal de Zelada. Painting by Rafael Mengs, 1728–1779. Note how the red in the costume is reflected in the facial shadows.

Figure J-13. John Tyler, 1859, detail. Painting by George Peter Alexander Healy. Note particularly the cheek and nose shadows and the color in the cheeks, on the nose and chin, and around the eyes.

Figure J-14. George Washington, 1795, detail. Painting by Rembrandt Peale. Note especially the red on the cheeks, nose, chin, and jowls.

J-15 J-16 J-17

J-18 J-19 J-20

Figure J-15. Mrs. Grace Dalrymple Elliott, c. 1778, detail. Painting by Gainsborough. The placement of the rouge shown here was fashionable at the time, as were the full, dark eyebrows.

Figure J-16. Vinnie Ream, c. 1870, detail. Painting by George Peter Alexander Healy. An illustration of natural, healthy coloring, in contrast to the pale, rouged faces fashionable in the 18th century.

Figure J-17. Madame de Caumartin as Hebe, 1753, detail. Painting by Nattier. The rouged cheeks on a pale or whitened skin were fashionable at the time. Note the difference in placement and shape of the rouged area between this portrait and the one in J-15.

Figure J-18. George Clymer, c. 1810, detail. Painting by an unidentified artist, after Wilson Peale. Note the color in the cheeks, nose, chin, and eyelids, as well as the shading in the cheeks and on the temples.

Figure J-19. Portrait of a Man, 1647, detail. Painting by Bartholomeus van der Helst. Note the unshaven effect on the cheeks and jowls and the color in the nasolabial folds, cheeks, and chin.

Figure J-20. Paul Wayland Bartlett, 1865-1925, detail. Painting by Charles Sprague Pearce. Note the extreme naturalness of the coloring—the red on the cheeks, nose, and ear lobes, and the subtle suggestion of a beard shadow.

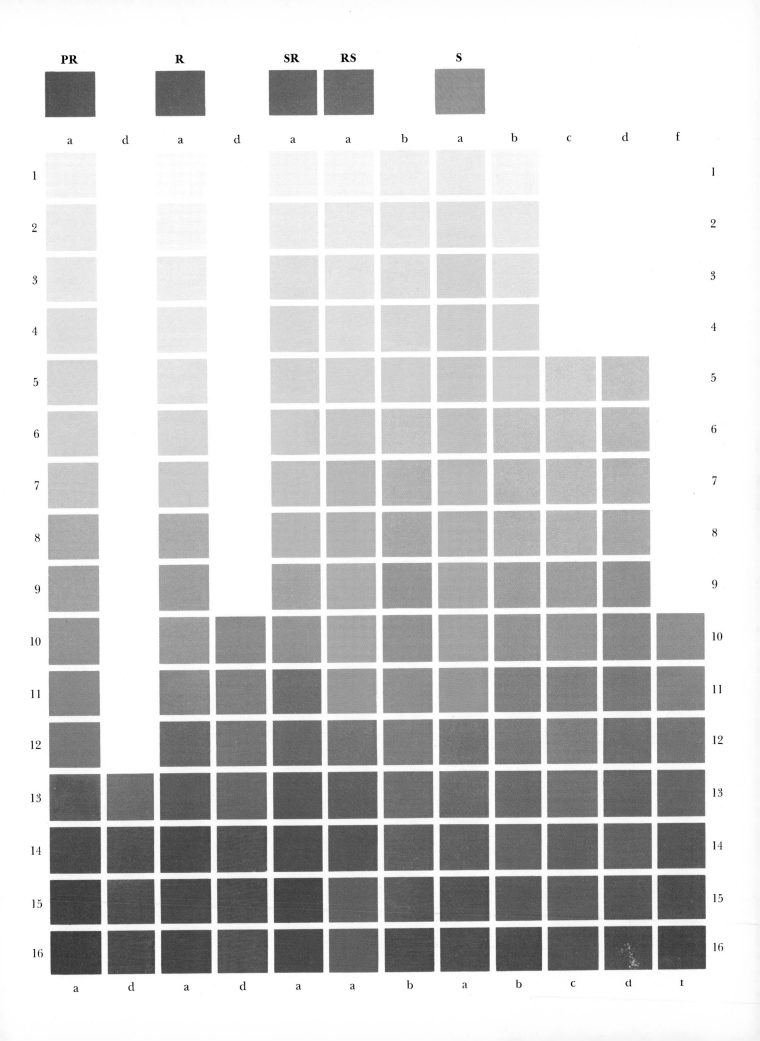

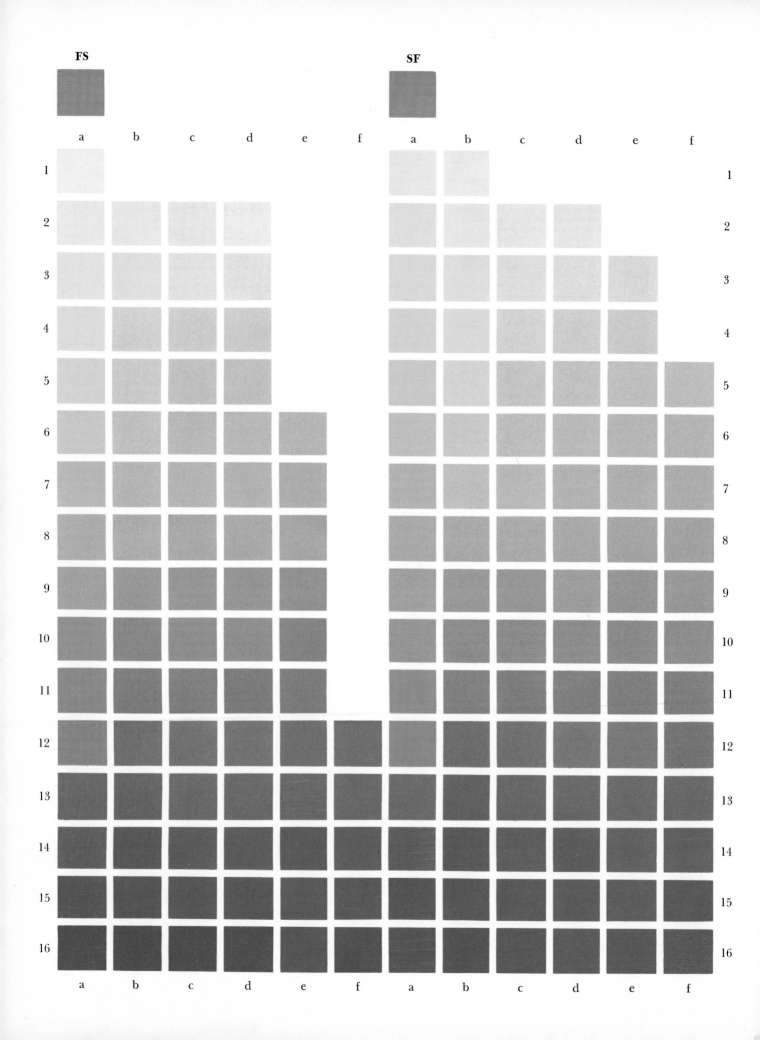

F

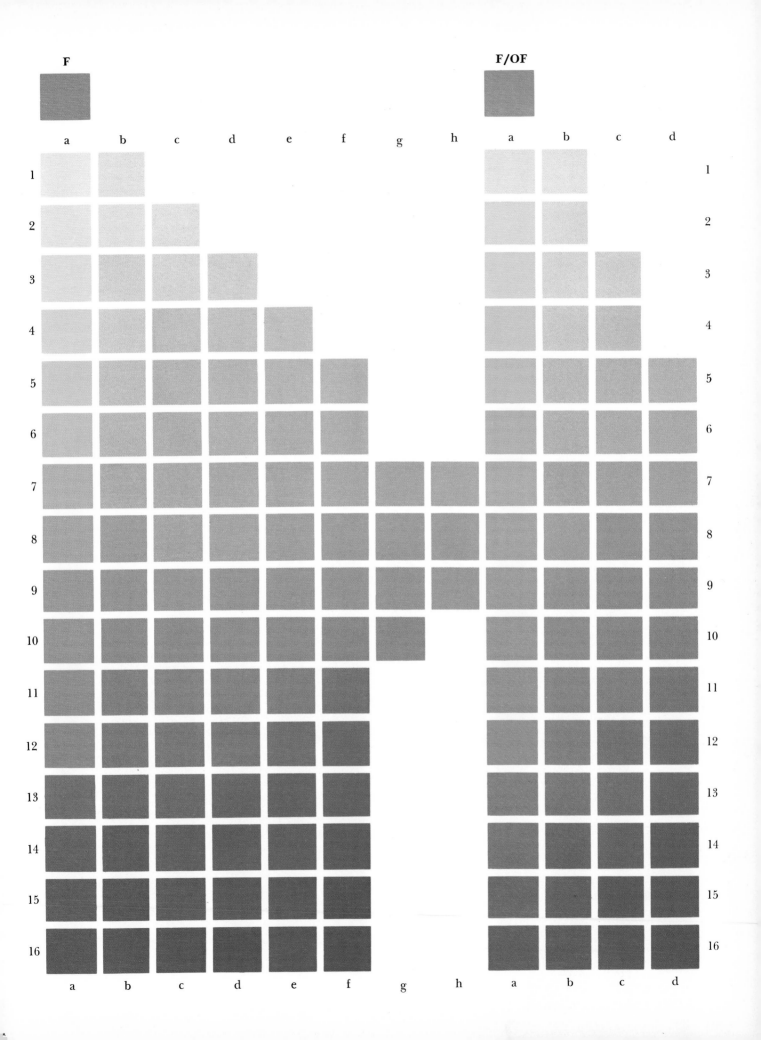

F/OF

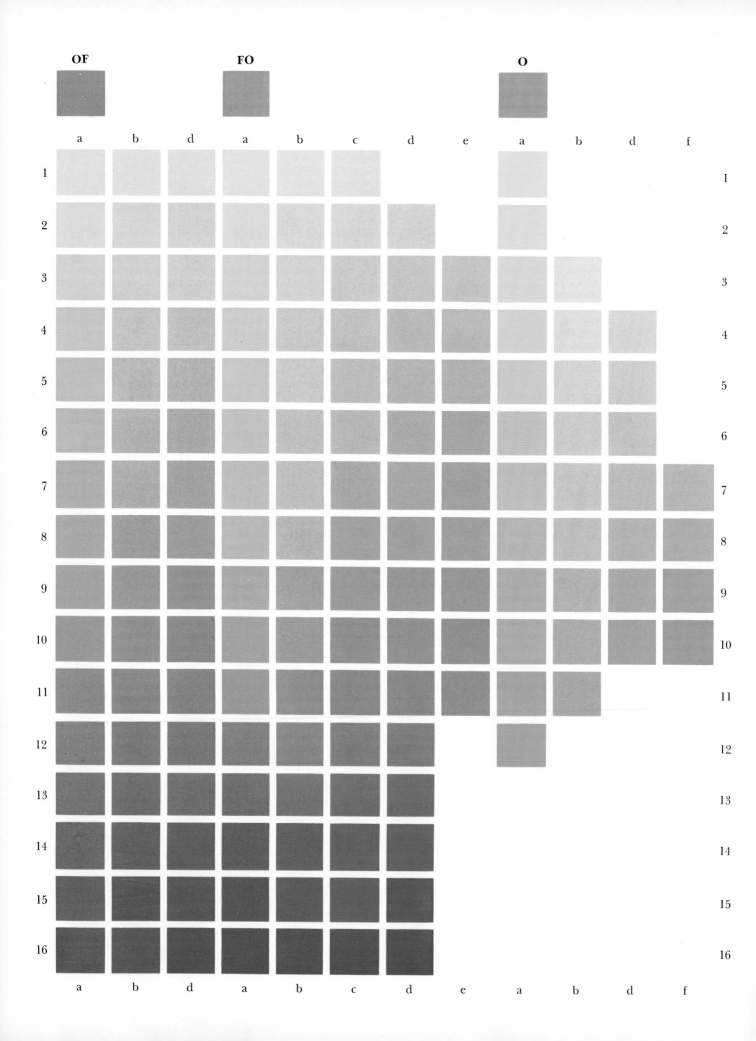

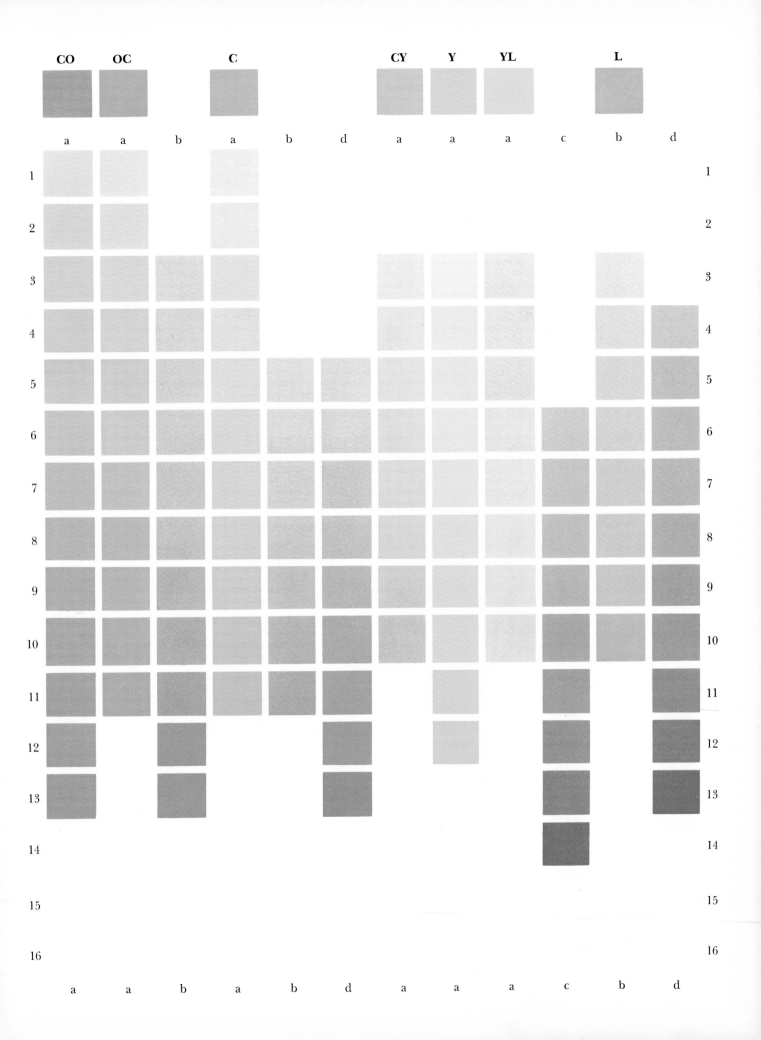

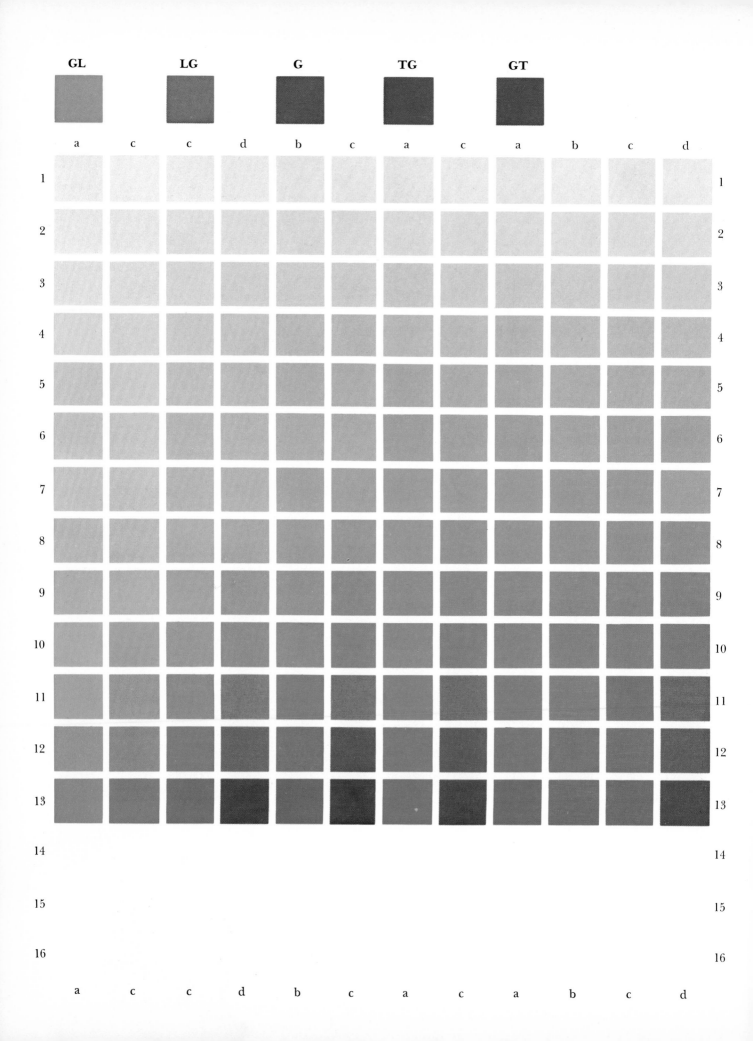

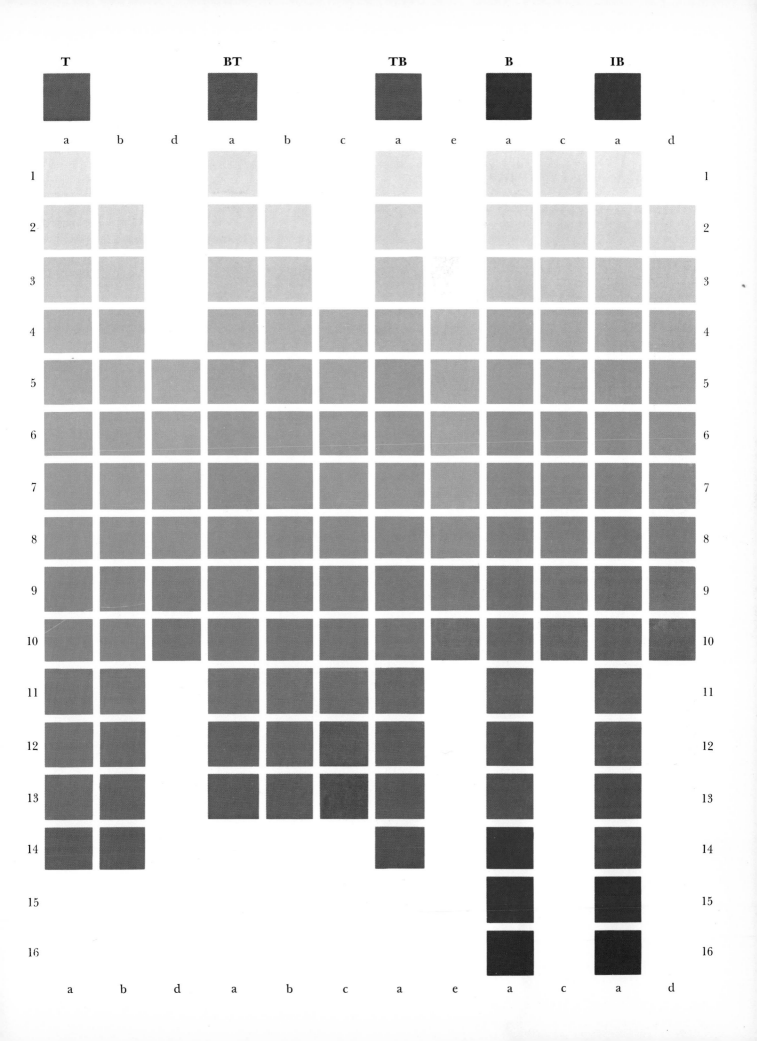

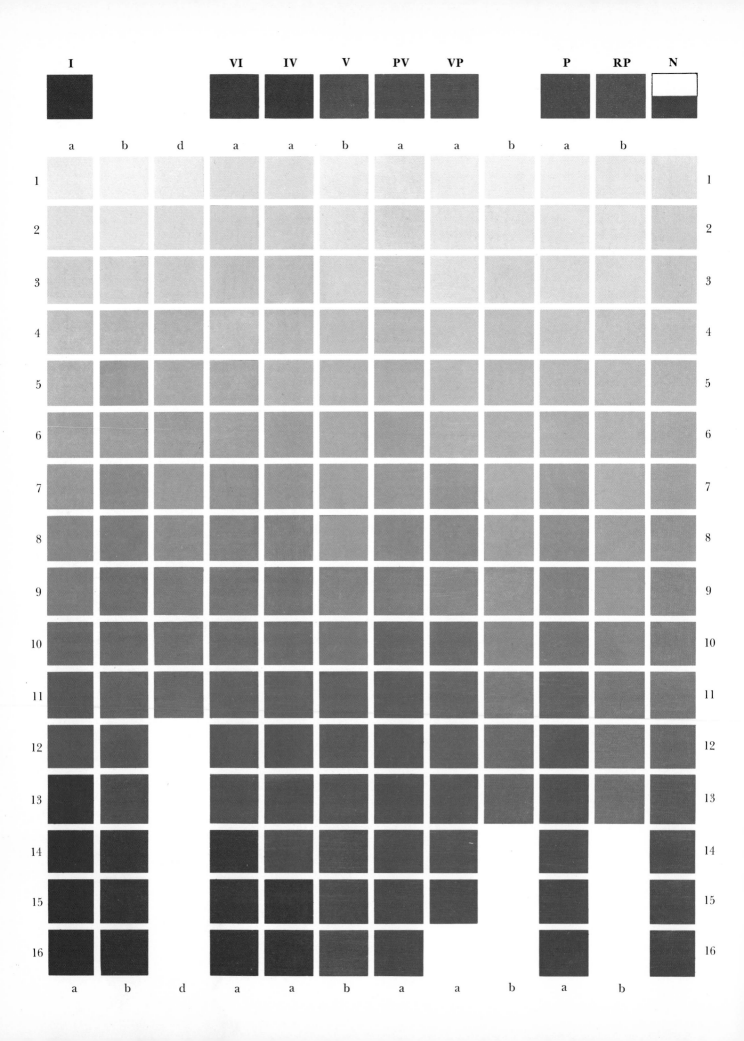

MAKEUP COLOR CHART

On the preceding pages, makeup colors from Bob Kelly, Kryolan/Braendel, Leichner, Mehron, Ben Nye, and Stein are indicated in chart form by actual color and by the standardized numbers by which the colors are referred to in this book. On the following pages the colors are listed by both standardized numbers and the numbers under which they are sold.

The color chart can be used in the following ways:

1. You can consult the chart to find the actual color makeup you need, along with the standardized number.

2. In studying the text, if you wish to know the exact color of a particular number referred to, the chart will give you that information.

3. When you want to find out what makeup paints correspond to a particular standardized number, consult Table 1 of Equivalent Colors, which lists the colors currently available, along with the makeup companies that make them and the number they use to designate them.

4. If you should want to know what color a certain commercial number represents, consult Table 2, which lists makeup by the manufacturer, along with the standardized numbers, then simply look up that number in the color chart.

5. If you wish to find the number of the paint in one brand of makeup that is equivalent to a certain number in another brand, refer first to the listing by manufacturer (Table 2) to find the standardized number, which will enable you to refer to Table 1, where you will find all equivalent paints listed.

In using the chart, keep in mind that although the color blocks and the makeup paints were equated as precisely as possible, makeup colors often change from batch to batch, occasionally in hue and more frequently in value. Therefore, the particular paint you are using may not be exactly the same as the one used in the analysis for the chart.

Keep in mind also that the colors shown represent as nearly as possible the color of the makeup on the skin, not in the cake, tube, or stick. The difference is sometimes quite marked. In addition to appearing considerably lighter or occasionally darker on the skin, a color may sometimes change in hue, often becoming noticeably redder.

Remember, however, that there are many more colors shown in the chart than there are makeup colors on the market. Any of these colors that do not currently have commercial equivalents can be mixed—provided you are using creme makeup or greasepaint.

In Tables 1 and 2 the following abbreviations are used:

f—foundation paint
c—cake makeup
cf—creme foundation
s—shading colors
ess—eyeshadow stick
ces—cake eyeshadow
cr—creme rouge
mr—moist rouge (grease or lanolin)
dr—dry rouge (cake or powder)
br—brush-on rouge
ur—under rouge
lr—lip rouge
l—lipstick
p—makeup pencils.

Table 1

THE STANDARDIZED COLOR NUMBERS AND THEIR EQUIVALENT COLOR NUMBERS USED BY THE VARIOUS MAKEUP COMPANIES

PR
PR-3-a
  MEHRON: *f* 2
PR-8-a
  KELLY: *dr* SRC-4
PR-10-g
  KELLY *cf* 32-E
PR-11-a
  KELLY: *p* Pink Red
  STEIN: *dr* 18
PR-13-a
  STEIN: *mr* 5, 7
PR-15-d
  KELLY: *s* SL-17

R/PR
R/PR-10-a
  MEHRON: *mr* 11
R/PR-11-b
  STEIN: *dr* 20
R/PR-16-a
  LEICHNER: *s* 25

R
R-3-e
  KRYOLAN: 072
R-6-a
  KELLY: *cr* SR-2
R-7-a
  KELLY: *br* Pink
R-9-a
  KELLY: *dr* Female
R-10-c
  KELLY: *dr* Male
R-11-a
  KELLY: *cr* SR-4, *l* LP-3
  NYE: *cr* Raspberry
R-11-a/b
  KELLY: *cr* SR-5
R-13-a
  KELLY: *p* Medium Red
  NYE: *l* True Red 14
  STEIN: *mr* 3, *dr* 16
R-15-a
  KRYOLAN: 082
  NYE: *s* Dark Maroon
R-16-a
  MEHRON: *lr* Crimson
R-16-a/b
  KELLY: *p* Maroon

R/SR
R/SR-14-a
  LEICHNER: *s* 322

SR
SR-9-a/b

MEHRON: *mr* 10
SR-10½-a
  STEIN: *dr* 14
SR-11-b
  KELLY: *l* Zebra
SR-12-a
  KELLY: *l* LP-4
  STEIN: *mr*-6
SR-13-a
  STEIN: *mr* 4
SR-14-a
  KRYOLAN: 083
  MEHRON: *lr* Cherry
  NYE: *s* Maroon
SR-14½-a
  MEHRON: *lr* Dark
SR-16-a
  KRYOLAN: 086
  STEIN: *s* 13

SR/RS
SR/RS-13-a
  KELLY: *p* Dark Red
  KRYOLAN: 081
SR/RS-14-a
  MEHRON: *lr* Medium

RS
RS-1-b
  KELLY: *cf* S-2
RS-1½-a
  LEICHNER: *f* 2
RS-4-a
  KRYOLAN: 03
RS-6-a
  LEICHNER: *f* 2½
RS-7-*a*
  KELLY: *l* LP-10
RS-9-a
  KELLY: *cr* SR-9
  KRYOLAN: 031
RS-10-a
  MEHRON: *mr* 9
RS-10-b
  KELLY: *cr* Bronze, *dr* Bronze
RS-11-a
  KELLY: *p* Orange-Red
  NYE: *dr* Raspberry
  STEIN: *mr* 8
RS-12-a
  KELLY: *cf* Red, *p* Red-Red
  KRYOLAN: 078
  MEHRON: *lr* Light
  NYE: *cr* Red, *dr* Red

STEIN: *f* 18
RS-13-a
  KRYOLAN: 080
  LEICHNER: *s* 320
  MEHRON: *f* Red
RS-13-c
  NYE: *l* 7
RS-13½-a
  LEICHNER: *s* 321
RS-14-a
  STEIN: *s* 14
RS-15-a
  STEIN: *s* 12

S
S-1-a
  MEHRON: *c* 1B
S-2-a
  MEHRON: *c* 2B
S-5-a
  KELLY: *cr* SR-1
S-6-c/d
  MEHRON: *f* 5
S-8-b/c
  MEHRON: *f* 9
S-9-a
  KELLY *l* LP-2
S-9-c
  MEHRON: *f* 7
S-9-d
  KRYOLAN: 160
S-9-f
  MEHRON: *f* 11
S-10-a
  NYE: *cr* Coral 31
S-10-d
  MEHRON: *c* 43
S-11-a
  KELLY: *cr* SR-3, *dr* DRC-1, *p* Light Red
  NYE: *l* Coral
S-11-a/b
  KRYOLAN: 012
S-11-f
  MEHRON: *c* 11B
S-12-a
  KELLY: *l* LP-9
  KRYOLAN: 079
  STEIN: *cf* 48
S-12-a/b
  NYE: *cr* Dark Technicolor
S-12-d
  KELLY: *s* SL-16
S-12-e
  MEHRON: *c* 37
S-13-a
  KRYOLAN: 416

STEIN: *s* 18
S-14-b
  MEHRON: *c* Red Brown
S-16-a
  STEIN: *cf* 9, *s* 22
S-16-b
  KRYOLAN: 046
S-16-c
  KRYOLAN: 050

FS
FS-1-a
  KELLY: *cf* C-1
FS-2-a
  MEHRON: *f* 1
FS-5-b
  LEICHNER: *f* 52
FS-5-d
  KELLY: *cf* S-3
FS-5-g
  KRYOLAN: 513
FS-6-b
  LEICHNER: *f* 53
FS-8-b
  MEHRON: *c* 9B
FS-8-e
  STEIN: *f* 13
FS-8½-c
  LEICHNER: *f* 3½
FS-9-a
  KELLY: *l* LP-5
FS-9-b/c
  MEHRON: *f* LM Dark Sunburn
FS-9-c
  KELLY: *cf* S-6, *br* Tawny
  MEHRON: *c* 7B
FS-9-d
  KELLY: *cr* SR-6
FS-9-d/e
  MEHRON: *c* 41
FS-10-a
  STEIN: *dr* 5
FS-10-b
  KELLY: *l* LP-6
  MEHRON: *c* 10B
FS-10-d/e
  MEHRON: *c* 42
FS-11-b
  MEHRON: *f* 10
FS-11-b/c
  KRYOLAN: 431
FS-11-d
  KELLY: *cf* S-5
FS-12-e

STEIN: *cf* 50
FS-14-d
  NYE: *cs* Character
    Shadow
FS-15-f
  MEHRON: *c* 38
FS-16-a
  MEHRON: *lr* Special 5
FS-19-d
  KELLY: *p* Dark Brown
FS-19-f
  NYE: *s* Beard Stipple

FS/SF
FS/SF-6-c
  KELLY: *cf* S-4
FS/SF-7-a
  KELLY: *cr* SR-10
FS/SF-8-b
  STEIN: *f* 7F
FS/SF-8-d/e
  KELLY: *cf* D.P.G.
FS/SF-9-a
  KELLY: *l* Coffee
FS/SF-9-b/c
  KELLY: *cr* SR-7
FS/SF-9-c
  MEHRON: *c* 29A
FS/SF-10-c
  MEHRON: *c* 30A
FS/SF-14-b
  KELLY:*cf* CVA-Red, *l*
    CVA-RED

SF
SF-1-b
  STEIN: *f* 1
SF-3-b
  KRYOLAN: 01s
  NYE: *s* Extra Lite
SF-3-f
  KRYOLAN: F7
SF-3½-b
  MEHRON: *c* 5B
SF-4-a
  STEIN: *f* 2½
SF-4-c
  KELLY: *cf* Dolly 3
  MEHRON: *c* 24A
  NYE: *cf* L-1
SF-4-d
  KELLY: *cf* Dolly 1
SF-4½-c
  MEHRON: *c* 3B
SF-5-b
  MEHRON: *f* 3
SF-5-c
  KELLY: *cf* Dolly 2
  MEHRON: *c* 25A
  NYE: *cf* L-2
SF-5-d
  KELLY: *cf* Deep Olive

SF-5-e
  KELLY: *cf* Olive
  STEIN: *cf* Tan Blush
SF-6-a
  KRYOLAN: 449
SF-6-b
  KELLY: *br* Peach
SF-6-c
  MEHRON: *c* 26A
  NYE: *cf* L-3
SF-6-d
  STEIN: *cf* Natural B
SF-6-e
  MEHRON: *c* 40
  STEIN: *cf* Natural Blush
SF-7-a
  KELLY: *l* LP-1
SF-7-b
  KELLY: *br* Amber
SF-7-c
  MEHRON: *c* 27A
SF-7-d
  KELLY: *cf* LL
  NYE: *cf* L-4
SF-7-d/e
  KRYOLAN: F4
SF-7-e
  KELLY: *cf* Coppertone
SF-7-f
  STEIN: *cf* Tan A
SF-7-g
  KRYOLAN: F5
SF-8-c
  KELLY: *cf* Dolly 4
  MEHRON: *c* 28A
  STEIN: *cf* 2
SF-8-d
  NYE: *cf* L-5
SF-8-e
  KRYOLAN: 438
SF-8-e/f
  KELLY: *cf* S-8
SF-9-c
  MEHRON: *c* 6½B, *f* 6½
  STEIN: *cf* 45
SF-9-d
  MEHRON: *c* 6B
SF-9-d
  LEICHNER: *f* 4½
SF-9-e
  NYE: *cf* M-1
  STEIN: *cf* Tan B
SF-10-d
  KRYOLAN: 035
  MEHRON: *f* 6
  STEIN: *c* 7
SF-10-d/e
  KELLY: *cf* S-14
SF-10-e
  NYE: *cf* M-2

SF-10-f
  NYE: *es* 42
SF-11-a
  KELLY: *cr* SR-8, *l* LP-8
SF-11-b
  LEICHNER: *f* 4
  MEHRON: *c* 12B, *f*
    LM 11
SF-11-c
  MEHRON: *c* 31A
SF-11-e
  KELLY: *cf* BK-6,
    CV-12W
  STEIN: *f* 10
SF-12-a
  STEIN: *mr* 1
SF-12-a/b
  LEICHNER: *f* 9
SF-12-b
  MEHRON: *f* 12
SF-12-d
  KELLY: *cf* S-10
SF-12-d/e
  KELLY: *cf* BK-2
SF-12-e
  KELLY: *cf* BK-1
SF-13-a
  NYE: *cr* Blush Coral 35
SF-13-a/b
  KRYOLAN: 075
SF-13-b
  KELLY: *cf* S-15
  NYE: *s* Sunburn Stipple
SF-13-c
  STEIN: *f* 9
SF-13-d
  KRYOLAN: 039
  STEIN: *cf* 38
SF-13-d/e
  MEHRON: *s* 9
SF-13-f
  STEIN: *ess* 2
SF-14-a
  KRYOLAN: 08
SF-14-a/b
  LEICHNER: *f* 8
SF-14-b
  KRYOLAN: 470
SF-14-b/c
  STEIN: *cf* 37
SF-14-c/d
  NYE: *l* 12
SF-14-d
  KELLY: *cf* BK-7
SF-15-c
  MEHRON: *s* 8½
  STEIN: *cf* 41A
SF-15-d
  KRYOLAN: 453
SF-16-f
  KRYOLAN: 047

SF-16-f
  KRYOLAN: 103

F
F-1-a
  LEICHNER: *f* 51
F-1-b
  MEHRON: *f* A
F-2-a
  STEIN: *f* 1½
F-2-b
  KELLY: *cf* S-21
  MEHRON: *f* B
  STEIN: *cf* Natural A
F-2-f
  STEIN: *ess* 1
F-3-a
  STEIN: *f* 2
F-3-b
  MEHRON: *f* C
  STEIN: *cf* Cream Blush
F-3-c
  KELLY: *cf* CV-1W
  STEIN: *cf* Cream B
F-3½-b
  STEIN: *cf* 44
F-4-a
  STEIN: *f* 3
F-4-b
  KRYOLAN: 02
  MEHRON: *f* D
F-4-b/c
  KELLY: *cf* Lady Fair
F-4-c
  KELLY: *cf* CV-2W
F-5-b
  MEHRON: *f* E
F-5-b/c
  MEHRON: *f* LM 5
F-5-c
  KRYOLAN: F2
F-5-d
  KELLY: *cf* CV-3W
F-6-b
  KRYOLAN: 033
  MEHRON: *f* F
F-6-c
  KELLY: *cf* CV-4W
F-7-b/c
  KRYOLAN: 034
F-7-c
  KELLY: *cf* CV-5W
  KRYOLAN: F3
F-7-c/d
  KELLY: *cf* Natural Tan
F-7-d
  KELLY: *cf* CV-6W
F-7-g
  KELLY: *p* Ash
F-8-a
  KRYOLAN: 030
F-8-b

MEHRON: *f* LM 8
F-8-c
  KRYOLAN: F16
F-8-c/d
  NYE: *cf* Tan 1
F-8-d
  KELLY: *cf* CV-7W
F-8-f
  NYE: *cf* Old Age
F-8½-e/f
  KRYOLAN: F10
F-9-b
  KELLY: *l* LP-7
F-9-b/c
  KRYOLAN: 017
F-9-c/d
  NYE: *cf* Tan 2
F-9-f
  KRYOLAN: F9
F-9-g
  KELLY: *p* Deep Ash
F-9-h
  KELLY: *cf* AL, *ces* SESC-7
F-10-b
  MEHRON: *f* 8
F-10-b/c
  MEHRON: *c* 8B
F-10-c
  KELLY: *cf* CV-11W
F-10-d
  KELLY: *cf* CV-9W
F-11-a
  KELLY: *l* Cinnamon
  MEHRON: *mr* 15
  STEIN: *dr* 12
F-11-d
  NYE: *cf* M3
F-11-e
  KELLY: *cf* S-23
F-11½-e
  NYE: *cf* Y-3
F-12-a
  KELLY: *l* Orange
  NYE: *s* Orange
F-12-c
  KELLY: *cf* S-22
F-12-c/d
  KELLY: *cf* S-17
F-12-d
  NYE: *cf* M-4
F-12-d/e
  KELLY: *cf* SC-50
  MEHRON: *c* 14B
F-12-e
  NYE: *cf* Y-5
F-13-d
  KELLY: *cf* S-12
  NYE: *cf* M-5
  STEIN: *s* 6
F-13½-d
  KELLY: *cf* S-11
F-14-a

STEIN: *cf* 41, *mr* 9
F-14-a/b
  KELLY: *cf* S-16
F-14-b
  STEIN: *cf* 42
F-14-b/c
  LEICHNER: *s* 30
F-14-d
  KELLY: *cf* SC-51
  NYE: *cf* 30
F-15-a
  STEIN: *s* 1
F-15-d
  KELLY: *cf* S-18
F-15-f
  MEHRON: *c* 17B
F-15-h
  KRYOLAN: 459
F-16-b
  LEICHNER: *f* 7
  STEIN: *s* 2, *es* 1
F-16-c
  KELLY: *p* Light Brown
F-16-d
  MEHRON: *f* 14
  NYE: *es* 44
  STEIN: *ess* 7
F-16-e
  LEICHNER: *f* 16
  NYE: *es* 43
  STEIN: *cf* 52
F-17-a
  STEIN: *s* 7
F-17-d
  KELLY: *p* Medium
    Brown
F-17-e
  KRYOLAN: 101
F-18-d
  LEICHNER: *s* 28
  MEHRON: *f* 17
F-18-e
  KRYOLAN: 102
F-18-f
  STEIN: *f* 11
F-19-c
  KELLY: *p* Midnight
    Brown

F/OF
F/OF-1-a
  STEIN: *f* 4
F/OF-1-b
  MEHRON: *c* 21
F/OF-2-a
  KRYOLAN: 576
F/OF-2-b
  KRYOLAN: 01
  MEHRON: *c* 22
F/OF-3-a
  STEIN: *f* 21

F/OF-3-b
  MEHRON: *c* 23
F/OF-3-c
  KELLY: *cf* Light Brunette
F/OF-4-b
  MEHRON: *c* 24
F/OF-4-c
  KELLY: *cf* Medium Olive
  MEHRON: *c* TV4
F/OF-5-b
  MEHRON: *c* 25
F/OF-5-b/c
  MEHRON: *f* 2½
  NYE: *s* Medium
F/OF-5-c
  KELLY: *cf* Medium
    Brunette
  MEHRON: *c* TV5
F/OF-6-b
  MEHRON: *c* 26
F/OF-6-c
  MEHRON: *c* TV6
  NYE· *cf* 22
  STEIN: *cf* Tan Blush 2
F/OF-6-d
  KELLY: *cf* Tantone
F/OF-7-b
  MEHRON: *c* 27, *fG*
F/OF-7-c
  MEHRON: *c* TV7
  NYE: *cf* 23
F/OF-7-d
  KELLY: *cf* Dark
    Brunette
  NYE: *s* Deep
F/OF-8-a
  STEIN: *f* 8
F/OF-8-b
  MEHRON: *c* 28
F/OF-8-c
  MEHRON: *c* TV8
  NYE: *cf* 24
  STEIN: *cf* Tan Blush 3
F/OF-8-d
  KELLY: *cf* BK-3
F/OF-8½-d
  KELLY: *cf* BK-4
F/OF-9-b
  MEHRON: *c* 29
F/OF-9-c
  KELLY: *cf* Golden Tan
  KRYOLAN: F17
  MEHRON: *c* TV9
  NYE: *cf* 25
F/OF-9-c/d
  KELLY: *cf* Bronzetone
  NYE: *s* 5 O'Sharp-Ruddy
F/OF-9-d
  KELLY: *cf* CV-8W
  NYE: 5 O'Sharp-Olive
F/OF-9-g
  KRYOLAN: F12

F/OF-10-a
  KRYOLAN: 032
F/OF-10-b
  MEHRON: *c* 30
F/OF-10-c
  KELLY: *cf* CV-10W
  MEHRON: *c* TV10
  NYE: *cf* 26
  STEIN: *f* 14
F/OF-10-d
  KELLY: *cf* BK-5
  MEHRON: *c* 4C
F/OF-11-b
  MEHRON: *c* 31
F/OF-11-b/c
  KRYOLAN: 09
F/OF-11-c
  NYE: *cf* 27
F/OF-11-d
  MEHRON: *c* 5C
F/OF-12-c
  NYE: *cf* 28
F/OF-12-d
  MEHRON: *c* 6C
  NYE: *cf* Indian 1
F/OF-13-c
  KELLY: *cf* S-7
  NYE: *cf* 29
F/OF-13-d
  KRYOLAN: 040
  MEHRON: *c* 7C
  NYE: *cf* Indian 3,
    Mexican 3
F/OF-14-b
  KRYOLAN: *cf* 045
  STEIN: *cf* 39
F/OF-14-c
  KRYOLAN: 468
F/OF-14-d
  MEHRON: *c* 8C
  NYE· *cf* Indian 5
F/OF-15-b
  STEIN: *cf* 36
F/OF-15-b/c
  STEIN: *cf* 35
F/OF-15-c
  KELLY: *s* SL-8, *p* Auburn
  STEIN: *cf* 32
F/OF-15-d
  MEHRON: *c* 9C
F/OF-16-b
  KELLY: *cf* S-19, SC-52
  STEIN: *f* 16
F/OF-16-c
  MEHRON: *f* 15, *s* 8
F/OF-16-d
  MEHRON: *c* 10C
F/OF-17-b
  KELLY: *cf* S-20, SC-53
  MEHRON: *f* LM Negro
F/OF-17-c
  KELLY: *cf* SC-54

OF
OF-2-a
  STEIN: *cf* Cream A
OF-3-b
  KELLY: *cf* Fairest
OF-4-b
  KELLY: *cf* Medium
    Fair
OF-6-a
  STEIN: *f* 3½
OF-6-a/b
  KRYOLAN: 05
OF-6-b
  KRYOLAN: 015
OF-6-c
  KRYOLAN: F8
OF-6-d
  STEIN: *f* 23
OF-7-a/b
  STEIN: *f* 7
OF-7-b
  KRYOLAN: 016
OF-7-c
  STEIN: *f* 24
OF-8-b
  KRYOLAN: 021
OF-8-b/c
  MEHRON: *f* H
OF-9-a
  STEIN: *f* 6
OF-9-c
  KRYOLAN: 466
OF-12-b/c
  KRYOLAN: 014
OF-12-c
  NYE: *cf* Mexican 1
OF-16-c
  KRYOLAN· 579
  STEIN: *f* 19
OF-17-c
  KELLY: *es* SES-2
  STEIN: *cf* 51
OF-18-d
  KRYOLAN: 462

FO
FO-½-b
  KRYOLAN: 406
FO-2-b
  NYE: *cf* Ultra Fair
  STEIN: *f* 22
FO-3-c
  KRYOLAN: F1
FO-5-a
  LEICHNER: *f* 50
  STEIN: *f* 5½
FO-5-c
  KRYOLAN: *cf* F18
FO-6-c
  KRYOLAN: 04a
  MEHRON: *c* 16B

FO-7-b
  KRYOLAN: 07
FO-7-c
  MEHRON: *f* 16
FO-7-d
  LEICHNER: *f* 6
FO-8-a
  KRYOLAN: 508
FO-8-b
  KRYOLAN: 06
FO-8-c
  KRYOLAN: 04
FO-9-b
  MEHRON: *f* K
FO-9-d
  KRYOLAN: F15
FO-10-b
  KRYOLAN: 010
  MEHRON: *f* L
FO-10-c
  KRYOLAN: F 11
FO-11-a
  MEHRON: *f* Orange
FO-12-d
  STEIN: *cf* 40
FO-13-a
  KRYOLAN: 421
FO-13-d
  KRYOLAN: 503
FO-14-a
  KRYOLAN: 024
FO-15-d
  KRYOLAN: 041
FO-16-b/c
  KELLY: *s* SL-7, *es* SES-1
FO-17-b
  STEIN: *f* 20
FO-17-e
  KRYOLAN: 043

O/FO
O/FO-3-b
  LEICHNER: *f* 5
O/FO-10-b
  KRYOLAN: 022a
  MEHRON: *f* M
O/FO-11-b
  KRYOLAN: 022
O/FO-11-c
  LEICHNER: *s* 28A

O
O-1-a
  MEHRON: *f* 4
O-5-d
  KRYOLAN: 522
O-6-c
  MEHRON: *f* LM
    Oriental

O-10-c
  STEIN: *cf* 39½
O-10-f
  LEICHNER: *f* 6½

CO
CO-1-a
  KRYOLAN: 521
CO-2-a
  KRYOLAN: 436
  MEHRON: *c* 4B
CO-3-a
  MEHRON: *c* 4½B
CO-3½-a
  MEHRON: *f* 4½
CO-11-d
  KRYOLAN: 507

OC
OC-4-b
  STEIN: *f* 5
OC-6-b
  NYE: *cs* Mellow Yellow
OC-7-a
  KRYOLAN: 303
OC-7-b
  KELLY: *s* SL-14
OC-9-a
  KELLY: *cf* S-9
OC-10-b
  KELLY: *s* SL-15
OC-11-a
  KRYOLAN: 305
OC-11-b
  KRYOLAN: 308
OC-12-c
  KRYOLAN: 452

C
C-9-a
  LEICHNER: *f* 59
C-9-b
  STEIN: *f* 12
C-10-a
  KELLY: *p* Yellow
  STEIN: *cf* 40½
C-10-d
  KRYOLAN: 477
C-12-d
  KRYOLAN: 607
C-13-d
  KRYOLAN: 504
C-13½-c
  KRYOLAN: 606

YC
YC-11-e
  KRYOLAN: 304

CY
CY-9-a
  NYE: *s* Yellow
CY-10-a

KELLY: *cf* Yellow
KRYOLAN: 509
STEIN: *s* 16

Y/CY
Y/CY-11-a
  MEHRON: *f* Yellow

Y
Y-3-a
  KRYOLAN: 523
Y-10-a
  MEHRON: *s* 11

LY
LY-12-a
  KRYOLAN: 534

YL
YL-11-c
  KELLY: *ces* SESC-8
YL-13-d
  KRYOLAN: 502

L
L-4-b
  KRYOLAN: 092
L-9-d
  KELLY: *ces* SESC-6, *p*
    Vivid Green
L-12-d
  KELLY: *s* SL-5
L-14-d
  KRYOLAN: 454

GL
GL-6-h
  KRYOLAN: 074
GL-9-c
  KRYOLAN: 511
GL-13-a
  STEIN: *s* 19, *es* 16
GL-14-b
  STEIN: *es* 17

LG
LG-12-c
  KRYOLAN: 512
LG-13-c
  NYE: *s* Green
LG-13-d
  KELLY: *es* SES-7
LG-15-a
  STEIN: *cf* 46

G
G-6-h
  KRYOLAN: 089
G-11-b
  KELLY: *cf* Green
G-13-c
  MEHRON: *s* 5

TG
TG-1-a
  KRYOLAN: 097
TG-5-a
  LEICHNER: *s* 334
TG-11-c
  MEHRON: *s* 4

GT
GT-9-c
  KELLY: *es* SES-6
GT-11-b
  LEICHNER: *s* 335
  STEIN: *ess* 11
GT-12-c
  KELLY: *p* Green
  KRYOLAN: 096
  MEHRON: *f* Green
GT-13-b
  KRYOLAN: 095
  LEICHNER: *s* 336
GT-13-d
  KELLY: *s* SL-6

T
T-3-d
  KELLY: *ces* SESC-4
T-9-b
  STEIN: *es* 6
T-11-a
  KELLY: *p* Turquoise
  STEIN: *es* 3

BT
BT-8-c
  STEIN: *ess* 6
BT-9-c
  MEHRON: *s* 2½
BT-11-c
  KRYOLAN: 094
BT-13-b
  STEIN: *s* 20

TB
TB-8-a
  KRYOLAN: 090
TB-9-e
  KRYOLAN: 193
TB-11-d
  KRYOLAN: 093

TB-13-a
  MEHRON: *s* 2
TB-16-a
  KELLY: *p* Blue

B
B-1-a
  MEHRON: *f* 19, *c* 19B
B-7-c
  KELLY: *cf* Blue
B-9-b
  KRYOLAN: 549
  MEHRON: *c* Blue
B-9-c
  KELLY: *ces* SESC-3
B-15-a
  KELLY: *p* Vivid Blue

IB
IB-5-a
  LEICHNER: *s* 326L
IB-6-a
  LEICHNER: *s* 325
IB-6-d
  STEIN: *ess* 5
IB-7-a
  KRYOLAN: 587
IB-10-a
  LEICHNER: *s* 326M
IB-13-a
  KELLY: *s* SL-2
IB-14-a
  KRYOLAN: 510

BI
BI-8-b
  STEIN: *s* 11
BI-13-a
  MEHRON: *s* 1

I
I-4-d
  KELLY: *ces* SESC-2
I-7-b
  MEHRON: *s* 3
I-8-b
  KELLY: *s* SL-1, *ces*
    SESC-1
I-9-a

STEIN: *s* 8, *es* 19
I-10-b
  KRYOLAN: 091
  STEIN: *ess* 3
I-11-a
  KELLY: *es* SES-5
  MEHRON: *f* Blue
  STEIN: *s* 9, *es* 2
I-11-c
  NYE: *s* Blue-Gray
I-12-a
  NYE: *s* Blue
  STEIN: *cf* 47
I-13-a
  STEIN: *es* 20, *s* 10
I-15-a
  KELLY: *s* SL-3
  LEICHNER: *s* 326D

VI
VI-8-a
  KRYOLAN: 483
VI-11-a
  MEHRON: *s* 6

IV
IV-5-a
  LEICHNER: *s* 337M
IV-8-b
  LEICHNER: *s* 337D
  STEIN: *cf* 49
IV-13-a
  KRYOLAN: 098
IV-15-a
  KRYOLAN: 545

V
V-1-f
  MEHRON: *c* 20B
V-3-b
  KRYOLAN: 481
V-5-b
  KRYOLAN: 087
V-5-f
  KRYOLAN: 173
V-10-b
  KELLY: *s* SL-4, *es* SES-8

PV
PV-11-b

STEIN: *s* 23, *es* 4
PV-13-a
  KELLY: *cf* Purple

VP
VP-3-b
  KRYOLAN: 482
VP-4-d
  MEHRON: *f* 20
VP-9-b
  STEIN: *ess* 8
VP-13-a
  STEIN: *s* 21, *es* 5
VP-13-b
  KELLY: *es* SES-9

RP
RP-11-b
  NYE: *s* Purple
RP-12-b
  KELLY: *p* Lilac

N
N-4
  STEIN: *cf* 34
N-5
  LEICHNER: *s* 31
N-8
  KELLY: *s* SL-10
  MEHRON: *f* 18
  STEIN: *s* 3
N-11
  KELLY: *es* SES-3
  NYE: *s* Gray
  STEIN: *es* 18
N-12
  MEHRON: *s* 7
N-13
  KELLY: *s* SL-11
  KRYOLAN: 517
  LEICHNER: *s* 32
  STEIN: *s* 4
N-14
  KELLY: *es* SES-4, *p* Gray
  KRYOLAN: 501
N-15
  KELLY: *p* Soft Gray
  KRYOLAN: 088
  MEHRON: *c* 18B
  STEIN: *s* 5

Table 2

MANUFACTURERS' MAKEUP COLOR NUMBERS AND THEIR EQUIVALENT STANDARDIZED NUMBERS

BOB KELLY CREME STICK:
S-1: White
S-2: RS-1-b
S-3: FS-5-d
S-4: FS/SF-6-c
S-5: FS-11-d
S-6: FS-9-c
S-7: F/OF-13-c
S-8: SF-8-e/f
S-9: OC-9-a
S-10: SF-12-d
S-11: F-13½-d
S-12: F-13-d
S-14: SF-10-d/e
S-15: SF-13-b
S-16: F-14-a/b
S-17: F-12-c/d
S-18: F-15-d
S-19: F/OF-16-b
S-20: F/OF-17-b
S-21: F-2-b
S-22: F-12-c
S-23: F-11-e
BK-1: SF-12-e
BK-2: SF-12-d/e
BK-3: F/OF-8-d
BK-4: F/OF-8½-d
BK-5: F/OF-10-d
BK-6: SF-11-e
BK-7: SF-14-d
Dolly-1: SF-4-d
Dolly-2: SF-5-c
Dolly-3: SF-4-c
Dolly-4: SF-8-c
D.P.G.: FS/SF-8-d/e
LL: SF-7-d
C-1: FS-1-a
AL: F-9-h
32-E: PR-10-g
CVA-Red: FS/SF-14-b
SC-50: F-12-d/e
SC-51: F-14-d
SC-52: F/OF-16-b
SC-53: F/OF-17-b
SC-54: F/OF-17-c
Fairest: OF-3-b
Medium Fair: OF-4-b
Lady Fair: F-4-b/c
Olive: SF-5-e
Medium Olive: F/OF-4-c
Deep Olive: SF-5-d
Light Brunette: F/OF-3-c
Medium Brunette: F/OF-5-c
Dark Brunette: F/OF-7-d

Tantone: F/OF-6-d
Natural Tan: F-7-c/d
Golden Tan: F/OF-9-c
Coppertone: SF-7-e
Bronzetone: F/OF-9-c/d
CV-1W: F-3-c
CV-2W: F-4-c
CV-3W: F-5-d
CV-4W: F-6-c
CV-5W: F-7-c
CV-6W: F-7-d
CV-7W: F-8-d
CV-8W: F/OF-9-d
CV-9W: F-10-d
CV-10W: F/OF-10-c
CV-11W: F-10-c
CV-12W: SF-11-e
Blue: B-7-c
Green: G-11-b
Purple: PV-13-a
Red: RS-12-a
Yellow: CY-10-a

BOB KELLY CAKE MAKEUP:
Because cake makeup shades (with the exception of the CV series) are supposed to match creme-stick shades, they are not listed separately.

BOB KELLY CREME SHADING COLORS (LINERS):
SL-1: I-8-b
SL-2: IB-13-a
SL-3: I-15-a
SL-4: V-10-b
SL-5: L-12-d
SL-6: GT-13-d
SL-7: FO-16-b/c
SL-8: F/OF-15-c
SL-9: Black
SL-10: N-8
SL-11: N-13
SL-12: White
SL-14: OC-7-b
SL-15: OC-10-b
SL-16: S-12-d
SL-17: PR-15-d

BOB KELLY CREME EYESHADOW:
SES-1: FO-16-b/c
SES-2: OF-17-c
SES-3: N-11
SES-4: N-14
SES-5: I-11-a
SES-6: GT-9-c
SES-7: LG-13-d
SES-8: V-10-b
SES-9: VP-13-b

BOB KELLY CAKE EYESHADOW:
SESC-1: I-8-b
SESC-2: I-4-d (Silver)
SESC-3: B-9-c
SESC-4: T-3-d
SESC-5: White
SESC-6: L-9-d (Gold)
SESC-7: F-9-h
SESC-8: YL-11-c

BOB KELLY CREME ROUGE:
SR-1: S-5-a
SR-2: R-6-a
SR-3: S-11-a
SR-4: R-11-a
SR-5: R-11-a/b
SR-6: FS-9-d
SR-7: FS/SF-9-b/c
SR-8: SF-11-a
SR-9: RS-9-a
SR-10: FS/SF-7-a
SR-Bronze: RS-10-b

BOB KELLY DRY ROUGE:
Female: R-9-a
Male: R-10-c
DRC-1: S-11-a
SRC-4: PR-8-a
Bronze: RS-10-b

BOB KELLY BRUSH-ON (BLUSH-ON) ROUGE:
Amber: SF-7-b
Peach: SF-6-b
Pink: R-7-a
Tawny: FS-9-c

BOB KELLY LIPSTICK:
LP-1: SF-7-a
LP-2: S-9-a
LP-3: R-11-a

LP-4: SR-12-a
LP-5: FS-9-a
LP-6: FS-10-b
LP-7: F-9-b
LP-8: SF-11-a
LP-9: S-12-a
LP-10: RS-7-a
Cinnamon: F-11-a
Coffee: FS/SF-9-a
Orange: F-12-a
Zebra: SR-11-b
CVA-Red: FS/SF-14-b

BOB KELLY MAKEUP PENCILS:
Auburn: F/OF-15-c
Light Brown: F-16-c
Medium Brown: F-17-d
Dark Brown: FS-19-d
Midnight Brown: F-19-c
Soft Gray: N-15
Gray: N-14
Light Red: S-11-a
Medium Red: R-13-a
Dark Red: SR/RS-13-a
Pink Red: PR-11-a
Orange Red: RS-11-a
Red Red: RS-12-a
Ash: F-7-g
Deep Ash: F-9-g
Yellow: C-10-a
Blue: TB-16-a
Vivid Blue: B-15-a
Turquoise: T-11-a
Green: GT-12-c
Vivid Green: L-9-d
Lilac: RP-12-b
Maroon: R-16-a/b

KRYOLAN MAKEUP COLORS:
The same Kryolan color numbers are used for all of their paints.

01: F/OF-2-b
01s: SF-3-b
02: F-4-b
03: RS-4-a
04: FO-8-c
04a: FO-6-c
05: OF-6-a/b
06: FO-8-b
07: FO-7-b
08: SF-14-a
09: F/OF-11-b/c
010: FO-10-b

012: S-11-a/b
014: OF-12-b/c
015: OF-6-b
016: OF-7-b
017: F-9-b/c
021: OF-8-b
022: O/FO-11-b
022a: O/FO-10-b
024: FO-14-a
030: F-8-a
031: RS-9-a
032: F/OF-10-a
033: F-6-b
034: F-7-b/c
035: SF-10-d
039: SF-13-d
040: F/OF-13-d
041: FO-15-d
043: FO-17-e
045: F/OF-14-b
046: S-16-b
047: SF-16-d
050: S-16-c
070: White
071: Black
072: R-3-e
074: GL-6-h
075: SF-13-a/b
078: RS-12-a
079: S-12-a
080: RS-13-a
081: SR/RS-13-a
082: R-15-a
083: SR-14-a
086: SR-16-a
087: V-5-b
088: N-15
089: G-6-h
090: TB-8-a
091: I-10-b
092: L-4-b
093: TB-11-d
094: BT-11-c
095: GT-13-b
096: GT-12-c
097: TG-1-a
098: IV-13-a
101: F-17-e
102: F-18-e
103: SF-16-f
160: S-9-d
173: V-5-f
193: TB-9-e
303: OC-7-a
304: YC-11-e
305: OC-11-a
308: OC-11-b
406: FO-1/2-b
416: S-13-a
421: FO-13-a
431: FS-11-b/c
436: CO-2-a

438: SF-8-e
449: SF-6-a
452: OC-12-c
453: SF-15-d
454: L-14-d
459: F-15-h
462: OF-18-d
466: OF-9-c
468: F/OF-14-c
470: SF-14-b
477: C-10-d
481: V-3-b
482: VP-3-b
483: VI-8-a
501: N-14
502: YL-13-d
503: FO-13-d
504: C-13-d
507: CO-11-d
508: FO-8-a
509: CY-10-a
510: IB-14-a
511: GL-9-c
512: LG-12-c
513: FS-5-g
517: N-13
521: CO-1-a
522: O-5-d
523: Y-3-a
534: LY-12-a
545: IV-15-a
549: B-9-b
576: F/OF-2-a
579: OF-16-c
587: IB-7-a
606: C-13½-c
607: C-12-d
F1: FO-3-c
F2: F-5-c
F3: F-7-c
F4: SF-7-d/e
F5: SF-7-g
F7: SF-3-f
F8: OF-6-c
F9: F-9-f
F10: F-8½-e/f
F11: FO-10-c
F12: F/OF-9-g
F15: FO-9-d
F-16: F-8-c
F17: F/OF-9-c
F18: FO-5-c

LEICHNER GREASEPAINT:
2: RS-1½-a
2½: RS-6-a
3½: FS-8½-c
4: SF-11-b
4½: SF-9-d
5: O/FO-3-b

6: FO-7-d
6½: O-10-f
7: F-16-b
8: SF-14-a/b
9: SF-12-a/b
12: Black
16: F-16-e
20: White
50: FO-5-a
51: F-1-a
52: FS-5-b
53: FS-6-b
59: C-9-a

LEICHNER SHADING COLORS:
22: White
25: R/PR-16-a
28: F-18-d
28A: O/FO-11-c
30: F-14-b/c
31: N-5
32: N-13
42: Black
320: RS-13-a
321: RS-13½-a
322: R/SR-14-a
325: IB-6-a
326L: 1B-5-a
326M: 1B-10-a
326D: I-15-a
334: TG-5-a
335: GT-11-b
336: GT-13-b
337M: IV-5-a
337D: IV-8-b

MEHRON CAKE MAKEUP:
21: F/OF-1-b
22: F/OF-2-b
23: F/OF-3-b
24: F/OF-4-b
25: F/OF-5-b
26: F/OF-6-b
27: F/OF-7-b
28: F/OF-8-b
29: F/OF-9-b
30: F/OF-10-b
31: F/OF-11-b
37: S-12-e
38: FS-15-f
40: SF-6-e
41: FS-9-d/e
42: FS-10-d/e
43: S-10-d
RB: S-14-b
24A: SF-4-c
25A: SF-5-c
26A: SF-6-c
27A: SF-7-c

28A: SF-8-c
29A: FS/SF-9-c
30A: FS/SF-10-c
31A: SF-11-c
1B: S-1-a
2B: S-2-a
3B: SF-4½-c
4B: CO-2-a
4½B: CO-3-a
5B: SF-3½-b
6B: SF-9-d
6½B: SF-9-c
7B: FS-9-c
8B: F-10-b/c
9B: FS-8-b
10B: FS-10-b
11B: S-11-f
12B: SF-11-b
14B: F-12-d/e
16B: FO-6-c
17B: F-15-f
18B: N-15
19B: B-1-a
20B: V-1-f
BLUE: B-9-b
TV4: F/OF-4-c
TV5: F/OF-5-c
TV6: F/OF-6-c
TV7: F/OF-7-c
TV8: F/OF-8-c
TV9: F/OF-9-c
TV10: F/OF-10-c
4C: F/OF-10-d
5C: F/OF-11-d
6C: F/OF-12-d
7C: F/OF-13-d
8C: F/OF-14-d
9C: F/OF-15-d
10C: F/OF-16-d

MEHRON RUBBER-MASK GREASEPAINT (MASK COVER):
LM 5: F-5-b/c
LM 8: F-8-b
LM 11: SF-11-b
LM Dark Sunburn: FS-9-b/c
LM Oriental: O-6-c
LM Negro: F/OF-17-b

MEHRON FOUNDATION COLORS:
1: FS-2-a
2: PR-3-a
2½: F/OF-5-b/c
3: SF-5-b
4: O-1-a
4½: CO-3½-a
5: S-6-c/d

6: SF-10-d
6½: SF-9-c
7: S-9-c
8: F-10-b
9: S-8-b/c
10: FS-11-b
11: S-9-f
12: SF-12-b
14: F-16-d
15: F/OF-16-c
16: FO-7-c
17: F-18-d
18: N-8
19: B-1-a
20: VP-4-d
A: F-1-b
B: F-2-b
C: F-3-b
D: F-4-b
E: F-5-b
F: F-6-b
G: F/OF-7-b
H: OF-8-b/c
K: FO-9-b
L: FO-10-b
M: O/FO-10-b
Red: RS-13-a
Blue: I-11-a
Green: GT-12-c
Yellow: Y/CY-11-a
Orange: FO-11-a

MEHRON MOIST ROUGE (BLUSHTONE):
9: RS-10-a
10: SR-9-a/b
11: R/PR-10-a
15: F-11-a

MEHRON LIP ROUGE:
Light: RS-12-a
Medium: SR/RS-14-a
Dark: SR-14½-a
Cherry: SR-14-a
Crimson: R-16-a
Sp. #5: FS-16-a

MEHRON SHADING COLORS (SHADO-LINERS):
1: BI-13-a
2: TB-13-a
2½: BT-9-c
3: I-7-b
4: TG-11-c
5: G-13-c
6: VI-11-a
7: N-12
8: F/OF-16-c
8½: SF-15-c
9: SF-13-d/e
11: Y-10-a

SB: I-8-c (Silver)
BP: VI-10-d (Bronze)
GG: L-13-d (Gold)
SG: T-9-e (Silver)

BEN NYE CREME FOUNDATIONS:
M-1: SF-9-e
M-2: SF-10-e
M-3: F-11-d
M-4: F-12-d
M-5: F-13-d
Y-3: F-11½-e
Y-5: F-12-e
L-1: SF-4-c
L-2: SF-5-c
L-3: SF-6-c
L-4: SF-7-d
L-5: SF-8-d
Tan 1: F-8-c/d
Tan 2: F-9-c/d
22: F/OF-6-c
23: F/OF-7-c
24: F/OF-8-c
25: F/OF-9-c
26: F/OF-10-c
27: F/OF11-c
28: F/OF-12-c
29: F/OF-13-c
30: F-14-d
Indian 1: F/OF-12-d
Indian 3: F/OF-13-d
Indian 5: F/OF-14-d
Mexican 1: OF-12-c
Mexican 3: F/OF-13-d
Old Age: F-8-f
Ultra Fair: FO-2-b

BEN NYE CREME SHADING COLORS (LINERS):
Maroon: SR-14-a
Dark Maroon: R-15-a
Purple: RP-11-b
Yellow: CY-9-a
Orange: F-12-a
Blue: I-12-a
Blue-gray: I-11-c
Gray: N-11
Character Shadow: FS-14-d
Green: LG-13-c
Five O'Sharp—Olive: F/OF-9-d
Five O'Sharp—Ruddy: F/OF-9-c/d
Beard Stipple FS-19-f
Sunburn Stipple: SF-13-b
Mellow Yellow: OC-6-b

BEN NYE CREME HIGHLIGHTS:
Extra Lite: SF-3-b

Medium: F/OF-5-b/c
Deep: F/OF-7-d

BEN NYE EYESHADOW:
Brown 42: SF-10-f
Dark Brown 43: F-16-e
Extra Dark Brown 44: F-16-d

BEN NYE CREME ROUGE:
Raspberry: R-11-a
Coral 31: S-10-a
Blush Coral 35: SF-13-a
Dark Technicolor: S-12-a/b
Red: RS-12-a

BEN NYE DRY ROUGE:
Red: RS-12-a
Raspberry: RS-11-a

BEN NYE LIPSTICK:
Coral: S-11-a
Natural 7: RS-13-c
Dark Brown 12: SF-14-c/d
True Red 14: R-13-a

STEIN GREASEPAINT:
1: SF-1-b
1½: F-2-a
2: F-3-a
2½: SF-4-a
3: F-4-a
3½: OF-6-a
4: F/OF-1-a
5: OC-4-b
5½: FO-5-a
6: OF-9-a
7: OF-7-a/b
7F: FS/SF-8-b
8: F/OF-8-a
9: SF-13-c
10: SF-11-e
11: F-18-f
12: C-9-b
13: FS-8-e
14: F/OF-10-c
16: F/OF-16-b
18: RS-12-a
19: OF-16-c
20: FO-17-b
21: F/OF-3-a
22: FO-2-b
23: OF-6-d
24: OF-7-c

STEIN CREME MAKEUP (VELVET STICK):
Natural Blush: SF-6-e

Natural A: F-2-b
Natural B: SF-6-d
Cream Blush: F-3-b
Cream A: OF-2-a
Cream B: F-3-c
Tan Blush: SF-5-e
Tan Blush #2: F/OF-6-c
Tan Blush #3: F/OF-8-c
Tan A: SF-7-f
Tan B: SF-9-e
2: SF-8-c
7: SF-10-d
9: S-16-a
32: F/OF-15-c
33: Black
34: N-4
35: F/OF-15-b/c
36: F/OF-15-b
37: SF-14-b/c
38: SF-13-d
39: F/OF-14-b
39½: O-10-c
40: FO-12-d
40½: C-10-a
41: F-14-a
41A: SF-15-c
42: F-14-b
43: White
44: F-3½-b
45: SF-9-c
46: LG-15-a
47: I-12-a
48: S-12-a
49: IV-8-b
50: FS-12-e
51: OF-17-c
52: F-16-e

STEIN CAKE MAKEUP:
Because cake makeup shades are supposed to match creme makeup shades, they are not listed separately.

STEIN SOFT SHADING (LINING) COLORS:
1: F-15-a
2: F-16-b
3: N-8
4: N-13
5: N-15
6: F-13-d
7: F-17-a
8: I-9-a
9: I-11-a
10: I-13-a
11: BI-8-b
12: RS-15-a
13: SR-16-a
14: RS-14-a

15: White
16: CY-10-a
17: Black
18: S-13-a
19: GL-13-a
20: BT-13-b
21: VP-13-a
22: S-16-a
23: PV-11-b

**STEIN MOIST
EYESHADOW:**
1: F-16-b
2: I-11-a
3: T-11-a

4: PV-11-b
5: VP-13-a
6: T-9-b
16: GL-13-a
17: GL-14-b
18: N-11
19: I-9-a
20: I-13-a

**STEIN EYESHADOW
STICK:**
1: F-2-f
2: SF-13-f
3: I-10-b
5: IB-6-d

6: BT-8-c
7: F-16-d
8: VP-9-b
11: GT-11-b

STEIN MOIST ROUGE:
1: SF-12-a
3: R-13-a
4: SR-13-a
5: PR-13-a
6: SR-12-a
7: PR-13-a
8: RS-11-a
9: F-14-a

STEIN LIPSTICK:
*Because lipstick shades
are supposed to match
moist rouge shades, they
are not listed separately.*

STEIN DRY ROUGE:
5: FS-10-a
12: F-11-a
14: SR-10½-a
16: R-13-a
18: PR-11-a
20: R/PR-11-b

INDEX

A

Abbott's wig, 201

Absorbent cotton, *see* Cotton, absorbent

Accenting the eyes, 78

Acetate, used for false fingernails, 151

Acetone, 105, 250; artificial dried blood removed with, 252; cleaning blenders with, 215, 222; cleaning brushes with, 253; cleaning hairlace with, 215; collodion diluted with, 146; collodion removed with, 151, 253; an ingredient in sealer, 262; nail polish removed with, 130; plastic film blended with, 106, 107, 151, 152, 210, *246**; scissors cleaned with, 180; sealer diluted with, 253; spirit gum removed with, 165, 180, 190

Acrylic paint, 243

Actor, Makeup and the, 3, 4

Adams, John, 316, *317, 355*

Adapting wigs, 217, 218

Adhesive, Dicor, 251; Duo, 84, 250, 254, 255; Flexol, 84, 250, 255; hairlace, 262; Slomon's Medico, 171, 243, 250, 263; surgical, *see* Adhesive, latex cream

Adhesive, latex cream, 84, 148, 165, 176, 237, 250, 254; false eyelashes attached with, 80; in prosthesis, 165, 176; sequins attached with, 237; stippling with, 148, 165, 215, 250

Adhesive powder for false teeth, 152

Adhesive tape, double-faced, 250; transparent, 250, *251; see also* Tape, adhesive

Adhesives, 250, *262; see also* Spirit gum

Aerial perspective, 29

Afro hair style, 330, *331*

Age, appearance affected by, 9, 10; hair styles influenced by, 200; modeling face, neck, and hands for, 87–130; skin texture effects for, *see* Skin texture

*Italic numerals refer to page numbers of illustrations.

Aging, method for subtle, 71

Aguecheek, Sir Andrew, 8

Ahab, Captain, 183

Akkadian, Semitic, 294, *295*

Albert, Prince, *355*

Albolene, 260

Alcohol, isopropyl, 260, 262

Alcohol, rubbing, 183, 250; collodion diluted with, 146; spirit gum removed with, 105, 142, 143, 144, 148, 165, 180, 183, 189

Alembert, Jacques d', 316, *317*

Alexander II, 322, *323*

Alexandra, Queen, 286

Alfonso V, 302, *303*

Alginate, 155, 159, 250, 257, 261; applying, *156, 157*

Alice in Wonderland, 69, 229, 230

Alpine races, 275

Amber light on makeup, 39

Analysis of characters, 5–12

Anatomy, facial, 20–26

Ancient civilizations, hair styles and makeup, 279, 290, *291, 292, 293, 294, 295, 296, 297*

Angel makeup, 231

Animal makeups, 231, *233, 234, 362*

Anne of Austria, 312, *313*

Anne of England, 318, *319*

Anthropometamorphosis, 283

Antimony sulfide, 279

Ape hair style, 334, *335*

Ape makeup, *232*

Apple cheeks, 30, 115, 117, 125, *360*

Applying the Makeup, 57–248

Aquacolor, 251, 260

Arabs, 275, 277

Aragon, Prince of, *200*

Arena theater, 144, 152

Armenoid races, 275

Art du Perruquier, 201

Artificial blood, 147, *251*, 252; dried, 252

Artificial eyelashes, *75, 79*, 80, 100, 255, *256*
Artists' modeling tools, *see* Modeling tools
Aryan races, 276
Assignment sheet for a short course in makeup, 273, 274
Assyrians, 279
Astringent, 183
Atomizers, 250
Audience, as a determining factor in makeup, 229
Augsburger, Christine, *238*
Augustus, Caesar, *24*
Austin, Lee, *135, 357, 362*
Awl, used in making Kabuki wig, *213*

B

Baby oil, 260
Bag wigs, 201, 316, *317*
Bald caps, 164, 209
Bald head, 196; soaping out hair for, *197, 198*
Bald pate, *198, 208*
Bald wigs, 164, 176, 209
Balding heads, *210*
Balkan races, 275
Balsa wood, 164
Bandage, plaster, *see* Plaster bandage; spray-on, 263; surgical gauze, 158
Bandeau d'amour, le, 318, *319*
Bandoline, 250
Barbarians, 298, *299*
Barber's basin, *207*
Barber's chair, 63, 66, 155, *156*
Barber's shears, 181, *184*, 188, *252*, 262
Barker, Sarah, *237*
Barrett, Edward Moulton, 48
Barrett, Elizabeth, 9
Barretts of Wimpole Street, The, 47
Barrie, Sir James, *113*
Barrymore, John, 328, *329*
Bartlett, Paul Wayland, *364*
Base, *see* Foundation color *and* Foundation paint
Beadex, 254
Beaks, *233*
Beans, *237*
Beard blocks, 186, 188, *189*, 250
Beard stubble, 183–85, *349, 364*; adhesive for, 183, *184*, 250, 264; applied with spirit gum, 183, 184; removing 183
Beards, ancient Egyptian, 279; ancient Greek, 292, *293*; Assyrian, 279; breakwater, 322, *323*; bush, 306, *307*; Byzantine, 298, *299*; construction of, 177–183; diagram for measurements, *216*; fifteenth-century, 302, *303*; Imperial, 324, *325*; made-to-order, 251; marquisette, 306, *307*; measuring for, 190; Medieval, 298, *299, 343*; metal, 279; needle, 310, *311*; nineteenth-century, 322, *323*, 324, *325*, *350*; Persian, 279; pique devant, 306, *307*, 310, *311*; ready-made, 251; round, 310, *311*; seventeenth-century, 283, 310, *311*; sixteenth-

century, 282, 306, *307*, *340*, *342*, *343*, *345*, *346*, *348*, *351*; square-cut, 310, *311*; stiletto, 310, *311*; Sumerian, 290, *291*; swallow-tail, 306, *307*, 324, *325*; twentieth-century, 328, *329*; Uncle Sam, 322, *323*; Vandyke, 310, *311*
Beards and mustaches, 177–91; applied over putty, 138; as a reflection of personality, 8, 177; buying, 177, 190; choice of style for, 177; constructing, 177–83; crepe hair, 177–83; diagram for applying, *180*; influenced by fashion, 8, 177; on latex, 182, 183; sketches of, 177; trimming and shaping, 181; unkempt, 182; used to widen the face, *126*
Beards and mustaches, ventilated, *126, 177, 184*, 185–91; adapting, 190; advantages of, 177; application of, 188, 189; color of, 188, 190; combing, 189, 190; construction of, 186–88; curling, 189; dirty-looking, 189; dressing of, 189; fluffy, 179, 180; materials for, 185, 186; measuring for, 190; patterns for, 186; ready-made, 177, 190; removal and cleaning of, 189, 190; storing, 190; trimming, 188
Beater, electric, 176
Beatle style, 328, *329*
Beauty patches, 279
Beehive hair style, 332, *333*
Beeswax, 294
Belch, Sir Toby, 8
Benzine, 216
Billy whiskers, 322, *323*
Birds, 233
Black tooth enamel, *see* Tooth enamel
Black wax, 84, 251; eyebrow pencil used as substitute for, 130
Blemishes, cover stick used over, 254; covering with greasepaint, 71; patches used for covering, 283
Blender wig, 208, 209, 221, 222; cleaning, 215, 222; constructing, 208; wearing and making up, 215, 222
Blenders, wig, 199, 208, 209, 217
Blending, of charcoal and chalk, 30; of derma wax, 138, 257; of greasepaint, 71; of nose putty, 133, 134, 135; of shadows and highlights, 70, 93, 111, 112, 114, *358*, *359*
Blending liquid for Scar Plastic, 245
Blending powder, *see* Face powder
Bligh, William, 316, *317*
Blind eye, casting, 147
Blindness, methods of simulating, 146, 147
Blocking out eyebrows, 105–8, *224*, 226, 234; *see also* Eyebrows
Blocking out hair, *135, 194, 195*, 196–98, *361*
Blood, artificial, 147, *251*, 252; creme rouge used to simulate, 150, *361*; dried, 252
Blot-out, 254
Blue light on makeup, 40
Blue-green light on makeup, 40
Bob wigs, 201, 314, *315*
Bobby pins, 196, *198*, 214
Bobs, twentieth-century, 332, *333*
Bodmer, Johann, Portrait of, *341*
Body makeup, 193, 252; hair grayed with, 196; metallic, 239, 260

Bone structure, importance of understanding, 20
Boss, Stuart, 129
Botticelli, 347
Bottom the Weaver, 15
Bowan, Gaye, *362*
Boyish bob, 332
Bradac, Tom, *117*
Brady, Matthew, 322, *323*
Brandes, Georg Morris Cohen, 328, *329*
Breakwater beard, 322, *323*
Brigadier wig, *201*, 314, *315*
Brilliantine, 108, 150, 152
Broadening the face, 82, 85
Broadening the forehead, 76
Broadening the nose, *76*, 109
Brooke, Rupert, 328, *329*
Brooks, Wilson, 219, *220*
Broughton, John, *14*
Brownie makeup, 236
Bruises, 147, *361*
Brunner, Richard, 51, 52, 53, *148*, 162, 176
Brushes, applying plastic with, *106*; camel's hair, 253; care of, 161; Chinese, 68, 72, 73, 93, 101, 252; drawing, 204; dye, 189, 252, 253; eyebrow, *252*, 253; eyeliner, 68, 72, 73, 101, *102*, 255; hair, 193, *252*; latex, 161; moulage, 253; oxhair, 253; powder, *252*, 253; rouge, 183, *252*, 253; sable, 72, *252*, 253, 255; shading, 68, 221, *252*, 253; stiff-bristled, 142, 189, 253; stippling with, *73*, 247; technique for using, 68, 70, 93, 114; water color, 253
Brush-on rouge, 70, 90, 91, 117, 262
Brutus, Marcus Junius, 292, *293*
Bucer, Martin, 306, *307*
Buckram, wig foundations of, 214
Bulwer, John, 283
Burgess, Debra, *237*
Burns, simulated, 147; ready-made, 258
Burnsides, 324, *325*
Burnt cork, 253
Burton, Warren, *45*
Bush, George, *14*
Bush beard, 306, *307*
Byron, Lord, *356*
Byzantine hair styles, 298, *299*, 300, *301*

C

Cabinets, makeup storage, *62*
Cadogan wig, 316, *317*
Caesar, Julius, 292, *293*, 337
Caesar cut, 328, *329*
Cage, The, 230
Cake makeup, *251*, 253; advantages and disadvantages of, 253; application of, 68–70, 105; brands of, 253; creating a sheen on, 176, 196; over derma wax, *150*; description of, 253; dulling hair with, 189, 193; graying eyebrows with, 109; graying hair with, 196; grease-

paint or creme makeup used with, 71–73, *200*; hands aged with, *144*; over latex, 139, 148, 165, 176; over lubricating jelly, 106, 108; under latex, 139; lubricating jelly over, 145; neck aged with, *127*; on putty, 135; removal of, 260; on scalp, 196; over soaped-out hair, *198*; over spirit gum, 105; under spirit gum, 180; stippling with, 70; under syrup and tissue, 144; in television, 242; on tissue and spirit gum, 145; over wax, 105
California State University at Long Beach, 62
Calvin, John, *355*
Camburn, Herbert, 195
Camel's hair brushes, 253
Camera, Polaroid, 55
Camille, 9
Campaign wigs, 314, *315*
Candle wax, used for blisters, 147
Capes, plastic, 155, *156*
Caps, latex, 155, 164, 209, 234, 258, *259*; plastic, 155, 196, 209, 215, 217, 234, 261
Card for mixing hair, 205
Carmine, used by ancient Egyptians, 279; in the eighteenth century, 284
Carroll, Lewis, 230
Casanova, 284
Cassius, 15
Cast shadows, 29, 30
Casting for rubber prosthesis, 154–61, *166*
Castor oil, 165, 253, 262; molds greased with, 175
Casts, plaster, *154*, 161, 250; negative, 159–61; positive 158, 159
Catalogs, makeup, 67
Caterpillar, flower with, *237*
Catherine the Great, *356*
Caucasian Chalk Circle, The, 228
Caucasians, foundation colors for, 74
Caul netting, 199
Cauliflower wigs, 314, *315*
Cavaliers, 283
Celtic races, 275
Centralization of value, 29
Cepero, Luis, *45*
Cereal, puffed, used for warts, 153
Chaillot, Madwoman of, *120*
Chairs, dentists', *62*, 64, 66, 155
Chalk, perfumed, 285
Chamois, 181, 189, 226, 253
Chamois stumps, 264
Character, and makeup, 4, 5; related to physical appearance, 13
Character analysis, 5–12, 90
Character makeup, 10
Characters, individuality of, 5, 6, 7
Charcoal and chalk, drawing with, *28*, 29, 30
Charles of Austria, 310, *311*
Charles I, *356*
Charles II, 283, 310, *311*, 338
Charles VII, 302, *303*
Chayefsky, Paddy, 223

Cheekbones, *112, 113*; conformation of, 21, *111*; effect of light falling on, 111; locating, 88, 111; modeling with paint, 87, 88, 220; nose putty used on, 133

Cheeks, aging of, 111; corrective makeup for, 81; foamed latex, *172, 244*; modeling with paint, 111, 112; planes of, *112*; puffy, 120; sponges or cotton used in, 119; sunken, 81; *see also* Rouge

Cheerfulness, 17

Cheshire cat, *230*

Chesterfield, Earl of, 282

Chiaroscuro, *see* Light and shade

Chien couchant, 320, *321*

Chiffon, used for blocking out eyebrows, 106

Chignons, 326, *327*

Chin, aging, 125, 164; building up, 135, 163, 164; cleft in, 220; corrective makeup for, 77; derma wax on, 239; double, 125; foam latex, *171*; modeling with paint, 88, 125; modeling with putty or wax, 133, 135; putty-wax, *229*; receding, 163; rubber prosthesis on, 163, 164

Chinese, 275, 277; eyes of an elderly, *103; see also* Orientals

Chinese brushes, 93, 100, 101, 114

Chins, *123*

Chopin, 322, *323*

Christian IV, 310, *311*

Clamps, for weaving sticks, 204, 205

Classes, makeup materials for, 61

Classic facial proportions, 75

Classification of reference material, 67

Classroom, makeup, *62*

Claudius, 292, *293*

Clay, modeling, 21, 22, 23, 24, 121, 147, 159, *160*, 161, 164, 175, 260, 261; ready for casting, *154, 167*; sculpting a head in, 22–25

Cleansing cream, removal of, before using greasepaint, 70; *see also* Makeup removers

Cleansing tissues, 253; dispenser for, 61; latex used with, 139–42, 147, *150*, 151, 152, 153; in mouth, 120; spirit gum used with, *144*, 145; syrup used with, *144*, 145; used in simulating scar tissue, *150*, 151, 152

Cleopatra, *356*

Clergyman's bob, 314, *315*

Clips, French, 215

Clock face, *238*

Closed molds, *65*, 175

Cloth, wigs of, 228

Clown makeup, 233, 234

Clown white, 233, 253

Club wig, 316, *317*

Clymer, George, *364*

Coat hangers, embedded in plaster, 159

Cold cream, 81, 108, 165

Coldness, 18

Colley, Peter, *45*

Collier, John, 350

Collodion, 253; brushes for, 253; and cotton, 145, 146; flexible, 105, 106, 146, 253; non-flexible, 151, 253, *361*; removal of, 151; scar made with, *361*; used in blocking out eyebrows, 105

Color, approaches to, 31; characteristics of, 31–33; effect of distance on, 29; source of, 31

Color chart for makeup paints, 35, 36, 90, 365–73

Color classification, a system of, 34, 35, 36

Color cone, *32, 33*

Color in light, 38; absorption and reflection of, 38; effect on pigment color, 38–40; primaries, 38; refraction of, 38; synthesis of, 38

Color in pigment, 31–40; characteristics of, 31–33; complements, 33; effects of light on, 38–40; hue, 31, 32; intensity, 31, 32, 33; loss of intensity in mixing, 33; mixing, 33; primaries, 33, secondaries, 33, source of, 38; value, 32, 33

Color Sprae, 257

Color tables, 374–82

Color television makeup, 242–48

Color triangle, *32*

Color wheel, 31, *32, 33*

Colors, complementary, 33; mixing, 36; primary, 33; secondary, 33; tables of equivalent, 35, 36, 374–82

Colors in makeup, analysis and classification of, 34–36, 373–82; chart for, 365–73; for cheeks and lips, 81, 82, 83; foundation, 74, 75, 90, 91; highlights, 91; hue, 34; inconsistency in commercial names and numbers, 34; intensity, 35; mixing of, 36; shadows, 91; value, 35; *see also* Shadows

Colorset, 255

Combing crepe hair, 177, 179

Combing wigs, beards, and mustaches on net, 189

Combs, 193, 253; in falls, 211; rat-tail, 214, 254; tortoise-shell, 332, *333*; wide-toothed, 177, 189, 253

Complementary colors, 33

Computer, 238

Condé, Princesse de, 284

Cone, powder, 207

Constantine the Great, 292, *293*

Conté crayon, 47, 52

Copper sheeting, *212*

Cordelia, 5, 100

Cork, burnt, 253

Corn husks, *228*

Corn Silk Micron Pressed Powder, 243

Cornmeal, used with latex, 143, 144, *145*

Cornstarch, 196, 254

Coronation of the Virgin, 27

Corot, Jean Baptiste Camille, *348*

Corrective makeup, 10, 74–86; for cheeks, 81; color in, 74, 75; contrasted with straight makeup, 10; for eyebrows, 80, 81; for eyes, 77–80; facial analysis for, 75; for the forehead, 76; for hair, 84–86; highlight colors for, 91; for lips, 82, 83; for neck, 83, 84, *85*; for the platform, 241; shadow colors for, 91; for teeth, 84; for television, 242, 243

Cosmetic, 236, 254

Cosmetics, used by men, 7, 279, 282, 284, 285

Costume, makeup colors related to, 81, 83, 100, 111

Cotton, absorbent, 250; combined with liquid plastic to simulate scar tissue, 146; used in cheeks, 120, 127; collodion used with, 145, 146; used with latex, 153; used with latex and tissue, 140, 142, 152

Cotton, latex, and spirit gum, for building up the face, 142–44; for burns, 147; for scar effects, 151, 152; for skin texture, 142–44

Coventry, Lady, 284

Cover stick, 254

Cowper, William, *350*

Cranach, Lucas, 349

Crane, Bruce, likeness of, *27*

Crawford, Joan, 121

Cream, cleansing, *see* Cleansing cream

Creases, deepening, 93

Credulity, 15

Creme makeup, *251*, 254; application of, 70, 254; brands of, 254; cake makeup used with, 71–75; hair whitened with, 196; shading with, 70; used in blocking out eyebrows, 105, 226; used in blocking out hair, *195, 197, 200*; used over syrup and tissue, 144; used for television, 242

Creme rouge, used for blood, 150; *see also* Rouge, creme

Creme Stick, Bob Kelly's, 254

Crepe hair, 177–85, 254; added to eyebrows, 108; for animal makeups, 233; application of, 180–83; beards, construction of, 177–83; beard stubble made with, 183; colors of, 177, 254; combing, 177, 179; curling, 179; eyebrows made of, 108, 185; on latex, 182, 183; mixing colors of, 177, *179*, 180; mustaches, construction of, 182, 183; preparation of, 177, 179, 180; pressing, 177; sideburns constructed of, 182; straightened, *179, 181*; straightening, 177, 179; on warts, 153; wavy, 179

Crew cut, 328, *329*

Cromwell, Oliver, 310, *311*

Crook, George, 322, *323*

Crows' feet, 100

Curl papers, *207*

Curling iron, use of, 179, 189, 193, 214

Curling stick, 179

Curling tongs, 279

Cuts, 147, *150, 361*

Cylinder, used in drawing, *28*, 29; related to modeling with makeup, 111, 121, 127, 129

Cyrano de Bergerac, 5; nose for, *154*

Czechoslovakians, 275

D

Danish, 275

Dark-skinned actors, highlight colors for, 91

Darwin, Charles, *350*

Death, 234, 235

Death Takes a Holiday, 234, 258

Demons, 235, *236*

Dental impression powder, 155

Dental stone, 157, 158, 159, 161, 175

Dental wax, 152

Dentists' cases, 59

Dentists' chairs, *62*, 64, 66, 155

Dep, 254

DePauw, Washington C., 322, *323*

Derma wax, 254; application of, 138; blending with alcohol, 138; blending with lubricating jelly, 257; blocking out eyebrows with, 105, 106; bruised and swollen flesh built up with, 147, *361*; compared with nose putty, 138; over cotton and collodion, 146; for deep cuts, 147, *361*; on the hand, *138*, 164; with latex and tissue, 140, 142; mixed with nose putty, 138; used over nose putty, 138; removal of, 105; scar tissue formed with, *150*, 151; sealer used over, 262; used over soaped-out hair, 196; spirit gum used with, 138; types of, 138; welts and warts constructed of, *150*, 152, 153; on wig blenders, 215

Designer, makeup, 43–46

Designing the Makeup, 41–55

Detergent, for cleaning wigs, 216

Determination, 18

Devils, 147, 235, *236*

Dicor adhesives, 251

Dioctylphthalate, 262

Dionysius the Elder, 290, 291

Director, approval of sketches by, 43

Disposition, appearance affected by, 5, 8

Disraeli, *354*; nose for, *154*

Dissipation, 18, 101

Distance, effect on color, 29

Doll makeup, 236, *237*

Donish, Christine, *228*

Doscher, Carol, *281*

Double chin, minimizing, 77

Double boiler, use of, 138, 155

Double knotting in wigmaking, 187

Double-faced adhesive, 250

Dracula, *355*

Dravidians in India, 276

Drawing brushes, used in wigmaking, 204

Drawing in light and shade, 29, 30

Drawing mats, 204, 254

Drawn parting, 199

Dressing room equipment, 61, *63*

Dressing tables, *61, 62*

Dressing wigs, 214, 215, 216

DuBarry, Madame, 318, *319*

Duchess, from *Alice in Wonderland, 230*

Dundrearies, 322, *323*, 324, *325*

Duo adhesive, used with lifts, 84; used as a sealer, 245; used to stipple edges of prosthetic pieces, 148, 250; used to stipple edges of wig blenders, 250; *see also* Latex cream adhesive

Dürer, Albrecht, 343, 346, 348, 350, 351

Dürer's father, *350*

Dürer's mother, *127*

Durfey, Thomas, *14*

Dutch, 275, 276

Dye, food coloring as, 161, 196, 254, 257; in latex compounds, 175; in liquid makeup, 258

Dye brushes, 189

Dye colors, 254

E

Ears, 147, 148; casting, 158; cauliflower, 163; elf, 236; gnome, 238; latex, 163, *172*; nose putty used on, 133; pointed, 147; putty wax used on, *148*; remodeling, 147, *148*; sprite, 147

East Baltic races, 275

Eastern Washington State College, 64

Eckermann, Johann Peter, 322, *323*

Edges, hard and soft, *see* Hard and soft edges

Edges, sharp, *see* Hard and soft edges

Egotism, 16

Egyptian bob, 332, *333*

Egyptians, ancient, 275; hair styles of, 279, 290, *291*, *292*, *293*; makeup of, 279

Eighteenth century, hair styles, 284; makeup, 279, 283, 284

Elastic, used with facial lifts, 84; used in wig foundations, 198, 199, 203

Elastic net, 198

Electric iron, use of, 177

Electric mixer, 175

Electric range, *62*

Elizabeth I, *135*, 282, *344*

Elliot, Marla, *114*

Elliott, Grace Dalrymple, *364*

Elves, 229, 236

Elvis style, 328, *329*

Emaciation, 100

Emerson, Ralph Waldo, 322, *323*

Endicott, John, 310, *311*

Energy, 15

English, 275

English cut, 328, *329*

Enthusiasm, 18

Environment, appearance affected by, 5, 10, 12

Epicanthic fold, 103

Epoxy mold, *168*

Epstein, Alvin, 223, *225*, 226

Equipment for makeup, 59–67

Equivalent colors, tables of, 35, 36, 374–82

Erace, 254

Erratic mind, 15

Erickson, Mitchell, 185

Eskimos, 276, *277*

Este, Isabella d', 304, *305*

Etruscan hair styles, 290, *291*, 294, *295*

Eugénie, Empress, 285

Eye, disfigurement of, *146*; planes of, 23, 24, *95*

Eye accents, 78

Eye dropper, 147

Eye makeup, ancient Egyptian, 279, *280*; color selection in, 78; optical illusions in, *78*

Eye pouches, casting, *160*; corrective makeup for, 77; foam-latex, *244*; modeling with cotton, 142; modeling with latex, 163; modeling with paint, 88, 101–3, *176*, *359*; ready-made latex, 258

Eyebrow brushes, 105, 189

Eyebrow covers, 105, 106, *107*, 108, 261

Eyebrow paste, blocking out eyebrows with, 105, 106, *107*, 142

Eyebrow-pencil sharpeners, 254

Eyebrow pencils, *see* Pencils

Eyebrow Plastic, Kryolan's, 255, *256*

Eyebrow wax, 255

Eyebrows, 80, 81, 104–9; adding hair to, 105; aging, 109; ancient Egyptian, 279, *280*; arched, 81; Assyrian, 279; blocked out with derma wax, 138, 142, 185, 281; blocked out with eyebrow paste, 142; blocked out with putty wax, 211; blocked out with soap, *108*, *362*; blocked out with spirit gum, 185, *211*, 281; blocking out, 105–8, *224*, 226, 234; bushy, 15; changing shape of, 105; in corrective makeup, 80, 81; covering with foam-latex pieces, 245; covering with latex, 139, 142, 163, *185*; crepe hair, 108, 143, 163, 177, 179, 185; darkening, 80; devil, 235; faint, 15; flattened with spirit gum, 244; grayed, 109; hair added to, 105; heavy, 15; high and arching, 15; importance in suggesting character, 15; on latex, 163; men's, *80*; nineteenth-century, 285; Oriental, 103; painted, 108, *357*; plucked, 7, 109, 281, 286, *287*, 288; plucking, 80, 81; reflection of character and personality, 15, 16; reshaping, 80, 81; shaggy, 81, 223; shaved, 281; slanting, 16, 81; smooth, 16; soaped out, *108*, *362*; straight, 16, 81; thick, 81, thin, 81; ventilated into latex, 163, *185*; ventilated on lace, 108, *224*, 226, *247*; women's, *79*; yak hair, *185*, youthful, *79, 80*

Eyelash adhesive, 80

Eyelashes, 78–80; beading, 254; coloring, 78, 80; false, *79*, 80, 100, 255, *256*; in optical illusions, 78; men's, 80

Eyelids, casts of, *154*; enlarging, 100; foam latex, *171*; latex, *154*, 162, 163; modeling, 100; Oriental, 148, 149, 155, 162; prominent, 78, 100; sagging, 149–51, *154*, 162, 163, 219

Eyeliner Seal, 255

Eyeliners, 255

Eyes, *79, 96, 97, 98, 99*; accenting, 78; aging, 94, *95*, 100–103, *359*; blind, 146, 147; casting, *155*; closely spaced, 77, 78; corrective makeup for, 77–80; deepset, 14, 15, 94; enlarging, 78; modeling in clay, 23, 24; modeling with paint, 90, 94–104; optical illusions applied to, 77, *78*; Oriental, 103, 104, 162; prominent, 14, 15, 100; reflection of character, 14, 15; small, 15; sunken, 100; weak, 100, *359*; widely spaced, 78

Eyes and eyebrows, character in, *15, 96, 97, 98, 99*

Eyeshadow, 255; ancient Egyptian, 279; application of, 70; color of, 78, 100; in corrective makeup, 78; metallic, 260; placement of, 78, 100

Eyeshadow stick, 255, 382

F

Fabric pattern, makeup based on, *229*

Face, areas of, 91; asymmetrical, how to correct, 75; bones of, 20, 21; broadening, 82, 85; classic propor-

Face (*continued*)
tions of, 23; counteracting roundness of, 86; counter-acting squareness of, 86; designs painted on, 228, *229,* 230; division into areas, *91;* lengthening, 85; planes of, *23;* round, 125–27; shortening, 83; widening, *126*

Face powder, 255; added to liquid plastic, 146, 152; application of, 70; dulling hair with, 189, 193; dusted on sticky fingers, 180; neutral, 70; removal of excess, 70, 144; translucent, 72, 73; used in blocking out eyebrows, 106, *107,* 108; used on latex, 139, 140, 159, 161, 163, 176, 183; used in the nineteenth century, 285; used over nose putty, 134, 135; used on plastic, 106, 150, 152; used on rubber-mask grease, 176, 196; used on spirit gum, 145; used over syrup, 144; white, 196

Faces, analysis of, 13, 14

Facial analysis, for corrective makeup, 75; for creating a likeness, 219

Facial anatomy, 20–26

Facial fuzz, protecting from latex, 139

Facial lifts, 83, *84, 85*

Facial proportions, classic, 75

Facial tissue, *see* Cleansing tissue

Factor makeup, 249

Fagin, 100

Fairies, 229, 237, 238

Falk, Peter, 48, 223, *224,* 226

Falls (hair), 198, 211, 217

False eyelashes, *75,* 78, *79,* 80, 147

False nails, 151, *173,* 235

False teeth, 121, 152, 238

Falstaff, 9, 100, *126*

Fangs, 238

Fashion, in corrective makeup, 74, 75, 81, 83; as a determining factor in hair styles, 8; as an environmental influence, 7; related to eye makeup, 100; related to lip makeup, 121; related to rouge, 111; related to temperament, 8

Fashions in Hair, 200

Fashions in makeup, 7, 279–88

Favorites, 318, *319*

Feathers, for bird makeups, 233; wigs made of, 228

Fielding, Henry, 314, *315*

Fifteenth-century hair styles, 302, *303,* 304, *305*

File, expanding, 67

Filing cabinets, 67

Filing system, development and use of, 67

Fillets, 292, *293*

Film, photographic, used for fingernails, 151

Fingernail polish, 130, 151

Fingernails, construction of, 151; false, 151, *173,* 235

Fingers, applying latex with 139, 143; shading for age, 129

Finian's Rainbow, 163

Finns, 275, 276

Firebird, 230

Firelight, effect on makeup, 38

Fishing tackle box, *60*

Fishskin, 255

Fixative, 135

Fixative A, 253, 262

Fixative spray, 255, *262*

Fixblut, Kryolan's, 252

Flattening the nose, 76

Flexible collodion, 105, 106, 146, 253

Flexol adhesive, 250, 255

Florentines, fifteenth-century, 339

Flowers, makeup for, *237,* 238

Fluorescent makeup, 234

Fluorescent paint, 234, 258

Fluorescent powder, 234

Foam sponge compounds, 258

Foamed latex, *65,* 154, 165–76, *232, 243–47;* cheeks of, *172, 176;* chin of, *171, 176;* curing, 176; difficulties in working with, 176; eyelids of, *171,* hands of, *173;* head piece of, *173;* neck of, *172, 176;* nose of, *171, 176;* shoulder hump of, *173*

Folds, nasolabial, *see* Nasolabial folds

Fontange, 312, *313,* 318, *319*

Food coloring, 161, 196, 254, 257

Fop, eighteenth-century, 7

Forcefulness, 15, 16, 18

Forehead, anatomy of, 20, 21; aging, 87, 92–94; corrective makeup for, 76; an indication of intellect, 13; lowering, 76; modeling with paint, 90, 91, 92–94; narrowing, 76; nose putty used on, 133; planes of, 92; raising, 76; rounding, 92; widening, 76

Foreheads, *92*

Fortrose, Lady, 284

Foundation color, affected by natural skin coloring, 74; average for men and women, 74; for corrective makeup, 74, 75; purposes of, 74; for racial groups, 275–78; selecting, 74

Foundation colors, available in commercial brands, 379, 380, 381

Foundation paint, and shading colors, *256;* application of, 68; on lips, 83; stippled, 72, 73

Fourment, Hélène, 312, *313*

Francesco de' Medici, 310, *311*

Francis I, *343*

Franklin, Benjamin, *112*

Frederick the Wise, *351*

Freeman, Jon, *237*

French, 275, 276

French clips, 215

Frontal bone, 20, 92; highlighting for age, 87

Frost, A. B., 230

Frowning wrinkles, 109

Fugger, Johannes, *340*

Full-bottom wig, 314, *315*

Fulvia, 296, *297*

Fuseli, Henry, 341

Fust, Johann, 302, *303*

G

Gackowski, Carol, *237*

Gainsborough, 364

Galileo, *356*

Gallup, Bonnie, *49*
Gautier, Marguerite, 5
Gauze, 185, 186, 187, 188, 198, 199, 208, 210, 255
Gauze, surgical, 255, 261; blocking out eyebrows with, 105, 106, 226, *229*; dipped in plaster, 255
Gee, John, 236
Gelatine, colors of, effect on makeup, 39, 40; use of, in lighting, 38; used over makeup lights, 61
Gelatine capsules, 252
Geniality, 18
George II, 314, *315*
George III, *14*
George IV, 322, *323*
Germans, 275, 276
Gibson girl, 332, *333*
Glass, latex painted on, 146, 151, 152; liquid plastic painted on, *106*, 146, *149*, 150, 151, 152, 153
Glass Menagerie, The, 9
Glass rods, 106
Glatzan, Kryolan's, *106*, 255, 261
Glitter, 228, *256*, 260
Goatees, crepe hair, 177, *235*; on latex, 164; ventilated, *225; see also* Beards and mustaches
Goblins, 238
God, 27
Gold dust, used on hair, 279
Gold threads, used in hair, 279
Goneril, 5
Gonzaga, Cicilia, 304, *305*
Gonzaga, Elisabetta, 304, *305*
Gouvernor, Maria Monroe, 326, *327*
Grafton, Duchess of, 283
Grant, U. S., *356*
Granville, Countess of, 284
Grapefruit skin, used for skin texture, 106, 142, 159
Gray, how to mix, 33
Graying the hair, 196
Greasepaint, 256; advantages and disadvantages of, 256; application of, 70, *71*; brands of, 256; combined with cake makeup, 71–73; designation by number, 379, 380, 381; listing of colors, 379, 380, 381; mixing colors of, 70; on putty, 135; removal of, 260; rubber-mask, *see* Rubber-mask grease; spirit gum used over, 180; stippling with, *see* Stippling; types of, 256; used in blocking out eyebrows, 105; used under latex, 139; used over soaped-out hair, *198*; used over syrup and tissue, 144
Great Britain, sources of makeup in, 267, 268
Grecque, 316, *317*
Grecque, à la, 320, *321*
Greek, 275, 276
Greeks, ancient, 276; hair styles and makeup of, 292, *293*, 294, *295*
Green light on makeup, 40
Green-blue light on makeup, 40
Green Pastures, The, 231
Group makeup, kits for, 59, 272
Guise, duc de, 306, *307*
Gustavus I, 306, *307*
Gwynne, Nell, 312, *313*
Gypsum, 175

H

Hackle, 205, *207*, 256
Hadlock, Pat, *117*
Hair, attached to latex, *169*; bleached, 282, 286; blocking out, *135*, *194*, *195*, 196–98; coloring and graying, 193, *194*, 196, 198; concealed with plastic, 246; corrective makeup for, 84–86; crepe, *see* Crepe hair; curled with tongs, 279; dirty-looking, 189; dulling, 189, 193; dyed, 186; facial, in optical illusions, *126*; fashions in, 7, 8, 289–335; flattened with spirit gum, *200*, *244*; gold dust used on, 279; graying, 196; human, 186, 189, 256; importance in makeup, 193; matted effect for, 193; mixing, 203, 205; natural, 193–96; painted, 279; parting, 193; plucked or shaved, 281; powdered, 284; real, 190; reflection of personality, 8; related to facial proportions, 85, 86; restyling, 85, 193; styles of dressing, 290–335; synthetic, 185, 186, 189, 190, 236, 256; soaping out, *194*, *195*, 196–98, *357*, *362*; synthetic, 214; thin at the crown, 196; teased, 288; ventilated into gauze, 208; ventilated into latex, 209; wavy, 214; weaving, 204, 205; yak, *185*, 186, 256; *see also* Hair styles
Hair and wigs, 193–218; *see also* Wigs
Hair coloring, 256, 257
Hair dressings, 189, 193
Hair dryer, 140, 143, 144, 158, 161, 163, 165, 176, 179, *194*, 196, 214, 244, 257
Hair dyes, 285
Hair goods, 266
Hair lacquer, 193, 215
Hair powder, *207*, 282, 283
Hair rollers, 193
Hair set, liquid, 193
Hair spray, 179, 189, 193, 196, 215, 257; colored, 216, 257
Hair styles, Afro, 330, *331*; age a factor in determining, 200; Ape, 334, *335*; Assyrian, 279, 290, *291*; barbaric, 298, *299*; beehive, 332, *333*; boyish bob, 332; Byzantine, 298, *299*, 300, *301*; corrective, 85, 86; Egyptian, 279, 290, *291*, 292, *293*; eighteenth-century, *201*, 284, 314, *315*, 316, *317*, 318, *319*, 320, *321*; Etruscan, 290, *291*; fashions in, 7, 289–333; fifteenth-century, *195*, *200*, *339*; Gibson girl, 332, *334*; Greek, 279, 290, *291*; Hittite, 290, *291*; influenced by fashion, 199, 200; length of, 7; marcelled bob, 332, *333*; Medieval, 298, *299*, 300, *301*, *343*; Natural, 330, *331*; nineteenth-century, 286, 322, *323*, 324, *325*, 326, *327*, *348*, *350*, *353*, *354*; page boy, 334, *335*; period, 199, 200, 289–335, 336–56; Persian, 279, 290, 291; Phoenician, 290, *291*; reflection of personality, 8; Renaissance, 302, *303*, 304, *305*, 306, *307*, 308, *309*; Roman, 279, 292, *293*, *337*; Semitic Akkadian, 294, *295*; seventeenth-century, 310, *311*, *338*; shingled bob, 332, *333*; Shirley Temple, 334, *335*; sixteenth-century, 282, 306, *307*, 308, *309*, *340*, *343*, *344*, *345*, *350*, *351*; social class reflected in, 200; Sosh, 330, *331*; Sumerian, 290, *291*, 294, *295*; twentieth-century, 7, 286, *287*, 288, 328, *329*, 330, *331*, 332, *333*, 334, *335*

Hair whitener, 109, 196, 257
Hairlace and net, 185, 198, 199, 205, 257, 261
Hairlace Adhesive, *262*
Hairline, plucked, 281; receding, 86; ventilated, *208*
Hairpieces, *69*, 198, 210, 211, 219
Hairpins, 214
Hand, severed, *138*
Hands, *128*; aging, 129, 130, *139, 144*, 145, 164, 165; bones of, *129*; casting, 164, 165; color of, 129, 130; delicate, 130; derma wax used on, 138; foamed latex, *173, 245*; latex used on, *139*; modeling with paint, 129, 130; rough, 130; rubber, 164, 165; spirit gum and tissue used on, 145; stippling, 130; syrup and tissue used on, 145; youthful, 129
Hangers, for plaster casts, 159
Hard and soft edges, 28, 29; in cheek modeling, 111, 112, *113*, 114, 119; in drawing, 29, 30; in eye makeup, 94, 100, 101, *102*; in modeling the forehead, 82, 83, *84*; in modeling jowls, 117, 119; in mouth wrinkles, 125; in nasolabial folds, 112, 114
Harris, Diane, *362*
Hawaiians, 276
Haweis, Mary, 286
Hayes, Gordon, 233
Head, construction of, 21–25; modeling in clay, 21–25; papier maché, 22; plaster, *166*; severed, *22*, shrunken, 159
Head form, plastic, *209*
Head molds, 164
Headbands, 209; elastic, 215
Health, appearance affected by, 5, 9, 12
Heinrich, Gottfried, 310, *311*
Henna, 286
Henri II, 306, *307*
Henri III, 282
Henry V, makeup for, *200*
Henry VIII, 16, 18
Heredity, appearance affected by 6, 10
Hérisson style, 320, *321*
Herman, Elaine, *6*, *228*
Highlight colors, 91
Highlights, application of, 68, 70, 71, 93, 114, *357*; color of, 91; importance of, 88; in corrective makeup, 76, 77; in drawing, 29, 30; for nonrealistic makeups, 91; placement of, 87–130; stippled, 70, *72*, 73, 91; in television makeup, 242
Highlights and shadows, intensity of, 112; in television, 242; variations in intensity in, 101
Hillstrom, Rondi, 362
Historical characters, source material for, 66
Historical periods, beard styles related to, 177
Hitler, Adolf, *355*
Hittite warrior, 290, *291*
Hoffman, Dustin, 65, *166–74*
Holbrook, Hal, *73*, 176, 220–23, *243–47*
Hollows of skull, 87
Holzschuher, Heironymus, 306, *307, 345*
Horft, Catherina, 312, *313*
Horseshoe toupee, 314, *315*
Howard, John, 316, *317*

Howard, Thomas, 310, *311*
Hue, 31, 32; in makeup, 34
Hues, primary and secondary, 33
Hurluberlu, 312, *313*

I

Iago, 16; makeup for, *126*
Illness, *see* Health
Imaginative makeup, 227–39
Imperial beard, 324, *325*
Inanimate objects, 238
Indians, American, 276, *277*
Indians, East, 276, *277*
Indians, Mexican, 276, *277*
Individual makeup kits, 59, 269–72
Individuality of dramatic characters, 5, 6, 7, 8, 9, 10
Infratemporal fossae, 21
Inge, William, 153
Ingres, Jean-Auguste-Dominique, likeness of, *27*
Inlay wax, 152
Inquisitiveness, 13
Intensity, loss of, in color mixing, 33; decreased in aerial perspective, 29; of pigment color, 31, 33
Introversion, 18
Irish, 175
Iron, curling, 179, 189, 193, 214; electric, 177
Isopropyl alcohol, 260, 262
Italian, 276

J

Japanese, 276, *277; see also* Orientals
Jaw line, aging, 88, 117–21, *359, 360*; corrective makeup for, 77
Jaw lines, *118*
Jawbone, conformation of, 119
Jaws, muscles of, *126*; planes of, *120*
Jean Valjean, 7
Jeanmaire, Zizi, 332, *333*
Jeanne de Saveuse, 304, *305*
Jefferson, Thomas, *355*
Jessop, Carl, *45*
Jester, Devil as, *236*
Jowls, 117, *119, 172*, 175, *244*
Julian Domna, 296, *297*
Juvenile makeup, *see* Corrective makeup

K

Kabuki wig, construction of, *212, 213*
Kalginate, 257

Karo syrup, 144, 145
Kaulbach, Friedrich von, *11*, 285
Kelly, Bob, 249, 250; makeup numbers, 379
Kidder, Donna, 194, 195
Kim, Randy, *104*
King Lear, makeup for, *185*
King Lear, 5
Kits, makeup, 59–65, 270–72
Klein, Howard, 43, 45, 229
Knotted wig, 201, 314, *315*
Knotting, double, 187
Knotting hair, *see* Ventilating technique
Knotting needles, *see* Ventilating needles
Knuckles, 129; derma wax used on, 138, *239*
Kohl, 279
Kollwitz, Käte, 229
Koreans, *277*
Kropotkin, Piotr, 328, *329*
Kryolan/Braendel makeup, 249, 250; numbers for, 279, 280
Kryolan transparent adhesive tape, *251*
Kulp, Larry, 129
K-Y lubricating jelly, *see* Lubricating jelly

L

Laboratory, makeup, *62*
Lacquer, hair, 182
Lady Macbeth, 9
Lafayette, Marquis de, 316, *317*
Lake, Veronica, 332, *333*
Lanolin, 249
Larynx, 127
Latex, 161, 257, 258, *262*; as adhesive, 165, 176; adhesive for crepe hair, 182, 183; blindness simulated with, 147; cake makeup used over, 139, 148, 165, 176; caps, 155, 164, 209, 234, 258, *259*; casting, *160*, 161, 163, 164, 165; clear, 151; coloring, 161; cornmeal used with, 143, 144, *145*, 238; cotton used with, 151, 153; cotton and spirit gum used with, 142–44; cream adhesive, 84, 148, 165, 176, 237, 250, 254; direct application of, 138, 139; ears of, *172*; eye pouch of, *160*; over eyebrows, 139, 185; foamed, *65*, 154, 165–76, *232*, 243, 244–47; foaming procedure for, 175, 176; on grapefruit rind, 159; over greasepaint, 138; greasepaint not used on; 165; on hands, *139*; hair attached to, *169*; irritating to the skin, 139, 142, 238; muslin ear tips coated with, 147; paper toweling used with, 139, *140*; pouring, *65*; powdering, 139, 140, 159, 161, 163, 176, 183; prosthesis with, 154–76; protecting skin from, 182; ready-made pieces, 258; removal of, 140, 142, 143, 165; for sagging eyelids, 151, 219; scar tissue of, *150*, 151; scars, 151, 152; for simulating burns, 147; for simulating cuts, 147; for skin texture, 139; spirit gum used with, 130, 183; stippling with, 139, 140; tissue used with, 139–42, 238; warts constructed of, 153; welts constructed of, 152
Lavater, John G., *14*

Lazar, Lydia, *229*
Lear, King, *185*
Leibnitz, Baron von, 314, *315*
Leichner makeup, 249, 250, 285; numbers for, 380
Lemon, used for skin texture, 106, 159
Lemon light on makeup, 39
Lengthening the face, 85
Lengthening the nose, *76*
Lenin, *355*
Lennox, Lady Sarah, 284
Leopard makeup, *362*
Leprechauns, 147
Les Misérables, 7
Life of Lady Sarah Lennox, 283
Life with Father, 6
Lifts, facial, 83, *84, 85*
Light, absence of, 87; absorption of, 31, 38, 39, 76; color in, 38; direction of, 92, *93*, 94, 111, 119, 125, 129; falling on cheekbones, 111; on makeup, 39, 40; mixing colors of, 38; on pigment, 38–40; primary colors in, 38; reflected, 26, 27, 28, 38, 39, 76; refraction of, 38
Light bulbs, non-heating, *62*
Light and shade, 3, 26–30; drawing in, 29, 30; principles of, applied to makeup, 87–130
Light source, 92, *93*
Lighting, stage, and makeup, 38–40
Lights, dressing room, 39, 61
Likeness, creating a, 219–26
Liles, Larry, *211*
Lincoln, Abraham, 18, *51, 53*, 163, *355*
Liners, *see* Shading colors
Lip rouge, *256*; application of, 83; color of, 83; colors used in TV, 242; determined by character, 121; for men, 83; *see also* Mouth
Lips, in age, 12, 121; aging, *120*, 121, *171*; bee-stung, 121, 286; classic, *82, 83*; color in, 18; coloring, 82, 83, 121; compressed, 18; corrective makeup for, 82, 83; firm, 18; foam latex, *171*; full, 18, 82; loose, 18; men's, *82*; over-painting, 82, 83; reshaping, 82, 83, 121, 220, *357, 362*; size of, 121; split, 233, *362*; texture of, 121; thin, 82; thinned, *120*
Lipscomb, Andrew, 322, *323*
Lipstick, 258; *see also* Lip rouge
Liquefying cream, *259*
Liquid Brightness, Kryolan's, 258
Liquid latex, *see* Latex
Liquid makeup, 258; application of, 258; on hair, 193; metallic, 260; removal of, 258; for statuary, 239; transparent, 241, 254, 258
Liston, Lady, 111, *363*
Little Big Man, 65, 166
Liver spots, painting, *170, 360*
Livia, 25
Long bobs, 314, *315*
Lorenzo de' Medici, 302, *303*
Lorraine, Henri de, 310
Lossing, Benson John, 322, *323*
LOTOL L-7176, 175
Louis II, 302, *303*
Louis XII, *340*
Louis XIII, 283

Louis XIV, 310, *311*
Love in a Wood, 283
Lovelocks, 310, *311*
Love's Labours Lost, 281
Lowering the forehead, 76
Lubricating jelly, 106, 108, 145, 176, 196, 198, 257, *262*; used with nose putty, 133, 134, 135
Lucrezia Borgia, 308, *309*
Luminous makeup, 234
Luminous paint, 258
Luther, Martin, *11*
Luther's father, 306, *307*
Luther's mother, *349*
Lynch, Paul, *150*
Lyttleton, Lord George, *14*

M

Mackenzie, Lady Caroline, 283
Mad Hatter, *69, 230*
Maddock, Gloria, *142*
Madwoman of Chaillot, 9, *120*
Magnetic container for pins, *263*
Major wig, 314, *315*
Makeup, and the actor, 3, 4; actor with and without, *3*; adaptation to the actor, 47, 48, 223; application of, 57–248; Assyrian, 279; brands of, 249, 250; cake, *see* Cake makeup; character, 10; and characterization, 223; color chart, 365–73; color in, *see* Color in makeup; color tables, 374–82; corrective, *see* Corrective makeup; creme, *see* Creme makeup; decorative, *see* Makeup, nonrealistic; dispensation for class work, 61; Egyptian, 279; eighteenth-century, 279, 283, 284; fashions in, 7, 279–88; fifteenth-century, 281; fluorescent, 234, 258; glamor, 100; Greek, 279; hypo-allergenic, 249; imaginative, 227–39; importance of, 3, 4; importance of planning in, 12, 223; inconsistency in colors of, 34, 36; light on, 39, 40; liquid, *see* Liquid makeup; luminous, 234; materials for, 249–65; Medieval, 279; metallic, *229, 237, 238, 239,* 260; nineteenth-century, 284–86; non-realistic, *227, 228, 229, 230, 231, 232, 233, 234, 235, 236, 237, 238, 239, 362*; Oriental, 230; for photography, 10, *242*; plan for a short course in, 273, 274; for the platform, 241, 242; and portrait painting, 26, 27; preparation for, 5; prosthetic, *see* Prosthesis *and* Prosthetic pieces; purpose of, 4, 5; quick-change, 49, 223, 226, 257; related to actor's face, 125; removal of, 105, *134, 135,* 165, 183, 215, 260; for Restoration plays, 282, 283; Roman, 279; seventeenth-century, 282, 283; short course in, 273, 274; sixteenth-century, 281; straight, 10; street, 7; styles of, 227; stylized, *6,* 230, *233, 235, 236, 237, 238, 239*; for television, 242–48; thirteenth-century, 281; three-dimensional, *69, 77, 108, 117, 126,* 133–53, 154–76, *185, 211,* 227, *229,* 233, *237,* 243–47, 248, *256, 357, 361*; transparent liquid, 183; twentieth-century, 286, *287,* 288; Victorian, 286
Makeup artist, function of, 4
Makeup artists, in the nonprofessional theater, 44, 46, 63, 217; in the professional theater, 43, 44, 46, 217
Makeup cape, 258
Makeup Center, 249
Makeup chairs, *62*
Makeup charts (worksheets), *50, 51, 52, 53*
Makeup classes, 64, 65
Makeup classroom, *62*
Makeup color charts, 365–73; use of, 35, 36
Makeup colors, *see* Colors in makeup
Makeup crew, 63
Makeup designer, 43–46
Makeup equipment, 57–63
Makeup kits, 59–61, 258, *259,* 269–72
Makeup laboratory, *62, 63*
Makeup materials, 249–65; for classes, 61; for the kit, 60, 61; sources of, 266–68; storage for, *62, 63*
Makeup morgue, *66,* 67
Makeup palette, 59, *60,* 258, *259*
Makeup removers, *259,* 260; liquid, 105, *259,* 260
Makeup room, 61–66
Makeup storage room, *63*
Makeup tables, *62;* portable, *64,* 65
Makeup worksheets, *50,* 51–54
Makeup workshop, 65, 66
Makeups, sketches for, *43, 48, 51, 52, 224, 225*
Malachite, green, 279
Mandible, 21, 117
Mannozzi, Giovanni, likeness of, 27
Marcelled bob, 332, *333*
Marie-Antoinette, 284
Marionettes, *237,* 239
Mark Twain Tonight, 243
Marquisette beard, 306, *307*
Mary Queen of Scots, 282, *344*
Mascara, 260; application of, 80; colors of, 260; in corrective makeup, 81; hair grayed with, 196; white, 109, 196, 257
Mask Cover, *256*
Masking tape, 165; used in wigmaking, 186, 250
Masks, 47, *228,* 231; bird and animal, *232, 233;* disadvantages of, 154; Etruscan, *231;* foamed latex, *166–74, 232;* French, *231;* grotesque, *231, 235;* latex, 154; Renaissance, *231*
Masonite, 21
Massey, Doug, *227*
Masslinn towels, 139, 160
Mat knife, for sharpening makeup pencils, 254
Materials, makeup, 249–65
Mathilde, Queen, 300, *301*
Matte plastic, 247
Mats, drawing, 204
Maxilla, 20, *21*
Maybelline, 252, 254
McKeen, Joseph, 322, *323*
Measuring for wigs, 216, 217
Medico Adhesive, 171, 176
Medieval hair styles, 298, *299,* 300, *301, 343*
Medieval sculpture, *336*
Mediterranean races, 276
Mehron makeup, 249, 250; numbers of, 380, 381

Melancholy, 18
Melanchthon, Philip, *340*
Men, cosmetics used by, 7, 279, 282, 284, 285
Mengs, Rafael, 363
Mephistopheles, *235*
Mercator, Geradus, 306, *307*
Metal, wigs made of, 228
Metallic flakes, 237, 260
Metallic makeup, *229*, 237, 238, 239, 260; warnings about using, 260
Metallic powders, 260
Metallic sprays, 260
Mexicans, 276, *277*
Meyer, Charles, 285
Meyer, Donna, 197, 198, *229*
Middle age, 10–12; *see* Age
Middle Ages, hair styles and makeup, 279, 281, 298, *299*, 300, *301, 343*
Military haircut, 328, *329*
Mill, John Stuart, *353*
Mimi, 9
Mineral oil, 260
Minor bobs, 314, *315*
Mirandola, Giovanni Pico della, 302, *303*
Mirrors, 59, 61, *62, 64*, 133, 134, 181, 260
Mr. Puff, 154
Mitchell, Edward, 324, *325*
Mixer, electric, 175
Mixing bowls, plastic, 155, 158
Modeling, with clay, 21–25; of cheeks with paint, 111, 112; of face, 87–127; of hands, *128, 129*, 130; of neck, 127–29; with paint, 69, 87–132, *358, 359, 360*; with putty and wax, 133, 134, 135, 138
Modeling clay, *see* Clay, modeling
Modeling tools, *22, 252*, 261; use of, 22, 24, 159, 196
Mohair wigs, 214
Moist rouge, 262, 271
Molds, closed, *65*, 175; epoxy, *168*; negative, 154–58, 175; positive, 175; split, 163; stone, 175, 176
Molière, 310, *311*
Mongolian race, 276, *277*
Monsters, 238
More, Sir Thomas, *350*
Morgue, makeup, *66, 67*, 162
Mortician's wax, *see* Derma wax
Mosaics, 228
Mother Courage, 43, 44, 46, 229
Mott, Lucretia, *14*
Moulage, 154, 155, 165, 261; applying, 155–58; brushes for, *156, 157*; mixing, 155; removing, 158; reusable, 155, 158, *159*; types of, 155
Mousseline de soie, 261; used for facial lifts, 84
Mouth, aging, 121, 125; contracted, 18; expanded, 18; large, 18; modeling, in clay, 23; modeling, with paint, *120*, 121–25; narrow, 83, 121; neglected, *143*; reflection of character, 13, 18; small, 18; straight, 18; turned-down, 18; turned-up, 18; wide, 83, 121; in youth, 10
Mouths, *122, 123, 124*
Mozart, 316, *317*
Muscles, neck and jaw, *126*; sagging, 119, 125; sterno-cleido-mastoid, 127

Muslin, used in making ear tips, 147
Mustache wax, 183
Mustaches, barbaric, 298, *299*; inverted, 306, *307*; real, *178, 188*
Mustaches, crepe hair, construction of, 182, 183; removing, 183; spraying, 182; waxing, 182
Mustaches, ventilated, *72, 183, 228*; application of, 188, 189; construction of, 186–88; dressing of, 189; made on gauze, *184*; made on net, *184*, 223, *224, 225, 247*; materials for, 186–88; pattern for, *188*; ready-made, 261; removal and cleaning of, 189, 190; trimming, 187
Mustaches and beards, 177–91, real, *178*; as a reflection of personality, 8; styles of, 290–331; trimming, 188; waxed, 283
Mutnezemt, Queen, 294, *295*

N

Nail polish, 130, 151
Nail polish remover, 250
Naissante wig, 316, *317*
Nansen, Fritdjof, 324, *325*
Na-ny, Princess, 294, *295*
Napoleon, *355*
Narrowing the face with rouge, 82
Narrowing the forehead, 76
Narrowing the nose, *76*
Nasal bones, 21
Nasolabial folds, *116*; analyzed in terms of light and shade, 112, *113*; constructed of foamed latex, *244*; modeling with paint, 88, 90, 112–17, *358*
Nattier, 364
Natural Affection, 153
Natural wig, *201*
Naturo Plasto, 254
Neck, in age, *118*; aged with cake makeup, *127*; color of, 129; corrective makeup for, 83, 84, *85*; foamed latex, *172, 244*; latex piece for, *154*, 164; modeling with paint, 88, 127–29; muscles of, *126*, plump, 129; prosthetic attachments for, *170, 172, 176, 244*; sagging, 125, *154*; scrawny, 127; wrinkled, 127, 129
Necker, Jacques, 316, *317*
Needle beard, 310, *311*
Needles, ventilating, 186, 187
Nefertiti, *280*
Negative moulage mold, 155–58; removing, 158
Negative stone or plaster cast, 159–61, 164, 165
Negroes, 276, *277*
Net (netting), 185, 186, 187, 188, 190, 198, 199, 205, 211, 261
Neville, Sir Henry, 306, *307*
Newcastle, Duchess of, 283
Nineteenth century, 284–86, 322, *323*, 324, *325*, 326, *327*
Nonflexible collodion, 151, 253, *361*
Nonrealistic makeup, 227, *228*, 229, *230*, 231, *232, 233, 234, 235, 236, 237, 238, 239, 362*; highlights for, 91
Nordic, 276
Norwegian, 276

Nose, aging, 109, 110; aquiline, 18; aristocratic, 18; broad, 17, 18; broadening, 109; broken, 109; building up with derma wax, *135, 361*; building up with putty, 133–35, *357*; building up with putty-wax, 77; casting, 158; character in the, 16–18; changing the shape of, 133, *135*; clay model for, *154*; coarsely formed, 18; concave, 18; convex, 17, 18; corrective makeup for, 76, 77; crooked, *76*, 109; crudeness in, 17; delicate modeling in, 17; drooping, 12, 111; flat, 109; flattening, 109; foamed latex, *171, 245*; Grecian, 18; importance in suggesting character, 13, 16, 17; inquisitive, 13, 14, 17; large, 17, 219; latex, 161, 162, 281; length of, 18; lengthening, *76, 126*; long, 17; modeled with putty-wax, *108, 142*; modeling with clay, 23; modeled with derma wax, *239*; modeling with paint, 76, 88, 109–11; narrow, 17; in old age, 115, 141; planes of, 23, 109; prosthetic, 161, 162; putty, *117, 153, 211, 237*; putty-wax, *227, 229, 282*; refined, 18; reflection of character, 16–18; retroussé, 18; Roman, 17; rouging, *361*; sharp, 109; short, 17, 18; shortening, *76*, 109; size of, 17; small, 18, 219; stippling, *361*; straight, 18; straightening, 76; strength of, 18; turned-down, 18; turned-up, 18; widening, *76*; width of, 18

Nose putty, 133–38, *256*, 261; application of, 133, *134*; application of foundation over, *135*; blending, 133, 134, 135; bruised and swollen flesh built up with, 147; cake makeup over, 135; chin built up with, 235; deep cuts made in, 147; ears built up with, 148; ears pushed out with, 220; hands built up with, 138; with latex and tissue, 140, 142; lubricating jelly used for blending, 257; modeling with, 133–38; nose built up with, *117, 153*, 235; preparation of, 133, 134; removal of, *134*, 135; softening, 133, 134; spirit gum used under, 134; warts and welts constructed of, 152, 153

Nose and Scar Wax, 254

Noses, *110, 136, 137*; latex, *154*; ready-made latex, 258

Nostrils, highlighting, 76, 88, 190, 219; rouging, 135; shadowing, 109; widening, 109

Nye, Ben, 249, 250; makeup numbers for, *381*

Nylon net, 185, 186, 198, 199, 205, 208, 210, 219

Nylon stocking, used in blocking out eyebrows, 106, *357*; used in blocking out hair, *194, 195*, 196, *197, 198*; hair ventilated into, *209*

O

Oberon, 237

Observation, importance of, 3

Occupation, appearance affected by, 5

Ogre makeup, 238

Old age, creating the effect of, with paint, 87–90; *see also* Age

On Stage makeup, 249, 254

Ophelia, 10

Optical illusions, *78*

Optimism, 16, 17

Orange, used for skin texture, 106, 159

Orange light on makeup, 39

Orangewood sticks, 106, 151, 152, 183, *252*, 261

Orbiana, 296, *297*

Orbis, 296, *297*

Orbital bone, highlighting for age, 87

Orbital fossae, 21

Organizing makeup colors, 34–38

Organza de soie, used in blocking out eyebrows, 106

Oriental actor as a Caucasian character, *104*

Oriental eyes, modeling with paint, 103, 104

Oriental head, *336*

Oriental mask, *228*

Oriental mask, makeup based on, *362*

Orientals, foundation colors for, 74; highlight colors for, 91

Oven, 175, 176

Oxhair brushes, 253

P

Paint, acrylic, 243; luminous, 258

Painting, portrait, compared to makeup, 26, 27

Paintings, reproductions of, 27, 345–54; used as source material, 88, 336

Palette, makeup, 59, *60*

Palette knife, use of, 61, 147, 151

Palmquist, Sally, *142*

Pan, head of, *336*

Pan-Cake makeup, 261

Panchromatic, colors, 242

Pan-Stik, 261

Paper, eyelashes made of, *237*; gummed, for patches, 283; tracing, *see* Tracing paper; wigs made of, 228

Paper stumps, 52, 264

Paper toweling, 139, *140*

Papier maché, 231

Paramount Theatrical Supplies, 249

Parrot, makeup for, *233*

Parting, double, 217; drawn, 199, *208*; horizontal, 217; ventilated, 208, 210

Passion of Josef D., The, 223–26

Pastels, 50

Patches, facial, 282, 283

Patriot for Me, A, 46; makeups for, *45*

Patterns, for Kabuki wig foundation, *212*; for ventilated beards and mustaches, 186; for wigs and toupees, 205, 211

Peale, Rembrandt, 363

Peer Gynt, 239

Pellinore, King, *52, 53*

Pen, felt-tipped, 196

Pencil, grease, 196; indelible, 155

Pencils, eyebrow, 186, 210, 211, 254, 258; used in corrective makeup, 81, 84, 86

Pencils, makeup, *252*, 258; colored, 50, 55, 226; listing of colors of, *379*; flat-cut, *94, 102, 252*; sharpening, 102; shaving, 102; used for eye accents, 78; used for marking wig line, 210, 211; used in blocking out teeth, 84, 130, 251; used in correcting hair line, 86;

Pencils (*continued*)
    used in eye makeup, 78; used over latex, 139, 140, 143; used in lip makeup, 83; used on scalp, 196; used for shadowing, *94, 102, 117, 358, 359*
Pencil sharpeners, eyebrow 102, *252*, 254
Pepys, Samuel, 282
Period hair styles, 199, 200, 189–335, 336–56
Persephone, 294, *295*
Perception, threshold of, 31
Persians, 275, 276, *277*; ancient, 279
Personality, reflected in beard styles, 177; reflected in hair styles, 200; related to physical appearance, 5
Perspective, aerial, 29
Perspiration, 144; simulated with mineral oil, 260
Pessimism, 16, 17, 18
Peter Owen Limited, 289
Petroleum jelly, used on eyebrows, 81, 108; used on hands, 165
Phantom of the Opera, *148*
Philadelphia, Here I Come, 48, 49
Philip IV, makeup for, *211*
Phoenecian hair style, 290, *291*
Phosphorescent paint or powder, 234, 258
Photographic film, used for fingernails, 151
Photographs, creating a likeness from, 223; light source in, 94; used as source material, 66, 67, 88, 92, 117, 121, 125, 162, 163, 177, 188
Photography, makeup for, 10, 242
Physical appearance, determining factors in, 5, 6
Physical bobs, 314, *315*
Physical tie wigs, 314, *315*
Physiognomy, 13–19
Picture collection, 336–56
Piero de' Medici, 302, *303*
Pierpont, John, 14
Pierrot, 238, 239
Pigment, color in, 31–33; light on, 38–40
Pigtail wigs, 201, 316, *317*; machine for binding, *207*
Pills, used for warts, 153
Pin curls, 189, 193, 214
Ping hammer, *213*
Pink light on makeup, 39
Pinocchio, *237*
Pins, magnetic container for, *263*; T-shaped, 186, 252, *263*, 264
Pipe cleaners, used in remodeling ears, 147
Pique devant beard, 306, *307*, 310, *311*
Pirkheimer, Wilibald, *340*
Planes, of cheeks, *112*; of eye, 94, *95*, 100, 101; of forehead, 92; of mouth and chin, 121; of nose, 109, 111
Plaster, used in casting, 154–61, 163, 164, 165, 175, 261
Plaster bandage, *155, 156*, 158, 261
Plaster casts or molds, 147, 164, 165, *166–69*, 175; used in ventilating beards, 186, 188, *189*
Plastic, liquid, 151, 196, 261; sagging eyelids made with, 149–51; scar tissue made with, 146, *151*, 152; painted over nylon stocking, *209*; warts made with, 153
Plastic, matte, 247
Plastic capes, 155, *156*
Plastic caps, 155, 196, 209, 215, 217, 234, 261; ventilating

hair into, 209
Plastic film, 261; application of, 106; blindness simulated with, 146; blocking out eyebrows with, 105, 106, *107*, 108; edges thinned with acetone, 106, 107, 151; sagging eyelids constructed with, 149–51
Plastic foam, 258
Plastic forehead piece or head band, 208, *246*
Plastic head forms, 261
Plastic makeup, 106, *107*, 146, 149, 150, 151, 152, 153, 209, 210
Plastic sealer, *see* Sealer
Plastic, sheets of, 155, 258
Plastici, Kryolan's, 261
Plastics, used in prosthesis, 255, 261
Plastolene, 21
Platform makeup, 241, 242
Platinum blondes, 286
Plumpers, 283
Plumpness, 125–27
Polaroid camera, 55
Polynesian races, 276
Polyvinyl butyral, 262
Pomatum, 318
Pompadour, Madame de, 318, *319*
Pompey, 292, *293*
Ponzuric, Lorie, *237*
Popcorn, *237*
Porta, J. B., *14*
Portrait collection, 336–56
Portrait painting, compared with makeup, 26, 27
Portraits, copying, 219
Portuguese, 276
Positive latex cast, 161
Positive plaster cast, *157*, 158, 159, 165
Pouches, eye, *see* Eye pouches
Powder, blending, *see* Face powder; hair, *207*, 282, 283
Powder bag, *207*
Powder brush, *195*
Powder cone, *207*
Powder puffs, *195, 207*
Preparation, importance of, 5
Primary colors, in pigment, 33, in light, 38
Prince of Aragon, makeup for, *200*
Principles of makeup, 1–40
Professional makeup kits, 59
Professional theater, makeup artist in, 217
Prophet Haggai, The, *338*
Proportions, classic facial, 75
Prosthesis, 154–76, 248; casting for, 154–61
Prosthetic pieces, *154*; advantages of using, 154; application of, 165, 176, *244–47*; casting of, 154–61; casts, *154*; cleaning, 165; hair ventilated into, 163, *185*; molds, *154*; removal of, 165; types of, 161–65; used in television, 242, 243, *244–47*, 248
Prosthetic work, electric range for, *62*
Puck, 163, *237*
Puff, Mr., nose for, *154*
Puritans, 283
Purple light on makeup, 40
Putty, *see* Nose putty

Putty-wax, 262; application of, *69*, 138; bruised and swollen flesh built up with, 147; ears built up with, *148*; eyebrows blocked out with, *211*; with latex and tissue, 140; mixing, 138; nose built up with, *77, 108, 126, 142*; on wig blenders, 215
Pygmalion, 8

Q

Queen of Hearts, *6, 108*, 230
Queensberry, Duchess of, 283
Quick-change makeups, 49, 223, 226, 257

R

Rabbits' paws, 262
Race, appearance partially determined by, 6, 7
Races, dark-skinned, selection of colors for, 74, 75
Racial characteristics, 275–78
Raisin in the Sun, 6
Raising the forehead, 76
Raleigh, Sir Walter, *356*
Rashomon, 7
Rat-tail comb, 214, 254
Razor blades, used for sharpening pencils, 102, 254, 260
Razors, eighteenth-century, *207*
Read, John Meredith, 322, *323*
Ream, Vinnie, *364*
Red light on makeup, 39
Reflected light, 26, 27, 28, 38, 39, 76
Refraction of light, 38
Remodeling the nose with paint, *76*
Removal of beards on latex, 183
Removal of collodion, 253
Removal of nose putty, *134*, 135
Removal of prosthetic pieces, 165
Removal of spirit gum, 215
Renaissance hair styles, 302, *303*, 304, *305*, 306, *307*, 308, *309*
Renting or buying wigs, 214, 264
Research, importance of, 223
Restoration period, 282, 283
Revolutionary period, *317*
Rice, *237*
Richard II, *343*
Richard III, 10, 16, 100
Rivets, for Kabuki wig, *212*
Rojas, Joseph, *150*
Robespierre, *356*
Rollers, hair, *214*
Romans, ancient, 25, 276, 279, 292, *293, 337*
Romeo, 15, 100
Roosevelt, Franklin D., *356*
Roosevelt, Theodore, *356*
Rope, wigs of, 228

Roth, Bert, 75, 85, 152, *157*, 232, *361*
Rotundity, 125–27
Rouge, affected by colored lights, 39, 40; application of, 70, 71, 81; brush-on, 70, 90, 91, 117, 262; cake, 70, 262; color of, 81, 111, 241; colors used in TV, 242; in corrective makeup, 81, 82; creme, 70, 90, 150, 262; dry, 91, 262; in the eighteenth-century, 283, 284; in eye makeup, 78, 100; grease, 70; lip coloring related to, 121; for men, 82; moist, 71, 262; natural, 111; in the nineteenth century, 284–86 placement of, 81, 82, 111, 117, 125; powdered, 152; related to character, 111; for rounding the face, 125; stippling with, 72, 134; used in shading, 81, 90, 91, 93, 94, 101, 114, 117, 119; in television makeup, 242; used on false ears, 148; used on hands, 129; used on the nose, 111, 134, 135; used on putty, 134
Round beard, 310, *311*
Roundheads, 283
Router bit, 175
Rubber, *see* Latex
Rubber caps, 155, 164, 209, 234, 258, *259*
Rubber gloves, 164, 165
Rubber-mask grease, *256*, 262; how to make, 253; molds greased with, 175; used in blocking out eyebrows, 105, 106, *107*; used over cotton and collodion, 146; used over latex, 139, 140, 142, 143, 144, 164, 165, 176, *247*; used with muslin ear tips, 147; used over nose putty, 135; used over soaped-out hair, 196; used in television, 242
Rubber prosthesis, 154–76, 243–47
Rubber prosthetic pieces, *see* Prosthetic pieces
Rudolf II, *345*
Russians, 275, 276

S

Sable brushes, 72, *252, 253*, 255
Safeguard bandage, 263
Saffron, 279
St. Barnabas, *347*
St. Philip, *346*
Salisbury, Ruth, *114, 362*
Samoans, 276, 277
Sample cases, 266
Sassoon, Vidal, 332
Savanarola, *355*
Saverio, Francesco, *363*
Scalp, coloring, 196
Scandinavians, 276
Scar Plastic, 262
Scar Plastic Blending Liquid, 245
Scar tissue, *146, 150*
Scarecrow, 228
Scarring Material, 253, *262*
Scars, *150*, 151, 152, *361*; ready-made, 258
Schmidt-Rottluff, Karl, 229
Schumann, Robert, 322, *323*
Scissors, 181, *252, 262*; cleaning, 180; sticky, 180

Scottish, 275, 276, 278

Scratch wig, 314, *315*

Scrooge, 16

Sea shells, *228*

Sealer, 253, 262; brushes for, 253; formula for, 262; muslin ear tips coated with, 147; removal of, 105, 135; substitute for latex, 139; used in blocking out eyebrows, 105; used in blocking out hair, *195, 196,* 198; scars made with, 152; used over derma wax, 147, 153, 215; used with facial lifts, 84; used over gauze, 106; used under latex, 139; used for wrinkling, 139

Secondary colors, 33

Secretiveness, 17

Semitic Akkadian, 294, *295*

Sensitivity, 18

Sequins, 237, 260

Servanius, Julius Ursus, 292, *293*

Seventeenth century, 282, 283, 310, *311*, 338

Severity, 18

Shades in color, *32, 33*

Shading brushes, *see* Brushes, shading

Shading colors, 256; application of, 68, 71; applied under the foundation, 68; cake, 68; creme, 70; grease, 70

Shado-liners, Mehron, *256*

Shadows, application of, 68, 70, 71, 221; cast, 29, 30; color of, 71, 91, 221; in corrective makeup, 76, 77; danger of overemphasis on, 88; in drawing, 29; how to lighten or soften, 70; placement of, 87-130; related to costume, 91; rouge used in, 91, 93, 101, 117; stippled, 70, 73

Shadows and highlights in television makeup, 242

Shag hair style, 334, *335*

Shakespeare, William, 310, *311, 356*

Shaw, George Bernard, *355*

Shears, barbers', 181

Shellac on plaster casts, 159

Shingled bob, 332, *333*

Shirting, used for blenders, 208

Shortening the nose, *76*

Shoulder hump, foamed latex, *173*

Shrewdness, 15

Shrunken head, 159

Siamese, 278

Sideburns, 177, 182; blocked out, *200*; concealing with hairpieces, 211; used in concealing facial lifts, 84; extending with crepe hair, 182; ventilated, *190*

Silk, filmed, *see* Filmed silk

Silk cloth, 189

Silk gauze, *see* Gauze, silk

Silk net or lace, 185, 186

Silver Hair Gray, Ben Nye's, 257

Silver powder, 260

Sinks, steel, *62*

Sixteenth century, 281, 282, 306, *307, 308, 309*

Sketches, of beards, 177; for historical characters, 223, *224, 225*; of noses, 133, 134

Sketches for makeups, *43, 48, 54,* 223, *224, 225, 233*; approval of, 43, 47, 51; final, 50, 51; importance of, 47; preliminary, 47

Skin, irritations of, 151; tightening, 83, 84, 85; trans-lucent, 226

Skin color, affected by age, 10, 12; affected by environment, 7; affected by health, 9; affected by race, 7, 275-78

Skin discolorations (liver spots), 145, 196, 223, *360*; cover stick used over, 254

Skin freshener, 70, 262

Skin texture, 121, 125, *141*, 223; affected by environment, 7; on clay models, 159, 162, 175; from grapefruit, 106, 134, 142; with latex, 139-44; with latex and cornmeal, 144; with latex, cotton, and spirit gum, 142-44; with latex and tissue, 139, 140, *142*; with latex and toweling, 139, 140; on nose putty, 134; with paint, 125, 134, 176; on prosthetic pieces, 154; in latex eye pouches, 163; with syrup and tissue, 144-45; stippling for, *359*; in television, 243; three-dimensional, 134

Skull, *20, 21, 234,* 235; locating bones of, 87

Skull cap, 234

Slater, William, 310, *311*

Slides, glass, used in dispensing makeup, 61

Slomon's Medico Adhesive, 171, 243, 250, 263

Slush mold, *163*

Slush technique used in casting, 161, 163, 164

Small Person with Flowered Hat, *228*

Smith, Bill, 22, 62, *150, 183,* 213, 233

Smith, Dick, *65, 120,* 166-74, 243-47

Smith, John, 310, *311*

Snow White and the Seven Dwarfs, 239

Soap, 263; blocking out eyebrows with, 105, 106, *108,* 263; blocking out hair with, *194, 195,* 196-98, 263, *281*; cleaning brushes with, 161

Socrates, *356*

Soft and hard edges, *see* Hard and soft edges

Soft Putty, Kryolan's, 254

Sothern, E. A., 322, *323*

Sousa, John Philip, 324, *325,* 328, *329*

Spanish, 276

Spanish leather, 283

Spanish papers, 281, 282

Spanish wool, 281, 283, 284

Spectacles, 217

Sperry, Watson, 322, *323*

Sphere, 30, 125

Spirit gum, 262, 263; application of, 180; attaching ear tips with, 147; attaching latex pieces with, 165; attaching plastic film with, 106, *107*; with beards on latex, 183; with blenders, 215; blocking out eyebrows with, 104, 226; bottle for, 262, 263; with cleansing tissues, *144,* 145, 238; with cotton and collodion, 145, 146; with cotton and latex, 142-44; with crepe hair, 180, 181; under derma wax, 138; diluted for spraying, 182, 250; eyebrows blocked out with, *211*; foamed latex attached with, 176, 245; over greasepaint, 180; hair flattened with, *200, 244*; with hairlace, 188, 189, 215; with latex, 139; matte, 183, 188, 263; with nose putty, 134, 135, 138, 142; nylon stocking attached with, *194, 195,* 196; plastic pieces attached with, 146, 152; removal of, 105, 165, 189, 190; scars applied with, 151, 152; sequins attached with, 237; sideburns blocked out with, *200*; used as spray, 182; used on

Spirit gum (*continued*)
  plastic caps, 209; used in attaching facial lifts, 84; used in attaching rubber pieces, 165, 176; used to attach false fingernails, 151; used to attach scars and welts, 153; used with derma wax, 105, 138, 142; used over makeup, 185; used with wigs, 199
Spirit gum remover, 105, 142, 143, 144, 148, 180, 183, 189, 190, 215, *259*, 260
Split mold, 163
Sponge applicator for eyeshadow, *252*
Sponges, for applying rubber-mask grease, 176; cellulose, *72, 73*; foam, 263; highlighting with, 111; plastic stipple, 72, 73, 142, 263; rubber, 70, 72, 73, 147, 263; silk, 68, 263; sterilized, 120; stippling with, 223; synthetic, 70, 263; used in applying cake makeup, 68, 71; used in applying dry rouge, 91; used in applying liquid makeup, 193; used in modeling cheekbones, 111; used in mouth, 119, 120, 127; used in stippling, 223, 263; use of, 263
Spotlights, used in the makeup room, 61, *62*, 65, 88, 93
Spray-on bandage, 182, 189, 263
Springs, steel, for wigs, 198
Sprites, 147
Square wigs, 314, *315*
Square-cut beard, 310, *311*
Stage lighting and makeup, 38–40
Stained glass, 228
Stalin, Josef, 48, 223, *224*, 226
Standardized makeup color numbers, 34, 35, 36, 374–78
Statuary, 239
Steam iron, 177, *179*
Stearns, James Hart, 228
Stein's makeup, 249, 250; numbers for, 381, 382
Stearn, Lea, 139
Sterno-cleido-mastoid muscles, 88, 127
Stevens, Harold K., 64
Stevenson, Robert Louis, 324, *325*
Stick greasepaint, application of, 71
Stick liner, 220; for whitening eyebrows, 109
Stiff-bristled brushes, 142, 189, 253
Stiletto beard, 310, *311*
Stipple-latex, 244, 245
Stipple sponge, 72, 73, 142
Stippling, for age, *72*, 90, *359*; on blenders, 215, 222; with brushes, 223; for burns, 147; with cake makeup, 70; colors used for, 73; with latex cream adhesive, 148, 165, 215, 250; with creme makeup, 71, *72, 73*, 196, *359*; with greasepaint, 71, *72, 73*, 142; over highlights and shadows, 91, 93, 101, *102*, 114; with latex, 139; materials for, 72; nose putty, 134, 135, 142; with rubber-mask grease, 176; with sponges, 223; derma wax, 142; over foam latex, *247*; over spirit gum and tissue, 145; over syrup and tissue, 144; in television makeup, 243; types of sponges used for, 70, *72, 73*; for unshaven beard, 226
Stone, dental, 263
Stone texture, *145*
Stoppelpaste, Kryolan's, 251, 264
Storage cabinets, *62*
Straight makeup, 10

Straightening crepe hair, 177, 179
Straw light on makeup, 40
Straws, used in casting, 158
Streaks n' Tips, 257
Streetcar Named Desire, A, 6
Stretch wigs, 199, 203
Stretcher, for Kabuki wig, *212, 213*
String, used in making scars, 152; used in making welts, *152*
Stuart, Gilbert, 363
Stubble paste, 264
Stubbornness, 18
Student makeup kits, 258, 269, 270
Stumps, chamois, 264
Stumps, paper, 52, 264
Style, contrasts in, *6*
Stylized makeup, *227*
Sudermann, Hermann, 324, *325*
Sulfur dispersion, 175
Sullivan, Sir Arthur, 324, *325*
Sumerian hair styles, 290, *291*
Superciliary arch, 20, 92; highlighting, for age, 87, 93, 94, 220
Surfaces, flat and curved, 27, 28
Surgical adhesive, *see* Adhesive, cream latex
Svengali, 100
Swallow-tail beard, 306, *307*, 324, *325*
Swedish, 278
Swinburne, Algernon Charles, 322, *323*
Swiss, 275, 278
Switches (hair), 198, *199*, 217
Synthetic hair, 214
Syrian, 275
Syrienne, à la, 318, *319*
Syrup, Karo, 144, 145
Syrup and tissue, 144, 145

T

Tables of equivalent makeup numbers, 373–82; use of, 35, 36, 373
Tackle boxes, 59
Taffeta, black, patches of, 283
Tahitians, 276, *277*, 278
Talcum powder, 161
Tammi, Tom, *45*
Tan Klear, 258
Tape, adhesive, 250; for Oriental eyes, 148, 149; for sagging eyelids, 149; for scar tissue, *150*
Tape, masking, used in wigmaking, 186, 250
Teeth, in age, 121, 130; blocking out, 130; corrective makeup for, 84; darkening, 130; false, 121, 152, 238; pointed, 130; shortening, 84; uneven, 130; whitening, 84, 130
Television makeup, 242–48
Temperament, appearance affected by, 6, 8, 9, 10, 12
Temple White, 257, 264

Temples, correcting sunken, 76; highlighting and shadowing for corrective makeup, 76; lifts used on, *85*; modeling for age, 92, 222

Temporal fossae, 21, 92

Tenacity, 18

Tenniel, Sir John, 229, *230*

Texas Dirt, 264

Texture effects, *see* Skin texture

Thomas, Susan, 194, 195, 197

Thread, use of, for removing putty, 135; in ventilating beards, 188

Threads, for weaving, 204

Three-dimensional makeup, 133–53; in television, 243–48

Three-faced Girl, *162*

Three Voices, The, illustration from, *230*

Threshold of perception, 31

Throat, cut, 147, *361*

Through the Looking Glass, 6, 229

Tibetans, 278

Tie wigs, 314, *315,* 316, *317*

Tiger makeup, *232*

Tinting brushes, *see* Shading brushes

Tints, 33

Tissue paper, for storing wigs, 216

Tissues, cleansing, *see* Cleansing tissues

Titania, 237

Titus Andronicus, 104

Titus cut, 320, *321*

Tones in color, *32, 33*

Tonsure, *208,* 217

Tools, wigmakers', 207

Tooth enamel, 84, 251; substitute for, 251

Toothbrushes, 189

Toothpaste, red, 252

Top Stick, 250

Toupee tape, 188, 215, 250

Toupees, 198, 199; constructing, 210, 211; for corrective makeup, 86; measurements for, 216, 217; putting on, 215; removing, 215

Towels, 181, 183, 185, 222, 244; lintless, 189; Masslinn, *see* Masslinn towels; paper, *see* Paper toweling

Toys, 239

T-pins, 186, 252, *263,* 264

Trachea, 127

Tracing paper, for beard patterns, 186; for reproducing photographs, 48, 50; for wig patterns, 211

Tramp-clown, 233, *234*

Treachery, 16

Trolls, *227,* 229, 238, 239

Trotsky, Leon, 223, *225,* 226

Tuffy head, 264

Tuplast, Kryolan's, *256,* 261, 264

Turks, 275, *277,* 278

Tussaud, Marie, *354*

Twain, Mark, makeup for, *73,* 220–23, *243–47*

Tweezers, 106, 108, 161, 183, 185, *244, 252,* 264

Twentieth century, 286–88; hair styles, 328–35

Tyler, John, *363*

Tyng, S. H., *14*

U

Ultraviolet light, 234, 258

Uncle Sam beard, 322, *323*

Underwood, Nancie, *239*

University of North Carolina, 64

Unshaven effect, *224, 226*

Upper lip, modeling with paint, 88, *120,* 121

V

Vacillation, 15

Valois, Marguerite de, 308, *309*

Value in color, 35; centralization of, 29

Van Buren, Martin, 285

Van de Passe, Crispin, 310, *311*

Van Dyck, Anthony, 310, *311*

Vandun, Cornelius, 306, *307*

Veins, of bosom, 279; of hands, 129, 130, 145, 164

Velvet Stick, Stein's, 254, 264

Ventilated hairpieces, 211

Ventilating needles, 186, 187, 203, 205, 208, 211, 264

Ventilating technique, 186, 187

Ventilating a wig, 203, 204, *209*

Ventilation, importance of good, 64

Venus, à la, 318, *319*

Verus, Lucius, 292, *293*

Vespasian, 292, *293*

Victoria, Queen, 120, *352, 356*

Vidra, Jan, *234*

Violet light on makeup, 40

Vitality, 18

Vlad, Prince, *355*

Voltaire, 314, *315*

VYNS, 262

W

Walpole, Horace, 283, 284

Warts, *152, 153,* 164, *227,* 239; ready-made, 258

Washington, George, 285, *355, 363*

Water color brushes, 253

Water color pencils, 50, 52

Water colors, 50, 52

Wave set, 133, 179

Wax, balls of, 283; black, 84; candle, 147; dental, 152; derma, *see* Derma wax; inlay, 152; mortician's, *see* Derma wax

Waxed paper, 149

Weak eyes, 100, 359

Weakness, 15

Wearing of wigs, 215, 216

Weaving frames, 264
Weaving hair, 204, *205, 206*
Weaving sticks, 204, 205; clamps for, 204
Webbing, for wig foundations, 198
Weft, 199, 204, 205; making, 205; used in making falls, 211
Welch, 275, 278
Welts, *150, 151,* 152, 153, 164
Wens, *152*
Werewolves, 238
Wieland, C.M., *14*
Wheat germ, used with latex, 144
Whip lashes, welts from, 153
Whiskers, animal, 233
White, Richard Grant, 322, *323*
White lead, 279, 283, 284
Whitener, *see* Hair whitener
Widening the face, 82, 85
Widow's peak, 210
Wig block holder, *203,* 251
Wig blocks, 164, 186, 203, 205, 211, 214, 216, 264
Wig cleaner, 216
Wig foundations, 198, 200, *202,* 203, *204,* 208; remodeling, 205, 208
Wig partings, 199, *208*
Wig shop, eighteenth-century, *206*
Wig springs, 264
Wig stands, 203, 264
Wig stays, 203
Wigmakers, 264, 266; supplies for, 266; tools for, *207*
Wigs, 198–218, 264; abbot's, *201;* adapting, 217, 218; *à la Grecque,* 320, *321; à l'enfant,* 316, *317;* bag, *201,* 316, *317;* bald, 164, 176, 209; blender, 208, 209, 221, 222; bob, *201,* 314, *315;* brigadier, *201;* buying, 264; cadogan, 316, *317;* campaign, 314, *315;* carrying case for, 202; cleaning, 216; club, 316, *317;* coloring, 217; combing, *224;* construction of, 198, 200–203, *204;* for corrective makeup, 86; cut, 314, *315;* diagram for measurements, *216;* dressing, 214, 215, 216; Egyptian, 279, 290, *291,* 292, *293;* eighteenth-century, 199, *201, 206,* 217, 284, 314, *315,* 316, *317, 351;* full-bottom, 314, *315;* and hair, 193–218; Kabuki, *212, 213;* knotted, *201;* lace front, *199;* major, 314, *315;* measuring for, 216, 217; mohair, 214; naissante, 316, *317;* natural, *201;* nineteenth-century, 284; physical, 314, *315;* pigtail, *201,* 314, *315,* 316, *317;* putting on, 215, *224;* ready-made, 264; removing, 215; renting, 214, 264; Samurai, *212, 213;* scratch, 314, *315;* seventeenth-century, 283, 310, *311,* 312, *313;* square, *201,* 314, *315;* storage of, 63; for street wear, 199; stretch, 199; synthetic hair, 214; stylized, 228; tie, 314, *315,* 316, *317;* ventilated, *183, 214, 224, 225, 246, 247;* ventilating, 203, 204, *209;* wearing, 215, 216; weight of, 203; yak hair, *185*
Wilde, Oscar, *356*
Wiles, Irving, 322, *323*
Wilson, Woodrow, 210, 219, 220, *356*
Wire, for hanging casts, 159
Wire frames, hair dressed over, 308, *309*
Wit Restored, 283
Witches, *153,* 239
Wittop, Freddy, 45
Wohlgemut, Portrait of, *348*
Wolsey, Thomas, *113*
Wood shavings, wigs of, 228
Worksheet for makeup, *50, 51, 52*
Worksheets, sketches and, 47–55
Workshop, makeup, *65,* 66
Wounds, 147
Wrinkles, *141,* 223; analyzed in terms of light and shade, 28; blending, 93; creating with latex, 138–44; around eyes, 100, 101; between eyebrows, 109; forehead, 92–94, 220, 222; minimizing in corrective makeup, 77; around mouth, 121, 125; modeling, 92–94, 100; neck, 127, 129; rouge used in modeling, 91, 93, *360; see also* Nasolabial folds
Württemberg, Count Ulrich von, 306, *307*

Y

Yak hair, 185
Yarn, wigs of, 228, *237*
Yellow light on makeup, 40
Young, Bryan, *45*
Youth, 10; *see also* Corrective makeup
Yugoslav, 278

Z

Zavala, Jeanne, *150, 237*
Zelada, Cardinal de, *563*
Zinc oxide dispersion, 175
Zinc stearate, 175
Zygomatic arch, 20, 21